Introduction to
International Political
Economy

Second Edition

Introduction to International Political Economy

Professor David N. Balaam
*Department of Politics and Government
and the International Political Economy Program*

Professor Michael Veseth
*Department of Economics
and Director of the International
Political Economy Program*

IN COLLABORATION WITH FACULTY
OF THE INTERNATIONAL POLITICAL ECONOMY PROGRAM
UNIVERSITY OF PUGET SOUND

Prentice
Hall

Upper Saddle River, New Jersey 07458

Library of Congress Cataloging-in-Publication Data

BALAAM, DAVID N., [date]
   Introduction to international political economy / DAVID N. BALAAM, MICHAEL VESETH.—
   2nd ed.
      p. cm.
   Includes bibliographical references and index.
   ISBN 0-13-018349-0
   1. International economic relations. I. Veseth, Michael.
   HF1359 .B33 2001
   337—dc21   00-028475

VP, Editorial Director: *Laura Pearson*
Executive Editor: *Beth Gillett Mejia*
Assistant Editor: *Brian Prybella*
Editorial Assistant: *Beth Murtha*
Director of Marketing: *Gina Sluss*
Editorial/production supervision: *Edie Riker*
Prepress and Manufacturing Buyer: *Benjamin D. Smith*
Cover Director: *Jayne Conte*
Cover designer: *Bruce Kenselaar*

This book was set in 10/12 Palatino by East End Publishing Services, Inc., and was printed and bound by Hamilton Printing Company. The cover was printed by Phoenix Color Corp.

 © 2001, 1996 by Prentice-Hall, Inc.
A Division of Pearson Education
Upper Saddle River, New Jersey 07458

Printed in the United States of America

10 9 8 7 6 5 4 3 2 1

ISBN   0-13-018349-0

Prentice-Hall International (UK) Limited, *London*
Prentice-Hall of Australia Pty. Limited, *Sydney*
Prentice-Hall Canada Inc., *Toronto*
Prentice-Hall Hispanoamericana, S.A., *Mexico*
Prentice-Hall of India Private Limited, *New Delhi*
Prentice-Hall of Japan, Inc., *Tokyo*
Pearson Education Asia Pte. Ltd., *Singapore*
Editora Prentice-Hall do Brasil, Ltda., *Rio de Janeiro*

Contents

5 Critical Perspectives on International Political Economy 87

PART II IPE Structures: Production, Finance, Security, and Knowledge 107

6 International Trade 110

9 The Global Security Structure   182

10 Knowledge and Technology: The Basis of Wealth and Power   208
by Professor Ross Singleton

16   The IPE of Multinational Corporations   346
by Professor Leon Grunberg

17   The IPE of OPEC and Oil   369

Preface

... the ideas of economists and political philosophers, both when they are right and when they are wrong, are more powerful than is commonly understood. Indeed the world is ruled by little else. Practical men, who believe themselves to be quite exempt from any intellectual influences, are usually the slaves of some defunct economist. Madmen in authority, who hear voices in the air, are distilling their frenzy from some academic scribbler of a few years back.[1]

John Maynard Keynes

The ideas, questions, issues, and problems that we study in International Political Economy (IPE) are increasingly important. It is hard to make sense of a newspaper, a business investment, or a government policy without an understanding of the theories, institutions, and relationships found in IPE. It is difficult, in other words, to understand our everyday lives without some understanding of IPE, so deeply are we now touched by international relations and global events.

We believe that IPE is so important that all college students need to understand it in a fundamental way. Our conviction is that it is possible to present this material in simple ways that retain the complexity of the global issues and intellectual problems we address, but without making the discussion fit only for graduate students. Our aim is to provide educational materials that will allow "beginners" (college freshmen and sophomores) to go from 0 to 60 in IPE in a single semester. Our hope is that these students will get excited about IPE as an element of lifelong learning and become better citizens and more knowledgeable individuals in the process.

OUTLINE OF THE BOOK

The book begins with five chapters designed to set out some basic tools for studying IPE. Chapter 1 introduces the fundamental elements of IPE. We will begin with relatively simple tools and ideas, then add layers and detail to make IPE real. Chapters 2, 3, and 4 explore three ways of looking at IPE that have been powerful forces in history and remain influential in today's world: mercantilism, liberalism, and marxism or structuralism. Chapter 5 introduces four theories (rational choice, feminist, green, and postmodern) that challenge our understanding some IPE questions and events.

The second section of the text examines the web of relationships or structures that tie nations and their citizens together. As a student sitting at your desk, you are linked to people and places around the world in a number of ways which you need to understand if you are to make good personal, business, and social choices. Chapter 6 looks at production and international trade. Chapter 7 looks at the monetary linkages that bind us together. Chapters 8, 9, and 10 examine, respectively, the debt connections, the security structure, and the ties created by knowledge and technology.

At the end of the first ten chapters, then, you should be able to imagine yourself as part of the international political economy and how you are linked to states and markets around the globe. You should have a fundamental understanding of what these linkages are, and an appreciation of the theories and perspectives that interpret these structures and guide our understanding of them.

The second half of the book looks at specific topics and problems in IPE that are essential to a sound understanding of the world today. Chapters 11 to 14 look at issues and events that are usually associated with the industrial nations of the North. We examine the European Union, the controversy over NAFTA, the IPE of Japan, and the problems of the formerly Communist countries making the transition to another form of political economy.

Problems and issues generally associated with the less developed countries of the South are discussed in chapters 15 to 17. These chapters look at the dilemma of Less Developed Countries (LDCs) and Newly Industrialized Countries (NICs), the nature of the multinational corporation, and the IPE of OPEC and oil.

Finally, the last three chapters examine global problems. The global environment and the food crisis are discussed. The very last chapter asks, "Where do we go from here?" After reviewing basic concepts and examining the fundamental tensions that shape today's world, we consider four scenarios for the future of IPE.

At the University of Puget Sound, where we teach, all of our students take a course in IPE, or something similar, in their sophomore year. We have written this text to help our students and to help ourselves serve their needs. We hope you find it a valuable educational resource.

WHAT'S NEW IN THE SECOND EDITION?

The world has changed a lot since the first edition of this textbook appeared in 1996 and the second edition has been thoroughly revised to reflect the dynamic environment of IPE. We have retained the basic format that has proved so successful: a survey of theoretical perspectives followed by an analysis of structural connections, leading to sections that explore state-market tensions, North-South relations, and global problems. Within this structure, each chapter has been carefully revised. A few chapters have received major overhauls; all of them have been updated. Here is a list of the most significant changes.

- Chapter 1 has been revised to make it a more user-friendly introduction to IPE for beginners (but not, as the popular how-to book series has it, for "dummies"). The U.S.-China case study has been retained and deepened somewhat. The notion of Waltz's three levels of analysis is introduced in this chapter to provide a basis for discussion in later chapters.
- Chapter 5 has been broadened significantly.[2] In place of a chapter on rational choice theory, Michael Veseth has written a new chapter that surveys four theories that, depending upon your viewpoint either challenge or enrich the traditional study of IPE: rational choice, feminist, green, and postmodern theories. We want this chapter to serve as a point of entry for professors who want their students to study one or all of these theoretical perspectives without fundamentally changing the format and focus of the book. We hope that professors who wanted to be able to teach these theories as part of IPE will find this chapter's summaries useful and will supplement them with other readings and assignments.
- Dave Balaam has written an entirely new chapter 9 on the global security structure, uprooting the discussion from the previous focus on the Cold War and asking students to consider security as a dynamic and many-layered problem.
- Chapter 13's analysis of state-market tensions in Japan has been thoroughly revised by Karl Fields and Michael Veseth to reflect more clearly the political and economic crises that Japan has confronted in the 1990s. The focus of this chapter is now the model of the developmental state and the question of whether this system of state-market relations is still valid.[3]
- The analysis of the transition from state to market by former communist countries has been strengthened through a revision authored by Patrick O'Neil, our colleague at Puget Sound, who joins the textbook team in the second edition. Professor O'Neil's revision adds detailed substance to the basic outline established in the first edition.
- Chapter 17's discussion of the IPE of energy and oil has also come in for a major revision. The focus of the chapter is now clearly on oil and the recent issues in the IPE of oil. Much of the historical analysis of the first edition chapter has been cut to make room for more recent events.[4]
- "Where do we go from here?" We have revised chaper 20 to make it less U.S.-centric and to address more directly the questions and concerns that students have when they reach the end of a textbook like this.
- All the chapters have been revised to take into account a number of important IPE events, especially the growing discussion of and concern about economic globalization, the financial crises in Asia and elsewhere, and the advent of a single currency in Europe, the euro.

ACKNOWLEDGMENTS

This textbook is truly a cooperative effort. We have benefited from the contributions and support of many persons, students, colleagues, family, and friends. We are especially grateful, however, to our colleagues in the International Political Economy program who have contributed directly to this work by writing chapters in their fields of expertise: David Sousa, Karl Fields, Ross Singleton, Leon Grunberg, Patrick O'Neil, and Sunil Kukreja.

The second edition of this text has especially benefited from the work of our colleagues who have taught IPE at the University of Puget Sound: Richard Anderson-Connolly, Matt Warning, Jan van der Veen, Elizabeth Norville, Lisa Nunn, Martyn Kingston, Arpad Kadarkay, Peter Loedell, and Nick Kontogeorgopoulos.

Finally, we owe debts we can never repay to our families and to our mentors. We love you.

We dedicate the second edition to the memory of Susan Strange, who taught IPE to all of us.

David N. Balaam and Michael Veseth
Tacoma, Washington

NOTES

1. John Maynard Keynes, *The General Theory of Employment, Interest, and Money* (New York: Harcourt Brace Jovanovich, 1964), p. 383.
2. Our thanks to Lisa Nunn, who wrote the rational choice chapter for the first edition.
3. Our thanks to Elizabeth Norville, who was co-author of this chapter in the first edition of the text.
4. Our thanks to Tim Amen, whose earlier work provided the foundation for this revised chapter.

PART I

Perspectives on International Political Economy

What is International Political Economy (IPE)? The first chapter of this book answers this question, stressing the fundamental nature of IPE and its multidimensional character. The chapters that follow in part I will broaden and deepen this basic understanding. Chapters 2 through 4 are the core chapters of part I, presenting ideas that are used everywhere in the text. These chapters explore the history of IPE through a discussion of the three main IPE viewpoints or perspectives—namely, mercantilism, liberalism, and structuralism. This discussion will provide students with a basic vocabulary and some theoretical tools that are useful in understanding any IPE issue. These chapters will also help students see more clearly the roots of IPE in the past and its relevance to the contemporary world. The first part of the text concludes with chapter 5, which examines four critiques of IPE thought, proving brief glimpses of alternative perspectives on IPE.

1

What Is International Political Economy?

OVERVIEW

What is international political economy? Chapter 1 answers this question in three ways: by example; by comparison, contrasting IPE with more familiar disciplines such as economics, political science, and sociology; and directly, through discussion of the fundamental principles of IPE.

In simple terms, we define IPE as the study of those international problems and issues that cannot adequately be addressed by recourse to economic, political, or sociological analysis alone. IPE is the study of international affairs that focuses on the elements of complex interdependence that define many of our most pressing problems today.

The need to study IPE arises because many important contemporary questions cannot adequately be addressed from the standpoint of a single discipline—economics, politics, or sociology—or by the analysis of actors and actions that take place on a particular level of analysis—individual, state, or international system. IPE breaks down the barriers that separate and isolate the traditional methods of analysis, seeking a comprehensive understanding of issues and events.

The main case study presented in this chapter examines the tension between the United States and China regarding two sets of issues—international trade and human rights—that are brought together in the international political economy. This case study illustrates the fundamental tension between and the dynamic interaction of two spheres of life, which we can variously call "society and individuals," "politics and economics," or "states and markets," the values they represent, and the ways those values and interests affect relations between nations and politics within them.

The world is a complicated place, characterized at all levels by elements of *interdependence*. We depend on one another in many ways and at many levels. Human existence is, therefore, filled with elements of tension, boundaries where differing and sometimes conflicting interests, points of view, or value systems come into contact with one another. It is the purpose of the humanities and the social sciences to improve our understanding of the human condition by analyzing the causes of these tensions and their consequences—how they are resolved. International Political Economy (IPE) contributes to this work by focusing on particular tensions that have traditionally been of interest to social scientists.

International political economy is both the past and the future of social science. It is the past because it represents a return to the origins of social science, before the study of human social behavior became fragmented into the discrete fields of economics, political science, sociology, history, and philosophy. It is the future because, in today's complex world, most important social problems clearly have an international or multinational aspect that is best understood through an integrated study drawing on a variety of tools and perspectives, not just one.

In an academic world full of fences that enclose disciplines and limit interaction, IPE represents a return to the idea that Susan Strange described as

> . . . a vast, wide open range where anyone interested in the behavior of men and women in society could roam just as freely as the deer and the antelope. There were no fences or boundary-posts to confine the historians to history, the economists to economics. Political scientists had no exclusive rights to write about politics, nor sociologists to write about social relations.[1]

Rowland Maddock put it in a slightly different way:

> . . . international political economy is not a tightly defined and exclusive discipline with a well-established methodology. It is more a set of issues, which need investigating and which tend to be ignored by the more established disciplines, using whatever tools are at hand.[2]

IPE does not replace the separate social science disciplines. It unites them into a fence-free, wide-open field, better to serve the needs of our complex society. IPE attempts to understand the world of human interaction in a comprehensive fashion, which is an ambitious undertaking but a necessary one for the people who live in the world and for future leaders who will have to deal with its economic, political, and social problems.

Why should a person study international political economy? We give three brief answers: because it is interesting, because it is important, and because it is useful.

IPE is interesting. To paraphrase Samuel Johnson, a person who is bored with IPE is bored with life! IPE is all about life and the many actions and interactions that connect human beings around the globe. The study of IPE is the opportunity to study some of the most interesting issues and questions in the world.

IPE is important. IPE makes the front pages every day because IPE events affect us all as citizens of the world, residents of particular nation-states, and daily participants in systems of markets that are increasingly global in nature. IPE events affect us all and it is important that we understand them and see how we connect to and can influence global affairs.

Finally, *IPE is useful.* Public and private employers increasingly seek out individuals who can think broadly and critically, who can understand complex and dynamic systems, and who can appreciate the impact of social conditions and alternative values. Employers, in short, seek out those who can understand the international and global context of human activity today. Heck, a person needs to understand a little IPE just to be able to make sense of the nightly newscast. IPE is the social science that most directly addresses these needs.[3]

IPE IN THEORY AND IN PRACTICE

What is IPE? Why should it be studied? How? This book is an introduction to IPE, written to help you understand the issues, forces, and problems that characterize today's interdependent world and to help you appreciate where you fit into the picture. This chapter gets you started by outlining the basics of IPE, using a case study to illustrate IPE's power and importance.

One way to understand the basics of IPE is to pick apart its name. It is first, therefore, *international*, meaning it deals with issues that cross national borders and with relations between and among nation-states. Increasingly today, people talk about *global* political economy, because more and more problems and issues affect the whole world, not just a few nations, and require a global perspective and understanding. This book will often take this global view of political, social, and economic problems.

Secondly, IPE is *political* in that it involves the use of state power to make decisions about who gets what, when, and how in a society. Politics is a process of collective choice, drawing in competing and often conflicting interests and values of different actors, including individuals, voluntary associations, businesses, and political parties. The political process is complex and multilayered, involving nation-states, bilateral and multilateral relations between and among nation-states, and many international organizations, regional alliances, and global agreements.

Lastly, IPE is about the *economy* or economics, which means that it deals with how scarce resources are allocated to different uses and distributed among individuals through the decentralized market process. Economic analysis and political analysis often look at the same questions, but economic analysis focuses less on issues of state power and national interest and more on issues of income and wealth and individual interest. Political economy, therefore, combines these two ways of looking at the world in order to grasp more fully society's fundamental nature.

The international, the political, and the economic do not interact in a vacuum. The social and cultural environments must be considered along with the values of the different actors. The historical development of important issues cannot be ignored either. IPE thus attempts to understand the complex interaction of real people in the real world, with the attitudes, emotions, and beliefs that they bring with them.

This textbook is an introduction to the formal study of IPE, but it is unlikely that it is the first time you have confronted the sorts of issues that IPE studies. Every day the newspapers and media are full of IPE because, in a way, the study of IPE is the study of modern life.

U.S. AND CHINA REACH TRADE PACTS BUT CLASH ON RIGHTS

WASHINGTON—President Clinton and the Chinese president, Jiang Zemin, engaged in a day of unexpectedly contentious talks on Wednesday that produced several significant commercial agreements but appeared to broaden the gulf between the two powers on human rights.

China agreed to buy $3 billion worth of American civilian airplanes and to make concessions that clear the way for American companies to compete to sell nuclear reactors to China. . . .

Jiang emerged from the summit talks as a recognized major world player, commanding one of the globe's most powerful armies and one of its largest and fastest-growing economies. He shared a stage as an equal with the president of the United States, and while he had to endure some stinging criticism of his country's human-rights record, he left with the grudging respect of official Washington for the forceful way he played his hand.[4]

by JOHN M. BRODER
New York Times, October 30, 1997

International political economy dominated the front page of the *New York Times* and most other newspapers in the United States on October 30, 1997. The issue was complex but clearly important. President Bill Clinton had to choose between two conflicting national interests. The economic interests of both China and the United States would be served best by granting Chinese goods favorable entry into the U.S. market, a condition generally termed *Most Favored Nation* (MFN) status, although it is sometimes called *Normal Trade Relations* (NTR) in the United States.[5] China, however, had a record of violating human rights as they are defined by Western culture. Since the height of the Cold War in 1961 it has been U.S. policy to deny MFN status to nations that violate U.S. human rights standards.[6]

The issue, therefore, is whether China's domestic policies on human rights should be a factor in United States economic policies toward that nation. The tension between the economic interests of the United States and its moral principles thus caused friction between these two mighty nations—a disagreement that U.S. President Clinton and Chinese President Jiang Zemin sought to resolve through face-to-face discussions.

In confronting this issue, Clinton and Jiang were unavoidably involved in IPE. They faced an *international economic* issue (U.S.-Chinese trade) with domestic and international *political* implications that was based on fundamental *social and cultural* differences between U.S. versus Chinese human rights traditions. Their political problem, as reported in newspapers around the world, was how to reconcile their common interests on trade with their opposing cultural human rights beliefs given that U.S. law links the former with the latter. President Clinton acknowledged China's progress in some areas of concern, which made it possible to announce a number of pending business deals between the two countries. The *New York Times* article continued, noting that

> But if the summit was a victory for commercial diplomacy, it did little to assuage American concerns about political and religious rights in China.
> Jiang stood beside Clinton at a joint news conference this afternoon and forcefully defended China's historic preference for order over personal freedom, even when it leads to the abridgement of individual rights.
> The Chinese president emphasized the mutual economic benefits of the relationship between the two countries and tried to minimize the "noises" he heard from human rights protesters gathered in Lafayette Park across from the White House.
> "President Clinton and I share the view that China and the United States enjoy a high degree of complementarity and a huge potential for cooperation in the economic and trade fields," he said in his opening remarks. But Clinton insisted that the Chinese could not expect to prosper while suppressing social and political freedoms. He said that the United States and China had "profound disagreements" on Beijing's treatment of its citizens even as it sought to broaden the two countries' business ties.[7]

In determining his policy towards China, President Clinton had to take into account the many types of interactions between China and the United States, and the impacts they have on other nations. He needed to consider as well the different points of view regarding those actions, and the different ways that they would affect the individuals, the two nations, and the international system. He had to weigh historical factors and consider deep cultural differences. The *New York Times* explained that

> At the earlier press conference, Jiang, 71, told a global television audience that a country of 1.2 billion could not progress toward economic reform and renewal without "social and political stability."
> "The concepts of democracy, of human rights and of freedoms are relative and specific ones, and they are to be determined by the specific national situation of different countries," Jiang said.

He offered no apologies for the brutal suppression of pro-democracy demonstrators in Tiananmen Square in 1989 or for his country's continued jailing of dissidents today. And he warned Clinton against interfering in China's internal affairs.

Clinton, responding to Jiang in a moment of drama that defined the distance between the United States and China on the fundamental question of human rights, declared the Chinese government to be "on the wrong side of history" in its response to the Tiananmen demonstrations and in its approach to personal liberties.

"I believe that what happened and the aftermath and the continuing reluctance to tolerate political dissent has kept China from politically developing the level of support in the rest of the world that otherwise would have been developed," Clinton said.[8]

In the end, President Clinton chose to extend MFN trade privileges to China, satisfying some economic and political interests, despite China's overall lack of progress on human rights, a temporary resolution to an issue that must be addressed each year under current federal law. The tension between what is in the interest of the economy (free trade) and what is in the broader national interest (a historical commitment to individual human rights), however, is in some respects fundamental. When an international issue is complex or important enough that it cannot be adequately understood as a simple matter of economics or politics or philosophy or sociology, it falls into the class of questions that are studied by the emerging discipline of *International Political Economy (IPE).*

Sometimes international political economy makes the front page, as it did here, but it is *always* in the news. We live in a rapidly changing world, where everyday concerns are increasingly global. As interdependence grows, economic issues are increasingly political in their nature and impact, and political issues are increasingly economic.

THE IPE APPROACH TO INTERNATIONAL ISSUES

The issue of China's MFN is typically IPE in its nature, since this issue deals with U.S. government policies that affect both commerce and social values in the United States and China. IPE is a social science that focuses on the set of problems, issues, and events where I, P, and E intersect, connect, or overlap, creating a rich pattern of interactions. In today's world, this is a growing and increasingly fascinating set of questions to study.

The IPE approach to social science is to synthesize methods and insights derived from economics, political science, and sociology as conditioned by an understanding of history and philosophy and an appreciation of the importance of culture. This synthesis is made necessary in part because of the tendency of the separate academic disciplines to focus on only certain elements of complex problems and, in part, on the tendency of interdependent real-world issues to expand beyond any particular set of intellectual boundaries.

The academic division of labor, where scholars focus on a narrow range of methods and issues, allows for intellectual specialization and the efficiency that goes with it, but it also promotes a sort of blindness that comes from staring too long at just one side of a multidimensional problem. IPE tries to take the methods and insights from the separate disciplines and pull them together into a more comprehensive analysis.

The U.S.-China dispute over MFN and human rights provides a good example of the relationship between IPE and the academic disciplines. Here is a short list of the ways that different academic disciplines might address the U.S.-China debate, each focusing on a particular element of this complex issue.

- *Microeconomics.* A microeconomist would think about how trade policy affects the decisions made by individual consumers, producers, and investors and how those choices would affect various markets. She might consider the individual winners and losers that would be created by granting permanent MFN status to China and attempt to calculate the welfare gains that would be caused by the increased efficiency of production and trade.
- *Macroeconomics.* A macroeconomist would think about the overall economic effects of MFN on the nation and its trading partner nations. He might speculate about the impact of MFN policy on the balance of trade between the United States and China and how this would affect production, income, and growth rates in the two countries. Changes in trade with China would also affect other nations, such as Japan and Thailand, which a macroeconomist would want to understand.
- *U.S. politics.* A U.S. politics specialist would think in terms of how domestic politics influences international politics and vice versa. She might consider how different special interest groups such as labor unions, banking associations, and multinational corporations might be affected by the MFN decision and then attempt to trace their political influence on the actions of the president and the congress.
- *Comparative Politics.* A comparative political scientist would be interested in how this case relates to similar political actions involving other countries. The U.S. policy of linking MFN to human rights, for example, can be considered an *economic sanction* designed to punish nations that do not abide by U.S. human rights policies by denying them preferential access to U.S. markets. Comparative politics would consider what makes this example of economic sanctions similar to or different from the sanctions that have been applied by the United States to Cuba in the years it has had a communist government and those that were applied to South Africa while its government supported a policy of apartheid. The South African sanctions were relatively effective because they enjoyed broad support among other major trading nations. Cuban sanctions, like those that might be applied to China, have done little to alter domestic politics in the target nation because of the lack of international solidarity on this issue.
- *International Relations.* Political scientists often consider that politics takes place at three levels: the level of the individual, the level of the state, and the level of the international system. Political scientists who specialize in international relations focus on nation-states and the nature of their interdependent relations with each other as conditioned by the nature of the international system. In international relations you might consider how MFN and human rights affect the security of the United States and China. The United States, for example, might seek to increase its national security by encouraging the growth of democratic movements within China, which would require the current Chinese government to liberalize its human rights policies. Such a policy would make sense in international relations if it is thought that a Chinese democracy would pose less of a threat to U.S. national interests than the current authoritarian Chinese government.
- *International Organizations.* A specialist in the study of international organizations might note that the political and economic interactions between the United States and China take place in a complex environment where there are many other actors.

There are international organizations such as the World Trade Organization that enter into this problem as well as a variety of *Nongovernmental Organizations (NGO)* that influence the two national governments and condition the environment in which their discussions take place.

- *Political Theory.* The focus for a political theorist might be on the philosophical foundations of the governments involved in this issue. The United States is based on the Jeffersonian principles of democracy and the individual. China's government is based on the political principles of Lenin and Mao. In both cases these principles have been modified in pragmatic ways over the years. The actions and reactions of these governments should reflect the principles on which they are founded. The political interaction of the two nations is thus a confrontation of two sets of very different political and social values.

- *Sociology.* A sociologist would be concerned with how class relations enter into this debate. Would increased trade with China be in the interests of the U.S. working class, the *proletariat*? Or would it mainly benefit the capital-owning class of the *bourgeoisie*? Issues of race, ethnicity, and gender might also enter into the sociological analysis of this problem.

- *Anthropology.* An anthropologist might focus on the cultural differences between the United States and China and how culture contributes to this debate. The United States defines human rights as the rights of the individuals while China defines them as the rights of the group or society. An anthropologist might see this as a clash of cultures or cultural values, not nations or economies, and consider how cultural elements might be influenced by any political or economic "solution."

- *History.* A historian of China might point out that imperialist Western governments have a long history of attempting to influence Chinese policies—generally not with the interests of China at heart. The hard-line Chinese reaction to U.S. MFN policy may be conditioned by these unpleasant historical experiences. A U.S. diplomatic historian, on the other hand, might ask us to look back to the original function of the MFN human rights policy—to try to force the communist USSR government to limit its repression of Soviet Jews—and how the relative success of this policy may have contributed to the eventual collapse of communism in the USSR.

Each of these different approaches is valid, but regarding issues as complex and important as U.S.-Chinese relations, not one of them by itself presents us with a comprehensive image of the actors, interests, and forces involved. An issue like this requires the IPE approach, where we attempt to draw together methods and insights from several different disciplinary perspectives and all three levels of analysis (individual, state, international system) in order to gain a comprehensive understanding of the issue. Put another way, an issue like this breaks down the artificial barriers that separate the academic disciplines and allows us to think about problems freed from the constraints that the academic division of labor imposes. IPE issues also break down the barriers that separate individual interests from those of the state and the international system.

The intellectual origins of IPE thus lie in problems and issues that break down arbitrary but traditional boundaries to intellectual inquiry and policy analysis. This makes IPE at once both very old and very new. It is very new because the necessity to pursue this sort of interdisciplinary, multilevel analysis has only recently been combined with institutional structures that systematically permit and encourage these activities—in the form of courses, majors, and graduate programs in IPE.

In another sense, however, IPE is very old. The division of the social sciences into distinct and separate disciplines is a phenomenon of the nineteenth and twentieth centuries. Before that time, it was not considered either wise or necessary to break knowledge into pieces for detailed study. The broad and encompassing study of social problems was given the name political economy. IPE today is the intellectual descendent of the borderless method of inquiry that began as political economy more than two centuries ago.

MULTIDIMENSIONAL INFORMATION ARBITRAGE

In his best-selling book about globalization, *The Lexus and the Olive Tree*, *New York Times* foreign affairs columnist Thomas L. Friedman explains how the demands of his job forced him to begin to think about the world in a broad and integrative way. What Friedman describes is the IPE way of thinking, although he never calls it that.[a]

In college Friedman studied Arabian and Middle East Studies, training that prepared him very well for his first assignment with the *New York Times* reporting on Arab-Israeli relations. As his career developed and his reporting "beat" expanded, however, he discovered that he needed to master new fields and learn how to explain them in clear and relatively simple ways. His work became more and more "multidimensional"—drawing on history, economics, politics, culture, environment, technology, and national security ideas.

Soon Friedman became skilled at what he calls "information arbitrage." In the world of finance, arbitrage is the practice of buying something in one market and selling it for more in another market—profiting from the ability to take advantage of differences in market prices in different places. Information arbitrage, as Friedman practices it, is the ability to profit from the use of concepts and theories from one academic field (say, history) to help explain forces or events in other areas (economics or politics).[b]

Multidimensional information arbitrage, Friedman writes, is

> . . . like putting on a new pair of glasses and suddenly looking at the world in 4-D. I saw news stories that I would never have recognized as news stories before. I saw causal chains of events that I never could have identified before. I saw invisible hands and handcuffs impeding leaders and nations from doing things that I never imagined before.[c]

It is a shame that Thomas Friedman invented such a cumbersome name—multidimensional information arbitrage—for this very useful and interesting way of thinking because a term already existed that captures exactly the essence of what he does: international political economy.

IPE is like Friedman's 4-D glasses, which reveal unexpected connections and make otherwise fuzzy relationships clear. Like any new pair of eyeglasses, IPE take a bit of getting used to, but once you are comfortable with it you will never be able to look at the world in the same way again.

---

[a]Thomas L. Friedman, *The Lexus and the Olive Tree: Understanding Globalization.* (New York: Farrar, Straus and Giroux, 1999).
[b]Ibid., pp. 17-18.
[c]Ibid., p. 17.

FUNDAMENTAL ELEMENTS OF IPE

IPE thus defines itself as the study of the problems and issues that require the interdisciplinary, multilevel IPE approach just discussed. This definition is correct, but it is also a bit vague. Perhaps the clearest definition of international political economy comes from Professor Susan Strange, who helped establish the modern study of IPE at the London School of Economics and Politics. Professor Strange has written that IPE

> . . . concerns the social, political, and economic arrangements affecting the global systems of production, exchange, and distribution and the mix of values reflected therein. Those arrangements are not divinely ordained, nor are they the fortuitous outcome of blind chance. Rather they are the result of human decisions taken in the context of man-made institutions and sets of self-set rules and customs.[9]

Several elements of this definition are worthy of note. This definition of IPE gives equal weight to social, political, and economic arrangements and stresses that IPE is not just the study of institutions or organizations, but also of the *values* they reflect. States and markets are connected by "global systems of production, exchange, and distribution," which this book terms the **structures** of the international political economy. IPE therefore looks at the ways that the individuals, states, and markets of the world are connected to one another and the arrangements or structures that have evolved to connect them. These arrangements reflect culture, history, and values. They change—and will continue to change in the future.

While Professor Strange's definition seems to focus narrowly on economic connections (production, exchange, and distribution), in fact these terms have much broader intent and meaning. While it is true that goods and services get produced, exchanged, and distributed, this is also true about other aspects of life, such as power, security, culture, and status. The production, exchange, and distribution of motion pictures, for example, is at once an economic enterprise and a cultural one that affects the values that people hold and the nature of social and political relations within and between nation-states. (Some nations limit access to foreign movies and television shows, for example, because they fear the influence of foreign ideas and images.) When the U.S. government wanted to try to weaken political support for the communist government of the USSR during the Cold War, it began by sending jazz musicians to Moscow. American jazz was intended to create the image of the United States as a free, creative, multiracial society and therefore to display to the Soviet people an image of American values that was distinctly different from the official Soviet party line.

The arrangements that IPE studies are the arrangements of lives, and the social, political, and economic institutions that condition those lives, with particular emphasis on their global character. Some persons, like some nations, are wealthier than others, are more powerful than others, or have higher status or greater authority than others. These conditions are in part the result of the global structures or arrangements that produce, exchange, and distribute social, political, and economic resources. These IPE structures provide a useful framework for the analysis of IPE problems.

Much of the study of IPE focuses on the interaction of two highly important social institutions, states and markets, and on the nature of their interaction within the international system (the international "rules of the game"). Robert Gilpin, for example, has defined political economy as "the field of study that analyzes the problems and questions arising from the parallel existence and dynamic interaction of 'state' and 'market' in the modern world."[10]

The state is the realm of collective action and decision. By *state* we usually mean the political institutions of the modern nation-state, a geographic region with a relatively coherent and autonomous system of government that extends over that region. The nation-state is a legal entity that has a well-defined territory and population, with a government capable of exercising sovereignty. France, for example, means the territory of France, the people of France, and the government of France and its policies, depending on context. We should, however, also consider the state more broadly, as the domain of collective or political behavior that takes place at many levels. The European Union (EU), for example, is not a nation-state; it is an organization of nation-states. Yet to the extent the EU makes choices or policies that affect the entire group of nations and their citizens, it demonstrates the properties of a state.

The market is the realm of individual actions and decisions. By *market* we usually mean the economic institutions of modern capitalism. The market is the sphere of human action dominated by individual self-interest and conditioned by the forces of competition. Although a market is sometimes a geographical location (such as the New York Stock Exchange or the Pike Place Market in Seattle), it is more often a *force*. That is, the force of the market motivates and conditions individual human behavior. Individuals are driven by the motive of self-interest, for example, to produce and supply scarce goods and services or to seek out bargain products or high-wage jobs. They are driven by the market force of competition to make products better, or cheaper, or more attractive.

We define political economy this way, knowing that states and markets are complicated systems of social organization. Society contains both state and market elements, which reflect the history, culture, and values of their social systems.

The parallel existence of states (politics) and markets (economics) creates a fundamental tension that characterizes political economy. States and markets do not always conflict, but they do overlap to such a degree that their fundamental tension is apparent. The tensions created by their differing interests or values can be resolved in different ways at different times, but the underlying conflicts remain and reappear throughout human history. The interaction of states and markets is *dynamic*, which means it changes over time. In particular, states influence markets and markets influence states, constantly changing the pattern of interests and values that political economists study.

WEALTH AND POWER: THE TENSION BETWEEN STATES AND MARKETS

What is the nature of the interaction between states and markets? Why do their parallel existence and dynamic interaction often create tensions? Where are the boundary lines drawn? States and markets embrace different basic values. They work in different ways to achieve different ends. They necessarily intersect and overlap, creating the subject we will study here.

Economists like to say that markets "allocate and distribute scarce resources." Markets are a highly decentralized and individualistic way to decide how scarce resources are used (allocation) and who gets them (distribution). Markets let the "invisible hand" of individual action make resource decisions. Decisions that affect resource use influence the creation of wealth and its distribution both within nations and among nations. There are ways other than markets of making choices about scarce resources. In "command economies," like the Soviet Union before 1989, allocation and distribution choices were made mainly by the state, based on the government's notion of national interest. In "mixed economies" such as the United States, markets make a great many resource decisions, but not all of them.

Political scientists often say that states "allocate and distribute power." Power is the ability to affect or determine outcomes. Hans Morgenthau defined power as the ability to control the minds and actions of others.[11] In its sphere of influence, a state may be said to be in the business of choosing where the power of collective action is used (allocation) and who gets to use it (distribution). Elections are all about the allocation and distribution of power. Elections are one way the state determines who has power and how it is used.

Since the exercise of power generally affects the allocation and distribution of resources, politics (power) and economics (wealth) are thoroughly intertwined. States and markets interact because the boundary between what happens to wealth (the sphere of the market) and what happens to power (the sphere of the state) is sometimes ambiguous and constantly shifting. People who can command resources in our society have power, so the market necessarily influences actions of the state. People who command power in our society can influence how and where resources go. A strict distinction between states and markets is therefore really arbitrary and artificial. If markets are yellow and states are blue, then most of the world is made up of the various shades of green that reflect the many degrees of relative influence of state and market forces. And, of course, the precise color depends upon the social and historical context.

When states and markets have similar goals or are driven by similar interests and values, their interactions tend to be relatively uncontroversial. It is more typically the case, however, that the motives of states and markets differ. Markets typically reflect the values and interests of the individuals that comprise them. Both buyers and sellers are typically self-interested; they take actions that they perceive will make them better off. Thus, workers try to negotiate the highest wages they can, subject to working conditions and other factors, in order to increase their command of scarce resources (food, clothing, housing, education, etc.). In the same way, employers find it in their interest to pay the lowest wages they can, subject to other concerns such as worker loyalty and workforce stability, so as to increase their profits and thus their own ability to command scarce resources. The outcome of the market reflects whatever compromise is reached between the often-opposing individual interests.

States also reflect social values, but in a very different way. In a market, an individual's voice is heard loudly or softly or not at all based on the value of the resources that person commands. The state engages in collective action—its laws, wars, and rules affect everyone—while the market is based on individual actions. How well the collective choices of the state reflect the general will and public interest depends on a large number of factors, such as voting rights, representation rules, and the nature of political institutions in a country. In the United States, for example, we employ an extremely complicated system of public choice, with a great many elected and appointed executive and legislative officials, deliberative bodies, and administrative agencies.

One problem with markets that is often noted is that no one negotiates with the public interest in mind.[12] That is, in the process of satisfying individual interests, the market may allocate and distribute resources (and therefore power) in ways that are not in the general interest of the population or different from the way the state would make these choices. In fact, states can sometimes be manipulated by a small group of "elites" or by the economic forces of special interests. Public interest can be sacrificed on the altar of narrow private interest.

A value that markets strongly hold is efficiency, the ability to use and distribute resources (and hence power) effectively and with little waste. The motivation of private self-interested action and the economy of decentralized decision making tend to promote efficiency. A value that states strongly hold is fairness (variously termed *equity* or *equality*) and state power is often used to promote fairness. Relations between and among individuals can be unfair or unequal if the power that individuals can exercise (either through states or markets) is unequally distributed.[13]

One value that both states and markets strongly hold is security. Security from fear or threat is a basic human need that we have both as individuals and collectively. Sometimes the need for security drives states and markets in the same direction. At other times, however, these two spheres conflict. Farmers in both the United States and in the European Union desire greater economic security, for example, and so demand subsidy payments from their governments. These subsidies, however, create problems on international food markets, which bring the states into conflict with one another, lessening security on this level.

To summarize, states and markets embody different *values* (such as efficiency versus fairness), they employ different *means* (decentralized markets and voluntary bargains versus collective action and force) and they therefore have different *goals*. It is unsurprising, therefore, that tension exists along the fault lines between states and markets. The controversy over human rights in China and the granting of MFN status to Chinese goods is just one example of the way that the pressure between differences in values and means contributes to the tensions that define IPE.

THE DYNAMIC NATURE OF STATE-MARKET INTERACTION

What makes IPE an especially interesting field of study is the dynamic nature of the interaction of states and markets. People live simultaneously in both states and markets, confronting at once the multiple constraints of wealth and power. It is not surprising, therefore, that change in one sphere of existence evokes change in the other. This dynamic interaction means that IPE is always in a state of transition. Cycles of change are transposed upon evolutionary paths. There is always something familiar, and always something new.

Changes in the state's domain—power—necessarily affects the individuals in the economy. In South Africa, for example, the decision to abandon apartheid and to increase the power of blacks in government rule necessarily also impacts the status of black people in the market. Their ability to command resources, earn incomes, and accumulate wealth will surely change as their political power increases. It may be some years before the full outline of the consequences of these interactions is clear.

Likewise, changes in the market's domain—wealth—necessarily affect the allocation and distribution of state power. In China, for example, changes in the economy have helped galvanize forces for political change in the state. In an attempt to improve the living standards of their people, Chinese leaders have introduced free market forces into some areas of China's economy. Free markets, profits, and private enterprise are seen as a way to speed growth.

The rise of self-interest in the market, however, has created problems for China's state. Individuals who follow the beacon of self-interest in the market may be less willing to be guided by the light of social interest as revealed through state policies. The 1989 Tianamen Square confrontation between state forces and members of the democracy movement in China illustrates vividly the tensions that exist between these changes in the two spheres of life. This fault line between individual interest and state power is seen as well in the most favored nation issue with which this chapter began.

DIMENSIONS OF INTERNATIONAL POLITICAL ECONOMY

The international political economy is a network of bargains between and among states and markets. These bargains determine the production, exchange, and distribution of wealth and power. Bargains can take many forms. Some are formal agreements, signed, ratified, and enforced. Other bargains are merely conventions, understandings, or rules of thumb. These bargains tend to be far less formal, but just as important.[14]

Perhaps the most important thing, however, about the bargains we study in IPE is that they are multidimensional. That is, they defy any attempt to oversimplify them—to make them simple one-dimensional issues. We have already seen in the U.S.-China case study the way that an economic issue (free trade) becomes a political problem (the need to set a U.S. policy and to deal with domestic and international politics) due to fundamental social and cultural differences (individual versus collective definitions of human rights). We hope you can see that treating this issue in one-dimensional fashion—as just a political problem or just an economic issue or just a social difference—would be a fundamental error.

One way to approach IPE, in fact, is to think about the different dimensions that important complex international problems exhibit in the same way that we think about the size, shape, color, and texture of multidimensional physical objects. This provides us with both a vocabulary to use in describing international issues and a set of analytical tools to increase our understanding of them. The most important dimensions of IPE, as we will discuss them in this textbook, are

- Three *levels of analysis*: individual, state, and international system.
- Two *types of power*: relational power and structural power.
- Four international power *structures*: security, production, finance, and knowledge.
- Three *perspectives*, which are different ways of looking at the IPE based on different systems of values or beliefs: realism or mercantilism, liberalism, and structuralism (or Marxism).

Three Levels of Analysis

Most significant IPE problems involve all three levels of analysis—individual, state, and international system—and it is often useful to think clearly about how each level is involved. In Kenneth Waltz's famous book on the causes of war, *Man, the State, and War*, for example, he determined that international conflict was sometimes caused by conflictual human nature (individual level), sometimes by aggressive national governments (state level), and sometimes by a risky and unstable international power figuration (international system level).[15] The power of Waltz's three-level analysis of war is that it forces us to think about the different causes of different conflicts and about how and why people can agree about the danger of war and yet disagree about how to deal with it.

When we approach IPE issues, it is generally a good idea to consider each of the three levels of analysis, bearing in mind that there are many different actors at each level. The U.S.-China case study, for example, illustrates how the system of international trade links the human rights policies of the state with the economic interests of individuals in different countries. The tensions and conflicts between the United States and China could be resolved by changing the U.S. laws that define the trading system (to "de-link" trade and human rights), by changing China's state policies regarding human rights, or by altering the pattern of individual economic transactions between the two countries. In IPE we are especially concerned about the three levels of analysis because IPE issues tend to break down the barriers that separate the levels. Inevitably, however, policies adopted at one level have impacts on the other levels of analysis.

Two Types of Power

If we think of IPE as a complex set of bargains, then we must recognize that bargains are negotiated and negotiations often involve the use of power, so we must consider the configuration of power in international affairs. Some IPE bargains reflect what Professor Strange calls ***relational power***, which is the power of one player to get another player to do something (or not do it). This is power as most of us normally think of it, especially when we think about sports like football, soccer, or chess. Relational power exists in its most potent forms at the individual and state levels of analysis.

Increasingly, however, what is important in IPE according to Professor Strange, is *structural power,* which she defines as "the power to shape and determine the *structures* of the global political economy within which other states, their political institutions, their economic enterprises and (not least) their scientists and other professional people have to operate."[16] Structural power is thus the ability to shape or condition the system level of analysis. In a sport stuctural power would be the power to affect the rules, the choice of playing field, or the way that players can be deployed.

Structural power is less direct than relational power, but it can be even more effective in some situations. Many IPE authors have observed, for example, that while the United States no longer has such a dramatic edge in relational power in the world today as it did in the early post-World War II years, it is still the leader of the industrial democracy nations and has lots of structural power at its command.

In the U.S.-China case study, for example, both countries have enormous amounts of relational power in the form of "sticks" to punish and "carrots" to persuade. Both the United States and China have *hard power* sticks in the form of large military forces and dangerous weapons. Both have *soft power* carrots, too, such as attractive market opportunities and valuable natural or technological resources. Much of the focus of the U.S.-China debate is on how each country mobilizes its hard and soft power resources to gain an advantage in bargaining relations.

But the United States has an advantage in terms of structural power in bargaining with China. The United States is well positioned to influence China's place in the international system through its influence within the World Trade Organization, the World Bank, and the International Monetary Fund, to give just three examples of international institutions that will be discussed later in this book. Structural power can supplement or be a substitute for relational power. In the delicate negotiations between superpowers such as the United States and China, structural power may be more effective than relational power simply because it is less confrontational and therefore is less likely to produce retaliation than the direct use of relational power. The existence of two different forms of power makes IPE more complex and more interesting.

Four Global Structures

The institutions, arrangements, and the "rules of the game" that govern the behavior of states and markets in the international political economy can be analyzed as four power structures, which together produce, exchange, and distribute wealth and power.[17] It is useful to think of these power structures as networks, bargains, or linkages that connect individuals and states and form international systems, and through which relational and structural power are exercised. In a way, you are tied to every other person on earth through the complex interaction of these four power structures.

The Security Structure. Security—from natural forces or, more important, from the threats and actions of others—is perhaps the most basic human need. When one person or group provides security for another (or contributes to that security), a security structure is created. The nature of this security structure depends on the kind of bargain that is struck among its participants. The security structure has been an important defining force in IPE in the twentieth century. The nature of a nation's production, finance, and knowledge of structural relationships during the Cold War depended critically on its status as a member of either the Soviet bloc (the Warsaw Pact nations and their allies), the U.S.-centered NATO bloc, or the group of nonaligned states.

The nature of the security structure was a contributing factor in the debate over China's MFN status in 1997. Sometimes China has been thought of as a threat to U.S. security interests; at other times it has been seen as a part of a trilateral balance of power along with the United States and the Soviet Union. Until the late 1970s, all trade with China was forbidden for national security reasons. Although the ban on China trade is gone, it is clear that fear, uncertainty, and doubt remain regarding what threat, if any, China represents to the United States. This security question tempers to some degree relations between the United States and China in all areas.

The Production Structure. "A production structure can be defined as the sum of all arrangements determining what is produced, by whom and for whom, by what methods and on what terms. It is people at work, and the wealth they produce by working."[18] Production is the act of creating value and wealth, and wealth is nearly always linked to power. The issue of who produces what for whom on what terms, therefore, lies at the heart of international political economy. Recent decades have seen dramatic changes in the production structure, with production of certain high-value items such as automobiles shifting from the United States to Japan and now to other countries, such as Korea, Mexico, Brazil—and possibly China. These structural changes affect the distribution of wealth and power in the world and, therefore, impact the other structures of IPE.

The Finance Structure. The finance structure is perhaps the most abstract set of linkages between and among nations. One way to describe the finance structure is to say that it is the pattern of money flows between and among nations. That is, this structure defines who has access to money, how, and on what terms. This definition's simplicity covers up two important points. First, we are not really interested in money so much as in what money can buy—scarce resources. So the finance structure is really a description of how certain resources are allocated and distributed between and among nations. In this respect, money is a means, not an end.

Second, we are at this point mostly interested in money to the extent that it creates an obligation between people or states. This occurs in several ways. For example, sometimes money moves from one nation to another in the form of loans, which must be repaid. At other times the money movement is in the form of direct investment, where a foreigner gains control directly over the use of resources by, say, purchasing a factory or a farm. Financial bargains create obligations, which join the interests of different nations. The nature of these obligations, and their effects, are important elements of IPE.

The Knowledge Structure. It is often said that knowledge is power. Knowledge is wealth, too, for those who can use it effectively. Who has knowledge and how it is used is therefore an important factor in IPE. Nations with poor access to knowledge in the form of industrial technology, scientific discoveries, medical procedures, or instant communications, for example, find themselves at a disadvantage relative to others. Increasingly in the world today, the bargains made in the security, production, and finance structure depend on access to knowledge in its several forms.

It may be difficult to overestimate the importance of the knowledge structure in the world today. Indeed, Robert Reich has written an influential book that envisions the future as a world where wealth and power are determined more by knowledge than by any other single factor.[19] One reason China desired MFN status in 1997 was that it hoped that increased economic interaction with the United States would give it greater access to industrial technology.Technology determines in large measure a nation's place in the production structure. To move up in the international division of labor, China needed to accelerate its acquisition of science, technology, and know-how from abroad.

Taken together, these four IPE power structures form the international system within which the interdependent relations of individuals and states occur. The international system is therefore a set of bargains and relationships—human arrangements—that condition how states and individuals behave and determine in part the mix of values that results from their dynamic interaction.

Three Perspectives and Three Sets of Values

Finally, there are a variety of theories that attempt to describe how states and nations should interact (normative theories that reflect a particular set of values) or how they really do behave (positive theories). These theories are like lenses that we can use to view and interpret the international political economy. They are also important in the history of IPE. Indeed, in many respects the history of international relations is a competition for dominance among opposing IPE theoretical perspectives and the values and beliefs that they represent.

The theories of IPE are not just abstract academic scribblings; they guide the thoughts and actions of men and women in all sorts of ways and so shape and condition the world. If we want to understand how people think about and behave within the spheres that define IPE, we must understand these theories.

Different people give different names to the main IPE theories, a problem that results from the "wide open spaces" that are also the strength of IPE. The three main IPE theories are often broadly termed:

- *Mercantilism,* or economic nationalism, which looks at IPE issues mainly in terms of national interest. Mercantilism is the IPE perspective that is most closely associated with political science, especially the political philosophy of *realism.*
- *Liberalism,* or economic liberalism, which looks at IPE issues mainly in terms of individual interests. Liberalism is most closely associated with the system of markets that are the study of economists.

- *Structuralism,* or *Marxism* or Marx-Leninism, which looks at IPE issues mainly in terms of class interests. Structuralism is most closely associated with the methods of analysis employed by many sociologists.

It would be a mistake to try to summarize or simplify these perspectives here, so the next three chapters will examine them in historical terms. Also, we will explore their development and their relationship to one another. These theories are important because they provide us with a frame of reference as we try to understand IPE and reconcile its many dimensions.

It is useful, in fact, to think of these IPE theories as "points of view" or "perspectives" because they are really exactly that. All IPE theories look at the same world of international problems, issues, and events. But each approaches it from a different angle with a different set of core beliefs and values, and so sees the multidimensional form in a different light. Each viewpoint reveals some aspects particularly well but may cast a shadow on other important points.

While many authors approach IPE from a single point of view that they feel is most revealing or useful for the problems they want to consider, this book takes a firm multidimensional stand. Most IPE problems, like most aspects of human existence, can be understood best if a variety of viewpoints are considered, not just one, reducing the chance of overlooking some important aspect. It is often true, however, that a given situation can be most revealingly understood from a particular perspective. Thus, while we encourage the consideration of many perspectives, we emphasize the right and obligation of individuals to make their own judgments about which view (or combination of perspectives) is best.

IPE IN THE BORDERLESS WORLD

The world we live in is changing very rapidly—this is so obvious that it hardly needs saying, yet it is important to say nonetheless because it is best reason to read the rest of this book. One aspect of this change goes by the name of globalization. It is commonplace to read that we now live in a "borderless world" where economic, social, and political forces increasingly act at the system level of analysis, far above and beyond the control of states and individuals. The sense that globalization is a driving force in the political economy today has spawned a raft of books such as *The Global Age, Market Unbound: Unleashing Global Capitalism, Globalization in Question, Has Globalization Gone Too Far?* and *Selling Globalization: The Myth of the Global Economy.*[20]

Globalization is very controversial. Optimists see globalization as the death of distance as a barrier to human interaction and the birth of a new, more efficient, more prosperous, more peaceful world order. Pessimists see globalization as the end of the state, the end of democracy, and the end of culture. For the pessimists, globalization replaces today's multicultural civilization with the civilization of the market—the brutal law of the jungle.

We think that globalization is neither so virtuous as the optimists hope nor so dangerous as the pessimists fear. The many sides of the globalization debate will appear throughout this text and, in the end, it will be up to you, the reader, to make up your own mind.

Of one thing we are sure, however. The various and multiple forces that comprise globalization are breaking down the traditional ways we understand international and global events. What will emerge from this process of creative destruction will be a new world order that we cannot yet see clearly and a way of thinking about it, which we call international political economy.

DISCUSSION QUESTIONS

1. Define the terms "state" and "market" and give examples of "state actions" and "market actions." Is the line between state and market clean and clear, or is it sometimes hard to determine? What is the relationship between politics and the state and economics and the market?
2. International political economy is sometimes defined as the set of questions and issues arising from the parallel existence and dynamic interaction of states and markets. Find an example of a current event that should properly be considered part of IPE (newspapers and newsmagazines are good sources for this information). How do state-market tensions and interactions figure in these events?
3. How do states and markets differ in their values and goals and the means with which they seek to achieve their goals? Discuss this question both in general and with respect to the current event topic in question 2.
4. What are the three levels of analysis used in international relations (and in IPE)? Use the U.S.-China issue to provide examples of potential impacts of MFN policy at all three levels of analysis.
5. How does the U.S.-China MFN issue illustrate the concepts presented in this chapter? Identify state and market interests, the tension between economics and politics, and the dynamic interaction of states and markets in this example. Which force seems to be stronger in this case: state or market? How is an understanding of history and culture useful in understanding this issue?

INTERNET LINKS

Each chapter of this textbook will include several suggested links to sites on the World Wide Web that can provide current information or greater depth for the interested reader. Internet addresses change frequently, however, so do not be discouraged if some of the addresses you find here are "broken" when you try them. An up-to-date set of Internet links as well as many other useful and interesting items can be found at the Internet home page for this textbook:

http://www.ups.edu/ipe/ipebook.htm

Home page for *The Lexus and the Olive Tree* by Thomas Friedman:

http://www.lexusandtheolivetree.com/

The IPE Network (sponsored by the IPE section of the International Studies Association):

http://csf.colorado.edu/ipe/

SUGGESTED READINGS

Kenneth E. Boulding. "Is Economics Necessary?" and "The Relations of Economic, Political, and Social Systems," in *Beyond Economics: Essays on Society, Religion and Ethics.* Ann Arbor: University of Michigan Press, 1970.

Michael W. Doyle. *Ways of War and Peace.* New York: W.W. Norton, 1998.

Milton Friedman. Especially chap. 1 in *Capitalism and Freedom.* Chicago: University of Chicago Press, 1982.

Thomas L. Friedman. *The Lexus and the Olive Tree: Understanding Globalization.* New York: Farrar, Straus and Giroux, 1999.

Robert Gilpin. Especially chap. 1 in *The Political Economy of International Relations.* Princeton, NJ: Princeton University Press, 1987.

Martin Staniland. *What is Political Economy? A Study of Social Theory and Underdevelopment.* New Haven, CT: Yale University Press, 1985.

Susan Strange. *States and Markets: An Introduction to International Political Economy.* New York: Basil Blackwell, 1988.

Kenneth N. Waltz. *Man, the State, and War: A Theoretical Analysis.* New York: Columbia University Press, 1959.

NOTES

1. Susan Strange, ed., *Paths to International Political Economy* (London: George Allen & Unwin, 1984), p. ix.
2. Rowland Maddock, "The Global Political Economy," in John Bayless and N. J. Rengger, eds., *Dilemmas of World Politics* (New York: Oxford University Press, 1992), p. 108.
3. More and more colleges and universities are now giving undergraduate students the opportunity to study IPE, either as special courses or as an academic major. IPE has also become an important area of graduate education. A gateway to the world of IPE on the internet can be found at http://www.ups.edu/ipe/
4. John M. Broder, "U.S. and China Reach Trade Pacts but Clash on Rights," *New York Times*, 30 October 1994, p. 1.
5. The use of the term *Normal Trade Relations (NTR)* is relatively recent and so far confined to some government statements in the United States, so we continue to use the more widely known term *Most Favored Nation (MFN)*. The switch in terminology may be an attempt to influence the debate about U.S.-China trade by changing the terms of discourse that both describe and color that debate.
6. Although the U.S. law regarding MFN is specifically framed in terms of human rights—a moral or ethical issue—there is another state value that is indirectly linked to it: national security. At least some of the drafters of the legislation probably believed that any nation that has a very different view of individual rights from the United States (such as the USSR in the 1960s or China in the 1990s) represents a potential threat to U.S. national security.
7. Broder, "U.S. and China."
8. Ibid.
9. Susan Strange, *States and Markets: An Introduction to International Political Economy* (New York: Basil Blackwell, 1988), p. 18.
10. This is the definition used by Robert Gilpin in his influential book, *The Political Economy of International Relations* (Princeton, NJ: Princeton University Press, 1987), p. 8.
11. Cited in Charles P. Kindleberger, *Power and Money* (New York: Basic Books, 1970), p. 55.
12. As we will see later, the public interest may be represented through the force of the market's "invisible hand." Economic liberals believe that, in a wide range of situations, the compromise that is reached in the market between opposing self-interests is ultimately also a reflection of the public interest.

13. These are not the only values that states and markets may hold, as will be discussed later. It is also true that markets value efficiency and states value fairness to much different degrees, at different times and different places.

14. The Cold War was a period when the United States and the USSR behaved according to a highly unstable "bargain"—not to launch an unprovoked "first-strike" nuclear attack. In the 1960s and 1970s, this agreement was backed only by the reality of "Mutually Assured Destruction" (MAD). Only in recent years have formal agreements started to replace the balance of terror as the organizing principle of nuclear weapons policy.

15. Kenneth N. Waltz, *Man, the State, and War: A Theoretical Analysis.* (New York: Columbia University Press, 1959). Waltz wrote about three "images" rather than three "levels" and both terms are used in discussions of this concept. We use the "levels of analysis" language only because it seems a bit more intuitive.

16. See Strange, *States and Markets*, pp. 24–25

17. Ibid., ch. 3–6.

18. Ibid., p. 62.

19. Robert B. Reich, *The Work of Nations* (New York: Alfred A. Knopf, 1991).

20. Martin Albrow, *The Global Age* (Stanford, CA: Stanford University Press, 1996); Lowell Bryan and Diana Farrell, *Market Unbound: Unleashing Global Capitalism* (New York: John Wiley, 1996); Dani Rodrik, *Has Globalization Gone Too Far?* (Washington DC: Institute for International Economics, 1997); Paul Hirst and Grahame Thompson, *Globalization in Question* (Cambridge: Polity Press, 1996); Michael Veseth, *Selling Globalization: The Myth of the Global Economy* (Boulder CO: Lynne Rienner, 1998).

2

Wealth and Power: Mercantilism and Economic Nationalism

OVERVIEW

Mercantilism is the oldest and from an historical standpoint perhaps the most important IPE theoretical perspective. The central focus of mercantilism is the problem of security and the role of the state and the market in providing and maintaining a nation's security in all its forms. This chapter begins by examining the three sides of mercantilism: mercantilism as a period in world history, as a political philosophy or worldview that arose during that period, and as a set of state policies and actions that derive from that philosophy.

Mercantilism has changed over the years as the economy and the nature of the problem of national security have changed and as the tools that can be used to achieve security have changed, too. This chapter therefore traces the history of mercantilist thought from its origins as classical mercantilism, to its development as economic nationalism, to its several forms of "neomercantilism" today.

As you read about mercantilism in its various flavors and colors, try to keep clear in your mind how and why the various forms of mercantilism differ and what there is about them that make them elements of a single IPE perspective.

Anglo-American theory instructs Westerners that economics is by nature a "positive sum game" from which all can emerge as winners. Asian history instructs many Koreans, Chinese, Japanese, and others that economic competition is a form of war in which some win and others lose. To be strong is much better than to be weak; to give orders is better than to take them. By this logic, the way to be strong, to give orders, to have independence and control, is to keep in mind the difference between "us" and "them." This perspective comes naturally to Koreans (when thinking about Japan), or Canadians (when thinking about the United States), or Britons (when thinking, even today, about Germany), or to Chinese or Japanese (when thinking about what the Europeans did to their nations).[1]

James Fallows (1994)

Our economic rights are leaking away . . . If we want to recover these rights . . . we must quickly employ state power to promote industry, use machinery in production, give employment to the workers of the nation . . .[2]

Sun Yat-Sen (1920)

Mercantilism is a theoretical perspective that accounts for one of the basic compulsions of all nation-states: to create wealth and power in order to preserve and protect their national security and independence. Wherever you find a concern about foreign threats to security—whether military, economic, or cultural—you will find evidence of mercantilist thought.

Typically, mercantilism is defined somewhat narrowly in terms of state efforts to promote exports and limit imports, thereby generating trade surpluses to create wealth and power.[3] In IPE, we like to think of mercantilism in somewhat broader terms, as a theoretical perspective that puts security at the center of national concerns. A nation's security can be threatened in many ways: by foreign armies, foreign firms and their products, foreign influence over international laws and institutions, and even by foreign movies, magazines, and television shows, which may weaken a nation's social and cultural cohesion.[4]

MERCANTILISM AS HISTORY, PHILOSOPHY, AND STATE POLICY

The term *mercantilism* tends to be used in three different ways in IPE discourse. Sometimes it refers to a period of history. Sometimes it denotes a theoretical perspective or philosophy of political economy. Most often the term is applied to a set of state policies and actions that aim to secure and maintain a nation's security and independence, especially with respect to its economy. We will survey these three sides of mercantilism and then move on to an examination of the ways that mercantilist thought and action have evolved and adapted over time.

The mercantilist period of history is inextricably linked to the rise of the modern nation-state in Europe during the fifteenth through eighteenth centuries.[5] This was a period associated with the idea of state building and intervention in the economy for the sake of security of the nation-state. A *nation* is a collection of people who on the basis of ethnic background, language, and history, or some other set of factors define themselves as members of an extended political community.[6] The **state** is a legal entity, theoretically free of external interference, that monopolizes the means of physical force in society and that exercises *sovereignty* (final political authority) over the population of a well-defined territory.[7]

The new nation-states had many needs that could be secured either through violent or peaceful means. The threat of war and violence was always real, as the history of European wars in this period makes clear. Security became the "number one job" for the state, since it was useless to achieve prosperity, justice, or domestic peace if all of this could be torn apart by foreign invaders. Security was expensive, however. Armies and navies were expensive to raise, equip, and maintain. The key to power, it became clear, was wealth. And the key to maintaining wealth was the power to keep it secure. Thus was born the political philosophy of mercantilism.

Wealth and power are intertwined in mercantilism. They can form a *virtuous* cycle, where power creates wealth, which increases power, which in turn increases wealth, thus making a nation secure and prosperous. But wealth and power can also form a *vicious* cycle. Inadequate power means loss of wealth to other states. The poorer the nation is, the weaker and more vulnerable. This vicious cycle of weakness and poverty, if left unaddressed by mercantilist action, proceeds to a situation as disastrous as the virtuous cycle is successful. Which would *you* choose: wealth, power, and security? Or poverty, fear, and subjugation?

Early European states followed mercantilist policies that sought to produce ¹⁺ʰ through trade, by promoting exports and limiting imports. The German

Becher said "that it is always better to sell goods to others
m others, for the former brings a certain advantage and the
age."[8] Trade surpluses, then, earned wealth and power, but
edly weakened a state—politically and economically.

nds were used to encourage the production of goods for
e, King Louis XIV's minister Jean Baptiste Colbert (1619–83)
ders from Holland to build ships and seaports; financed road
provided tax exemptions, subsidies, and import tariffs to
of France's most expensive items such as silk, tapestries, and
er source of wealth for the king and his treasury was gold and
quired from colonies in the New World.

form of mercantilism, which focused narrowly on gaining wealth
xports and discouraging imports, is called *classical mercantilism* to
om later strains of mercantilist thought. As trade increased between
ions, so did the opportunity for economic and political rivalry. The
en employed a variety of protectionist trade and monetary measures
ther economic devices to increase their wealth and military power.
ies one monarch adopted to generate and protect national wealth and
re often perceived to be at the expense of another state.

in an economically competitive and politically hostile environment,
gains by one state were likely to be perceived by competing states as
nferring on mercantilism a *zero-sum* worldview. Likewise, because there
so much bullion, states felt better off having more than less of it. This

outlook of tending to see power in terms of absolute gains and losses related to trade and treasure also contributed to the idea that war was a permanent feature of the international political economy.

Colonialism, supplemented by the state military power, became an important instrument in mercantilist efforts to control trade. Colonies served as exclusive markets for the goods of the mother country, a source of raw materials or goods that would have been bought from a competitive country, or a source of cheap labor. Thomas Mun, a successful trader and director of the East India Company, argued for "the overridding need for England to pursue a positive balance of trade."[9] In so doing the growing merchant class supported a strong state that would protect its interests, and in return the state sanctioned monopolistic merchant control over certain industries related to the profit merchants and the state shared via commercial trade.

Mercantilism thus refers to a period of history when newly emerging nation-states faced the problem of security. The political philosophy of mercantilism told national leaders how they could create a virtuous cycle of power and wealth that would allow them to achieve security and prosperity. Mercantilist policies included restrictions on imports, "encouragements" to exports, such as subsidies, and the development of colonial empires. These classical mercantilist policies were not ends in themselves but rather means to the end of wealth, power, and national security.

MERCANTILISM AND REALISM: COMPLEMENTARY PERSPECTIVES

Quite often the ideas of mercantilists and *realists* have been lumped together, because like mercantilism, realism accounts for some of the ways that politics, power, and the state impact the economy and markets. Realism has been the dominant *Weltanschauung* (worldview) of most world leaders and foreign policy officials since World War II.[10] In many ways these two approaches incorporate some of the same assumptions, yet in some ways they differ. A brief sketch of realism reveals that many of the forces that drive the international political economy and generate economic nationalism are the same conditions that compel states to seek security for themselves and groups within their jurisdiction.

For realists, as for mercantilists, the nation-state is the primary actor in the international system because it is the highest unit of sovereign political authority. One of the tenets of realism is that the international system of nation-states is in a constant state of potential anarchy given that conflicting national interests force states to compete with one another for limited amounts of resources. Power is the ultimate arbiter of conflict. Power stems from natural resources, geographic location, and national characteristics and traits that go into the production of wealth and military weapons and other national capabilities. For realists the capabilities of states and the global distribution of power determine the manner in which rival states deal with one another in a self-help international state system. For realists state competition also results in a zero-sum game where relative gains for one state may be perceived as absolute losses by other states. Both realists and neomercantilists today assume that measures taken to enhance the security of one state necessarily detract from the security of others because of the relatively fixed amount of power resources in the world.

One difference between realists and modern neomercantilists is the stress realists put on military instruments and similar state capabilities to render the state secure. When push comes to shove, realists feel strongly that military power and capabilities are crucial if a state is to either defend itself against the aggressive tendencies of other states or, if necessary, overcome its enemies. On the other hand mercantilists and economic nationalists stress not only that conflict is economically driven, but that a viable economy is essential if a state is to be able to purchase the weapons necessary to secure the state.

The tension between the pursuit of wealth and power by the state is usually settled in favor of one or the other from time to time, or both simultaneously. Jacob Viner's often cited dictum that "wealth and power are each proper and ultimate ends of national policy"[11] has become the credo of most economic nationalist and neomercantilist public officials. Furthermore, in an international system where states must ultimately rely on themselves for security, the economy remains one of several instruments the state uses to accomplish a variety of domestic and foreign policy objectives.

ECONOMIC NATIONALISM

Mercantilism evolved and adapted to changing conditions in the economic and political environment. An important example of this evolution is the development of *economic nationalism* as a form of mercantilism in the late eighteenth and nineteenth centuries.

Whereas classical mercantilism focused on gaining wealth and power through unequal foreign trade, economic nationalism focused on the internal development of the national economy. In an important sense, economic nationalism was a reaction to economic liberalism. As Great Britain grew rich and powerful, other nations such as the United States and the German principalities grew concerned about their independence and adopted economic nationalist policies as a way to protect themselves from what they perceived as Britain's aggressive liberal politics. Here are the details of this rise of economic nationalism.

Improvements in production technology and transportation gradually created economies that were truly national in scope (as opposed to local or regionally based). The political borders of the state and the market borders of the economy began to coincide to a greater degree. To a certain extent, the line between wealth and power began to blur, too, since either one could be used to gain the other. To be an independent political power, some thought, it was necessary to be an independent economic power, too. But markets, left to their own devices, naturally link up into domestic and international patterns of trade that were viewed by mercantilists as webs of dependency. How can a nation be independent of, say, Great Britain, if it depended upon that nation for manufactured goods and as a market for agricultural exports?

If, as mercantilists believed, unregulated markets fostered economic dependency, then it was up to the state to turn market linkages inward and develop the domestic economy as a strong and independent engine of wealth and power. The idea that the economic interests of the nation should be put ahead of the economic interests of the individual and fostered through strong state action has come to be called economic nationalism.

The most famous proponents of economic nationalism were the American Alexander Hamilton (1755–1804) and the German Friedrich List (1789–1846). In the United States Alexander Hamilton[12] felt that a strong manufacturing and industrial base for the nation required an active state along with trade protection for U.S. infant industries. In his *Report on the Subject of Manufactures* to the first Congress, he wrote in terms that are familiar even today when he argued both for trade protection and also for a strong role for the state in promoting domestic industries. Hamilton saw U.S. economic security threatened by the mercantilist policies of other nations and he saw the necessity of strong state actions to beat back foreign economic invaders. He favored subsidies to make U.S. goods more competitive at home and abroad (to offset subsidies granted by foreign states). Hamilton reluctantly favored the use of tariffs to limit imports. He wrote that

> It is well known . . . that certain nations grant bounties [subsidies] on the exportation of particular commodities, to enable their own workmen to undersell and supplant all competitors in the countries to which those commodities are sent. Hence the undertakers of a new manufacture have to contend not only with the natural disadvantages of a new undertaking, but with the gratuities and remunerations which other governments bestow. To be enabled to contend with success, it is evident that the interference and aid of their own government are indispensable.[13]

The nineteenth century German political economist Friedrich List was an even more vigorous proponent of economic nationalism. Exiled from his German home, ironically for his radical free-trade views, List came to the United States and, in a sense, saw the results of Hamilton's economic nationalist policies. Here was a nation that had built itself up and achieved independence and security, List thought. Writing in the 1840s, List came to view that state action was needed to promote productive power in the form of education, technology, and industry. According to List, "The *power of producing* is ... infinitely more important than *wealth* itself ...".[14] He also offered many reasons for why manufacturing and not agriculture was a more desirable basis for national wealth and power. His argument that manufacturing developed greater human skills and opportunities is still popular today. He wrote:

> If we regard manufacturing occupations as a whole, it must be evident at first glance that they develop and bring into action an incomparably greater variety and higher type of mental qualities and abilities than agriculture. Manufactures are at once the offspring, and at the same time the supporters and the nurses, of science and the arts.[15]

The writings of Hamilton and List incorporate a spirit of patriotic economic nationalism to the extent that they both support state policies that furthered the national interest by assisting in the industrialization of the economy. Their views tie together the important notions of national interest, a positive role for the state in the economy, and sacrifice for future gain. Many regard these ingredients as a key element in the classical formula for nation building. Indeed, Robert Reich writes that "the idea that the citizens of a nation shared responsibility for their economic well-being was a natural outgrowth of this budding patriotism."[16]

This kind of patriotic political economy is still found everywhere in the world today. For example many officials in developing nations as yet view the development and nation-building processes as one of "catching up" to the Western industrialized nations. In so doing, quite often they look to the state to promote domestic industries and/or to protect their "infant" industries against the more mature industries and protectionist policies of the industrialized nations.

In the 1980s and 1990s a popular academic trend was to contrast the economic success of Japan and the some of the Newly Industrialized Countries (NICs) to that of the United States and other industrialized nations. The economist Lester Thurow wrote that the Japanese secret is found in the fact that they "tapped a universal human desire to build, to belong to an empire, to conquer neighboring empires, and to become the world's economic power."[17] The ambition to protect one's industries as well as to get ahead of others, to gain more and more security in an unpredictable world are some of the emotions that drive mercantilism, even today.

Although the goals of economic nationalism seem relatively benign—to build domestic economic power in order to gain security and independence—improvements in technology, communication, and transportation eventually changed the impact of these policies significantly. By the end of the nineteenth century a nation's ability to produce manufactured goods often far exceeded the ability of its domestic markets to absorb these items. The focus of economic nationalism turned from developing domestic *productive power* to finding foreign markets for the goods that productive power produced. The key to security changed from a strong domestic economy to an extensive foreign economic empire capable of supplying scarce resources to the home country and purchasing the output of its industries. In short, economic *nationalism* helped generate foreign *imperialism*.

As many different nations adopted similar policies to, first, develop domestic industries and then, second, to expand into foreign markets, it was inevitable that national interests would clash. It can be argued that to a certain degree the global conflicts of World War I and World War II had at their root the international competition among nations that economic nationalism promoted.[18]

THE RISE OF NEOMERCANTILISM

International *economic interdependence* has gradually reached an all time high in the years since World War II (and especially since the collapse of communism in 1989).[19] International organizations such as the General Agreement on Tariffs and Trade (GATT), the World Trade Organization (WTO), and the Asian-Pacific

Economic Conference (APEC) promoted free trade and open markets (these institutions are discussed in chapter 6). The logic of this movement was that free trade and open markets would prevent the sort of mercantilist conflicts that had plagued the recent past and caused so much human suffering.

Free trade and open markets, however, create a dilemma for the state. As Robert Gilpin has written,

> Whereas powerful market forces in the form of trade, money and foreign investment tend to jump national boundaries, to escape political control, and to integrate societies, the tendency of government is to restrict, to channel, and to make economic activities serve the perceived interests of the state and of powerful groups within it. The logic of the market is to locate economic activities where they are most productive and profitable; the logic of the state is to capture and control the process of economic growth and capital accumulation.[20]

Their commitment to this worthy international goal of peaceful trade therefore did not prevent individual nations from also being concerned about their own economic security and national independence. They sought ways of protecting their economic security within an international political and economic environment that increasingly discouraged classical mercantilist policies, especially tariffs and quotas. We give the name *neomercantilism* to the policies that more recently are essentially mercantilist policies adopted by individual nations in an insecure international economic environment.

Contrary to the use of overt protectionist trade barriers such as import tariffs, after World War II neomercantilist policies were often craftily designed to appear as being less than protectionist. Many of them created political and economic advantages for national industries or private enterprises while others were employed to counter the advantages other states gave their industries.

If you want an example of how economic interdependence has lead to neomercantilism, look no further than your car, truck, or sport-utility vehicle. In 1973, (and again in 1979 in the case of price hikes), the Organization of Petroleum Exporting Countries (OPEC) oil cartel raised the price of oil, embargoed oil shipments to the United States and the Netherlands, and reduced oil shipments to the rest of the world by 25 percent. The resultant increase in the price of oil and transfer of massive amounts of currency to oil-rich countries was thought to have economically weakened the West and made OPEC a political economic power with which to reckon. The dependency of the West on oil imports, and on OPEC in particular, helped push the issue of *economic security* higher on the policy agenda of oil importing nations everywhere in the world. At the time, U.S. President Carter went so far as to say that efforts to combat oil dependency were "the moral equivalent of war."

The result was a campaign by many of the industrialized states to decrease dependency on oil imports in order to increase economic security. The United States sponsored the development of a strategic petroleum reserve and promoted development of the North Slope oilfields in Alaska. Other national policies included tax breaks to people who adopted measures to cut home energy use, a 55-mph speed limit, and state funds for the development of alternative energy resources. Congress even imposed fuel mileage requirements on automobile manufacturers to force them to design more fuel-efficient cars.[21] In a sense, what you drive, how you drive it, and where the gas for your car or truck comes from today have all been conditioned by neomercantilist policies dating from the 1970s designed to reduce economic dependence on oil imports.

The case of international economic interdependence also applied to a number of other natural resources and raw materials that were in great demand in the industrialized nations—often referred to as *strategic resources*— such as special alloys and minerals used in aircraft production or uranium used for atomic weapons. Both realist and neomercantilist explanations of IPE hold that, at some point, dependence upon foreign suppliers for strategic resources is an unacceptable security risk.

Realists and neomercantilists also believe that interdependencies are not always symmetrical (felt equally) between states. The suppliers of oil and other needed resources or commodities tended to view their capacity and the resultant dependence as something positive that improved their power and security. In many cases, the relatively high cost of oil, coupled with supplier threats to cut it off to client states, made the issue of dependency on any resource or vulnerability to a supplier of that resource synonymous with a national security threat.[22] Ideally, only complete self-sufficiency would make a nation-state politically and economically secure. In the real world however, states were constantly trying to minimize their dependence on others while fostering conditions that made others dependent on them.

Many states found themselves torn between their international obligation to promote and protect free trade and open markets versus their natural desire to safeguard their nation's independence and economic security. Faced with this dilemma a variety of new (neomercantilist) protectionist techniques emerged and have been with us since the 1970s. Many of these actions and policies were not covered by international trade agreements, for instance, and therefore were *legally* designed to protect national industries, while others were intended to overcome the negative connotations associated with trade protection all the while subtly accomplishing that objective. Still others were meant to counter the unintentional protectionist policies other states had adopted under difficult circumstances.

Some states employed *export subsidies* to lower the price of goods, making them more attractive to importers. The United States routinely subsidized its agricultural exports, it claimed, to counter the subsidies the EU used to increase its share of agriculture export markets. (See Banana Trade War box.) Likewise, a number of methods were developed to limit consumer spending on imports. While the multilateral GATT negotiations after World War II successfully curtailed the use of import *tariffs* (i.e., taxes on imports) on industrial products, many nations resorted to the use of *import quotas* to steer consumers away from imported goods. These quotas specified the quantity of a particular product that could be sold locally. The United States still uses import quotas to limit the amount of sugar its consumers can buy from abroad, which helps its sugar producers compete with foreign sugar producers.

Another way to limit imports from abroad is the *Voluntary Export Restraint* **(VER)** or Voluntary Export Agreement (VEA). This policy amounts to a negotiated quota or "gentlemen's agreement" between an exporter and importer whereby the exporter "voluntarily" restricts sales of his products in the importing country. Exporters feel compelled to comply with the importer's request for fear the importer may impose some more costly form of protection on their exports. More sophisticated import barriers include an array of *Nontariff Barriers* **(NTBs).** For instance, a series of complex government regulations pertaining to health and safety standards, licensing and labeling requirements, and domestic content requirements have been known to either block or distort the sales or distribution of imported goods (see chapter 6).

Still other measures states have more routinely used to assist select industries include *loans, regional infrastructure development programs, investment promotions,* and even *direct public ownership* of certain industries. Many governments also helped certain companies market their products overseas. The embassies of most developed countries routinely employ officials whose responsibility it is to monitor national political economic conditions and to assess their potential impact for the businesses of his/her home country just as, in earlier days, they would have kept track of troop deployments and arms buildups.

MILITARY VERSUS ECONOMIC SECURITY

The central concern of mercantilists is security. Once upon a time security meant military security, plain and simple. Today, however, national security is much more complicated and, to be really secure and independent, a nation needs to be secure from military, economic, terrorist, environmental, and even cultural threats (the security structure will be discussed in more detail in chapter 9). The world is still a dangerous place and it is hard to be secure from its many threats.

Sometimes an attempt to gain one type of security results in a loss in other types of security so that it is difficult to tell whether the nation has in fact benefited. The United States wishes to maintain its military security, for example, by restricting access to military technology secrets. High-tech military systems are key elements of the U.S. national security strategy and it is important to stay one step ahead of potential adversaries. At the same time, however, the United States also desires to promote sales of high-technology products abroad, according to the mercantilist way of thinking, so as to strengthen U.S. industries and keep foreign competitors from taking markets from us.

In the spring of 1999 two U.S. Congressional committees along with a presidential advisory board simultaneously studied what many U.S. officials feel is a growing problem of Chinese espionage to secure U.S. technology about nuclear warheads, mobile missile systems, the neutron bomb, and satellite technology. The Select House Committee released a 700-page report on June 25 that accuses the Chinese of "a pattern of systematic and successful Chinese espionage to learn American nuclear secrets" over the last 20 years.[a] The Senate committee accuses the Energy Department of lax monitoring[b] of satellite technology transfers to Beijing. The Senate committee also studied the issue of China's attempt to influence government officials, especially in the form of campaign contributions made to the Clinton administration in the 1996 election.

The Select House Committee report accused the Clinton administration of promoting exports at risk of security—tilting too much toward commerce and not enough to national security. The report specifically criticizes two corporations for their "bottom-line" outlook of putting exports before security: the Hughes Electronics Corporation (a subsidiary of General Motors) and the Loral Space and Communications Corporation.

What China supposedly secured from the United States was sensitive information about U.S. warheads, especially the new W-88, and the neutron bomb. Some officials believe that China stole plans for all seven U.S. nuclear warheads. Some U.S. military experts believe that China has sought this missile technology and information in order to produce smaller more mobile nuclear weapons, and also to be able to survive a U.S. retaliatory second strike.

In particular, China was accused of targeting three major U.S. Department of Energy laboratories—at Los Alamos and Sandia, New Mexico, and the Lawrence Livermore Laboratory in California for this information. The press focused a good deal of attention on Wen Ho Lee, a research mathematician at the Los Alamos nuclear weapons laboratory who was dismissed for security violations.[c] He supposedly downloaded information about miniature and mobile ballistic missiles and may then have transferred this information to Chinese officials while vacationing in Asia.

China denied all of these charges and accused the United States of being "bossy." Meanwhile China built up its missile deployments along its border with Taiwan while criticizing the United States for covering Taiwan with its new missile defense system.

Democrats on the House committee lead by Congressman Norm Dicks (D., WA) claimed that these cases present no damage to long-term U.S. national security. China has only 18 ICBMs. Dicks and other Democrats have blamed the Reagan and Bush administrations for initiating technology transfers to China in the early 1980s. Republicans led by the chairman of the committee, Congressman Christopher Cox (R., CA) claimed that U.S. national security has been damaged. The Republicans blame the aggressive export enhancement policies of the Clinton administration (last year's trade deficit with China was $57 billion), and especially the Commerce Department for approving licenses for technology transfers without sufficient review.

Several measures have been adopted by different agencies to deal with this situation. In February 1999 the Clinton administration seemed to reverse its policy of helping businesses promote exports by rejecting the sale of $450 million worth of satellite technology to a Singapore-based business group with ties to senior Chinese military officers.[d] While not wanting to quarantine nuclear scientists, Secretary of Energy Bill Richardson has attempted to improve security at labs, including the use of counterespionage to deal with the problem. The administration has also come out in favor of the Commerce Department's once again taking the lead in approving licenses for commercial exports.

Some officials worry that China may seek to purchase these technologies from the European Union (EU) in particular. Others worry that the accusation of espionage and cancellation of sales may hurt U.S. efforts to bring China into the WTO. And still others worry that U.S. accusations may cause efforts to improve human rights conditions in that country to worsen. Everyone, it seems, worries about the problem of security and the difficult task of achieving security in the complex and interdependent IPE of today.

---

[a] See "Spying Charges Against Beijing Are Spelled Out by House Panel" *New York Times*, 26 May 1999, p. A1.

[b] See "Lax Monitoring Let China Improve Missiles, Panel Says" *New York Times*, 7 May 1999, p. A19.

[c] See "Suspect in Loss of Nuclear Secrets Unlikely to Face Spying Charges" *New York Times*, 15 June 1999, p. A1.

[d] See "Citing Security, U.S. Spurns China on Satellite Deal" *New York Times*, 23 February 1999, p. A1.

For most modern neomercantilists the capacity of the nation-state to generate wealth is as important as its capacity to produce military weapons. Industrial capacity (including defense industries) benefit the state in at least three ways. First, it generates military weapons and defense-related technologies and products. Secondly, the effects of industrial production spill over into other parts of the national political economy, generating jobs and stimulating the production of consumer goods such as computers and laser technology. Finally, a nation's industrial capacity increases its self-sufficiency and political autonomy, to the extent that the nation does not become dependent on external sources of raw materials for security or imports to satisfy consumer demands.

Finally, many neomercantilists today would argue that to accumulate and maintain their wealth and power states are more than ever tempted to intervene in and influence developments not only in their domestic economies but also in other nations' economies and the international economy itself. In effect, many states—often in support of their own industries—try to restructure the international economy in their favor. One way to do so is to influence or even control the political and economic rules of the game.

JAPAN: BENIGN OR MALEVOLENT MERCANTILIST?

Robert Gilpin makes a useful distinction about many of the neomercantilist policies states employed after World War II to assist not only their industries but also to maintain their power and security. According to Gilpin *malevolent mercantilism* is a more hostile version of economic warfare and expansionary economic policies associated with the practices of such countries as Nazi Germany and imperial Japan. Malevolent nations employ a variety of measures to expand their territorial base and/or political and economic influence intentionally at the expense of other nations' beyond what is regarded as reasonable to protect themselves.

On the other hand *benign mercantilism* is more defensive in nature as "it attempts to protect the economy against untoward economic and political forces."[23] As one would expect, however, what one states regards as benign, another easily regards as malevolent mercantilism, especially when the policies of the first state play serious havoc with the political and economic interests of the second.

An interesting question is whether Japan has been a benign or a malevolent mercantilist in the postwar era. After World War II Japan adopted a carefully thought out strategy of strengthening its domestic industry along the lines recommended by Hamilton and List. Officials from the Ministry of Trade and Industry (MITI) worked closely with corporate officials and Liberal Democratic Party (LDP) members to carefully guide the development of the economy. The United States accepted Japanese import barriers as a cost of basing U.S. troops in Japan and using it as one of its geopolitical pillars in its campaign against communism. In a sense, Japan was able to adopt overtly mercantilist policies to promote its economic security because a strong Japan was in the military security interests of the United States.

With the end of the Cold War between the United States and the Soviet Union, however, things changed. The United States gradually put more pressure on Japan not only to lower its trade barriers but to also open its markets to more foreign competition. The United States and Japan have confronted one another in a series of trade disputes covering a variety of items from rice to semiconductors.

In essence, the U.S. government has accused Japan of engaging in malevolent mercantilism designed to weaken the economies of other nations while Japan maintains that it has sought only to strengthen its own national security through benign mercantilist policies. It is difficult to determine who is right here. Even the experts disagree. For example, Chalmers Johnson has argued that Japan's state-dominated style of capitalism has made use of an *industrial policy* whereby the government has chosen certain industries for state and bank subsidies in an effort to make them more competitive with U.S. and European firms, which may be viewed as a benign effort.[24] Others like Clyde Prestowitz[25] add that Japan has *also* employed a *strategic trade policy* whereby in the case of lacking a natural comparative advantage in the production of certain products, it has used a combination of state assistance and industry efforts to purposefully *create* such an advantage in favor of its industries, which might be viewed as a more aggressive action.

The reaction to Japan's policies in the post-Cold War environment has been predictable. Neomercantilist policies tend to provoke retaliatory actions that can lead to trade wars regardless of whether the "first shot" fired was benign or malevolent in its intent.[26] Thus, Japan is coming under increasing pressure both at home and abroad to conform more closely to the international norms of free trade and open markets.

Ironically, then, one nation's defensive mercantilism can be perceived by other nations as an aggressive action and trade wars may result. This is one way, for example, to interpret the United States-European Union banana war, discussed in the box below. The EU's banana regime may be viewed as a defensive policy designed to cushion nations with historic links to Europe from the harsh effects of economic globalization. The United States, however, may interpret this as an offensive action and challenge to the principles of free trade and open markets on which globalization depends. A trade war which neither side desires may be the outcome.

BANANA WARS

Slipping on a banana peel is one of the oldest and most reliable comedy gimmicks around. The banana war between the European Union and the United States, however, shows clearly that what is silly slapstick on the silver screen is far more serious in IPE.

In March 1999 the United States began imposing trade sanctions worth some $520 million on the EU because it has been limiting imports of bananas produced by the U.S. multinationals Chiquita and Dole for the past six years. This is only the latest in a series of trade disputes between the United States and EU over a variety of items including agricultural and food products going back to the 1950s. This time, however, the dispute resulted in a trade war.

The latest dispute began in 1993 when, in an effort to support a number of ex-British and French colonies in the Caribbean, the EU restricted imports of bananas into the EU from other areas of the world. The United States[a] brought the issue before the World Trade Organization (WTO) dispute panel in 1995 and again in 1997, which on both occasions found that the EU was illegally restraining imports of Latin American-grown bananas into Europe.[b]

The United States felt that time had run out and requested that the WTO begin imposing trade sanctions worth $520 million annually (the amount U.S. companies have lost due to EU discriminatory policies) on the EU. Because the EU failed to comply with the WTO finding, the Clinton administration took the step of imposing 100 percent duties on imports originating in the EU on such items as cashmere sweaters, pork, wine, cheese, fruit, and toys. In return EU officials vow to retaliate with duties on U.S. goods, thus risking to further escalate what has in effect become a trade war between the United States and EU.

What in the world could have caused the United States and the EU to go to war (a trade war, admittedly, not a shooting war) over something as seemingly trivial as whether European consumers will buy Caribbean versus Latin American bananas? Although bananas are big business, the real roots of this dispute reach far beyond the plantation.

From the EU perspective, much more than bananas are at stake. The core issue from this point of view is the ability of the EU to control the types of goods that it allows to enter its borders—an issue of sovereignty and self-determination. The EU banana regime is, in a way, a test case for the EU to determine whether it has the ability to pursue food security policies within the context of the WTO agreement.[c] This is an important issue in Europe, where genetically modified foods and hormone-enhanced beef are viewed with great suspicion. If the EU can not keep out Central American bananas, Europeans worry, how can they keep out other food imports? Now bananas, then hormonally-modified beef—then what?

Other analysts argue that the tough stance by the United States, and in particular the Clinton administration, is driven by domestic political concerns that have little to do with trade or the EU. The banana war, from this perspective, is just the byproduct of the U.S. domestic political economy situation. It may not be an accident, for example, that the banana wars came to a head during the period when President Clinton was facing impeachment proceedings in Congress. Perhaps the administration used bananas to gain public support by being openly tough and strongly "presidential" tough during the impeachment hearings. President Clinton was under pressure to "stand up robustly for U.S. interests in trade disputes" given his failure in 1997 to secure from the U.S. Congress "fast track" authority to negotiate trade agreements.[d] Furthermore, the head of Chiquita—Carl Lindner—is known to have made large contributions to Washington officials and is generally regarded as an effective lobbyist.[e] Perhaps U.S. banana policies have more to do with campaign finance than tropical fruit trade.

The banana dispute is yet another a case where one nation's political and business interests conflict with the practices of other states or with international political economic conditions. The loss of banana and beef sales to the EU is not going to make or break the U.S. or the EU's balance of trade, but because trade is linked to security, even relatively trivial issues can have great symbolic importance or set precedents that ultimately have significant impact.

---

[a] While the United States itself does not produce bananas, Chiquita Brands International and Dole Food are regarded as U.S. companies.
[b] See "Banana Talks with Europe Turn Nasty," *New York Times*, 26 January 1999, p. C.6.
[c] Because the EU is made up of 15 countries, for many of them the banana issue constitutes a "national sovereignty" problem.
[d] See "Market Disputes: Trade Goes Bananas" *Financial Times*, 26 January 1999, p. 19.
[e] Ibid.

MERCANTILISM AS ECONOMIC MANAGEMENT: STATISM

Another development that contributed to the growing use of neomercantilist policies was **statism**. Because states have some influence over economic activity, and because they influence market forces to some degree, political arrangements are the foundation upon which both domestic and international markets function. Statism refers to the continuation and also intensification of an earlier trend of states subordinating economic policies to political objectives. Communist states come closest to this ideal. In relatively open economies, states allow markets a good deal of leeway in setting prices for goods. On the other hand, in relatively closed economies, states severely restrict markets and set prices according to some ideological or nationalist objective.

In the 1970s and 1980s states everywhere increasingly took on more responsibility for providing "wealth and welfare" benefits to its citizens. In order to better macro- and micromanage their economies, the industrialized states became less willing to allow market forces to determine their policy objectives and shape the size of their public programs. In response to the demands of domestic groups, and also in response to increasing international economic interdependence, protectionist trade, finance, and monetary policies proliferated. Many states felt compelled more than ever to resort to using a variety of neomercantilist policies and measures to insulate and protect their economies and certain industries. Many of these industries employed large numbers of people or occupied strategic positions in the economy—that is, they made military weapons or items some of the major powers did not want to be dependent on importing from other nations. Likewise during the 1970s and 1980s, aside from some of the NICs that adopted the Japanese export-led growth model, the states of many developing nations adopted a variety of protectionist measures in response to intensive domestic pressure on their governments to manage the economy (see chapter 15).

GLOBALIZATION AND DEFENSIVE MERCANTILISM

It has become a cliché to say that we live in the age of globalization. Certainly in the last several years the international political economy (made up of linkages connecting nation-states) has become much more of a global political economy (where linkages transcend state boundaries). Not unexpectedly, some mercantilists view economic globalization as a security threat, potentially a threat to the fundamental sovereignty of the nation-state itself.[27] As we noted before, markets tend naturally to link together, seeking efficiency through an international or global division of labor, but this also creates interdependency, which is often viewed as a security threat to states. This is a fundamental dilemma. What is economically efficient may sometimes threaten the state's ability to protect and defend its economic security.

How can states facilitate the efficiencies of globalization while also attempting to limit some of its most damaging effects?[28] One answer is what we might call *defensive mercantilism* which seeks to protect the national interest against the global expansion of markets more than the malevolent actions of other nations. The difference between defensive mercantilism and other types of mercantilist action lies more in its intent or motivation than in its specific form. In practice, it is difficult tell the difference between a defensive policy that is designed to protect a domestic industry from the negative effects of globalization and an offensive policy that is designed to help gain market shares from foreign sellers. Both defensive and malevolent policies will favor domestic over foreign or international competitors.

INDUSTRIAL ESPIONAGE

Since the end of the Cold War, espionage—the business of spying and gathering secret intelligence—has not disappeared, as some expected it might, but has shifted its focus from military security to economic security. As nations find themselves drawn into more intensive economic competition in an international political economy marked by increasing international economic interdependence, many of the industrialized nations have looked to industrial espionage as another tactic for states and businesses to use to acquire information and technology.

The end of the Cold War produced a large number of agents in the West and in the former Soviet Union with well-established contact networks who were well versed in the art of spying and intelligence gathering. A number of businesses have sprung up, mainly in the industrialized countries, that specialize in providing industries and governments with intelligence, counterintelligence, and security services.

The U.S. Federal Bureau of Investigation (FBI) is "investigating instances of foreign intelligence services stealing U.S. information on robotics, high-tempered materials, advanced ceramics and biogenetics."[a] The FBI estimates that in the United States alone some 50 nations conduct economic spying. Twenty of those nations including Japan, France, England, Canada, Germany, South Korea, Sweden, and Israel have been considered to be "allies" of the United States. And in the cases of Germany, Japan, South Korea and France, the United States assisted these nations in setting up their intelligence services. Edwin Fraumann has estimated that the cost of information stolen each year amounts to between $24 and 100 billion.[b]

Fraumann goes on to describe some of the national intelligence operations of different nations. France's Directorate General of the External (the equivalent of the U.S. CIA) has been known to bug Air France flights from New York to Paris. Even if France has one of the world's strictest laws on the abuse of personal data, its intelligence services are not held accountable to these laws. Japan's External Trade Organization (JETRO) with offices in some 59 countries and the Ministry of International Trade and Industry are leading agencies in gathering economic intelligence from other countries. Japan also has an economic espionage school. China focuses on the same sort of intelligence and is also known to use visiting students and professors in nonintrusive ways to penetrate academic and corporate labs.[c] China has set up three institutes to monitor intelligence. And Germany spends a good deal of time and money on computer espionage—by gaining access into the computer bases of other nations and businesses. The Germans have a computer-hacking school in Frankfurt.

Just some of the practices governments (including the United States) have been accused of using to gather intelligence include electronic eavesdropping, bugging hotel facilities and the flights of executives of large companies such as Boeing, IBM, NCR, and Texas Instruments; attempting to bribe U.S businessmen with intelligence-trained prostitutes; infiltrating congressional offices and even the White House; organizing spy networks in conjunction with foreign military or national security and intelligence operations; recruiting spies in the U.S. military; and, monitoring database networks of large companies. Most experts on the subject of industrial espionage estimate that approximately 75 percent of commercial intelligence is acquired rather easily through computers, publications, and research or business journals. "In the information age, there's very little that an adversary can't dig up with a computer."[d] On the other hand many companies are known to have warded off spies and their clandestine practices with such counterintelligence methods as filing false patents for inventions.

To counter the efforts of states and businesses to acquire information covertly, nations have adopted a number of measures. In the United States some nine federal agencies have been provided with the authority to deal with economic espionage. In 1996 the U.S. Congress passed the Economic Espionage Act of 1996 making it a federal crime to steal trade secrets. Other countries have adopted similar measures. Fraumann also estimates that in 1995 over 700 counterintelligence investigations involved economic espionage.[e]

Since the end of the Cold War, international conflict has centered more on economic competition than on traditional high-security issues. As long as nations fear for their military, economic, social, or cultural security, mercantilist policies will exist.

---

[a] See "Cold War Spies Turn Their Skills to Corporate Data," *Seattle Times*, 13 June 1993.
[b] Edwin Fraumann, "Economic Espionage: Security Missions Redefined," *Public Administration Review* 57 (July-August 1997), pp. 303-318.
[c] For a more detailed description of some of these national intelligence gathering agencies and processes, see Fraumann, "Economic Espionage."
[d] "Cold War Spies."
[e] Fraumann, "Economic Espionage."

CONCLUSION

Of the three ideological perspectives most often used to explain IPE, namely mercantilism, liberalism, and structuralism, mercantilism is the oldest and arguably the most powerful. If List were still around, he would likely argue that as long as states are the final source of political (sovereign) authority, the economy and markets cannot be divorced from the effects politics and the state have on them. States can be expected to use the economy as a means to generate more wealth and power.

List would also likely argue that free trade is a myth. As long as states exist, they will give first priority to their own national security and independence, including economic security and economic independence. We are all mercantilists—even nations like Great Britain in the nineteenth century and the United States in the twentieth century—that advocate free trade. These nations will only promote free trade, List might say, as long as doing so promotes their national interest. The rise of neomercantilism is proof positive that states favor free trade when it benefits them and protection when it doesn't.

Responsibilities and objectives related to increasing and maintaining state wealth and power have proliferated since World War II due to the growing interdependence of nations and globalization of the international political economy. Economic "statecraft" remains a complicated task that befuddles politicians and academics alike.[29] As states and national industries become more dependent on external sources of revenue and markets, they also feel more vulnerable to developments in the international political economy. Protectionist trade, finance, and monetary policies have proliferated everywhere as states have attempted to better macro- and micromanage their economies. Pragmatic mercantilism is a fact of life, which is why the mercantilist perspective is so powerful.

DISCUSSION QUESTIONS

1. Each of the IPE perspectives has at its center a fundamental value of idea. What is the central idea of mercantilism? Explain how that central idea is illustrated by the mercantilist period of history, mercantilist philosophy, and mercantilist policies.
2. Mercantilism has evolved and adapted to changing IPE environments. Briefly explain how and why these forms of mercantilism differ: classical mercantilism, neomercantilism, defensive mercantilism.
3. What is the difference between benign mercantilism and malevolent mercantilism in theory? How could you tell the difference between them in practice? Explain.
4. How is it possible for a state simultaneously to be a member of the World Trade Organization, which promotes free trade and open markets and also provide subsidies to domestic firms to help them compete with foreign producers?
5. Would you agree or disagree with the assertion that, in today's world, economic security is more at risk than is military security? Explain.
6. Is economic globalization a threat? Make a brief list of the positive and negative potential effects of a more global economic system and explain the basis for your opinion.

INTERNET LINKS

Japan's Ministry of International Trade and Industry:
   http://www.miti.go.jp/index-e.html
Office of the U.S. Trade Representative:
   http://www.ustr.gov/
Friedrich List and *The National System of Political Economy:*
   http://www.ecn.bris.ac.uk/het/list/index.htm

SUGGESTED READINGS

James Fallows. *More Like Us: Putting America's Native Strengths and Traditional Values to Work to Overcome the Asian Challenge.* Boston: Houghton Mifflin, 1990.
James Fallows. *Looking at the Sun.* New York: Pantheon, 1994.
Edwin Fraumann, "Economic Espionage: Security Missions Redefined," *Public Administration Review,* 57 (July-August 1997), pp. 303-318.
Alexander Hamilton. "Report on Manufactures," in George T. Crane and Abla Amawi, *The Theoretical Evolution of International Political Economy: A Reader.* New York: Oxford University Press, 1991, pp. 37-47.
Eli F. Heckscher. *Mercantilism.* Rev. ed., 2 vols. New York: Macmillan, 1955.

Robert Kuttner. *The End of Laissez-Faire*. New York: Knopf, 1991.

Friedrich List. *The National System of Political Economy*. New York: Augustus M. Kelley, 1966.

Robert B. Reich. *The Work of Nations*. New York: Knopf, 1991.

Martin and Susan J. Tolchin. *Selling Our Security: The Erosion of America's Assets*. New York: Penguin Books, 1992.

Lester Thurow. *Head to Head: The Coming Economic Battle Among Japan, Europe, and America*. New York: William Morrow, 1991.

Jacob Viner. "Power versus Plenty as Objectives of Foreign Policy in the Seventeenth and Eighteenth Centuries," *World Politics* 1 (Oct. 1948), pp. 1-29.

John Zysman and Laura Tyson. *American Industry in International Competition: Government Policies and Corporate Strategies*. Ithaca, NY: Cornell University Press, 1983.

NOTES

1. James Fallows, *Looking at the Sun,* (New York: Pantheon, 1994), p. 231.
2. Sun Yat-sen (1920), cited in Robert Reich, *The Work of Nations,* (New York: Knopf, 1991), p. 30.
3. See, for example, the "Mercantilism" entry of Randy Epping, *A Beginner's Guide to the World Economy* (New York: Vintage Books, 1992), p. 139.
4. Of course nations vary in how much they feel threatened by these things.
5. The rise of the nation-state was very uneven. Venice was already a "nation-state" in the fifteenth century, whereas Germany and Italy were not consolidated into the national entities that we know today until the second half of the nineteenth century.
6. The concepts of nation and nationalism are the focus of the classic work by Hans Kohn, *The Idea of Nationalism* (New York: Macmillan, 1944) and E.J. Hobsbawm, *Nations and Nationalism Since 1780*, 2d ed. (Cambridge: Cambridge University Press, 1992).
7. The classic definition of the state is Max Weber's, which emphasizes its administrative and legal qualities. See Max Weber, *The Theory of Social and Economic Organization* (New York: Free Press, 1947), p. 156.
8. Cited in Erich Roll, *A History of Economic Thought,* (Upper Saddle River, NJ: Prentice Hall), p. 68.
9. Robert Heilbroner, *Teachings from the Worldly Philosophy* (New York: W.W. Norton, 1996), p. 25.
10. There are a variety of subdivisions within realist thought. Two of the classic works in the field are Hans Morgenthau, *Politics Among Nations: The Struggle for Power and Peace* (New York: Alfred Knopf, any edition) and Kenneth Waltz, *Theory of International Politics* (Reading, MA: Addison-Wesley, 1979).
11. Jacob Viner, "Power versus Plenty as Objectives of Foreign Policy in the Seventeenth and Eighteenth Centuries," *World Politics* 1 (October 1948), p. 2.
12. For a detailed account of Hamilton's works, see J.C. Hamilton, ed., *The Works of Alexander Hamilton* (New York: C.S. Francis & Company, 1851).
13. Alexander Hamilton, "Report on Manfucturers," in George T. Crane and Abla Amawi, *The Theoretical Evolution of International Political Economy: A Reader* (New York: Oxford University Press, 1991), p. 42.
14. Friedrich List, *The National System of Political Economy* (New York: Augustus M. Kelley, 1966), p. 144. Italics are ours.
15. Ibid., pp. 199-200.
16. Reich, *The Work of Nations*, p. 18.
17. Lester Thurow, *Head to Head: The Coming Economic Battle Among Japan, Europe, and America* (New York: William Morrow, 1991), p. 118.
18. See the discussion of John Maynard Keynes in chapter 3 and V.I. Lenis's views in chapter 4.
19. Kenneth Waltz argues that interdependence was actually greater after World War I than in the 1970s. See Waltz, *Theory of International Politics*, pp. 141-143. By some measures,

however, economic interdependence reached a peak in the late nineteenth century that has not yet been surpassed.

20. Robert Gilpin, *The Political Economy of International Relations* (Princeton, NJ: Princeton University Press) p. 11.

21. Ironically, this instead gave auto firms an incentive to design and market new trucks, minivans, and sport-utility vehicles, which are not covered by the fuel mileage requirement (nor, at current writing, by many auto safety rules). The best selling vehicle in the United States today is a truck, which is perhaps an unintended consequence of the OPEC-driven neomercantilism of the 1970s.

22. For a more detailed discussion of dependency and interdependency, see Robert Keohane and Joseph S. Nye Jr., *Power and Interdependence* (Boston: Little, Brown, 1977).

23. Gilpin, *The Political Economy of International Relations*, p. 33.

24. See, for example, Chalmers Johnson "Introduction: The Idea of Industrial Policy," in his *The Industrial Policy Debate* (San Francisco, CA: ICS Press, 1984), pp. 3-26.

25. See, for example, Clyde Prestowitz, *Trading Places: How We Allowed Japan to Take the Lead* (New York: Basic Books, 1988).

26. See for example, John Zysman and Laura Tyson, *American Industry in International Competition: Government Policies and Corporate Strategies* (Ithaca, NY: Cornell University Press, 1983). A former trade advisor to President Clinton, Laura Tyson elsewhere argued that in an international environment where states increasingly consciously adopted measures to artificially enhance the competitiveness of their industries, the United States should adopt these kinds of practices because U.S. industries found it exceedingly difficult to be competitive without state assistance. See "As Economist Snipe, Adviser Gets to Work," *New York Times*, 15 March, 1993, p. A8.

27. See, for example, Robert Wade, "Globalization and Its Limits: Reports of the Death of the National Economy are Greatly Exaggerated," in Suzanne Berger and Ronald Dore, eds. *National Diversity and Global Capitalism* (Ithaca, NY: Cornell University Press, 1996), pp. 60-88.

28. For a provocative essay that makes this argument see Ethan Kapstein, "Workers and the World Economy," *Foreign Affairs* 75 (May/June, 1996), pp. 16-37.

29. For a sophisticated discussion of the problems associated with economic statecraft, see David A. Baldwin, *Economic Statecraft* (Princeton, NJ: Princeton University Press, 1985).

3

"Laissez-Faire, Laissez-Passer": The Liberal IPE Perspective

OVERVIEW

This chapter outlines the liberal perspective on international political economy, linking today's rise of the liberal view to its historical roots. We trace liberalism from eighteenth-century France, through nineteenth-century England, to today's world of the twenty-first century. Along the way we listen to the words of some of the most famous political economists, Adam Smith, David Ricardo, John Maynard Keynes, Friedrich Hayek, and Milton Friedman, and to some noteworthy practitioners of political economy such as Václav Havel. This chapter contains an unusual number of direct quotes from the works of these authors because the grace and power of their writings are irresistible.

Liberalism, like many other terms we use in IPE, suffers from something of a personality disorder. The same set of letters means different things in different contexts. In the United States today, for example, a "liberal" is generally one who believes in a strong and active state role in society, helping the poor and solving social problems. It is ironic, therefore, that liberalism, as we will study it here, means almost (but not exactly) the opposite of this.

Liberals, in the classical sense used here, fear the heavy hand of government and seek to liberate the individual from state oppression. Liberals believe in freedom, individual rights, and free markets. It is no accident that liberal and liberty have the same Latin root. In other words, liberals have much in common with people who are now called "conservatives" in the United States and other countries.

Liberalism arose and evolved in reaction to important trends and events in the real world. In plotting liberalism's path from its origins to the present day, we will necessarily pause to consider the events that shaped this point of view. A case study of the Corn Laws will illustrate the political economy of liberalism in the context of nineteenth-century Britain.

This chapter also introduces the important notion of hegemony. A hegemon is a rich, powerful nation that organizes the IPE. Britain was hegemon in the nineteenth century, and the United States in the twentieth century. Is a hegemon necessary? What are its motives? These are critical questions in IPE today.

Though my heart may be left of centre, I have always known that the only economic system that works is a market economy, in which everything belongs to someone—which means that someone is responsible for everything. It is a system in which complete independence and plurality of economic entities exist within a legal framework, and its workings are guided chiefly by the laws of the marketplace. This is the only natural economy, the only kind that makes sense, the only one that can lead to prosperity, because it is the only one that reflects the nature of life itself. The essence of life is infinitely and mysteriously multiform, and therefore it cannot be contained or planned for, in its fullness and variability, by any central intelligence.

The attempt to unite all economic entities under the authority of a single monstrous owner, the state, and to subject all economic life to one central voice of reason that deems itself more clever than life itself, is an attempt against life itself. It is an extreme expression of the hubris of modern man, who thinks that he understands the world completely—that he is the apex of creation and is therefore competent to run the whole world; who claims that his own brain is the highest form of organized matter and has not noticed that there is a structure infinitely more complex, of which he himself is merely a tiny part: this is, nature, the universe, the order of Being.[1]

Václav Havel

Václav Havel's elegant words praise the market and condemn the state. The market is natural, the essence of life, while the state is arrogant and monstrous. In this essay, Havel's state was, of course, the rigid and authoritarian communist regime that fused state and market in his native Czechoslovakia before 1989. For Havel, then, the market represents the individual freedom that the communist state denied.

If you listen carefully, you might hear an echo as you read Havel's text aloud. It is the echo of François Quesnay (1694–1774), leader of a group of French philosophers called the Physiocrats or "les Économistes." Quesnay condemned government interference in the market, holding that, with few exceptions, it brought harm to society. The Physiocrats' motto was "*Laissez-faire*, laissez-passer," meaning "let be, let pass" but said in the spirit of "Hands off! Leave us alone!"

The echo reappears in the writings of Adam Smith (1723–1790), a Scottish contemporary of Quesnay, who is generally regarded as the father of modern economics. Compare these lines from Smith's *The Wealth of Nations* (1776) with the views of Václav Havel printed above. Speaking of the free individual, the *entrepreneur*, Smith said that

> Every Individual is continually exerting himself to find out the most advantageous employment for whatever capital he can command. It is his own advantage, indeed, and not that of society, which he has in view. But the study of his own advantage naturally, or rather necessarily, leads him to prefer that employment which is most advantageous to society.[2]
>
> The Statesman, who should attempt to direct private people in what manner they ought to employ their capitals, would not only load himself with a most unnecessary attention, but assume an authority which could safely be trusted, not only to no single person, but to no council or senate whatever, and which would nowhere be so dangerous as in the hands of a man who had folly and presumption enough to fancy himself fit to exercise it.[3]

Adam Smith and Václav Havel explore common themes in these brief passages. On the one hand, they display respect, admiration, almost affection for the market. It is Smith's "invisible hand" and Havel's "essence of life." The other side of this love of market is a distaste for the state, or at least for the abusive potential of the state. Smith's state is dangerous and untrustworthy. Havel's is arrogant and "monstrous." Smith and Havel share affection for the same market, the "laissez-faire" world of individual initiative, private ownership, and limited government interference, but their fear and loathing are directed toward very different sorts of states.

The state that Smith argued against in 1776 was the mercantilist state of the eighteenth century, a strong state established on the principle that the national interest is best served when state power is used to create wealth, which produces even more power. For Adam Smith, the individual freedom of the marketplace represented the best alternative to abusive state power. As we look around the world today, we see that many nations are seeking to replace restrictive, mercantilist systems of political economy with new regimes that put more stress on market and less on state control. India and Mexico are just two examples of nations that look to market reforms to stimulate economic growth and raise living standards. Even China is using the market to infuse its political economy with the spirit of individual initiative.

The state that Havel criticized in 1992 was the communist state that dominated Czechoslovakia (and other Soviet bloc nations) from the end of World War II until 1989. This communist state engulfed the market, replacing most market activities with rigid and centralized state planning. The state owned the shops and factories and natural resources, for the most part, and ordered their use in ways that fit the planners' notion of the national interest. This centralized state-market system was powerful, but it proved to be terribly inefficient in its ability to create wealth. In embracing the marketplace, then, Havel seeks both to gain individual freedom from state power and also to gain prosperity through the market's flexibility and dynamism.

Today's news is filled with stories of the transition from rigid communist state to flexible free markets. The states of the former Soviet Union, including Russia, and former members of the Warsaw Pact, including Hungary, Poland, East Germany, and the Czech and Slovak republics, are all moving toward greater emphasis on markets and less stress on state control. Taken together, over half of all the human beings on earth are now coming to terms with the liberal ideas of Quesnay, Adam Smith, Havel, and others of their stripe. We are living in the time of a great market surge. By all appearances, this is the liberal hour.

ROOTS OF THE LIBERAL PERSPECTIVE

Liberalism is "a simple, dramatic philosophy. Its central idea is liberty under the law."[4] The liberal perspective sees individuals and states in a decidedly different light from the mercantilist perspectives discussed in the last chapter. The liberal point of view reveals clearly some parts of political economy that mercantilists miss but necessarily loses other valuable insights in the shadows.

The liberal perspective focuses on the side of human nature that is peaceful and cooperative, competitive in a constructive way, and guided by reason, not emotion. To the extent that individuals and states behave in this way, the liberal perspective holds. Although liberals believe that people are fundamentally self-interested, they do not see this as a disadvantage because they think that broad areas of society are set up in such a way that competitors can all gain, through peaceful and cooperative actions. This contrasts with the mercantilist view, which dwells on the side of human nature that is more aggressive, combative, and suspicious.

While the cooperative side of human nature is highlighted by the liberal perspective, it tends to focus on the abusive aspects of the state. Indeed, it might not be too strong to consider liberalism as an antistate school of thought. Early liberals condemned the abuses of state authority and promoted reforms, such as democratic systems of government, that weakened central power while promoting individual liberty. The dual nature of liberal thought—embracing individual liberty and wary of state abuses—is fundamental to liberalism and can be seen clearly in the earlier quotations from Smith and Havel.

It is easy to imagine why one might fear state abuses; one need only read the U.S. Declaration of Independence to gain an appreciation of this side of liberalism. But it may be more difficult to appreciate the liberal tendency to view individual actions as cooperative and constructive, not competitive and destructive. In the jargon of political economy, liberals think that society is a *positive-sum game*. In a positive-sum game, everyone can potentially get more out of a bargain than they put in. Love is one example of a positive-sum game, and market exchanges of goods or services that are mutually advantageous are another.

If you prefer apples to pears, and I prefer pears to apples, then we can swap fruit and both potentially benefit from the exchange. Mercantilists, on the other hand, tend to view life as a *zero-sum game,* where gains by one person or group necessarily come at the expense of others. Poker is one example of a zero-sum game, and dividing up a pizza pie is another. If one gets more, someone else gets less.

Liberals view the fundamental tension between state and market as a conflict between coercion and freedom, authority and individual rights, autocratic dogma and rational logic. Appalled by the abuses of church and state authority dating from feudal days, the early liberals saw a kind of salvation in individual freedom, voluntary association, and rational thought. The market, in their view, was an admirable distillation of the values and characteristics that they advocated.

The liberal view, then, comes down heavily on the side of the market when choosing sides between state and market, a fundamental tension that characterizes political economy. A free market is just one element of the liberal view (democratic government is another), but it is a very important one.

MORE THAN JUST GREED: THE ECONOMICS AND POLITICS OF LIBERALISM

The liberal perspective on political economy is perhaps best summarized by the phrase *laissez-faire* or "let be." Free individuals are best equipped to make social choices. Liberalism is, in short, very conservative, as we understand liberal and conservative politics today. The role of the state is to perform the limited number of tasks that individuals cannot perform by themselves, such as establish a basic legal system, assure national defense, and coin money. People sometimes talk about liberalism as "classical liberalism" to differentiate it from the "modern liberalism" of today.

The liberal view of human nature shows up in Adam Smith's writings. He believed in the cooperative, constructive side of human nature and gave it the famous name the "invisible hand."

> He generally, indeed, neither intends to promote the public interest, nor knows how much he is promoting it. By preferring the support of domestic to that of foreign industry, he intends only his own security; and by directing that industry in such a manner as its own produce may be of the greatest value, he intends only his own gain, and he is in this, as in many other cases, led by an invisible hand to promote an end which was no part of his intention. Nor is it always the worse for the society that it was no part of it. By pursuing his own interest he frequently promotes that of society more effectually than when he really intends to promote it. I have never known much good done by those who affected to trade for the public good.[5]

It is clear that Smith sees people working in harmony, even when they are competing for the same customers or products. For the most part, then, Smith's liberal philosophy sees no need for the heavy hand of the state in individual and market activities. Indeed, as we have seen, Smith was suspicious of the motives and methods of those who would use state power in the "public interest."

Some writers paint Adam Smith as unrealistic in his optimistic view of human nature, but he was no romantic Pollyanna. Smith knew that any individual or group that gains power also gains the potential to abuse it. This is true even in the market. Smith wrote that "people of the same trade seldom meet together, even for merriment and diversion, but the conversation ends in a conspiracy against the public, or in some contrivance to raise prices."[6]

Adam Smith has been quoted frequently in these pages; it would be hard to overstate the importance of his writings and his ideas in the development of political economy. Smith's works struck the right note at the right time and so gained a measure of respect and influence that is rare. It is important, however, to think of both sides of Smith's writings when considering the liberal view. It is not so much that liberals such as Adam Smith love wealth, perhaps, than that they fear and loathe power.[7] In a way the title of Smith's book, *The Wealth of Nations*, makes it appear that liberalism is concerned only with economics and wealth, when in fact it is perhaps more profoundly a view of politics, power, and freedom.

Adam Smith's economic writings were part of a broader intellectual movement that was intensely political. Liberal politics are represented by the writings on John Locke in England and those of Thomas Jefferson in the United States. Economic theorists may think of laissez-faire in terms of markets. "Political theorists, however, identify Liberalism with an essential principle, the importance of the freedom of the individual. Above all, this is a belief in the importance of moral freedom, of the right to be treated and a duty to treat others as ethical subjects, not as objects or means only."[8] This philosophy implies that citizens need to have certain negative rights (freedoms *from* state authority, such as freedom from unlawful arrest), positive rights (unalienable rights and freedoms *to* take certain actions, such as perhaps freedom of speech or freedom of the press), and the right of democratic participation in government without which positive and negative freedom cannot be guaranteed.[9] If these liberal political ideas sound familiar, they should be. They are embedded firmly into the U.S. Declaration of Independence and the Bill of Rights.

If liberals are falsely accused of thinking of wealth and not power, they are also wrongly often said to believe that people never disagree, that life is always a positive-sum proposition. In fact, however, liberalism understands that disagreements cannot be avoided. The question is: How will they be resolved? If power is concentrated , either by monopolies in the market or by tyrants in the state, then conflicts tend to be resolved in unfair ways and freedom is sacrificed in the process. Liberals believe that with power diffused in both state and market and rights and freedoms guaranteed, conflicts can be resolved through peaceful civil means. Liberals are optimistic about human nature and the potential for individual action, as long as power is diffused so that its corrupting influence is diminished.

THE LIBERAL VIEW OF INTERNATIONAL RELATIONS

The liberal view of human nature extends to an analysis of international affairs. Liberals tend to focus on the domain where nation-states show their cooperative, peaceful, constructive natures through harmonious competition. International trade is therefore seen as mutually advantageous, not cutthroat competition for wealth and power. What is true about individuals is true about states, in this view. Or, as Smith wrote, "What is prudence in the conduct of every family, can scarce be folly in that of a great kingdom. If a foreign country can supply us with a commodity cheaper than we ourselves can make it, better buy it of them with some part of the produce of our industry, employed in a way in which we have some advantage."[10]

Liberals like Smith generally opposed most state restrictions on free international markets. The tariffs that mercantilists saw as tools for concentrating wealth and distilling power, for example, were condemned by Smith: "Such taxes, when they have grown up to a certain height, are a curse equal to the barrenness of the earth and the inclemency of the heavens. . . ."[11]

David Ricardo (1772–1823) followed Smith in adopting the liberal view of international affairs. Ricardo was a true *political* economist who pursued successful careers in business, economics, and as a member of Parliament. Ricardo was a particular champion of free trade, which made him part of the minority in Britain's Parliament in his day. Ricardo opposed the *Corn Laws* (see the box on page 52), which restricted agricultural trade. This passage shows Ricardo's liberal point of view on trade issues:

> Under a system of perfectly free commerce, each country naturally devotes its capital and labour to such employments as are most beneficial to each. The pursuit of individual advantage is admirably connected with the universal good of the whole. By stimulating industry, by rewarding ingenuity, and by using most efficaciously the peculiar powers bestowed by nature, it distributes labour most effectively and most economically: while, by increasing the general mass of productions, it diffuses general benefit, and binds together, by one common tie of interest and intercourse, the universal society of nations throughout the civilized world.[12]

A close reading of Ricardo's words throws new light on the liberal perspective on IPE. Free commerce makes nations efficient, and efficiency is a quality that liberals value almost as highly as freedom. Individual success is "admirably connected" with "universal good"—no conflict among people or nations is envisioned here. The free international market stimulates industry, encourages innovation, and creates a "general benefit" by raising production.

Most important, perhaps, is the notion that it "binds together, by one common tie of interest and intercourse" the nations of the world. In other words, free individual actions in the production, finance, and knowledge structures create such strong ties of mutual advantage among nations that the security tie is irrelevant, or nearly so. The nations of the world become part of a "universal society" united, not separated, by their national interests. This statement reflects the liberal view of international politics as well as economics. There is no reason why the state of nature for nations need be war any more than the state of nature for individuals is merciless conflict. International institutions, such as perhaps the United Nations, that provide freedoms from, freedoms to, and a system of democratic governance have the potential, in the liberal view, to provide an environment for international peace and prosperity.

BRITAIN'S CORN LAWS

Britain's Parliament enacted the Corn Laws in 1815, soon after the defeat of Napoleon ended the long years of war. The Corn Laws were a system of tariffs and regulations that restricted food imports into Great Britain. The battle over the Corn Laws, which lasted from their inception until they were finally removed in 1846, is a classic IPE case study in the conflict between liberalism and mercantilism, market and state.

Why would Britain seek to limit imports of food from the United States and other countries? The "official" argument was that Britain needed to be self-sufficient in food, and the Corn Laws were a way to ensure that it did not become dependent on uncertain foreign supplies. This sort of argument carried some weight at the time, given Britain's wartime experiences (although Napoleon never attempted to cut off food supplies to Great Britain).

There were other reasons for Parliament's support of the Corn Laws, however. Parliament was constituted along different lines in the nineteenth century. The right to vote was not universal, and members of Parliament were chosen based on rural landholdings, not the distribution of population. The result was that Parliament represented the largely agricultural interests of the landed estates, which were an important source of both power and wealth in the seventeenth and eighteenth centuries. The growing industrial cities and towns, which were increasingly the engine of wealth in the nineteenth century, were not represented in Parliament to a proportional degree.

Seen in this light, it is clear that the Corn Laws were in the economic interests of the members of Parliament and their allies. They were detrimental, however, to the rising industrial interests in two ways. First, by forcing food prices up, the Corn Laws indirectly forced employers to increase the wages they paid workers. This increased production costs and squeezed profits. Second, by reducing Britain's imports from other countries, the Corn Laws indirectly limited Britain's manufactured exports to these markets. The United States, for example, counted on sales of agricultural goods to Britain to generate the cash to pay for imported manufactured goods. Without agricultural exports, the United States couldn't afford as many British imports.

The industrialists embraced the liberal view of IPE, that free markets and minimal state interference were in the nation's interest. (It was clearly in their interest to do so!) Adam Smith's ghost was repeatedly summoned to support their assaults. David Ricardo, the liberal political economist, grew wealthy enough from his financial affairs to acquire landholdings and a seat in Parliament, from which he railed against the Corn Laws.

Clearly, the industrialists favored repeal of the Corn Laws, but they lacked the political power to achieve their goal. The Parliamentary Reform Act of 1832, however, revised the system of parliamentary representation in Britain, reducing the power of the landed elites, who had previously dominated the government, and increasing the power of representatives of the emerging industrial centers. This Reform Act began the political process that eventually abolished the Corn Laws by weakening their political base of support.

The Corn Laws were repealed in 1846, in an act of high political drama, which changed the course of British policy for a generation. While this act is often seen as the triumph of liberal views over old-fashioned mercantilism, it is perhaps better seen as the victory of the masses over the agricultural oligarchy. Britain's population had grown quickly during the first half of the nineteenth century, and agricultural self-sufficiency was increasingly difficult, even with rising farm productivity. Crop failures in Ireland (the potato famine) in the 1840s left Parliament with little choice. It was either repeal the Corn Laws or face famine, death, and food riots.

The repeal of the Corn Laws was accompanied by a boom in the Victorian economy. Cheaper food and bigger export markets fueled a rapid short-term expansion of the British economy. Britain embraced a liberal view of trade for the rest of the century.

Given Britain's place in the global political economy as the "workshop of the world," liberal policies were the most effective way to build national wealth and power. Other nations, however, felt exploited or threatened by Britain's power and adopted mercantilist policies in self-defense.

The Corn Laws illustrate the dynamic interaction of state and market. Changes in the wealth-producing structure of the economy (from farm to industry, from country to city) eventually led to a change in the distribution of state power. The transition was not smooth, however, and took a long time, important points for us to remember as we consider states and markets in transition today.

J. S. MILL AND THE EVOLUTION OF THE LIBERAL PERSPECTIVE

It is tempting to stop here with our discussion of the liberal perspective. A view of IPE that says, basically, "hands off the market" is easy to memorize and apply. And there are political economists today who adopt what is fundamentally this classical liberal view of state-market relations. But political economy is a dynamic field, and the liberal view has evolved over the years as the nature of state market interaction has changed. The liberal view today is more complex and interesting, a set of variations on Adam Smith's powerful tune, not an endless repetition of it.

A critical person in the intellectual development of liberalism was John Stuart Mill (1806–1873).[13] Mill inherited the liberalism of Smith and Ricardo, as transmitted by his father, the political economist James Mill. His textbook *Principles of Political Economy with Some of Their Applications to Social Philosophy* (1848) more or less defined liberalism for half a century.

Mill held that liberalism had been an important *destructive* force in the eighteenth century—it was the intellectual foundation of the revolutions and reforms that weakened central authority and strengthened individual liberty in the United States and in Europe. This was an important accomplishment, in Mill's view, but he wanted more. Mill wanted a philosophy of social progress that was "moral and spiritual progress rather than the mere accumulation of wealth."[14] He proposed, therefore, that the state should take limited and selective action to supplement the market, correcting for market failures or weaknesses better to achieve social progress.

Mill believed that the state should "laissez-faire" in most but not all areas of life. He advocated limited state action in some areas, such as educating children and assisting the poor, where individual initiative might be inadequate in promoting social welfare. In general, Mill advocated as much decentralization as was consistent with reasonable efficiency; the slogan was centralize information, decentralize power, so that central government could advise and assist, but not preempt local initiative. An application of Mill's approach is easily found in his own views on education. Parents had a duty to educate their children, and might be legally compelled to do so; it was obviously intolerable to make them pay for this education if they were already poor; it was dangerous for the state to take over education as a centralized activity. The remedy was to enforce the duty on parents, give grants to individuals to pay the charges of schools, leave most education in private hands, but set up some state schools as models of good practice.[15]

This statement of Mill's views on education illustrates effectively the development of the liberal view. Parents had a duty or moral obligation to educate their children. This social duty was so important, he believed, that it outweighed the rights of individual parents. Hence, the state was justified, in Mill's view, to use its coercive power to require the education of children. But Mill also acknowledged the problems created by the market's inherent inequality—some parents might not be able to educate their children as moral obligation and state regulations required—so he advocated government grants to make education of poor children possible. Too much state involvement in education was "dangerous," but some state action, the operation of "model schools," for example, was desirable.

Mill's views on education, as on other similar social issues, reflect the evolution of liberalism in his time. The guiding principle was still "laissez-faire"; when in doubt, state interference was to be avoided. But, within a political economy based on markets and individuals, some limited government actions were desirable. The questions, for Mill as for liberal thinkers since his time, are when, how, and how far? When is government's visible hand justified as an assistant to or replacement for the invisible hand of the market? How should the state act? How far can the state go before its interference with individual rights and liberties is abusive?

Many liberals today believe that the state has some role to play in equalizing income, although there is much disagreement about how much redistribution is desirable and how much is too much. Many liberals also see advantages in state actions to preserve the environment, to promote education and training, to improve transportation and communication, and to advance science and the arts. The *degree* of state action needed in each case remains controversial, however, even among liberals.

THE WAR, DEPRESSION, AND MR. KEYNES

John Maynard Keynes[16] (pronounced "canes") stands out in the development of IPE and in the evolution of the liberal perspective. Keynes (1883–1946) developed an interesting and subtle strain of the liberal perspective that we call the ***Keynesian Theory*** of economics or perhaps Keynesian political economy. The Keynesian version of liberalism (and there are many liberals who would not include Keynes in their ranks!) combines state and market influences in a way that, while still in the spirit of Adam Smith, relies on the "invisible hand" on a narrower range of issues and sees a larger, but still limited, sphere of constructive state action.

Keynes's political economy was shaped by his experiences with three of the defining events of the twentieth century: World War I, the rise of the Marxist-Leninist Soviet Union, and the worldwide Great Depression of the 1930s. From World War I, Keynes learned the dangers of undiluted mercantilism. The Great War and its unstable aftermath were, in his view, the result of nationalism, greed, and vengeance. Clearly states could go much too far in the name of national interest!

Keynes's experiences in and with the Soviet Union discouraged any thought he might have had of adopting a Marxist or communist point of view. Keynes viewed Leninism as a religion, with a strong emotional appeal that capitalism lacked, not a theory of political economy. He found the Soviet regime repressive, its disregard for individual freedom intolerable.

Because Keynes rejected mercantilism, like Adam Smith, and communism, like Václav Havel, it might appear that Keynes would necessarily be a liberal. But Keynes was critical, too, of the cult of the market that extreme liberalism represents. Here he was influenced by the Great Depression of the 1930s, which he interpreted as evidence that the invisible hand sometimes errs in catastrophic ways. As early as 1926, Keynes wrote:

> Let us clear from the ground the metaphysical or general principles upon which, from time to time, *laissez-faire* has been founded. It is *not* true that individuals possess a prescriptive "Natural liberty" in their economic activities. There is *no* "compact" conferring perpetual rights on those who Have or on those who Acquire. The world is *not* so governed from above that private and social interest always coincide. It is *not* so managed here below that in practice they coincide. It is *not* a correct deduction from the Principles of Economics that enlightened self-interest always operates in the public interest. Nor is it true that self-interest generally *is* enlightened; more often individuals acting separately to promote their own ends are too ignorant or too weak to attain even these. Experience does *not* show that individuals, when they make up a social unit, are always less clear-sighted than when they act separately.[17]

In Keynes's view, individuals and markets tended to make decisions that were particularly unwise when faced with situations where the future is unknown and there is no effective way to share risks or coordinate otherwise chaotic actions. It is possible for individuals to behave rationally and in their individual self interest, Keynes thought, and yet to have the collective result be both irrational and destructive—a clear failure of the invisible hand. Here Keynes seems to foresee the Great Depression that came just a few years later.

> Many of the greatest economic evils of our time are the fruits of risk, uncertainty, and ignorance. . . . Yet the cure lies outside the operations of individuals; it may even be to the interest of individuals to aggravate the disease. . . . These measures would involve Society in exercising directive intelligence through some appropriate organ of action over many of the inner intricacies of private business, yet it would leave private initiative and enterprise unhindered.[18]

A classic example of this problem is called the ***paradox of thrift.*** Suppose that you were concerned that you might be unemployed next year. What would it be rational for you to do? One rational response to uncertainty about your future income would be to spend less and save more, to build up a cushion of funds in case you need them later. This is fine for you, but what if everyone behaves rationally in this way? If everyone spends less, then there is less purchased, less produced, fewer workers needed, and less income created. The recession and unemployment that everyone feared will come to pass—*caused* by the very actions that individuals took to protect themselves from this eventuality.

And, just as no individual caused the recession, no individual can reverse or prevent it either. Only collective action—through the state—can make a difference. Keynes argued that the state should spend and invest when individuals would not to offset their collective irrationality. In principle, he wrote, the state could spend on anything—even putting money into old bottles, burying them at the bottom of old coal mines, then hiring the unemployed to dig them out—as long as its rational program offset the collective irrationality of individuals.[19]

In other words, Keynes thought that the state could and should use its power to fortify and improve the market, but not along the aggressive, nationalistic lines of mercantilism, and not with the oppressive force of communism. Keynes was, at heart, still a liberal, who believed in the positive force of the market but saw the need for state action where rational individual choices were most likely to produce irrational collective outcomes.

> These reflections have been directed towards possible improvements in the technique of modern Capitalism by the agency of collective action. There is nothing in them which is seriously incompatible with what seems to me to be the essential characteristic of Capitalism, namely the dependence upon the intense appeal to the money-making and money-loving instincts of individuals as the main motive force of the economic machine.[20]
>
> For my part, I think that Capitalism, wisely managed, can probably be made more efficient for attaining economic ends than any alternative system yet in sight, but that in itself is in many ways objectionable. Our problem is to work out a social organization which shall be as efficient as possible without offending our notions of a satisfactory way of life.[21]

Keynes's perspective on IPE finds strengths and weaknesses in both state and market. While he advocated free markets in a wide domain, including international trade and finance, for the most part, he still believed that positive government action was both useful and necessary to deal with problems that the invisible hand would not set right. These problems included especially the macroeconomic diseases of inflation and unemployment.

Keynes also doubted that people are invariably rational in their behavior. The stock market, he said, was influenced by the "animal spirits" of traders. The stock market crash of 1929 showed what can happen when investors are spooked and stampede.

Keynes developed a new and somewhat complex strain of IPE that was liberal on the international front but recognized a need for firm state action internally to overcome the obstacles of risk, uncertainty, and ignorance. Keynes's ideas formed and shaped many modern institutions, ranging from the system of international trade and finance, on one hand, to the programs of unemployment insurance, social security, and bank deposit insurance on the other.

THE KEYNESIAN COMPROMISE

Keynes's complex view of political economy shaped the world's IPE for a generation when it became embedded in the post–World War II *Bretton Woods system* of international political and economic arrangements and institutions. Near the end of World War II, leaders of the Allied nations met at a hotel in Bretton Woods, New Hampshire, to forge global structures that would change the course of history from the war-depression-war pattern of the first half of the twentieth century. Keynes headed the British delegation to Bretton Woods, and the Bretton Woods system, while not Keynes's plan, certainly reflected many of his ideas.

The postwar *Bretton Woods* system has been called the **Keynesian compromise** or a system of "embedded liberalism." This system envisioned a liberal international system, with open markets and free trade. Within this system, however, individual nations would be able to undertake the sorts of domestic policies that Keynes advocated for moderating inflation, controlling unemployment, and encouraging economic growth. In other words, the state had a fairly important macroeconomic role *within* each nation, but free markets were intended to dominate relations *between* nations. Bretton Woods can thus be thought of as something of a compromise between a strong market and a strong state (hence "Keynesian compromise"), or as a strong state embedded in a strong market ("embedded liberalism").

The Bretton Woods system will be discussed in greater depth later in this book (especially in chapters 6 through 8). For now, however, it is important to note that Bretton Woods represented a fundamental change in liberalism. After Keynes and Bretton Woods, liberals no longer viewed IPE as state versus market. Rather, liberals sought the right degree and nature of state intervention within an overall system of open markets. The difference between liberalism and mercantilism, while still clear in general, became blurred in places.

THE LIBERAL VIEW OF HEGEMONY

The theory of **hegemonic stability** is another variation on the liberal theme, different from Keynes but clearly reflecting the Keynesian spirit.[22] This theory looks at the role of state and market in the global economy and observes that international markets work best when certain international **public goods** are present.[23] These public goods include such things as free trade, peace, and security, or at least a balance of powers, and a sound system of international payments.

Each of these public goods is costly to provide, and each suffers from what economists call the **free-rider problem.** Individuals and nations that do not contribute to the cost of providing these public goods will still be able to benefit from them. Under these circumstances, it will often be the case that the world economy will suffer, since no nation will be willing to bear all the costs of enforcing free trade, sound money, and so on, while others derive benefits without paying. At certain times, however, one nation that dominates the world economy emerges. That nation finds it in its own interest to provide international public goods, even taking free riders into account. The *hegemon* benefits so much from the growth and success of the world economy that it is willing to bear the costs of providing international public goods to smaller or weaker states which find it in their interest to cooperate in order to preserve their "free ride."

The liberal theory of hegemonic stability asserts that when a hegemon arises, the world economy tends to grow and prosper, as the benefits of free trade, peace and security, sound money, and so forth, stimulate markets everywhere. When the hegemon fails, however, these public goods disappear and the world economy stagnates or declines. Political economists generally recognize three instances of hegemonic stability in modern history: The United Provinces (Holland) was the hegemon in the eighteenth century, Great Britain was the hegemon in the nineteenth century, and the United States performed the hegemon's function for much of the postwar era.

The hegemonic stability theory has stimulated a great deal of discussion. Scholars ask, What happens when there is no hegemon? Is the United States still a hegemon? If the United States is a "hegemon in decline" (like Great Britain before World War I), then is some sort of group hegemon possible, involving the European Union or perhaps a U.S.–Japan "bigemony"?

Scholars also debate the motives and effects of hegemony. Is the hegemon unselfish, draining itself dry in the end as it tries to keep the international system running? Or is the hegemon selfish and imperialistic, draining the rest of the world to fill its coffers?

Like the Keynesian viewpoint, the liberal theory of hegemonic stability is based on the strength and resiliency of the market as a form of social and economic organization. Whereas Keynes thought that the state needed to be active within nations to assure economic growth and stability, hegemonic stability theory asserts that some state—the hegemon—needs to shoulder an international role if markets are to achieve their potential. Where Keynes called for domestic policy, then, hegemonic stability focuses on international policies.

THREE PERSPECTIVES ON HEGEMONY

Few ideas in IPE have generated as much discussion and debate as has hegemony. Who are the hegemons? What are their motives? How do they behave? What effect do they have on the IPE? This chapter introduced the idea of hegemony in the context of the liberal theory of hegemonic stability as developed in the postwar period. This brief box provides a glimpse of some alternative views of hegemony.

A hegemon is created when the richest and most powerful nation within some sphere of the international political economy assumes responsibility for organizing a system of international political and economic relations. Most IPE scholars identify three instances of hegemony in the modern period of history: the United Provinces (Holland) in the eighteenth century, the United Kingdom in the nineteenth century, and the United States since the end of World War II. In the years between hegemons, as during the period between World Wars I and II, no single nation-state dominates or organizes the international system.

Liberals, as noted in the text, generally view the hegemon as the key to a positive-sum game. The hegemon supplies the public goods, such as security and free trade, that make the international system function more efficiently. This increases the range and degree of mutually advantageous transactions that take place. The *benevolent hegemon* bears most of the costs of maintaining this system but also reaps most of the gains, since its own success is so tightly bound to the success of its partner nations. The hegemon is guided by what we might call enlightened self-interest—its self-interest is best served by maintaining the security and prosperity of others. Liberal scholars thus view the behavior of the United States in the postwar IPE, including its role in the Bretton Woods monetary system (see chapter 6) and the NATO security system (see chapter 9) as examples of an enlightened hegemon at work. The problem with hegemony, in the liberal view, is that the costs of hegemony tend to rise and weaken the hegemon's base of wealth and power. If this condition persists, the security and prosperity of the IPE are threatened.

The notion of the benevolent hegemon, however, is challenged from two intellectual directions. Realists see hegemony as part of a mercantilist strategy of dominance. Proponents of the *modern world system* view (to be developed in chapter 4) see hegemony as part of a grand cycle of history. All three views of hegemony provide important insights into the nature of IPE relations.

Nation-states are guided by self-interest, according to the realists (see chapter 2). The realist analysis of hegemony, therefore, focuses on the *selfish hegemon*. As the richest and most powerful nation, the hegemon is able to call the tune, to set the rules of the game for international political and economic relations. It is only natural, realists argue, for the hegemon to establish rules and relationships that will favor it over its partners and competitors. The hegemon uses its dominant position to gain wealth and power from others in the international system, which is a logical extension of the mercantilist view of IPE.

The temptations of selfish hegemony are great, according to realists, and it is to be expected that the hegemon will eventually overreach, seeking more international influence than it can maintain. "Imperial overreach" weakens hegemony and leads to its decline.[a]

Political realists view the United States as a classic example of a selfish hegemon. The United States established the postwar "rules of the game" with a built-in bias in favor of U.S. interests. Through the General Agreement on Tariffs and Trade (GATT) and the World Trade Organization, for example, the United States supported a system of free world trade. This might have benefited other countries, realists argue, but it benefited the United States most of all since, in the days following the end of World War II, the United States was the largest industrial producer and so got the lion's share of the gains from a free trade system.

In the same way, realists argue that the United States was the selfish hegemon on monetary fronts. The Bretton Woods monetary system put the U.S. dollar at the center of global finance. This arrangement burdened the United States with special obligations but also gave it opportunities to abuse the system. For a time, the United States could run up international debts and pay for them by simply printing dollars—an advantage that other debtor nations, who had to pay with real resources, were not permitted.

Realists look at U.S. security policy in the same light. They focus on the extent to which the postwar security structure, the so-called **Pax Americana** that included NATO, served U.S. interests more than the interests of its allies. The pattern of the selfish hegemon can be found throughout the IPE. The decline of the United States in recent decades is seen as the result of its "imperial overreach" during the 1960s and 1970s.

A third perspective on hegemony is provided by the *Modern World System* (MWS) theory (which will be explored in chapter 4). Briefly, MWS theory looks at the IPE as the interaction of an industrial *core* and an agricultural *periphery* taking place within the global system of capitalism. MWS theory focuses on the long-term nature of IPE relationships and thus views hegemony as part of a long-term cycle within the industrial core. Christopher Chase-Dunn notes

> a fluctuation of hegemony versus multicentricity in the distribution of military power and economic competitive advantage in production among core states. Hegemonic periods are those in which power and competitive advantage are relatively concentrated in a single hegemonic state. Multicentric periods are those in which there is a more equal distribution of power and competitive advantage among core states. In only a very rough sense is this a cycle because its periodicy is very uneven.[b]

An oversimplified MWS account of the hegemonic cycle might go like this: A rich and powerful nation gains control over the core following a world war. Eventually, however, the hegemon falls into decline, leading to a period where there may be several important core nation-states held in a *balance of power*. The balance eventually breaks down, war follows, and a new hegemon rises from the ashes. Hegemony in this view is neither benevolent nor selfish as much as it is part of the nature of capitalist international relations. The postwar hegemony of the United States is part of the larger pattern of capitalism in the MWS view.

An active scholarly controversy exists about the nature and consequences of hegemony. As is often the case, however, the three viewpoints presented here help illuminate different aspects of the situation, so we do not necessarily need to *choose* a single view of hegemony but can gain insights from its many-sidedness. One scholar who has taken this position is David P. Calleo, who has described the benevolent hegemon and the selfish hegemon as two stages in a larger hegemonic cycle. Calleo notes that

> while the [liberal] hegemonic view served well enough to inspire the creation of the *Pax Americana*, it also carried troubling implications for its future, the future that now seems fast upon us. Hegemony has a tendency to break down because of the absolute or relative weakening of the hegemonic power itself. A hegemon in decay begins to exploit the system in order to compensate for its progressing debility.[c]

Two important questions regarding hegemony will appear repeatedly in this book. The first is the question of decline—is the United States a hegemon in decline (or decay, to use Calleo's term)? If so, what does this mean for the United States and for the world? The second question follows from the first: If the United States *is* a declining hegemon, then *what next?* Is this the end of hegemony and the start of a new multicentered system, as the MWS theorists would suggest? Or will some other hegemon rise up to take the place of the United States? If so, *who?*

---

[a]See Paul Kennedy, *The Rise and Fall of the Great Powers* (New York: Random House, 1987) for a historical account of this viewpoint.
[b]Christopher Chase-Dunn, *Global Formation* (Cambridge, MA: Blackwell, 1989), p. 50.
[c]David P. Calleo, *Beyond American Hegemony* (New York: Basic Books, 1987), p. 149

CONSERVATISM: THE RESURGENCE OF CLASSICAL LIBERALISM

The Keynesian flavor of liberalism, markets swirled with a distinct state stripe, became the mainstream IPE view in the industrial world during the years from the 1930s to the 1970s. In some places, such as Hong Kong, the market was emphasized to a greater extent, creating a dynamic, free-wheeling, free-market system. In other places, such as Sweden, the role of the state was emphasized to a greater degree, creating a more socialist system.[24] Generally, however, the industrialized nations balanced state and market forces along the lines of the Keynesian compromise, using state power to supplement, strengthen, and stabilize the market economy, within the liberal Bretton Woods system of international institutions.[25]

During this period, the term *liberal* in political discourse came to mean something different than what it means historically in IPE. *Liberal* came to be associated with the stronger state role that the Keynesians and eventually the socialists advocated. In other words, *liberal*, a view that emphasizes the market, came to mean an emphasis on the state. The opposite of the new "liberalism" is the "old liberalism," which came to be called conservatism! In most respects, contemporary conservative views mirror those of the classical liberals, such as Adam Smith.

During the 1960s, for example, state policy in the United States became much more active than in previous decades. The federal government took strong steps at home and abroad in such varied areas as space exploration, the Vietnam War, civil rights, the "Great Society" antipoverty programs, Medicare medical insurance for the elderly, and regulation of business and the environment. Especially during this period, the term *liberal* became associated with advocates of a strong state.

The rising influence of the state in socialist countries and in "liberal" industrial nations stimulated a resurgence of "conservative" classical liberal views. Two influential leaders of this movement were the Austrian Friedrich A. Hayek (1899–1992) and the American Milton Friedman (1912–), both economists and both Nobel prize winners in their field. Hayek and Friedman renewed Adam Smith's call for laissez-faire in a world where the goals of state intervention were much different than in Smith's day, but many of its methods (taxation, regulation, etc.) were the same.

Hayek's most influential work was *The Road to Serfdom* (1944), where he argued that socialism and growing state influence represented fundamental threats to individual liberty. In Hayek's view, the growing role of government to provide greater economic security was the first step on a slippery slope. A little economic security soon leads to demand for even more security, he wrote, and before you know it you've slid all the way—the role of the state has grown so large that individual freedom and liberty have disappeared, as in Fascist Germany. Looking at the world of the 1930s, he wrote that

> If we want to form a picture of what society would be like if, according to the ideal which has seduced so many socialists, if was organized as a single great factory, we have only to look to ancient Sparta or to [Hitler's] Germany . . .
>
> In a society used to freedom it is unlikely that many people would be ready deliberately to purchase security at this price. But the policies which are now followed everywhere, which hand out the privilege of security, now to this group and now to that, are nevertheless rapidly creating conditions in which the striving for security tends to become stronger than the love of freedom. The reason for this is that with every grant of complete security to one group the insecurity of the rest necessarily increases. . . . And the essential element of security which the competitive system offers, the great variety of opportunities, is more and more reduced.[26]

Hayek argued that the only way to have security *and* freedom was to limit the role of government and draw security from the opportunity that the market provides to free individuals.

Friedman built upon Hayek's foundation. In *Capitalism and Freedom* (1962) he reacted directly to the progovernment policies of President John F. Kennedy, who said in his inaugural address that citizens should "ask not what your country can do for you—ask what you can do for your country." Friedman wrote that

> The free man will ask neither what his country can do for him nor what he can do for his country. He will ask rather "What can I and my compatriots do through government" to help us discharge our individual responsibilities, to achieve our several

goals and purposes, and above all to protect our freedom? And he will accompany this question with another: How can we keep the government we create from becoming a Frankenstein that will destroy the very freedom we establish it to protect? Freedom is a rare and delicate plant. Our minds tell us, and history confirms, that *the great threat to freedom is the concentration of power*. Government is necessary to preserve our freedom, it is an instrument through which we can exercise our freedom; yet by concentrating power in political hands, it is also a threat to freedom. Even though the men who wield this power initially be of good will and even though they be not corrupted by the power they exercise, the power will be attract and form men of a different stamp.[27]

Here Friedman consciously returns to the classical liberalism of Adam Smith. A state that takes the citizens' freedom through actions based on Keynesian ideas is no better than one that seizes freedom guided by mercantilist, socialist, or fascist notions of security. Power naturally concentrates in the state and the great threat to freedom is the concentration of power. Capitalism, with its free competitive market, diffuses power and so preserves freedom. Friedman's title, *Capitalism and Freedom,* stresses the classical liberal view that the market preserves and protects liberty. Together with others writing in the same vein Hayek and Friedman laid out an intellectual framework and policy agenda that was distinctly in the spirit of Adam Smith, in direct opposition to the prevailing Keynesian ideas of the 1960s and 1970s.

As the Keynesian compromise broke down in the 1970s, classical liberal ideas like those of Hayek and Friedman became increasingly popular and powerful. These forces reached their zenith in the 1980s as classical liberalism became a dominant political ideology.

REAGAN, THATCHER, AND THE NEOCONSERVATIVES

In the 1980s, the classical liberal view of IPE asserted itself forcefully through a movement that is often called *neoconservatism* (which could just as well have been termed *neoliberalism*!). The chief practitioners of neoconservative IPE were Prime Minister Margaret Thatcher of Great Britain and U.S. President Ronald Reagan. These two strong leaders advocated free markets at home and on the international front, and minimal state interference in all spheres of activity except security, where a strong anticommunist stand was advocated. This view of IPE owes far more to Adam Smith, Friedrich von Hayek, and Milton Friedman than to Maynard Keynes.

The neoconservative policies of Reagan and Thatcher were designed to reduce state control of private sector activities. In the United States, this took the form of tax cuts and deregulation of markets. The top income tax rate in the United States was cut in stages from 70 percent in 1980 to 33 percent in 1986. Telephone, commercial airline, and trucking industries were subject to dramatic deregulation, allowing greater competition and freedom to set prices.

Deregulation in Britain was accompanied by a dramatic reduction in state ownership of business and assets. Publicly owned firms and publicly held housing were "privatized," reducing the size of government and its influence on individual decisions.

The success of these classical liberal policies in the United States and Britain, combined with the collapse of communism in Eastern Europe, has led to a dramatic renewal of liberal policies around the world. Deregulation and privatization were widespread policies in the 1990s; the influence of Reagan and Thatcher can be seen today all over the world, from Africa to Europe, from South America to Asia. The neoconservative perspective on IPE remains influential. It calls for a reduced state role in the market through such actions as deregulation of industry, privatization of state-owned enterprises, and lower tax burdens on businesses and individuals. To an important extent, the "conservative revolution" of classical liberalism continues today, although the perennial problems of the balance between state and market remain everywhere controversial.

LIBERALISM TODAY

With the collapse of communism and the increasing influence of liberal views and market forces around the world today, this would seem to be the dawn of the liberal era. Liberalism today, however, retains all the stripes and variations of its past, which makes it complex and interesting. There are many variations of the "liberal" perspective on IPE. The classical "liberal" views of Smith and Ricardo exist alongside the very similar "conservative" ideas of Reagan and Thatcher and the somewhat more "progressive" views of Keynes.

Václav Havel reflects a modern liberal's view of these matters. Writing about energy policy in the former Czechoslovakia, he calls for greater use of the market than in communist times, but

> Even so, I think—and I am newly persuaded of this every day—that there are problems that the marketplace cannot and will not solve by itself. . . . One doesn't need to be an expert to understand that the marketplace alone cannot decide which direction Czechoslovakia should take. . . . Clearly the state will play a diminishing role in guiding the economy and deciding where, by whom, how, and how much. . . . Its role will be to come up with appropriate legislation and economic policies to encourage development in the desired direction, that direction being towards decentralization, plurality of sources, efficiency, ecological soundness, and diversification of foreign suppliers.[28]

In fact, as president of the Czech Republic, Havel worried that the emphasis on the market might go *too* far, with disastrous social results for both market and state. Moving from too strong a state (communism) to too weak a state might risk a backlash and a return to authoritarian rule. Here Havel warns against adopting liberal policies to an unwise extreme:

> The market economy is as natural and matter-of-fact to me as air. After all, it is a system of human economic activity that has been tried and found to work over centuries (centuries? millennia!). It is the system that best corresponds to human nature. But precisely because it is so down-to-earth, it is not, and cannot constitute, a world view, a philosophy, or an ideology. Even less does it contain the meaning of life. It seems both ridiculous and dangerous when . . . the market economy suddenly becomes a cult, a collection of dogmas, uncompromisingly defended and more important, even, than what the economic system is intended to serve—that is, life itself.[29]

So what can we conclude about liberalism today? It is possible to be as optimistic or as pessimistic about liberalism as you care to be. You can look at the newspaper and find plenty of evidence supporting liberalism's success or its failure.

On one hand you can celebrate the triumph of capitalism and democracy over communism and proclaim, along with Francis Fukuyama, the "end of history" in the sense that the historic struggle to determine the best system of political economy has ended and liberalism is the winner. Certainly there is a remarkable global consensus that economic decentralization is desirable and that concentrated power corrupts. Globalization, the worldwide expansion of the market, puts increasing pressure on states to adopt liberal economic policies (although liberal political institutions do not always follow). In many respects this *is* the "liberal hour," the clear dawn when freedom's blossoms all burst into bloom.

On the other hand, on closer inspection, both capitalism and democracy turn out to be surprisingly fragile flowers. It is difficult in practice to create the social environment that these liberal institutions need to thrive. In Russia, for example, citizens equate the market with the Mafia because of the power that organized crime has taken in the new markets there. Democracy in Russia is off to a shaky start, too. Many nations are learning that markets can be an unstable foundation for domestic society (see the discussion of currency crises in chapter 7). With the end of the Cold War, we have observed the rise of conflicts and divisions based on tribal, ethnic, racial, and religious differences. It is not clear that even Adam Smith's invisible hand can point the way to freedom in this landscape of fear and hate.

Liberalism today is therefore something of a paradox. It is more accepted than ever as a theory of how society can and should work if freedom and prosperity are sought. But liberalism is difficult to transplant and hard to maintain. The challenge for liberals today is to learn how to create civil society, the society of individual rights and freedoms from and freedoms to, on which to build a liberal world of capitalism and freedom.

DISCUSSION QUESTIONS

1. Adam Smith and Václav Havel are both liberals in the sense this term is used in IPE. Explain what views Smith and Havel share regarding the market, the state, human nature, and power.
2. How do liberals such as David Ricardo view international trade? Why do they hold this opinion? Explain how the Corn Laws debate in nineteenth-century Britain illustrates the conflict between mercantilist and liberal views of international trade.
3. John Stuart Mill and John Maynard Keynes thought that government could play a positive role in correcting problems in the market. Discuss the specific types of "market failures" that Mill and Keynes perceived and the types of government actions they advocated. If Mill and Keynes favored some state action in the market, how can we consider them liberals? Explain.

4. The term "liberal" in IPE means something different from what it means in everyday political discussions. Explain the difference and briefly explain how and why the term took on its current meaning.
5. Compare and contrast the liberal perspective on IPE with the mercantilist perspective in terms of the following factors: level of analysis, view of human nature, attitude toward power, notion of the proper role of government, and view of the nature of the international system.

INTERNET LINKS

Adam Smith and the *Wealth of Nations*:
> http://bized.ac.uk/virtual/economy/library/economists/smith.htm

David Ricardo:
> http://bized.ac.uk/virtual/economy/library/economists/ricardo.htm

John Maynard Keynes:
> http://bized.ac.uk/virtual/economy/library/economists/keynes.htm

Milton Friedman and Friedrich von Hayek:
> http://bized.ac.uk/virtual/economy/library/economists/monetarist.htm

SUGGESTED READINGS

Milton Friedman. *Capitalism and Freedom*. Chicago: University of Chicago Press, 1962.

Michael W. Doyle. Especially Part II: Liberalism, in *Ways of War and Peace*. New York: W.W. Norton, 1997.

John Kenneth Galbraith. Especially "The New World of Adam Smith" and "John Maynard Keynes", in *Economics in Perspective*. Boston: Houghton-Mifflin, 1987.

Václav Havel. *Summer Meditations*, trans. Paul Wilson. New York: Knopf, 1992.

John A. Hall. *Corecion and Consent*. Cambridge: Polity Press, 1994.

Friedrich A. Hayek. *The Road to Serfdom*. Chicago: University of Chicago Press, 1944.

John Maynard Keynes. *Essays in Persuasion*. New York: W. W. Norton, 1963.

Kent Mathews and Patrick Minford. "Mrs Thatcher's Economic Policies. 1979–87," *Economic Policy* (October 1987), pp. 57–102.

Thomas K. McCraw. "The Trouble with Adam Smith," *The American Scholar* (Summer 1992), pp. 353–373.

David Ricardo. *The Principles of Political Economy and Taxation*. London: Dent, 1973.

Adam Smith. *The Wealth of Nations*. New York: Dutton, 1964.

Daniel Yergin and Joseph Stanislaw. *The Commanding Heights*. New York: Simon & Schuster, 1998.

NOTES

1. Václav Havel, "What I Believe," in *Summer Meditations*, trans. Paul Wilson (New York: Knopf, 1992), p. 62. Havel was president of the Czech and Slovak Federal Republic when these words were written, and they must be interpreted in the context of Czechoslovakia's overthrow of its communist government. In 1992, Czechoslovakia split into the separate Czech and Slovak Republics.
2. Adam Smith, *The Wealth of Nations* (New York: Dutton, 1964), p. 398. *The Wealth of Nations* was first published in 1776, a noteworthy year in liberal IPE. Do not confuse Adam Smith, the classical liberal, with "Adam Smith," the contemporary business journalist who uses this famous pen name.
3. Ibid., p. 400.

4. Ralf Dahrendorf, "Liberalism," in John Eatwell, Murray Milgate, and Peter Newman, eds., *The New Palgrave: Invisible Hand* (New York: W. W. Norton, 1989), p. 183.

5. Smith, *The Wealth of Nations*, p. 400.

6. Ibid., p. 117.

7. To Smith, the "state" meant Britain's Parliament, which represented the interests of the landed gentry, *not* the entrepreneurs and citizens of the growing industrial centers. Not until the 1830s was Parliament reformed to distribute political power more widely. As a Scot without landed estates, Smith had some reason to question the power structure of his time.

8. Michael W. Doyle, *The Ways of War and Peace* (New York: W.W. Norton, 1997), p. 207.

9. Ibid.

10. Smith, *Wealth of Nations*, p. 401.

11. Ibid., p. 410.

12. David Ricardo, *The Principles of Political Economy and Taxation* (London: Dent, 1973), p. 81.

13. J. S. Mill's dates place him between the life spans of Adam Smith and J. M. Keynes, which is roughly where he falls, as well, in the development of liberal thought.

14. Alan Ryan, "John Stuart Mill," in *The New Palgrave: The Invisible Hand*, (New York: W.W. Norton, 1989) p. 201.

15. Ibid., p. 208.

16. He was known as Maynard Keynes, to distinguish him from his father, the economist John Neville Keynes.

17. John Maynard Keynes, "The End of Laissez-Faire," in *Essays in Persuasion* (New York: W. W. Norton, 1963), p. 312.

18. Ibid., pp. 317–318.

19. Of course Keynes did not actually advocate wasteful spending, but his point was that what was needed was spending, pure and simple, not spending on some particular item.

20. Ibid., pp. 319.

21. Ibid., pp. 321.

22. The American economist Charles Kindleberger is generally credited as the originator of the hegemonic stability theory. See his *Money and Power: The Economics of International Politics and the Politics of International Economics* (New York: Basic Books, 1970).

23. A *public good* is a good or service which, once made available to someone, can be consumed or used by all without cost. The classic example of a public good is a lighthouse, which warns ships of a hazard.

24. Socialism is a system of political economy that puts particular emphasis on equality of distribution.

25. This discussion refers to the nations of Western Europe and North America, for the most part. The communist nations and less developed countries were generally organized along different lines.

26. Friedrich A. Hayek, *The Road to Serfdom* (Chicago: University of Chicago Press, 1944), pp. 127-128.

27. Milton Friedman, *Capitalism and Freedom* (Chicago: University of Chicago Press, 1962), p. 2. Italics added.

28. Havel, *Summer Meditations*, pp. 72–73.

29. Ibid.

4

Marx, Lenin,
and the Structuralist
Perspective

OVERVIEW

Karl Marx is one of the most imposing figures in the history of political economy. With the collapse of communism in Russia and Eastern Europe, it is tempting to conclude that "Marx is dead" and to move on to other, easier pursuits. However, ideas that originated with Marx remain very much alive today. Theories that incorporate notions of class struggle, exploitation, imperialism, and technical change, to name just a few, remain important tools of IPE analysis.

This chapter explores a number of theories, ideas, and concepts whose roots are located in *Marxist* and *Leninist* thought. The general heading *structuralism* accounts for some of the more recent theories and concepts that incorporate a number of Marx's and Lenin's ideas.

Modern structuralists often ask questions that others tend to overlook or downplay. Indeed, there are many problems in IPE that cannot be understood or completely appreciated without considering Marx's viewpoint and the more recent structuralist perspectives he helped pioneer. The underlying notion uniting the ideas of what we will call structuralism is that structure conditions outcome. Since capitalism was primarily a national phenomenon in Marx's time, he focused most of his analysis on national economies and how the class structure resulted in exploitation, conflict, and crisis within nation-states.

V. I. Lenin expanded Marx's study to account explicitly for imperialism, manifest in the dominant and exploitative relationship of industrial countries with their colonial possessions.

More recently, a number of structuralists focus on a variety of issues associated with imperialism or, otherwise, with the relationship of developing to developed countries. Two concepts that are integral to these studies are the dependency of Third and Fourth World countries on industrialized First World countries, and the modern world system theory, which assigns nations a role in the international division of labor.

Those who hold structuralist views see the global political economy in ways fundamentally different from liberals and mercantilists. The keys for them are the national and international economic structures, which they consider to be the driving force behind IPE. "Economics determines politics," as the saying goes. Likewise, whereas liberals and mercantilists make individuals and the state their respective basic units of analysis, structuralists focus on class and the global political economy (often referred to as the modern world system).

The history of all hitherto existing society is the history of class struggles.[1]

Karl Marx and Friedrich Engels

Imperialism is capitalism in that stage of development in which the domination of monopolies and finance capital has established itself; in which the export of capital has acquired pronounced importance; in which the partition of all the territories of the globe among the great capitalist powers has been completed.[2]

V. I. Lenin

The Third World countries of today were drawn into the capitalist world market under regimes of formal and informal colonialism, as appendages of the metropolitan nations to supply raw materials and exotic commodities to the industrial center.[3]

Joan Robinson

On January 1, 1994, a small army of peasant guerrillas seized six towns in the poor Mexican state of Chiapas. The "Chiapas Awakening," as it was called by some, was a protest against a political and economic system that the peasants saw as fundamentally biased against them. The date of the revolt was carefully chosen for its symbolic value. New Year's Day 1994, was the date when the North American Free Trade Agreement (NAFTA) came into force, uniting Mexico with Canada and the United States in a huge open market. NAFTA, the rebels believed, would serve to increase their exploitation by the capitalist system. In revolting against the Mexican system of political economy, they were revolting against the inherent inequality of certain kinds of economic development.

The Chiapas Awakening clearly was neither liberal nor mercantilist in nature. The rebels protested against both the force of the market and the collective power of the state. The intellectual forefather of the Chiapas rebellion was Karl Marx, not Adam Smith or Friedrich List. The Chiapas Awakening reflected the third perspective on IPE, which we term *structuralism*.

This chapter explores the intellectual family tree of structuralism from its historical roots in the industrial revolution to its several branches in the world today. The quotations that opened this chapter, by Karl Marx, V. I. Lenin, and Joan Robinson, hint at where the discussion in this chapter will take us. We will first explore the early roots of the structuralist perspective in the writings of Karl Marx. Marx thought that power was rooted in the ownership of production capital (the means of production), which shaped the relationship among different classes within a nation. Lenin saw imperialism—the domination of industrializing nations over dependent colonial possessions—as a necessary stage of capitalism. Later in the chapter, we will explore a number of contemporary structuralist viewpoints that incorporate variations on these themes.

Some people tend to look at all of IPE from the structuralist perspective, rejecting as hopelessly biased the other viewpoints we have discussed so far. In the same way, economic liberals and mercantilists usually reject the structuralist view as fatally flawed.

In this book, we take a firm stand on middle ground. The structuralist perspective forces us to analyze problems, issues, and events that might be overlooked if we limited ourselves to the liberal and mercantilist viewpoints alone. For example, issues of class, exploitation, the distribution of wealth and power, dependency, and global aspects of capitalism take center stage.

Moreover, this perspective is, at its roots, a critical one, raising challenges to the existing state of affairs. First, many see in structuralism not only the tools to conduct a scientific analysis of existing capitalist arrangements but also the grounds for a moral critique of the inequality and exploitation that capitalism produces within and between countries. Second, this framework of analysis is the only one that allows us to view IPE "from below," that is, from the perspective of the oppressed classes and poor, developing Third World nations. In contrast to mercantilism and liberalism, it gives a voice to the powerless. Finally, structuralism focuses on what is dynamic in IPE, seeing capitalism and other modes of production as driven by conflict and crisis and subject to change. What exists now is a system and set of structures that emerged at a particular time and will eventually be replaced by a new and different system of political economy.

We should make it clear at this point that a good many of the more recent structuralists do not subscribe to Marx's or Lenin's views in a prescriptive sense—that is, they do not ideologically agree with many of the political implications that flow from Marxist or Leninist ideas. However, these structuralists base a good deal of their analysis of IPE on many of Marx's and Lenin's more well-known perceptions and arguments.

MARX AND HISTORY

The first great scholar to pioneer a structural approach to political economy was Karl Marx (1818–1883). Born in Trier, Germany, Marx did his greatest work while living in England, spending hours in research at the British Museum in London. Many of his views reflect things he and his collaborator Friedrich Engels studied about English mills and factories at the height of the industrial revolution. Adults and children often labored under dreadful working conditions and lived in abject poverty and squalor. Marx's theory of history, his notion of class conflict, and his critique of capitalism must all be understood in the context of nineteenth-century Europe's cultural, political, and economic climate.

A word of caution is in order concerning Marx and Marxism. Marx wrote millions of words; in so vast a body of work, he necessarily treated the main themes repeatedly, and not always consistently. What Marx "said" or "thought" about any interesting issue is, therefore, subject to some dispute. In the same way, Marxist scholars have interpreted Marx's writings in many ways. There is not, therefore, a definitive reading of Marx, any more than there is a definitive interpretation of the Bible or performance of a Beethoven sonata. Marxism is at once a theory of economics, politics, sociology, and ethics. For some, it is also a call to action.

Marx understood history to be a great, dynamic, evolving creature, determined fundamentally by economic and technological forces. Marx believed that through a process called *historical materialism*[4] these forces can be objectively explained and understood just like any other natural law.

Historical materialism takes as its starting point the notion that the *forces of production* of society (i.e., the sum total of knowledge and technology contained in society) set the parameters for the kind of system of political economy, or *mode of production*, that is possible. As Marx put it, "the hand mill gives you society with the feudal lord, the steam mill society with the industrial capitalist."[5] The economic structure (what Marx called the *relations of production*, or class relations) that emerge from such a mode of production in turn determines the social and ethical structures of society.

It is in the contradictions or conflicts between the forces of production and the relations of production in a society that Marx sees the mechanism for evolutionary and revolutionary change. Marx sees the course of history as steadily evolving. The process of change from one system of political economy (or mode of production, in Marx's words) to another is rooted in the growing contradiction between the forces of production (technological development) and the class or property relations in which they develop.

Since class relations change more slowly than technological development, social change is impeded, fostering conflict between the classes. An example today would be computers, which open up possibilities of different class relations and more free time for workers. But because capitalists control how technology is used, many of the computer's potential gains are not realized. When that conflict becomes so severe as to block the advance of human development, a social revolution sweeps away the existing legal and political arrangements and replaces them with ones more compatible with continued social progress.

In this way, history has evolved through distinct epochs or stages: primitive communism, slavery, feudalism, capitalism, socialism, and finally arrival at pure communism. In each of these modes of production, there is a dialectical process whereby inherently unstable and tortured opposing economic forces and counterforces lead to crisis, revolution, and to the next stage of history. And for Marx, the agents of that change are human beings organized in conflicting social classes.

MARX AND CLASS STRUGGLE

> For Marx, power was the inescapable fact of economic life; it proceeded from the possession of property and was thus the natural inevitable possession of the capitalist.[6]

Caught in history's capitalist era, Marx tried to understand the nature of the political economy and the forces pushing toward crisis and for change. Marx did not approach the questions of political economy from the perspectives of either the liberals or the mercantilists. He did not frame his questions in terms of the individual (market) versus society (state). Rather, influenced by the human relationships that he saw in his factory visits, where the capital-owning *bourgeoisie* seemingly exploited the laboring *proletariat*, Marx looked at social change from an angle that revealed deep class cleavages. For Marx, a *class* was a set of persons who stood in the same objective relationship to the means of production. According to Buchholz,

> Each system of production creates ruling and ruled classes. Each epoch is marked by a particular way of extracting income for the rulers. In Roman times, whoever owned a slave owned a claim on output. In feudal times, lords owned a claim on the output of serfs. Under capitalism, owners of factories and land owned a claim on the output of their wage laborers.[7]

Critical for Marx is the fundamental imbalance of power between the classes. To a liberal, the bourgeoisie and proletariat should be capable of forming a peaceful and mutually advantageous relationship. To Marx, however, the bourgeoisie and the proletariat are trapped in a decidedly one-sided relationship, with an "unemployed army" of workers frustrating the ability of the labor force to organize itself, and giving the capitalists the upper hand in all negotiations. The pressure of competition and profit-maximization drive the bourgeoisie to ruthlessly exploit the workers they employ. According to Marx and Engels,

> Modern industry has converted the little workshop of patriarchal master into the great factory of the industrial capitalist. Masses of laborers, crowded into the factory, are organized like soldiers. As privates of the industrial army they are placed under the command of a perfect hierarchy of officers and sergeants. Not only are they slaves of the bourgeois class, and of the bourgeois state; they are daily and hourly enslaved by the machine, by the overlooker, and above all, by the individual bourgeois manufacturer himself. The more openly this despotism proclaims gain to be its end and aim, the more petty, the more hateful and the more embittering it is.[8]

Marx argued that the concentration of wealth in the hands of fewer and fewer capitalists leads to the impoverishment of greater numbers of laborers. At the same time, new technology gradually replaces labor, driving up the reserve army of unemployed and driving down the pay workers receive. Ultimately, this process results in a mass of proletarian misery, setting the stage for revolution. A popular saying attributed to Marx and Engels was that capitalism produces its own "gravediggers."[9]

Marx is critical of the bourgeoisie for the callous manner in which the proletariat are treated. In *The Communist Manifesto*, he and Engels assert that the bourgeoisie

> has left no other bond between man and man than naked self-interest. . . . It has drowned the most heavenly ecstasies of religious fervor, of chivalrous enthusiasm, of Philistine sentimentalism, in the icy water of egotistical calculation. It has resolved personal worth into exchange value, and in place of the numberless indefeasible chartered freedoms, has set up that single, unconscionable freedom—Free Trade. In one word, for exploitation, veiled by religious and political illusions, it has substituted naked, shameless, direct brutal exploitation.[10]

MARX AND THE CRISIS OF CAPITALISM

Marx's attitude toward capitalism and exploitation can be frustrating, even if you believe that his views are fundamentally correct. Although he points out the abuses of capitalism, he also finds merit in its effects. Capitalism is, for Marx, more than an unhappy stop on the road to socialism; it is also a *necessary* stage, which builds wealth and raises material living standards. For Marx, it is the dynamic nature of market capitalism that lies at the heart of political economy. Rational men, driven by fierce competition, assault the status quo where they find it, transforming the world.

According to Marxian analysis, capitalism has an historic role, which is to transform the world. In so doing, capitalism accomplishes two goals at once. First, it breaks down slavery and feudalism, which are its historical (and dialectical) antecedents. Second, it creates the social and economic foundations for the eventual transition to a "higher" level of social development.

> The bourgeoisie has through its exploitation of the world market given a cosmopolitan character to production and consumption in every country. . . . The bourgeoisie, by the rapid improvement of all instruments of production, by the immensely facilitated means of communication, draws all nations, even the most barbarian, into civilization. The cheap prices of its commodities are the heavy artillery with which it batters down all Chinese walls, with which it forces the barbarians' intensely obstinate hatred of foreigners to capitulate. It compels all nations, on pain of extinction, to adopt the bourgeois mode of production; it compels them to introduce what it calls civilization into their midst, i.e., to become bourgeois themselves. In a word, it creates a world after its own image.[11]

It would seem, then, that the Marxian vision foresees the triumph of capitalism over other world orders.[12] In fact, Marx believes that capitalism is fundamentally flawed. As was discussed above, capitalism contains the seeds of its own destruction. The crisis of capitalism is inevitable. He identified three objective laws of this mode of production.

The law of the falling rate of profit holds that as capitalists try to gain a competitive advantage by investing in new labor-saving and productive technologies, unemployment increases and the rate of profit decreases. Surplus value (or profit) can only come from living labor and not machines, and since production is increasingly based on less labor, even with very high rates of exploitation of those still working, the rate of profit tends to fall.

The law of disproportionality (also called the *problem of underconsumption*)[13] argues that capitalism, because of its anarchic, unplanned nature, is prone to instability. For a variety of reasons, capitalism is subject to overproduction or, the obverse side of the same coin, underconsumption. That is, capitalists are not able to sell everything they produce at a profit and workers cannot afford to buy what they make. This disproportionality between supply and demand leads to wild fluctuations in the history of capitalism, with periodic booms and busts. This increases the likelihood of social unrest and the prospects for revolution and change. In response, capitalist governments have often stepped in to smooth out the development of the economy by, for example, creating a large military-industrial complex.

The law of concentration (or *accumulation of capital*) holds that capitalism tends to produce increasing inequality in the distribution of income and wealth. As the bourgeoisie continue to exploit the proletariat and weaker capitalists are swallowed by stronger, bigger ones, wealth and the ownership of capital become increasingly concentrated in fewer and fewer hands. This, then, makes more visible the inequality in the system and exacerbates the effects of the law of disproportionality, since the mass of impoverished consumers lack purchasing power.

The curse of capitalism, seen in this light, is its deceptive logic. Workers and business owners are indeed all rational individuals, as Adam Smith would have us believe, acting primarily in their own self-interest. In this case, however, the invisible hand does not benignly guide everyone so that all of society benefits. Rather, individual rationality adds up to collective irrationality. Increasing numbers of the proletariat are driven to cutthroat competition for jobs, driving wages and working conditions down to shocking levels, trading even their children's youthful vigor for a little more money. The bourgeoisie, equally driven by competitive forces, check their moral and ethical beliefs at the factory door and, for the sake of efficiency and productivity, thoroughly exploit their fellow citizens.

MARX AND STRUCTURALISM

So far, we have just scratched the surface of Marx and Marxism, and a deeper analysis of Marx's work and its influence lies well beyond the scope of this text.[14] Let us pause, then, and briefly attempt to restate Marx in a way that will help us in later sections.

Marx's analysis finds a home under the general heading of *structuralism* (or perhaps **economic structuralism**) because he views the economic structure to be the strongest single influence on society.[15] Marx focused on the *production* structure inherent in capitalism, seeing in it a dynamic that produces classes, leads to class struggle, and generates crises that lead to revolution and the next stage in history. For Marx, it is the structure that dominates events, more so than ideas, nature, or military generals. Marx saw people trapped in a production structure that shaped them and that they could change only by acting collectively and heroically.

Marx, then, sees IPE in terms of class exploitation driven by market forces. Where is the state in Marx's view? Where the state is a powerful force to mercantilists, and a dangerous force to liberals, to Marx it is *not* an *independent* force. In Marx's view, the state and the bourgeoisie are intertwined to such an extent that the two cannot be separated. The state exists to support and defend the interests of the dominant class of capitalist bourgeois owners.

MARX AND CULTURE

Although Marx wrote about economics and class conflict, he was interested in something much larger: society, the social relations that comprise society, and the dynamic that drives it. Marx thought that the most important factors in understanding all of this were production and private property. The basic social relations, including of course class relations, were determined by the relationships established at the office, factory, or store. Certainly his classes, the bourgeoisie and the proletariat, are defined this way.

In general, Marx's influence on culture takes the form of an understanding that what happens to individuals is a surface phenomenon, like the surface geology of the earth, which is conditioned by much deeper internal structures. Marxian cultural analysis looks through the surface of society to reveal the structural relationships, much as an X-ray looks through the skin to see the muscles, organs, and bones. Herewith are three admittedly shallow examples of Marxian cultural analysis.[a]

If you have taken an art history class, you have had a chance to see how Western art was transformed during the Italian Renaissance. In the Middle Ages, paintings and sculptures were more symbolic than representative of the natural world. Human figures were wooden and stylized, two-dimensional, and out of perspective. Figures standing together were given size and weight according to their symbolic importance, not according to their actual physical stature. A saint, for example, appears to be 11-feet tall when standing next to a 5-foot tall feudal lord, who looks down upon a 2-foot tall shepherd. It is hard for untutored modern eyes to look closely at these works of art and appreciate them, even the great ones, because they are so alien to our everyday experiences. They are symbols, to be read like a visual code, not photographs. They are meant to display social and religious images, not the simple ones you observe directly.

With the Renaissance, however, art began to display real people, presented in realistic perspective and proper proportion. You can feel the power in the muscles of Michaelangelo's David, for example; he is *so* real.

Why did art change and become more realistic during the Renaissance? It changed, a Marxian scholar would say, because in Renaissance Italy the means of production changed from the feudal farm to the urban textile factory. The elite class changed, too, from the hereditary aristocracy to the newly rising class of bankers, traders, and factory owners—the early capitalists. The new bourgeoisie had "cruder" tastes – they wanted to see people like themselves in buildings like their own and they wanted them to be something they could understand. They were not interested in visual codes. They wanted the Renaissance equivalent of photographs. The art did change, too, in just this way, as changing production structures shifted power relations between and among the classes. In a Marxian analysis of art, the answer is fairly clear. Art is expensive and it is produced to please those who can afford to commission and buy it. Artists produce, generally, what art patrons want to buy. Who could afford expensive art during the Middle Ages? The answer is the elite landowners who formed a hereditary and therefore nearly impenetrable aristocratic class of the Middle Ages. *They* were the big figures in those paintings, not so large as Christ or St. Francis, maybe, but surely a lot bigger than a peasant or a shopkeeper. *They* had the leisure, as well, to study and interpret these art works. The great art of the Middle Ages is great because it served the purposes of the aristocrat class.

Marxian analysis of Renaissance art therefore focuses on how the rise of proto-capitalism in the Italian city-states and the fall of the feudal system changed the dominant socioeconomic class from feudal lords to people like the Medici, rich urban bankers and factory owners with "bourgeois" tastes. This fundamental change in the nature of production is the deep structural change that is important. The transformation of Western art is a surface phenomenon that could not have happened except through the influence of the deeper structural movements.

Let us shift to literature. Literature tells stories about people and we usually consider the characters and what they think, how they feel. It is no great leap, however, to consider that the characters are elements of classes and that their place in society and what happens to them is determined by social structures. The stories of these people can be interpreted in light of the structural forces and class issues that are revealed in the story. Thus we can read a story on two levels—the individuals in the story and the structures and classes they represent. This is not very hard to do in, for example, John Steinbeck's classic novel of the Great Depression, *The Grapes of Wrath* or Tom Wolfe's best-selling novel of the 1980s, *The Bonfire of the Vanities*. When you read these books for the first time, Fate seems to be the main character. In both cases the reader senses early on that a tragedy is in the works—even the book's characters seem to understand this. What is Fate to the people on the surface, however, is in Marxian analysis the force of the deep structures of production and finance, which conditions the outcomes experienced by both the Dust Bowl "Okies" and the Wall Street "Masters of the Universe."

Third, films and theater can be subjected to Marxian-type analysis with interesting results. It is not so hard, for example, to see class struggle symbolically represented by the main characters in the movie *Titanic*. In fact, isn't that what the movie is really all about, not some icy boat versus iceberg confrontation? Although Titanic: The Historical Event is a complex tragedy that wraps together nature, technology, and human folly, Titanic: the Movie is a tragedy of class struggle. What separates the lovers and is the source of their tragedy is not an iceberg but social class, the difference between first class and steerage, bourgeoisie and proletariat.

What about *The Lion King*, the Disney animated classic? Deep structures are what are important here, too, not the surface tale of singing zoology. Is it difficult to see that the lions in this film are the feudal aristocracy class in the precapitalism era? Certainly they behave like feudal lords and ladies, relying on power to maintain power—they control the local geography, which is their means of production—and their society is even organized as a hereditary monarchy. You cannot get much more feudal than this.

This ruling class is inevitably brought into conflict with the rising capitalist class—played by the "lower" animals in the cartoon (after all, the lions *eat* them—peaceful class relations shouldn't be expected under these circumstances!). The hyenas, who have the least "refined" taste of all the animals in the film, are the future bourgeoisie (just like the Ferenghi in the *Star Trek* films). Marx would tell us that it is their role to rise up and destroy the feudal lion kingdom so as to make way for the next stage of history: capitalism. For Marx, deep structural forces make history a straight line of change: feudalism $\Rightarrow$ capitalism $\Rightarrow$ socialism $\Rightarrow$ communism. The feudal lions, however, want to hold onto what they've got, so they sing about a "circle of life," which keeps coming back around, always with them on the top and the other animals on the bottom.

If Marx were writing *The Lion King*, the lions would have been overthrown in the film, as the feudal lords were in real life, and the "lower" animals would have taken over. The melodious critters on the screen are just surface phenomena and their individual stories aren't what's really important: The real story is about structural change and class conflict. In Marxian analysis, the hyenas inherit the earth, but then the story goes on. Soon a class-based hierarchy is established among these animals, based on ownership of the means of production and the crisis of capitalism begins to loom over the African landscape. (Can you see George Orwell's *Animal Farm* falling into place at this point?).

In Marx's *Lion King*, lions lose, the king dies, the hyenas take their place, and history moves on to its next stage. The Disney studios wanted a happy ending, however, so the lions win, Simba is King, and the circle of feudal exploitation continues. This makes the lions happy, presumably, but it seems unlikely that Marx and Engels would give it "two thumbs up."

---

[a] In this box we discuss Marxian cultural analysis; some elements of this analysis are called structuralism, just as we call the the overall IPE perspective discussed here structuralism, and often the general approach is the same: Structure conditions outcome. But we will intentionally avoid using the term structuralism in this box because its use in cultural studies is not consistently the same as or similar to its use in IPE. That is, there are some structuralist theories that are based on different concepts of structure than those we consider in IPE.

LENIN AND IMPERIALISM

V. I. Lenin (1870–1924) is best known for his role in the Russian Revolution of 1917 and the founding of the Soviet Union. Lenin symbolized for many people the principles and ideas of the 1917 Revolution. In fact, in many ways, Lenin turned Marx on his head by placing politics over economics when he argued that Russia had gone through its capitalist stage of history and was ready for a second, socialist revolution.

Here we focus on Lenin's ideas about imperialism more than on his revolutionary strategies. Lenin developed a perspective on IPE that took Marx's class struggle, based on the mode of production, and used it to explain capitalism's international effects as transmitted through the production and finance structures of rich industrial countries to the poorer developing regions of the world. Lenin's famous summary of his views is *Imperialism: The Highest Stage of Capitalism* (1917).[16]

Marx said that capitalism, driven by its three laws, would come to revolutionary crisis and suffer internal class revolt, paving the way for the transition to socialism. Lenin observed that capitalist nations had avoided this crisis by *expanding* the pool of workers they exploited. Capitalism, he argued, "had escaped its three laws of motion through overseas imperialism. The acquisition of colonies had enabled the capitalist economies to dispose of their unconsumed goods, to acquire cheap resources, and to vent their surplus capital."[17]

In short, Lenin added to Marx what Robert Gilpin has called a "fourth law" of capitalism, which we might call the *law of capitalist imperialism*: "As capitalist economies mature, as capital accumulates, and as profit rates fall, the capitalist economies are compelled to seize colonies and create dependencies to serve as markets, investment outlets, and sources of food and raw materials. In competition with one another, they divide up the colonial world in accordance with their relative strengths."[18]

To Lenin, imperialism is another portion of the capitalist epoch of history (referred to as the highest stage of capitalism) that the world must endure on the road to communism. According to Lenin; "Monopoly is the transition from capitalism to a higher system."[19]

The critical element fueling imperialism, according to Lenin, was the decline of national economic competition and the growth of monopolies. Based on Marx's law of concentration, what emerged was an aggregation of market power into the hands of a few "cartels, syndicates and trusts, and merging with them, the capital of a dozen or so banks manipulating thousands of millions." Lenin goes on to argue that

> Monopoly is exactly the opposite of free competition; but we have seen the latter being transformed into monopoly before our very eyes, creating large-scale industry and eliminating small industry, replacing large-scale industry by still larger-scale industry, finally leading to such a concentration of production and capital that monopoly has been and is the result.[20]

The key for Lenin was that because monopolies concentrated capital, they could not find sufficient investment opportunities in industrial regions of the world. They therefore found it necessary to export capital around the globe to earn sufficient profits.

Lenin argued that imperialist expansion allowed capitalism to postpone its inevitable crisis and metamorphose into socialism. It also created new, serious problems for the world. Lenin viewed World War I as an imperialist war, caused by tensions that arose from the simultaneous expansion of several European empires. As nations at the core of capitalism competed to expand their exploitative sphere, their interests intersected and conflicted with one another, producing the Great War.

Lenin's role in the Revolution of 1917 was to help defeat liberal political forces that sought to keep Russia within the European capitalist system. Under Lenin's leadership, Russia essentially withdrew from Europe and its imperialist conflicts, and resolved to move quickly and on its own toward a communist system free of class conflict and imperialist wars.

LENIN AND INTERNATIONAL CAPITALISM

Lenin's imperialist theory of capitalism has been very influential, so it is worthwhile considering briefly a few other aspects of his analysis. Lenin sought to explain how it was that capitalism shifted from internal to international exploitation, and how the inequality among classes had as its parallel the law of uneven development among nations.

For Lenin, profit-seeking capitalists could not be expected to use surplus capital to improve the living standards of the proletariat. Therefore, capitalist societies would remain unevenly developed ones, with some classes prospering as others were mired in poverty. The imperial phase of capitalism simply transferred this duality of wealth and poverty onto the world stage, as capitalists, seeking to maintain and even increase their profits, exported to what contemporaries of Lenin called "backward" regions of the world. These poor peripheral countries were now integrated into the world economy as the new "proletariat" of the world. According to Lenin,

> Monopolist capitalist combines—cartels, syndicates, trusts—divide among themselves, first of all, the whole internal market of a country, and impose their control, more or less completely, upon the industry of that country. But under capitalism the home market is inevitably bound up with the foreign market. Capitalism long ago created a world market.[21]

The uneven development of society within a nation now took place on an international scale.

Lenin saw imperial capitalism spreading through two structures of the IPE: production and finance. Both of these structures were so constituted, under capitalism, as to create dependency and facilitate exploitation. Cutthroat competition among poorer nations made them easy targets for monopolies in the production structure in the capitalist core. The same forces were at work within the finance structure, where the superabundance of finance capital, controlled by monopolistic banks, was used to exploit less developed countries.

The bottom line of *imperialism*, for Lenin, was that the rich capitalist nations were able to delay their final crisis by keeping the poorer nations underdeveloped and deep in debt, and dependent on them for manufactured goods, jobs, and financial resources. It is not surprising, then, that Lenin's theory of imperialism has been very influential, especially among intellectuals in the less developed countries, where his views have shaped policy and attitudes toward international trade and finance generally.

We include Lenin's imperialism under the general heading of "structuralism," as we did with Marx's theories, because its analysis is based on the assumption that it is in capitalism's nature for the finance and production structures among nations to be biased in favor of the owners of capital. While, in theory, the relationship between capital-abundant nations and capital-scarce nations should be one of *interdependence*, since each needs the other for maximum growth, in practice the result is *dependence*, exploitation, and uneven development. The same forces that drive the bourgeoisie to exploit the proletariat ultimately drive the capitalist core nations to dominate and exploit less developed countries.

No attempt to consider the IPE of North-South relations is complete without taking imperialism's perspective into account. To some extent, Lenin's ideas are the basis of the theories of dependency and of the modern world system, to which we will shortly turn.

OTHER ASPECTS OF THE STRUCTURALIST PERSPECTIVE

The fundamental notion of structuralism is that economic structure heavily influences the distribution of wealth and power. According to this viewpoint, institutions associated with global capitalism are inherently biased in favor of the dominant powers, creating a web of dependency that mirrors, in some ways, the relationship of nineteenth-century mother countries to their colonial possessions.

Marx focused on the biases inherent in the production structure under capitalism that caused the bourgeoisie to exploit the proletariat. Lenin expanded this point of view to take into account exploitation of the structure of international finance and ways in which exploitation is transmitted internationally through imperialism. Other structuralists have continued along this line of reasoning, exploring the biased character of the security structure and the knowledge structure.

Structuralists argue that security structures linking rich countries with poorer ones are another aspect of imperialism. The security links between the

Soviet Union and its Warsaw Pact allies prior to 1989 are one example. The communist governments of East Germany and Hungary were dependent on Moscow for security, a fact that Soviet leaders used to systematically exploit the citizens of these countries. Structuralists argue, as well, that Less Developed Countries (LDC) regimes that are dependent on the United States for security create a structure that fosters exploitation.

From the structuralist perspective, imperialist exploitation also works through the knowledge structure. Capitalist countries control access to technology, which they use to their own advantage. Less developed countries tend to acquire low-end technology, which limits their productivity and growth, while factories in the capitalist core states retain the most advanced technology, which gives them a monopoly in the most valuable products. Because LDCs rarely get advanced technology, they rarely acquire the resources they need to advance further. They remain dependent on others for technology and so are unable to break the ties that exploit them.

This perspective, then, sees systematic exploitation and imperialism in each of the four IPE structures: production, finance, security, and knowledge. A nation's place in the world thus depends on its access to production capital, finance capital, security resources, and technological advances. Given the biases in these structures, there is little a nation can do to alter its global status.

MODERN WORLD SYSTEM THEORY

The structuralist perspective has many variants in the modern world. These different viewpoints share the basic idea that the structure of the global economy strongly influences the IPE. Beyond this, however, they differ in many important ways.

One fascinating contemporary variant of the structuralist perspective focuses on the way in which the global system has developed since the middle of the fifteenth century. This is the *modern world system (MWS)* theory[22] originated by Immanuel Wallerstein and developed by a number of scholars, including Christopher Chase-Dunn. Capitalist in nature, the world system largely determines political and social relations, both within and between nations and other international entities.

For Wallerstein, the world economy provides the sole means of organization in the international system. The modern world system exhibits the following characteristics: a single division of labor whereby nation-states are mutually dependent upon economic exchange; the sale of products and goods for the sake of profit; and, finally, the division of the world into three functional areas or socioeconomic units, which correspond to the role nations within these regions play in the international economy.

From the MWS perspective the capitalist *core* states of northwest Europe in the sixteenth century moved beyond agricultural specialization to higher-skilled industries and modes of production by penetrating and absorbing other regions into the capitalist world economy. Through this process, Eastern Europe became the agricultural *periphery* and exported grains, bullion, wood, cotton, and sugar to the core. Mediterranean Europe and its labor-intensive industries became the *semiperiphery* or intermediary between the core and periphery.

It would be easy to define the core, periphery, and semiperiphery in terms of the types of nations within each group (such as the United States, China, and Korea, respectively), but the MWS is not based primarily on the nation-state. In this theory, the core represents a geographic region made up of nation-states that play a partial role in the modern world system. The force of bourgeoisie interests actually exists, in varying degrees, in every country. Every nation has elements of core, periphery, and semiperiphery, although not equally so. In common with Marx, then, the MWS theory looks at IPE in terms of class relations and patterns of exploitation.

According to Wallerstein, the core states dominate the peripheral states through unequal exchange for the purpose of extracting cheap raw materials instead of, as Lenin argued, merely using the periphery as a market for dumping surplus production. The core interacts with the semiperiphery and periphery through the global structure of capitalism, exploiting these regions and also transforming them. The semiperiphery serves more of a political than an economic role; it is both exploited and exploiter, diffusing opposition of the periphery to the core region.

Interestingly, on some issues, Wallerstein attempts to bridge mercantilism (and political realism) with Marxist views about the relationship of politics to economics. For instance, as a mercantilist would, he accepts the notion that the world is politically arranged in an anarchical manner, that is, there is no *single* sovereign political authority to govern interstate relations. However, much like a Marxist-Leninist, he proposes that power politics and social differences are also conditioned by the capitalist structure of the world economy.

According to Wallerstein, capitalists within core nation-states use state authority as an instrument to maximize individual profit. Historically, the state served economic interests to the extent that "state machineries of the core states were strengthened to meet the needs of capitalist landowners and their merchant allies."[23] Also Wallerstein argues that "once created," state machineries have a certain amount of autonomy.[24] On the other hand, politics is constrained by economic structure. He asserts, for instance, that strong (core) states dominate weak (peripheral) ones because placement of the nation-state in the world capitalist system affects its ability to influence its global role. As Wallerstein puts it; "The functioning then of a capitalist world economy requires that groups pursue their economic interests within a single world market while seeking to distort this market for their benefit by organizing to exert influence on states, some of which are far more powerful than others but none of which controls the world-market in its entirety."[25]

Wallerstein's conception of the modern world system has gained a good deal of notoriety in the last 20 years. He offers us a recipe of ideas and concepts that are relatively easy to understand and that account for a large part of the relationship of Northern developed to Southern developing nations. "Semiperiphery" also seems to fit the status of the Newly Industrialized Countries (NICs). Furthermore, the MWS approach to structuralism sees exploitation as an inherent element of the capitalist structures both within and among core, periphery, and semiperiphery.

One thing that is problematic about Wallerstein's views is precisely what makes them so attractive: his comprehensive yet almost simple way of characterizing IPE. Many criticize his theory for being too deterministic, both economically and in terms of the constraining effects of the *global* capitalist system. Nation-states are not free to choose courses of action or policies. Instead, they are relegated to playing economically determined roles. Finally, Wallerstein is faulted for viewing capitalism as the end product of current history.

DEPENDENCY THEORY

Another contemporary variant of the structuralist perspective is called ***dependency theory.*** A wide range of views can be grouped together under this heading. Their differences, however, are less important to us here than what they have in common, which is the view that the structure of the global political economy essentially enslaves the less developed countries of the "South" by making them dependent on the nations of the capitalist core of the "North."[26] Theotonio Dos Santos has written:

> By dependence we mean a situation in which the economy of certain countries is conditioned by the development and expansion of another economy to which the former is subjected. The relation of interdependence between two or more economics, and between these and world trade, assumes the form of dependence when some countries (the dominant ones) can expand and can be self-sustaining, while others (the dependent ones) can do this only as a reflection of that expansion, which can have either a positive or a negative effect on their immediate development.[27]

Dos Santos sees three eras of dependence in modern history: colonial dependence (during the eighteenth and nineteenth centuries), financial-industrial dependence (during the nineteenth and early twentieth centuries), and a structure of dependence today based on the postwar multinational corporations.

One dependency theorist in particular has focused a good deal of attention on the effects of imperialism in Latin America. Andre Gunder Frank rejects the Marxist notion that societies go through different stages or modes of production as they develop. However, he supports the imperialism thesis that connections between developed and developing regions of the world resulted in exploitation of peripheral regions by metropolitan capitalist countries.

Frank is noted for his "development of underdevelopment" thesis. He argues that developing nations were never "underdeveloped" in the sense that one might think of them as "backward" or traditional societies. Instead, once great civilizations in their own right, the developing regions of the world *became* underdeveloped as a result of their colonization by the Western industrialized nations. Along with exploitation, imperialism produced underdevelopment: "Historical research demonstrates that contemporary underdevelopment is in large part the historical product of past and continuing economic and other relations between the satellite underdeveloped and the now developed metropolitan countries."[28]

How are developing nations to develop if in fact they are exploited by the developed capitalist industrial powers? Dependency theorists have suggested a variety of responses to this trap. A number of researchers—for example, Andre Gunder Frank—have called for peripheral nations to withdraw from the global

litical economy. In the 1950s and 1960s, the leadership of many socialist movements in the Third World favored revolutionary tactics and ideological mass
movements to change not only the fundamental dynamic of both the political
and economic order of their society, but also the world capitalist system.

More recently, dependency theorists have recommended a variety of other
strategies and policies by which developing nations could industrialize and
develop. Raul Prebisch, an Argentinean economist, was instrumental in founding, under the auspices of the United Nations, the United Nations Committee on
Trade and Development (UNCTAD). The developing nations that have joined
this body within the UN have made it their goal to monitor and recommend policies that would, in effect, help redistribute power and income between Northern
developed and Southern developing countries. These and other dependency theorists, however, have been more aggressive about reforming the international
economy and have supported the calls for a New International Economic Order
(NIEO) which gained momentum shortly after the OPEC oil price hike in 1973.

The important point to make here is that dependency theories have served
as part of a critique of the relationship of the metropolitan to satellite, or core to
peripheral, nations. Whether or not that relationship can—or even should—be
equalized is a matter developed elsewhere. These theories will be important to
our discussion of "the development dilemma" in chapter 15.

STRUCTURALISM IN PERSPECTIVE

To an important extent, the twentieth century has been defined by the political,
economic, and intellectual forces of economic nationalism, liberalism, and structuralism. Structuralism has had a profound influence on world events in this
period.

In Russia, Joseph Stalin implemented the ruthless and rigid system of centralized political and economic control in an attempt to achieve a transition to
communism without the necessary intermediate steps of capitalism, imperialism,
and socialism. In China, Mao Zedong led a revolt and fashioned another communist state within a completely different cultural context. In Cuba, Fidel Castro
created a communist state that in most respects is cut off from the global economy in an attempt to avoid the dependency dilemma. Structuralist views are influential in all regions of the world, perhaps especially in Latin America.

The fact that so much of the world's population has been governed by leaders who have been influenced by structuralism demonstrates the importance of
this perspective. The tension between the forces of national interest, self-interest,
and class-based dependency are fundamental to the world and to political economy.

This chapter began with Marx and ends with Dos Santos. What ties these
writers together and links them with the many authors and ideas that came in
between? The tie that binds here is the notion that the different structures of the
IPE do not benefit everyone, as liberals believe, nor are they tools that enable, or
tools that enhance state power, as mercantilists believe. Rather, the structuralist
perspective holds that in the system of global capitalism that dominates the
world today, these structures are systematically and inherently biased in favor

of certain classes of individuals and nations; the Marx-Lenin laws of capitalism tend to hold on at a global level.

Some people ask if studying Marxism or structuralism in the postcommunist era is worthwhile. The answer is yes. The structuralist perspective encompasses far more than the Soviet model of communism. This perspective on IPE is revealing and represents a powerful intellectual and political influence.

Indeed, the noted historian Eric Hobsbawm has recently observed, in his introduction to the one hundred-fiftieth anniversary edition of Marx and Engel's *Communist Manifesto,* that it makes more sense to consider Marx's ideas now than at any previous time in history![29] Marx looked ahead and saw what capitalism would do to the world, including the class conflicts that would unavoidably arise. But the world of 1848, when the *Manfiesto* was written, was not yet the world of the crisis of capitalism. But,

> We now live in a world in which this transformation has largely taken place . . . In some ways we can even see the force of the Manifesto's predictions more clearly than the generations between us and its publication. . . . In short, what might in 1848 have struck an uncommitted reader as revolutionary rhetoric—or, at best, plausible prediction, can now be read as a concise characterization of capitalism at the end of the twentieth century. Of what other document of the 1840s can this be said?[30]

STRUCTURALISM TODAY:
THE MANIC LOGIC OF GLOBAL CAPITALISM

It is commonplace today to say that Marx died with the fall of the Berlin Wall. The collapse of communism has put to an end the grand social experiment that began more than 150 years ago with *The Communist Manifesto* (1848). Although it is not the aim of this book to predict the future, it is almost certainly true that it is too soon to bury Marx. There are at least three good reasons to study Marx and the structuralist perspective built upon his analysis of class struggle.

First, Marx presents us with powerful ideas that are worth studying as theory or philosophy or, as we saw earlier, cultural critique. Marx was the first political economist to present a theory of the dynamic development of society, which sought to explain not only politics and economics, but also the social relationships on which they are based. Serious students of political economy must study Marx to understand and appreciate the power of theory to shape our understanding of everyday events.[a]

Second, it is important to understand that communism is not the same as Marxism. Communism, as practiced in the former Soviet Union and elsewhere, was an economic, political, and social organization that, although rooted in the theoretical writings of Marx and Lenin, had relatively little to do with these ideas in practice. (See chapter 14 for a more thorough analysis of the communist system of political economy.)

The practical problems of constructing a modern socialist state from the available feudal raw materials forced Lenin and then Stalin to institute many pragmatic policies that would surely have drawn scorn from Karl Marx. Marxian methods were sacrificed in an attempt to deal with critical short-term problems. The harsh international environment of World War II and the Cold War forced further deviations from Marx's goal of the withering away of the state. The bottom line is that communism at the end had little to do in practical terms with Marxian philosophy. The collapse of communism should be seen as the rejection of a particular system of political economy and social relations, not necessarily a refutation of Marx's ideas.

The third reason to study Marx today is that some people believe that the process of globalization that we can see everywhere around us today is constructing a world that looks more and more like the world that Marx and Lenin wrote about. This is the thesis of William Greider's recent book *One World, Ready or Not: The Manic Logic of Global Capitalism* (New York: Simon & Schuster, 1997). Greider writes that "Marxism is dead, the Communist system utterly discredited by human experience, but the ghost of Marx hovers over the global landscape, perhaps with a knowing smile. The gross conditions that inspired Karl Marx's original critique of capitalism in the nineteenth century are present and flourishing again. The world has reached not only the end of ideology, but also the beginnings of the next great conflict over the nature of capitalism."[b] Greider's analysis makes fascinating political economy. Keynesian economic policies (see chapter 3) postponed the crisis of capitalism in the Great Depression of the 1930s. But the renaissance of classical liberalism in the 1980s and the 1990s removed many of the state policies that had for 50 years tempered the "manic logic" of Marx's three laws of capitalism.

Now unfettered capitalism is engulfing the world in the form of "globalization." The essence of globalization, Greider proposes, is the desire to produce more and more for less and less in search of profit. It is competition that is ultimately destructive to all parties, as Marx predicted.

What is the likely result of this vicious cycle of greater output, surplus, lower prices, lower wages, and falling profits? In the long run the crisis of capitalism looms as one possibility, Greider thinks. Faced with global recession, he believes that people will seek political solutions that could lead to the sort of radical nationalism that drove the Fascist parties in Europe in the 1930s. Indeed, one doesn't have to look too hard to see early indicators of this trend in some nationalist and racist political movements around the world today.

But in the short term the exploitation of labor is the real problem. Thus he calls for a twentieth century version of "workers of the world unite" in the form of global unions. Only global unions would have the power to deal with global firms in global markets. Even so, there would still be the need for some sort of "global Keynesiansim" to try to balance global demand with global supply and control capitalism's propensity to rational irrationality.

In the end, Greider cannot help but be a pessimist. Like Marx, he sees the forces driving the global economy to its own destruction as inevitable. But Marx accepted this as part of the great plan of history. Having seen the misery that nationalism, racism, and religious fundamentalism can produce, Greider cannot be as sanguine as Marx.

Maybe the right state policies will be enacted and the right global institutions created to prevent the collapse of civilization into the pit of humankind's darkest fears and motives. "In fact, there is not much evidence from economic history of societies that have acted in an alert, timely manner to avert similar catastrophes. Usually, it is the opposite story. Contractions and instabilities accumulate, but no one in power has the presence to act. Warnings are sounded, but pass by unheeded. . . . neither technological invention nor economic revolution has managed to eliminate folly and error from the human condition."[c]

---

[a]See Joseph Schumpeter, *Capitalism, Socialism and Democracy* (New York: Harper Torchbooks, 1942). Special attention should be given to part I: The Marxian Doctrine.
[b]William Greider, *One World, Ready or Not: The Manic Logic of Global Capitalism* (New York: Simon & Schuster, 1997), p. 39.
[c]Ibid., p. 53.

DISCUSSION QUESTIONS

1. After reading the chapter compare and contrast structuralism with mercantilism and liberalism in the following areas:
   a. the dominant actors
   b. political versus economic motivation behind actor behavior
   c. the role of the state in the economy
2. How did Marx's and Lenin's views shape those of structuralism? Be specific and give examples from the reading.
3. Outline the essential characteristics/features of Marxism, dependency theory, and the modern world system approach.
4. Employing a structuralist approach, outline the significant changes that have occurred in the relationship of the Northern industrialized nations to the Southern developing countries since the late 1960s.

INTERNET LINKS

One Hundred-fifty Years of the Communist Manifesto:
   http://www.marxist.com/150years/index.html
World Systems Network:
   http://csf.colorado.edu/wsystems/index.html
Fernand Braudel Center for the Study of Economics, Historical Systems, and Civilizations:
   http://fbc.binghamton.edu/

SUGGESTED READINGS

Anthony Brewer. *Marxist Theories of Imperialism: A Critical Survey*, 2d ed. New York: Routledge, 1990.

Christopher Chase-Dunn. *Global Formation: Structures of the World Economy*. Cambridge, MA: Basil Blackwell, 1989.

Benjamin J. Cohen. *The Question of Imperialism*. New York: Basic Books, 1973.

Theotonio Dos Santos. "The Structure of Dependency." In George T. Crane and Abla Amawi, eds., *The Theoretical Evolution of International Political Economy*. New York: Oxford University Press, 1990.

John Kenneth Galbraith. *Economics in Perspective*. Boston: Houghton-Mifflin, 1987. See especially chap. 11.

William Greider. *One World, Ready or Not: The Manic Logic of Global Capitalism*. New York: Simon & Schuster, 1997.

V. I. Lenin. *Imperialism: The Highest Stage of Capitalism*. New York: International Publishers, 1939.

Karl Marx. *Capital*, Friedrich Engels, ed. Chicago: Encyclopedia Britannica, 1952.

Karl Marx and Friedrich Engels. *The Communist Manifesto: A Modern Edition* (with an introduction by Eric Hobsbawm). New York: Verso, 1998. Be sure to read Hobsbawm's introduction.

Joan Robinson. "Trade in Primary Commodities." In Jeffry A. Frieden and David A. Lake, eds., *International Political Economy: Perspectives on Global Power and Wealth*, 2d ed. New York: St. Martin's Press, 1991.

NOTES

1. Karl Marx and Friedrich Engels, *The Communist Manifesto*, Samuel Beer, ed., (New York: Appleton-Century-Crofts, 1955), p. 9.
2. V. I. Lenin, *Imperialism: The Highest Stage of Capitalism* (New York: International Publishers Co., 1939).

3. Joan Robinson, "Trade in Primary Commodities," in Jeffrey A. Frieden and David A. Lake, eds., *International Political Economy*, 2d ed. (New York: St Martin's Press, 1991), p. 376.

4. For a discussion of Marx's methodology, see Todd G. Buchholz, *New Ideas from Dead Economists* (New York: New American Library, 1989), pp. 113–120.

5. Karl Marx, *The Poverty of Philosophy* (New York: International Publishers, 1963), p. 122.

6. John Kenneth Galbraith, *Economics in Perspective* (Boston: Houghton-Mifflin, 1987), p. 133.

7. Buchholz, *New Ideas from Dead Economists*, p. 115.

8. Marx and Engels, *The Communist Manifesto*, p. 17.

9. Ibid., p. 22.

10. Ibid., p. 12

11. Ibid., pp. 13–14

12. See the comments by Václav Havel regarding the "cult of the market" in chapter 3 for an indication of this viewpoint.

13. A more analytical definition of disproportionality and its place in Marx's theory can be found in Paul M. Sweezy, *The Theory of Capitalist Development* (New York: Monthly Review Press, 1970), chap. 5.

14. See the suggested readings on Marx and Marxism at the end of this chapter.

15. We have used the term *structuralism* in a general sense here. At a more advanced level, "economic structuralism" is differentiated from "political structuralism." In economic structuralism, it is the structure of economic relations that influences society most. In political structuralism, it is the structure of political power that is most influential.

16. Lenin, *Imperialism*.

17. Robert Gilpin, *The Political Economy of International Relations* (Princeton, NJ: Princeton University Press, 1987), p. 38.

18. Ibid., p. 39.

19. Lenin argues that "this is a new stage of world concentration of capital and production, incomparably higher than the preceding stages." Lenin, *Imperialism*, p. 68.

20. Ibid., p. 88.

21. Ibid., p. 68.

22. Immanuel Wallerstein, "The Rise and Future Demise of the World Capitalist System: Concepts for Comparative Analysis," *Comparative Studies in Society and History*, 16 (September 1974); pp. 387–415.

23. Ibid., p. 402.

24. Ibid.

25. Ibid., p. 406.

26. Dependency theory is thus seen as an interpretation of North-South IPE relations.

27. Theotonio Dos Santos, "The Structure of Dependence," *American Economic Review* 60 (1970); pp. 231–236.

28. Andre Gunder Frank, *Capitalism and Underdevelopment in Latin America: Historical Studies of Chile and Brazil* (New York: Monthly Review Press, 1967), p. 9.

29. "Introduction," by Eric Hobsbawm in Karl Marx and Friedrich Engels, *The Communist Manifesto: A Modern Edition* (New York: Verso, 1998), pp. 3-29.

30 Hobsbawm, "Introduction," pp. 17-18.

5

Critical Perspectives on International Political Economy

OVERVIEW

IPE is about states and markets, but it is about *more than* states and markets, as the analysis of the past four chapters should have made clear. Still it is deceptively easy to oversimplify IPE. Liberalism is about laissez faire, free markets, and greed. Economic nationalism is about states, state power, and security. Structuralism is about how capitalism pushes states and markets into class warfare. Each of these oversimplifications contains a kernel of truth, but much is lost in the process of simplifying, too. As Einstein said, it is important to make things as simple as possible, but no simpler.

An important intellectual initiative within IPE is the movement to expand the field and make it more inclusive of different ideas and to keep it from being oversimplified. This chapter presents four critiques of mainstream IPE theory (economic, nationalism, liberalism, and structuralism) that, taken individually or together, expand IPE's domain and make it even more relevant and interesting.

We begin with the rational choice perspective, which holds that IPE is not about states and markets; it is about individuals and their interests. The rational choice perspective, an application of economic methodology to political issues, is both influential and controversial within the political science community. Rational choice IPE reminds us of the power of the individual and his or her importance in the world today.

Next we examine the green perspective on IPE, which looks at the world not as states and markets so much as in terms of a global biosphere. Green IPE is concerned about the balance of nature, both on environmental issues and for IPE issues generally. Green IPE reminds us of the importance of the natural and human environments in the world today.

The feminist critique considers that the IPE reflects dominant gender roles and values. Feminist IPE is concerned about the status of women and the intellectual biases that are introduced when we look at the world through gender-tinted glasses. Feminist IPE reminds us of the importance of the family, of the family's security, and of reproductive (not just productive) resources in today's world.

Finally, postmodern analysis challenges us to cast off obsolete ways of thinking about the world. In particular, postmodern IPE asks us to reconsider the relevance of the nation-state in today's increasingly fragmented, multilevel, and multidimensional world. Postmodern IPE reminds us that we live in a world of change, where yesterday's ways of thinking, based on yesterday's social institutions, may no longer be relevant.

The world is a complicated place, characterized at all levels by elements of interdependence. We depend on one another in many ways and at many levels. Human existence is, therefore, filled with elements of tension, boundaries where differing and sometimes conflicting interests, points of view, or value systems come into contact with one another.

The mainstream IPE theories of economic nationalism, liberalism, and structuralism frame IPE issues in particular ways that capture some of the most important elements of IPE today, but not all of them. One of the main intellectual projects of contemporary IPE is to expand its domain to include actors, frameworks, and ways of thinking that cannot easily be classified under the three main perspectives. The goal of this project is a broader, more inclusive IPE—an IPE truly "without fences"—that can confront honestly a broader range of issues that are important to today's world without necessarily abandoning IPE's intellectual roots.

This chapter presents four critiques of mainstream IPE: rational choice IPE, green IPE, feminist IPE, and postmodern IPE. Each of these four critiques asks us to think of IPE in a different and generally a broader way. IPE in the twenty-first century, however it may develop, will necessarily be conditioned by *all* these critiques.

Before we begin, a word of caution is in order. Each of these four IPE critiques is complex and controversial. Different points of view can be found within each of the critiques, so it is either bold or foolhardy to try to concisely and simply sum up any of these schools of thought. The analysis presented here, however, *is* concise and therefore intentionally incomplete and necessarily superficial. Experts in any one of these theories will find our discussion hopelessly flawed.

But this chapter is not written for experts; it is written for IPE beginners. Our aim here is to stimulate fresh ideas among those who confront these ideas for the first time and perhaps to encourage them to look a little deeper into these perspectives. We think it is better to introduce these ideas, albeit concisely, than to ignore them as others have done. We apologize in advance to experts in these fields and invite them to suggest to us better ways of presenting these ideas. With this warning in mind, proceed.

THE RATIONAL CHOICE CRITIQUE

The traditional IPE perspectives tend to frame questions in terms of states, markets, and classes. States act in the national interest, markets are driven by the invisible hand of individual self-interest, and class conflict results from diverging class interests. The *rational choice critique* of this way of thinking is based on the idea that states do not think, make decisions, or "do" things; *people* do. There is no distinct "national interest"; there are only the interests of the individuals who make and influence national policies and the ways that these interests are resolved in the political marketplace.

People—individuals—are the appropriate level of analysis for IPE, according to the rational choice critique. To understand how states and classes behave, it is necessary to understand how the individuals who comprise them behave within the prevailing system of social constraints.[1]

The rational choice critique is essentially an application of the methodology of economics to the analysis of problems of politics and society. Within the political science discipline this study is called **rational choice theory** although within the economics discipline it goes by the name of *public choice analysis.* By either name, this school of thought focuses on the actions of elected and appointed government officials, their self-interests, and the nature of their relations with various client groups, including especially voters and campaign contributors. In simple terms, the rational choice critique is built upon the following ideas.

- *Who Are the Actors?* The actors are individuals. Government policies are made by elected officials and appointed bureaucrats who make choices in a world of scarce resources. They are influenced by each other, by their relations with foreign officials, and by voters, campaign contributors, political party leaders, and a variety of other individuals such as union officials, corporate executives, community leaders, and journalists who have a direct or indirect stake in public policies. The political marketplace is made up of the individuals who "demand" certain types of public policies and those who "supply" them.
- *What Are their Interests?* The actors are rational and self-interested. They are motivated to make themselves better off, just as they are in market activities. This sounds bad. It sounds as if elected officials are corrupt and will sell their votes to the highest bidder or provide government benefits in exchange for campaign contributions or election endorsements. In fact, some government officials *are* corrupt—political corruption scandals are uncomfortably familiar news. But the rational choice critique does not assume that government officials are corrupt generally. An elected

official has a strong self-interest in reelection, for example, so that self-interest may drive him or her to do an exceptionally good job of representing the interests of voters in the district. Self-interest here can be seen to motivate good government, not bad government. The self-interest motive is complicated because individuals are complicated. A given elected official may be motivated by the need to raise funds for the next election campaign, the desire to please voters and give them sound public service, a personal philosophy or set of beliefs about what is best for the nation, and perhaps even a yearning for a prominent place in the history books. Public policy depends on these complex interests, according to the rational choice critique, not simple images of "national interest."

- *What Is the Institutional Environment?* Public policy is conditioned by the institutional structure of the political marketplace. The institutional structure can be thought of as the "rules of the game"—the ways that political choices are made. The structure of political decisionmaking, combined with the interests of the actors and the resources they command, determines what government policies are enacted and how they are implemented. Thus, as we will see below, *how* political choices are made influences *what* political choices are made.

The rational choice critique can shed light on many issues we study in IPE. For example, rational choice analysis helps us understand the debate between liberals and mercantilists regarding tariffs and quotas and other protectionist trade policies. Liberals since David Ricardo have argued that protectionism is generally counter to the national interest because it is inefficient while mercantilists, in the spirit of Friedrich List and Alexander Hamilton, tend to argue that trade barriers promote the national interest by building domestic economic strength. The rational choice critique points out that national interest may have little to do with government policy—individual interests can be far more powerful.

To see this, suppose that the House of Representatives is today considering a tariff on inexpensive imported sports shoes. Let us suppose that this tariff would benefit a small number of domestic shoemaking firms, their owners and employees, but that it would harm the nation overall by reducing the real incomes of many millions of households by a small amount each. The protectionist gains are assumed to be very small in absolute amount and highly concentrated compared to the costs of protectionism, which are typically large, but highly diffused. The winners gain a lot per person and the losers each lose only a little. But the number of winners is so small compared with the vast majority of losers that the nation overall loses, too.

In other words, the tariff redistributes income from a large group in society to a much smaller one, but in a very inefficient way. The losers lose much more than the gainers gain. Only part of the transfer goes from loser consumer to protected winner industry; the rest disappears in the form of economic inefficiency.

If we had a system of direct democracy, where every voter cast a ballot on each issue, the shoe tariff would be voted down in an enormous electoral landslide. But we have a system of representative democracy, where we elect representatives to serve our interests. How will Congress vote on this issue?

The "national interest" would seem to be served by a "no" vote in this example, since we have assumed that the total losses outweigh the total gains, yet rational choice analysis predicts a "yes" vote by Congress even if elected officials are uncorrupt. Here is the logic behind this conclusion. In a representative democracy like ours it is costly to attempt to follow what Congress is doing and to influence votes that affect our individual interests. We tend to remain rationally ignorant of most government actions, which have little direct bearing on our lives, and pay attention to only the small number of items that are likely to impose high costs or provide high benefits. Your representative is therefore unlikely to get much mail opposing the shoe tariff, because most of the voters who would be harmed by it are rationally ignorant of the bill. But domestic shoe interests have a much stronger incentive to lobby representatives, send them mail, make campaign contributions, and commission studies and reports that stress the jobs and other benefits that a protected domestic shoe industry would provide. Listening honestly to the "voice of the people," your busy representative might conclude that shoe tariffs are a good idea because the voices of those who would benefit are much louder than the voices of the (rationally ignorant) persons who would be harmed.

The bottom line of this rational choice analysis is that representative democracy is biased *in favor* of government policies that favor special interests and biased *against* policies that benefit society broadly, if they impose concentrated costs on some well-organized interest group. This bias may not result in government policies that are *always* undesirable, because political leaders and elected officials take into account many different factors in choosing how to vote. They are often too sophisticated to be taken in by a special interest letter-writing campaign, for example. But representative democracy is not perfect, as this example indicates, and one should not always assume that the "national interest" that public policies reflect is actually the same as the interest of a majority of the nation's citizens.

One of the more useful aspects of rational choice analysis is its ability to help us understand change in the international political economy. Changing national policies, viewed this way, are not necessarily based on changing national interests but rather occur due to some combination of changes in the actors, their interests, and the institutional environment of the political marketplace. This provides a well-structured framework for analysis.

For example, how can one explain why the United States, which was highly protectionist during the Great Depression, became such a strong advocate of free trade after the Second World War and, in fact, was a leading force in the GATT and WTO trade negotiations that reduced tariff and quota barriers through the world? How and why did U.S. policy change so dramatically? Rational choice analysis asks us to look at the actors, their interests, and the institutional environment.

The implementation of the Bretton Woods agreements in the years immediately following World War II had many important effects. In the *trade regime,* the General Agreement on Tariffs and Trade was established as a system of multilateral negotiations aimed at reducing protectionism. Although the GATT had no real enforcement powers, causing it to be dubbed by cynics "The Gentlemen's Agreement to Talk and Talk," it was still an important actor. This is because, in part, it is better to "Talk, talk" than to "Tariff, tariff" (to paraphrase Winston Churchill), and also because GATT's rules altered the domestic political environment.

The GATT rules specified that each trade negotiation round be multilateral, with many countries participating, and that tariff reductions be reciprocal, so when the United States lowered tariffs on, say, the shoes that it imports, other countries would simultaneously reduce tariffs on, say, the wheat that the United States exports. Thus if Congress were to vote against a GATT treaty in an attempt to protect domestic shoe firms and workers, it would also necessarily be voting to damage the interests of U.S. exporting sectors such as agriculture.

This, clearly, had the effect of bringing new interests—the interests of exporting firms—into the political marketplace. Whereas before GATT the concentrated interests of protection-seeking firms often dominated the interests of the majority of consumers, the GATT environment had the effect of mobilizing countervailing export interests. Those seeking protection from foreign competition now had to contend with firms that wanted freer access to foreign markets. We should not be surprised that GATT, the new actor, by creating a new political environment, allowed new interests to be represented and so changed national policy regarding trade.

One of the most important insights that rational choice analysis provides to IPE involves the concept of *rent-seeking behavior.* In economics, the term "rent" is often used to describe unearned income that a person or firm receives because of scarcity. If a monopolist is able to restrict supply and drive up prices, for example, the extra profits are termed "rents." David Ricardo used the term "rent" for the income that landlords received from their ownership of land—a scarce resource with fixed supply.

Some resources are scarce by nature, but other resources are scarce because of human action. Diamonds, for example, are really a relatively abundant mineral. They are expensive, however, because of diamond cartels which keep the supply of gem-quality diamonds artificially limited in order to keep prices and profits high. The cartel creates scarcity so that it can earn rent. Governments have the ability to create artificial scarcity of some items through the policies that they adopt. Individuals who wish to profit from a government-created scarcity are called *rent-seekers.* When these individuals try to influence public policy so as to gain rents, they are engaged in rent-seeking behavior. Basically, they are looking for ways to use public policy to create private profits for themselves.

If the United States were to impose a quota on automobile imports, for example, imported cars would become scarce and their price would rise. The government would distribute import licenses to certain dealers, giving them the right to import cars and sell them at the higher price. Dealers not favored with import licenses wouldn't be able to benefit directly from the import car shortage. This is how most import quotas work.

Rent-seeking behavior can occur at several points in the political system when an import quota is enacted. First, of course, politically well-placed auto dealers may begin to lobby members of Congress to impose a quota so they can receive rents—this is the classic rent-seeking behavior that lies at the heart of the matter. But they may not get all the rents that would be available. Some elected officials are especially well placed to influence trade legislation because of their committee assignments and other factors. These officials, even if they are honest and upright, will end up collecting some of the rents available as they receive campaign contributions, gifts, or other favors from individuals seeking their influence over legislation.

Rents can also be dispersed within the bureaucracy. It may be that an Office of Auto Import Licenses is created, for example, to handle applications by various auto dealers for the right to bring cars into the country. In this case, some of the focus of rent-seeking behavior may fall on those who have some influence over the issuance of import licenses. A corrupt official may be able to demand bribes in exchange for considering an application for an import license. Even an honest official may get some benefits from the position in the form of favors, gifts or discounts on car purchases. Individual rent-seeking behavior has the direct effect of distorting government policy and the indirect effect of creating an environment where corruption is possible and profitable and therefore more likely to exist.

In summary, the rational choice critique reminds us that public policies are made by private persons. The public interest always reflects the private interests of at least some persons. The actors, the interests, and the institutional environment must be considered if we are to understand what happens in the IPE.

RENT-SEEKING IN MEXICO

Rent-seeking behavior and the environment of corruption that it fosters comprise one of the most serious problems facing less developed countries today. A recent study by Paul Craig Roberts and Karen LaFollette Araujo has drawn attention to the role of rent seeking in explaining Mexico's uneven path toward prosperity in the postwar era.[a]

Mexico has long been a paradox to those who study international affairs from narrow disciplinary perspectives. For a country to be prosperous, many people believe, you need abundant economic resources and political stability. Mexico has both. From the economic standpoint, it has many valuable natural resources, a talented and creative population, and access to foreign investment and technology. It also has had a stable political system, long dominated by the Institutional Revolutionary party (PRI), which has held the reigns of government power in Mexico since 1929. And yet Mexico has failed to achieve self-sustaining economic growth. What holds back Mexico?

The answer, according to Roberts and Araujo, is at least in part the structure of government and the perverse incentives that structure created. The PRI has until very recently had little competition from other political parties and has enjoyed a virtual monopoly on domestic power. Within the PRI, power was concentrated at the top, in the hands of the president. Power was distributed like a pyramid, with the political elites holding most of the control and the masses having just a little (the power of the vote and sometimes—when elections were rigged—not even that).

The rational choice approach asks us to consider how this power structure affects the incentives of the people of Mexico. With small chance of being turned out of office, Mexican officials needed to pay only nominal attention to the voting masses. It was in their interests to use their power to enrich themselves. "Within the government, the modus operandi was 'robar pero obrar,' which means literally 'steal and build.' . . . Someone would say 'PRI functionary so-and-so stole millions,' while another person would reply, 'Yes, but he built the municipal buildings and opened the local state-owned sugar mill.'"[b] It is estimated that ex-Mexican President José López Portillo (1976–82) accumulated $1–$3 billion via top-level robar pero obrar.[c] The total amount that was extracted at all levels by the political elites through bribes, corruption, and crime, is uncounted, but it is surely an enormous sum, especially compared to the low living standards of many Mexican citizens.

This corruption has many roots. In part, the ethics of Mexico's government may reflect values and practices inherited from past colonial rule and administrations. "Like European aristocrats of former times, Mexican elites built mansions, the modern equivalent of castles, and felt few qualms about enriching themselves from public coffers. For the most part, they did not wear the look of the guilty. Indeed, they did not regard themselves as wrongdoers. Plunder has always been the job of the Mexican ruling class."[d]

Roberts and Araujo, however, note that Mexico's constitution concentrated power in particular ways, without many checks and balances, creating a monopoly environment that encourages self-interest that violates the public trust. Mexican presidents, for example, may serve only a single six-year term. Since they cannot gain through reelection, their self interest necessarily drives them to gain through other means, some of them corrupt. Thus, in a way, the corrupt officials are only doing what the rational choice critique predicts that they will do: rationally promote their self-interest given the incentives and constraints they face.

It would have been bad enough if Mexico's only problem was a corrupt government sector, but rent seeking is contagious. As the government took over a larger and larger part of the economy, to increase their gains, rent seeking and corruption became increasingly prevalent. Even in the nongovernment sector, rent seeking became the surest way to individual prosperity. Business executives found it more important to keep up contacts and favorable relationships with the PRI than to invest in new factories and technology. The PRI could, perhaps, throw vast profits their way by enacting favorable regulations or import restrictions, whereas investing in the market economy was risky and—if someone else got to the PRI first with a gift or a bribe—perhaps even economically fatal.

"A fish rots from the head," it is said, and when rent seeking begins at the top, as it did in Mexico, it eventually spreads all the way through. Crime, corruption, and bribery paralyzed Mexico making it, in Roberts and Araujo's term, "the blocked society." Nothing much could happen to mobilize Mexico's vast resources and wonderful people with a bribe and so the wealth went to the crooks, not to the people.

Significantly, Roberts and Araujo are optimistic about Mexico's future. Mexico's severe debt crisis, which came to a head in the early 1980s, forced the government to reduce its influence in the country's economy. (See discussion of the Latin American debt crisis in chapter 8.) And the PRI is facing more and more competition from other parties for power, although at this writing they still seem to have a firm grip on the presidency. So perhaps these reforms can reduce rent seeking in Mexico and change the blocked society and the culture of corruption, with elites skimming the cream, to a flexible and productive commercial and political culture that can benefit the masses.

---

[a] Paul Craig Roberts and Karen LaFollette Araujo, *The Capitalist Revolution in Latin America* (New York: Oxford University Press, 1997). See especially chap. 3, "The Blocked Society," pp. 52-101. Special thanks to Ross Singleton for suggesting this topic for treatment in this chapter.
[b] Roberts and Araujo, *Capitalist Revolution,* p. 56.
[c] Ibid., p. 75.
[d] Ibid., p. 75.

THE GREEN CRITIQUE OF IPE

Humans and human institutions dominate our thinking about IPE as they do in so many other things. The missing actor in the IPE drama is nature. The green critique of IPE is an attempt to remedy this situation. The discussion of the green critique of IPE presented here is based on the essay "International Political Economy and the Greens" by Eric Helleiner.[2]

Markets are hard on nature and hard on the environment. Mainstream economic analysis recognizes that otherwise efficient markets may cause inefficient environmental damage. If a paper mill, for example, removes pollution from its waste water before returning it to a river, it bears a higher cost than a firm that simply dumps tainted water back into the environment. Unregulated competition will tend to drive all paper mills to pollute. Any firm that fails to do so will have higher costs, higher prices, or lower profits and will be driven from the marketplace by competitive forces. In economic terms, the firms pass the *external cost* of making paper on to society in the form of pollution. The invisible hand pollutes; the visible hand of government may be necessary to correct the situation. Mainstream economic theory suggests that there are several effective strategies of government intervention to deal with the problem of external cost.[3]

Experience has demonstrated that the only thing that is harder on Nature than the market is the State. Just as the market tends to put the interests of individuals above the interests of Nature, so we have observed that in many situations states put the "national interest" above natural interest. The strong, highly focused state of the USSR, for example, undertook shockingly irresponsible environmental policies driven by the desire to maximize national security in a world of very scarce resources. Noncommunist governments often have deplorable environmental track records, too. The problem may be that the environment belongs to everyone, which means that it belongs to no one, which means that while everyone has a general interest in preserving and protecting Nature, no one has a special interest in doing so. If the rational choice theorists are right and special interests often dominate the political marketplace, then we should not be surprised to observe that the general interests of nature are not well represented in state policy.

The green critique of IPE is, at one level, an attempt to make Nature an actor in our analysis, to make the environment a value that we consider along with security, freedom, and justice. IPE writers have played a fairly important part in this intellectual movement, as chapter 19 indicates. But, as Eric Helleiner argues, the green critique goes beyond a view that IPE should pay attention to Nature and environmental issues. The green critique asks IPE to consider far more seriously the fundamental nature of human arrangements. Helleiner writes that

> Despite their growing prominence in debates and political struggles concerning IPE issues, the greens' normative project in the international political economy is still poorly understood. To understand it better, we must investigate the slogan that best summarizes the project: 'think globally, act locally.' Despite the popularity of this slogan, the meaning originally ascribed to it by the greens has often been forgotten as it has proliferated not just on car bumper stickers but also in corporate strategy sessions. . . . I suggest that the slogan highlights the greens' commitment to a project of constructing what international relations scholars would call a 'neo-mediaeval' world political-economic order.[4]

What does it mean to "act locally"? The green critique begins with the notion that the most important human relationships are distinctly local in nature. Families, neighborhoods, communities—these are the human arrangements that really matter. These arrangements grow naturally from human needs and interactions.

They have existed for as long as humans have lived together in social groups. They embody the green desire to live life on a natural scale where the value of nature can be sensed and honored. Green IPE is therefore about natural environments, both Nature with an upper case N meaning the land, water, and air, but also lower case nature meaning human nature and a natural way of living. Helleiner writes that

> "Act locally" is meant to convey the idea that people should focus their energies primarily on improving the quality of life and solving problems within the local communities where they live. The phrase reflects a deep commitment to the decentralization of political-economic life and the strength and value of local communities. Behind these sentiments also rests a critique of the large-scale nature of social life in the industrial era. . . . the industrial age is seen to have ushered in a condition perhaps best captured by the Hopi work "koyaanisqatsi," a world that translates roughly as 'life out of balance.'[5]

Big states and big markets, in the green critique, create a world out of balance with ordinary life. The greens seek to restore a balanced life, where people can live in an environment that is human in scale and where their economic, political, and social relationships can be more natural and personal.

Many political economists were introduced to this point of view through E.F. Schumacher's enormously influential book *Small is Beautiful: Economics as if People Mattered.*[6] Schumacher advocated a more balanced view of human activity. He suggested, for example, a return to biologically sound agricultural techniques that built soil instead of depleting it, the adoption of small-scale appropriate technology "with a human face," and forms of business, such as communal ownership, that make workers real participants in the process of creating wealth, not production-line drones. In a famous chapter, Schumacher considered "Buddhist economics"—how an economy would work if it were organized along Buddhist principles that emphasize balance and human development over consumption and materialism.

How does "think globally" fit into this framework? In one sense, it makes the point that the increasingly global structures of production, finance, security, and technology—particularly global patterns of industrialization—threaten local human-scale environments everywhere. The need to act locally is therefore made much more urgent when we think about the global processes that are at work. Thinking globally also means that we must consider that the challenge of maintaining ecological balance in the global biosphere is beyond the competence of the modern nation-state. Increasingly, environmental issues are *global* not just national. Global problems require global thinking—but local action.

The green critique thus forges a local-global nexus. Global problems, local solutions. The greens seek a life that is balanced on a human scale in a global environment. To the traditional analytical levels of individual, class, nation-state, and international system, the greens add community and global biosphere.

THINKING GLOBAL AND ACTING LOCAL ON THE GANGES RIVER

An interesting case study of green IPE appeared recently in "A Reporter at Large: The Ganges' Next Life" by Alexander Stille.[a] The article tells the story of a man named Veer Bhadra Mishra, a devout Hindu who swims nearly every day in the dangerously polluted waters of the Ganges River in the holy city of Varanasi, India.

The Ganges River is sacred to Hindus and to them has great powers of purification. For this reason Hindus make the pilgrimage to Varanasi to perform five full immersions. They come here to die, too, so their ashes can be scattered on the river and carried straight to Heaven.

The Ganges may be pure to the faithful, but it is also terribly polluted in a scientific sense, filled with raw sewage, industrial waste, and decomposing animal and human remains. It is a real act of faith, many would say, to believe in the cleansing powers of such water. Perhaps that is the miracle and the mystery of the River. The region of the Ganges bears the burden of a huge population (one of twelve people in the world live in the Ganges basin!) and raw human sewage accounts for much of the problem.

Veer Bhadra Mishra's role in the story is an interesting one. He is the mahat (head) of Sankat Mochan Temple, one of the city's principal temples. He is also a professor of hydraulic engineering at Banaras Hindu University. He believes in the river's purity and at the same time understands its deadly potential. He thinks globally, in the world of science and health research, and acts locally, immersing himself in the brown waters each day. He is a good person to study if you want to learn about green IPE.

Cleaning the Ganges, as you might imagine, is a huge task. Beginning in 1985, the Indian government began an initiative to clean the river using Western-type waste treatment technology. High-technology wastewater plants were built along the river at a cost of $150 million—a princely sum especially in a poor country like India. They were not a very effective solution. Because such plants are so expensive, only a few of them can be built, and so only a small fraction of all polluted water can be treated. The plants require electricity to operate and electrical supplies in India, as in many less developed countries, are famously unreliable. When the power goes off, the plant shuts down and sewage flows into the river. The plants also shut down when flooded by monsoon rains and when local government authorities run out of money to keep them open.

The wastewater treatment plants are ineffective, but they are also unpopular. They don't fit into the culture of the people of the Ganges River basin. The very idea of wastewater plants contradicts the fundamental Hindu religious belief in the purifying power of the Ganges River, so there is little public support.

Veer Bhadra Mishra enters the story because of work he is doing to replace these high-tech plants with simple systems of ponds that will remove pollution naturally and at low cost. The system he favors uses four sets of ponds to purify wastewater. The first ponds are deep and dark and decompose heavy solid wastes. The second are shallow and use algae and photosynthesis to kill dangerous bacteria. The water goes next to deep ponds, where the algae settles and is harvested to feed farm animals. Finally, the water goes into storage reservoirs that supply the needs of irrigated agriculture. The pond system is cheap, efficient, natural, and can handle large quantities of polluted water. It is a low-tech local solution to a low-tech local problem. If adopted on a global scale, these ponds could have a global impact on water quality.

The best thing, Veer Bhadra Mishra notes, is that the pond system fits easily into the context of Hindu religious belief. "There are three gods: Brahma, the creator, Vishnu, the sustainer, and Shiva, the god who provides us happiness in this world, which is decaying every day."[b] The ponds are part of Shiva's domain and therefore a natural part of Hindu life.

---

[a] Alexander Stille, "A Reporter at Large: The Ganges' Next Life," *New Yorker* 19 January 1998, pp. 58-67.
[b] Ibid., p. 67.

THE FEMINIST CRITIQUE

The feminist critique of IPE begins with the point that the world is not made up of states and markets, or proletariat and bourgeoisie; it is made up of men and women. The interactions of men and women take place in social settings that are frequently disadvantageous to women and within socially constructed institutions that reflect male dominance. The feminist critique is complex and still developing. This short summary will highlight just a few of its contributions to IPE analysis.[7]

The feminist critique invites a gendered analysis of IPE issues which has a particular meaning in this context. When we talk about *sex* in this section, we are discussing biological differences between men and women, which are relevant to many IPE issues. But when we talk about *gender*, however, we refer to the

> . . . associations, stereotypes, and social patterns that a culture constructs on the basis of actual or perceived differences between men and women. Women's lesser average brain weight than men, for example, is a biological characteristic. The nineteenth-century interpretation of this fact as implying that women are therefore less rational is an example of a social belief, that is, a construction of gender.[8]

The goal of some feminist IPE theorists is to take account of the degree to which IPE is dominated by male gender attitudes and stereotypes, and then either to take the gender out or to build a female gender element into the theory. Either way, this is a big job. So deep have male patterns of thought and action rooted themselves in social science theory that we accept them without thinking or realizing their existence. Here is an example of how IPE theories become gendered.

If you want to find male-gendered theory, start with national security theory! After all, men are from Mars (according to the popular book series) and Mars is the god of war and, hence, the muse of national security scholars like Kenneth Waltz. Among Waltz's many contributions to IPE is the idea of the three levels of analysis: individual, state, and system. War, Waltz suggested in his classic *Man, the State, and War: A Theoretical Analysis* can be caused by human nature, the nature of the state, or the nature of the international system in which states exist.[9] This concept was introduced in chapter 1 and it is a useful framework of analysis.

So what is particularly *male* about it? Well, consider what this analytical framework leaves out. One important thing that is missing here is nurturing, upbringing, development, and growth. Man's (*man's!*) nature is taken as a given. Man is taken to emerge into society all at once, his attitudes, interests and behaviors fully formed.[10] In fact, we all know that humans aren't really like this. We believe that attitudes and behaviors are formed gradually as we grow up and are conditioned by our early experiences and perhaps especially by family matters. Instead of man's nature, shouldn't we be talking about human development and how it may cause war or not? In other words, is one source of war man's *nature* or is it man's *nurture*?

The same criticism can be applied to the state and to the system levels of analysis. States and systems also develop and are the results of complicated interactions. Shouldn't the IPE theory talk about the developmental process that shapes states and systems, rather than taking the outcomes of their development for granted?

Why are these particular issues ignored in social science theories? The feminist critique answers that it is because raising a family and nurturing human development is women's work and it is therefore assigned lower value in making theories than other factors that are not associated with women. Social science theories reflect the values of society and, in this case, the low status of women and the low value of women's work translate into a particular bias in our understanding of the ways of war and peace.

The general cultural linking of value (superior/inferior) and gender (masculine/feminine) is a serious matter. Julie A. Nelson has written that

> Any reader who might question the asymmetry of this linking, preferring, perhaps, to think of gender differences in terms of a more benign complementarity, should ponder some of the more obvious manifestations of asymmetry in the social domain. Rough "tomboy" girls are socially acceptable and even praised, but woe to the gentle-natured boy who is labeled a "sissy" ... The sexist association of femininity with lesser worth implicit in such judgements should be noted, not as a matter of isolated personal beliefs but rather a matter of cultural and even cognitive habit.[11]

In other words, because society values stereotypical masculine attitudes and behaviors over the feminine kind, this can result in lifelong reinforcement of certain individual and social patterns. *Society* produces the aggressive individuals and the aggressiveness that Kenneth Waltz described in his theory, not nature. His three-level theory of IPE is aggressively male in its values and approach precisely because the society that he describes is, too. But these attitudes are not "natural"; they are socially constructed and we do not have to accept them. What can be socially constructed can be socially changed.

The feminist critique also takes aim at the deep influence that neoclassical economics has had on the way the IPE has developed. Economic analysis focuses on self-interested individual choice, drawing on the methods of scientific inquiry to produce simple cause-and-effect narratives. What is left out of economics, and therefore left out of political economy in many cases, is intuition, emotion, feeling, belief, and the complex and ambiguous senses that we usually associate with the humanities. These senses are not coldly rational, but they are hardly irrational, either. They are human, but often associated with women and, therefore, dismissed as unimportant by economists and others more attuned to a male-conditioned mode of thought.

Neoclassical economics focuses on production and accumulation, but the feminist critique argues that this ignores important issues of reproduction and provisioning. One result of this way of thinking is that paid work gets a great deal of attention and economic development success is sometimes measured by the ability of states and markets to create "jobs." These jobs, until relatively recently, were men's jobs and the emphasis given them reflects the structural power of men in states and markets. Unpaid jobs, such as raising children, growing and cooking food, providing services to family and community, are seen as backward and unproductive, reflecting the social status of the women who perform them. The feminist critique requires that we rethink the idea of production and the concept of social value so that we perceive the worth in women's work, not just the money that men make.

One of the most important structural changes in IPE over the last 20 years has been the rise of the market and the expansion of market forces. Some countries are experiencing a transition from state to market, other countries from traditional social arrangements to market-driven relationships. This transition to the market has many effects. An important element of this is the transition from the production of goods ("men's work") to greater production of services ("women's work"). Greater female participation in the labor force, combined with the need for a more "flexible" labor force (which women often provide) goes hand-in-hand with economic development. The growth of the market, therefore, is also a change in the status and power of women. Market transition is thus a social and cultural transition within these societies. Mainstream IPE generally focuses on the economic and political consequences of this transition. The feminist critique proposes that the focus should be on the gender issues.

So far we have focused on how feminist scholars critique IPE. What would a true feminist IPE look like? The answer is that it is really too soon to tell. Feminists have been working on gender issues in the economic development area for the longest period of time, and it is here that they have made the greatest progress (although much remains to be done, as the next section will show). Women's

---

WOMEN AND DEVELOPMENT: UNEXPECTED CONSEQUENCES

What does the globalization of economic activity have to do with the number of women being treated in the burn unit of the Dhaka Medical College Hospital in Bangladesh? Nothing, according to the usual way of thinking. Quite a lot, according to the feminist critique.

Take the case of Asma Begum, a 21-year old female who works in a clothing factory, as reported by *The Economist*.[a] When she returned late to her home in the slums, her rickshaw-driver husband was waiting for her. He was furious there was no food on the table when he came home. He stalked out, but returned later with a vial of sulphuric acid, which he threw on her as she slept, severely burning her face, arms, and chest.

This story is repeated over and over again in Dhaka. *The Economist* found 16 women in the hospital burn unit, all suffering from acid burns, all telling just about the same story. Some died from their burns. Each week more female burn victims are admitted in an increasing flow of pain and misery.

It is perhaps impossible to understand such brutality, but it is hard not to search for explanations. One theory is that the trend toward acid burns is a backlash against the rising status of women. The globalization of economic activity creates new opportunities for women in factories and shops, draws them out of the home, gives them increased independence, and generally shakes up traditional gender roles. Microlending schemes, which provide start-up loans for women's cooperative enterprises, also provoke male backlash. Males are often left behind during the transition to a more modern economy, as the example of the rickshaw-driving husband suggests. "Progressive" economic development initiatives can have unexpected, and often tragic, consequences when they are mixed with rigid attitudes in a previously male-dominated society.

By focusing on states and markets, traditional IPE analysis overlooks the differential impact of economic, political, and social change on men and women. This is a great mistake. The solution to problems like those reported here begins with the search for an understanding of them, which the feminist critique provokes.

---

[a] "Acid Horrors," *The Economist*, 17 January 1998, pp. 35-36.

attitudes and women's work are increasingly taken into account in analysis of the problems of less developed countries, although it must be said that male dominance still prevails generally. In other fields, however, the work is just beginning.

As the status of women changes within rigid male-dominated cultures, many important tensions are created that need to be considered formally within the framework of IPE. The box on page 100 makes this point brutally clear.

POSTMODERNISM AND IPE

> Post-modernism haunts social science today. In a number of respects, some plausible and some preposterous, post-modern approaches dispute the underlying assumptions of mainstream social science and its research product over the last three decades. The challenges post-modernism poses seem endless.[12]

Postmodernism is a powerful but undefined critique on patterns of contemporary thought that, having originated in the humanities, now also challenges the social sciences and the natural sciences to reconsider fundamental assumptions and beliefs. Postmodernism lacks a coherent definition. Indeed, one of the most-often cited attempts to define this term took the form not of a definitive essay but of a statistical analysis of how the term was used by others![13] Very well, just as we can define mathematics as "what mathematicians do," so we will define postmodernism as what postmodernists do.

What *do* they do? Well, they do a great many different things that have only a very few things in common, really. Generally, postmodernists are engaged in efforts to undermine the "modern" way of thinking about the world. In literature, for example, the modern way to read a book is to think about what the author was trying to say. The postmodernist approach is to focus on the text itself, independent of the author, and examine instead the reader's reaction. It is the reader, not the author, who creates meaning, in this way of thinking. The author created only a text.

The social sciences are a very modern enterprise, so postmodernist social scientists have a lot of work on their hands. The ways that social scientists think about the world and the theories they use to frame their thoughts are heavily conditioned by specific modern notions and the unquestioned acceptance of certain modern institutions and relationships. The postmodern critique attempts to question these givens and undermine obsolete modes of thought. Postmodernism is naturally controversial, since it challenges so many vested interests. It is also a thought-provoking antidote to sloppy analysis and lazy reasoning, and so it belongs in this chapter.

To a certain extent, IPE is postmodern itself. As discussed in chapter 1, IPE challenges the notion that some important aspects of society can best be understood by modern "disciplinary" analysis—economists doing economics, political scientists doing political science, sociologists doing sociology, and so on, and so on. IPE asks whether there are not questions that can only be answered by breaking down disciplinary walls. IPE, in this sense, undermines the modern division of labor in the academic world and the notion, which dates from Adam Smith, that division of labor, because it increases output, is progressive.

IPE is postmodernist in this sense, but most of the IPE that you will read is still very firmly rooted in modes of thought that are at least 100 years old. IPE defines itself around such modern institutions as classes, states, and markets, for example. But these institutions, and particularly "the state," are hardly well-defined creatures these days. The authority of the state has been fragmented again and again, divided up among different layers of government, transferred to various public, private, and semi-autonomous groups, conditioned by treaties, regional organizations, and global initiatives. In some respects the news media has as much authority as the state. Certainly CNN has more influence than most states in some situations. In some respects the community or the neighborhood is a more meaningful form of social organization.

The problem with the state is that society is very fragmented, existing simultaneously on many levels at once, and the state is only really important on a few of those levels at any one time. Each layer of our complex society is organized differently, with different authority frameworks and different sets of values. The layers are woven through each other. For a postmodernist, it is hard to see how it is meaningful to talk about national interest and "the state." The same sort of critique could be applied to "the market" or "the international system" or "capitalism." We use these words because they are convenient descriptions of what we think we mean, but they are based on a way of seeing society that does not always apply today. We are in danger, the postmodern critique suggests, of misunderstanding society because of the icons (like "state" and "market") that we mentally manipulate in thinking about it.

Susan Strange probably does not think of herself as a postmodernist, but her recent work provides a concrete example of the postmodern critique of IPE. Her most recent book, *The Retreat of the State: The Diffusion of Power in the World Economy*, makes clear her view that authority is now diffused far beyond the state through a series of case studies of non-state actors that now wield some state power.[14] These case studies include telecommunications firms, organized crime syndicates, insurance and accounting firms, and nongovernmental organizations. There is no way to get a mistaken impression from the title of this book! It is clear that Professor Strange thinks a single-minded focus on the state is now passé.

To get a better feel for the postmodernist critique, let us try it ourselves. The notions of hegemony and hegemonic cycles are among the most durable and powerful ideas in IPE. As we saw in chapter 3, mercantilists, liberals, and structuralists all have their own versions of the hegemonic fable. Thousands and thousands of words have been written in recent years all built upon premises inspired by the idea of hegemony. Some have worried that the United States might be weakening—a declining hegemon—and speculated whether the United States could regain its strength, if some other country could rise up to take the hegemonic crown, and what chaos would result if no country did. Others have spilled ink crowing that the United States is as strong as ever and that the world is in good order because a hegemon is in place. When U.S. President George Bush sent U.S. troops into Kuwait and then Iraq in the early 1990s, he was fulfilling his role as a hegemonic leader, conditioned by hegemonic theory.

Here is the basic story of hegemony presented using some stylized facts. Out of a period of disorder there arises one country that is the richest and most powerful. This nation-state, if it assumes the rights and responsibilities of the hegemon, organizes the world system, supplying public goods such as sound money, free trade, and security in return for whatever benefits it gains from its position at the center of the world system. Inevitably, however, its greed or its obligations begin to overreach its resources. The hegemon has trouble making ends meet. It becomes cranky and selfish, or perhaps it is just weak. In any case, it loses its great wealth and its moral authority. Meanwhile, other contenders rise up and gain strength. Eventually they quarrel with each other or with the hegemon, but in any case the hegemon cannot preserve the peace and chaos again rules. Return to the beginning of the paragraph, but with a new hegemon in place.

This is a pretty good story and it can be associated with facts very effectively and very persuasively. The historian Paul Kennedy, for example, turned it into the influential book, *The Rise and Fall of the Great Powers*.[15] This was a good book, well-researched and reflecting excellent scholarship, but of course hopelessly trapped in modern modes of thought. With only a little bit of work to change the cast of characters, however, the hegemon story can also be told of King Arthur, Sir Lancelot, and Lady Guinevere. Arthur is the old hegemon, Lancelot is a rising new one, and the Lady is symbolic of peace and prosperity. The Knights of the Round Table get bit parts. You can fill in the rest of the plot. Or you can retell the story as Walt Disney did in the *Lion King*. The Lion King is the hegemon who weakens and is trampled, only to have a new hegemon arise phoenix-like to restore peace and stability. Each story ends with the peaceful hegemon restored (Lion King) or with chaos in a hegemonless void (see King Arthur's England in *Camelot*). It is a good story line; no wonder it is so appealing when told about felines, medieval monarchs, or modern nation-states.

What's wrong with hegemonic stability theory? Nothing, postmodernists say, as a *story*, but everything as a framework for understanding the world. The postmodern critique of hegemonic stability theory faults it for the following errors.

- It is a grand theory of history when history does not obey grand theories. History is messy, mangled, and still under construction. It moves in many directions on many levels. You can't expect to tell its story as if it were a fairytale.
- It looks for cycles where there are none. Cycles are an old and superficial way of thinking about life, suitable for infants, not adults. Life doesn't loop back on itself any more than it follows a straight theoretical line. If we are going to understand the world we must understand that where we go depends on where we have been and where we are now, and we have never been *here* before. The future is always a mystery. Progress is an illusion.
- The focus is on the nation-state, which is an outmoded concept. Hardly any important IPE question can be addressed solely from the standpoint of the behavior of nation-states.
- The point of this story is to understand the world system and why it is sometimes peaceful and sometimes chaotic. But there is no single world system, so the whole point of hegemonic analysis is moot. The world does not have a center or a single organizing principle. It is aimless to try to understand the world as if it did.
- Hegemonic stability theory aims to understand the circumstances so that the world system reaches some sort of stable equilibrium, a balance of forces that leads to peace and prosperity. Equilibrium is a useless concept in the social sciences, however, where things constantly change and are transformed. Equilibrium might usefully describe two rocks sitting on opposite sides of a scale, but it is just plain wrong to think of society in the same way. The world is fragmented, relationships are unstable, progress is illusive. Deal with it.

THE POST-MODERN STATE AND THE WORLD ORDER

A recent article in *The Economist* applied an interesting postmodern critique to an analysis of foreign policy issues.[a] The article compared the "modern state" of the type that emerged from the Treaty of Westphalia in 1648 and the "postmodern state" that emerged from the collapse of communism in 1989. The differences are worth noting here.

The modern state, first and foremost, is about security and plays a role in some sort of balance of power system. *The Economist* writes that "The modern states are more familiar creatures. They believe strongly in state sovereignty and its corollary—non-interference by one country in another's internal affairs. The moderns . . . are nationalist, and they may well be willing to pursue their national interests by force; they are therefore susceptible to containment through a balance of power like the one, for instance, that before the Iran-Iraq war kept the Gulf in some sort of equilibrium."[b]

The postmodern state is far more open and relies on different mechanisms for security. "The postmoderns are altogether different. These states have largely shed their hang-ups about sovereignty. They operate in a system that encourages mutual interference in each other's domestic affairs and invites constraints and surveillance in military affairs. . . . For their security, these postmodern countries depend not on the balance of power but on international constraints on each other's military capacity."[c]

The change from modern to postmodern states has many implications for the conduct of foreign affairs. First and foremost, it changes the nature of diplomacy itself. Modern diplomacy was about balance and state power. Postmodern is about overlapping layers of international agreements, regional arrangements, and cooperative initiatives. It is the security that comes from many small things, not one big thing. It is lace, not steel. It is a net to constrain and ensnare, not a knife that drives for the heart.

One important problem, however, is that the transition from modern to postmodern is far from complete. Modern states, aggressive and powerful, still walk the earth. Modern states like Korea and Iraq, to name just two, complicate matters and introduce elements of risk and doubt into the postmodern analysis of national and global security. There are even premodern states still around, based on tribal and ethnic relations. *The Economist* advises that the postmodern state must do what it can to encourage openness and cooperation during this time of transition "without ever dropping its guard, if it is wise, against whatever thunderbolts moderns and pre-moderns may throw at it."[d] In short, the postmodern state cannot wholly kick off its modern security roots.

---

[a] "Not Quite a New World Order, More a Three Way Split," *The Economist* (20 December 1997) pp. 41-43. This is based on "The Post-Modern State and the World Order" by Robert Cooper.
[b] "Not Quite a New World Order," p. 42.
[c] Ibid.
[d] Ibid., p. 43.

CONCLUSIONS

As the previous section has tried to demonstrate, the postmodern critique of IPE and of social science generally challenges the givens with force and more than a little attitude. It is up to the reader to determine whether postmodern analysis is the gateway to wisdom or a dead-end road. Whatever it is, is must be taken seriously, because postmodernism takes ideas seriously and tries to get us to take our own ideas more seriously than we usually do.

Ideas *should* be taken seriously. The critiques of rational choice, green, feminist, and postmodern IPE *all* challenge us to think about IPE in new ways, or at least to consider if there are new ways that we *should* think about IPE. This is important because ideas are very powerful. As John Maynard Keynes noted famously in the closing pages of his *General Theory*,

> . . . the ideas of economists and political philosophers, both when they are right and when they are wrong, are more powerful than is commonly understood. Indeed the world is ruled by little else. Practical men, who believe themselves to be quite exempt from any intellectual influences, are usually the slaves of some defunct economist. Madmen in authority, who hear voices in the air, are distilling their frenzy from some academic scribbler of a few years back.[16]

DISCUSSION QUESTIONS

1. How does the rational choice critique explain the existence of tariffs and other mercantilist policies? How does this critique explain liberal policies such as trade barrier reduction? What determines whether a nation is liberal and mercantilist from this point of view?
2. Is the green critique of IPE only about the environment, or does it extend further? How does green IPE view capitalist industrialization, for example, differently from a mercantilist, a liberal, or a structuralist?
3. How would the feminist critique of IPE approach mercantilism, liberalism, and structuralism? Explain.
4. Apply the postmodern critique to List's view of the role of the state and Marx's view of class relations.

INTERNET LINKS

The Canadian Electronic Feminist Network:
   http://www.unb.ca/web/par-l/index.html
People-Centered Development Forum:
   http://iisd1.iisd.ca/pcdf/
Positive Futures Network:
   http://www.futurenet.org/

SUGGESTED READINGS

Robert A. Denemark and Robert O'Brien. "Contesting the Canon: International Political Economy at UK and US Universities," *Review of International Political Economy* 4:1 (Spring 1997), pp. 214-238.

Eric Helleiner. "International Political Economy and the Greens," *New Political Economy* 1:1 (March 1996), pp. 59-78

Bruno S. Frey. *International Political Economics.* New York: Basil Blackwell, 1984.

Phillip I. Levy. "A Political-Economic Analysis of Free-Trade Agreements," *The American Economic Review* 87:4 (September 1997), pp. 506-519.

Julie A. Nelson. "Feminism and Economics," *The Journal of Economic Perspectives* 9:2 (Spring 1995), pp. 131-148.

Paul Craig Roberts and Karen LaFollette Araujo. *The Capitalist Revolution in Latin America.* New York: Oxford University Press, 1997.

Pauline Marie Rosenau. *Post-Modernism and the Social Sciences: Insights, Inroads, and Intrusions.* Princeton, NJ: Princeton University Press, 1992.

E.F. Schumacher. *Small Is Beautiful: Economics as if People Mattered.* New York: HarperPerennial, 1973.

Alexander Stille. "A Reporter at Large: The Ganges' Next Life." *New Yorker*, 19 January 1998, pp. 58-67.

Susan Strange. *The Retreat of the State: The Diffusion of Power in the World Economy.* Cambridge: Cambridge University Press, 1996.

Georgina Waylen. "Gender, Feminism and Political Economy," *New Political Economy* 2:2 (July 1997), pp.205-220.

"Not Quite a New World Order, More a Three Way Split," *The Economist* 20 December 1997 pp. 41-43.

NOTES

1. A classic application of this approach to IPE can be found in *International Political Economics* by Bruno S. Frey (New York: Basil Blackwell, 1984).
2. Eric Helleiner, "International Political Economy and the Greens," *New Political Economy* 1:1 (March 1996), pp. 59-78. The green critique of IPE does not necessarily represent the views of the green political parties that exist in many countries, most notably in Europe. See Helleiner's analysis for a more thorough analysis.
3. See Michael Veseth, *Public Finance* (Reston, VA: Reston Publishing Company, 1984), pp. 45-57.
4. Helleiner, "IPE and the Greens," p. 60.
5. Ibid., pp. 60-61.
6. E.F. Schumacher, *Small Is Beautiful: Economics as if People Mattered.* (New York: HarperPerennial, 1973).
7. This discussion of the feminist critique draws mainly on "Gender, Feminism and Political Economy" by Georgina Waylen, *New Political Economy* 2:2 (July 1997), pp. 205-220 and "Feminism and Economics" by Julie A. Nelson, *The Journal of Economic Perspectives* 9:2 (Spring 1995), pp. 131-148.
8. Nelson, "Feminism and Economics," pp. 132-33.
9. Kenneth Waltz, *Man, the State, and War: A Theoretical Analysis* (New York: Columbia University Press, 1959).
10. Julie A. Nelson calls this the "mushroom man" phenomenon, because these men pop up full formed over night, like mushrooms in the garden.
11. Nelson, "Feminism and Economics," p. 134.
12. Pauline Maris Rosenau, *Post-Modernism and the Social Sciences: Insights, Inroads, and Intrusions* (Princeton, NJ: Princeton University Press, 1992), p. 3.
13. Allan Megill, "What Does the Term 'Postmodern' Mean?" *Annals of Scholarship* 6 (1989), pp. 129-151.
14. Susan Strange, *The Retreat of the State: The Diffusion of Power in the World Economy* (Cambridge: Cambridge University Press, 1996).
15. Paul Kennedy, *The Rise and Fall of the Great Powers* (New York: Random House, 1987).
16. John Maynard Keynes, *The General Theory of Employment, Interest, and Money* (New York: Harcourt Brace Jovanovich, 1964), p. 383.

PART II

IPE Structures:
Production, Finance,
Security, and Knowledge

The first five chapters of this book have provided you with an intellectual foundation upon which to build a sophisticated understanding of the international political economy. In them we covered many of the basic ideas and fundamental
assumptions about international political economy, the three principal IPE perspectives that are most often used to analyze and interpret IPE interactions, and
several new perspectives that account for developments outside the three most popular IPE perspectives. The next five chapters look at the sets of relationships or
"structures" that tie together nation-states and other actors and that link national
and global markets in the IPE. Professor Susan Strange, a leading IPE thinker, proposed that in thinking about the main elements and arrangements of the international political economy we focus on the four core structures of production,
finance, security, and knowledge.

A word of explanation is useful at this point concerning the use of the term
"structure" here and its relationships to "structuralism" discussed in chapter 4. Each
of the four main IPE structures is a network of bargains, agreements, institutions,
and other relationships that connect the people of the world in various ways. You

can think of a structure such as a computer network, for example, in the sense that people are connected in particular ways by the "hardware" (institutions and their structural power) and "software" (individual bargains and personal arrangements with their relational power) of the network's current setup. We propose to study how the four main structures of IPE connect the people of the world and condition the behavior of states and markets. This is a general framework of analysis that can be approached from many different points of view.

Structuralists believe that the best way to understand IPE is to focus specifically on the capitalist elements of the IPE structures. They believe that the structures of capitalism condition or determine the outcomes of IPE. In other words, structuralists believe that the answer to the question *cui bono?* is determined by the structures of capitalism—a viewpoint that puts especially great importance on the study of these structures.

Each structure accounts for a set of relationships or arrangements and distinct rules (if not tacit understandings) between and among different political, economic, and social actors in each of these areas. In looking at the characteristics of each structure Strange also encourages us to ask the simple question, "*cui bono?*" (who benefits?). Asking this question forces us to go beyond description to analysis—to identify not only the structure and how it works, but what benefit it provides to those who founded it or to those who manage it today. What sources of power did they use to create the structure and how has it been managed since? Strange also encourages us to ask questions not only about the role of each structure in the international political economy, but, also about the relationship of one structure to another. Perhaps the most interesting thing about IPE is the fact that states and markets along with an increasing number of other important actors are generally involved in a number of simultaneous structural relationships, often on different terms, and usually with different partners. In the international political economy elements of one structure routinely influence developments in another structure. A good example here is the way many officials promote trade (an element of the production structure) as an "engine to growth" and at the same time often attempt to use it as a means or tool of foreign policy to punish another nation (an element of the security structure) by withholding it from that nation.

This section's information is important in it own right, but it will be especially useful to us in the second half of the text, when we tackle international and global problems. In these later sections, we will build upon the foundation of the IPE perspectives and structures to construct a clear yet sophisticated understanding of some of the most important issues of yesterday, today, and tomorrow.

We begin with the production structure, which encompasses a number of critical issues about international trade. The production structure accounts for who produces what, where, under what conditions, and how it is sold, to whom, and on what terms. Some scholars have characterized the production structure as the *international division of labor*, but it means much more than simple categories of nations that produce different types of goods given their local resources and labor conditions. In IPE, the production structure most frequently accounts for issues involving international trade. The issue of trade (chapter 6) deals with a number of controversies surrounding where goods are produced (at home or abroad), who gains as a result of this production, and what terms or conditions prevail when it comes to the sale or exchange of these goods. Because of their connection to earning income, a politically charged issue in particular, questions of production and trade are among the oldest, most controversial, most timely, and most important in IPE.

We next analyze the finance structure, which is most effectively divided into two parts: the analysis of the international monetary system (chapter 7) and international finance and debt (chapter 8). Here we will learn how individuals and nations are interconnected by monetary linkages. Each of these chapters really has two parts. Part of each chapter is devoted to introducing the specialized vocabulary of international finance, so you can understand what it means when you read about exchange rates or the balance of payments. The second part of each chapter analyzes the networks that money creates, how those networks have changed, and how they all affect states, markets, and you.

The security structure or network of war and peace defines the sets of relationships and rules of behavior that affect the safety and security of states, groups, and individuals within the IPE. Hardly anything is older or more important than this problem that increasingly affects and is effected by international economic developments. Some parts of the security structure are easy to recognize, such as the formal security alliances that comprise NATO (the North Atlantic Treaty Organization). Other aspects such as the role of terrorists for example, are less visible or certain, but important nonetheless.

Finally, states and markets are also linked by a set of relationships involving knowledge, ideas, and technology (chapter 10). Who has access to knowledge and technology, and on what terms, is a question of growing importance in the study of IPE today. More and more, knowledge and technology represent the ability to "do things" that dramatically affect the balance of power between and among actors in the finance, production, and security spheres of life. Knowledge is power, it is said, but who has this power and how will it be used?

6

International Trade

OVERVIEW

International trade is one of the international political economy's oldest and most controversial subjects. International trade is considered to be part of the production structure of the international political economy.[1] To review, the production structure is the set of relationships between states and other actors such as international businesses that determine what is produced, where, by whom, how, for whom, and at what price. Together with the international financial, technological, and security structures, trade links nation-states and other actors, furthering their interdependence, and some believe globalization—conditions that benefit but are also sources of tension between states and different groups within them. Controversies about international trade stem from the compulsion of nation-states and also business enterprises to capture the economic benefits of trade while limiting its negative political, economic, and social effects on producer groups and society in general.

This chapter surveys a variety developments and changes that have occurred in the post-World War II trade system where officials in the northern industrialized developed nations have sought ways to liberalize (i.e., to reduce the level of protectionist barriers) in the international trade system. The United

States and its allies created the General Agreement on Tariffs and Trade (GATT) to promote liberal trade values and objectives commensurate with U.S. political and military strategic objectives. In an effort to further liberalize world trade, in 1995 the World Trade Organization (WTO) replaced the GATT. Despite some success these organizations have had in promoting free trade, the result is an impasse of sorts whereby simultaneously both protection and free trade are promoted by a growing number of actors with an interest in trade policy.

The chapter concludes with a survey of a number of other important trade problems and issues including the role of developing nations in international trade; the growing number of regional trade blocs or alliances; the role of strategic trade policies some states use to enhance the competitiveness of their goods; the use of trade as an instrument of foreign policy; and finally, several "new" complicated trade issues that are linked to issues about human rights, the environment, jurisdictional and "trade diplomacy" problems that make trade one of IPE's most complex and politically contentious issues.

In the absence of a world government, cross border trade is always subject to rules that must be politically negotiated among nations that are sovereign in their own realm but not outside their borders.[2]

Robert Kuttner

Trade is *always* political, Robert Kuttner tells us. The economics of trade cannot be separated from its political aspects. In fact, many IPE theorists would say that no topic is more quintessentially IPE than trade, and it is no surprise that for hundreds of years the time and talents of many IPE scholars and practitioners focused on trade issues. If anything, Kuttner's words understate the issue; trade is more political than ever now. Not only does trade continue to gain in importance for national officials, but also the number of political actors and institutions outside the nation-state that shape developments in this area has grown significantly since the end of the Cold War in the late 1980s.

International political economists term the network of human arrangements that determine what is produced, how, by whom, for whom, and on what terms the ***production structure.*** When elements of that structure cross international boundaries, the result is international trade, one of the oldest and most contentious areas of IPE. Although the production structure is still largely domestic in the sense that most of the goods and services consumed in nations today (measured by their value) are produced domestically, international trade has been growing dramatically. This reflects the increasing internationalization or globalization of production.

During the period 1960 to 1995, for example, world trade increased from a total of $629 billion to more than $5 trillion (both figures in constant 1995 dollars). While world production increased at an annual rate of 3.8 percent over this period, international trade rose by an annual rate of 6.1 percent.[3]

Trade ties countries together, and in so doing, generates a good deal of economic and political interdependence. Because trade plays such an important, if not large, role in most economies, states are more than ever compelled to regulate it so as to capture its benefits and limit its costs to their economies.

THREE PERSPECTIVES ON INTERNATIONAL TRADE

The system of international trade pulls in three directions at once. There is a large (but far from universal) consensus that a liberal international trading system is desirable. Within that liberal structure, however, individual nation-states try to pursue mercantilist policies while worrying about becoming dependent and being exploited by other nations. Thus it is possible for national leaders apparently to believe in all three IPE perspectives at once: a global system of free trade (liberal), but protection for domestic firms and workers (mercantilist) by promoting high-wage or high-technology (core-type) industrialization (structuralist). No wonder international trade policy is so controversial.

During the mercantilist period from the sixteenth through eighteenth centuries (see chapter 2), for example, early European states aggressively sought to generate trade surpluses as a source of wealth for local producers and for royalty and later the bureaucratic state. To help local industries get off the ground, imports of intermediate goods were discouraged if they meant people would purchase imports instead of buying locally produced goods. For mercantilists, trade was also one among many instruments the state tried to use to enhance its wealth and thus its power and prestige in relation to the power and prestige of other states. The territories the Europeans colonized provided them with gold, silver, and other precious metals, adding to their national wealth. The Europeans often used this wealth to help pay for the many wars they fought with one another on and around the continent. This dynamic relationship between wealth and power lies at the heart of the mercantilist and much of the structuralist theories of international trade.

Reacting to what they viewed as mercantilist abuses, in the late eighteenth century Adam Smith and David Ricardo proposed a distinctly liberal theory of trade that dominated British policy for over 100 years and is still very influential today. Smith, of course, advocated *laissez-faire* policies generally. Ricardo went one step further; his work on the *law of comparative advantage* demonstrated that free trade increased efficiency and had the potential to make everyone better off. It mattered little to liberals, who produced the goods, where, how, or under what circumstances as long as individuals were free to buy and sell them on open markets. The world was becoming a global workshop, where everyone benefited, guided by the "invisible hand" of the market.

The law of comparative advantage is deceptively simple. When people and nations produce goods and services, they have to give up something to get them. We normally think that the "something" we give up is money, but that misses the point. What we really give up are the other goods and services that could have been produced instead. This is what economists call an *opportunity cost*.

The law of comparative advantage holds that we gain when we find ways to minimize the opportunity cost that we pay. Thus, for example, if we give up more when we produce oil at home than what we have to give up in exchange when we buy it from another country (say, Saudia Arabia), we are better off.

The law of comparative advantage invites us to compare the opportunity cost of producing an item ourselves with the opportunity cost of buying it from others and to make a logical and efficient choice between the two. In Ricardo's day, as we saw in chapter 2, the law of comparative advantage specified that Great Britain should import food grains rather than produce them at home because the cost of imports was comparatively less than the cost of domestic production. This was controversial, of course, because of the political influence of property owners whose interests were tied to domestic grain farming. Ricardo proposed that free trade could benefit all trading partners and, by causing goods to be produced where their opportunity costs were the lowest, thus increase the wealth of nations (and of people).

If trade were only about comparative advantage and whether nations are better off trading versus the extreme of being self-sufficient, it would not be so controversial. However, the question *"cui bono?"* remains. According to economic liberals, the issue of who benefits the most from these efficiencies depends upon whether the **terms of trade**[4] favor the importer or the exporting nation. If the price of oil is high compared to wheat, then Saudi Arabia will reap more of the gains from trade. If oil is relatively cheap, then the United States will derive more gain. Trading partners, like the United States and Saudi Arabia in this example, both gain from trade, so they are encouraged to trade. Yet each struggles to get a little larger share of the efficiency gains that trade creates. For developing nations trade often serves as an "engine to growth" and is looked to as one of the most important elements of economic development.

First Alexander Hamilton and then Friedrich List challenged what became accepted liberal doctrine about trade (see chapter 2). From their mercantilist perspective, liberalism and free trade policies were nothing more than an academic justification for England to maintain its dominant advantage over its trading partners on the continent and in the New World. Hamilton argued that U.S. infant industries and national independence and security required the employment of trade protectionist measures.[5] List argued that liberalism manifested unequal power among nations. In order for free trade to work it must be preceded by greater equality between states, or at least a willingness on their part to share the benefits and costs associated with trade. Furthermore, List argued that in a climate of rising economic nationalism, protectionist trade policies such as import tariffs and export subsidies were necessary if Europe's infant industries were to compete on an equal footing with England's industries.[6]

Mercantilists then challenged the assumption that comparative advantage unconditionally benefits both parties. The national production structure generates goods for trade. Yet this structure reflects a distribution of national resources such that people are employed in different sectors of the economy. While comparative advantages are theoretically dynamic—that is, shifts in a nation's resources and capabilities generate new opportunity costs, people employed in those industries are likely to resist moving into other occupations. This helps explain why farmers seek trade protection for their agricultural commodities—because they like to farm—even if commodity surpluses drive down food prices and weaken the demand for their commodities.

Mercantilists also stress the *politics* of trade. Liberal trade theories do not wash in the real political world. States naturally desire to *protect* themselves and their businesses from the negative effects of trade. Any number of domestic groups and industries may appeal to the state for protection—and receive it. Farmers often get trade protection for a number of reasons. First, even though they are relatively small in number compared to the size of other industries, they have tended to be overrepresented in national legislatures in the United States, Western Europe, and Japan. Trade protection takes many forms: policies designed to encourage exports, and policies designed to discourage imports (see box on page 115).

Second, nation-states *fear* becoming too dependent on others for certain goods. Based on security concerns, many nations prefer being relatively self-sufficient when it comes to food and natural resources and raw materials that sustain a nation's basic industries. Mercantilists are very much aware of the protectionist trade policies one state or group of states such as a regional trade alliance such as NAFTA or the European Union (EU) (discussed below) use to help its industries and that can unintentionally disrupt another economy through trade. Finally, as in the recent case of the United Nations' effort to cut off all trade with Iraq during the Persian Gulf War, mercantilists also recognize the extent to which nations will often turn to trade embargoes or boycotts, among other economic sanctions, to punish or otherwise hurt other nations.

By the turn of the twentieth century, protectionist trade policies were on the rise as the major powers once again raced to stimulate industrial growth. After World War I, some states adopted two different types of trade protectionism.[7] In conjunction with expansionist foreign policies, Italy, Germany, and Japan supposedly used trade protectionism in a *malevolent* or aggressive manner to dominate the colonial possessions they acquired. The other European powers and the United States are supposed to have acted in a more *benign* manner, by adopting protectionist trade policies in an attempt to counter the protectionsist policies others employed to insulate their economies. During the Great Depression of the 1930s, trade protectionism spiraled upward while international trade significantly decreased. Between 1929 and 1933, worldwide trade declined by an estimated 54 percent, strangled in part by the Smoot-Hawley tariffs in the United States and similar onerous trade barriers enacted elsewhere.[8] Many historians argue that the trade situation and the depressed international economy associated with it helped generate the bleak economic conditions ultranationalist leaders such as Mussolini and Hitler reacted to.

Structuralists look at the mercantilist period quite differently than do mercantilists and liberals. First, they label the early mercantilist period as one of ***classical imperialism.*** Imperialism of the major European powers originated in their own economies. Mercantilist policies that emphasized exports became necessary when industrial capitalist societies experienced economic depression. Manufacturers overproduced industrial products and financiers had a surplus of capital to invest abroad. Colonies served at least two purposes. They were a place to

---

THE VOCABULARY OF INTERNATIONAL TRADE POLICY

Some of the more important and most often used protectionist measures include

- *Tariffs* A tax placed on imported goods to raise the price of those goods, making them less attractive to consumers. Tariffs are used at times to raise government revenue (particularly in LDCs). Tariffs are more commonly a means to protect domestic industry from foreign competition.
- *Import Quotas* A limit on the quantity of an item that can be imported into a nation. By limiting the quantity of imports, the quota tends to drive up the price of a good at the same time it restricts competition.
- *Export Quotas* These international agreements limit the quantity of an item that a nation can export. The effect is to limit the number of goods imported into a country. Examples include *Orderly Marketing Arrangements* (OMAs), *Voluntary Export Restraints* (VERs) or *Voluntary Restraint Agreements* (VRAs). The *multifibre agreement* establishes a system of textile export quotas for less developed countries, for example.
- *Export Subsidies* Any measure that effectively reduces the price of an exported product, making it more attractive to potential foreign buyers.
- *Currency Devaluations* The effect of devaluing one's currency is to make exports cheaper to other countries while imports from abroad become more expensive. Currency depreciation thus tends to achieve the effects, temporarily at least, of both a tariff (raising import prices) and an export subsidy (lowering the costs of exports). Currency changes affect the prices of all traded goods, however, while tariffs and subsidies generally apply to one good at a time.
- *Nontariff Barriers (NTBs)* Other ways of limiting imports include government health and safety standards, domestic content legislation, licensing requirements, and labeling requirements. Such measures make it difficult for imported goods to be marketed or significantly raise the price of imported goods.
- *Strategic Trade Practices* Efforts on the part of the state to *create* comparative advantages in trade by methods such as subsidizing research and development of a product, or providing subsidies to help an industry increase production to the point where it can move down the "learning curve" to achieve greater production efficiency than foreign competitors. Strategic trade practices are often associated with *state industrial policies*, that is, intervention in the economy to promote specific patterns of industrial development.
- *Dumping* The practice of selling an item for less abroad than at home. Dumping is an unfair trade practice when it is used to drive out competitors from an export market with the goal of creating monopoly power.
- *Countervailing Trade Practices* Defensive measures taken on the part of the state to counter the advantage gained by another state when it adopts protectionist measures. Such practices include antidumping measures and the imposition of countervailing tariffs or quotas.
- *Safeguards.* Another defensive measure used when, after tariffs are reduced, a product is imported in quantities that threaten serious injury to domestic producers of like or directly competitive products.

---

dump these goods and a place where investment could be made in industries that profited from cheap labor and access to plentiful (i.e., inexpensive) quantities of natural resources and mineral deposits. Trade helped colonial mother countries dominate and subjugate the undeveloped colonial territories of the world. Lenin argued that national trade policies benefited most the dominant class in society—the bourgeoisie. According to Lenin, in the period of *modern imperialism* toward the end of the nineteenth century, capitalist countries used trade to spread capitalism into underdeveloped regions of the world. The "soft" power of finance as much as the "hard" power of colonial conquest helped establish empires of dependency and exploitation.

During the early colonial period, developing regions of the world remained on the periphery of the international trade system. They provided their "mother" countries with primary goods and mineral resources along with markets for manufactured products. Structuralists argue that industrializing core nations converted these resources and minerals into finished and semifinished products, many of which were sold to other major powers and back to their colonies. From the perspective of many structuralists, trade to this day continues to play a key role in helping the imperialist industrialized nations subjugate the masses of people in developing regions of the world.

Andre Gunder Frank and other theorists who apply structuralist ideas and arguments to analyze the internal effects of colonialism and imperialism on such countries as Brazil, argue that trade helped generate dependency of peripheral regions and nations on the industrialized core nations. While particular sectors (enclaves) of core economies have developed, political and economic conditions for the masses of people within peripheral nations and regions *have become underdeveloped* since contact with the industrialized nations through trade.[9]

Likewise, modern world system structuralists, such as Immanual Wallerstein, stress the linkage between capitalist core countries and periphery and semi-periphery regions of the world. Patterns of international trade are largely determined by an *international division of labor* that accompanies capitalism. Within these different structuralist perspectives there are a number of views as to how trade might help more fairly distribute or even redistribute income among the nations of the world. Solutions to trade problems between the rich and poor vary from policies of autarchy (i.e., no trade at all) to rather cautious opinions that, for the most part, nations should be able to solve their trade problems amicably with one another.

Contemporary trade policy is deeply conditioned by all three IPE perspectives on trade. As noted earlier, there is a consensus in favor of a liberal international trade system. Within that liberal system, however, nations tend to behave as mercantilists when their national interests are threatened. And there is a general concern (both in LDCs and in industrialized nations) that trade may be more exploitative than mutually advantageous.

GATT AND THE LIBERAL POSTWAR TRADE STRUCTURE

The postwar structure of much of the capitalist world's political economy was designed and established in 1944 at the *Bretton Woods conference*. There, allied leaders, led by the United States and Great Britain, tried to create a new economic order that would prevent many of the interwar economic conflict and problems that led to World War II. In conjunction with this effort, the United States also promoted the establishment of an *International Trade Organization (ITO)* that was to oversee new liberal (open) trade rules applied to tariffs, subsidies, and other protectionist measures. The idea was that the ITO would serve as an international counterbalance to domestic tendencies toward protectionism. Membership in the ITO would establish an international obligation to keep trade lines open, which would, it was hoped, offset domestic mercantilist tendencies.[10]

The ITO never got off the ground because a coalition of protectionist interests in the U.S. Congress forced the United States to withdraw from the agreement, effectively killing it. President Harry Truman advanced a temporary alternative structure for multilateral trade negotiations under the *General Agreement on Tariffs and Trade (GATT).* In 1948, GATT became the primary organization responsible for the liberalization of international trade.[11] The GATT sought to liberalize trade through a series of multilateral negotiations, called rounds, where the main trading nations of the world would each agree to reduce their own protectionist barriers in return for freer access to each other's markets.

The GATT was based on the principles of *reciprocity* and *non-discrimination*. Trade concessions were reciprocal—all member nations agreed to lower their trade barriers together. This principle was conceived as a way to discourage or prevent nations from enacting unilateral trade barriers. The loss in protection of domestic industry was thus offset by freer access to foreign markets. The principle of nondiscrimination required that imports from all countries be treated the same—imports from one nation cannot be given preference over those from another. This is called Most Favored Nation (MFN) trading status. This principle was designed to prevent bilateral trade wars.

These two principles proved potent during the early years of GATT negotiations. Member nations slowly peeled away the protectionist barriers they had erected in the 1930s, allowing international trade to expand dramatically.

But it was impossible to divorce politics from trade, even under GATT rules. Some nations were not willing to automatically grant this privilege to their trading partners. In mercantilist fashion they often selectively granted it to those they politically favored or wanted to assist while withholding it from other states for any number of reasons. MFN became a carrot and stick instrument used by many nations. The GATT also allowed *exemptions* from generalized trade rules for certain goods and services, including agricultural products and quotas. These exemptions allowed many of the war-ravaged nations to resolve balance-of-payments shortages. In the case of agriculture they reflected food shortages in Europe and the need for financial assistance to farmers. GATT's membership was theoretically open to any nation, but until the 1980s most communist countries refused to join it, viewing GATT as a tool of Western imperialism.

MERCANTILIST POLICIES IN A LIBERAL TRADE SYSTEM

During the 1960s and early 1970s the pace at which the Western industrialized economies grew after the war began to slow appreciably. The OPEC oil crisis began in 1973 and would soon result in economic recession throughout many of the Western industrialized nations. Throughout this period international trade continued to grow, but not at the rate at which it had earlier. Under increasing pressure to stimulate economic growth, many nations reduced their tariff barriers. At the same time however, they devised new and more sophisticated ways of protecting their exports and otherwise limiting imports. By the time the Tokyo round of GATT (1973–1979) got underway, the level of tariffs on industrial products had decreased to an average of 9 percent. The Tokyo GATT round tried to deal with a growing number of *Non Tariff Barriers (NTBs)* that many believed were stifling world trade. Rules or codes covered a range of discriminatory trade practices, including the use of export subsidies, countervailing duties, dumping, government purchasing practices, government imposed product standards, and custom valuation and licensing requirements on importers. Some new rules were also devised that covered trade with developing nations.

Many liberal trade theorists at the time argued that the Tokyo round did not go far enough, especially in dealing with the growing problem of NTBs. In the 1970s and 1980s, the industrialized nations were encountering a number of old but also new kinds trade problems. Trade among the industrialized nations quadrupled from 1963 to 1973, but increased only two and one-half times in the next decade. Meanwhile, trade accounted for increasingly higher percentages of Gross Domestic Product (GDP) in the industrialized nations in the 1980s: around 20 percent for the United States, 20 percent for Japan, and an average of 50 percent for members of the European Union (EU). To put it mildly, trade policy continued to be a serious issue of disagreement among the industrialized nations, reflecting their increasing dependence on it to help generate and maintain economic growth.

Japan was the quintessential mercantilist nation during this period. It benefited from the liberal international trade system while erecting mercantilist policies domestically. By the 1970s, Japan's export-led growth trade strategy began to bear fruit. The Ministry of International Trade and Industry (MITI) helped pick corporate winners it and other government officials felt would prosper in the international economy from state assistance (see chapter 13). Most of these industries were high-employment, high-technology firms whose future looked bright. Working closely with their national firms, the Japanese and the Newly Industrialized Countries (NICs) began assisting their firms in ways that would put them in a strong competitive position.

The term *strategic trade policies* became synonymous with state efforts to stimulate exports[12] or block foreign access to domestic markets. The practice of strategic trade then included "the use of threats, promises, and other bargaining techniques in order to alter the trading regime in ways that improve the market position and increase the profits of national corporations."[13] In the United States, for instance, the Omnibus Trade and Competitiveness Act of 1988 produced "Super 301," legislation that required trade officials to list "priority" countries that unfairly threatened U.S. exports. Aside from export subsidies and the use of a variety of import limiting measures, proactive strategic trade policy measures included extended support for "infant industries" complemented by import protection and export promotion measures. Some states went out of their way to form joint ventures with firms in the research and development of new technologies and products. An example was U.S. government assistance to Microsoft Corporation in an effort to crack down on Chinese computer software pirates.[14]

One step at a time, the liberal GATT system was compromised. *Free trade* was slowly replaced as the central principle with the notion of *fair trade* or a "level playing field." States sought to level the playing field by enacting mercantilist policies to counteract those of their trading partners. Trade policy moved from the multilateral arena of GATT to a series of bilateral discussions, as between the United States and Japan and the United States and the European Union. It was time, some thought, to reassert the liberal vision of free trade. Thus was born the Uruguay round of the GATT.

THE URUGUAY ROUND AND THE WTO

The eighth GATT round—the Uruguay round—got underway in 1986 in Punta del Este, Uruguay. Meeting routinely in Geneva, Switzerland, but also occasionally in other cities, the Uruguay round appeared to be headed for failure when it was finally completed on December 15, 1993. Generally speaking liberals tend to view the Uruguary round as a success related to the impact it and past GATT rounds have had on the volume and value of international trade. According to a *Financial Times* survey the eight GATT rounds produced "a reduction in the tariffs of the industrialized nations to less than 4 percent on average, a tenth of their level" in 1948.[15] Many import quotas have been done away with and export subsidies brought under control. This same survey also reports that since 1948 merchandise exports have increased 16 times or three times the growth in world output. Foreign direct investment has surged alongside this growth in trade tying national economies into an "interdependent global network."

Specifically, the final agreement of the Uruguay round resulted in the establishment of new rules and regulations on the trade of older trade items including agriculture and textiles and such protectionist measures as dumping and the use of state subsidies. However, the Uruguay round went beyond previous trade rounds to cover a number of newer commercial items such as services (e.g., insurance), Trade-Related Intellectual Property rights (so-called TRIPs) that include such items as copyrights, patents, and trademarks on computer software, and Trade-Related Investment Measures (TRIMs). By packaging negotiations on some 15 items together, agreements often reflected deals nations or groups of nations made with one another after considering the political and economic trade-offs trade policies generated.

For the first time of any significance, GATT trade negotiations dealt with the contentious issue of agriculture.[16] All of the major producers and importers of agricultural products routinely employed subsidies and other measures that, according to liberal critics, distorted agricultural trade. Agricultural issues had been intentionally absent from previous GATT rounds because they were too contentious—too hot to handle—and would prevent progress in areas where agreements were possible. Instead of once again leaving agriculture off the table, trade officials made the issue of agriculture assistance and reform one of the main objectives of the round.

During the Uruguay round, the United States, the Cairns Group (composed of Australia and 13 other pro free trade countries), and at times Japan, led an effort to phase out all agricultural subsidies. At first the Reagan administration held out the possibility of completely eliminating such subsidies to U.S. farmers. The U.S. farm program had slowly been shifting to allow for market forces to play a greater role in determining farm prices and the level of farm assistance programs. After resistance by some farm groups and government officials, the United States agreed to gradually eliminate its domestic farm programs and agricultural trade support measures. Farmers in the EU (especially in France) were more critical of efforts to decrease support for agriculture from the outset. EU efforts to significantly reduce agricultural subsidies were complicated by a farm program—the Common Agricultural Policy (CAP) that reflected the combined interests of 15 member states. Bringing the EU's farm program in line with GATT reform proposals would be a politically contentious and complicated process that took almost five years.

Agricultural trade then remained one of the major sticking points of the Uruguay round, deadlocking the entire negotiations on several occasions. Final agreement on agricultural trade was reached at the eleventh hour in November 1993, opening the way for agreement on all other issues. The final agreement of the round was finally approved in late 1994 and came into effect in early 1995. Many U.S. exporters expected big gains, namely 20,000 jobs for every $1 billion increase in exports, and access to overseas markets for U.S. semiconductors, computers, and a variety of U.S. agricultural commodities.[17]

It remains to be seen just how much the new rules for agriculture will decrease protection in this trade sector. While countries agreed to reduce their use of agricultural export subsidies and level of domestic assistance gradually over a period of years, the new rules allow them to convert nontariff import barriers into tariff equivalents, which are then to be reduced in stages. However, because of the way tariff equivalents are calculated, in some cases new tariff levels may legally be higher than previous assistance levels, effectively nullifying efforts to reduce farm assistance. For now though, most liberal critics of agricultural assistance are happy that reductions in agriculture assistance can be negotiated in future rounds.

Of major significance to international trade, the final agreement of the Uruguay round launched the new World Trade Organization (WTO). Comprised of 135 members (as of 1999) with 30 countries seeking membership,[18] the WTO accounts for over 90 percent of world trade and is headquartered in Geneva, Switzerland. Its primary job is to implement the latest GATT agreement and act as a forum for negotiating new trade deals, help settle trade disputes, review national trade policies, and assist LDCs in trade policy issues by technical assistance and training programs. Theoretically, WTO decisions are taken by the members themselves seeking consensus. The WTO's decision-making structure includes a *ministerial conference* that meets at least once every two years and a *general council* composed of ambassadors and delegation heads that meet several times a year in Geneva. These councils include a goods, services, and intellectual property (TRIPs) council. Numerous specialized *working groups* deal with the environment, development, membership applications, regional trade agreements, the relationship of trade to investment, the interaction between trade and competition policy, and the transparency in government procurement.

One of the more controversial WTO institutions is the *dispute-settlement mechanism* designed to have more teeth in it—including the authority to impose trade sanctions on member states that violate trade agreements—than the GATT mechanism for settling trade disputes. The WTO's dispute-resolution board chooses an impartial panel of experts to oversee cases submitted to it for resolution. Members can appeal the findings of the expert panel after following a carefully mapped out set of procedures. By March 1999 some 167 cases had been brought before the dispute panel. Several cases that have gained a good deal of press attention are a judgment against the EU's attempt to limit imports of hormone-fed U.S. beef into the EU. Likewise the WTO ruled against the EU's banana import program which seeks to curtail imports of bananas produced by U.S. companies in the Caribbean (see box, chapter 2). Meanwhile the WTO ruled in favor of some developing countries and against U.S. programs that rescued dolphins caught in tuna nets as well as the U.S. ban on sales of shrimp caught in nets that do not allow sea turtles to escape. So far it seems that nations have been willing to abide by the dispute panel decisions rather than withdraw from the WTO when such decisions go against them. Because so much appears to be at stake for each nation by way of expected economic gain that would result from further liberalizing trade, states have felt compelled to participate in the rule-making exercise rather than being left out of it.

A good deal of political controversy surrounds the WTO. Many of its economic liberal supporters view it as a positive step given that the WTO extends the provisional treaty status of GATT to a full-fledged international organization whose job it is to not only bring down barriers but also settle the terms of global competition. GATT promoted side agreements on national dumping and the subsidy policies of a limited number of states for example, but the WTO administers a unified package of agreements to which all members are committed. The WTO also signifies a multinational effort to manage the entire international trade system without the necessity of a national hegemon imposing order on the trade system. As the focus of the WTO has shifted from bringing down barriers to setting the terms of global competition, some economic liberals have criticized the latest GATT agreement for, in essence, accepting in principle the idea of fair trade over free trade. Other liberal critics focus on the WTO's failure to reach consensus on measures that deal with such new issues as the movement of "cultural products" (e.g., movies), insurance companies, security firms, banking across national borders, and protectionist "local content" legislation.

It is hard to determine how successful the effort to liberalize international trade will be under conditions where multilateral trade negotiations have become quite complicated and politicized. Critics of all ideological persuasions have raised questions about the ability of the WTO to produce new agreements that cover not only old and new trade items but that also deal with the connection between trade and such topics as investment, competition policy, the environment, workers' rights, and an assortment of human rights and other ethical issues. Protestors representing these and other interests helped disrupt the November 1999 WTO ministerial meeting in Seattle in the United States.

Many trade experts argue that certainly the effort to liberalize trade will continue related to economic growth and other benefits associated with international commerce. Yet, domestic protectionist pressure can also be expected to mount given the dislocating effects trade continues to have on different societal groups. National delegates often feel the need to stay in touch with domestic groups as the political and economic stakes associated with different agreements have important consequences for a wider and more disparate range of interest groups.

Likewise, many experts note that it is also hard to make and implement new trade rules and regulations given the growing number of political actors, especially *Nongovernmental Organizations (NGOs)* with an interest in trade policy. For example in 1996 the World Federation of Sporting Goods Industries (comprised of representatives from Nike, Reebok, and Adidas) agreed to improve working conditions for child laborers and low-wage workers in LDCs. In Singapore WTO members agreed to promote better working conditions for some 250 million children in LDCs and to uphold internationally recognized labor standards. Meanwhile Greenpeace and other NGOs have sponsored "alternative trade" meetings held alongside multilateral trade negotiations. And a number of NGOs have also sponsored international campaigns against corporations such as Occidental Petroleum in Colombia and Shell Oil in Nigeria for failing to do more to counter human rights violations in these countries.

NORTH-SOUTH TRADE ISSUES

In the Uruguay round the industrialized developed states made a concerted effort to further involve the developing nations in the trade negotiation process and to further entrench them in the international trade system. This effort reflects a recognition of the important role LDCs have come to play in the international trade system. Since World War II there has been a tremendous amount of economic growth in many LDCs, due in part to an emphasis on manufactured goods produced for export. Much of the recent geographic shift in the production of manufactured products by Multinational Corporations (MNCs) for instance, has occurred in developing regions of the world. And many LDC governments have adopted complementary economic liberal development strategies and trade policies.

Despite the economic success of mainly Asian economies, a number of controversial issues still surround the issue of LDCs and trade. Trade accounts for as much as 75 percent of many LDCs' foreign exchange earnings. LDCs have nearly tripled their percentage share of world merchandise exports from 7 percent in 1973 to 20 in 1995. However, as many structuralists and critics of the WTO would point out, the vast majority of the world's nations still account for only about one-fifth of the world's trade in manufactured goods. Some 40 percent of those exports have come from the NICs (especially the "Asian Tigers"). During this same period the share of LDC trade in agricultural and mining products and fuel declined. Meanwhile, many LDCs, especially the Least Developed LDCs (LLDCs) in Africa and also in Latin America, suffer chronic trade deficits and the effects of large international debt.

Many LDCs accuse the developed nations of hypocrisy when it comes to living up to the principles of the liberal international trade system. Countries like the United States favor free trade when it benefits them, they argue, but not when it might benefit LDC producers instead. From the perspective of many LDCs, the developed nations have an extensive history of using protectionist trade measures to promote their economic growth. Furthermore, the GATT and now the

WTO's liberal trade policy objectives, regulations, and procedures have usually reflected the interests of the richest and most powerful Northern industrialized nations. The industrialized nations used the GATT and now the WTO and other trade and finance organizations, together with direct pressure, to bring down LDC tariff barriers, exposing their infant industries to competition with the more mature industries of the industrialized nations.

Many LDC officials believe that one of the main reasons the United States and other developed nations supported the GATT Uruguay round was their fear of losing Third World export markets and their desire for even greater access to LDC resources and raw materials. In the Uruguay round an agreement was reached between the industrialized developed and developing nations whereby LDCs gained more access to the markets of the industrialized nations for many of their raw materials and semifinished and finished products in exchange for developed nation access to LDC markets for some of their new trade goods such as telecommunication technology and services.

The latest WTO agreements include a number of special provisions for LDCs that include longer time periods for implementing agreements and commitments; provisions requiring WTO members to safeguard the interests of LDCs; and several measures to help developing countries build their infrastructures, handle disputes, and implement technical standards. The WTO suggests that LDCs are likely to benefit from new trade rules to the extent that these rules provide them with access to the markets of other countries and make transparent and predictable the trade rules themselves. Furthermore, to the extent they remain committed to the new rules, LDCs are likely to attract new foreign and domestic investors. The share of total world Foreign Direct Investment (FDI) did jump from 15 to 35 percent between 1986 and 1994, yet the share of investment in LLDCs remained stagnant, while 10 LDCs received almost 80 percent of FDI in developing countries. The WTO does suggest that it is time for the international community to recognize the need to address the LDC debt burden by new methods and approaches.

Has the WTO done enough when it comes to improving the terms of trade for LDCs? The reasoning of the WTO continues to be that LDCs can benefit from trade if they continue to reform their economies and trade policies along economic liberal lines. According to the WTO, "countries which have experienced strong export growth have lower levels of import protection than countries with stagnant or declining exports."[19] Many economic liberals also believe that by the late-1980s LDCs had become so well integrated into the international trade system that international economic integration was breaking down the North-South division between nations.

Many structuralists, however, argue that the Uruguay round and efforts by the WTO have not fundamentally changed the relationship of the dependent South on the North. If anything, Northern development policies continue to result in economic growth for the few, often at the expense of political liberal (i.e., democratic) values in many places. This kind of argument is made by Walden Bello of the University of the Philippines. Bellow claims that new trade rules for agriculture have hurt small rice farmers in Malaysia and rice and corn farmers in the Philippines. Further liberalization serves the interests of the U.S.

agricultural "dumping lobby" and a "small elite of Asian agro-exporters."[20] Interestingly, Bello argues that protection of small farmers can be justified on the basis of agriculture's "multifunctional" role, that is, "it protects biodiversity, guarantees food security, promotes rural social development, (and) is part of a nation's cultural heritage and enhances the regional landscape."[21]

REGIONAL TRADE BLOCS

Some trade experts argue that regional trading blocs will play a major role in shaping future trade rules and regulations. Trade blocs promote internal free trade while retaining trade barriers with nonmember nations. The North American Free Trade Agreement (NAFTA) and the European Union (EU) are the two largest trade blocs. Other trade blocs include

- the European Free Trade Association
- the Latin American Free Trade Association
- the Caribbean Free Trade Association
- the Central American Common Market
- the Andean Group
- Mercosur
- the Association of Southeast Asian Nations
- the Arab Cooperation Council
- the Economic Community of West African States
- the Southern African Development Coordination Conference
- the Economic Community of West Africa
- the Organization of African Unity
- the Asian Pacific Economic Cooperation Forum

From a technical standpoint, regional trade groups violate the GATT and WTO principles of nondiscrimination. By permitting internal free trade while still imposing trade restrictions on external trade, regional trade blocs obviously discriminate in favor of trade within the bloc versus trade outside the bloc.[22] Imports of beer from Mexico, for example, are treated differently by the United States under NAFTA than are imports of beer from the Philippines, which is not a NAFTA member. There is considerable debate among political economists concerning the desirability of regional trade blocs. Some see them as a natural way to extend the realm of free trade one *region* at a time while others suggest that they undermine the WTO process and its ultimate goal of *world* free trade.

Liberals dislike the extent to which blocs employ a variety of measures to assist local producers. These measures often generate more trade protectionism and neomercantilist practices on the national, regional-bloc, and global levels. For example, one of the arguments President Clinton made to support U.S. efforts to help organize NAFTA was that the United States should be able to penetrate and secure Mexican markets before the Japanese.[23] If the United States did not quickly bring Mexico into its trade orbit in 1993, Japanese investments in Mexico would negate U.S. influence over Mexico's future trade policies. For liberals, trade blocs tend to be a double-edged sword. Some liberals fear that they exacerbate international tension and, as in the case of imports of U.S. bananas and hormone-fed beef into the EU, can result in trade wars between different blocs or bloc members and nonmembers. Other liberals see trade blocs as stepping stones toward the gradual reduction of trade barriers and hold out for the possibility of a global free trade zone.

The most developed and integrated bloc, the European Union, was founded on the liberal principle of enhancing production specialization and efficiency and liberalizing trade between union members (see chapter 11). Internal trade barriers between member states have gradually been reduced over the years. However, competitors from outside the EU have found it difficult to penetrate its markets. Other trade blocs—some of which are quite developed—are actively competing with the EU and with NAFTA, founded in 1993 when the United States, Canada, and Mexico extended what previously had been a free trade area between the United States and Canada. As yet NAFTA is not as integrated a bloc as is the EU. Many believe that there is every reason to believe that increased trade and other financial transactions among the United States, Canada, and Mexico will gradually enhance political economic cooperation and even integration. A move is also underway to expand NAFTA to include such South American countries such as Chile, Colombia, Venezuela, Peru, Ecuador, and Bolivia.[24]

The Asia-Pacific Economic Cooperation (APEC) FTA attempts to integrate 18 Pacific and Asian nations into a nonbinding arrangement that would gradually remove trade barriers among members by 2020. As promoter of the agreement, the United States hopes to further liberalize trade among the members while accelerating economic growth in the Pacific-Asia region.[25]

There is little doubt about the growing influence of regional trade blocs. It remains to be seen, however, whether these blocs will be stepping stones on the path to global free trade or whether they will end up as tools of regional protectionism. They stand clearly, however, as examples of how the contemporary trade system simultaneously embraces both the principle of free trade and the practical need for protectionism.

TRADE AS A FOREIGN POLICY TOOL

Another mercantilist compulsion of states is the use of trade as an instrument of foreign policy. If wealth is power, then trade is both—a fact as old as history. Athens may have sparked the Peloponnesian wars when it tried to restrict imports from one of Sparta's allies, Megara.[26] Trade sanctions take many forms, including boycotts, import restrictions, and embargoes that prohibit exports to another country. They are one kind of penalty states use to reward other states, coerce a competitor, or punish an enemy. In the 1980s, the Reagan administration applied a series of economic sanctions that included trade restrictions on several Third World nations it felt were either supporters of communist revolutionary movements (e.g., Nicaragua), sponsors of terrorism (e.g., Libya, Iran, Cuba, Syria, and the People's Democratic Republic of Yemen), or nations that were reluctant to give up the practice of apartheid (e.g., South Africa). At the same time, the U.S. Department of Commerce handed out Generalized Systems of Preferences (GSPs)—reductions of trade restrictions on certain goods—to Caribbean countries that supported U.S. anticommunist foreign policy objectives in the region. The commerce department also kept a "black list" of those nations that for any political reason were not to receive GSPs. The objective in these cases was to impose an intolerable hardship on a society and to break the will of its people and leaders to carry on some type of unacceptable behavior. Finally, international organizations like the United Nations have used trade and other sanctions to punish aggressive or uncooperative states as in the case of UN-sponsored efforts to limit trade with Iraq after the Persian Gulf war.

A good deal of debate surrounds the question of the effectiveness of trade sanctions of all sorts. Generally, the conclusion is that they have a limited effect on the behavior of the intended target. It is hard to determine what precisely the aims of those imposing the sanctions were and what would have happened had they not been employed in the first place. Experts have argued that a number of conditions must be present if nations are going to use trade restrictions successfully to punish a nation. Governments must be able to control its businesses or prevent certain goods from being shipped to another country as a third-party nation will often find it profitable to provide that country with boycotted goods. Businesses and governments can often get around trade sanctions because goods produced in one country are hard to distinguish from those produced in another. It is also difficult to determine how the target state will adjust to an embargo or boycott. When the United States imposed its grain embargo on the Soviet Union in 1980, not only did the Soviet Union turn to other suppliers for grain, but it also cut back on meat and feed grain rations for its own people. Finally, as Richard Haas and others report, trade sanctions usually never punish government leaders as much as they do the unintended local population.[27] In the case of Nicaragua in the 1980s and Iraq in the 1990s, U.S. economic sanctions helped generate popular resistance and support for the government to oppose imperial aggressors.

These and other cases that employ trade as a mechanism to change the behavior of states or other actors demonstrate that, despite the few instances in which it has worked, nations will continue to be tempted to employ trade as a weapon or tool of foreign policy. The box on trade sanctions demonstrates that some evidence exists that the United States and other nations are turning away from using trade as much as a stick and more as a carrot. Quite often this reflects pressure on a state by domestic interest groups that have an interest in promoting trade. Also a number of proposals have been put forward in the WTO to outlaw trade sanctions. This shift also reflects a changed international security environment where increasingly more emphasis has been put on economic growth as opposed to military defense (see chapter 9).

CUBA, VIETNAM, AND CHINA: THE SHIFTING USE OF TRADE SANCTIONS

In the case of each of these three countries the United States used trade sanctions of one sort or another to either change or control political conditions within each country, or between it and the United States. The extent to which trade successfully served this purpose differs depending on a variety of domestic and international political and economic conditions.

In the case of Cuba, since the late 1950s, the United States has stuck to its guns so to speak and used a trade embargo of Cuba as a stick to punish and bring down President

Fidel Casto's communist regime. In 1949 and 1951, the U.S. Congress passed the Export Control and Battle acts that outlawed trade between U.S. businesses and the Soviet Union and Communist bloc countries. When Castro came to power in 1959 the United States canceled its quota of sugar from Cuba. Cuba then turned to the Soviet Union to buy much of its sugar, thereby minimizing the harm of U.S. economic sanctions on the country. In 1963, the United States gradually increased its trade sanctions on Cuba to the level of a total embargo, dealing Cuba a crippling blow to its trade and economy. Since then relations between the United States and Cuba have been acrimonious, to say the least.

In 1961 the United States helped a small army of Cuban exiles invade Cuba at the Bay of Pigs. When U.S. military support was not forthcoming, Castro defeated the invaders and jailed those who weren't killed on the beach. In 1962 Cuba let the Soviet Union build launching platforms and support facilities for its medium range ballistic missiles in Cuba. The United States and Soviet Union nearly went to war over the situation, which resulted in President Khrushchev's withdrawing Soviet missiles from Cuba. After President Kennedy's assassination in 1963, the CIA is alleged to have tried to assassinate President Castro on several occasions. Likewise, some who have studied the matter argue that Castro may have had a hand in President Kennedy's death.

During the Cold War most other countries in the world traded with Cuba. Suffice it to say that throughout the rest of the Cold War and until just recently, the United States did not back off from attempting to use trade as a weapon in its war on Cuba. In 1996 the U.S. Congress passed the Helms-Burton Act, imposing even tougher economic sanctions on Cuba and companies that deal with the Castro regime. Much of the pressure to continue the embargo emanated from the Cuban American National Foundation (CANF), a strong lobby in the U.S. Congress that successfully challenged efforts to halt funding of Radio Marti (the anti-Castro station in south Florida) and appointments to the U.S. State Department. Many of its members live in Cuban communities in and around Miami and New Jersey. Because of its large number of electoral votes, Florida is an important state in any presidential election. Also the chair of the U.S. Senate Foreign Relations Committee is an avid anticommunist and "cold warrior" who has resisted efforts over the years to improve United States-Cuba relations. Simply put, despite changed international circumstances, domestic political pressure to change United States-Cuba policy has not been that influential until recently.

The Clinton administration tried to change United States-Cuba policy so as to ease the hardships of the Cuban people and to allow certain Americans to visit Cuba and send the Cubans money, food, and medicine, all within the law.[a] Arguing that it doesn't want to be held hostage by interest groups, the administration's efforts appear to be backed up by a number of groups including businesses, farmers, religious groups, and younger Cuban-Americans.

The use of trade sanctions on Vietnam stands in marked contrast to their use in Cuba. In the Vietnam War the United States lost some 58,000 servicemen and women. In 1975 the United States banned trade with Vietnam in response to the defeat of South Vietnam by North Vietnam. Washington used a trade embargo to pressure Hanoi into releasing information about more that 2,200 United States military personnel listed as "Missing in Action" (MIAs) during the Vietnam War. In the late 1980s, the very poor country of Vietnam gradually abandoned Marxist economic theories and employed more market principles to stimulate economic growth and investment in the nation. Asian and European businesses began investing in an economy that exhibited high growth rates. Following this lead, a number of U.S. businesses lobbied the administration and Congress to rescind the 1975 legislation that disallowed trade with Vietnam.

In the summer of 1993 the Clinton administration decided not to veto loans and aid the IMF and World Bank proposed to offer Vietnam. It became increasingly clear that more and more U.S. goods were getting into Vietnam via third parties and middlemen who profited a great deal from the sales. Slowly the U.S. Senate began to show signs of willingness to rescind the trade embargo, even if some MIA families and veteran groups actively lobbied the administration not to drop the embargo until Vietnam was more forthcoming about the MIAs.

In retrospect it seems clear that the president and some of his administrators were in favor of lifting the embargo all along but were nervous about the president's potentially being embarrassed by his antiwar record.[b] In early February 1994, the president announced that the ban on trade with Vietnam would be rescinded and that he hoped that Vietnam would continue to provide the United States with information about the MIAs. U.S. companies immediately began making arrangements to set up shop in Vietnam.

Clearly the case of Vietnam demonstrates that the United States increasingly found itself caught in a bind—between the political objective of not trading with a former enemy that was being uncooperative and forsaking the economic benefits of trade with a fast-growing Third World economy. One could argue that the benefits of trade eventually won out over political considerations—that more immediate U.S. business interests prevailed over long-term U.S. foreign policy objectives. However, it might also be argued that in dropping the embargo, the United States merely gave up using trade as a stick and employed it as a carrot. The United States reconciled its conflicting trade and foreign policy objectives and interests under changed international political and economic circumstances by dropping the embargo and using trade as part of an effort to try and shape the behavior of Vietnam.

As Michael Veseth points out in chapter one, the case of the United States' granting MFN status to China is not only a good one to help explain what IPE means, but it has become a classic case of some of many problems surrounding the use of trade sanctions. To review briefly, until 1997 the United States was reluctant to grant China MFN trade status given its poor (at least from a Western perspective) record on human rights. The United States cut off trade with China during the Cold War but reopened trade with it in the late 1970s when China adopted its modernization program and began importing large amounts of goods from the Western industrialized nations. Many businesses in these countries saw China as the "last market frontier" and pressured their governments along with international trade and finance institutions to grant China MFN status and do what they could to develop and gain access to China's markets and raw materials. Other U.S. firms invested in production facilities in China because these ventures paid high returns, and MFN status would open U.S. markets for these industries.

MFN status would allow China's products to enter the vast U.S. marketplace on equal footing with goods from other nations. Open access to the U.S. market meant greater sales, higher incomes, and more jobs to China's workers and businesses. Of course, being denied MFN status would mean that imports from, in this case China, would face additional trade barriers that discouraged their purchase.

One event in particular clouded U.S.-China relations more than any other in recent history—the Tianamen Square massacre in 1989. The Bush administration found itself caught between the proverbial rock and hard place when it tried to reconcile its displeasure over the way the Chinese government handled the prodemocracy movement with the U.S. objective of furthering trade with China. The U.S. Congress imposed on the Clinton administration the requirement that China make significant progress on a number of issues including human rights if it were to be granted MFN status. These issues included the release of political prisoners, recognition of Tibet's "distinctive cultural heritage," permission for international radio and television broadcasts into China, more humane practices in the use of prison labor, progress on nuclear nonproliferation, and the elimination of trade barriers.

In 1997, in spite of critical reports on China's human rights record, the Clinton administration granted China MFN status. One could argue that in many ways U.S. treatment of China constituted a rejection of longstanding U.S. policy with Cuba, all the while extending to China the policy the United States adopted with regard to Vietnam. How do we account for U.S. willingness to give China "the benefit of the doubt" and even appear to bend over backwards to increase trade with it, while being so reluctant to trade with Cuba?

Part of the answer lies in the ideas associated with economic liberalism. Back in 1993 the influential British newsweekly *The Economist* took a strong stand in favor of open trade with China and argued that Western nations should do all they can to draw China into the world market system. "China's rush to capitalism is also a rush to individual liberty: a chance to choose not just fancy clothes and fast cars but how to live, where to live, and who to be ruled by. China remains a repressive place. . . . But economic reform is passing power from central governments to the provinces, and from repressive institutions to individual enterprises."[c] From the liberal perspective of the Clinton administration, trade or what his advisors labeled "commercial diplomacy" with China would not only benefit U.S. businesses but would help to eventually change China's political institutions. While human rights violations certainly should not be overlooked, there was more for the United States to gain by fostering trade with China than by punishing it with a trade embargo for its violations of human rights. We should be clear, however, that the administration's decision was not a case of economics over politics, but economics and one political objective over another political objective that also hurt trade.

More recently, the United States and the other industrialized states have made an effort to bring China into the WTO. In November 1999 China and the United States reached an agreement whereby China would soon be admitted to the WTO. Because China is such a large market for both goods and services and because so many nations and their businesses buy goods produced in China, everyone stands to benefit from China's playing by the same WTO trade rules as everyone else. On this issue however, U.S. policy makers are still divided for a number of reasons. Some Republicans and Democrats argue that the case of alleged long-term Chinese spying on U.S. nuclear facilities and China's hostile reaction to the mistaken bombing of its embassy in Belgrade, among other things, raise suspicions about China's intended use of computer and other technologies it may import from the United States and other Western industrialized nations. As discussed in chapter 9, a number of security experts feel that China may be using some of this technology to modernize, if not significantly increase, the size of its nuclear arsenal. On the other hand U.S. businesses such as the Intel Corporation have actively promoted China's entry into the WTO. Intel Corporation chairman Andrew Grove argues that restrictions on trade with China will force the Chinese to develop their own computers and processes.[d] Ironically, Mr. Grove and a number of political leaders argue that those who support increased trade with China have had to reverse their strategy of tying trade to politics. Many of them now argue that trade is *not* connected to politics in the form of U.S. security interests and that considerations of U.S. security interests and trade should be separated from one another.

What we can conclude from these cases is that the use of trade embargoes and other sanctions reflects a variety of political and economic pressures on trade officials that have their source in all three *levels of analysis* (see chapter one). Presidents and other important state officials as well as businessmen have a vested interest in trade policy. The influence of domestic producer groups or those interested in trade policy varies a good deal depending on how much they support U.S. political and economic foreign policy objectives. Finally, international system conditions can either constrain or provide officials and businessmen with new opportunities. Since the end of the Cold War U.S. officials have sought to gradually move beyond the use of trade as a punishing weapon to using it more often as a means of generating both political and economic opportunity. The cases of Cuba and China in particular, demonstrate that political interests and considerations as yet play a major role in trade policy.

---

[a] See "U.S. Quietly Opening More Doors to Cuba," *Tacoma News-Tribune*, 7 July, 1999, p. A2.
[b] See "Clinton Continues to Tiptoe through Vietnam Minefield," *New York Times*, 3 February 1994, p. A1.
[c] See "China Belongs to Me," *Economist*, 29 May 1993, pp. 13-14.
[d] See David E. Sanger, "Trade Status with China: Risky Vote Tomorrow," *New York Times*, 2 June 1999, p. A5.

CONCLUSION: THE FUTURE OF INTERNATIONAL TRADE

Many economic liberals applaud the completion of the Uruguay round and creation of the WTO as two of the biggest developments in the international trade system since the end of the Cold War. The WTO is seen as a move in the right direction—toward fulfilling the dream many officials had at the end of World War II as part of the Bretton Woods Agreement (see chapter 7) to create a world trade organization with the authority to compel nations to reduce, if not eliminate, their protectionist trade barriers and otherwise open up the international trade system. Many of those liberal objectives have been achieved since World War II, resulting in dramatic increases in the volume and value of trade. However, a number of countertrends coexist with this liberal trade order, suggesting that the values of the order are not shared by all states, nor are they shared equally by all members.

What we should expect in the future then is a continuation of the effort by the industrialized nations in particular to push the liberalization of international trade rules and regulations on past old goods and on to many new goods and services associated with information and communication systems and technological products, many of them digital in nature. Efforts to solve trade problems are likely to take place in multilateral forums like the WTO.

However, a number of developments and circumstances are likely to make it difficult for the WTO to maintain cohesion among an increasing number of members at different development levels needed to advance the liberal objective of global economic integration. The involvement of more actors like MNCs and NGOs with an interest in trade is likely to complicate "trade diplomacy" carried on by nation-states in the WTO. Also complicating the negotiation processes are likely to be agriculture and a variety of scientific issues associated with the use of new technologies in global telecommunication systems, information products, pharmaceuticals, and financial services. Finally, trade negotiations are likely to be obscured by the connection between trade and such other structural issues as monetary, finance, national security, and environmental problems (see chapter 19). Production and trade activities impact the environment in ways states and businesses never anticipated as the demand for more energy resources increasingly makes the true cost of trade incalculable. Liberal free trade ideals are also likely to come under increasing attacks by antiglobalizations groups that have mounted campaigns and challenged many of the assumed benefits of free trade. Probably the two most popular arguments put forth by these critics are the undermining effect the WTO and liberal trade has on the authority of the nation-state and local and regional laws, especially on democratic societies.

Under these circumstances and despite limited success of the GATT and WTO along with bilateral efforts to liberalize trade and trade practices, the ideal of free trade has gradually given way to fair trade. A *managed trade system* best describes and accounts for the mixture of liberal and mercantilist trade practices that have become the objectives of most states but also the new WTO itself. Trade liberalization can be expected to go forth but must be reconciled with the political reality of protectionist forces that exist in the world. The tension between domestic needs and international responsibilities, which was created at Bretton Woods in 1944, continues to dominate the IPE of trade today.

DISCUSSION QUESTIONS

1. Discuss and explain the role of trade in the international production structure. Why is the issue of trade so controversial?
2. Outline the basic ways that mercantilists, economic liberals, and structuralists view trade. (*Note:* Think about the tension between the politics and economics of trade.)
3. Which of the three IPE approaches best accounts for the relationship of the Northern industrialized nations to the Southern developing nations when it comes to trade? Explain and discuss.
4. Outline and discuss the most important issues of the GATT Uruguay round.
5. Outline and discuss the most important features of the WTO. Are you hopeful the WTO will be able to continue to liberalize international trade? Why? Why not?
6. How have the United States and other nations used trade as a tool to achieve foreign policy objectives? Be specific and give examples. Research some other examples.

INTERNET LINKS

World Trade Organization:
> http://www.wto.org

Institute for International Economics:
> http://www.iie.com

Office of the U.S. Trade Representative:
> http://www.ustr.gov

United States APEC Index:
> http://www.apec.org

Jagdish Bhagwati's home page:
> http://www.columbia.edu/~jb38/

Robert Kuttner's home page:
> http://epn.org/prospect/39/39kuttfs.html

SUGGESTED READINGS

Jagdish Bhagwati. *Protectionism*. Cambridge, MA: MIT Press, 1991.

John M. Culbertson. *The Dangers of "Free Trade."* Madison, WI: 21st Century Press, 1985.

Arghiri Emmanuel. *Unequal Exchange: A Study of the Imperialism of Trade*. New York: Monthly Review Press, 1972.

Brian Hocking and Steven McGuire (eds), *Trade Politics: International, Domestic and Regional Perspectives* (London: Routledge, 1999)

Congressional Quarterly, Inc. *Trade: U.S. Policy Since 1945*. Washington, DC: Congressional Quarterly Inc., 1984.

Robert Kuttner. *The End of Laissez Faire*. New York: Knopf, 1991.

Stefanie Ann Lenway. *The Politics of U.S. International Trade: Protection, Expansion and Escape*. Marshfield, MA: Pittman Publishing, 1985.

Lester Thurow. *Head to Head: The Coming Economic Battle Among Japan, Europe, and America*. New York: William Morrow, 1992.

NOTES

1. For a more detailed discussion of the international production structure, see Susan Strange, *States and Markets: An Introduction to International Political Economy* (New York: Basil Blackwell, 1988).
2. Robert Kuttner, *The End of Laissez Faire* (New York: Knopf, 1991), p. 157.
3. *Economic Report of the President 1997*, (Washington DC: President's Council of Economic Advisors, 1997), p. 243.
4. The *terms of trade* are the relative prices of goods in international trade. In the U.S.-Saudi Arabia example, the terms of trade would be the amount of wheat paid for each barrel of oil (or the quantity of oil paid for wheat). The terms of trade are generally measured in items of commodities (as opposed to ordinary money prices) to overcome the difficulties posed by exchange rates.
5. See Jacob E. Cooke, ed., *The Reports of Alexander Hamilton* (New York: Harper & Row, 1964).
6. See Friedrich List, "Political and Cosmopolitical Economy," in *The National System of Political Economy* (New York: Augustus M. Kelley, Reprints of Economic Classics, 1966).
7. Robert Gilpin, *The Political Economy of International Relations* (Princeton, NJ: Princeton University Press, 1987), pp. 31–33.
8. Cited in Stefanie Ann Lenway, *The Politics of U.S. International Trade: Protection, Expansion and Escape* (Marshfield, MA: Pittman Publishing, 1985), p. 65.
9. Andre Gunder Frank, *Latin America: Underdevelopment or Revolution* (New York: Monthly Review Press, 1970).
10. The key element of the entire Bretton Woods system is that it created a conflict between domestic needs and international responsibilities.
11. Technically, GATT was not an international organization but rather a "gentlemen's agreement" whereby member parties (nation-states) contracted trade agreements with one another.
12. For a sophisticated account of strategic trade policy, see Paul Krugman, *Strategic Trade Policy and the New International Economics* (Cambridge, MA: MIT Press, 1986).
13. Gilpin, *The Political Economy of International Relations*, p. 215.
14. "U.S. Aids Microsoft in War on Software Piracy by Chinese," *Tacoma News Tribune*, 22 November 1994, p. E5.
15. See "Success Brings New Challenges," *Financial Times*, 18 May 1998, p.1.
16. For a more detailed discussion of agriculture's role in the Uruguay round see David N. Balaam "Agricultural Trade Policy" in Brian Hocking and Steven McGuire (eds), *Trade Politics: International, Domestic, and Regional Perspectives* (London: Routledge, 1999), pp. 52-66.
17. "U.S. GATT Flap Reverberates around the World," *Christian Science Monitor*, 23 November 1994, p. 1.
18. See http/www.wto.org.
19. Ibid., p. 3.
20. See Walden Bello, "Rethinking Asia: The WTO's Big Losers," *Far Eastern Economic Review*, June 24, 1999, p. 77.
21. Ibid., p. 78.
22. This type of trade discrimination is allowed under GATT/WTO rules only when economic integration is intended to serve as a foundation for political unification. While this *may* be the case with the European Union, for example, it is clearly not true about NAFTA and most other trade groups.
23. "Will Treaty Give U.S. Global Edge?" *Christian Science Monitor*, 17 November 1993, p. 3.
24. "U.S. Plans Expanded Trade Zone," *New York Times*, 4 February 1994, p. D1.
25. "Asia-Pacific Countries Near Agreement on Trade," *New York Times*, 15 November 1994, p. A1.
26. David Baldwin, *Economic Statecraft* (Princeton, NJ: Princeton University Press, 1985).
27. See Richard Haas, "Sanctioning Madness," *Foreign Affairs* 76:6 (November/December 1997), pp. 74-85.

7

The International Monetary System

OVERVIEW

The international political economy comprises nation-states and markets that are connected by a framework of simultaneous relationships or *structures* that condition their behavior and interaction. The finance structure describes the set of monetary or financial relationships in which states and markets exist. These financial relationships affect all the other types of interactions of states and markets to some degree.

The financial structure exists within what is called the international monetary system, one of the most abstract and enigmatic parts of IPE. The international monetary system can best be thought of as a set of rules and practices that govern how debts are honored and paid between and among nations. As always, there is the question *cui bono?*—who benefits from the way that world finances are organized? This chapter focuses on the international monetary system, which is an important element of the financial framework of the IPE. (Chapter 8, which looks at international debt, will continue this analysis of the finance structure.)

The other commonly discussed structures of IPE are relationships based on security, production (and trade), and access to knowledge and technology. These sets of relationships will also be discussed in upcoming chapters. At any given time, a set of relationships or structures exist that link states and markets in the spheres of finance, production, security, and knowledge.

This chapter will examine the IPE of exchange rates and the international monetary system, focusing on its post–World War II history and the problems and issues that dominate the contemporary world of international finance. Along the way we will stop to survey the most important international financial institutions (the IMF and World Bank) and consider the special case of the CFA franc, an example of the problems of soft currency countries in "French Africa."

. . . in exact proportion to the power of this system is its delicacy—I should hardly say too much if I said its danger. Only our familiarity blinds us to the marvelous nature of the system.[1]

I am by no means an alarmist. I believe our system, though curious and peculiar, may be worked safely; but if we wish to work it, we must study it. We must not think we have an easy task when we have a difficult task, or that we are living in a natural state when we are really living in an artificial one. Money will not manage itself, and Lombard Street has a great deal of money to manage.[2]

Walter Bagehot (1873)

Lombard Street is a short stretch of road in the city of London, the original square mile closest to Tower Bridge. Lombard Street is lined with banks and finance houses that today still display the colorful banners of the Italian traders who pioneered banking in medieval and renaissance England, giving it something of the feeling of the busy small-scale market street it once was. In the nineteenth century, Lombard Street was the center of the financial world. International monetary transactions involving states and markets throughout the globe were tied to or influenced somehow by the activities of the people and institutions on Lombard Street.

When Walter Bagehot[3] wrote about Lombard Street in the nineteenth century, he was really writing about the world's finance system and the framework or structure that conditioned the many relationships among states and markets. In the passages above, he stresses the power and also the delicacy of the financial structure, and the need for it to be managed effectively. Lombard Street is still a significant center of international finance, even though it is no longer the center of the monetary universe.

The biggest difference between the finance structure in Bagehot's time, more than 100 years ago, and the finance structure today is that in Bagehot's day it was possible to go to a place like Lombard Street and meet the people who were part of the tangible structure of world finance. By spending a day in a bank office or stock market trading floor in London, one could see what the world of financial IPE was all about. Today this world is far more decentralized and increasingly global, with computer networks and telecommunications replacing the person-to-person relationships of Bagehot's time. It is harder, therefore, to actually observe the financial network, or to see the framework of the international monetary system. It exists just the same, however. This chapter will help you perceive its outlines and understand how it has evolved. In chapter 8, we will examine another aspect of the financial structure—international debt—which operates within the financial environment created by the international monetary system.

This chapter has two main parts. The first section looks at the sometimes confusing world of foreign exchange and explores the causes and consequences of changing exchange rates. The second part of the chapter focuses on the international monetary system, the system that governs financial relations among nations. Here we will focus on the problem of creating an international monetary system that can satisfy the needs of states and markets in a dynamic and changing world. The goal of this chapter is to enable the student to understand what the international monetary system is and how foreign exchange works so we can understand today's most important monetary problems and issues and appreciate how they affect us, as individual citizens, nation-states, or business firms.

A STUDENT'S GUIDE TO FOREIGN EXCHANGE

Just as people in different nations often speak different languages (requiring translation to understand one another), they also tend to transact business in different currencies, requiring conversion from one type of money to another. To understand the international monetary system and how it affects the various structures of IPE, we must first understand a little about the exchange rate and become familiar with some of the special vocabulary of international finance.

Most people are first exposed to the vagaries of *foreign exchange (FX)* and the exchange rate when they travel abroad and face a purely practical problem: How many of my dollars will it cost to buy the pesos, pounds, marks, or yen that I need for my travels? People quickly become accustomed to FX math—using the exchange rate to convert from foreign currency into dollars and back again. Thus, if the *exchange rate* is $1.50 per British pound sterling, it follows that a £10 cheap theater ticket in London really costs $15 in U.S. currency (£10 x $1.50 per £ equals $15). In the same way, that ¥1,000 caffè latte at the airport in Tokyo really costs $10 if the yen–dollar exchange rate is ¥100 per US$ (¥1000 ÷ ¥100 per $ equals $10). Before long, tourists find themselves able to perform complex mental gymnastics to convert from one money to another using the FX rate.

Table 7–1 shows the exchange rates of selected currencies relative to the dollar on August 12, 1999. Exchange rates are determined for the most part by market forces and thus change every day as trends and events in IPE alter the supply and demand for one currency relative to another.

TABLE 7–1 Foreign Exchange Rates for August 12, 1999. Selected Countries.

COUNTRY	FOREIGN CURRENCY	FX RATE	UNITS
Brazil	Real, R$	1.86	R$ per US$
Canada	Canadian dollar, C$	1.47	C$ per US$
Côte d'Ivoire	CFA, franc	620.70	CFA fr per US$
European Monetary Union	Euro, €	1.05	US$ per €
France	Franc, FFr	6.20	FFr per US$
Germany	Deutschemark, DM	1.85	DM per US$
Hungary	Forint, £	239.58	£ per US$
Italy	Lira, £	1832.00	£ per US$
Japan	Yen, ¥	115.90	¥ per US$
Malaysia	Ringgit, M$	3.80	M$ per US$
Mexico	New peso, N$	9.39	N$ per US$
Poland	Zloty	3.98	Zloty per US$
South Korea	Won	1206.00	Won per US$
Spain	Peseta, Pta	157.44	Pta per US$
Thailand	Baht, Bt	38.02	Bt per US$
Turkey	Lira, £	437,750.00	£ per US$
United Kingdom	Pound sterling, £	1.60	US$ Per £

Source: Financial Times, 16 August 1999, p. 20.

Each exchange rate can be stated in two mathematically equivalent ways. The exchange rate between the U.S. dollar and the Mexican peso, for example, can be stated as either 9 pesos per dollar or about 11 cents per peso.[4] For some currencies, such as the British pound, many people find it easier to keep track of the exchange rate in dollar terms (about $1.60 per pound) while other currencies, such as the Japanese yen, can be easier to understand using the other view— about 116 yen per U.S. dollar.[5] For some currencies, such as the Polish zloty or the Mexican peso, both ways are about equally easy to understand.[6]

Although many people find it interesting that some currency units are seemingly worth so much more than others (a pound is more than a dollar, while a yen is about a penny), this is really not an important aspect of exchange rates. The exchange rate is just a way of converting values from one country's unit of measurement to another. It doesn't really matter what units are used. What *does* matter, however, is whether the measurement is valid and how it changes over time.

THE FX TICKET: A CURRENCY'S VALUE DEPENDS ON WHAT IT CAN BUY

It is useful to think of a nation's money as a ticket that can be exchanged for goods and services in the country that issues it. There are two types of tickets. Hard currency tickets are issued by large countries with reliable and predictable economic systems and stable internal and external political relations. They are traded widely and have well-known values. You can exchange a hard currency ticket in most other countries for the local currency. The countries that issue the "hardest" currencies today are the United States (dollar), the EU (European euro), Japan (yen), Britain (pound), and Switzerland (Swiss franc).[7]

Soft currency tickets are not as widely accepted; a soft currency tends to be used in its home country, but not elsewhere because its value may be too uncertain or the volume of possible transactions insufficient to support an international trading network. Less developed countries and former Eastern bloc states generally have soft currencies because their political relations are less stable than some other countries; in addition, their economies are small relative to the world market and face an uncertain future. A soft currency country must usually acquire hard currency (through exports or by borrowing) in order to purchase goods or services from other nations. A hard currency country, on the other hand, can generally exchange its own currency directly for other hard currencies, and therefore for foreign goods and services, a distinct advantage. Because only hard currencies get much international use, we'll focus on hard currencies in this chapter.

One important feature of the FX "ticket," unlike other types of tickets, is that it can be exchanged for so many different things. A ticket to *Phantom of the Opera*, for example, can be exchanged only for a chance to see a particular performance of this show. But a £ ticket can be exchanged for a £'s worth of British goods, services, or investments. You could even treat a £ ticket as a lottery ticket, buying it on speculation, hoping it will go up in value and earn a profit.

The value of a £ ticket or a $ ticket (to people in other countries) depends on what it can be traded for in terms of goods, services, investments, and potential lottery winnings. A currency generally rises and falls in value, therefore, with the value of the goods, services, and investments that it can buy on its home market. The powerful forces of supply and demand translate the $ ticket's worth into an exchange rate in worldwide foreign exchange markets.

While many economic forces affect exchange rates, two of the most important are the inflation rate and interest rate changes. All else being equal, a nation's currency tends to depreciate when that nation experiences higher inflation rates. Inflation, a rise in overall prices, means that currency has less real purchasing power within its home country. This makes the currency less attractive to foreign buyers. The currency therefore tends to depreciate on foreign exchange markets to reflect its reduced real value at home. In the same way, if nation A has a lower inflation rate than nation B, its currency tends to appreciate, reflecting the relatively higher purchasing power of its money.

Interest rates also affect exchange rates because they influence the value and desirability of the investments that a particular currency can purchase. If interest rates rise in the United States, for example, then the demand for dollars to purchase U.S. government bonds and other interest-earning investments also increases, pushing the dollar's FX value higher. In the same way, lower interest rates can lead to a lower demand for the dollar, as dollar-denominated investments become less attractive to foreigners.

While this simple relationship between interest rates and exchange rates generally holds true, there are important exceptions that should be considered, as when several related forces all act at once on the FX market. Sometimes, for example, accelerating inflation rates within a country drive up interest rates there; the force of inflation pushing the dollar down would then typically surmount the ability of interest rates to push it up. Economists say that what matters with respect to exchange rates is the ***real interest rate*** (adjusted for inflation's affects), not the ***nominal*** (unadjusted) ***interest rate***. Only higher real interest rates can reliably increase a currency's value.

Nations can influence the FX rate through policies that affect their currency's value relative to other currencies. Interest rate changes, tax laws, domestic inflation rates, and a variety of regulations, therefore, affect the FX rate. Since a dollar is really a $ ticket, a ticket that can be exchanged for goods, services, or investments in the United States, the $ ticket's price (the FX rate) depends on the value of what the $ ticket buys. In other words, the FX rate of the dollar depends on the dollar's ability to buy U.S. goods, services, and investments and the worth of these resources to foreigners.

In today's world, with a global financial marketplace, a hard currency nation can most effectively vary the FX rate of its currency through manipulation of interest rates. If interest rates rise (or fall) in the United States, interest-earning investments in the United States become worth more (or less) to foreigners. All else being equal, this increased (or decreased) value will be reflected in the FX rate. In 1993, for example, long-term interest rates fell in the United States. This made the $ ticket for investment less attractive for foreigners, since interest-earning assets in the United States then were less lucrative. It follows that the dollar depreciated or fell in value in 1993 relative to many other currencies.[8]

A special vocabulary is used in discussing changes in the FX rate. When a currency becomes more valuable relative to other currencies, we say that it ***appreciates***. When it becomes less valuable relative to other currencies, we say it ***depreciates***. Suppose, for example, that the British pound currently trades at $1.50 per £. If the pound appreciates (becomes more valuable), then it takes more dollars to buy a pound, so the exchange rate might change to $1.60 per £. The pound has appreciated and the dollar depreciated (is less valuable relative to the pound).[9] These exchange rate changes are a little confusing until you get used to them. What would you say about the yen and the dollar if the FX rate changed from ¥120 per $ to ¥130 per $?[10] (See the footnote for the answer.) What would you say about the Mexican peso and the dollar if the exchange rate changed from 11 cents per peso to 15 cents per peso?[11]

Exchange rates tend to change over time in complex and often unexpected ways. Table 7–2 shows how several selected currencies varied in value relative to the dollar between 1995 and 1999. If you study the table carefully you will note that some currencies appreciated relative to the dollar, others depreciated, and some varied in different directions at different times. A few of these trends deserve brief explanations.

Compare Turkey with Argentina. Argentina's exchange rate was extremely stable relative to the dollar, with less than 1 cent variance over four years. Turkey, on the other hand, experienced *massive* depreciation. Both are soft currencies. Why such a large difference? The answer is that both Argentina and Turkey have had recent experiences with inflation. Turkey has failed to find a solution to their problem. Price increases within Turkey have been spectacular and the lira buys less and less within Turkey each year. If it is worth less inside Turkey, its foreign

TABLE 7–2 FX Rates over Time. Selected Dates and Countries.

FOREIGN CURRENCY UNITS PER DOLLAR

CURRENCY	*8/17/99*	*6/25/98*	*3/30/98*	*3/15/96*	*2/24/95*
Argentina	0.99	0.99	0.99	1.00	1.00
Canada	1.47	1.46	1.42	1.36	1.39
France	6.24	6.02	6.18	5.04	5.15
Germany	1.85	1.79	1.84	1.47	1.46
Italy	1842.49	1772.00	1820.00	1562.00	1626.00
Japan	114.05	142.30	132.00	105.93	97.00
Malaysia	3.80	3.99	3.62	2.54	2.55
Mexico	9.31	8.95	8.51	7.52	5.68
Thailand	37.98	41.16	37.75	27.45	24.93
Turkey	438,700.00	263,765.00	239,695.00	67,942.50	41,353.07
UK	0.62	0.59	0.59	0.65	0.62

Source: New York Times, various dates.

exchange value should fall too, according to the purchasing power parity idea, and so it has, from about 41,000 lira per dollar in 1995 to more than 400,000 lira per dollar (!) in 1999. In a way, for Turkey, the exchange rate is like a thermometer and it shows that prices in Turkey are burning up the value of its money. Argentina, on the other hand, effectively reduced its inflation rate through the use of a *currency board* system. The currency board controls domestic inflation by linking a soft currency as directly as possible to a hard currency—the dollar. For most practical purposes, Argentina is on a dollar standard and has succeeded both in reducing inflation and in stabilizing its exchange rate as a result.

Malaysia, Mexico, and Thailand all suffered rather sharp and dramatic depreciations of their currencies over the period covered by the table—not as sharp as in Turkey, but nearly a 50 percent change in each case. Inflation was not the problem in these countries, however. Malaysia, Mexico, and Thailand are examples of countries that suffered *currency crises.* Essentially, a currency crisis is a sudden and dramatic shift in market activity. Demand for a currency disappears and supply rushes in, forcing the price down. Currency crises are a problem that will be discussed in more detail later in the chapter.

Finally, Japan's yen shows how FX values can rise and fall over time. The yen depreciated steadily from 1995 to 1998, but appreciated (from 142 yen per dollar to 114 yen per dollar) between 1998 and 1999. The long period of depreciation reflects in part Japan's deep economic recession in the 1990s. There was so little demand for investment funds in Japan during the late 1990s that interest rates fell to less than 1 percent. Obviously, investors looking for high returns would not buy yen and invest in Japan; they would sell yen and invest elsewhere, in the booming U.S. economy, perhaps. For Japan, then, the exchange rate was like a blood pressure gauge and the falling yen showed that there was not a very strong pulse in this economic system. The United States and Japan have tried to boost the yen in 1999 by intervening and buying yen on the international markets—a controversial policy that is discussed later in this chapter.

THE EFFECTS OF FX CHANGES

Tourists quickly learn the rules of the foreign exchange game. As a tourist interested in maximizing purchasing power and minimizing cost, you want whatever currency you hold the most of to appreciate! If you were visiting Tokyo, for example, you would want the dollar to appreciate (and the yen to depreciate) from ¥100 to ¥120, since you would get more yen and therefore more value for each dollar you have. A Japanese student visiting the United States, however, would hope that the dollar would depreciate, so that the yen's purchasing power in terms of dollars would rise.

A change in the exchange rate, then, has a relatively simple and predictable effect on foreign visitors. Life is more complex for nation-states and international businesses, because a change in the FX rate has many different effects on them. To see this, and to see how nations may try to use the FX rate to their advantage, let's work through an example.

For a simple example, consider two countries, the United States and Malaysia, with two currencies ($ and ringgit, which uses the M$ symbol), and focus on just one traded good, fine cotton sports shirts, which are meant to represent generally the goods traded between these countries. Suppose that the price is $30 for shirts made in the United States and M$60 for shirts made in Malaysia (see Table 7–3). (It is natural that shirt manufacturers would price their goods in terms of their home-country currencies.) What does a U.S.-made shirt cost in Malaysia? What would a Malaysian shirt cost in the United States? The answer to these questions depends critically on the exchange rate between the two currencies.

Suppose, for simplicity, the current exchange rate is M$2 per dollar, or 50 cents per ringgit. At this exchange rate, the shirts manufactured in Malaysia and the United States are priced very competitively. Indeed, adjusting for the exchange rates, they are equally priced in both countries. The M$60 Malaysian shirts should sell for $30 in the United States, the same as U.S.-made shirts.[12] The $30 U.S.-made shirts should sell for M$60 in Malaysia. The shirts of the two nations are equal values if there are no style or quality differences to cause buyers to favor one over the other.

This starting point is an example of *purchasing power parity (PPP)*, where money has the same purchasing power outside a nation as within it. At the PPP exchange rates, equally efficient producers in different countries tend to be equally competitive in international markets.[13] Put more simply, a person with $30 could buy one shirt, either U.S.-made or Malaysian, whether in the United States or Malaysia. At the PPP exchange rate, the significance of the FX rate effectively disappears. Purchases are made for reasons other than the FX value.

TABLE 7–3 Price Comparison of Two Sports Shirts

ITEM	PRICE IN UNITED STATES	PRICE IN MALAYSIA
U.S.-made shirt	$30.00	M$60.00
Malaysia-made shirt	$30.00	M$60.00

Note: Exchange rate $1 = M$2.00

A change in the exchange rate tends to alter the competitive balance between nations, making one country's goods a better value than another. Suppose, for example, that the dollar appreciated relative to the ringgit, from M$2 per dollar to M$4 per dollar. (This is equivalent to the ringgit's depreciating from 50 cents to 25 cents per M$.) This change in the FX rate will have, in fact, rather large impacts on shoppers and consumers in *both* Malaysia and the United States. Table 7–4 shows the initial impacts.

While the domestic prices of the two shirts stay the same ($30 for the U.S. shirt, M$60 for the Malaysian shirt), their prices abroad are altered. The $30 U.S. shirt now costs M$120 in Malaysia. Since the dollar is more expensive in terms of ringgit, the U.S. product is more expensive, too. Assuming equal style and quality, we can expect Malaysian shoppers to switch away from the U.S. goods and buy more Malaysian products.

A similar situation will prevail in the United States. The Malaysian shirt still costs M$60, but each ringgit now costs 25 cents, compared to 50 cents at the previous exchange rate. The Malaysian shirt therefore costs $15.00 in the United States (M$60 ÷ M$4 per dollar = $15.00). Buyers in the United States will also switch their purchases in favor of the Malaysia products and away from the relatively more expensive U.S.-produced goods.

The appreciation of the dollar and equivalent depreciation of the ringgit alter the relative prices of goods in both countries. Buyers switch in favor of goods priced in the relatively cheaper currency. As purchases of Malaysian goods increase, production, jobs, and incomes rise in the Malaysia. As the demand for U.S. goods falls, production, jobs, and incomes fall in the United States. Thus a change in the exchange rates redistributes jobs and income between countries, all else being equal. This effect is relatively small for the United States, because its domestic economy is large relative to its participation in global trade, but it would very significant for a country like Malaysia with a relatively larger traded goods sector.

The FX rate affects shirts, as the example here indicates, and it also affects *everything else* that a nation buys or sells on international markets. The FX rate is thus the one price that affects virtually all other prices. The impact of the FX rate on a nation's wealth and power can, therefore, be significant.[14]

When a currency's FX value is less than the PPP value that equalizes international prices, we say that it is **undervalued**. This would be the situation for the ringgit in this example, since the PPP exchange rate is 50 cents per ringgit, but the market currency's value has fallen to 25 cents. As you can see, there is considerable temptation for a mercantilist nation (or a political leader facing an important election) to attempt to achieve an undervalued currency by manipulating FX markets in some way. The undervalued currency would shift production and

TABLE 7–4   Price Comparison after Ringgit Depreciation.

ITEM	PRICE IN UNITED STATES	PRICE IN MALAYSIA
U.S.-made shirt	$30.00	M$120.00
Malaysia-made shirt	$15.00	M$60.00

Note: Exchange rate $1 = M$4.00.

international trade in its favor. Having an undervalued currency is clearly good for domestic industries, since imports are discouraged and exports increase. There is a dark side to currency depreciation, however. Goods that *must* be imported will cost more when your currency is undervalued. If a nation imports many vital items, such as food or oil, this currency effect can tend to reduce living standards and retard economic growth, as well as cause inflation. In most cases, it is wrong to conclude either that a cheaper currency is good for a nation or that it is bad. Rather, changes in exchange rates tend to unleash a series of changes in external economic relations, some positive and some negative. The net effect is often hard to calculate.

Sometimes less developed nations try to gain some advantage from the FX rate by *overvaluing* their currency to get access to cheaper imported goods, shifting the terms of trade in their favor. The cost of imported products, including perhaps food, arms, and manufactured goods, is artificially low if a currency is overvalued. A less developed nation might try this overvaluation strategy if it were having trouble paying for imported technology, for example, or a vital resource such as oil. Although its own goods would become less competitive abroad, it could at least enjoy some imported items at lower cost.

In practice, it is very hard for LDCs to reap the gains of overvaluation in any meaningful way because their currencies are usually quite soft, which means that they are not used much in international business and finance. This does not stop them from trying, however, and many LDC currencies end up being systematically overvalued in an attempt, like as not, to buy imported military hardware for a little less. This almost invariably winds up choking domestic production, leaving the LDC dependent on foreign sellers and lenders for help.

CRISIS IN THE CFA FRANC ZONE

Fourteen African nations (Benin, Burkina Faso, Côte d'Ivoire, Mali, Niger, Senegal, Togo, Cameroon, the Central African Republic, Chad, Congo, Equatorial Guinea, the Islamic Republic of Cormoros, and Gabon) form a unique international financial structure called the Central African franc zone or the *CFA franc zone*. The currencies of these Third World nations are pegged to the French franc, providing a stable foreign exchange relationship between France and nations that were once within its colonial sphere.

Membership in the CFA is a mixed blessing for these African nations. On one hand, they benefit from a much more stable exchange rate and hence more stable external economic relations than if their currency were allowed to "float" against other currencies. In essence, the members of the CFA zone, soft currency countries in every objective respect, gain some aspect of "hard" currency by formally linking their money to the French franc. There are costs to this strategy, too, however. One important cost is that the value of their currency relative to, say, the U.S. dollar is determined by the relationship between the U.S. and French economies, not by factors relating to their own economies, which may be especially relevant in particular situations.

Over time in the 1980s and early 1990s, the CFA franc became overvalued. While the value of the franc, and therefore the CFA franc, might well have reflected the value of a French franc "ticket" in international trade, it did not reflect the corresponding value of a ticket to purchase the goods or services from these African nations' economies.

The fact that the CFA franc became overvalued created winners and losers within the CFA nations. The agricultural sector of the economy, for example, suffered from the currency imbalance. The fact that the CFA franc was overvalued made agricultural exports from these nations uncompetitive on international markets (since the CFA franc was relatively costly, their produce was costly to foreign buyers). At the same time, however, agricultural imports into the CFA zone were relatively cheap, since other currencies were undervalued relative to the CFA franc, putting pressure on African farmers to cut prices in order to compete. Important sectors—like agriculture—of the CFA nations were therefore disadvantaged by the CFA franc's high value.

Luxury goods, military weapons, oil, medicines, and other imported goods were made artificially cheap due to the CFA franc's condition, benefiting the minority of the population in the CFA zone who purchased large quantities of these items.

On January 12, 1994, the CFA franc was devalued by 50 percent relative to the French franc—a traumatic event indeed, since the FX rate is the one price that affects all other prices within a nation. The price of imported French goods doubled overnight for these African nations, and the cost of their own goods halved for foreign buyers, in terms of the French franc. Franc-denominated debts doubled in local currency terms. Although this financial action was intended to make the overvalued CFA nations competitive with other countries, in fact a wide net of winners and losers was created. In general, persons who exported goods and services outside the CFA zone found themselves more competitive, as did persons who produced goods that competed with imports. The cheaper CFA franc gave their products an advantage in the marketplace over more expensive foreign goods. Persons who purchased large quantities of imports, however, were worse off, as were those who owed foreign debts denominated in a hard currency such as the French franc, which was now much more expensive.

The impact on the African countries was sudden and dramatic as the cost, in terms of local currency, of imports from France (and other hard currency nations) shot up. The alternative to this devaluation, however, was also dismal. The *Financial Times* of London reported that "the alternative to devaluation was not rosy. French aid would have been entirely swallowed in helping CFA states to service their foreign debt because without devaluation these states would not have got fresh credit from the International Monetary Fund, the World Bank, and other donors. The relationship between the CFA members and France would have been increasingly like 'that of Cuba and the old Soviet Union. . . .'"[a]

The *New York Times* report also saw the CFA regime as a remnant of nineteenth-century imperialism. "The nub of the French post-colonial relationship is economic. The Ivory Coast, for example, buys about 40 percent of its imports from France and the French own a third of the country's manufacturing industries. Elsewhere, more than half of French foreign aid goes to Africa, making France the continent's foremost patron."[b]

The sudden devaluation left many in France and in Africa "fuming," according to the *Financial Times*. "Politically, they accuse the French government of betraying its old colonies and friends in Africa. Economically, they see an end to a market in which African ability to purchase French goods was kept artificially high by a parity unchanged since 1948. Financially, they are reeling from the implications of having their African assets halved and cash flow severely disrupted."[c]

The *New York Times* reported that "people are trying to adapt to increases for nearly everything they eat and drink. Prices for pharmaceutical products, nearly all of which are imported, have soared. The cost of drugs for malaria, the continent's biggest killer, have nearly doubled in some places, putting them out of the reach of many Africans."[d]

The case of the CFA franc illustrates several important points about the financial structure as it relates to less developed countries such as these French-speaking African nations. Clearly, the foreign exchange rate matters; it affects the cost of precious imports, the price competitiveness of their exports, the value that foreigners assign to their assets, their ability to gain international support (IMF and World Bank backing) for their debts, and all manner of other issues. Exchange rates "count" for LDCs. A second point is that soft currency LDCs are at a disadvantage in international finance. The CFA nations benefited from their fixed rate against the franc for over 45 years, but at the critical moment in 1994 this was no protection from financial chaos.

"The measures that have been taken after the devaluation—IMF and World Bank decisions, the French forgiveness of debt—are all quite encouraging," according to Citibank official Robert Thornton, as quoted in the *New York Times* article. But considerable short-term pain must be endured in the form of falling material living standards before long-term gains due to expanding exports and rising levels of economic growth can be realized.

The CFA franc will enter a new era early in the twenty-first century. When France enters the European monetary system and trades the franc for the euro, the CFA zone will follow suit and peg its currency to the euro, too. It is too soon to tell if the "CFA euro" will be an effective monetary tool for the states and citizens of Central Africa.

[a] "Disquiet Over CFA Franc Fall," *Financial Times*, 28 January 1994, p. 6.
[b] "French Currency Move Provokes Unrest in Africa," *New York Times*, 23 February 1994, p. 6.
[c] "Disquiet Over CFA Franc Fall," p. 6.
[d] "French Currency Move Provokes Unrest in Africa," p. 1.

EXCHANGE RATE INSTABILITY

Since the exchange rate is the one price that affects *all* the prices in a country (to foreign buyers), it is important that the FX rate be stable in the short run and be able to adjust smoothly to changing economic and political conditions. It is significant, therefore, that many of the world's most important currencies have experienced great instability in the past ten years. Unstable FX rates have caused significant economic and political tensions within and between nations. Unstable exchange rates sometimes force governments to choose between domestic needs and their responsibilities to the international trade and monetary systems.

Inflation and PPP Exchange rate instability is not due to any one single factor but results from a number of factors that build up to create an unstable pattern of FX movements. For simplicity, let us think about these forces as layers. The first layer is based on international price and inflation differences. Over the long run, the purchasing power parity rule tends to apply. If nation A has lower inflation than nation B, then people will prefer A's goods over B's and so buy those goods, along with A's currency. So, in the long run, we expect A's currency to appreciate and B's currency to depreciate. This is a necessary and useful exchange rate movement. But inflation is not the only factor that will affect the exchange rate.

Economic Policy Changing interest rates and economic policy will be a second independent factor influencing the exchange rate between A and B. If, for example, B's central bank raises interests rates in the short run (perhaps to reduce its inflation rate), this causes investment funds to flow into B, appreciating its currency. Thus the long-term depreciation of B's currencies is interrupted by a short-term appreciation. *Central banks* are the national monetary authorities that represent nation-states in the international arena. The Federal Reserve System, for example, is the U.S. central bank. If you look at U.S. currency, you will see that dollars are actually Federal Reserve notes, issued by the Federal Reserve. The Federal Reserve regulates the availability of money and credit within the United States, plays a role in regulating the banking system, and works with other countries' central banks.

Asset Price Bubble Under certain circumstances, B's economic policies may trigger an investment bubble. This occurs when international investors begin to pour funds into the country, encouraged by good economic news or expectations of improved performance. As a wave of foreign funds enters the country, it can drive up the prices of stocks and other investments in the country and, simultaneously, also push up the value of the currency. This creates very large "paper profits," as investors calculate how much they have made from the combination of asset and exchange rate changes.

The profits from the first investment wave encourages further investment, and wave after wave floods the economy, pushing up both the currency and asset prices. The problem, especially in a less developed country, is that there may not be enough prudent investment opportunities to absorb all these foreign funds. At some point, foreign investors become concerned that their investments are not as secure as they seem. The bubble can burst, with dramatic effect. As investors sell out and take their funds home, both asset prices and exchange rates crash. This affects the investors, of course, but even more it affects the other parts of the economy that are affected by trade and finance and creates political and social problems as well.

The collapse of Mexico's peso in 1994-95 was due to an investment bubble like the one just described. Although you would think that international investors would learn from this experience, apparently their memories are very short term, because another investment bubble, this time in Asia, caused the crash of the Thai bhat in 1997 and contributed to the Asian economic crisis that followed.[15]

Central Bank Intervention Perhaps, at this point, A's central bank is concerned about the fact that the long-term appreciation of its currency is making its export businesses less competitive than those in B. If so, it could take some currency from its stockpile of reserve and *intervene* in the exchange market, selling its currency to drive down the exchange rate and appreciate B's currency instead. If this takes place, then we might see a very large shift in the exchange rates in the *opposite direction* of the long-term PPP movement. This could be a good and useful thing if it addresses legitimate short-term economic and political problems. But it might cause the exchange rate to vibrate or oscillate, inviting speculation.

Speculation Speculators are individuals and firms that bet on which direction the exchange rate will move next. If they think that A's currency will depreciate tomorrow, they will sell it today, hoping to be able to buy it back tomorrow at a lower price, profiting from the difference in the exchange rate. (If they guess wrong, of course, they lose). Such speculation is often actually constructive, helping the market move more efficiently to the market equilibrium. At other times, however, speculation is tremendously damaging and disrupting, especially when it takes the form of a *speculative attack*.

Speculative Attack A speculative attack is essentially a confrontation between a central bank, which pledges to maintain its country's exchange rate at a certain level, and international currency speculators, who are willing to wager that the central bank is not committed to its exchange rate goal. The speculators attack the currency by borrowing huge sums of it and then selling them on the currency market. The central bank can keeps its pledge by using its currency reserves to buy up the currency that the speculators are selling. If the central bank keeps its pledge, the speculators have little to lose because they can buy back the currency to repay their loans at about the same rate at which they sold it. If, however, the central bank is not willing to intervene to keep its currency stable, or if it runs low on the reserves it needs to do this, then the currency will fall. The speculators will be able to buy back their currency at a lower price and have great profits left even after they've paid back their loans.

Speculative attacks were responsible for the collapse of the Indonesian rupiah and the Malaysian ringgit in 1997–1998 as well as the British pound and the Italian lira in 1992–1993.[16] As long as investment capital is freely mobile between countries, the sorts of currency crises that are caused by speculative attacks and investment bubbles are likely to occur. Exchange rates, therefore, can be expected to display a variety of patterns over time, including stability, cycles, booms, and crashes. The problem of the international monetary system is to provide ways for nations to deal with this complex financial environment.

INTRODUCTION TO THE INTERNATIONAL MONETARY SYSTEM

The international monetary system is the set of relationships that determine how international payments are made and how international debts are settled.[17] Since international payments generally involve foreign exchange transactions—converting dollars, for example, into yen in order to pay for goods imported from Japan—it is convenient to think of the international monetary system as the system that organizes foreign exchange.

The FX system organizes the terms and conditions for international payments and sets the method for determining the exchange rate between different countries' currencies (the FX rate). The three main types of systems that are important to us are

- *Fixed* or *"pegged" exchange rates*, where the FX rate is most heavily influenced by state actions;
- *Flexible* or *"floating" exchange rates*, where international FX markets are the principle determinants of exchange rates; and
- *Managed* or *"coordinated" FX rates*, where states and markets are both important determinants of the FX rates.

In the twentieth century, we experienced each of these different systems. Each of these exchange rate systems attempts to achieve simultaneously three different and often conflicting goals: stability, flexibility, and credibility.

Stable FX rates and a stable FX system are necessary conditions for international trade and investment. Instability discourages individuals and nations from establishing close linkages and encourages nations to act in their own narrow self-interest. The "correct" FX value of one currency relative to another, however, tends to change over time as the economies of nations move in different directions at different speeds.

The FX system, therefore, must also be flexible enough to value different currencies effectively over time, which means that no currency can be allowed to be persistently overvalued (priced too high) or undervalued (priced too low) relative to other currencies. A currency that is consistently misvalued creates a distortion in international economic relations, which often leads to distorted political relations. During the 1981–1985 period, for example, the U.S. dollar was persistently overvalued, which made U.S. goods less competitive in international marketplaces (an economic distortion). Congress threatened trade barriers and other measures against our political allies (political distortion) in an attempt to deal politically with an economic disequilibrium.

The FX system must also be flexible enough to deal with the inevitable unexpected events in the IPE. Changing international economic and political structures tend to distort financial flows from their historical patterns, and the FX systems need to be able to accommodate these changes, whether they are long term or transitory. In the 1970s, for example, the rise of OPEC and the corresponding surge in oil prices dramatically changed the pattern of international payments, shifting billions of dollars toward oil-exporting nations. In the 1990s, adjustment problems involved integrating countries such as Russia and China, which for political reasons previously had little involvement in international financial markets, into the global monetary system with a minimum of unnecessary distortions elsewhere.

Finally, the FX system needs to be credible, which in this context means that it is reasonable to believe that the actors in the system, such as the central banks, will honor the agreements they have entered into and, generally, will play by the "rules of the game." If the system lacks credibility, then speculators will tear it apart, betting that central banks will do what is in their interest and not what they have publicly pledged to do. The lack of credibility is one cause of the speculative attacks that have caused currency crises in the 1990s.

The exchange rate system, therefore, must be stable, flexible, and credible. It should be stable enough to encourage long-term commitments among and between nations, but it must be flexible enough to change smoothly with the times. You probably won't be surprised to discover that we have not yet found the perfect system to achieve these dual objectives, although several different approaches have been tried including fixed exchange rates, market-based exchange rates, and managed exchange rates.

How well has the international monetary system achieved these three goals? We begin this discussion with the Bretton Woods system and examine its evolution and transformation in the postwar era.

THE BRETTON WOODS SYSTEM

Post–World War II IPE was born in Bretton Woods, New Hampshire, and students of IPE necessarily become familiar with what is often called the ***Bretton Woods system.*** The Mount Washington Hotel in Bretton Woods was the site of an economic conference in 1944 that brought together the economic leaders of all the Allied nations. Their task, which they took very seriously, was to create a postwar economic order that would be stable and flexible, promote economic growth and development, and avoid the nationalistic pressures that led to two world wars in a single generation. It was a big job.

What came out of Bretton Woods was a set of international institutions and a particular form of international monetary system. The World Bank, the International Monetary Fund, and the General Agreement on Tariffs and Trade[18] were the institutions that evolved from these critical meetings, along with the Bretton Woods FX system, which characterized world monetary affairs from 1946 to about 1973.

The *International Monetary Fund* is the central bankers' central bank. The IMF is an international organization that tries to create stable and responsive international financial relations among nations, just as central banks seek to create a favorable financial climate within each country's borders. The IMF has, since its creation at Bretton Woods, played an important role in the international monetary system.

The IMF's most controversial function is to serve as a *lender of last resort* in international finance. That is, the IMF stands ready to make loans to keep debtor nations from collapsing under the weight of their obligations, possibly causing panic and chaos throughout the international financial system. The IMF's help, however, is "conditional." Countries that seek the IMF's help must be willing to accept the sorts of austere policies that it generally recommends—higher taxes, reduced government spending, cuts in subsidies, and the like. These policies tend to reduce living standards in a nation in the short run, but they are often effective in restoring fiscal stability. The IMF-sponsored reforms in Mexico, begun in the mid-1980s, achieved some success in providing a more stable foundation for Mexican economic growth, although Mexico's 1995 fiscal problems and currency crisis suggest that the mid-80s reforms did not achieve all their goals. Mercantilists, however, often see the IMF as acting in the interests of the United States, its largest shareholder, and structuralists see the IMF as part of the capitalist core's systematic exploitation of the periphery.

The *World Bank* is another creation of Bretton Woods. The official name of the World Bank is the International Bank for Reconstruction and Development (IBRD), which is a bit more descriptive. In the period immediately after World War II, the World Bank funded efforts to reconstruct the economies of war-torn Europe. Since the 1950s, the World Bank has concentrated on the problems of less developed countries, making loans to LDCs at terms that are generally far better than they could get directly from international capital markets.

Like the IMF, the World Bank is controversial and its motives have been questioned. The bank makes loans for economic development purposes; it can make loans to improve railways or irrigation systems, for example, since such projects stimulate economic growth, but it cannot make loans to improve social justice or reduce income inequality unless a financial return is likely. In recent years, the World Bank has been criticized for funding projects with undesirable environmental impacts—economic growth is often hard on nature—but it has recently begun "green" initiatives to promote environmentally friendly economic development in LDCs.

The Bretton Woods system was an attempt to construct a set of IPE structures built on pluralistic international institutions, not solely the strength of a hegemonic power. The United States wanted an orderly system of international relations, but it was unwilling to assume the role that Great Britain had played in the nineteenth century, with its many burdens. Thus, whereas London's Lombard Street had been the center of the gold standard FX system, the multilateral international monetary system was meant to be the center of the Bretton Woods monetary system.

The Bretton Woods FX system can be thought of as a *fixed exchange rate* system built on a gold–dollar standard. Formally, each nation established a fixed value of its currency in terms of gold. The United States also established a gold value for its currency at the rate of $35 per ounce. In practice, however, this established a fixed FX rate between the dollar and other currencies, and the dollar became the medium for international transactions. It is convenient to think of the Bretton Woods FX system as a wheel with the dollar at its hub. It was thus the task of the United States, despite its reluctance to do so, to bear the hegemon's burden, regulating the dollar so as to provide financial stability and also the necessary degree of flexibility.[19]

This system worked well in the 1950s and the early 1960s, when the United States was clearly the world's strongest economic power. The United States supplied dollars to the world system, which stimulated economic growth in Europe and Japan, creating new and larger markets for U.S. goods and services. The period of Bretton Wood's greatest success was a time of unusually vigorous worldwide prosperity and growth.

Eventually, however, the United States became uncomfortable in the role of hegemon. As Europe and Japan expanded and achieved self-sustaining growth, they no longer required the large inflows of dollars. But the United States found it difficult to stem this flow, since sending dollars abroad (to purchase foreign goods or investments) was an effective way to manage an increasingly complex domestic situation. As David P. Calleo has argued, the United States changed from a "benevolent hegemon" to a "selfish hegemon," using its place at the center of things to preserve wealth and power, as the costs of hegemony weakened it.[20]

By the late 1960s, the United States was faced with a domestic war on poverty, an international war on communism (in Vietnam), and the burden of Bretton Woods hegemony, which called for greater financial discipline. Eventually, U.S. leaders were forced to choose between national interest and international responsibility, which is a fundamental tension in IPE. The key decision was made in 1971, when President Richard Nixon formally broke the link between the dollar and gold. The world slowly shook off its system of fixed exchange rates. By the time of the oil shocks of 1973–1974, a system of flexible exchange rates had been established.

THE LESSONS OF BRETTON WOODS

What are the lessons of the Bretton Woods FX system? This is a controversial question in IPE. For pure Adam Smith liberals, the history of Bretton Woods illustrates the futility of trying to set exchange rates through state action rather than market forces. The state-based system was doomed from the start, according to liberals, because no government can know as much as well as the market can.

Others view Bretton Woods as an example of the important role of a benev-olent hegemon in IPE. The world thrived as long as the United States was effec-tive in its role as monetary hegemon, it seems. Since the collapse of the Bretton Woods system, world growth has been much slower and uneven. Scholars who take this point of view talk of the need for a new Bretton Woods agreement and a renewed hegemonic structure to manage the international monetary system. Another lesson taken from Bretton Woods illustrates the temptations of hege-mony. All hegemons, this realist argument goes, eventually become overextend-ed and exploit their position for national gain or to preserve wealth and power.

There are also those who see in the results of Bretton Woods an example of selfish nationalistic action by the United States or even ruthless capitalist exploitation. The United States was the principal beneficiary of Bretton Woods, they argue, gaining economically at the expense of other countries. For them, Bretton Woods is an example of how power can be abused in IPE.

Barry Eichengreen has argued that the key to Bretton Woods was its initial ability to isolate international monetary politics from domestic economic poli-tics.[21] A key element of Bretton Woods was a system of *capital controls* — con-straints on international transfers of investment funds. Keynes called these short-term financial flows *hot money* because they could get passed back and forth among nations in an unstable and excited manner familiar to anyone who played "hot potato" as a child. Controlling these capital flows gave each nation the ability to adjust interest rates and economic conditions to meet the needs of *domestic* political forces without inducing massive hot money flows that would undermine *international* economic agreements. The separation of domestic poli-tics from international economics is the heart of what was called in chapter 3 the *Keynesian compromise* between domestic needs and international obligations.

The breakdown of Bretton Woods, in this analysis, occurred as internation-al capital began to find ways around the state controls built into the Bretton Woods system (the globalization of finance is discussed in detail in chapter 8). With hot money fully mobile internationally, *domestic* political choices had *inter-national* consequences. In essence, the United States and other nations were forced to choose which was more important: the interests of domestic voters and businesses or the interests of the Bretton Woods system. Unsurprisingly, they all at some point found themselves placing domestic interests over international obligations, cutting interest rates, for example, when this created domestic jobs, even though it also caused international monetary instability. As more and more nations made this understandable choice, the Bretton Woods system broke down.

FLOATING EXCHANGE RATES AND THE UNHOLY TRINITY

Flexible or "floating" exchange rates are set by pure market forces, with a minimum of direct state influence. The hard currency FX system moved from fixed to flex-ible in the early 1970s, which was a time of enormous structural change in the world. Under a system of flexible FX rates, a nation's FX rate depends on the expected value of its FX ticket (to goods, services, and investments) relative to the tickets of other nations. The FX rate changes daily as economic and political conditions change. The dollar has mostly floated since 1973.

The flexible FX rate was intended to resolve the tension between domestic needs and international responsibilities by putting the market in charge of the international system, leaving states to look after their domestic political and economic priorities. Flexible exchange rates were also intended to replace the unwise or erratic state action of a hegemon with the smooth, logical, efficient action of the market. This, however, has not turned out to be the case. For one thing, it is impossible to isolate markets from states, since state actions necessarily influence the value of an FX ticket. Neither stability nor appropriate flexibility nor government credibility has been achieved to the extent that the architects of the flexible FX system envisioned.

One reason for the failure of floating exchange rates to achieve their goals is that the FX market is an instrument that has too many functions under a floating FX system. It cannot reliably perform them all at once. The FX ticket is a claim on a number of different items. The dollar FX ticket buys U.S. manufactured goods, natural resources, physical assets (such as hotels or office buildings), business assets (such as RCA stock), and it is also a lottery ticket for speculators who bet for or against currencies on the international markets. It is probably too much to ask the FX rate to set the "right price" for the dollar so as to balance all these markets. Almost necessarily, some imbalance will occur.

In the mid-1980s, for example, the U.S. dollar was in high demand on currency markets as a ticket to purchase U.S. investments, such as government bonds and corporate shares. The dollar's FX price reflected this demand, rising to an FX rate of more than ¥250 during one period. This investment FX equilibrium threw international trade all out of balance, a problem from which the United States has not yet fully recovered. The high price of the dollar made U.S. goods and services very costly abroad, and foreign goods were artificially cheap for U.S. consumers. Imports increased and exports began to dry up. The U.S. trade imbalance soared.

In the 1990s, the dollar-yen exchange rate was under a different sort of pressure. Financial problems within Japan in the early 1990s caused Japanese firms to bring some of their investment funds back home to stabilize the domestic economy. As Japanese investors converted dollars into yen, they caused the dollar to depreciate and the yen to appreciate. At one point in 1995, the dollar fell to nearly ¥80 per dollar. This made U.S. goods inexpensive in Japan, but Japanese products more costly abroad. Japan's exports fell, making their domestic economic problems even worse. By 1998, the exchange rate was back to about ¥140. Forecasters believe that the yen could fall as far as ¥200 per dollar in the short run or rise as high as ¥75 in the long run.

It should be clear from this one example that whatever its advantages in theory, *in practice* floating exchange rates have proved to be so flexible in so many ways as to be unstable. The case of the dollar's swing from an overvalued ¥250 to an undervalued ¥80 is an extreme example, but a relevant one nonetheless, since U.S.-Japanese relations are so important in IPE today. The short-run political and economic decisions that are made based on FX fluctuations are unlikely to be in the long-run interest of the states and markets involved. In other words, if states consider *only* their domestic economic and political needs, there is no one to look after the international system, which becomes a "nonsystem."

The period of floating exchange rates has been dominated by the problem that Benjamin J. Cohen calls the "unholy trinity."[22] The idea of the *unholy trinity* is that the actors in the international monetary system desire (among other things) these three things:

- the ability to respond to domestic political forces (this is sometimes called *monetary autonomy*),
- international *capital mobility* (necessary for efficient international finance), and
- stable *exchange rates* (desirable for smooth international trade and investment).

The problem is that these three goals are mutually inconsistent. You cannot have all three, but if you give up any one of them, then the other two are possible.[23]

In the Bretton Woods system, for example, capital controls eliminated international capital mobility. This allowed states, for a time at least, to respond to domestic political forces without causing exchange rate instability. Hot money could not rush in or out of a nation in response to domestic policies, so it could not disturb international exchange rate instability.

In the floating exchange rate era, however, capital controls have proved impossible to enforce. There are just too many ways to use technology and ingenuity to transfer funds from one country to another. This fact means that states must choose, when they are given the choice,[24] between stable exchange rates and the ability to set their own domestic economic agenda. The United States and Japan, for example, have opted for domestic autonomy and scarificed exchange rate stability. This is perhaps rational for these nations because they are both relatively "closed" economies, which means that they depend less on international trade and finance than most other countries for jobs, income and growth.[25]

On the other hand, countries like Argentina and Hong Kong, which are more dependent on the international economy, have made the choice to take stable exchange rates and sacrifice domestic autonomy. Both these countries peg their currencies to the U.S. dollar. This makes their exchange rates more stable but limits their ability to respond to domestic economic and political problems.

What seems to be impossible, however, is the missing middle ground: managed exchange rates that allow some ability to respond to domestic political forces but without giving up too much exchange rate stability. The key to managed exchange rates is *policy coordination*. States, through their central banks, must agree to cooperate with each other, to avoid taking domestic actions that might provoke international instability. The idea is that if two national economies are going in the same direction at about the same speed, then their FX rates should remain fairly constant because the value of one FX ticket relative to the other should not change dramatically. This system works as long as both nations keep their pace and avoid temptations to speed up or slow down or change course, even if there are strong domestic interests in favor of changing speed or direction.

In other words, the practical problem with managed exchange rates is that policy coordination requires the state, at some point, to be willing to sacrifice what seems to be their national interest in order to preserve a stable international financial structure. The classic tension between individual (nation) and group (nations) appears. Self-interest and national interest are powerful forces, so policy coordination in the long run is not guaranteed.

Nations that attempt to retain political autonomy while intervening to preserve some measure of exchange rate stability seem inevitably to run into problems of credibility. At some point, they are caught in a situation where they must choose between domestic needs and international obligations. In this situation they may swear on a stack of *Wall Street Journals* that they will do what is necessary to keep the exchange rate stable, but speculators will not hesitate to launch speculative attacks that create a currency crisis. This happened to Great Britain in 1993-94 and to Indonesia in 1997-98 and to a long list of other countries, too. The Keynesian compromise is no longer feasible, it seems. We have entered the Age of Extremes.[26]

THE AGE OF EXTREMES

If this analysis is correct, then states must deal with the unholy trinity as best they can. Taking international capital mobility (and the currency speculation that goes with it) as a given, states must choose between domestic autonomy and stable exchange rates. The choice, which is also the choice between politics and economics or states and markets to a certain degree, is not an easy one. This choice strikes at the heart of the dilemmas that define international political economy.

The Age of Extremes has produced in the European Union one of the great IPE experiments of the twenty-first century: the euro. Some of the nations of the European Union have taken the ultimate step toward exchange rate stability: They have traded their own separate currencies for a single European currency the euro (see chapter 11 for a more complete discussion of this event). This is the ultimate step to stabilize exchange rates (and sacrifice domestic autonomy) *within* Europe. It is unclear how effective this choice will prove to be, however. A single currency effectively stabilizes exchange rates *within* Europe, of course, but how stable will the euro be relative to the dollar and the yen? Until *all* nations make the same choice, the unholy trinity will pose political and economic problems.

This chapter does not end on a comforting note. The finance structure is of critical importance to the IPE, but we have seen that there are many unresolved issues and unsolved problems. The world clearly needs a stable FX system that is able to adapt effectively to changing structural conditions. Postwar history, however, provides few insights into how such a system can be designed and implemented. This is important since, as we have seen, problems in the financial structure can create or exacerbate problems elsewhere in the IPE.

The international monetary system interacts with other structures of IPE. The recent instability of this aspect of IPE has created both economic and political tensions, straining the trade, security, and technology structures that, together with the finance structure, link the nations and peoples of the world.

The problems of a world monetary order thus remain. We cannot take for granted the stability and adaptability of our financial structure, an important consideration as we turn to face the additional challenges of the future. In this sense, there is great stability in the international monetary system. Recall Walter Bagehot's comment on the financial structure of his day:

> I am by no means an alarmist. I believe our system, though curious and peculiar, may be worked safely; but if we wish to work it, we must study it. We must not think we have an easy task when we have a difficult task, or that we are living in a natural state when we are really living in an artificial one. Money will not manage itself, and Lombard Street has a great deal of money to manage.[27]

DISCUSSION QUESTIONS

1. Explain the difference between a hard currency and a soft currency. What disadvantages does a soft currency nation have when engaging in international trade? Explain.
2. What does it mean for a nation's currency to be overvalued? How does an overvalued currency affect that nation? Use the example of the CFA franc zone to explain the costs and benefits of an overvalued currency and the difficulties that arise when an overvalued currency is devalued.
3. The U.S. dollar depreciated dramatically relative to the Japanese yen in 1995. What impact would this event likely have on consumers and businesses in each country? Is a falling dollar good or bad for the United States? Explain.
4. What are the characteristics of a good international monetary system? Which system of exchange rates has met these goals—fixed FX, flexible FX, or managed FX? Explain.

INTERNET LINKS

CNN Currency Converter:
    http://cnnfn.com/markets/currencies/
The World Bank:
    http://www.worldbank.org
The International Monetary Fund:
    http://www.imf.org
The Financial Times (London):
    http://www.ft.com
The Economist:
    http://www.economist.com
Historic Photos of the Bretton Woods Conference:
    http://www.mtwashington.com/hotel/monetary.html

SUGGESTED READINGS

David P. Calleo. *The Imperious Economy*. Cambridge, MA: Harvard University Press, 1982.
Benjamin J. Cohen. *The Geography of Money*. Ithaca NY: Cornell University Press, 1998.
Kenneth W. Dam. *The Rules of the Game*. Chicago: University of Chicago Press, 1982.
Barry Eichengreen. *Globalizing Capital: A History of the International Monetary System*. Princeton NJ: Princeton University Press, 1996.

Guilio M. Gallarotti. *The Anatomy of an International Monetary Regime.* New York: Oxford University Press, 1995.

Paul De Grauwe. *International Money: Post-war Trends and Theories.* New York: Oxford University Press, 1989.

———. *The Economics of Monetary Integration.* New York: Oxford University Press, 1992.

Barry Eichengreen, ed. *The Gold Standard in Theory and History.* New York: Methuen, 1985.

Yoichi Funabashi. *Managing the Dollar: From the Plaza to the Louvre.* Washington, DC: Institute for International Economics, 1988.

International Monetary Fund and Kennedy School, Harvard University. *Exchange Rate Analysis with a Case Study on Poland.* CD-ROM for PC and Mac. Washington DC: International Monetary Fund, 1998.

Charles P. Kindleberger. *International Capital Movements.* New York: Cambridge University Press, 1987.

———. *A Financial History of Western Europe,* 2d ed. New York: Oxford University Press, 1993.

Michael Veseth. *Selling Globalization: The Myth of the Global Economy.* Boulder CO: Lynne Rienner, 1998. See chap. 4, "Currency Crises."

Paul Volcker and Toyoo Gyohten. *Changing Fortunes.* New York: Times Books, 1992.

NOTES

1. Walter Bagehot. *Lombard Street: A Description of the Money Market* (Philadelphia: Orion Editions, 1991), p. 8.
2. Ibid., p. 10
3. Walter Bagehot (1826–1877) was editor of the *Economist* from 1860 to 1877 and one of the most influential writers on political economy of his day.
4. The symbol for the dollar is $. What is the symbol for the peso? It is $ or N$ since the Mexican government redefined the peso creating the new peso a few years ago. Most monetary symbols have long histories. A number of European currencies use the £ sign to signify currency. This sign goes back at least as far as the unified system of silver coinage established by Charlemagne. Why does Mexico use the dollar sign $ for its currency? The answer is that they do not! We use the peso sign $ for the dollar. The peso sign, which is hundreds of years older than the U.S. dollar, came into use in the Southern colonies as a general symbol for monetary value in the colonial days and the practice has continued to this day.
5. For the Turkish lira, which traded at 262,980 per dollar in 1998, it is difficult to state the exchange rate any other way without resorting to scientific notation.
6. By FX market tradition, the exchange rate is stated as the "softer" currency in terms of the "harder" currency. Thus tradition holds that we always give the exchange rate as (soft) Turkish lira per (hard) U.S. dollar. This tradition is often broken in specific cases, however, when concerns of accuracy or convenience arise.
7. See chapter 11 for a complete discussion of the European Monetary Union and the euro. At this writing, the UK is not a member of the European Monetary Union, although there is speculation that it could join in the coming years.
8. What really matters is inflation-adjusted interest rates in one country compared with similar inflation-adjusted interest rates in another country. If U.S. interest rates fall, for example, and interest rates fall equally in Great Britain, then the FX rate between the two nations is unlikely to change significantly.
9. Exchange rates always change inversely because we are comparing one against the other. If the exchange rate fell to $1.30 per £, we would say that the pound has depreciated (become less valuable), so the dollar has appreciated (become more valuable relative to the pound).
10. The yen depreciated, since it takes more yen to buy a dollar. The dollar has appreciated or gained in relative value.
11. The peso appreciated and the dollar depreciated.
12. These calculations ignore additional costs associated with foreign sales, such as transportation, tariffs, and so on.

13. This is part of the "level playing field" that people in business and economics believe is necessary in international trade and finance. For the most part, however, the "level playing field" refers to nondiscriminatory trade barriers, such as tariffs, quotas, and subsidies.

14. All countries are not equally affected by FX changes at all times. Very "open" nations, like Great Britain, experience much greater FX effects than more "closed" economies, such as the United States. The impact of an FX change also depends on the cause, direction, and magnitude of the change, and the coincident actions, if any, of other countries.

15. See Michael Veseth, *Selling Globalization: The Myth of the Global Economy* (Boulder CO: Lynne Rienner, 1998) pp. 75-89.

16. Ibid., pp. 89-98.

17. The international monetary system is in fact a "structure" of IPE in the sense used in this text. Since it is most commonly referred to as a "system," however, we use this terminology here.

18. The Bretton Woods agreements did not actually include the GATT. Proposals that emerged from Bretton Woods included a much stronger institution, the International Trade Organization (ITO), which was never implemented. The ITO would have had considerable authority to implement free trade policies. Its powers were probably greater than nations were willing to grant in the early postwar period. The weaker but still successful GATT emerged a few years later to fill the gap left by the ITO as an institution promoting open markets and free trade.

19. The International Monetary Fund lacks adequate resources to allow it to be the multilateral "lender of last resort" that was envisioned by the Bretton Woods architects.

20. See David P. Calleo, *The Imperious Economy* (Cambridge, MA: Harvard University Press, 1982) and *Beyond American Hegemony* (New York: Basic Books, 1987).

21. Barry Eichengreen, *Globalizing Capital: A History of the International Monetary System* (Princeton NJ: Princeton University Press, 1996).

22. See Benjamin J. Cohen, *The Geography of Money* (Ithaca NY: Cornell University Press, 1998).

23. There are other unholy trinities. For example, we would like food to be good, fast, and cheap, but generally you can have only two of these at a time, not all three.

24. David Balaam observes that sometimes the choice is only theoretical. In practical terms, states sometimes have no choice because of relational power politics or structural constraints.

25. People are usually surprised to discover how small Japan's imports and exports are relative to its domestic economy.

26. This is the title of a recent book by Eric Hobsbawm, who uses this excellent phrase in a somewhat different context.

27. Bagehot, *Lombard Street*, p. 10.

8

Debt: The Political Economy of International Finance

OVERVIEW

It was not an accident that, when Charles Dickens wanted to write a story about how much people depend upon each other and how tightly our lives are linked, he made his main character a money lender named Scrooge. The story, of course, was *A Christmas Carol*, and it was based on the paradox that a creditor needs the people who are his debtors as much (more!) than they need him.

Debt creates a bond of unusual strength and complexity. Financial connections can be mutually advantageous avenues of economic intercourse, clever levers that raise wealth and power for all. It can also be a forceful weapon or even a snare that entraps borrower, lender, or both.

Financial connections have always been both local and global, involving both states and markets. In the past 20 years, however, technological change and liberal market reforms have essentially globalized the international debt structure, placing debt dynamics increasingly outside the jurisdiction of nation-states. These factors have changed both the nature of international debt and the state's role in the international financial structure.

This chapter has four purposes. The first is to introduce the vocabulary of international finance and survey the world of the balance of payments and the basic institutions that deal with debt on the international level. The second purpose is to outline three perspectives on international finance. We will briefly examine the international finance structure as seen from the liberal, mercantilist, and structuralist viewpoints.

A third section focuses on the changing nature of international finance in a world of instantaneous global telecommunications. We will examine the ways that the finance structure has changed and explain why. The LDC debt crisis of the 1980s is discussed as an example of the development of the global financial structure.

A theme that emerges from this discussion is the importance of cooperation among nation-states on issues involving international debt. This chapter ends, therefore, with an analysis of the "prisoners' dilemma" and the problem of achieving cooperation in a world beset by self-interest.

Twenty years from now economists will think of the 1980s not as the decade of the international debt crisis, nor of the dollar's boom and bust, still less of Reaganomics and "monetarism." All these mattered, but none of them marked a decisive change in the forces that drive the world economy. Yet the 1980s did witness such a change. During those years many of the boundaries between national financial markets dissolved and a truly global capital market began to emerge. It is for this that the past decade will be remembered. And, in all likelihood, the next one will be remembered for the world's struggles to cope with it.

The Economist (19 September 1992)[1]

Debt is one aspect of the international finance structure that demands special attention. Debt creates a set of important relationships that affect all aspects of IPE. Where a nation stands in the web of international finance affects its behavior. In this chapter, we will become acquainted with the peculiar language of international finance, examine the nature of international debt relationships, and begin to understand how this important part of the IPE is changing and what the consequences of change might be.

In simple terms, the finance structure comprises the set of relationships, institutions, and practices that bind together creditors and debtors, borrowers and lenders. These relationships exist within the framework provided by the international monetary system, which was discussed in chapter 7. The finance structure creates a pattern of rights and obligations that conditions the behavior of nations, businesses, and individuals. To a very important extent, what happens to trade, security, and technology in the IPE today depends on finance.

The finance structure deals in debt—the formal or informal obligations that link creditor and debtor. For most people, debt is largely a local concern, involving family, friends, or the bank up the street. The finance structure, however, has been international in its scope for hundreds of years. As early as the fourteenth century, for example, the Florentine banking firms of the Bardi and the Peruzzi were engaged in complex financial transactions throughout Europe.[2] The modern era of international finance can be dated to 1817, when London's Baring Brothers created an international financial structure to accommodate the massive indemnity payments imposed on France by the Treaty of Paris.[3]

Today, the international financial system is undergoing rapid and dramatic change. Finance is increasingly a *global* structure, where nation-states are less important and global markets a more powerful force. The *globalization* of finance is the single most important trend in finance today.

This globalization of finance both magnifies the tensions within the financial structure and causes these stresses to spread, like earthquake tremors, to the other structures of international political economy: trade, security, and knowledge. The fact that finance is increasingly global, for example, has accelerated the growth of global business firms, which produce and sell everywhere. Global finance makes global business possible. The changes we will discuss in this chapter are accelerating the pace of change throughout the international political economy.

THE NATURE AND SIGNIFICANCE OF FINANCE

Finance is sometimes perceived as a sterile enterprise. Plato, for example, condemned income earned through moneylending as unjust, since he could not see any goods or services being produced through financial paper shuffling. To see finance this way, however, is to look only at shadows and miss the real action. Financial transactions involve both shadow and substance. Real resources—the stuff of wealth and power, the difference between subsistence and luxury—form the substance. The paper trail that these resources leave behind as they move from one use to another—the checks, forms, certificates, and receipts—are the shadows of resources on the move.

Here is a paradox of finance. We tend to think of finance as sterile because we see the shadows and miss the movements of real resources, which take place far away from the paper involved. But the real substance here depends on the existence of its shadow (not the other way around, as in everyday life). Real resources are not easily moved from person to person or place to place under ordinary circumstances, so the development of efficient forms of finance (clever shadows!) is a necessary condition for the sorts of relationships that lie at the heart of international political economy.

The sets of relationships that form the financial structure bind together those who pay and those who receive. As with other IPE structures, the nature of these ties is complex and controversial—the question *cui bono?* must always be asked. The answer to this question is not always as one would expect. This is another paradox of finance. John Maynard Keynes once noted that if he owed the bank a hundred pounds sterling and couldn't pay it, he was in trouble. But if he owed a hundred thousand pounds and couldn't pay, the *bank* was in trouble. The character of a financial relationship thus depends on the quantities involved as well as the nature of the connections it creates.

THE VOCABULARY OF INTERNATIONAL FINANCE

Like most other fields, international finance has a specialized vocabulary that it uses to describe the world. The traditional view of international finance uses the nation-state as its frame of reference, and its lexicon reflects this fact. At this level, the ideas of international finance are built around the concept of the *balance of payments.*

Balance of Payments

The balance of payments is a statistical record of all the international transactions undertaken by the residents of one nation with those of other nations in a given year, measured in current dollars. In simple terms, the balance of payments measures the inflows and outflows of money from one nation to other nations. Each international transaction involves both substance and shadow, which gives the balance of payments a dual importance. The substance—the goods, services, and ownership claims that move from country to country—are what really count, but they are too hard to quantify in themselves and pretty much impossible to add up and analyze in their natural state (this is a "mixing apples and oranges" problem). So the balance of payments records the shadows—the equal and opposite money movements—that accompany the real resource transfers. When a car is imported from Japan, for example, money moves from the United States to Japan (the shadow) and the automobile resource moves from Japan to the United States (substance). The money outflow from the United States is therefore the shadow of the inflow of a real resource.

The balance of payments is divided into two parts, which reflect the impact of international transactions on current income and on national wealth. The *current account* measures the way international transactions affect current national income. The *capital account* measures the impact of international transactions on a nation's wealth. Each balance of payments account can take one of three possible forms:

- A *surplus*, where money inflows exceed money outflows;
- A *deficit*, where money outflows exceed money inflows; or
- An *equilibrium*, where money inflows and outflows just balance.

The Current Account

The current account is an indicator of the impact of international transactions on a nation's income. Much of the language of international finance is British, and in Britain a "current account" is what we in the United States call a "checking account." Thinking of the current account as a nation's checking account is helpful in seeing its real meaning. Like a checking account, the current account records "deposits" or money inflows that derive from sales of currently produced goods and services, receipts of profits and interest from foreign investments, plus unilateral transfers from other nations.[4] These deposits are offset by money outflows due to purchases of goods and services from other countries and payments of profits and interest to foreign investors (plus unilateral transfers to other nations).[5] Examples of these transactions are given in Table 8–1.

TABLE 8–1 Balance of Payments Transactions

	EXAMPLES OF MONEY INFLOWS	EXAMPLES OF MONEY OUTFLOWS
Current account	Money received for exports of goods and services to foreign buyers, profit and interest received from U.S.-owned foreign assets, and unilateral transfers from other nations	Money paid for imports of goods, services, profit, and interest paid to the foreign owners of U.S. assets, and unilateral transfers to foreign persons
Capital account	Money received from foreign buyers for sale of U.S. bonds, stocks, real estate, patents, or other assets	Money paid to foreign sellers for purchase of foreign bonds, stocks, real estate, patents, or other assets

If a nation has a *current account surplus*, it means that the "deposits" or earnings are greater than the "withdrawals" or expenditures, so that on net these international transactions have increased national income, measured in dollar terms. If a nation has a *current account deficit*, on the other hand, it means that outflows or withdrawals are greater than inflows or deposits in a particular year, and that the net effect of these international transactions is to reduce the national income of the deficit country.

The Capital Account

The capital account is an indicator of the impact of international transactions on a nation's wealth. The capital account measures international transactions involving the existing resources that make up a nation's wealth—the ownership of its physical, intellectual, and natural resources. Examples of capital account transactions are given in Table 8–1. When a nation has a *capital account surplus*, therefore, it means that the flow of funds into a country, purchasing these assets, is greater than the flow of funds out of the country buying foreign assets. When a nation has a capital account surplus, it ends up with more money, but fewer assets and less wealth measured in these terms. Put another way, a nation with a capital account surplus is a *borrower* nation, or has experienced a net increase in foreign ownership of its wealth. In this situation, the money shadows accumulate, while the substance is transferred abroad!

A nation with a *capital account deficit*, on the other hand, experiences money outflows (to purchase foreign assets) that exceed money inflows (to buy domestic assets). It has a net outflow of money but a net increase in its wealth, measured in these terms. Put another way, a nation with a capital account deficit is a net creditor nation, or experiences a net increase in its ownership of foreign wealth. The interpretation of the current account and capital account conditions are summarized in Table 8–2.

The current account and the capital account are the key concepts in understanding a nation's standing in the international finance structure. Since these terms are fairly technical, however, it isn't unusual for speakers and writers to

TABLE 8–2 Interpretation of Balance of Payments Accounts

	SURPLUS	DEFICIT
Current account	Net increase in national income due to international transactions	Net decrease in national income due to international transactions
Capital account	Increase in foreign ownership of domestic assets; "net debtor" nation	Increase in domestic ownership of foreign assets; "net creditor" nation

substitute more common but less exact terms. Sometimes, for example, a person will say that a nation has a "balance of payments" deficit, which is impossible in fact, since the balance of payments by definition, balances. Usually, this person means that there is a current account deficit, with payments for goods, services, and transfers exceeding the corresponding receipts.

The Balance of Trade

It is common to find reference to the *trade deficit* in discussions of international finance. This refers to the balance of trade, which is included in the current account. The *balance of trade* measures the dollar value of payments and receipts for goods and services. Information about the balance of trade is important and gets plenty of attention in the press, usually as an indication of the nature of international competition. The balance of trade is an incomplete measure of the impact of international transactions on the economy, however, since it does not take into account payments and receipts of investment income and unilateral transfers. The current account, which includes these items in addition to those in the balance of trade, is therefore a better indicator of how international economic relations impact a nation. Sometimes people will discuss the *trade balance* when they really mean the *current account balance*. It is important not to confuse the two different but related concepts.

Table 8–3 presents data on the balance of payments of the United States for 1996. These figures indicate that the United States imported $191 billion of goods more than it exported, but sold $80 billion more services than it bought. Its balance of trade was thus a deficit of $111 billion. The United States received a net $3 billion of investment income but paid a net $40 billion of unilateral transfers. Summing the figures for merchandise trade, trade in services, investment income, and unilateral transfers results in a current account deficit of $148 billion. On net, international transactions reduced U.S. national income by $148 billion in 1996.

A capital account surplus of $195 billion offset the current account deficit. Foreigners purchased U.S. assets by $195 billion more than U.S. residents gained ownership of foreign assets. On net, then, U.S. ownership of wealth decreased by $195 billion in 1996. In theory, the capital account surplus should exactly offset the current account deficit. In practice, however, it is impossible actually to monitor

**TABLE 8-3   1996 Balance of Payments Position of the United States
(all figures are $ billions)**

PAYMENTS ACCOUNT	BALANCE	$ INFLOWS	$ OUTFLOWS
Merchandise trade	-$191	+$612	-$803
Trade in services	+$80		
Balance of trade	-$111		
Investment income	+$3	+$206	-$203
Unilateral transfers	-$40		
Current account	-$148		
Capital account	+$195	+$547	-$352
Statistical discrepancy	-$46		

Source: Economic Report of the President, 1998, Table B–103. Figures may not sum due to rounding.
   Capital Account = Current Account + Statistical Discrepancy.

all transactions involving the nations of the world. The $46 billion statistical dis-crepancy seen here is not uncommon in balance of payments records.

The relatively large 1996 U.S. current account deficit had a variety of caus-es. On the current account side, U.S. consumers purchased many imported items because strong economic growth in the United States provided them with high-er disposable income. At the same time, however, slow economic growth in other countries, particularly Japan, reduced U.S. exports. On the capital account side, the booming U.S. stock market attracted investment funds from abroad, account-ing for at least part of the capital account surplus.

HOW INTERNATIONAL PAYMENTS BALANCE

Under normal circumstances, a surplus in one account must be offset by a deficit in the other.[6] This is the "balance" in the balance of payments. A nation that has a current account deficit, for example, must either borrow funds from abroad or sell off assets to foreign buyers to pay its international bills and thus achieve an overall payments balance. A current account deficit therefore requires a capital account surplus. In the same way, a nation with a current account surplus has excess funds to purchase foreign assets, creating a capital account deficit.

Why does the balance of payments balance? The technical reason is that double-entry account books must always balance. The practical reason is that each international transaction involves foreign exchange, and for the foreign exchange markets to balance (make supply and demand equal), it is necessary for inflows and outflows of a currency to balance.[7] When a dollar leaves the Unit-ed States to pay for a foreign good or service (creating a current account deficit), for example, it must normally return in some offsetting transaction. Either it will return as a current account transaction (balancing the current account) or it will return as a capital account transaction, balancing the current account outflow with a capital account inflow.

For most of the past 20 years, Japan and the United States have had mirror-image balance of payments positions.[8] The United States has experienced persistent deficits in the current account, which have been offset by borrowing and sales of assets, which provide a surplus in the capital account. Japan, on the other hand, has experienced persistent capital account deficits, due to its high savings rates, which produce funds for foreign investment. This capital account deficit for Japan is offset by a current account surplus.

ANATOMY OF A BALANCE OF PAYMENTS CRISIS

What limits a nation's ability to run a current account deficit? Essentially a nation can continue to experience a deficit in the current account as long as it can obtain the necessary funds through a capital account surplus—that is, as long as it is able to borrow funds from abroad or to find foreign buyers for its assets. When these assets are exhausted or—more realistically—when foreign lenders are unwilling to extend additional credit, a predictable but unfortunate chain of events is set in motion.

The initial effects of a balance of payments crisis can be quite dramatic. The lack of foreign lending can create a crisis in the country's banking system, sending interest rates shooting up and inducing "capital flight," a condition where many people try to transfer their bank accounts out of the country to "safe harbor" nations. Together, these factors create an extreme shortage of funds in the debtor nation. These financial problems are compounded by reactions in the international trade sector of the economy. Because of the iron logic of the balance of payments, a nation that is unable to borrow (capital account) cannot afford to import (current account). International trade is disrupted and needed imports are often impossible to obtain.

A balance of payments crisis is a bad thing, both for the nation that experiences it and for the other nations of the world, since trade and international finance relationships are distorted by such a crisis. It is conceivable that crisis in one nation, along with that nation's attempts to deal with its problems, could spawn additional crises elsewhere. Economic peril can spread from nation to nation, much as it did during the Great Depression of the 1930s.

Although a balance of payments crisis is, fundamentally, an economic problem, it quickly translates into a political problem, since it usually falls to the state and its political leadership to propose and implement the frequently harsh policies that may be necessary to bring international payments back into balance. International economics thus affects domestic politics, and vice versa.

To prevent international debt calamities, the architects of the postwar Bretton Woods system of international finance sought to provide a *lender of last resort*, a term that refers to a hegemonic state or international institution that continues to lend after all others cease in order to provide the international financial structure with additional stability in times of crisis. In today's international monetary system, there is no individual country or international institution that can be relied upon to play this role consistently because the magnitude of international capital flows dwarf the financial reserves of any state or organization. The International Monetary Fund (IMF), however, is often called upon to be lender of last resort for certain types of balance of payments problems.[a]

The IMF enters the picture when it is clear that a balance of payments debt crisis is looming, either when a nation experiences increasing difficulties financing its current account deficit or, as in the case of Mexico in 1982, when outright default on existing debt seemed imminent. The IMF provides credit or *liquidity* to get the debtor nation through a period of adjustment, so that it can eventually achieve sustained growth. IMF loans are subject to stringent conditions.[b] IMF *conditionality* is controversial. A typical IMF debt plan involves a number of politically unpopular policies designed to restore economic balance, including

- *Currency Devaluation* The value of the nation's currency is reduced relative to other major currencies. This makes imports more expensive but reduces the cost of exports to foreign buyers, thus reducing the current account deficit.[c]
- *Price Stability* Restrictive policies are enacted in an attempt to bring the inflation rate down. Since high or unpredictable inflation can scare off foreign investors or lenders, lower and more stable inflation rates improve the investment climate.
- *Fiscal Austerity* The government is typically required to cut spending and subsidies, raise taxes, and "privatize" publicly owned enterprises. These policies reduce government borrowing, which is often an important cause of the nation's capital account problems.
- *Tariff Liberalization* Restrictive trade policies are reduced or eliminated, encouraging both imports (especially of raw materials and unfinished goods) and exports.
- *Social Safety Net* Because many of the policies already discussed reduce living standards and can be especially hard on the poor; it is generally necessary to construct sound social programs to reduce the negative impacts of such things as higher import prices, reduced subsidies, and higher taxes.

The logic of the IMF's policies is to reduce the current account deficit in the short run by increasing exports and reducing imports and simultaneously to help finance the capital account needs by stemming capital flight and limiting new borrowing needs. In the long run, these policies are also intended to encourage economic growth, making the nation better able to pay its old debts and less dependent on credit in the future.

Especially in the short run, "austerity" policies create tremendous political pressures because the debtor-nation government must enact policies that lower living standards and impose hardship. In essence, the government must sacrifice domestic autonomy for the sake of its international financial stability. The "austerity" measures that are required are never popular and generally fall harder on some groups than on others. These problems often weaken the state's ability to achieve its policies, which can lead to a further escalation of international financial problems. In short, international financial crisis thus leads to domestic political crisis, which can exacerbate and deepen the economic crisis. A debt crisis can therefore be a political and economic nightmare, which makes the IMF an even more important international institution.

Although the IMF and the debtor-nation government work together to deal with the debt crisis in theory, in practice the relationship can be conflictual, with the IMF responsible for international financial stability and the debtor-nation government responding to domestic political forces. The negotiations between them require some diplomacy, since a strong state is needed if IMF-approved austerity policies are to be implemented, but some programs tend to create political turmoil and weaken the existing government. Resolving a debt crisis is thus a delicate matter, with international economic stability balanced against domestic political realities.

The IMF is frequently criticized for ignoring political priorities, putting too much emphasis on economic balance relative to social justice and the needs of the poor. "Austerity programs" often hit the poor far harder than the rich. The alternative to IMF conditional aid, however, is that a nation must withdraw essentially from international economic relationships, a fate generally worse than whatever policies are necessary to receive IMF adjustment assistance.

Recently, however, the IMF has been criticized for a different reason. Traditional IMF policies are meant to deal with crises causes by unsustainable levels of debt. When a country's total indebtedness reaches crisis proportions, the IMF enters the picture and administers "tough love," forcing the country to gets its internal and external finances in order. In recent years, however, the problem has not been indebtedness so much as currency instability, as discussed in chapter 7 and also at the end of this chapter. A nation can also experience a current account crisis as a result of an international investment bubble or a speculative attack. It is not at all clear that traditional IMF austerity programs are the most effective policies in these cases.

Take, for example, the international investment bubble that lead to Thailand's financial crisis in 1997 (and started the Asian financial crisis of 1997–98). Foreign investors flooded Thailand with huge amounts of funds—more money than could prudently be invested. When the bubble burst, of course, many of the investments were busts and the Thai bhat collapsed. The result is that Thailand has large international debts that it is finding difficult to repay. But the question is, are traditional IMF policies the right way to deal with the problem?

Many observers wonder whether international investment controls, along with policies to improve "transparency" that would provide an early warning of another bubble, might not be a better solution than austerity. These policies might prevent a crisis from forming, not just sweep up the debris afterward. In other words, we must ask whether the role of the IMF should be reconsidered now that finance is less a *domestic* matter, caused by internal actions and remedied by internal reforms, and more a *global* problem.

[a] See discussion of the IMF and the World Bank in chap. 7.
[b] The IMF can provide credit in a number of ways, including the issuance of *special drawing rights* (so-called "paper gold"), which are special reserves used in international transactions between central banks.
[c] See discussion of depreciation of a currency in chap. 7.

THE GLOBAL FINANCIAL STRUCTURE

One of the most profound changes in the IPE is the increasingly *global* nature of the financial structure. That is, finance is less and less a structure that links nations, often through official lending by governments, and is more and more a concern of the global market, dominated by private capital flows, where national borders and regulations are relatively unimportant. Richard O'Brien writes:

> The end of geography, as a concept applied to international financial relationships, refers to a state of economic development where geographic location no longer matters in finance, or matters much less that hitherto.... The end of geography is a challenge to all participants in the world economy, to developing as well as developed economies, to public and private policymakers, to producers and consumers of financial services. It involves the debate over the role of the nation-state, integration of nations, and the disintegration of existing federations.[9]

The key idea here is that finance is a way of moving resources from person to person and from place to place—the "clever shadows" mentioned at the start of this chapter. Once these shadows are able to move freely everywhere and anywhere, it means that resources are equally free to move, since shadow and substance are linked. To the extent that "national interest" is identified with control over these resources, it follows that global finance reduces the state's ability to locate and protect its interests.

The movement from *international* finance to *global* finance may seem a bit obscure, but it is significant. To simplify, we can think of international finance as a system of financial markets, each centered in a nation-state and regulated by that state. International transactions are between and among these centers. Global finance, on the other hand, refers to a system of financial relationships with no real center in any state. Global financial markets, which transcend national borders, are the form and substance of the global financial structure. Global finance goes on 24 hours a day. Individual nations can influence the pattern of global finance but have little ability to control it, since global markets, like flooding rivers, find ways over and around any obstruction.

What caused the rise of the global financial structure? At least three forces can be identified with the emergence of global markets: structural economic change, a shift in IPE philosophy, and technological change. Together, these three sets of forces changed the pattern of international financial relationships.

Several changes in the international economic structure created the conditions for the emergence of global finance: the rise of Japan and Europe, the growth of the NICs, and the advent of the Organization of Petroleum Exporting Countries (OPEC). Beginning in the 1970s, Japan began to experience rising living standards and high rates of economic growth that dramatically changed its status in the world economy. Along with the increasingly prosperous nations of the European Community,[10] Japan became a major economic player. The rise of Japan and Europe created new centers of international finance, reducing somewhat the importance of New York and London in this regard. At the same time, the Newly Industrialized Countries (NICs) began to emerge, creating additional patterns of international financial activity.

The largest single event, however, was undoubtedly the rise of OPEC and the tremendous shifts in the pattern of international financial flows that followed the oil price increases of the 1970s. Almost overnight, the pattern of postwar finance changed, with billions of dollars being transferred along previously non-existent financial channels. Just as the Baring loan of 1817, which financed France's indemnity to England and its allies after Napoleon's defeat, led to the modern system of *international* finance, the OPEC oil crisis of 1973–1974 can be viewed as the event that ultimately created the *global* financial network. Responding to the demands of recycling OPEC "petrodollars" and accommodating the financial needs of a world economy where Japan, Europe, and the NICs were increasingly important, the financial markets developed the basic tools of global finance.

These tools would not have been sufficient to create global finance, however, if government regulations had not also changed. As noted earlier, the postwar system of international finance was based on the ability of a nation-state to regulate economic activities within its geographic area. In some nations, these regulations were mercantilistic in their intent, or even based on the notion that finance could cause dependency. In the United States and Europe, however, postwar financial policies were heavily influenced by the experience of financial collapse during the Great Depression of the 1930s. These policies therefore reflected a Keynesian view—that strong state influences were used to protect financial markets, limiting potentially destructive competition, and especially regulating international financial movements. During the Great Depression, financial panic and collapse was transmitted by markets from one nation to others. It was thought that by isolating each nation's financial system and then regulating it, global financial crisis and collapse could be avoided.

This pattern of financial regulation, already strained by the structural economic changes mentioned earlier, gave way to a change in political philosophy in the early 1980s. In Britain and the United States, national leaders emerged who swept aside the prevailing Keynesian orthodoxy in favor of a return to the classical liberal "laissez-faire" ideas of Adam Smith. Margaret Thatcher and Ronald Reagan championed the deregulation of financial markets, both within their nations and in the international arena. The result of the rise of liberal policies was a growth of the market as the driving force in international finance.

The final step in the creation of the global financial system was technological: the electronic communications revolution that has produced superfast computers, instantaneous worldwide communications, and the ability to link people and machines in communications networks of awesome power and efficiency. Equipped with a notebook computer and a modem, an individual can access financial markets around the world. This technological revolution spelled the "end of geography" so far as finance was concerned. By the 1990s, with the end of the Cold War removing some of the last important barriers to international transactions, it mattered relatively little "where" a transaction was made. What mattered were the what, how, and why—information to be digitized and transmitted anywhere in the world.

The financial structure did not "go global" all at once. Indeed, national policies and state actions still carry a good deal of weight, so geography does matter, after all. Indeed, Michael Veseth has argued that the extent to globalization is often vastly exaggerated—the IPE was about as "global" in 1998 as it was in 1898.[11] Globalization, he argues is frequently used as a promise of a threat to gain political changes that would otherwise be forthcoming. The *threat* that global investors may pull out their funds, for example, can be used to extort domestic political changes even when the actual likelihood of capital flight is quite low. It is important to view the specific claims made about the effects of financial globalization with skepticism, then, but it is also important to understand that the general process of financial globalization is real. But the globalization of finance has changed the nature of finance, making it far less state-based and more market oriented.[12]

Table 8-4 compares private and official capital flows to *emerging market economies* to show the impact of the global financial structure.[13] Private capital flows in the 1990s dwarfed offical flows (lending by the IMF, World Bank, and individual national governments). In 1996, to take an extreme example, net private capital flows amounted to $327 billion compared to net official flows of only $4.7 billion.

Private capital flows take four forms: direct investments (such as investments by multinational corporations), portfolio investments (such as purchases of foreign stocks by an international mutual fund), commercial bank lending, and nonbank lending. Of these four private flows, Table 8-4 shows that direct investment is the largest and most stable. Portfolio investment and commercial bank by comparison display considerable instability, which is both a cause of international financial crises and a reflection of their effect. Vast sums can flow into nations one year and flow out suddenly the next.

The *global* financial structure, then, can be characterized as follows. There are more international capital flows than in earlier years. These flows are predominantly private versus official money flows. Private capital flows are relatively unstable, especially portfolio investment and commercial bank lending, introducing an additional element of risk to the international financial system and those who depend upon it.

TABLE 8–4   Capital Flows to Emerging Market Countries ($ billions)

		1995	1996	1997	1998*	1999**
Net Private Flows		**228.9**	**327.7**	**262.8**	**143.3**	**140.9**
of which	• Direct investment	81.3	93.3	116.1	120.4	103.3
	• Portfolio investment	24.4	35.7	25.7	2.4	21.5
	• Commercial bank lending	98.7	119.7	32.0	-29.0	-11.8
	• Nonbank lending	24.4	78.9	89.0	49.0	27.9
Net Official Flows		**40.9**	**4.7**	**36.7**	**50.8**	**33.5**
of which	• International financial institutions	20.7	7.0	28.3	35.3	19.1
	• Bilateral loans	20.3	-2.3	8.4	15.5	14.3
Net Total Flows		**269.8**	**332.4**	**299.5**	**194.0**	**174.4**

Key: * estimate. ** forecast.

Source: "Capital Flows to Emerging Markets," Institute of International Finance, April 25, 1999, p. 1.

THE IMPACT OF GLOBAL FINANCE ON IPE

It may be too soon to tell the ultimate impact of the globalization of finance on the international political economy. It is clear, however, that this change in the financial structure will transform, to some degree, each of the other IPE structures discussed in this book.

Global finance, for example, has accelerated the tendency toward global production. The logic of international trade changes when resources can be moved more easily from place to place, creating new factories, stores, and communications networks. What is produced, where, for whom, and how—the key issues of the production structure—must all be reevaluated in this new light.

In the same way, the set of relationships that make up the knowledge structure are influenced by the globalization of finance. Knowledge and technology are becoming increasingly diffused, by the communications revolution and the globalization of production that is taking place. The financial revolution is at once a product of this trend and is accelerated by it.

Even the security structure is changing under the influence of global finance. Global investment opportunities are channeling resources to China and Vietnam, for example, countries that were until recently isolated from the United States because of security concerns. Increasing financial interconnectedness seems to be eroding the factors that divide nations.

It would seem that the emergence of the global financial structure marks the triumph of the market over the state. With resources free to move anywhere in the world, and government regulations nearly powerless to influence them, it would seem that the state is increasingly an irrelevant actor in the financial structure. This appearance is deceptive, however. Paradoxically, just when markets seem to dominate financial relationships, the role of the state has increased even as it has changed.

The events of the 1990s showed that the global financial structure was fragile, subject to debt crises, financial bubbles, and speculative attacks (see chapter 7). Some system of global governance seems needed to promote greater stability in the global financial structure. This can be seen through an examination of the LDC debt crises of the 1980s and the financial bubbles of the 1990s.

THE LDC DEBT CRISIS

By most counts, the LDC debt crisis began in 1982, when Mexico announced that it would default on its bank debt, and lasted until 1994, when Brazil, the largest LDC debtor, successfully resolved its financial problems. The news was reported in matter-of-fact style.

> **BRAZIL CLOSES CHAPTER RE DEBTS**
>
> NEW YORK (April 16, 1994)—Brazil Friday completed its external debt financing package covering approximately $49 billion in commercial bank debt, Citibank's vice-chairman and Brazil's Minister of Finance said in a joint statement.
>
> "Brazil today achieved an important milestone in its continuing programme of economic reform," said Ruben Ricupero, Brazil's Minister of Finance in the statement.
>
> "Today's closing is an historic day for Brazil in allowing it to normalize relations with its external creditors and giving further momentum to its programme of economic opening and reform," said William Rhodes, vice-chairman at Citibank. "Brazil should now have easier and less expensive access to the international capital markets," Rhodes said.
>
> Rhodes said the closing of the Brazil debt deal marks the end of the international debt crisis among Latin America's major economies, which began in 1982 when Mexico announced that it was no longer able to service its external debt.[14]

The history of the LDC debt crisis illustrates several important points about the international finance structure and raises important questions about the stability of this key part of the international political economy.

The LDC debt crisis was a consequence, in part, of the early stages of the globalization of finance. As financial flows became increasingly global in the late 1970s, powered by changing economic structures, market deregulation, and technological change, financial centers in the industrial North increasingly sought high returns wherever they could be found. Banks and other financial institutions turned their attention to the less developed South, which had previously received financial resources more through official and government sources rather than through the markets. LDCs thought that conditions were advantageous to take on new debt, especially since inflation rates were running ahead of interest rates on loans, creating negative *real* interest rates, which traditionally favor borrowers.[15] In theory, these loans should have achieved the success that the liberal perspective predicts: economic growth and higher returns for both borrower and lender. In practice, however, the uncoordinated actions of the market created a trap for both debtor nations and their creditors. In retrospect, it appears that too much was loaned by too many.

As many countries tried to expand their exports at once (to gain income to repay the loans), commodity prices collapsed, leaving the nations worse off than before the loans, in many cases. This problem was exacerbated in the early 1980s by a recession that slowed down economic activity throughout the industrialized North, shrinking the market for LDC exports. The banks continued to make additional loans, to provide even more resources for economic development and also to pay interest on the earlier loans. The debt grew exponentially, both in terms of the burden on the LDC nations and as a risk to the solvency of the financial institution involved. Soon Keynes's paradox of finance was clear: With so much debt outstanding, it was the banks that were in as much trouble as the debtor nations. The debtor nations owed more than they could reasonably be expected to repay, yet they continued to borrow more and more in order to meet their short-run obligations. The banks had lent so much to the LDCs that they faced disaster if the debtors declared default, so they made even more loans to keep the old loans from being declared worthless. A vicious cycle of debt and more debt had been created.

How serious was the LDC debt crisis at its worst point? Looking back over modern history, the nearest parallel is probably the condition of Germany after World War I. The German economy was in shambles, its political system in chaos, yet the Treaty of Versailles imposed an enormous debt in the form of war reparations owed to the Allied victors. The cause of the debt was different in these two cases, but the potential impact was much the same.

External debt was still a very serious burden for many LDCs in 1995 as Table 8–5 shows. Brazil's total foreign debt was 36.9 percent of its national income, for example, and the annual interest burden amounted to over 17 percent of its export earnings. While Brazil and Mexico had the largest debts, Argentina, Nigeria, Chile, and Nicaragua faced perhaps the greatest debt burdens.

The creditor nations in the 1980s feared for the economic consequences of a default on the loans—which would have removed the LDC debtors from access to world credit markets and caused a crisis in the banking systems of Japan, Europe, and the United States. But they feared, too, the consequences to the international political economy if the LDCs were to do what was necessary to repay

TABLE 8–5 Financial Indicators of Selected Debtor Nations, 1995

NATION	TOTAL EXTERNAL DEBT($ BILLIONS)	DEBT AS PERCENT OF GDP (%)	DEBT SERVICE AS PERCENT OF EXPORTS(%)
Mozambique	$5.7	443.6	35.3
India	$97.3	28.2	27.9
China	$118.0	17.2	9.9
Haiti	$0.8	386.8	45.2
Russian Federation	$120.4	37.6	6.6
Poland	$42.2	36.1	12.2
Mexico	$165.7	69.9	24.2
Brazil	$159.1	24.0	37.9
Nicaragua	$2.1	589.7	38.7

Source: World Bank, *World Development Report,* 1997.

the loans in full. To honor such huge debt and interest burdens would have required harsh austerity policies to restrict imports and expand exports, which would create problems in the industrialized nations that rely on LDCs as markets for their manufactured goods. The political consequences of repayment were perhaps even more frightening. The discipline and sacrifice that would have been necessary for the LDCs to service their debt would have created great social and political unrest: riots, revolt, revolution. Adolf Hitler's National Socialist (Nazi) party emerged in post–World War I Germany under conditions like these. The market's invisible hand clearly failed in the deregulated global financial markets of the 1980s.

Given the situation just described, it seems obvious that everyone—borrowers and lenders, too—would benefit from debt relief. Debt relief takes many forms, but the basic idea is for creditors to reduce the burden of debt on debtors, to adjust that burden down to levels that can reasonably be paid. Interest rates can be reduced, repayment schedules stretched out farther into the future, and some debt can be forgiven, written off by the creditor as a uncollectable debt.

Debt relief would obviously help the debtor nations, by reducing their international obligations, but it would also help the creditor banks, by clearing their books of bad loans and reducing the risks they faced from default. The banks, however, found themselves unable to grant debt relief because they were caught in a situation that is called the ***prisoners' dilemma***. The problem was that debt relief, which was in their collective interest, was not in the individual self-interest of each bank. Every bank wanted the others to forgive debt, but they were unwilling to do so themselves. This is because the banks that *cooperate* and grant relief would bear a cost, but the gains would be shared by all the banks, even those that gave up nothing. Under these circumstances, each bank had the incentive to be a "free rider" and let someone else bear the burden of debt relief. It is unsurprising, given the high stakes and the intensely competitive nature of international finance, that no one was willing to forgive LDC debts, and the vicious cycle of LDC debt continued.

THE PRISONERS' DILEMMA

Two burglars are captured by the police near the scene of a theft. The police are certain that they worked as a team to commit the robbery, but the only evidence they have is some of the loot, which the crooks did not have time to sell or hide.

The criminals are put into separate cells. Each is told the following. "We have enough evidence to charge you with possession of stolen merchandise. It is certain that you will go to jail for six months, but we'd like to make a deal. If you will give evidence against your partner so that he can be convicted of the more serious crime of burglary, and if no other evidence against you appears, we will recommend that you be released on probation, a very minor punishment. Your guilty partner, however, will spend three years in jail. Which do you choose: six months in jail, or probation?"

Most people would rather go free than go to jail, and a short jail term is preferable to a long one. This is a situation, therefore, where it is in the individual interest of each prisoner to give evidence and take the lighter sentence. It is clearly better to be free on probation than to spend six months in prison. When *both* prisoners give evidence, however, *both* receive the heavier punishment of three years in prison. But while it is in their collective interests to *cooperate* and keep quiet, it is in their individual interests to *defect* and take action that benefits one and harms the other. Because of the nature of the incentives that the prisoners face, it is likely that they will choose the actions (defect/defect) that leave them both with the worst possible outcome.

Though the plight of the prisoners is sad, it is not one that is likely to make honest citizens lose much sleep. The conflict of collective and individual interests that it illustrates, however, is not limited to crooks. Rather, the prisoners' dilemma is part and parcel of everyday life and, therefore part of the international political economy.

The nuclear standoff of the Cold War, for example, is a case of the prisoners' dilemma where mutual interests were well served. Cooperation, in this case, meant not using nuclear weapons. To "defect" in this context would be to launch a preemptive nuclear strike against the other power. For a number of reasons, including the high stakes involved and the uncertainty of survival, neither the United States nor the Soviet Union ever chose to defect from their deadly equilibrium.

In other IPE situations, however, the dismal logic of self-interest seems to rule. Many less developed countries have experienced dramatic deforestation in recent decades. Trees are cut and forests destroyed for fuel to heat and cook and sometimes to sell as hardwood lumber. As the forests are destroyed, the resource base shrinks, land erodes, farming productivity falls, and wood for heat and cooking becomes even harder to find. It would clearly be in the collective interest of the population to limit tree cutting and stop the loss of the forest. But to each individual, cutting another tree is beneficial personally, since the loss, which is shared with the rest of society, is more than offset by the private gain.

Can cooperation be assured, or at least encouraged? Or are defection and disaster the general fate of people and nations? Political economists have studied the prisoners' dilemma in some detail because of its important role in many aspects of life.[a] Several lessons have been learned. The first is that cooperation is more likely when the persons involved are part of long-term relationships, where they will face the consequences of their actions again and again. Defection is more likely when the situation is a "one-shot" relationship, unlikely to be repeated. Cooperation is also more likely when the number of individuals is small and the impact of any defection correspondingly high on all involved. In large groups, with costs and benefits widely diffused, free-riding and defection are far more likely. Finally, cooperation can be encouraged by "side payments," where potential gainers bribe likely defectors to go along. Such side payments are most likely to succeed if one participant is so large (and its share of the gains from cooperation so great) that it is always in its interest to promote cooperation. This "player" becomes, in essence, a hegemon, willing to bear the costs of organizing a cooperative effort because its share of the resulting gains are so great.

---

[a]See, for example, Robert M. Axelrod, *The Evolution of Cooperation* (New York: Basic Books, 1984).

CREATING COOPERATION: THE BRADY PLAN

Many attempts were made to solve the LDC debt problem, but the prisoners' dilemma of LDC debt was finally broken in the late 1980s by the *Brady Plan*, named for Nicholas Brady, U.S. Secretary of the Treasury in the Bush administration. The Brady Plan is complex in detail, but simple in concept. The United States government stepped into the negotiations and offered to refinance the external debt of Mexico provided that *all* lenders accepted specific measures of debt relief, including interest rate cuts, payments rescheduling, and some measure of forgiveness. Under the Brady Plan, private banks exchanged their Mexican debt for a lesser amount of U.S. government securities—"Brady bonds"—that are backed by corresponding Mexican obligations. Mexico pays the United States, which pays the creditors. Under this scheme, Mexico benefits from debt relief, the banks reduce the risk of default, and the United States government avoids the possibility of financial instability.

The U.S. government used the power of the state to break the destructive standoff that the prisoners' dilemma created. The government was able to change the game, by threatening those who failed to cooperate with a total loss. Suddenly it was in everyone's interest to support debt forgiveness. Only the state, acting in the collective interests of the banks and the debtor nations, could have achieved this result.[16]

The Brady Plan was successful in resolving the prisoners' dilemma in Mexico (although it could not prevent Mexico's subsequent balance of payment problems) and has been applied to many other LDC debtor nations. With their impossible debt burdens reduced, many of these nations have achieved greater economic success and political stability. By the time Brazil's debt problem was addressed in 1994, the pattern of cooperation was so firmly established that no Brady bond intervention was necessary. The creditors and debtors were able to work out a scheme for debt relief without intervention by the U.S. government.

It may be years before the effects of the LDC debt crisis are forgotten, but we can hope that even then the lessons of this situation will remain. The debt crisis shows that market competition can sometimes backfire when competition is caught up in a prisoners' dilemma like this one.

What can we say about LDC debt today? Tables 8–5 and 8–6 provide information about the external debt conditions of several less developed countries for 1995. Some countries, such as Mozambique, Haiti, and Nicaragua are still at the crisis level of indebtedness. Nicaragua's foreign debt stood in 1995 at almost six times its national income! Other countries have seen their debt service costs rise dramatically. Mali's annual debt service grew from 6.2 percent in 1980 (Table 8–6) to almost 50 percent of its export earnings.

TABLE 8–6 LDC Debt Progress, 1980-1995, Debt Service as Percent of GDP, Selected Countries.

NATION	DEBT SERVICE /EXPORT RATIO 1980 (%)	DEBT SERVICE /EXPORT RATIO 1995 (%)
Mexico	44.4	24.2
Brazil	63.3	37.9
Bangladesh	23.7	13.3
Argentina	37.3	34.7
Nicaragua	22.3	38.7
India	9.3	27.9
Mali	6.2	45.2

Source: World Bank, *World Development Report,* 1997.

Other countries such as Mexico and Brazil, which have gone through the Brady Plan process, are no longer suffering from a debt crisis, but they still face a very substantial debt burden in the upcoming years. In 1995, for example, Brazil still owed annual payments to foreign creditors equal to more than 37 percent of its export earnings. This is much less than the 63 percent it had to pay in 1980 (Table 8–6), but it still substantially reduces Brazil's ability to use export revenues to promote equality and growth at home.

It is fair to say, then, that although the general debt *crisis* of the 1980s has been addressed, the *problem* of managing international debt has not gone away and the *potential* for future debt crises remains real. This problem has been exacerbated by the rise of global finance, the decline of state authority, and the relatively limited flexibility of international institutions like the IMF in adjusting to this changing environment.

BUBBLES: THE CRISES OF GLOBAL FINANCE[17]

The Latin American debt crisis of the 1980s may have been the *last* crisis of the era of *international* finance, while Mexico's 1994–95 "peso panic" was probably the first crisis of the new era of *global* finance. Global investment patterns, not national economic policies, are increasingly the cause of instability in the financial structure. Global financial flows are more volatile and harder to regulate than nationally based financial issues.

Mexico's peso panic is an example of an international investment bubble. Currency crises are so much a natural part of international markets that it is perhaps true that the only way to eliminate them is to eliminate currencies themselves by regressing to a barter system or to eliminate exchange rates by adopting a single world currency. Money and exchange rates will always be a feature of the international system, according to Hyman Minsky and Charles Kindleberger, and so therefore will currency crises.[18]

The seven common features or stages in the development of a financial crisis are

1. Displacement
2. Expansion
3. Euphoria
4. Distress
5. Revulsion
6. Crisis
7. Contagion

Imagine for a moment a market for investments that has reached some sort of equilibrium, where investment flows are consistent with the information known to and expectations held by the market's participants. Financial crises can appear and then develop through the following stages.

Displacement refers to an external shock or some "news" that fundamentally alters the economic outlook in a market, shifting expectations concerning future profits in some significant way. Displacement in this sense of change that affects expected profits happens all the time, of course, and seldom leads to panic, crisis, or instability of any sort. The sorts of displacement we are concerned with create an object of speculation, some asset or financial instrument that becomes the focus of investors based upon the news, creating a "boom."

Speculative objects appear and disappear with great frequency in financial markets, seldom creating panics or crises. So speculation and crisis may be related, but they are not the same phenomenon. Expansion is a necessary prerequisite for a financial crisis to rise out of a speculative episode. Expansion is the stage where the boom is fed by an increase in liquidity, which provides the means for the boom to grow, perhaps becoming a bubble. Although Kindleberger focuses on increases in bank credit as a common source of expanding liquidity, there are many potential sources. Financial innovations, increased leverage, margin buying, and other techniques can stretch more buying power from a given monetary base.

Perhaps the most obvious form of expansion is the widening of the pool of potential investors or speculators, from a set of "insiders" to a larger group of "outsiders." Walter Bagehot, the great nineteenth-century political economist, suggested that panics formed when an object of speculation attracts the greed of authors, rectors, and grandmothers. "At intervals, from causes which are not to the present purpose, the money from these people—the blind capital, as we call it, of the country—is particularly craving; it seeks for some one to devour it, and there is a 'plethora'; it finds some one, and there is 'speculation'; it is devoured, and there is 'panic.'"[19]

Expansion becomes euphoria when trading on the basis of price alone takes the place of investment based on fundamentals. The purpose of buying is to sell and take a capital gain as the price rises up and up. The new buyer's motives are the same, and this euphoria continues as long as expectations do not change and liquidity holds out. This is the period of what Adam Smith called "over-trading" and Kindleberger terms "pure speculation"—that is speculation on the basis of rising prices alone. A bubble (that will burst) or a mania (driven by wild-eyed investor maniacs) may here be created.

Distress is the next stage of a classic crisis. Distress is the stage between euphoria and revulsion and when there is concern that the strength of the market may be fragile or that the limits of liquidity may be near. Distress is an unsettled time and the reactions to this unsettled environment often deflate the bubble and defuse the mania. Distress can persist for lengths of time until the crisis is averted, or it can turn sharply into revulsion.

Revulsion is a sharp shift in actions and expectations caused by new information or a significant event. "Insiders" realize the importance of the news and sell first, perhaps at the top of the market, while "outside" authors and rectors are still buying. Liquidity dries up, especially bank lending, causing "discredit."

In Minsky's model, revulsion and discredit lead to crisis, as outsiders join insiders in selling off. Kindleberger proposes the image created by the German term *Torschlusspanik*, gate-shut panic, to describe the rush to liquidity. The falling prices feed on themselves creating self-fulfilling prophecies. The result is a crisis, which may also be crash (collapse in price), or panic (sudden needless flight).

The crisis may be confined to a single market or it may spread, which is termed contagion. We are especially concerned with crises that spread from nation to nation through international linkages such as capital, currency, money, and commodity markets, trade interdependence effects, and shifting market psychology. Paul Krugman reserves the term "contagion crisis" for a financial crisis that spreads internationally to the extent that it causes a worldwide depression.[20]

What brings the crisis to an end? There are three possibilities, according to Kindleberger. The crisis may turn into a fire sale, with prices falling until buyers are eventually brought back into the market. Or trading may be halted by some authority, limiting losses. Or, finally, a *lender of last resort*, of which we will hear more soon, may step in to provide the liquidity necessary to bring the crisis to a "soft landing."

Mexico's peso panic followed this pattern fairly closely. Mexico's entrance into NAFTA (North American Free Trade Agreement—see chapter 12) may have been the displacement that started the bubble in this case. Certainly NAFTA altered the views of many regarding Mexico's prospects for political stability and economic growth. Capital began to flow into Mexico to take advantage of the new opportunities people thought were about to open up.

Expansion followed, driven by many factors. By the 1990s financial markets were well organized to mobilize the funds of authors, rectors, and grandmothers to invest in foreign countries that many would be hard-pressed to find on a map. The era of "global" and "emerging markets" mutual funds was here, creating the conditions for a classic speculative bubble. A modest recovery in economic prospects from the dismal 1980s led to large capital gains for those few investors who had been willing to put money into Third World markets. Their success led other investors to jump in, driving prices up still further. And by 1993 or so, "emerging markets funds" were being advertised on the television and the pages of some popular magazines.[21] As speculation on price alone took off, even fund managers became uncritical of their investment decisions, driven as they were to invest the huge sums coming in from authors and rectors every day. "We went into Latin America not knowing anything about the place," one of them noted after the Mexican crisis. "Now we are leaving without knowing anything about it."[22] You can see how disconnected investment became from any analysis of the realities involved.

Euphoria came next. "During the first half of the 1990s," according to Paul Krugman, "a set of mutually reinforcing beliefs and expectations created a mood of euphoria about the prospects for the developing world. Markets poured money into developing countries, encouraged both by the capital gains they had already seen and by the belief that a wave of reform was unstoppable."[23]

Distress can be located in March 1994, with the assassination of the ruling party's presidential candidate Donaldo Colosio, which raised significant doubts among foreign investors about the political stability of Mexico. The era of political stability and economic expansion that President Carlos Salinas had engineered was suddenly threatened. Insiders began to shift funds out of Mexico; this was the stage of distress.

Revulsion came in November 1994 as Mexican authorities found themselves in a position where they had to choose between their international financial responsibilities and their domestic political survival at a time when pressure was rising both inside and outside the country. They wanted to keep their exchange rate fixed to the dollar, but that required raising domestic interest rates to keep capital from fleeing. But raising domestic interest rates would have been damaging both to Mexican borrowers and their banks and would also have created a political crisis just as the presidential vote was taking place. It was too much to risk. Inevitably, domestic issues were found to be more important and the peso was allowed to fall in value. Insiders caught the scent of a crisis and ran for the shutting gate doors.

Contagion occurred both within Mexico and between Mexico and other countries. The effects of peso depreciation, domestic inflation, and higher interest rates caused Mexico to experience a severe recession. Unemployment rose sharply from just 3.2 percent in December 1994 to 7.6 percent in August 1995 before falling somewhat to about 6.0 percent in 1996. Inflation, as measured by monthly changes in the national consumer price index, rose from 3.8 percent per month in January 1995 to 8.0 percent in April, then fell back to a 2–3 percent per month range in 1996. Interbank interest rates soared, reaching 86.03 percent in March before falling back, although they remained above 40 percent until April 1996.

While the peso crisis recession in Mexico turned out to be relatively short, it was also relatively deep and its effects may be long lasting. Mexico's GDP fell dramatically in 1995, effectively wiping out the short-run gains from the NAFTA boom and leaving Mexico's citizens not much better off, if at all, than in the old days before market reforms. Recovery was highly concentrated in the export sector, which benefited from the peso's lower value. Mexico's internal economy, that part not directly affected by exports, remained deeply depressed by a combination of high interest rates, credit shortages, and general poverty.[24]

International contagion also occurred, notably to other "emerging market" nations that suffered from the "tequila hangover" effect. Krugman took a pessimistic view that because ". . . the 1990–95 euphoria about developing countries was so overdrawn, the Mexican crisis is likely to be the trigger that sets the process in reverse."[25] Krugman, however, overestimated the memories of international investors. Within a couple of years they were back into emerging markets again, but in Asia this time. The bubble they created there is one of the contributing factors to the Asian financial crisis of 1997-98.

How can bubbles be prevented? The classical solution, which Walter Bagehot presented over 100 years ago, is an international lender of last resort that will lend when no one else will, that will hold open the shutting gate and so stop the panic. You would imagine that the IMF would be the international lender of last resort, based on its central role in the international monetary system, but in fact that has not been the case. The IMF lacks the resources and institutional commitment to perform this task effectively.

In the 1990s, it was the United States that sometimes performed the lender of last resort's duties, usually in cooperation with other countries and with international organizations. It is unclear, however, how long or how often one nation can play this role before its will is exhausted or its resources run out. The IPE remains vulnerable to bubbles and other global financial crises for the foreseeable future.

STATES AND MARKETS IN GLOBAL FINANCE

In this chapter we have seen how the forces of global finance have developed and grown. It would be easy to say that the market has triumphed over the state, as many do in fact say, or to say that the state is powerless. On closer inspection, however, we also see the necessity of the state. The state is needed to regulate internal finance, to coordinate austerity programs in the case of traditional debt problems, to break the prisoners' dilemma in extreme cases, and to act as a lender of last resort in case of financial bubbles. It is too late to write off the state, it seems. If the state did not already exist, we would need to invent it in order to coordinate global financial markets in areas (especially the prisoners' dilemma and the lender of last resort) where they clearly cannot coordinate themselves.

The globalization of financial markets has created increased interdependence among nations, since all are linked to the global market. These strong market forces seem to require equally strong—and coordinated—state actions to balance them. The global markets already exist, but a system of coordinated state actions is still at an early stage of development.

DISCUSSION QUESTIONS

1. The United States has recently experienced the condition of a current account deficit and a capital account surplus. Explain the meaning and significance of this condition for the United States. Is this combination of current account and capital account balances an expected or unexpected event (i.e., is it more likely to have deficits or surpluses in *both* accounts simultaneously, rather than a surplus in one account and a deficit in another)? Explain.
2. What is the International Monetary Fund (IMF)? The IMF recommends what specific policies to nations that experience persistent current account deficits? How would these policies affect the United States if they were implemented in that country? Explain.
3. The financial structure has become increasingly globalized in recent years. Compare and contrast the mercantilist, liberal, and structuralist viewpoints of the finance structure. Which of these perspectives do you find most persuasive? Explain.
4. The prisoners' dilemma illustrates an important conflict between individual and group interests. Discuss the meaning and significance of the prisoners' dilemma and explain how it applies to the LDC debt crisis of the 1980s.
5. What are the seven stages of a bubble and how do these stages apply to the Mexican peso panic? How can a lender of last resort prevent the collapse of an investment bubble?

INTERNET LINKS

IMF Survey (biweekly report):
        http://www.imf.org/external/pubs/ft/survey/surveyx.htm
Institute of International Finance (capital flows analysis):
        http://www.iif.com/CapFlows.htm

Rolf Englund's Debt Crisis page:
　　http://www.internetional.se/ldc.html

Paul Krugman's home page:
　　http://www.mit.edu/people/krugman/index.html

Financial Times Asian Crisis survey:
　　http://www.ft.com/asia/

Nouriel Roubini's Asian Crisis Page:
　　http://www.stern.nyu.edu/~nroubini/asia/AsiaHomepage.html

The IMF explained:
　　http://www.imf.org/external/pubs/ft/survey/sup0998/contents.htm

SUGGESTED READINGS

Robert M. Axelrod. *The Evolution of Cooperation*. New York: Basic Books, 1984.

Barry Eichengreen. *Globalizing Capital*. Princeton NJ: Princeton University Press, 1996.

Eric Helleiner. *States and the Reemergence of Global Finance*. Ithaca NY: Cornell University Press, 1994.

Charles P. Kindleberger. *International Financial Movements*. Cambridge: Cambridge University Press, 1987.

————. *The International Economic Order*. Cambridge, MA: MIT Press, 1988.

————. *A Financial History of Western Europe*, 2d ed. New York: Oxford University Press, 1993.

————. *Manias, Panics, and Crashes: A History of Financial Crises*. New York: Basic Books, 1978.

Paul Krugman. "Dutch Tulips and Emerging Markets," *Foreign Affairs*. 74:4 (July/August 1995).

V. I. Lenin. *Imperialism: The Highest Stage of Capitalism*. New York: International Publishers, 1939.

Richard O'Brien. *Global Financial Integration*. New York: Council on Foreign Relations, 1992.

Sweder Van Wijnbergen. "Mexico and the Brady Plan," *Economic Policy* 12 (April 1991): pp. 13–56.

Michael Veseth. *Mountains of Debt*. New York: Oxford University Press, 1990.

————. *Selling Globalization*. Boulder CO: Lynne Rienner, 1998.

NOTES

1. "Fear of Finance" supplement, *Economist*, 19 September 1992, p. 1.
2. Michael Veseth, *Mountains of Debt*, (New York: Oxford University Press, 1990), p. 31. Both these firms collapsed in 1343 when England defaulted on a series of war loans, an event that shows that international financial crisis is at least as old as international finance itself.
3. Ibid., pp. 126–127.
4. Unilateral transfers include governmental foreign aid and private gifts from persons and organizations in one country to those in another country.
5. Although unilateral transfers appear last on the list of current account transactions, they are sometimes very important items. Earlier in this century, for example, the United States experienced huge transfer outflows as immigrants from abroad sent funds back home to their families, many of whom also eventually emigrated to the United States. The Marshall Plan transfers of the early postwar period were also an important international transfer, which aided in rebuilding Europe. More recently, the United States received large transfers from its allies in the Persian Gulf War, to help defray U.S. military costs.
6. The money inflows and money outflows correspond to the demand and supply of the foreign exchange for a currency. Since these two must balance under normal circumstances, the payments that they represent must also balance.
7. The intuitive reason is this: Imagine a dollar going out of the country to purchase imported coffee (current account outflow). Logically, that dollar must return to the United States, to be "redeemed" for a good or service, or asset. If the dollar does not return to

buy a good or service, which would balance the current account, it must return to purchase an asset, creating an offsetting transaction on the capital account.

8. Although the United States and Japan are compared here, it is important to understand that the balance of payments measures a nation's economic transactions with the *rest of the world*, not with any single foreign country.

9. Richard O'Brien, *Global Financial Integration: The End of Geography*, (New York: Council on Foreign Relations Press, 1992), p. 1.

10. Now the European Union (EU).

11. Michael Veseth, *Selling Globalization: The Myth of the Global Economy* (Boulder CO: Lynne Rienner, 1998).

12. How have these market-driven financial systems performed? This is a controversial question, as are so many in IPE. Certainly, global financial markets have grown quickly, exhibiting the dynamic nature of markets, but they have also experienced a number of crises, leading some to believe that these markets may not be as stable as the system of regulated financial markets they replace.

13. The Institute of International Finance includes the following countries in the list of "emerging market economies": China, India, Indonesia, Malaysia, Philippines, South Korea, Thailand, Argentina, Brazil, Chile, Colombia, Ecuador, Mexico, Peru, Uruguay, Venezuela, Bulgaria, Czech Republic, Hungary, Poland, Romania, Russian Federation, Slovakia, Turkey, Algeria, Egypt, Morocco, South Africa, Tunisia.

14. "Brazil Closes Chapter re Debt," from Reuters, 16 April 1994, copied from the Prodigy® service.

15. Negative real interest rates exist when inflation rates exceed the interest rate over the term of a loan. In simple terms, this benefits the borrower because loan repayments have less purchasing power (*lower real value*) than the amount borrowed. The borrower gains purchasing power under these circumstances, even accounting for interest payments made.

16. See discussion in Krugman, *The Age of Diminished Expectations* 2d ed. (Cambridge: MIT Press, 1994).

17. This section is based on Veseth, *Selling Globalization*, chap. 4.

18. The best place to learn about currency crises in particular and financial crises in general is a little book by Charles P. Kindleberger, *Manias, Panics, and Crashes: A History of Financial Crises* (New York: Basic Books, 1978). Kindleberger synthesizes the theoretical model of Hyman P. Minsky with his own deep understanding of financial history and experience of contemporary international economics.

19. Walter Bagehot quoted in Rudiger Dornbusch, "International Financial Crises," in Martin Feldstein, (ed.) *The Risk of Economic Crisis*, (Chicago: University of Chicago Press, 1991), p. 117.

20. Paul Krugman, "Financial Crises in the International Economy," in Feldstein *The Risk of Economic Crisis*, p. 100.

21. Paul Krugman, "Dutch Tulips and Emerging Markets." *Foreign Affairs*, 74:4 (July/August 1995), pp. 36-37.

22. Quoted by Moisés Naím, "Latin America the Morning After," *Foreign Affairs* 74:4 (July/August 1995), p. 51.

23. Krugman, "Dutch Tulips," p. 39.

24. Lesley Crawford, "Survey of Latin American Finance and Investment: Only Zedillo Optimistic," *Financial Times*, 25 March 1996, p. 4.

25. Krugman, "Dutch Tulips," p. 43.

9

The Global Security Structure

OVERVIEW

One of the most important structures of the international political economy is the security structure, or the configuration of military and economic power formed when some 200 nation-states protect and defend themselves. Linkages between a growing number of political economic actors and institutions form an arrangement or order that helps determine how secure nation-states and also international organizations and other actors are from the variety of threats and risks.

This chapter has three parts. The first compares the current developing security structure to the previous Cold War structure (1947–89). Second, we explore some of the features of the new emerging security order including the growing number of actors who play key roles in that structure and the impact economic forces and conditions have on them and on structural conditions. This chapter argues that the end of the Cold War has not in fact left the nations of the world and other political actors more secure. National security is perhaps more important than before yet more difficult to achieve because these actors find it increasingly difficult to defend themselves against a variety of political and economic risks and threats that are increasingly global in scope. Finally, we attempt to draw some conclusions about the shape of the emerging global security structure.

> There is nothing stable in the world; uproar's your only music.
>
> John Keats[1]

> If you live among wolves you have to act like a wolf.
>
> Nikita Khrushchev[2]

The international security structure is a multifaceted network of political and economic actors and institutions with conflicting interests and strategies that together help establish how safe or free from physical danger, fear, and anxiety these actors are in the world today. For realists (many of whose ideas are shared by mercantilists—see chapter 2) security sits atop the hierarchy of both individual and societal needs. It is the state's highest priority. The security structure is arguably the most important power structure in IPE. One could argue that trade, finance, and technology linkages matter little if nation-states, businesses, and other actors do not have a relatively stable and secure foundation upon which to function and operate.

Since the end of the Cold War in the late 1980s, a significant shift has occurred in the way academics and officials think about the international security structure related to a transformation that has occurred in the basic features of that structure. In this chapter we discuss how elements of the previous Cold War "inter-national" security arrangement have changed enough so as to produce a qualitatively different kind of security order, one we label a "multilayered global" order. The very nature of the threats to national security continue to change from a combination of military and economic sources to far more complex types of problems related to such things as the ease with which states and terrorists can acquire *Weapons of Mass Destruction* (WMD), environmental concerns, and human rights issues. Some of the security threats nations faced during the Cold War are still with us and, when mixed with newer ones, help intensify the severity of the problem. In the emerging global security structure a number of economic forces, including the cost of defense, increasing interdependence (aka globalization), the availability of new weapons technology, have also helped broaden the global security agenda. These forces have also helped render nation-states relatively less autonomous when it comes to managing global security issues. In many cases states are more than ever compelled to share management functions of the security structure with a variety of other political and economic actors including international organizations, international businesses, transnational and subnational groups, and nongovernmental organizations.

In the conclusion of this chapter we discuss some of the consequences of these developments for thinking about IPE. Despite the economic liberal hope that integrative features of the international economy will produce more cooperation and peace in the new global security structure, we believe that violent conflict and war are likely to remain integral parts of this new arrangement.

IMAGES OF THE CHANGING SECURITY STRUCTURE

Sometimes art imitates life and movie images can sometimes capture abstract notions better than the scribblings of academic authors. The late film director Stanley Kubrick captured the essence of the Cold War security structure in his 1964 film *Dr. Strangelove, or How I Learned to Stop Worrying and Love the Bomb*, which starred Peter Sellers. The security structure today is much different, perhaps (to pick an extreme case) more like the *Mad Max* movies of the 1980s, directed by George Miller and starring Mel Gibson. These films have become cult classics. What can they tell us about the changing problem of national and global security?

Dr. Strangelove is a film about the Cold War where there are two main political actors, the United States and the Soviet Union. These nation-states are powerful forces and the source of their power is clear: military might in general and nuclear weapons in particular. The two superpowers are locked in a face-off; each is capable of destroying the other hundreds of times over with its nuclear weapons. Kubrick shot the film in black and white, which is a powerful metaphor for the mindset of many officials, experts, and even the public during the Cold War: black and white, good guys and bad guys, pure and simple! In *Dr. Strangelove* the relatively stable military balance between the United States and the USSR is destabilized when a rogue U.S. military officer launches an unauthorized nuclear attack on the Soviet Union that cannot be stopped. The result? Well, we don't want to give away the ending. And if you see it, pay close attention to what the Soviet Union did in the movie (and also in real life) to counter this possibility.

The *Mad Max* movies are completely different from *Dr. Strangelove*, both artistically and in terms of their IPE message. Security is not national, but personal or sometimes tribal. Color cinematography makes the images very real, with lots of different hues and nuances. Security is not a cerebral pseudoscience, but a real-time dirty business. There are lots of threats to many different actors and plenty of violence and action (not of the nuclear MAD variety) and not much hope of real security in the end (if there *is* an end). Although the security structure today is not a *Mad Max* world of primitive motivations mixed with a variety of ancient and modern weapons, it is in some senses closer to that world of chaos than the clear and simple structure of the Cold War.

THE COLD WAR

Cold War tensions and hostility between the two superpowers shaped developments in the international security structure more than anything else in the second half of the twentieth century. In the late 1940s and 1950s the United States and Soviet Union mirrored each other in ways that helped entrench a *bipolar* security structure whereby the two dominant military powers organized political, military, and economic alliances against one another. The United States extended protection over Western Europe and other countries like Canada that belonged to the *North Atlantic Treaty Organization (NATO)*, while the Soviet Union organized the Warsaw Pact composed of Central and East European socialist states. The essence of the conflict between the two superpowers was ideologically based but featured a military component where nuclear weapons of mass destruction played a key role.

The role of the atomic bomb in the U.S. and Soviet arsenals added to the already hostile relations between the two superpowers and helped create a rather unique security dilemma or nuclear conundrum from which neither could escape by building bigger or more effective nuclear weapons. The more nuclear weapons one side built the more insecure the other side felt. The nuclear weapons and strategies each side employed produced a psychology and logic many labeled absurd.[3] By the 1960s, under conditions of *mutual assured destruction* (*MAD*) in order to deter (i.e., prevent) an opponent from initiating an attack, the other side would be able to launch a retaliatory attack that destroyed not only the enemy, but quite possibly itself. According to strategic (nuclear) doctrine, rationally, no one would start a war because there would be virtually nothing left to gain.

The MAD world of the bipolar nuclear standoff had a redeeming quality as an international security structure in that it succeeded somehow in preventing nuclear war between the United States and the Soviet Union. Perhaps as *Dr. Strangelove* suggests, to even consider fighting a nuclear war was insane.[4] Or, maybe we just got lucky. The United States and the Soviet Union did square off indirectly in *proxy wars* between their allies and client states. In these proxy wars the two superpowers also competed for political influence and allies in Asia, Africa, South America, and the Caribbean, often resulting in violent and destructive conflicts where thousands of people died.

We usually think about the Cold War in military terms, but the deeper underlying motives of the major powers were often more economic than military in nature. From the start the United States found it to be cheaper (and necessary) to defend Europe from Soviet threats by extending nuclear deterrence over its allies rather than deploying expensive conventional weapons and troops in Europe. In effect, it could be argued that the savings associated with this strategy drove the nuclear arms race and eventually led to the proliferation of nuclear weapons outside the two superpowers.

The United States also used its economic wealth and clout after World War II in consideration of a number of Cold War objectives. For example, in 1947 and 1948 U.S. Marshall Plan aid provided Western Europe with $13 billion in financial aid and trade concessions in an effort to contain the USSR and international communism.[5] Likewise, the United States gave its Third World allies financial aid along with technological and military assistance. Mercantilists and realists would also credit U.S. multinational corporations (MNCs) with helping to tie together the Western industrialized capitalist nations and carrying on the fight against communism.[6] Finally, the International Monetary Fund (IMF), World Bank, and General Agreement on Tariffs and Trade (GATT), in particular, all served the U.S. objective of separating East from West and constructing an international economic order favorable to it and its allies.

Both the United States and the USSR had the guns (military weapons, especially nuclear ones), but the U.S. economy could produce those guns and more butter (economic benefits for U.S. citizens and our allies) more cheaply than could the USSR. The Cold War ended in 1989 when these guns and butter facts became apparent to all.

TOWARD A POST-COLD WAR SECURITY STRUCTURE

For many realists the Cold War bipolar configuration of political and economic power lasted until the mid 1970s when that structure tended to loosen and became more *multipolar* in character. After the Vietnam War, the national security advisor to President Nixon, Dr. Henry Kissinger, promoted the idea of a coordinated pentagonal *balance of power* between the United States, USSR, Japan, the European Community, and the People's Republic of China (PRC). The economy played a major role in this pentagonal order as a tool the United States used to tie the major powers together in an interdependent political economic relationship. Among other things, the United States sold grain to the USSR and made a series of trade agreements with the PRC to further the modernization of the Chinese political economy.

In many ways the security structure has changed dramatically since the end of the Cold War, but in other ways it has changed much less. The high drama of the bipolar nuclear standoff diverted our attention from the fact that, even during the Cold War, the security structure comprised many different actors with many different political and economic motivations, operating in a complex IPE environment. The collapse of the Soviet Union has eliminated much of the confrontation between the two superpowers as the fundamental organizing principle of the security structure.

A hotly debated topic among historians, political economists, and political scientists is the nature of the security structure since the end of the Cold War.[7] What appears to be emerging is a security structure that is not as sharp as the proceeding structure in terms of hard structural characteristics. Some argue that the new arrangement has some definite multipolar qualities. The United States and also Great Britain, Germany, France, and increasingly China, have all played a major role in settling security disputes in one form or another. Others argue perhaps more convincingly that the United States remains in a global political and economic *hegemonic* position.[8] Even if Russia still possesses some nuclear weapons, in effect there is just one superpower, the United States, which has the means to back up its global security interests.

It may be too early to determine who will emerge as the dominant actor(s) of the new security order. For now though we have labeled the emerging security arrangement a multilayered global security structure. This arrangement manifests at least three features that increasingly distinguish it from the previous order. First is a proliferation in the number of political actors inside and outside the nation-state whose security concerns make for a much broader security agenda. These actors include *international organizations (IOs)* such as the United

Nations, whose interests include world "peace and security" and also deals with many of the ethnic and regional conflicts in developing regions of the world; regional organizations like NATO that wrestle with a variety of political-security issues in close geographic proximity; transnational but also subnational actors like terrorist groups that have access to and may be willing to use weapons of mass destruction; *nongovernmental organizations (NGOs)* that may, for instance, be working on decommissioning land mines in worn-torn LDCs; business firms, some of which either engage in war directly or profit from sales of weapons; and finally the media.

A second feature of the new security structure is the different and not always complementary roles played by a variety of economic forces and issues. Many states have incurred great costs purchasing new weapons and weapons systems. In many cases defense budgets constrain policy-maker choices about defense issues and strategies. New information, communication, and weapon technologies have significantly changed the face of warfare in the new security structure. Quite often new technologies are transferred between nations as part of arms sales and transfers. In the new security arrangement states and other actors have at times felt threatened by a variety of economic intimidations and issues such as the related problems of increasing international economic interdependence and globalization. Likewise an assortment of threats to national and transnational actors center on a number of ecological issues such as resource scarcity as well as environmental destruction.[9] The important point here is that these economic conditions often aggravate international relations and trigger cross-border conflicts.

While these economic forces and activities have all helped transform the old international security structure to some degree, they have also helped recast the nature of conflict within the new global security order.[10] For instance, some of the biggest political and economic changes that have occurred in the transformation of the security structure have occurred in the production of weapons and weapons technology. The noted military expert Eliot Cohen argues that today we are witnessing a revolution in the nature of warfare brought on by new technology, especially in the capability of the major powers to use supercomputers and electronic communication and intelligence gathering systems.[11] Many of these changes are occurring both inside and outside military establishments, influencing national preferences for a variety of land, air, and naval weapons platforms. Miniaturized weapons play a greater role in military strategy, in part because they are less costly than the standard weapons of the Cold War. The cruise missile for example, is a small winged rocket that can navigate across thousands of miles after being launched from a ship, submarine, airplane, or from the ground. Nations like France have put conventional arms on them. In 1993 the U.S. president used them to bomb Iraqi intelligence headquarters. The United States and NATO also used them against the Serbs in Bosnia. Small states have attempted to acquire them. And their components can easily be smuggled in a car, boat, or even a diplomatic pouch.

Developments in electronics—especially related to command and control over weapons—have produced changes in and have also increased the strategic importance of communication and information acquisition systems. The electronic countermeasure stealth or radar absorbent materials are routinely used on ships, missiles, and aircraft. On the battlefield radio waves, radar, and infrared systems help soldiers see into the dark and fog and illuminate the battlefield, while electromagnetic signals help improve communication. Likewise, a revolution has been occurring in the use of digital communication systems which compress data. Global Positioned Satellites (GPSs) make more exact guidance and navigation possible. A single screen can display any weather, as well as the position and type of every vehicle within an area 200 kilometers (125 miles) square.

Some argue that the advantage here goes to states that can afford these sorts of weapons. These weapons are likely to be effective to the extent they can be applied by their creators in a situation for which they were designed and in which opponents do not possess adequate countermeasures. That is precisely one of the main problems of the new global security structure: War cannot always be fought on the terms of the major powers. Lawrence Freedman phrases the problem nicely when he states that "a vision of a victimless, virtual war is developing suitable for a postheroic age, in which casualties on all sides, but especially our own, are kept to a minimum."[12] Freedman and other experts understand that technology creates both advantages and disadvantages. His main point is that in the future the United States and other major powers should expect at a minimum to "become bogged down in irregular forms of warfare over extended periods . . ."[13]

A third feature of the new global security structure then deals with managing that order or solving a variety of political and economic problems associated with it. Nation-states remain the dominant actors in the international system based on their claim over sovereignty, that is, to be the final authority over developments within their designated territory. However, questions continue to be raised about the utility of force and the extent to which the economy may undermine the authority of the nation-state in the new security structure.[14] Increasingly in the new security structure, states are not as autonomous as they have been when it comes to managing these issues. In many cases they have chosen—but increasingly have been compelled—to share structure management functions with other political actors.

Nation-States

A traditional analysis of national security takes the modern nation-state as its unit of analysis. States are still the most important actors in the security structure, if for no other reason than they control armed forces, develop military strategies, and set foreign policies. Even if the United States were the only superpower in the world today, more than likely it would not have any sort of monopoly on military power or the use of force. Global security depends upon interests and power that various nation-states have and how they choose to use this power to further those interests.

A growing number of nation-states and other international actors have a large stake in this structure. Some countries, like Japan, lack military *hard power* but still wield considerable economic *soft power*. Other countries, like Russia, India, Pakistan, Israel, and China, either have or will soon have nuclear weapons, even though they may lack long-range delivery systems. They and other countries have strong conventional military forces or control of strategic natural resources (such as oil).

Many security experts no longer worry so much about war between the major powers (although that is certainly still a possibility) as the possibility that any type of war will be generated by the so-called *rogue states* that often choose not to conform to international norms and values. Lists of rogue states are arbitrary but often include Iran, Iraq, North Korea, Syria, and Cuba. Rogue states are countries whose governments are usually authoritarian, ideologically hostile, and devoted to disrupting the international political economy.

THE PERSIAN GULF WAR

An example of rogue state behavior was Iraq's action in the Persian Gulf War. On August 2, 1990, Iraq surprised Kuwait when it invaded and took control of the whole nation in a few short hours. Iraq's leader Saddam Hussein wanted Kuwait's oil and decided to take it by force. Iraq's invasion of Kuwait destabilized the entire region and threatened the United States and its allies' influence over the production of oil in the region. The response on the part of the United States and its allies was at first carefully measured. Operation Desert Shield was limited to deploying a multilateral force to stabilize the region while deterring Saddam Hussein from attacking Saudi Arabia or any other nation. Concern mounted as to the capabilities of Iraq's forces and the number of deaths that could be expected from an encounter between the allies and the Iraqis. The allies and members of the U.S. Congress often split over how successful an attack on Iraq would be—how much it would cost in lives and dollars. After nearly four months of intense deliberation in national capitals and in the United Nations, the UN sanctioned a U.S.-led coalition of forces to liberate Kuwait. Operation Desert Shield became Operation Desert Storm when the allies moved in to liberate Kuwait. Once the attack began, it took a little over 100 hours for allied forces to militarily defeat Iraq, driving it out of Kuwait. The allies lost approximately 325 soldiers, while the Iraqis lost an estimated 20,000-70,000 soldiers and civilians.[a]

In some unexpected ways, however, the allied victory proved to be a hollow one. The United States and the coalition of other nations did use force to successfully maintain a good deal of influence over oil production in the Middle East, but a number of critics argue that the United States and its allies may have been more lucky than good when it came to defeating Iraq. First, had Saddam Hussein attacked Saudi Arabia, allied forces may have had a more difficult task prosecuting the war. According to Robert Lieber, "At best, this might have triggered a longer, less successful, and more costly war."[b] Iraq did launch Scud missile attacks against Israel, but at the request of the United States and other countries, Israel did not strike back. Second, Saudi Arabia made up much of the difference in Middle East oil that was not produced during the war. The International Energy Agency also released stored oil from supply stocks helping to keep oil prices in line. Even so prices were not kept low enough to prevent inflation and a new round of economic recession in the industrialized North. In effect, the industrialized nations were lucky not to have found themselves facing yet a third oil crisis.

Third, other critics argue that the allies were lucky that the terrain and topography of Kuwait were appropriate for the kinds of weapons the United States most wanted to use in the war. The Vietnam war had demonstrated to the major powers that wars in developing regions of the world would not always be easy to win and that under the right circumstances, small weak nations could defeat large strong nations. The Gulf War presented the military establishments of many of the industrialized nations with an opportunity to test their ability to defeat a Third World country with appropriately trained forces and an assortment of technologically advanced weapons including the latest jet fighters, the U.S. B-1 bomber, new helicopters, tanks, personnel carriers, and guided missiles such as the U.S. Patriot missile.

Fourth, a critic of intervention in the Persian Gulf charges that the war raised yet another issue related to the ecological damage to the environment Saddam Hussein inflicted on the region when he torched over 500 Kuwaiti oil fields in a last minute act of desperation.[c] Oil fires burned countless millions of barrels of oil per day and contributed to high levels of air pollution and lower daytime temperatures in affected areas. Other effects of the war included oil spilled into Gulf waters, which destroyed marine ecosystems while damaging fish and other wildlife. To what extent are other states likely to adopt similar environmentally damaging measures in an effort to win future wars?

Success of the allies in the Gulf War also raised a number of other significant issues that have yet to be settled to this day.For almost a decade now Saddam Hussein has remained a source of continuing tension in the region and frustration to all but a few. Citing a UN resolution that limited his authority, President Bush did not pursue Saddam Hussein in Iraq itself, effectively leaving Iraq's leadership in tact after the war. Since then the UN and United States have implemented a number of strategies in an effort to undermine Saddam's authority and to get the Iraqi people to drive him from office. The UN, pressed by the United States, imposed an embargo on Iraqi oil exports and most consumer goods coming into the country. Most experts concur that these sanctions have not had their intended effect of personally hurting Saddam Hussein as much as they have the majority of the nation's poor people. In many cases humanitarian food and medicine remains stored in government warehouses, while the number of sick and malnourished children and elderly continues to mount. Indeed, some argue that these sanctions may have backfired and rallied otherwise unsupportive Iraqi citizens around an unpopular leader standing in opposition to the United States and UN.

On an number of occasions the United States and the UN Special Commission (UNSCOM) assigned to inspect Iraqi weapons facilities found that Iraq had failed to abide by the terms of the 1990 Gulf War peace settlement whereby Iraq would allow UN inspections of their weapons facilities. As a show of resolve in 1994 the United States struck a number of Iraqi military and defense installations with cruise missiles. In 1998 the issue of weapons inspection once again came to a head dividing UN Security Council members as well as members of the UN inspection team. The International Atomic Energy Agency (IAEA) came out and said that there was "no evidence that Iraq has nuclear weapons or nuclear weapons-usable materials or the capability to produce such items."[d] The United States maintained that Iraq was hiding weapons and also loading some its missiles with the nerve gas VX. Swiss tests on Iraqi materials contradicted this finding. Meanwhile, the French said it was a possibility. Three countries agreed that the Iraqis had used detergent with trace elements of VX in it to wash down their missiles. Twenty-one scientists from seven nations said that it was hard for scientists to be sure—to conduct accurate tests on Iraqi weapons.

Even so the United States threatened once more to use military force to compel Iraq to allow UNSCOM to inspect its weapons facilities. UN Secretary-General Kofi Annan then helped broker a deal whereby Iraq would allow for UN weapons inspections. After reports of Iraq's failure to comply with this agreement, allied forces once again attacked Iraqi military installations in late 1998. At this writing these attacks have continued on an almost daily basis without Iraqi agreement to allow for weapons inspections.

Short of occupying Iraq itself, the allies have found the strategy of threatening Iraq with military strikes much less productive than hoped for. Much to the chagrin of the leaders of the Western industrialized states it has been difficult to compel Iraq and its leadership to abandon its strategy of disrupting the new global security structure by not complying with its agreements with the UN to allow for weapons inspection. Clearly, the Persian Gulf War was not as clean a victory as CNN and other media sources portrayed it to be. For our purposes here, however, we would argue that it stands as a prelude to the complexity of political and economic issues surrounding problems of managing rogue state behavior in the new global security structure.

---

[a] For a more detailed discussion of the numbers killed in the Gulf War, see John G. Heidenrich "The Gulf War: How Many Iraqis Died?" *Foreign Policy* 90 (Spring 1993), pp. 108-125.
[b] Robert J. Lieber, "Oil and Power after the Gulf War" in Theodore Rueter, ed., *The United States in the World Political Economy* (New York: McGraw-Hill, 1994), pp. 193-194.
[c] For a more detailed discussion of the ecological damage done to the Gulf region see Michael G. Renner, "Military Victory, Ecological Defeat" *World Watch* (July/August 1991), pp. 27-33.
[d] "Iraqis Hope for Easing of Sanctions," *New York Times*, 18 October 1998, p. A8.

Many security experts argue that one condition that accounts for the aggressive behavior of some rogue states and other states as well is their ability to easily acquire weapons through commercial and also noncommercial channels. The term "arms sales" usually accounts for the export and purchase of conventional weapons.[15] Realists argue that these sales may in some cases enhance peace by balancing the forces of two nations. In many other cases, however, they destabilize relations between nations, heightening security anxieties and compounding political tensions between two or more states. During the Cold War the United States and USSR eagerly provided their allies with an assortment of conventional and mainly nonnuclear military weapons. Toward the end of the Cold War spending for arms peaked in 1987 at $70 billion. In the 1990s spending for arms continued to decrease because of a drop-off in Russian arms production, Iraq's inability to purchase arms after its defeat in the Gulf War, and budget difficulties in general.

In the new global security structure, however, in an effort to stimulate trade and generate wealth, a growing number of nations—both developed and developing—have been eager to sell conventional weapons and sophisticated technologies to almost any other nation or international business. In some cases the drive to export arms is associated with threat perceptions, threats to allies, and other foreign policy interests. In most cases, however, sales are driven either by some combination of commercial export interests and the job interests of arms production and manufacturing groups. The developed states account for roughly 92 percent of total arms exports. The United States alone accounted for over 50 percent of the market in the late 1990s. Developing nations—especially in the Middle East and East Asia—accounted for nearly 80 percent of all arms imports by the mid-1990s. Many developing countries have used arms purchases to modernize their forces, while China, India, and Pakistan, among others, have attempted to extend their regional influence.

For the industrialized states in particular then, the issue of national security appears to have shifted to reflect not so much less attention on hard military threats as a greater need to deal with some of the softer intimidations stemming from the international economy. Some academics, for instance, have gone so far as to suggest that among the industrialized nations "war has become obsolete."[16] As yet however, many officials in developing nations still think of national security narrowly, that is, as their nation-state having a hard shell[17] around it, much the way the industrialized nations thought about the problem until the early 1970s. In many cases, problems associated with low-income growth or abject poverty, overpopulation, and an array of other economic and environmentally threatening issues face developing nations and exacerbate tension between them and the nations of the industrialized North. In cases of intense regional and ethnic conflicts that have occurred recently in Somalia, the Balkans, and Africa, for example, some security experts argue that what accounts most for them is a lack of either a clear balance of power structure or economic hegemon to establish clear "rules of the game" that would constrain state and group behavior.

International Organizations

International organizations are increasingly important in the security structure today as security problems often transcend the ability of individual nation-states to cope with them. International organizations allow nation-states to form cooperative solutions to security issues. Perhaps the most important international organizations in the global security structure today are the United Nations (UN) and the North Atlantic Treaty Organization (NATO). Significantly, organizations such as the UN and NATO were created at the end of World War II in an attempt to deal with the security issues that existed then. The challenge that these and other international organizations face is to adapt to the changing political and economic environment. The UN is evolving from an organization that acted largely as a forum for East-West and North-South discussion and debate toward a multinational organization capable of more forceful action. NATO seems to be evolving from a Cold War alliance toward a pan-European cooperative security arrangement (albeit one that still includes the United States as a major partner).

Promoting peace and security has always been one of the UN's primary objectives. During the Cold War the five permanent members of the UN Security Council (the United States, USSR, Great Britain, France, and China)[18] often deadlocked over the issue of when to act collectively to punish aggression. Failure to adopt collective security measures would mean authorizing a coalition of forces from the five permanent powers to deal with aggression. Until the Persian Gulf War in 1990 the UN's Security Council sanctioned collective security only once—in the case of the Korean war in 1950.[19] This situation primarily reflected U.S.-Soviet rivalry and the superpowers' reluctance to adopt measures that would push them and the other major powers into war with one another. Superpower approval of arms control agreements and significant disarmament measures were for the most part not forthcoming in the United Nations until the early 1970s when the United States and USSR agreed to a détente (period of reduced tensions). The Strategic Arms Limitations Agreement (SALT I) in 1972 reflected efforts to stabilize political relations between the two superpowers at a time when they appeared to be losing control over the arms race.

Despite these limits during the Cold War, the UN did play an important but indirect role in promoting peace and security by serving as a forum for negotiations that resulted in several treaties covering different security issues. First was the Non Proliferation Treaty (NPT) of 1968, obligating states with nuclear weapons not to transfer them to other states, and obligating nonnuclear states not to receive nuclear weapons or devices from any state. Today the NPT has been signed by 85 percent of the world's nations. George Perkovich argues that the NPT has been quite successful in conditioning state behavior when it comes to nuclear proliferation. While the big five—the United States, Russia, China, Great Britain, and France—all have nuclear capabilities, the list of potentially threatening nations that have them has been kept to a relatively low number of approximately seven: India, Pakistan, Israel, Iran, Iraq, Libya, and North Korea. Countries such as Argentina, Belarus, Brazil, Kazakhstan, South Africa, South Korea, and Ukraine have recently abandoned their nuclear programs.[20]

Critics charge that many developing countries continue to see the NPT as an effort on the part of the nuclear *haves* to prevent the *have-nots* (mainly developing countries) from acquiring nuclear weapons. At the same time others argue that the treaty cannot be expected to limit the proliferation of either nuclear weapons or knowledge about how to build them and other weapons of mass destruction given easy access to public and even private sources of information. Rogue states and terrorists can easily acquire these weapons via the expanding sources of suppliers willing to market weapons and information. The breakup of the Soviet Union accompanied by economic and political instability in Russia today increases the chances that some of these weapons and information may be sold to the highest bidder.

Another security issue dealt with by the UN is recent efforts to limit the testing of nuclear weapons—the Comprehensive Test Ban Treaty (CTB) signed in 1996. France and China were reluctant to sign the first Limited Test Ban Treaty. China has been slow to come to terms over the CTB because it has been developing a new generation of ballistic missiles and has wanted to test them in order to catch up with the other nuclear powers. Russia and also the United States, have yet to ratify the CTB. This treaty has been popular because it outlaws the testing of nuclear weapons under any conditions. However, some critics worry that it is basically moot, given that that many weapons do not need to be tested or can be tested under laboratory conditions.

A series of conferences held in Paris and Geneva in 1993 produced a Chemical Weapons Convention (CWC) that went into effect in 1997. Some 157 countries pledged to eliminate all chemical weapons by the year 2005 and never to develop, produce, stockpile, or use chemical weapons. Some critics of the treaty are suspicious that nations such as Russia may continue to develop chemical weapons as a relatively cheap way of countering U.S. conventional and nuclear superiority. Israel, Egypt, Syria, Libya, North Korea, and Iraq in particular have not signed the treaty but appear to be interested in pursuing such a program. For many developing countries chemical weapons are the equivalent of the "poor man's atomic bomb" because they easily help balance their arsenals with the arsenals of their neighbors or the nuclear countries.

Experts warn that one of the problems of implementing this treaty is the use of the chemicals for nonweapon purposes and the difficulty of detecting trace amounts of chemical agents. New information and communication technologies along with market conditions that favor importers also make it easy to access chemical weapons and technology.

The Biological and Toxic Weapons Convention (BWC) of 1972 was easily endorsed by more than 100 nations at the time, including the United States and Soviet Union that recognized the lethality of biological weapons and feared their ability to control them in war. The BWC restricts research on biological weapons to defensive measures. Yet, biological weapons are easy to hide. Recently, Iraq, Libya, and Syria are suspected of making them. UN inspectors have found evidence of Iraq making anthrax. Russia is also suspected of continuing its biological production program. Sixteen other countries are suspected of conducting research in this area. Management of this problem requires a big degree of cooperation on the part of the world's politicians as well as its military and medical officials, if they want to contain the threatened use of biological weapons.

One area in which the UN has tried to make significant inroads is the proliferation of conventional weapons. Ballistic missiles can be used to deliver conventional, chemical, and nuclear warheads—as Iraq did when it used Scud missiles to attack Israel during the Persian Gulf War. Some of the technologies used for launching space satellites can also be used for delivering warheads. Since 1987 countries capable of producing long-range missiles have worked on a convention to prohibit the export of missiles and related technology—the Missile Technology Control Regime (MTCR). China has come under pressure to adhere to this agreement and has, despite selling missiles to Pakistan and maybe to Iran. Under pressure to penalize China, the United States has at times responded by prohibiting sale of satellite technology to China. In 1994 the United States and China agreed to limit missile sales to those with a range shorter than 185 miles or weighing less than 1,000 pounds.

A number of conditions make it difficult to implement this and other agreements to limit the proliferation of weapons because in many cases that objective often conflicts with a state economic objective of marketing missiles and other technologies that can be used to produce weapons. These exports may also be connected to political objectives the seller may have via the recipient. In many cases, if the recipient is a developing nation, it may resent attempts to limit its ability to acquire such weapons. Likewise, sellers are reluctant to place any kind of sanctions on violators because it is usually too hard to condition the buyer's behavior via these sales or for fear the buyer will purchase from other producers.

Overall, since the end of the Cold War, the UN has been engaged in an assertive effort to create new rules and conventions related to the sales of conventional weapons and also conditions surrounding the production and sale of WMD and their component parts. If anything, these efforts increase awareness about these programs, making them more transparent, thereby enhancing political and security conditions.

The UN has routinely been involved in another kind of security management; that is, peacekeeping, or the periodic use of member state troops to help settle disputes and resolve conflicts.

UN PEACEKEEPING FUNCTIONS

Early in the Cold War, the UN created peacekeeping forces as a mechanism for dealing with aggression and conflict in the international system. UN peacekeepers were to serve as a neutral force between warring states, policing cease-fires, enforcing borders, and maintaining order when states requested their presence. Two of the oldest UN peace-keeping operations have been in operation since 1949 between India and Pakistan and the forces stationed in Cyprus since 1964. Most of these forces in some 42 other operations over the life of the UN have been made up of specially trained soldiers from countries regarded as neutral such as Canada, Ireland, and Sweden, but also from some developing countries such as India and Pakistan.

Toward the end of the Cold War the UN's role in peace and security began to change markedly in accordance with efforts by the major powers to give it more authority. On many occasions President George Bush suggested that in the "New World Order" a more effective UN was needed to promote peace as the United States was no longer willing to be the world's policeman. In 1992 secretary-general of the UN Boutros Boutros-Ghali suggested that UN peacekeeping forces should play a more proactive role in peacemaking. Because the post-Cold War world exhibited more nationalistic, ethnic and religious conflict, poverty, disease, and environmental problems, it was necessary to shift the objectives of UN peacekeepers to a more assertive position. Blue-helmeted (UN) soldiers, including soldiers from the United States, Great Britain, France, and increasingly from developing countries, would be able to defend themselves when fired upon. Peacekeepers would be rapidly deployed to hot spots, most of them in developing regions where post-Cold War ethnic rivalries and regional conflict occurred more often.

In essence, peacekeeping would be transformed from a passive "keep the peace" role to an active "peacemaking" or "peace-enforcement" (i.e., intervening and imposing cessation to hostilities if need be) role. The secretary-general also recommended that an "on call" force of 100,000 troops and support equipment be made available to him to quickly dispatch to world hotspots if needed. More importantly, Secretary-General Boutros-Ghali wrote that "while respect for the fundamental sovereignty and integrity of the state remains central, it is undeniable that the centuries-old doctrine of absolute and exclusive sovereignty no longer stands, and was in fact never so absolute as it was conceived to be in theory."[a]

In the late 1980s and early 1990s the UN did increase its operations in many different parts of the world including Angola, Liberia, Rwanda, Haiti, Tajikistan, Georgia, Bosnia, Croatia (two operations), Macedonia, Iraq/Kuwait, Somalia, and Cambodia, to name only a few of the more well-known efforts at peacemaking. More UN peacekeeping operations were authorized in the first five years after the Cold War—14 new operations—than during the entire Cold War period. In a few cases (e.g., Cambodia) these missions were deemed successful, while in most they were not well received. In the case of Somalia the UN operation shifted from humanitarian assistance to pursuing a Somali clan leader (Mohammad Faraah Ahdeed) who resisted the UN humanitarian operation of feeding hungry Somalis. When the number of UN casualties began to rise, the UN withdrew and lost a good deal of its reputation because it took sides in a domestic conflict.

Increasingly critics questioned the UN's ability to produce peace in a civil war environment. UN operations in Somalia, Bosnia, and Rwanda generated more criticism that the UN often arrived too late to make a difference in many of these internal conflicts. Furthermore, the cost of operations often exceeded estimates, member states used the UN to substitute for their more expensive campaigns, and due to complex conditions and factors that generated these regional conflicts, UN peacekeepers could not easily find political, let alone military, solutions to them.[b]

The new Secretary-General Kofi Annan has backed off from promoting peacemaking as aggressively as his predecessor did. The major powers in the UN failed to establish a significant presence during the conflict in the former Yugoslavia in the early 1990s because the major powers sided with different national groups involved in the fighting. Two rather small contingencies were eventually deployed there to protect several war-free zones and airports. And apart from UN Security Council sanctioning of NATO's efforts, the UN was purposely not sought out to play a major role in the recent conflicts in Kosovo (discussed later) or in East Timor.

---

[a] See Boutros Boutros-Ghali, "Empowering the United Nations," *Foreign Affairs* 71 (Winter 1992/93), pp. 98-99.
[b] See David Reiff, "The Illusions of Peacekeeping," *World Policy Journal* 11 (Fall 1994), pp. 1-18.

If anything, the global security structure reflects a situation where a number of security problems have become too complex for any one or group of states to manage alone. Paradoxically, member states have gradually been more willing and also compelled to transfer more authority to the UN to manage a variety of peace and security issues. Accompanying this shift in authority from individual nation-states to the UN in the area of security has been the establishment of two War Crime tribunals that reflect some amount of international agreement about the conduct of nations and even individuals in war. These tribunals are located in The Hague, the Netherlands, and in Kenya. So far a number of indictments for war crimes has been handed down against various soldiers accused of atrocities in the early 1990s in the Balkans and in Rwanda in 1994 and 1995 when the Hutus and Tutsis went to war. Several soldiers, officers, and even the Serbian leader Slobodan Milosevic have been indicted for crimes against humanity and other war crimes in Kosovo since the beginning of 1999.

Several realist critics point out that the new tribunals lack the authority to compel compliance to international laws and conventions that deal with the conduct of war given that they have no real power when it comes to punishing nations or groups within them for violating these laws. In some cases the tribunal can also complicate international relations. For instance, in the Balkans war U.S. and NATO officials were reluctant to arrest some of those charged with war crimes for fear of the impact these arrests would have on the local population or on peace talks. Establishment of the tribunals, on the other hand, signifies that the issue of the conduct during war has moved up on the agenda of states. UN member states may as yet be unwilling to transfer more of the authority they have reserved for themselves to a war crimes tribunal.

NATO as Regional Peacekeeping Effort

At the level of geographic regions, organizations such as NATO played a large role in international security issues during the Cold War. In many ways one would expect that NATO's role would have diminished after the Cold War, given the expense of maintaining coalition forces in the face of no clear enemy. However, NATO did not die, as did its counterpart the Warsaw Pact. If anything, it appears to be an organization still in search of either a clarified or new set of missions. While NATO's primary objective has always been the defense of Western Europe, its political objectives have included fostering cooperation among its members. Pursuant to this objective, since the early 1990s NATO has sought to extend membership to its former enemies in Central and Eastern Europe. In 1994 NATO's Partnership for Peace (PFP) program was announced with the intention of increasing confidence and reinforcing stability all throughout Europe. Twenty-five nations signed the PFP accords, committing themselves to maintaining good relations with Russia, assisting the independence movement in Eastern Europe, helping integrate Central Europe and the Baltic states (Latvia, Lithuania, and Estonia) into the West, and preserving democracy in the region.[21] In March 1999 Poland, Hungary, and the Czech Republic formally joined NATO, bringing the number of members to 19.

Some would like to see NATO ultimately bring Russia into its fold, thus eliminating the source of many of its security concerns. Some suggest that NATO continues to link the United States to Europe and provides a certain amount of political stability that other political and security organizations cannot. Still others have suggested that NATO should look to the South and Southeast and extend membership to a number of North African and Mediterranean nations with an eye to Islamic fundamentalists and terrorists.[22]

Critics of both NATO and its enlargement have raised many concerns about its military and political objectives, along with its cost.[23] Many have charged that NATO is simply too expensive, given the more subdued East-West environment in which it now exists. The respected analyst George Kennan opposed extending NATO much further into Eastern Europe for fear that it would put the Russians on the defensive and make them feel encircled by the West.[24] Others go so far as to suggest that pushing NATO further east may even help foster another cold war. Many suggest that now is the perfect time for the United States to decouple itself from the costs and political burdens associated with defending—and extending nuclear deterrence—over Western and now a much larger Europe. "Let the Europeans protect themselves" is often heard in the halls of the U.S. Congress. Others question whether NATO states would be willing to protect states they have little in common with. Furthermore, would a larger NATO be willing and able to act as a coherent unit under military duress? NATO members failed to demonstrate resolve in the early 1990s when the situation in Bosnia-Herzegovenia deteriorated and NATO members argued about what to do on NATO's "Eastern flank."

NATO efforts to deal with the situation in Kosovo seem to have given it a reprise, if not new life. Clearly, no one nation or small group of nations could handle management of this conflict, nor were the United States and Europe willing to let the UN play a role greater than sanctioning the actions and policies of the major powers. After failing to secure agreement to have Serbian forces withdraw from Kosovo, in October 1998 NATO authorized air strikes on Serbian military targets. In the spring of 1999 Kosovar refugees began pouring into Eastern Europe. Behind reports of ethnic cleansing and other atrocities, an estimated 750,000 refugees sought asylum in Macedonia and Albania. After more peace talks between Kosovo Albanians and Serbs failed in late March, NATO began bombing Serbian targets in Kosovo, gradually extending bombing to targets in Serbia itself. NATO bombing lasted 72 days, until early June when Serbia finally agreed to withdraw its troops from Kosovo.

In the early stages of the conflict NATO came under a good deal of criticism for having both an unclear military strategy and political endgame.[25] NATO bombing tactics also led to divisions between some NATO member states, within different national NATO military establishments, and in U.S. and European public opinion. The majority of public opinion seemed to support the bombing strategy in response to alleged atrocities and also the reluctance of national leaders to send ground forces into Kosovo proper. Despite some opposition in their nations, the United States and Great Britain consistently supported bombing Serb targets in Kosovo and also military targets in Serbia. Germany, Finland, Italy, and Greece were more adamant about diplomacy and negotiations. President Clinton promised not to send U.S. ground forces into Kosovo. Critics charged that Clinton's promise undermined NATO's efforts to get Milosovic to quit Kosovo, allowing Serbia to hold out in Kosovo much longer than many expected it to.

NATO was the basis for cooperative security actions in Kosovo, but questions linger about its ability to organize the national security interests of its member states. Its role in the future is not clear nor to be taken for granted. Many issues remain to be settled including who pays for it and how much, its relationship to a planned European defense organization, and the role of United States in it. Is the United States still willing to lead NATO, and are other members willing to go along with this arrangement?

Still bigger issues exist that NATO must be able to deal with. What about nationalism, and ethnic and religious rivalry in the Balkans and elsewhere, especially in nations that are not members? And what strategy should NATO adopt to deal with civil wars and other forms of unconventional war that have become more prevalent since the end of the Cold War? While NATO's bombing strategy may be effective in some places, can NATO deal with drugs, terrorism, weapons proliferation, and immigration issues, just to name a few other pressing security issues?

Nongovernment Organizations (NGOs)

One of the clearest trends in contemporary IPE is the growing importance of NGOs. NGOs include groups such as the Red Cross and Red Crescent, Amnesty International, Greenpeace, and Worldvision, to name only a few. NGOs are motivated by a variety of humanitarian, ideological, and practical concerns and are gaining greater influence in all aspects of IPE today. There is probably no better example of the potential impact of NGOs on IPE than the case of the international ban on land mines (see box below).

The significance of the International Campaign to Ban Land Mines (ICBL) goes beyond the immediate success of its members. It also demonstrates the ability of NGOs, and even individuals, to generate international norms in a short period of time and also to shape and redefine state interests and international standards pertaining to peace and security. In this case NGOs have become actors to reckon with in the new global security structure, and increasingly states must share management of that structure with not only other public institutions but also private organizations that have a stake in global security issues.

BANNING LAND MINES[a]

A weapon that has recently gained a good deal of public attention around the globe is the land mine. The campaign to ban land mines grabbed international headlines in 1997 when Ms. Jody Williams, head of the International Campaign to Ban Land Mines (ICBL) won the Nobel Peace prize. The death of Princess Diana of England has also helped advertise the campaign as it was one of her favorite causes. The case of Antipersonnel land (APLs) directly connects the issue of personal security to the growing role of NGOs in the new global security structure.

Land mines have a long history of use in conventional wars as well as in guerrilla and low-intensity conflict settings. APLs are hockey-puck size containers buried in the ground and exploded when someone steps on them or drives over them. Often regarded as the poor man's weapon, they are relatively inexpensive (about $3 each). After the Cold War APLs also came to be regarded as weapons that unnecessarily threatened people after a war had ended in that, according to one official, they "do not distinguish between civilians and combatants; indeed, they probably kill more children than soldiers."[b] There are presently an estimated 110 million active mines in 64 countries, most of them in developing countries such as Angola, Afghanistan, Cambodia, and Mozambique that injure an estimated 25,000 people (a third of them children) every year. The cost to the international community of disposing of land mines is estimated to be about $100–300 each.

Established in 1991, the ICBL is an umbrella organization pulling together a number of NGOs into an antiland mine advocacy campaign cosponsored by the Vietnam Veterans of America Foundation and Medico International.[c] The ICBL gained a full head of steam in 1995 at the Review Conference of the Convention on Conventional Weapons (CCW) when a number of states and individuals abandoned the CCW's effort to control the use of land mines because the treaty contained too many loopholes. In a very short time the ICBL produced a comprehensive treaty that completely bans the use of land mines. Created under the auspices of the UN, the treaty calls on signatories to "never under any circumstances" "use," "develop, produce, otherwise acquire, stockpile, retain or transfer to anyone" antipersonnel mines. Each party also undertakes "to destroy or ensure destruction of all antipersonnel mines." Some 122 nations signed the treaty in December 1997 in Canada, and as of September 1998 some 40 nations had ratified the treaty, bringing it into effect in March 1999.

One of the interesting elements of the campaign itself was the method the NGOs used to further their cause. The International Committee of the Red Cross (ICRC) commissioned an analysis of the military utility of APLs by a retired British combat engineer who found them to be unnecessary and not as useful as often assumed. A number of NGOs also conducted extensive education campaigns to inform the public and state officials of their horrible effects, all the while lobbying, and also, in some cases, shaming state and military officials who resisted their discontinuance.

The Clinton administration claims to support the treaty, but the United States did not sign it for reasons related to the use of APLs in South Korea near the Demilitarized Zone (DMZ). The US did give $7 million in demining assistance to 14 countries including Afghanistan, Angola, Cambodia, Eritrea, Ethiopia, Laos, Mozambique, Namibia, and Rwanda, along with $15 million for demining efforts in Bosnia-Herzegovina. Russia and Japan have signed the treaty, but China, Poland, Spain, and Kuwait have not. China has been a major supplier of cheap land mines, especially to African nations.[d]

---

[a] Many thanks to our student Meredith Ginn who helped research this issue.
[b] Warren Christopher, "Hidden Killers: US Policy on Anti-Personnel Landmines," U.S. Department of State Dispatch 6, 6 February 1995, p. 71.
[c] For an excellent discussion of the politics of the ICBL, see Richard Price, "Reversing the Gun Sights: Transnational Civil Society Targets Land Mines," *International Organization* 52 (Summer 1998), pp. 613-644.
[d] "Land Mine Treaty Takes Final Form Over U.S. Dissent," *New York Times*, 18 September 1997, p. A1.

The Media

One reason why NGOs have become more important actors in the security structure has been the rise of another nonstate player: the media, especially the news media. The *fact* of media influence on security policy is nothing new. The Spanish-American war, for example, was partly the result of media influence on U.S. foreign policy. To the extent that the news media can influence public opinion, media influence has always been with us. What is different now, and what makes the media a major player in the security structure, are the power and immediacy of global media coverage of security issues and the way this coverage conditions security policy. Some have called this the *CNN effect*. When NATO bombs fell in Belgrade in 1999, for example, the world saw both their military and personal impacts live on CNN and other global news networks. What the CNN effect has done is to bring the security structure down to the level of the individual. Security problems that are abstract and hard to visualize fade into the background when compared to concerns that have a clear, compelling human face. The fact that the media can so clearly display the impact of land mines on individual human lives is one reason why NGOs were so successful in changing this aspect of global security policy.

Terrorist Groups

When it comes to media coverage of compelling human faces, there is nothing as frightening to people all over the globe as terrorism. The traditional system of treaties, alliances, and international organizations that characterized the Cold War security structure were all based on the idea that the principal threat to security would be state centered and could, therefore, best be addressed at the state or international system level of analysis. Terrorist groups exist outside any such legal or organizational structure. They may be centered in one particular location, but their agendas are not those of any state.

Many people believe that terrorism has replaced nuclear war as the biggest physical and military threat to peace. According to one expert, the post-Cold War security structure appears to be rife with one form or another of "shadowy extremist groups, religious fanatics, and assorted crazies"[26] whom state officials fear will strike almost anywhere at anytime. The Japanese cult Aum Shinrikyo ushered in a new era in terrorist activity when it introduced sarin nerve gas into the Tokyo subway system in 1995. Until then many experts believed that terrorists were not inclined to use weapons that would kill large numbers of people because it might cause them to lose support for their cause. However, public officials everywhere increasingly fear that given the availability of weapons of mass destruction and the intensity of the terrorist groups' cause, terrorists are gradually becoming more willing to commit murder on a grand scale. Two recent instances to support this claim were the bombing of the federal building in Oklahoma City, Oklahoma, in 1995 and the terrorist attacks on U.S. embassies in Nairobi, Kenya, and Dar Es Salaam, Tanzania, in 1998.

Terrorism is defined as "the use of violence for purposes of political extortion, coercion, and publicity for a political cause."[27] As subnational (i.e., within nation-states) and increasingly transnational groups, terrorists have come to play a more demonstrative and important role in the new security structure. Terrorism has an extensive history, although it appears to actually be on the decline since the late 1980s. John Deutch reports that global terrorist incidents peaked in 1987 at 665 and dropped to 296 in 1996. In that year 25 percent of attacks were directed at the United States or its citizens abroad while Great Britain, Israel, Peru, and Sri Lanka, among others, incurred a large number of these attacks.[28]

Terrorist groups are hard to categorize given the different causes they support and objectives they seek to achieve. State-sponsored terrorists are usually financed or otherwise supported by governments seeking to affect the behavior of another nation. Iran, Iraq, North Korea, Sudan, and Syria, among others, have earned reputations as sponsors of terrorism. For instance, Iran has been accused of supporting Hizb'allah operations in Lebanon along with the murder of four Kurdish dissidents in Berlin. Other types of terrorists include those who want to create a new state (the Chechens); destroy an existing state (Hamas, or the white supremacists who bombed the U.S. Federal Building in Oklahoma City in 1995 along with the Tamil Tigers in Sri Lanka); liberate territory from others (the Irish Republican Army—IRA, Basque independence; Kashmiri separatists, and Palestinian Marxists); and those who would subvert a state (the Shining Path in Peru or Huks in the Philippines). Magnus Ranstrop argues that religious terrorists make up one-fourth of all terrorist groups, but that religious reasons for practicing terrorism are often hard to separate from ideological reasons such as the right to self-determination, which is the case of the Kach movement extremists in Israel who have accused Israeli officials of selling out by agreeing to give back territory to the Palestinians. Likewise both religion and politics are behind Hizb'allah, Hamas, and Islamic Jihad operations in Lebanon and Palestine.[29]

Finally, another breed of terrorism appears to be emerging, namely ecoterrorism, or efforts by national and transnational groups to deter or punish those who would harm either the environment or animals. In October 1998 a group called the Earth Liberation Front (ELF) claimed responsibility for firebombing a ski lodge and other buildings on a Vail, Colorado (U.S.) mountain causing some $12 million in damage. ELF was protesting the construction of new ski facilities that would interfere with plans to reintroduce the lynx into the region.[30] ELF was founded in 1992 in Britain by Earth First! members who wanted to take action against states and corporations "who continue to exploit and destroy the Earth." Other groups protecting animal rights such as the Animal Liberation Front have allied with some of these environmental groups and in some cases adopted violent methods of terrorizing people or corporations. In most cases these activists have no formal training and get much of their strategic information from books or the Internet.

Recently many states, international organizations, and NGOs have recommitted themselves to dealing with terrorism in a cooperative manner largely because the weapons that are available to terrorists are now so easy to acquire, sophisticated, and lethal. Many states, but also nonstate actors like terrorist groups, have easy access to weapons of all types via the market and channels of sophisticated information and technology. Many of the major producers have promoted the sale of old equipment or "off the shelf" items much like auto parts that can be combined with other items to produce rather sophisticated weapons systems. Essentially, it is getting easier all the time to produce weapons of mass destruction that include nuclear, biological, and chemical agents.

This is a long-term trend that shows no signs of slowing down. Former U.S. CIA Director John Deutch argues that the United States and other industrialized nations must reorganize their defense agencies so as to deal with special terrorist problems such as the protection of communication facilities and information, military forces deployed abroad, businesses and citizens abroad, and security for air travel and commerce. The U.S. Counter Terrorist Center (CTC) was created in 1986 and centralizes intelligence from other agencies dealing with terrorism. Sophisticated technologies dealing with satellites and communications surveillance are likely to be employed as tools against terrorists. Germany has tried to restrict access to the Internet by groups that support terrorism. And in order to protect private and public financial transactions, the U.S. government is promoting a "key recovery" system that would permit law enforcement officials to have access to encrypted records or communications.[31] The Clinton administration recently announced plans to stockpile vaccines around the United States for civilian protection. Some 40 U.S. executive agencies are reported to have made counterterrorism one of their top priorities.

National interest therefore dictates that nations make scientific security a high priority in an attempt to keep high-tech information out of the hands of potential enemies. As military and civilian technology has become increasingly sophisticated, two new security dilemmas have become increasingly important. The first is that the valuable technology that the state may want to keep under domestic control is often exactly the sort of thing that the nation's businesses want to produce and export widely. The goal of military security through technically sophisticated defense systems, therefore, can conflict with the goal of economic security through the development of technically sophisticated industries. There is no general rule to follow in choosing one type of security over the other. In the global security structure, it is as important, in some respects, to have a national technology policy as it is to have a foreign policy – in the sense that mistakes in either area can have monumental consequences.

The second dilemma is that the same forces that make it more important to be able to control access to critical technologies are sometimes the same forces that make it impossible (or very difficult) to control them. The Internet, for example, was originally conceived as a communications system for use by scientists doing national defense research. Everyone is aware of how the Internet has expanded, both in terms of the information available on it and the number of persons who have access to it. Its increasing breadth and sophistication now make it harder to keep information on it secure. Technological advances can sometimes undermine their own security in this way.[32]

Business Firms

One actor that increasingly plays a greater role in the global security structure all the time is (multinational) business firms. Because many of them are private enterprises, they are able to operate outside the control of states and international organizations. Businesses in general have a strong interest in a secure and stable

IPE because war disrupts the natural interconnectedness of markets. War doesn't pay, it is said. Quite often though security does pay, in a number of ways. The business of providing arms and military technology is a big business. There are strong business interests within every country that lobby for higher levels of security spending, both for the national security of the country and for the economic security of the particular firms that supply the weapons and defense systems involved. A "feeding frenzy" by nations and corporations exists for weapons and technology. Among the U.S. companies often involved in these transactions are Vector Microwave Research Corp, Electronic Warfare Associates, Science Applications International Corp, Loral Corp, McDonnell Douglas (now part of Boeing), and GM Hughes Electronics Corp. Many of these companies use former U.S. defense officials to help them sell and acquire new technologies. The point here is that if U.S. companies can purchase these weapons and technologies, so can others. In the 1980s Japan sold Russia advanced materials for quieter subs. More recently, journalists have covered the story of how the Russians have been more than willing to sell much of their weapons technologies given the lack of a central authority to govern such sales.[33]

More recently still other businesses have directly entered the business of war. David Shearer argues that "the increasing inability of weak governments to counter internal violence has created a ready market for private military forces."[34] Companies like Executive Outcomes of South Africa and Sandline International of Great Britain have provided training and strategic advice to both Angolan and Sierra Leone's armed forces. The company Military Professional Resources Incorporated has assisted the forces of Bosnia-Herzegovina and Croatia. These companies do not want to be labeled mercenaries because they argue they are not always directly involved in fighting even if they fulfill a variety of security functions. Shearer links their increased use to political and economic conditions that necessitate their use after the withdrawal of major powers from developing regions, especially Africa, and the ineffectiveness of the UN. Shearer also suggests that for reasons related to the growing cost of national security, private armies are likely to become an accepted feature of the global security order.

CONCLUSION: IMAGES OF THE GLOBAL SECURITY STRUCTURE

The global security structure of today results from the interaction of many actors with many interests in a world that is changing economically, politically, and technologically and that is increasingly interconnected. The drama that results from this interaction is complex and uncertain—and important to say the least.

An element of the complexity of security that has already been mentioned but is repeated here for emphasis is that national security is now multidimensional. Military security often overlaps economic security, for example, and both of these depend very much on the international structure of knowledge and technology (the topic of chapter 10) and also on the other two economic structures. For example, efforts to generate economic growth, along with market forces that make available both conventional and increasingly nonconventional weapons, condition the global weapons trade and technology transfer problems. While the economy helps make some states more physically and financially secure, it also helps make others as well as the entire global security structure less secure—physically, economically, and even psychologically.

It can be argued that the complexity of this system makes it more stable because the large number of simultaneous relationships that states engage in today make it more costly for them to take aggressive action. This is a version of what is called the "McDonald's theory of world peace." The McDonald's theory observes that countries that have networks of McDonald's stores do not go to war.[35] This theory is based on the argument that countries that are tightly woven into the global web of states, markets, international organizations, NGOs, and the like (and that, therefore, have McDonald's fast food stores) have too much to lose from military conflict and, therefore, will never go to war.

On the other hand, it can be argued that the large number of actors and overlapping layers of security policy that exist today create more potential for conflict and make it more difficult for decisive action to be taken in case of disagreement or against rogue states and terrorist groups. The large number of actors who must be consulted slows down the action of states. Media coverage adds a disincentive to strong action because harm to individual innocent bystanders and civilians can easily and effectively be communicated. The loss of a single soldier, an everyday occurrence in war, can be a national media event today. This fact may give rogue states and terrorist groups greater room to maneuver, making them a different and potentially more serious threat to security than in the past.

Because nations face trade-offs between different dimensions of national security, it is more difficult for them and other actors to be secure in all respects. Security may be more important than ever, but it is harder than ever to attain. The focus of the global security structure has changed. *Geopolitics*, the emphasis on national borders and the ways that nations, like chess pieces, could strategically be arranged against an organized opponent, is seemingly less important today than it once was. The case of land mines, for example, demonstrates that national borders do not seem to mean as much as they once did given the overlap between national and also individual interests on almost a global scale. More important now are economic and technological issues along with a host of other human problems that can be communicated powerfully on videotape and broadcast via satellite around the world.

The sharper focus on economics, technology, and human rights seems to diminish the role of the state in the global security structure. This is particularly true when we also observe the increased relevance of international organizations and nongovernment organizations in international relations. Yet the state remains the most important actor in security matters—the one actor who must put security concerns above all others. What we are left with may eventually look like *Mad Max*, with no states, just tribes, alliances, and back-stabbing self-interest. More than likely the security structure promises to reflect a mix of many of the elements of the conflict in Kosovo that are discussed in this chapter: rogue state (Serbia) versus international organization of states (NATO); a strong emphasis on human rights compared with geopolitics; highly technological military action and CNN coverage of the war from start to finish. And, for all its post-Cold War shine, Kosovo had this in common with all previous wars: Many people suffered, many people died.

DISCUSSION QUESTIONS

1. Outline and discuss some of the main differences between the structural features of the Cold War international security structure and the emerging multilayered global order.
2. Outline and discuss the way in which economic forces and activities helped transform the security structure such that it has become a multilayered global arrangement.
3. Outline and discuss what you think the new security structure will look like in the early twenty-first century in terms of
   a. polarity (the number of regional or global hegemons and their allies).
   b. the prevalence of military, economic, political, or other issues.
   c. how much nation-states will manage this structure alongside other political and economic actors.

INTERNET LINKS

Landmine Home Page:
    http://www.vvaf.org/htdocs/landmine/freeworld.html
NATO Home Page:
    http://www.nato.int/
Index of International Organizations:
    http://www.foreignpolicy.com/Resources/iiorgs.htm
Index of Nongovernmental Organizations:
    http://www.foreignpolicy.com/Resources/ttanks.htm

SUGGESTED READINGS

Edgar Bottome. *The Balance of Terror: Nuclear Weapons and the Illusion of Security 1945-1985*. Boston: Beacon Press, 1986.
John Deutch. "Terrorism," *Foreign Policy* 108 (Fall 1997), pp. 10-22.
Lawrence Freedman. "International Security: Changing Targets," *Foreign Policy* 110 (Spring 1998), pp. 48-64.
Aaron L. Friedberg, "The Changing Relationship Between Economics and National Security," *Political Science Quarterly* 106 (Summer 1991), pp. 265-276.
Ethan B. Kapstein. *The Political Economy of National Security: A Global Perspective*. New York: McGraw-Hill, 1992.
Robert J. Lieber. "Oil and Power after the Gulf War." In Theodore Rueter, ed., *The United States in the World Economy*. New York: McGraw-Hill, 1994.
Joseph S. Nye, Jr. "The Changing Nature of World Power," *Political Science Quarterly* 105 (Summer 1990), pp. 177-192.
David Shearer. "Outsourcing War." *Foreign Policy* 112 (Fall 1998), pp. 68-81.
Kenneth Waltz and Scott Sagan. *The Spread of Nuclear Weapons: A Debate*. New York: W.W. Norton, 1995.

NOTES

1. See *Letters of John Keats*, no. 37, letter of 13-19 January 1818 to his brothers George and Thomas Keats, *Columbia Dictionary of Quotations*, (New York: Columbia University Press, 1998).
2. Quoted in *Observer* (London), 26 September 1971. From *Columbia Dictionary of Quotations*, 1998.

3. There are many well-known critics of this dimension of the arms race. See, for example, Solly Zuckerman, *Nuclear Illusion & Reality*, (New York: Vintage Books, 1982); Nigel Calder, *Nuclear Nightmares: An Investigation Into Possible War* (New York: Penguin, 1982); and Helen Caldicott, *Missile Envy: The Arms Race and Nuclear War* (New York: Bantom Books, 1986).

4. It should be pointed out that during the first Reagan administration (1981–1984) a number of his advisors and strategic experts argued that nuclear war should be thought of as "thinkable" and "winnable," not only because Soviet motives were suspect, but also because newer more sophisticated weapons technology compelled each side to consider fighting "limited" nuclear wars. For a more detailed discussion of this issue, see Spurgeon M. Keeny, Jr., and Wolfgang K. H. Panofsky, "MAD versus NUTS: Can Doctrine or Weaponry Remedy the Mutual Hostage Relationship of the Superpowers?" *Foreign Affairs* 60 (Winter 1981/82), pp. 287-304.

5. For a more detailed description of the connection between U.S. political and economics interests, see Benjamin J. Cohen, "The Revolution in Atlantic Economic Relations: A Bargain Comes Unstuck" in Wolfram Hanrieder, *The United States and Western Europe: Political, Economic, and Strategic Perspectives* (Cambridge, MA: Winthrop, 1974), pp. 106-133, and David Calleo, *The Imperious Economy* (Cambridge, MA: Harvard University Press, 1982).

6. See Robert Gilpin, *U.S. Power and the Multinational Corporation: The Political Economy of Foreign Direct Investment* (New York: Basic Books, 1975), pp. 6-7.

7. For an interesting and insightful article that discusses the many possible security configurations of power since the end of the Cold War, see Charles W. Kegley, Jr., and Gregory A. Raymond, "Great-Power Relations in the 21st Century: A New Cold War, or Concert-Based Peace?" in Charles W. Kegley, Jr., and Eugene R. Wittkopf, *The Global Agenda* (Boston, MA: McGraw Hill, 1998), pp. 170-183.

8. The noted expert Samuel P. Huntington labels the current security structure a "strange hybrid, a *uni-multipolar* system with one superpower and several major powers." See his "The Lonely Superpower," *Foreign Affairs*, 78 (March/April 1999), p. 36.

9. See, for example, Thomas Homer-Dixon, "On the Threshold: Environmental Changes as the Cause of Acute Conflict, *International Security* 16 (Fall 1991), pp. 76-116.

10. For an insightful discussion of this shift in the focus of security studies, see Lawrence Freedman, "International Security: Changing Targets" *Foreign Policy* 110 (Spring 1998), pp. 48-64.

11. See Eliot Cohen, "A Revolution in Warfare," *Foreign Affairs* 75 (March/April 1996), pp. 37-54.

12. Freedman, "International Security: Changing Targets," p. 60.

13. Ibid., p. 61.

14. See for example, Joseph A. Camilleri and Jim Falk, *The End of Sovereignty?: The Politics of a Shrinking and Fragmenting World* (Aldershot, England: Edward Elgar, 1992), especially chap. 6, pp. 139-170.

15. This section borrows from Frederic Pearson and J. Martin Rochester, *International Relations: The Global Condition in the Twenty-First Century*, 4th ed., (New York: McGraw-Hill, 1998), pp. 413-423.

16. See John Mueller, "The Obsolescence of Major War," *Bulletin of Peace Proposals* 21 (1990).

17. The concept of a hard shell around the nation-state is explored in John Herz's classic piece "The Territorial State Revisited: Reflections on the Future of the Nation-State," *Polity, The Journal of the Northeastern Political Science Association* I (1968), pp. 12-34.

18. The China seat on the UN Security Council was occupied by Nationalist China (Taiwan) until 1973 when the seat went over to the People's Republic of China.

19. Then the Soviet Union was absent from the Security Council vote in protest over the Republic of China (Taiwan) representing China on the Council.

20. George Perkovich, "Nuclear Proliferation," *Foreign Policy* 112, (Fall 1998), pp. 12-13.

21. For a more detailed discussion of the PFP program, see Geoffrey Lee Williams, "NATO's Expansion: The Big Debate," *NATO Review* (May 1995).

22. A number of Islamic and other critics are concerned that focus on these potential kinds of threats are misdirected and only invite efforts to make new enemies.

23. See, for example, Amos Perlmutter and Ted G. Carpenter "NATO's Expensive Trip East," *Foreign Affairs* 77 (January/February 1998), pp. 2-6.

24. See George Kennan, "NATO: A Fateful Error, "*New York Times*, 5 February 1997, p. A19.

25. See, for example, David Rieff, "What Bombs Can't Do," *New York Times*, 25 March 1999, p. A31.

26. Ehud Sprinzak, "The Great Superterrorism Scare," *Foreign Policy* 112 (Fall 1998) p. 112.

27. Pearson and Rochester, *International Politics*, p. 452.

28. John Deutsch, "Terrorism," *Foreign Policy*, 108 (Fall 1997), p.10.

29. For a more detailed discussion of religious terrorism, see Magnus Ranstrop, "Terrorism in the Name of Religion," *Journal of International Affairs* 50 (Summer 1996), pp. 41-62. Ranstrop argues that a number of cults have recently appeared whose focus is the millenium or some messianic cause of one sort or another whereby salvation is achieved via Armageddon. These groups tend not to strike out at others. Instead the members of California's Heaven Gate and France's Order of the Solar Temple, for instance, believed in salvation gained through suicide rather than violence against nonmembers.

30. "Eco-terrorists wage 'war' to protect nature," *Tacoma News-Tribune*, 23 October 1998, p. A1.

31. Deutch, "Terrorism" p. 20.

32. The Internet has also made possible a new threat to the security of individuals, businesses, and even nations: the Internet virus.

33. See "Paying a Price for Russia's Military Technology," *Washington Post National Weekly Edition*, 2-8 January, 1995, p. 17.

34. See David Shearer, "Outsourcing War," *Foreign Policy* 112 (Fall, 1998), p. 70.

35. The 1999 war between Serbia and the NATO forces over Serbian action in Kosovo is an exception to this rule.

10

Knowledge and Technology: The Basis of Wealth and Power

By Professor Ross Singleton

OVERVIEW

Throughout history, but particularly in today's world, wealth and power flow from access to and control of knowledge and technology. In this chapter we examine the creation and diffusion of knowledge and technology. Who controls this process and how?

We begin by defining terms. What is technology? What is the nature of technological innovation? We then consider the notion of dynamic comparative advantage—the idea that countries can *create* comparative advantage given sufficient access to knowledge and technology.

The role of intellectual property rights, which control access to knowledge and the diffusion of technology, will be considered from the liberal, mercantilist, and structuralist perspectives. Do these rights further the development of the world market, thereby enhancing the benefits of specialization and trade? Do these rights provide a basis for national advantage in a struggle for wealth and power among nations? Or do these rights limit the transfer of technology to developing countries, thereby deepening their dependency?

The efforts of the United States to control the flow of technology beyond its borders using trade laws and the GATT and WTO processes are examined in detail. These efforts include enhancing the international protection of intellectual property rights (patents, trademarks, and copyrights).

Efforts to harmonize the treatment of intellectual property rights across national boundaries and conflicts among developed countries (particularly between the United States and Japan) regarding this process will also be considered. Finally, we will analyze the important process of the transfer of technology from developed to developing countries.

> The power of machinery, combined with the perfection of transport facilities in modern times, affords to the manufacturing State an immense superiority over the mere agricultural State. . . . in a manufacturing State there is not a path which leads more rapidly to wealth and position than that of invention and discovery.[1]
>
> Friedrich List

> Economic change and technological development, like wars or sporting tournaments, are usually not beneficial to all. Progress, welcomed by optimistic voices from the Enlightenment to our present age, benefits those groups or nations that are able to take advantage of the newer methods and science, just as it damages others that are less prepared technologically, culturally, and politically to respond to change.[2]
>
> Paul Kennedy

Students of IPE today find themselves in the midst of a technological-information revolution that will have political, economic, and social impacts, many believe, even more profound than the industrial revolution of the nineteenth century. Scientists and engineers have made it possible for us to do things that were not just impossible a few years ago; they were also absolutely unimaginable. Science fiction barely keeps ahead of science fact.

The industrial revolution had enormous impact on the international political economy because it altered global patterns of wealth and power. This makes the current revolution in science and technology an even more important factor in IPE because, compared to the industrial revolution, the changes in science and technology today are broader—affecting more aspects of life, faster, and more globally. What happens to IPE in the future increasingly depends on how the world's states and markets accommodate scientific and technical changes today.

The common notion that "knowledge is power" has therefore taken on profound significance. Individuals, business firms, and nations that control access to knowledge in the form of scientific understanding and technological innovation can often enjoy a clear competitive advantage in the world market, allowing them to dominate political and economic processes.

Three important trends have become apparent over the last 20 years.

- First, knowledge and technology have become increasingly important as determinants of wealth and power. Economic success and political influence increasingly require technological prowess more than just natural resources.

- Second, the pace of technological change has quickened. Computers and machines have long physical lifetimes, but very short economic lives, given the speed with which more powerful and useful replacements are produced.
- Finally, knowledge and technology are increasingly dispersed. The computer and communications revolutions make it possible for complex data and ideas to move instantaneously from desk to desk within a business and from country to country around the world.

These three trends mean essentially that knowledge is wealth and it is power—for those who have access to it and can control it. Those individuals, firms, and nations that are unable to acquire advanced technology, or cannot innovate at a competitive rate, will necessarily fall behind. In his book *The Work of Nations*, Robert Reich imagines a world where knowledge and technology create an international class system.[3] Persons and nations are "haves" or "have-nots" based on how they "plug in" to the "global web" of the future. One needn't go so far as Reich in order to understand the importance of knowledge and technology in the future.

THE INTERNATIONAL KNOWLEDGE STRUCTURE

The international *knowledge structure* is the set of relationships that govern access to knowledge and technology around the world. It is a web of rules, practices, institutions, and bargains that determine who owns and can make use of knowledge and technology, where, how, and on what terms. This structure is rapidly growing and changing, which adds an exciting dynamic element to its nature.

The knowledge structure establishes a set of linkages between and among states and markets in just the same general way as the production, finance, and security structures that have been discussed in this part of the textbook. To an important extent, a nation's position within the international political economy is determined by where it falls in the overlapping web that these four structures create.

What makes the international knowledge structure especially important today is the extent to which it interacts with the other IPE structures and thus conditions all the IPE relationships. Indeed, it would be hard to overstate the importance of knowledge and technology today. The role of knowledge and technology in the security structure was noted in chapter 9. To an important extent, the IPE of the Cold War was driven by technology. The strategy of nuclear deterrence was chosen by the United States in the early postwar years in part because technology made nuclear weapons appear to be a less costly strategy than conventional weapons. The high costs of the arms race, which was also a technology race, contributed to the pressures that brought the Cold War to an end in the 1980s. It seems likely that knowledge and technology will continue to influence the security structure in the years to come.

Knowledge and technology have had a tremendous impact on the international financial structures discussed in chapters 7 and 8. Advances in computer and communications technology have resulted in a global financial system by making national borders and regulations almost irrelevant. As technology continues to advance, it will no doubt influence the financial structure in new ways. Today, for example, financial markets increasingly trade complex instruments called derivatives (because their value is derived from movements of other financial items, such as interest rates and exchange rates). Derivatives can be so complex that supercomputers, such as those used to track missiles, must be used merely to calculate their value. Technological change has made markets in these financial instruments possible; further advances are sure to shape financial relationships in future years.

The impact of knowledge and technology on international trade and the production structure (see chapter 6) is especially significant and will, therefore, be the focus of most of the rest of this chapter. The production structure is the set of relationships that determine what is produced, where, how, for whom, and on what terms. Each and every aspect of the production function is now affected in important ways by technology and technological change. Advances in science and technology mean that new goods and services are being produced, in new and unexpected places, in ways different from the past, and distributed in new ways to new patterns of consumers. The knowledge structure and the production structure are now so intertwined that it is almost impossible to separate them in practice as we do here for analytical purposes.

Consider some of the consequences of rapid technological change within the production structure. Individuals who have the educational background and ability to understand and use sophisticated technologies, those whom Robert Reich has christened the "symbolic analysts," are in great demand wherever they are located.[4] Motorola, Digital Equipment, and other U.S. corporations have recently located software development subsidiaries in India to take advantage of the plethora of software engineers that country's universities produce.

Because of their global reach and their control of knowledge and technology, business firms in some respects now rival states for command of scarce resources and for control of wealth and power. Firms in today's competitive world market find themselves on an innovation treadmill. Success requires the constant development of new product and process technologies. The ability to protect technological innovations from immediate imitation is therefore critical. Without patent, trademark, and copyright protection, firms would find it difficult to recoup investment in new technologies.[5] Firms that are able to develop and control technology can produce and market their products and services throughout the world. Revolutions in data processing, transportation, and communications have made global reach a reality. Firms have become paramount actors in the international political economy arena.

Nations also struggle to become or remain competitive in the new world economy. Countries as diverse as El Salvador, China, Hungary, Russia, and the United States share the common desire to grow and prosper by competing in the world market. Power in international relations now depends in large measure on a nation's ability to generate technological innovation and wealth.[6] The name of the economic and political game for governmental leaders and the managers of firms is winning and maintaining a large market share of high value-added goods and services.[7] Clearly, winning or even holding their own in this game will require nations to develop or have access to the newest and best technology.

THE NATURE AND IMPACT OF TECHNOLOGICAL INNOVATION

Technology is the knowledge of how to combine resources to produce goods and services. Technological innovation comes in two varieties—product and process innovation. *Product innovation* is the development of new or better products. Product innovation can create entirely new markets and enormous benefits to consumers. The personal computer, ATM (cash) machines, and a whole range of pharmaceutical products come readily to mind as recent examples of product innovation. *Process innovation* is the development of more efficient, lower-cost production techniques. The robotics revolution led by Japanese producers and managerial innovations (also by Japanese producers) are perhaps the most dramatic recent examples of process innovation.

Technological innovation is largely the product of investment in research and development by individual firms. But governments can clearly also play an important role in the process. Governments recognize that technological growth has historically been a key determinant of economic growth. For example, "advances in knowledge" accounted for an estimated 68 percent of increase in labor productivity and 28 percent of the growth in U.S. income between 1929 and 1982.[8] Governments also recognize the significance of technological innovation in the creation of comparative advantage. Therefore, governments have attempted to encourage technological growth in a variety of ways. Governments often subsidize basic science research within universities or research institutes. Governments sometimes subsidize research and development by firms or encourage the formation of research consortia among firms. And governments provide protection for intellectual property in the form of patents, trademarks, and copyrights.

Rapid technological change has many important effects on the world around us. Two that are worth special mention here are the *product life cycle*, which illustrates how technological change leads to globalization of production and the ability of a nation to *create* comparative advantage through strategic investment in knowledge and technology.

The Product Life Cycle

The product life cycle was described in the 1970s by political economist Raymond Vernon (see chapter 16 for further discussion of this topic). Vernon observed that some products the United States once produced and even exported were eventually produced abroad and became imports. This life cycle (from export to import) is in part based on the interaction of product and process innovation. The United States, with its individualistic liberal IPE perspective, has for years been especially strong in product innovation. U.S. firms invent new products, develop them for the home market, and eventually export some of their production to other countries with similar needs.

Other nations, however, such as Japan, have shown greater success in process innovation. They find better ways to make existing products, often improving the basic goods in the process. As process innovation is applied, production is shifted abroad from U.S. factories. The new producer may be an especially innovative firm in Japan, or it could be a low-cost producer in a Newly

Industrialized Country (NIC) or Less Developed Country (LDC), especially if innovation has standardized the product and simplified its construction. The United States then imports at low cost the item it once exported.

One of the most famous examples of the product life cycle is the videocassette recorder (VCR). VCR technology was invented by a U.S. firm to provide recording facilities for television stations. European and Japanese firms took this product, designed for a limited market, and used process innovation skills to create the mass market electronic device we know today.

Once upon a time, it was probably enough to be successful in product innovation—new products could be produced, supplying profits and jobs for years and years. Today, however, with the rapid pace of technological change and the speed with which new ideas are diffused around the globe, process innovation has become perhaps the more important technological advantage.

Creating Comparative Advantage

The post–World War II Japanese experience and the more recent experience of the Asian "Tigers"—Hong Kong, South Korea, Taiwan, and Singapore—demonstrate the ability of nations to create comparative advantage in the production of high value-added goods. Unwilling to accept their "natural" role in the world economy as producers of unskilled labor-intensive goods, these nations have, through partnerships between government and business, developed their technology base sufficiently to become producers and exporters of high-technology goods and services. These countries have all invested in the educational infrastructure necessary to support high-tech production. They have also acquired technology from foreign sources and have developed their own capability to create new process and, to a lesser extent, product innovation. Firms in these countries now compete head to head for world market share in high value-added goods with U.S. and European firms.[9]

The transfer of technology from developed-country firms played a key role in the success of Japan and the Asian Tigers. Many developing countries are eager to follow this same path to development. Whether or not this model will succeed in Latin America, Africa, and Eastern Europe remains to be seen, but the transfer of technology will be a dominant issue in international political economy for some time to come. Clearly, firms within the developed countries own and control most of the technology that is so vital to international competition and the future of less developed countries. A technological leader among developed nations, the United States has, understandably, taken the lead in defining the terms and conditions under which the transfer of technology will occur.

THE IPE OF TECHNOLOGY AND INTELLECTUAL PROPERTY RIGHTS (IPRs)

If we stop for a moment and look back over the last few pages, an interesting dilemma appears. Knowledge and technology have become increasingly important in the IPE in many ways. With the rapid pace of technological change, new products and new processes are especially valuable to individuals, business firms, and nations because of the wealth and power that derive from them. To gain the maximum advantage, however, one needs to control access to new knowledge and technology—to keep others from using the products of research and innovation without paying in full for the right. At the same time, however, the computer and communications revolutions are making it easier and more efficient to move information around, making the control of access harder and harder. In short, precisely when the control of technology is of greatest value, it has become much more difficult and cumbersome.

It is unsurprising, given all the potential wealth and power that are at stake here, that the control of information has become a very important issue in international political economy. The vocabulary of this part of IPE is somewhat technical, but the issues are important enough to make learning the new terms worthwhile. What is at stake, after all, is the technological future.

The key concept in the IPE of the knowledge structure today is *Intellectual Property Rights (IPR)*. *Property rights* (generic term) are the rights to control the use of something, such as a house, or car, or a book. It is possible to make markets in these things because their property rights are well defined and well enforced. That is, it is possible to determine who owns a house and who doesn't, and a person who uses a house that belongs to someone else without first concluding a bargain will be punished. We can feel secure in our ownership of everyday goods because this system of property rights works relatively well.

Intellectual property rights are the rights to control use of intellectual property—an invention, or creative work such as a novel or poem. Patents, copyrights, trademarks, and other systems of intellectual property rights are the mechanisms normally used to control access to new ideas. Intellectual property rights are most effective when the state defines and enforces them strictly. This creates a problem, however, since there are many different states which may have many different rules regarding intellectual property rights. The inventor of a new process may be unable to stop a firm in another country from using his or her ideas if that country has less strict rules regarding patents, for example.

Intellectual property rights have thus become a critical issue for both those nations that own patents, copyrights, and so on, and those nations that seek to use them to produce goods and earn incomes. One goal of the Uruguay round of the GATT negotiations was to reach some agreement regarding intellectual property rights, but there is still much progress to be made on this front.

THREE PERSPECTIVES ON INTELLECTUAL PROPERTY RIGHTS

In the liberal view, property rights are fundamental to the functioning of a market system. Property rights create a powerful incentive to use resources efficiently. Property rights establish a direct link between effort and reward.

A privately owned farm, for example, is efficiently operated because the owner of the farm is legally entitled to all of the income that farm generates. The farmer strives to maximize the productivity of his land in order to maximize his own income. Now imagine a farm where property rights are not private and individually held, as in the farm above, but are collective or socially owned. On this farm there would be no direct link between effort and reward. A farm worker who was very diligent and hard-working would not have the right to any more of the farm's output than another worker who shirked and was a *freerider.*

Clearly, there is less incentive for individuals to work hard under the system of collective property rights than under the system of private property rights. The private farm would be much more productive and efficient. Similarly, individuals and firms have a powerful incentive to innovate and invent when they are legally entitled to the income associated with that process. Intellectual property rights—patents, trademarks, and copyrights—create the link between effort and reward.

Invention and innovation (commercialization of an invention) involve the creation of knowledge. And knowledge, by its nature, is nonrival. That is, the knowledge one firm uses can also be used by other firms. (By contrast, the ton of steel that one firm uses cannot also be used by other firms. Steel is a rival good.) The knowledge that one firm develops in the form of product and process innovation can also be used by other firms. Consequently, unless firms can legally deny the use of newly created knowledge to other firms, rapid imitation will eliminate the profits from innovation necessary to recoup the original investment in Research and Development (R&D) that created the new knowledge. The efforts necessary to develop new technology would not be rewarded. Without intellectual property rights, insufficient resources would be devoted to R&D, and far fewer new and lower-cost products would be available to consumers.

From the liberal perspective, then, international protection of IPRs is essential if the world market economy is to enjoy the extraordinary benefits of rapid technological growth. International IPR conventions should be strengthened to guarantee the effective protection of technological innovation. The winners in this process will ultimately be consumers the world over who will enjoy the availability of an astonishing variety of new products—from genetically engineered foodstuffs and medicines to educational and entertainment multimedia software. The only real losers will be those firms and individuals who will no longer profit from copying the creative, innovative efforts of others.

Mercantilists see the process of technological innovation in a much different light. Knowledge is a source of national wealth and power. Recall, according to this school of thought discussed in chapter 2, that production, not consumption, is critical to the national interest. The ability to produce is the true measure of a nation's wealth and power. Technology, then, the knowledge of production, largely determines a nation's place in the world. Nations must develop and then closely guard their own technology, and technology controlled by other nations must be acquired. Technological dependence must be avoided.

The protection of IPRs for *domestic* firms is clearly appropriate in order to foster domestic technological innovation. Equal protection for technology owned by foreign firms, however, is unlikely to be in the national interest. Rather, government policy in this area should facilitate the acquisition of foreign-owned technology at the lowest cost possible. Increased international protection of IPRs is, then, not necessarily in the national interest. Protecting intellectual property of national firms in domestic and foreign markets is appropriate, but reciprocal protection for foreign firms in domestic markets should be resisted—recall that trade is, according to this view, a zero-sum game. One nation's gains in international market share come at the expense of some other nation's losses. The battle for markets will be won by the nation that can best exploit its technological advantages.

An additional insight provided by mercantilist thought regards imbalances in stages of national development. List and Hamilton, early mercantilists, argued that free trade benefits the most developed manufacturing nation(s) at the expense of less developed nations. Similarly, international conventions that protect intellectual property rights will benefit those nations with the most advanced technological capabilities at the expense of less technologically developed nations. In this regard, mercantilist and structuralist thought is similar.

Structuralists contend that IPRs increase the dependency of the periphery on the core. IPRs are tools of dependency. The developed nations use IPRs to maintain their technological advantage over Third World countries. Patents, trademarks, and copyrights are used to monopolize Third World markets, to extract and repatriate excessive profits from Third World countries, and to deepen and legitimate dependency.

From the point of view of dependency theorists, then, the winners from more stringent international enforcement of IPRs are clearly the developed countries and their firms. The losers are the people of Third World countries who pay monopoly prices for many goods and services and who receive the benefits of technological transfer only on terms dictated by firms of the developed world. We will consider further the North-South aspects of IPRs in a later section of this chapter. First, it is appropriate to review the efforts of the United States to protect IPRs and then consider the degree of cooperation and conflict among developed countries regarding IPRs.

U.S. EFFORTS TO PROTECT INTELLECTUAL PROPERTY RIGHTS

> The increased significance of technological diffusion and the increasingly arbitrary nature of comparative advantage as well as military security concerns are causing the United States to make the protection of its high technology industries an important priority. In addition to its own effort to slow down the outflow of industrial know-how, the U.S. has placed the international protection of intellectual property rights on the agenda of trade negotiations.[10]
>
> Robert Gilpin

U.S. firms have played a major role in elevating the protection of Intellectual Property Rights (IPRs) to the status of a major U.S. foreign policy issue. The Intellectual Property Committee, an ad hoc coalition of 12 major U.S. corporations representing the entire spectrum of industries, was established in 1986 with the goal of increasing the international protection of IPRs.[11]

The Intellectual Property Committee contends there is a direct link between the protection of IPRs and U.S. international competitiveness. Without adequate protection of IPRs, U.S. firms would find it difficult to profit from product and process innovation. Foreign firms that infringe on IPRs have lower development costs, since they are merely copying original technological innovations. Consequently, these infringing firms can underprice the U.S. firms that incurred the original development costs. A new generation of semiconductors can cost $100 million or more to develop, and yet these same chips can be copied for less than $1 million. A popular software package that sells for $500 in the United States has been copied and sold for as little as $7.50 in foreign countries.[12] Piracy of U.S. entertainment media, including tape recordings and video tapes, has become epidemic in many parts of the world. The U.S. International Trade Commission has estimated that the overall loss to U.S. business from foreign infringement of IPRs in 1986 alone was between $43 billion and $61 billion.[13] Responding to pressure from U.S. businesses, the U.S. government has attempted to increase the international protection of IPRs through unilateral, bilateral, and multilateral means.

Under U.S. trade law, the government can impose unilateral retaliatory trade sanctions against countries that fail to adequately protect IPRs. Special Section 301 of the 1988 Omnibus Trade and Competition Act, generally called Super 301, requires the United States Trade Representative (USTR) to retaliate against countries that "deny adequate and effective protection of intellectual property rights" or "deny fair and equitable market access to United States persons that rely upon intellectual property protection."[14] Super 301 requires the USTR to create a list every year of priority foreign countries that have failed to adequately protect IPRs. After investigating the acts, practices, and policies of the offending country, the USTR may institute immediate trade sanctions, including the elimination of trade concessions and the imposition of import restrictions or duties. Or the USTR may choose to negotiate a bilateral agreement with the offending country to eliminate the cause of the action.

In 1989, the USTR identified no priority countries. Instead, a watch list was created, of 25 countries "whose practices deserve special attention." Eight countries—Brazil, India, Republic of Korea, Mexico, People's Republic of China, Saudi Arabia, Taiwan, and Thailand—were placed on a priority watch list as countries that formally met the criteria of priority foreign countries, but that were making satisfactory progress in bilateral and multilateral negotiations to address shortcomings in the protection of IPRs.[15]

On May 1, 1998, for example, Charlene Barshefsky, the USTR, announced the results of that year's review process. Bulgaria, Israel, Macao, Argentina, Ecuador, Egypt, the European Union, Greece, India, Indonesia, Russia, Turkey, Italy, Dominican Republic, and Kuwait were placed on the priority watch list and 32 other countries were included on the watch list.[16]

Section 337 of the Tariff Act of 1930 as amended by the Omnibus Trade and Competitiveness Act is designed to eliminate the importation into the United States of goods that infringe on IPRs. Under the amended Section 337, the complainant must merely demonstrate that an infringement of an IPR occurred rather than substantial injury, as the original law required. The International Trade Commission can issue an exclusion order or a cease and desist order in response to complaints.[17]

The unilateral trade sanctions made possible by U.S. trade laws have been criticized by its trading partners as violations of GATT (and now WTO) provisions. In fact, Section 337 has been challenged before a GATT tribunal.[18] U.S. efforts to negotiate bilateral agreements to improve the protection of IPRs are much less controversial.

With the stick of unilateral trade sanctions firmly in hand, the United States has been quite successful in negotiating bilateral agreements with many countries to improve the protection of IPRs. Negotiated changes in the treatment of IPRs have occurred in several countries, including Singapore, Malaysia, Thailand, the People's Republic of China, Taiwan, and South Korea. Bilateral disputes and negotiations continue between the United States and Brazil, India, Thailand, Japan, and the European Union.[19]

In 1991, while negotiating the North American Free Trade Agreement (NAFTA) with the United States, Mexico enacted comprehensive patent and copyright laws. The final NAFTA agreement "locks in" these Mexican reforms. As a result of the NAFTA negotiations, Mexico will now give copyright protection to software programs, satellite transmissions, and audio and video recordings. Better patent protection and protection of trade secrets and proprietary information in Mexico and Canada are also major accomplishments of NAFTA.[20]

The 12 U.S. firms that constitute the Intellectual Property Committee urged U.S. trade negotiators to place the protection of IPRs on the agenda for the Uruguay round of the GATT negotiations. The multilateral approach (described below) to the international enforcement of IPRs had, in the opinion of these U.S. firms, largely failed to provide adequate protection. More effective enforcement of IPRs, it was hoped, could be negotiated by linking the protection of IPRs to multilateral trade negotiation.

Multilateral agreements to protect IPRs include the Berne Convention, concluded in 1886 to define copyright protection, and the Paris Convention signed by the United States in 1887, which ostensibly provides protection for patents, trademarks, and industrial designs. In 1967, the World Intellectual Property Organization (WIPO), a United Nations agency, was created to monitor adherence to the Berne and Paris conventions. WIPO has been roundly criticized by firms in developed nations because its defined minimum standards of protection are inadequate and because it lacks effective enforcement and dispute resolution mechanisms. Developed country firms are pessimistic that WIPO will ever provide meaningful IPR protection because the policy and agenda of this United Nations agency are controlled by developing countries that, arguably, generally oppose IPR reforms.[21] We will explore developing country attitudes toward IPR protection later in this chapter.

The GATT agreement concluded in 1993 did include, at the insistence of the United States and other developed nations, provisions regarding Trade-Related Intellectual Property Rights (TRIPs). TRIP negotiations centered on effective enforcement of IPRs, on the definition of multilateral dispute resolution mechanisms, and on acceptable minimum standards of national protection.[22] These provisions have become part of the fundamental structure of the WTO, which succeeded the GATT as the forum for multilateral trade negotiations. Special concessions were also negotiated for developing countries that need time to create or amend IPR laws in order to conform to the minimum standards that will be required as a condition for their continued participation in the WTO's multilateral trade negotiations.[23]

COOPERATION AND CONFLICT AMONG INDUSTRIALIZED COUNTRIES

The developed nations of the world have, not surprisingly, supported the efforts spearheaded by the United States to enhance the international protection of IPRs, including the inclusion of TRIPs. Current discussions are underway within WIPO to enhance protection of performers, producers of sound recordings, and broadcasters. Enhanced trademark protection in the form of the Madrid Protocol is also under discussion.[24] There has also been a concerted effort among these nations to reach agreements to "harmonize" IPR laws across national boundaries.

One example of the need for harmonization involves the issue of "first to file" versus "first to invent" with respect to the awarding of patent rights. The United States finds itself at odds with most other countries by granting patents on a "first to invent" basis. In Japan, Sankyo, a Japanese firm, was granted the patent on a new anticholesterol drug, whereas in the United States, Merck, a U.S. firm, was granted a patent on the same drug. Merck was able to verify prior invention even though Sankyo had been the first to file in both countries.[25] This kind of conflict will be avoided when developed countries succeed in "harmonizing" IPR laws.

In December 1996, a diplomatic conference convened by WIPO produced two new treaties that harmonize the protection of IPRs on the Internet and thereby promote international electronic commerce. The WIPO Copyright Treaty supplements the Berne Convention by clarifying that the digital transmission and the distribution of literary or artistic works will receive copyright protection. This treaty also reconciles differences between the United States and European copyright protection systems. A second treaty, the WIPO Treaty on Performances and Phonograms, represents the first global efforts to protect sound recordings from exploitation by means other than simple physical reproduction.[26]

Although developed countries are cooperating in important ways, conflict between and among them over IPRs still exists to a significant degree. The basis of competitive advantage among developed countries in high-technology industries is knowledge.[27] Patterns of trade reflect the success national firms have had in developing new products and processes. And the success of national firms depends in large measure on the national organization of competition and policy toward knowledge creation.[28] Disputes among developed nations involving the treatment of intellectual property are to be expected given the centrality of knowledge and technology to competitive advantage. Conflict over the treatment of IPRs between Japan and the United States has been particularly serious in the past and continues to be a major foreign policy concern for both countries.

In the mid-1980s, the U.S. government, in response to its trade deficit with Japan, instituted bilateral trade talks with the Japanese called the market-oriented, sector-specific talks, designed to increase U.S. access to Japanese markets. These discussions in the case of electronics focused on the protection of U.S. technology, particularly semiconductor chip design and software created in the United States. As a result of these talks, the Japanese did adopt legislation extending 50-year copyright protection for software and 10-year protection for original chip design, thereby bringing Japanese practices into harmony with U.S. standards.[29]

In the late 1990s, however, the United States continued to blame its ongoing huge trade deficit with Japan largely on Japan's discriminatory treatment of IPRs. Whereas the U.S. grants exclusivity to Japanese innovators, thereby allowing them to develop strong brand names and market niches in the United States, according to Assistant Secretary of Commerce and Commissioner of Patents and Trademarks Bruce Lehman, U.S. firms are denied true exclusivity in Japan. According to Lehman, "If U.S. companies are fortunate enough to survive the gauntlet and the years of delay of the Japanese Patent Office, the most they can hope for—given the Japanese system of dependent patents—is royalty revenue from their Japanese competitors, rather than the true exclusivity which is necessary to open that market to competition."[30] Japan's discrimination against U.S. firms is certainly a clear example of the mercantilist approach to IPRs. Japan has been placed on the Super 301 watch list (discussed earlier in this chapter) because it is suspected of not adequately enforcing IPRs.

One would expect that Japan will at some point adopt a more liberal attitude toward IPR protection, either in response to U.S. and European pressure or in the realization that a more liberal approach both befits and benefits a major technologically advanced trading nation.

PATENTING LIFE—THE INTERNATIONAL HARMONIZATION OF BIOTECHNOLOGY PROTECTION

In April 1988, a white mouse made history by becoming the first animal ever to be patented in the United States. The "Harvard mouse," as it is known, was developed by Philip Leder of Harvard University and his colleague Timothy Stewart, now at Genentech, Inc., using genetic engineering. They "invented" the extraordinary mouse by inserting a human cancer gene into mouse egg cells. The mouse satisfied the requirements for protection as an invention under U.S. patent law because of its novelty and its usefulness in cancer research.

Microbes, plants, and, lately, other animals have also received patent protection from the U.S. Patent Office. In response to pressure from the United States and from its own biotechnology industry, the European Union is currently considering proposals to create comparable biotechnology protection. Developing countries are also being pressured by the United States to extend IPR protection to biotechnology via bilateral negotiations and multilateral negotiations under the GATT agreement.[a]

Many countries offer very limited protection, if any, for biotechnology because the agricultural, pharmaceutical, and medical products and processes that result from biotechnological innovation are considered fundamental rights and needs of the people. About 35 countries offer no patent protection for food products, among them Denmark, Brazil, China, Finland, Colombia, Egypt, New Zealand, and Venezuela. Animal and plant varieties are excluded from patent protection in 45 countries, including the EU member countries, Brazil, Canada, Ghana, Colombia, Cuba, Israel, Kenya, Malaysia, Nigeria, South Africa, Switzerland, and Thailand.[b] Many countries offer only process patents for pharmaceutical products, intending to create a powerful incentive for rival firms to develop different processes to produce the new and unpatented product. The reduced level of patent protection for biotechnology in many countries also reflects to some degree their greater reliance on government-sponsored, university biotechnology research, which does not require patent incentives.

The efforts of the U.S. government to increase the international protection of biotechnology arises from political pressure brought to bear by U.S. biotechnology firms that want to protect their competitive advantage in international markets. Many other developed and developing country governments are also beginning to feel the same pressures from their own budding biotechnology industries. But there are many thorny issues associated with the protection of biotechnology that must be resolved before international harmonization can occur.

The primary controversial issue has been whether or not living organisms are patentable. In the 1980s, the U.S. Supreme Court handed down several key decisions (in 1980 for an engineered microorganism; in 1985 for a maize plant and its components; and in 1988 for the aforementioned mouse) that set new precedents in this regard. The issue, according to the Court in the 1980 case, is not living versus nonliving but rather products of nature, living or not, versus human interventions.[c] Presumably, products of nature are not patentable, whereas products of human intervention may be. Although this legal issue appears to be resolved in the United States, many other controversial legal, technical, economic, and ethical issues remain.

If the international harmonization of biotechnology protection can be accomplished, great benefits might be forthcoming. A farmer anywhere in the world might buy a seed that has a U.S. company's disease resistance gene, an Egyptian company's drought resistance gene, and a Brazilian company's nutritional enhancement gene. Of course, the consequences of harmonization will likely be very different when viewed from a mercantilist or structuralist perspective.

---

[a] John A. Barton, "Patenting Life," *Scientific American* 264 (March 1991), p. 41.
[b] Bifani, "The International Stakes of Biotechnology and the Patent War: Considerations after the Uruguay Round," p. 48.
[c] Ibid., p. 50.

NORTH-SOUTH CONFLICTS OVER INTELLECTUAL PROPERTY RIGHTS

Many developing nations opposed the TRIP provisions of the WTO. They argued that WIPO was the appropriate forum for discussing the norms and standards of IPRs. And, more fundamentally, they argued that the efforts by the United States and other developed countries to strengthen the international protection of IPRs has focused on the enhancement of the proprietary aspects of IPRs, thereby reinforcing monopoly privileges, while weakening the aspects of IPRs that promote the prompt and widespread diffusion of new technology.[31] For example, the TRIP provisions broaden the scope and duration of patent protection and therefore of monopoly privilege, while enervating working requirements that foster technological diffusion.

The basic premise of developing nations in granting a patent is that the firm granted the patent will produce the patented product or use the patented process in the country granting the patent.[32] When the patent is "worked" locally, technological spillovers are generated. Scientists, technicians, and engineers in the patent-granting country become familiar with the technology. And, domestic firms may be called on to supply inputs into the production process, thereby upgrading their technological sophistication. As the technology is diffused throughout the domestic economy, it may become the basis for *domestic* technological innovation.

This premise is certainly consistent with the fundamental rationale for patents in any context. Patents represent a trade-off. The innovator is granted an exclusive right to produce the new product or use the new process. In exchange, the new knowledge the innovator has created is disclosed and made public in the patent application process so that others have access to this knowledge and can thereby create additional new knowledge. If patent rights were not available, innovators would attempt to keep new knowledge secret to avoid imitation. Patents and the working of patents facilitate the diffusion and creation of new knowledge.

The Paris Convention states that failure to work a patent is an abuse of patent rights. A compulsory license can be issued to another firm to guarantee local production. Firms from developed countries have argued that imports of the patented product or the product made with the patented process constitute working the patent. Developing countries have long opposed this notion. From their point of view, imports do not generate the same spillover benefits that domestic production would. Imports do not result in the transfer of technology— only local production accomplishes that.[33] Some analysts have gone so far as to oppose the creation of patent systems in developing countries on this basis. The granting of patents by developing countries, they argue, is akin to granting exclusive import rights to certain foreign firms allowing them to monopolize the local market and eliminate other (especially local) firms.[34] However, against the protests of many developing nations, the United States and other developed nations prevailed. The WTO rules expressly permits imports to constitute the working of a patent.[35]

The South Commission argued forcefully, but ultimately unsuccessfully, that the inclusion of IPRs under the GATT would have "significant adverse effects on the pace of generation, absorption, adaptation and assimilation of technical change in the developing countries."[36] C. Niranjan Rao summarized the sentiment of many critics of the TRIPs provisions of the WTO/GATT agreement as follows:

> By asking for a GATT based agreement on IPRs, the developed countries are seeking to bring in a system which fits into their trade strategies and preserves their technological superiority. These proposals are much tougher and pro-patentee than the Paris Convention. Such an agreement, given the concentration of ownership of patents in large multinational corporations from highly developed countries, will make the third world free playground for the trade and investment decisions of these MNCs.[37]

An additional area of contention between developed and developing countries concerns copyright protection. The developed countries, led by the United States, have recently been demanding stronger international copyright protection. The mind-set of developing countries in this regard can be best understood by considering the historical role of the United States in international copyright protection. Early on, the United States was more a consumer of works produced by foreign authors than a producer for foreign markets. Consequently, the United States refused to sign the Berne Copyright Agreement or even respect foreign copyrights until forced to do so by the growth of its own artistic and literary community. In fact, the United States did not sign the Berne Agreement until 1989. The United States, then, is a "Johnny-come-lately" when it comes to the international enforcement of copyright protection.[38]

Even though most developing countries are also consumers of works by foreign authors and artists more than producers of these works for other countries, they are being pressured by the United States and other developed countries to respect foreign copyrights.

There are no guarantees that developing countries will benefit from strengthening their systems of IPR protection. However, for those countries attempting to follow outward-oriented development strategies, the risk of trade retaliation and the need to attract foreign direct investment provide strong incentives to comply with developed country demands for stronger IPR protection.[39]

ASIAN DEVELOPING COUNTRIES—TIGERS OR COPYCATS?

"Ralph Lauren" polo shirts sell for $4 in Bangkok and "Rolex" watches (that have a wrist-life of six months) cost $8 each. Pirated video and audio tapes, sometimes with misspelled names, are available by the truckload at very low prices. Walt Disney released the film *Aladdin* in the United States in November 1992, and pirated copies were on sale in Bangkok within two weeks. In May 1993, Microsoft found pirated versions of MS-DOS 6 on sale in Singapore before the product's official release in the United States.[a] The worldwide sales of pirated compact discs doubled to 73 million from 1992 to 1993 primarily because of unauthorized production in China.[b]

The International Intellectual Property Alliance, noted in the text, estimates that U.S. companies lost $2 billion in potential sales in 1992 to the ten worst-offending Asian countries. This figure may well underestimate the loss because some imitations are very hard to distinguish from the real thing. Microsoft's own managers could not identify pirated copies of their Windows and MS-DOS products sold in Taiwan. Even the hologram placed on the software to prohibit copying had been counterfeited by a university in China.[c]

Inadequate protection of trademarks is probably the most important violation of intellectual property.[d] A trademark is a sign or symbol (including logos and names) registered by a manufacturer or merchant to identify goods and services. Protection is usually granted for ten years and is renewable as long as the trademark is effectively used.

In a broader sense, trademarks are essential for the efficient functioning of the market. Trademarks convey information and protect investments in the production of quality goods and services. Trademarks help consumers select products of high quality and reliability. Consumers come to rely on trademarked products. Consequently, search costs are reduced. Trademarks also motivate producers to maintain quality standards. Producers who do so know they will be rewarded with repeat purchases by consumers who have come to trust their trademark. Without adequate trademark protection, then, consumers will necessarily spend more hours attempting to discern quality differences, and producers will be discouraged from investing in the production of quality goods and services.

Copyrights protect the expression of an idea, not the idea itself. Copyright protection is provided to authors of original works, including literary, artistic, and scientific works. Software and databases are also afforded copyright protection in a growing number of developed and developing countries. Copyrights generally allow the owner to prevent the unauthorized reproduction, distribution (including rental), sale, and adaptation of original work. Protection lasts for the life of the author plus 50 years.[e] Copyrights, like patents, are necessary to encourage innovation. Without this protection, rapid reproduction by rivals would diminish the return on investment in the creation of new computer software, computerized databases, literary, artistic, or scientific work.

Intense pressure is being brought to bear by the United States on Asian countries to increase their protection of trademarks and copyrights. Thailand, for example, was listed as a "priority foreign country" by the United States Trade Representative in 1992 (under Super 301 provisions as described in the text) and therefore is subject to retaliatory trade sanctions. Thailand fired the official in charge of the enforcement of intellectual property rights on April 20, 1993, and launched a series of raids on counterfeiters resulting in public burnings of pirated materials as the April 30 deadline approached for the USTR's new watch lists.[f]

China made a substantial formal commitment to copyright protection in October 1992 by issuing regulations to protect foreign works consistent with the requirements of the Berne Copyright Convention. But, over the ensuing years, China's inability or unwillingess to actually enforce copyright and other IPR protections led the United States to threaten the imposition of 100 percent tariffs on more than $1 billion of Chinese imports if a satisfactory bilateral enforcement agreement could not be reached by February 26, 1995. On that very date, the USTR announced that such an agreement had been reached, thereby averting a crisis in U.S.- Chinese relations. China is currently designated by the USTR for "Section 306 monitoring" to ensure that it complies with IPR enforcement commitments it has made to the United States Section 306 of the Trade Act of 1974, as amended, allows the USTR to impose trade sanctions if such commitments are not met. Since 1996 China has shut down 64 CD production lines and largely reduced the export of IPR-protected products. China has imprisoned more than 800 individuals as a result of illegal IPR piracy activities. But the current USTR, Charlene Barshefsky, has stated that China still needs to decrease its illegal importation of CD and VCD products, as well as crack down on illegal reproduction of software products, retail piracy, and trademark counterfeiting.[g]

---

[a] "Caveat Vendor," *Economist* 1 May 1993, p. 33.
[b] "Worldwide Pirate Disc Sales Double to 75m," *Financial Times* 2 June 1994, p. 4.
[c] "Caveat Vendor," p. 33.
[d] Carlos M. Correa, *Intellectual Property Rights and Foreign Direct Investment* (New York: United Nations Publication ST/CTC/ERS.A/24, 1993), p. 14.
[e] Ibid., p. 8.
[f] "Caveat Vendor," p. 33.
[g] "USTR Announces Results of Special 301 Annual Review," Office of the United States Trade Representative, May 1, 1998. Online. Internet. Available: http://www.ustr.gov/releases/1998/05/98-44.pdf (26 August 1998).

CONCLUSION

The issues surrounding the development and control of knowledge and technology clearly play a central role in international political economy. Whether viewed from a liberal, mercantilist, or structuralist perspective, knowledge and technology form an increasingly critical basis of wealth and power. In this era of global competition, individuals, firms, and nations understand that knowledge and technology confer competitive advantage. That the protection of intellectual property rights has risen to the status of a major foreign policy concern for the United States and many other countries is not surprising. The knowledge structure, like the production structure, the finance structure, and the security structure, clearly constrains the options and conditions the behavior of individuals, firms, and nations, and therefore affects the wealth and power they enjoy.

DISCUSSION QUESTIONS

1. What are Intellectual Property Rights (IPRs) and why are they important in today's global markets? Briefly compare and contrast the mercantilist, liberal, and structuralist views of IPRs.
2. What three trends have become apparent over the last 20 years regarding the role of knowledge and technology in IPE? Explain.
3. Trade-Related Intellectual Property Rights (TRIPs) were a controversial issue raised in the GATT's Uruguay round. Explain what TRIPs are and discuss briefly the issues raised in these GATT negotiations.
4. Discuss the product life cycle phenomenon, with emphasis on the role of technology and knowledge in this process. What issues regarding IPRs are raised by the product life cycle business pattern? Explain.
5. Describe any two elements of the U.S. Trade Law the United States uses unilaterally to enforce intellectual property rights.

INTERNET LINKS

WTO Intellectual Property Page:
  http://www.wto.org/wto/intellec/intellec.htm
World Intellectual Property Organization:
  http://www.wipo.org/

SUGGESTED READINGS

Paolo Bifani. "The International Stakes of Biotechnology and the Patent War: Considerations after the Uruguay Round," *Agriculture and Human Values* (Spring 1993).

Carol J. Bilzi, Esq. "Towards an Intellectual Property Agreement in the GATT: View from the Private Sector," *Georgia Journal of International and Comparative Law* 19:2(1989).

John T. Masterson, Jr., "Intellectual Property Rights: A Post Uruguay Round Overview." Office of the Chief Counsel for International Commerce, U.S. Department of Commerce, April 20, 1998. Online. Internet. Available: http://www.ita.doc.gov/legal/ipr.html (26 August 1998).

Michael Porter. *The Competitive Advantage of Nations*. New York: Free Press, 1990.

C. Niranjan Rao. "Trade Related Aspects of Intellectual Property Rights: Question of Patents," *Economic and Political Weekly*, 13 May 1989.

Brent W. Sadler. "Intellectual Property Protection through International Trade," *Houston Journal of International Law* 14:393(1992).

W. E. Siebeck, ed. *Strengthening Protection of IP in Developing Countries: A Survey of the Literature*. World Bank Discussion Paper no. 112, Washington, DC, 1990.

Susan Strange. *States and Markets: An Introduction to International Political Economy*. New York: Basil Blackwell, 1988.

Laura D'Andrea Tyson. *Who's Bashing Whom?: Trade Conflict in High-Technology Industries*. Washington, DC: The Institute for International Economics, 1992.

NOTES

1. Friedrich List, *The National System of Political Economy* (New York: August M. Kelley, 1966), pp. 201–202.
2. Paul Kennedy, *Preparing for the Twenty-first Century* (New York: Random House, 1993), p. 15.
3. Robert Reich, *The Work of Nations* (New York: Knopf, 1991).

4. Ibid., pp. 177–180.
5. Patents are issued by a government conferring the exclusive right to make, use, or sell an invention for a period generally ranging from 15 to 20 years (counted from date of filing). Trademarks are signs or symbols (including logos and names) registered by a manufacturer or merchant to identify goods and services. Protection is usually granted for 10 years and is renewable. Copyrights protect the expression of an idea, not the idea itself. Copyright protection is provided to authors of original works of authorship, including literary, artistic, and scientific works. Copyrights are also issued for software and databases in a growing number of countries. Copyrights prohibit unauthorized reproduction, distribution (including rental), sale, and adaptation of original work. Protection lasts for the life of the author, plus 50 years. For more detailed descriptions of these and other intellectual property rights, see Carlo M. Correa, *Intellectual Property Rights and Foreign Direct Investment* (New York: United Nations, Publication ST/CTC/SER.A/24, 1993), pp. 8–9.
6. Thomas D. Lairson and David Skidmore, *International Political Economy* (Orlando, FL: Harcourt Brace Jovanovich College Publishers, 1993).
7. Susan Strange, "An Eclectic Approach," in Craig Murphy and Roger Tooze, eds, *The New International Political Economy* (Boulder, CO: Lynne Rienner Publishers, 1991).
8. Edward F. Denison, *Trends in American Economic Growth, 1929–1982* (Washington, DC: Brookings, 1985), p. 30.
9. This is one theme of Lester Thurow's best-selling book, *Head to Head: The Coming Economic Battle among Japan, Europe, and America* (New York: William & Morrow, 1991).
10. Robert Gilpin, *The Political Economy of Intentional Relations* (Princeton, NJ: Princeton University Press, 1987).
11. Carol J. Bilzi, Esq., "Towards an Intellectual Property Agreement in the GATT: View from the Private Sector," *Georgia Journal of International and Comparative Law* 19:2(1989), p. 343.
12. Ibid., p. 345
13. Richard A. Morford, "Intellectual Property Protection: A US Priority," *Georgia Journal of International and Comparative Law* 19:2(1989), p. 336.
14. Omnibus Trade and Competitiveness Act of 1988, tit. I, subtit. C, pt. 1, § 1303, Pub. L. No. 100–418, 102 Stat. 1179–81 (codified at 19 S.S.C. § 2242 [1992]).
15. Brent W. Sadler, "International Property Protection through International Trade," *Houston Journal of International Law* 14:393(1992), p. 416.
16. "USTR Announces Results of Special 301 Annual Review." Office of the United States Trade Representative, May 1, 1998. Online. Internet. Available: http://www.ustr.gov/releases/1998/05/98-44.pdf (26 August 1998).
17. Sadler, "International Property Protection through International Trade," p. 408.
18. Ibid.
19. See the International Trade Administration's (U. S. Commerce Department) trade agreement database for succinct summaries of the many bilateral and multilateral trade agreements the United States has negotiated over the last two decades at: http://www.mac.doc.gov/tcc/treaty.htm.
20. Gary Clyde Hufbauer and Jeffrey J. Schott, *NAFTA: An Assessment* (Washington, DC: Institute for International Economics, 1993), p. 85.
21. Sadler, "Intellectual Property Protection through International Trade," p. 401.
22. Critics of the TRIPs proposal argue that the effort to impose new international uniform standards at higher levels for IPR protection contradicts the GATT's traditional commitment to the principle of national treatment. By requiring reciprocity, the TRIPs proposal would violate existing GATT provisions that refer to the nonreciprocity of trade relationships between developed and developing countries. See Paolo Bifani, "The International Stakes of Biotechnology and the Patent War: Considerations after the Uruguay Round," *Agriculture and Human Values* (Spring 1993), p. 56.
23. Bilzi, "Toward an Intellectual Property Agreement in the GATT," p. 346.

24. Bruce Lehman, Assistant Secretary of Commerce and Commissioner of Patents and Trademarks, remarks before the Section of Patent, Trademark and Copyright Law, American Bar Association, New York, 10 August 1993, p. 6.

25. Dennis W. Carlton and Jeffrey M. Perloff, *Modern Industrial Organization,*2d ed. (New York: HarperCollins, 1994), p. 675.

26. *Chair's Bulletin*, American Bar Association Section of Intellectual Property Law, Vol. 1, No. 5, January 1997.

27. Laura D'Andrea Tyson, *Who's Bashing Whom?: Trade Conflict in High Technology Industries* (Washington, DC: Institute for International Economics, 1992), p. 18.

28. See Michael E. Porter, *The Competitive Advantage of Nations* (New York: Free Press, 1990) for a discussion of how differences in national organization of competition and policies toward knowledge creation affect competitive position in international trade and investment.

29. Tyson, *Who's Bashing Whom*, p. 59.

30. Bruce A. Lehman, remarks before the American Bar Association, p. 5.

31. Ibid., pp. 55–56.

32. C. Niranjan Rao, "Trade Related Aspects of Intellectual Property Rights; Question of Patents," *Economic and Political Weekly*, 13 May 1989, p. 1053.

33. Ibid., p. 1055.

34. See R. Vayrynen, "International Patenting as a Means of Technological Dominance," *International Social Science Journal* 30 (1978), pp. 315–337.

35. John T. Masterson, Jr., "Intellectual Property Rights: A Post Uruguay Round Overview." Office of the Chief Counsel for International Commerce, U.S. Department of Commerce, April 20, 1998, Online. Internet. Available: http://www.ita.doc.gov/legal/ipr.html (26 August 1998).

36. Rao, "Trade Related Aspects of Intellectual Property Rights," p. 1056.

37. Ibid.

38. Lewis Shapiro, "The Role of Intellectual Property Protection and International Competitiveness," *Antitrust Law Journal* 58 (1989), p. 577.

39. C. A. Primo Braza, "The Developing Country Case for and against IPP," in W. E. Siebeck, ed., *Strengthening Protection of IP in Developing Countries: A Survey of the Literature*, World Bank Discussion Paper No. 112.

PART III

State-Market Tensions Today

Part III presents four case studies of IPE analysis: the European Union, NAFTA, Japan, and nations in transition from communism to capitalism. While these studies are informative about four important sets of nations, they are intended to have broader application. Each study poses a particular question or explores a particular theme that applies around the globe. Students are challenged, therefore, to master the specific applications and at the same time appreciate the more general themes that derive from them.

Chapter 11 examines the specific case of economic and political integration in Europe, which was one of the most important IPE events of the twentieth century. This study raises a larger question: Which force is stronger—the political forces that divide nations or the global market forces that unite them? The tension between economics and politics is critical to Europe's development, but it conditions international behavior in all parts of the world.

The North American Free Trade Agreement (NAFTA) is the topic of chapter 12. On the surface, one might expect a good deal of overlap between this chapter and the previous one. NAFTA is also a program of economic and political integration, similar in nature but weaker in degree. The tensions between integrating economies and disintegrating politics exist here, too. But this chapter develops a different theme. Global markets diminish the state's sovereignty and pose something of a challenge to democracy. This tension between market processes and democratic processes is particularly clear in NAFTA but once again has nearly universal application. It is a fundamental tension of IPE.

Readers will learn a lot about Japan and the global IPE in chapter 13. This chapter's discussion of the capitalist developmental state, however, raises broader questions about the roles of states and markets in national development strategies.

Finally, chapter 14's analysis of states and markets in transition focuses specifically on Russia, Central Europe, and China—three regions that are moving from systems of classical socialism to more market-oriented and, in the case of Russia and Central Europe, more democratic systems of political economy. How do such fundamental changes in states and markets interact? Do political reforms encourage economic change or hinder it? How do economic reforms affect political decisions? These questions are critical in Russia, Central Europe, and China but are equally so to a long list of other nations around the world.

11

The European Union: The Economics and Politics of Integration

OVERVIEW

This chapter examines the political economy of economic integration, which is one of the most powerful dynamics of this era in world history. Increasingly, nations are driven to unite their economies for greater efficiency and growth. Integrated markets do not necessarily mean integrated states, however. The fundamental tension between economics and politics is revealed in heightened relief in the process of integration. This chapter examines the IPE of economic integration by looking at its most important example, the integration of Europe.

The European Union formally began life in 1957 as the European Economic Community (EEC), often called the *Common Market*. In the 1980s, the economic element in the group's name was eliminated, creating the *European Community* (EC) or often just "the Community," not so much because the economic function was diminished, but because the political and social functions were growing. In 1993, the name changed again to the *European Union* (EU), further evidence that integration was spreading from the economic sphere to the political and social spheres of European life.

The European Union is the product of over 40 years of political and economic activity aimed at creating a cooperative and growing environment for

Europe. It is, on one hand, arguably the largest and richest unified market in the world—a postwar success story. It is, on the other hand, arguably the weakest of political alliances imaginable, ever on the verge of collapse. The fundamental question that the European Union seeks to answer in our day is whether economics is more important than politics. That is, whether the dynamic individualistic motives of the market matter more than the unifying social values of the nation or state. Significantly, this is still an unanswered question at the start of the twenty-first century.

This chapter presents an interpretive history of economic integration in Europe (chapter 12 examines NAFTA and economic integration in North America). Monetary integration, a complex but important topic, is treated as a boxed case study. The chapter ends in speculation about how the forces of economics and politics will shape Europe's future.

> The European Community, if it were to become politically cohesive, would have the population, resources, economic wealth, technological, and actual and potential military strength to be the preeminent power of the twenty-first century.[1]
>
> Samuel P. Huntington

This chapter explores a powerful IPE theme that is illustrated in the most vivid of colors by the history of Europe in the post-World War II period. How can economic cooperation be used as a *means* to achieve the *end* of peaceful political cooperation? The question is important because peaceful cooperation remains an unfulfilled goal in much of the world where nationalism and division drive peoples apart. The answer will tell us whether the market and economics can solve problems that states and politics cannot.

As we will see, Europe has been perhaps the world's largest science project experiment in testing the hypothesis that economic benefits can reduce political divisions. This is important to Europe, obviously, but the significance extends far beyond Europe's borders. The process of globalization is making the world more economically interdependent. What will be the political consequences of wider and deeper global economic cooperation? This is a question that affects us all and that we can begin to answer it here.

The need to cooperate or avoid conflict was especially obvious in Europe in the twentieth century, the most violent century in history, with much of the violence located on European soil. European nations faced two common enemies: the external threat of the Soviet Union during the Cold War and the internal threat of a return to the divisions and conflicts that created war and instability in Europe in the past. Peaceful cooperation has been necessary in Europe, but it has also been very difficult precisely because of the burden of history and the forces of *nationalism* that drive nations apart and make them suspicious of one another.

Europe has been able to achieve a noteworthy degree of political cooperation and even unity by using economics as a political tool. Europe has used the benefits of economic cooperation to pave the way for political cooperation. In

other words, *economic integration* has been used to create an environment conducive to otherwise impossible acts of *political integration.* The results, as we will
see, have been remarkable, but the challenges to European unity in the post-Cold
War world are perhaps the most difficult since World War II. The question that
we face is whether this theme still holds or whether the logic of European cooperation is breaking down. Can Europe continue to use economic policies to solve
political problems?

The chapter is organized in the following manner. First we briefly survey
the logic of economic integration to see how and why economic cooperation create benefits. This discussion provides the foundation for a historical survey of
the European unity movement, with emphasis on the relationship between economic means and political ends. This survey builds toward the critical questions
facing Europe today.

THE LOGIC OF ECONOMIC INTEGRATION

Economic integration is the process by which a group of nation-states agree to
ignore their national boundaries for at least some economic purposes, creating a
larger and more tightly connected system of markets. There are several degrees
of economic integration that nations can attain. A *Free Trade Area (FTA)* involves
a relatively minimal degree of integration. Nations in a FTA agree to eliminate
tariff barriers to trade for goods and services they produce themselves. Each
nation, however, retains the right to set its own tariff barriers with respect to
products from outside the FTA. The fact that some goods are tariff free in FTA
transactions, but other goods are still subject to differential trade barriers com-
plicates intra-FTA trade and therefore limits the effective degree of integration.

The *North American Free Trade Agreement (NAFTA)* is an example of a
FTA. When NAFTA is fully implemented, goods from the United States, Canada,
and Mexico will be traded freely within the NAFTA borders. Goods from other
countries, however, will be subject to the differential tariff barriers of these three
countries. If, for example, Canada has a lower tariff on French wine than does
the United States, then any shipments of French wine that happen to flow
through Canada to the United States will be subject to an additional tariff upon
entering the United States To be sure that proper tariffs are collected, all goods
will be accompanied by some sort of certificate of origin.

The next level of economic integration is called a *customs union. (Customs* is
another word for a tariff.) Under a custom union, a group of nations agree both
to tariff-free trade within their collective borders and to a common set of external
trade barriers. If NAFTA were to evolve into a customs union, for example, the
United States, Canada, and Mexico would need to agree to a unified set of tariff
barriers that would apply to products from other countries. The Treaty of Rome,
which created the original European Economic Community, was based upon the
idea of a custom union.

The movement to a customs union is an important step in terms of economic and political integration. The nations involved give up some degree of
their sovereignty or national political autonomy, since they can no longer set
their own trade barriers without consulting their economic partners. What they

gain from this is a far greater degree of economic integration. Products flow more easily within a customs union, with no need for border inspections or customs fees because of the unified trade structure. In practice, of course, the elimination of trade barriers is not as complete as theory would suggest, since member nations retain the right to impose some nontariff trade barriers, such as health and safety standards, for example. Still, a customs union is an effective means of increasing market size and stimulating growth and efficiency.

An *economic union* is the final stage of economic and political integration. In an economic union, nontariff barriers are eliminated along with tariff barriers, creating an even more fully integrated market. The degree of integration in an economic union goes further than this, however. Member nations in an economic union agree to four "freedoms" of movement: of goods, services, people, and capital. These four freedoms represent significant limitations on national sovereignty, but they can also have significant effects on economic activity. The European Union, when its current plans are fully implemented, will become an economic union.

The free movement of goods is more complicated than it may seem for it goes beyond the elimination of tariff barriers. Free goods movement requires a variety of governmental health, safety, and other standards and regulations to be "harmonized" so that, at least in theory, a product that can be sold somewhere in the economic union can, in fact, be sold everywhere in it (aside from obvious technical barriers that can prevent sale, such as differences in electrical systems among nations, or the difference between left-hand drive and right-hand drive automobile systems).

Free movement of services is also more complex than it may seem. The service sector of international trade includes many industries, such as banking and finance, traditionally subject to heavy regulation that varies considerably among nations. Free movement of people requires a unified immigration policy, since a person free to enter and work in one member of the economic union would, in theory, be able to live and work anywhere in the area. Finally, free movement of capital means that individual nations give up their ability to regulate investment inflows and outflows. Many nations have traditionally imposed capital controls to encourage domestic investment, promote financial stability, or reduce foreign exchange variations. These controls are not eliminated in an economic union, but they must be "harmonized" so that national regulations are similar enough so they do not become a barrier to economic activity.

The most successful economic union in the world is the United States, if we consider it an alliance of the separate states. Consider how freely goods, services, people, and capital move from one state to another. This gigantic single market has been remarkably flexible and dynamic, making it a model for other developed nations. Consider, however, the degree of political complexity that is inherent in such a system as the United States. The elaborate system of economic and political federalism that characterizes the U.S. political economy is much different from relations that typically exist among and between autonomous nation-states. Economic integration is thus as significant politically as it is economically.

Economic integration is appealing because it is a way for nations to achieve greater *efficiency* in their use of scarce resources and higher rates of economic *growth*. In the lingo of economics, integration produces ***static efficiency*** gains and ***dynamic efficiency*** gains.

Economic integration promotes greater static efficiency for two main reasons. First, with completely free trade within the area, each member nation is able to specialize in producing the goods and services in which it is most efficient. Protective barriers that preserve inefficient industries and promote redundancy are eliminated. Economists believe that these gains from efficient specialization are significant. Second, the creation of a larger, integrated market promotes efficiency in certain industries where large-scale production or long production runs are possible. These gains from "economies of scale" make products cheaper and more competitive.

These static gains are important, but they tend to reach their potential fairly soon after economic integration occurs. The more important economic benefit of integration occurs in the long run, as *dynamic efficiency* promotes economic growth. The logic here is that a larger and more competitive market is likely to be more innovative. As internal trade barriers are removed, previously protected firms are forced to compete with one another. Firms become more efficient and "nimble."

If economic integration is successful, economic growth rates tend to increase, which raises living standards. Even a small rise in growth can be significant. If, for example, economic integration causes the long-term rate of economic growth to rise by one or two percentage points, the long-run impact would be that at the end of a single generation, the living standard could be about double what would have occurred without integration! Thus, economic integration need produce only a little extra growth to have a considerable long-term effect on people's lives.

SOVEREIGNTY AT RISK:
THE POLITICS OF INTEGRATION

> It is not simply for economic reasons that great attention ought to be paid to Europe's future. It is engaged in a political experiment of the highest importance concerning how human societies think about themselves and relationships with others.[2]
>
> Paul Kennedy

Most of the discussion of economic integration tends to focus on the benefits of a larger market. There are, however, many political impacts that must be considered. There is, to some degree, a trade-off between economic benefits and political costs. The closer the economic ties among nations, the closer their political ties. When nations agree to cooperate closely in the economic sphere, they commit themselves to closer political cooperation, too. Thus, for example, the economic efficiency and growth promised by an economic union requires that a nation negotiate a new immigration policy, safety standards, methods of financial regulation, and adopt a harmonized system of investment controls. These important political choices are no longer influenced mainly by the preferences and interests of domestic voters and groups—now the wishes of groups in other member countries must also be considered. Some observers have complained that economic integration creates a "democracy deficit" by breaking the link between political choices and the electorate.

The fundamental political problem posed by economic integration is the loss of sovereignty that occurs when nations form regional trade blocs. These pluralistic organizations necessarily place constraints on the actions of sovereign nation-states. At some point, each member state risks being forced to ignore national interests—political, economic, social, or cultural—as a consequence of maintaining its international obligations. This tension between national interest and international obligations is fundamental to multinational institutions and poses a severe dilemma for states, which tend to value security and autonomy above all else. Given the importance of this political tension, the extent of integration we observe in the world today should perhaps surprise us more than it does.

Economic integration creates political tensions in another way. As markets merge, the location and intensity of economic activity change. Some industries in a particular nation expand, while others contract. Some unions gain members and power; others lose them. The changing geography of wealth and power within each member nation necessarily changes the political landscape.

The view that economic integration weakens political power is not shared by all. Another school of thought holds that integration weakens the hold of national interest groups on political decisions. Broad multinational policies are less likely to benefit specific interest groups in each country, in their view, since their ability to influence legislation is watered down in international negotiations. The resulting policies may better reflect the public interest and be less influenced by special interests. It has been argued, for example, that labor unions in France have undue influence on public policy, which is leavened in a useful way when policies are made at the European Union level, rather than at the national level. This concern, of course, assumes that the "public interest" of the different members of the integrated group are not dissimilar.

There is also the view that individual nations may gain political power, especially in relations with other nations, by being members of a powerful economic alliance. This is the argument that Belgium, for example, is a more potent political presence as a leading nation of the European Union than if it were simply a small but autonomous European nation making its own way in international politics. It is also argued that smaller countries are far more powerful as members of a larger group than they would be as separate, unaffiliated individual nations.

THE BIRTH OF THE EUROPEAN ECONOMIC COMMUNITY

The idea of the economic integration of Europe is not a new one, but Europe's postwar leaders had good reason for putting integration at the top of their agenda. The history of Europe in the twentieth century had been dominated by war, depression, and revolution. Although each of these events was complex in itself, each demonstrated the cost of failure to achieve cooperation on economic and political matters (and the danger of aggressive mercantilist behavior by big nations on a small continent).

The movement toward a united Europe was founded upon two important ideas. The first and most important, which we can trace to the philosopher

Immanuel Kant, is that it is possible for nations to live in a state of "perpetual peace" under a federal system of governance, where each yields some sovereignty and sacrifices some national interests in return for like action by others. Kant wrote that

> It can be shown that this idea of federalism, extending gradually to encompass all states and thus leading to perpetual peace, is practicable and has objective reality. For if by good fortune one powerful and enlightened nation can form a republic (which is by nature inclined to seek perpetual peace), this will provide a focal point for federal association among other states. This will join up with the first one, thus securing the freedom of each state in accordance with the idea of international right, and the whole will gradually spread further and further by a series of alliances of this kind.[3]

Clearly, however, it is difficult to transform an environment of nearly perpetual war (which was Europe from 1914 to 1945) into one where Kant's vision of perpetual peace could take hold. Here is where the second profound idea enters the picture. Ricardo had thought that

> Under a system of perfectly free commerce, each country naturally devotes its capital and labour to such employments as are most beneficial to each. The pursuit of individual advantage is admirably connected with the universal good of the whole. By stimulating industry, by rewarding ingenuity, and by using most efficaciously the peculiar powers bestowed by nature, it distributes labour most effectively and most economically: while, by increasing the general mass of productions, it diffuses general benefit, and binds together, by one common tie of interest and intercourse, the universal society of nations throughout the civilized world.[4]

Thus, in theory, economic cooperation and the gains therefrom would strengthen the cooperative ties that bind European nations together. Kant and Ricardo together thus provide the intellectual foundation for the strategy of economic means to achieve political ends that has more or less defined the European unity project for 50 years.

More than perpetual internal peace was desired. Postwar Western leaders sought to create strong, democratic, capitalist nations to provide a firm wall of resistance to the spread of communism. The Soviet Union was the common enemy that united the nations of postwar Europe and caused them to seek a solution to their problems. The threat of communism gave them the courage to use Ricardo's economics to build Kant's peaceful league of nations.

The *Marshall Plan (1948)* was perhaps the first formal postwar step toward building an integrated European economy. General George Marshall (President Harry S Truman's secretary of state) called upon the nations of Europe to form a continentwide economic market—like the mass market of the United States. Marshall Plan aid was designed to hasten economic recovery by providing a resource base on which to build a European economy. This U.S. aid may have discouraged European nations from adopting the "beggar thy neighbor" policies that limited cooperation after World War I and so contributed to the global conflict that followed. An integrated Europe could never succeed as a U.S. initiative, however; European leadership was necessary.

Many visions of a more united Europe were expressed in the early postwar period. Winston Churchill's vision of a United States of Europe was discussed alongside Charles De Gaulle's less ambitious "Europe of States." It was Jean Monnet, a French political economist who held many positions during a long and distinguished career, who provided the key intellectual guidance.[5] Although Monnet talked of a grand political vision of a United States of Europe, he proposed a much narrower alliance along functional economic lines: a zone of free trade uniting the heavy-industry regions that spanned the French-German border. This plan, for the *European Coal and Steel Community (ECSC)*, was implemented by Robert Schuman, a French statesman, in 1950. The ECSC was the critical test case for economic and political cooperation between France and Germany. It was, by all accounts, a great success and thereby provided a model for further efforts at integration in Western Europe.

A fuller measure of economic integration was achieved in 1957: the Treaty of Rome created the *European Economic Community (EEC*, or the Common Market), a customs union that brought together the markets of Italy, France, Belgium, Luxembourg, the Netherlands, and West Germany. This union of "the Six" was a great success because these nations were natural trading partners that could, therefore, benefit from the static and dynamic benefits of economic integration. Indeed, it would be hard to find a set of nations that might be more suited, economically, to open markets.[6] Their limited but still very important economic union also benefited, however, from global trends of the time. Postwar recovery soon gave way to a global economic boom, which only served to strengthen the ties of prosperity that united Europe against the political and social forces that always act to drive nations apart.

Great Britain participated in the negotiations for the Treaty of Rome but decided in the end to stand apart from the EEC. There were many reasons for this decision, which was eventually reversed at some cost to Britain. The British were concerned, first of all, about the loss of political and economic autonomy that necessarily accompanies economic integration. British politicians (and probably most British citizens) were hesitant to cede decision-making power to others or to share it with the French and the Germans. Britain was forced to weigh the trade-off among self-determination, domestic democracy, and economic growth, which presented a constant tension in economic integration. Britain was also unwilling to give up either its "imperial preferences"—preferential trading relations with the Commonwealth nations—or its "special relationship" with the United States that it so highly valued.

Britain balked, therefore, at its first opportunity to enter the EEC, but it dared not be isolated from free trade in Europe. It organized, therefore, a weaker alliance of trading nations called the European Free Trade Area (EFTA). The EFTA brought together Denmark, Sweden, Austria, Switzerland, Portugal, and the United Kingdom. A free trade area, as noted earlier in this chapter, imposes fewer restrictions on national policy than does a customs union like the EEC, but it can also provide fewer opportunities for economic gain. In fact, the nations of the EFTA offered only limited opportunities for the static and dynamic gains that the EEC experienced. Geographical separation, deep cultural divisions, huge economic gaps between rich nations (Switzerland, Great Britain) and poor (Portugal) all combined to limit trade and growth. The EFTA never was and never would be the engine of economic growth that the EEC offered. It was inevitable, then, that EFTA members would eventually seek EEC membership.[7]

Despite its remarkable success in gaining cooperation from nations that had engaged in two world wars, it would be wrong to paint an overly rosy picture of the EEC. Trade among member nations was never entirely free. Nontariff barriers to trade abounded, and sometimes nations would simply refuse to accept imports of any items from another member, in open violation of the Treaty of Rome, because of domestic political or economic concerns. It was also necessary to create an elaborate system of agricultural subsidies across the EEC to defuse political opposition from powerful farm groups. The *Common Agricultural Policy (CAP)* provided for a complex pattern of payments to farmers in all EEC nations (although not equally in each). A far cry from free trade and laissez-faire liberalism, the CAP was seen as a necessary evil: Subsidies to farmers were one price of achieving greater liberalism and cooperation in other spheres of economic life. Besides, a unified system of farm payments was an improvement over the pattern of destructive competition in subsidies that might otherwise result. The CAP may have been necessary to the creation of the EEC, but it became a ticking time bomb, with ever growing costs, that eventually exploded in the 1980s, creating a budget crisis.

The EEC changed names in 1967, becoming the *European Community (EC)*. The EEC formally joined with the ECSC and Euratom, another pan-Europe organization, to create an institution with broader responsibilities. The change in name signaled an intention to move beyond purely economic issues, although economic concerns continued to dominate EC discussion.

THE COMMON AGRICULTURAL POLICY

The Common Agricultural Policy (CAP) is one of the most controversial and divisive elements of economic and political integration in Europe. The CAP is an EU-wide system of agricultural subsidies, financed through value-added taxes imposed by EU member nations. The CAP is far and away the largest item of expenditure of the European Union and has been a point of contention both within the EU and in its relations with other nations.

The CAP is a perfect example of the use of economic means to achieve political ends. When the EEC was first being formed, farm interests were a major political obstacle. Each nation's farmers feared that they would suffer if the market for agricultural goods were made more competitive. Farm groups could have potentially blocked the European integration or weakened it. The CAP effectively defused this threat, however, but creating a unified system of farm subsidies that insulated farmers from many aspects of competitive market forces. In a way, you can think of the CAP as a system that collected some of the economic gains of European integration in the form of taxes that were then paid to farmers in exchange for their political support. In this case, a cynic would say, economic gains essentially purchased political cooperation.

Almost every nation subsidizes or protects its farm interests to some extent, a fact that reveals the economic significance and political clout of agriculture, even in this "postindustrial" era. The CAP provides Europe's farmers with high prices through a system of price supports. The EU purchases excess farm produce to keep prices from falling and farm incomes from declining—a system that benefits farmers at the expense of the taxpaying public. Over the years, the CAP's guarantees have encouraged European farmers to expand production to a vast degree, creating "mountains" of dairy products and "lakes" of wine and olive oil, for example. These mountains and lakes owe their existence entirely to the CAP, since without it, prices would decline and surplus production would be eliminated.

Although the original purpose of the CAP was to smooth the road for political cooperation, it is now a source of deep political disagreement. First, as the EU has expanded, the cost of maintaining agricultural subsidies has grown. Rising costs have pitted nations that are net recipients of CAP funds against nations that are net payers of the taxes that fund the program.

Second, the prospects of the EU's future expansion into Central and Eastern Europe have created additional pressures. The countries that believe that they (unfairly) pay the bills are worried that the bills will grow larger and larger as the EU expands. At the same time, current EU members are fearful that more subsidies to new EU members will come at the expense of payments to their own farmers. Thus there is disagreement concerning the size of the CAP pie, who will pay the bill for it, and how it will be divided.

Finally, the EU is under pressure from the United States and other countries to reduce agricultural subsidies generally as part of the World Trade Organization's process of trade liberalization. If the EU cuts farm subsidies, then other countries can do so too without making their farmers uncompetitive. Thus external political pressures add to the internal political divisions over CAP. The CAP has thus become more of a political liability than an asset and therefore it is unsurprising that plans are in the works to reduce this program of agricultural subsidies. It remains to be seen, however, whether these political forces will eliminate the CAP or just make it smaller and more focused on a few particular regions or types of producers. Farm interests may be less powerful politically today than they were in the 1950s, but they must still be reckoned with as part of the political economy of European integration.

BROADER AND DEEPER: THE EC, 1973–1993

The second stage in the development of the European Union lasted from 1973 to 1993 and had two distinct stages. The EC broadened in all respects—geographically, economically, socially, and politically—from 1973 to 1986. Then it engaged in a dramatic experiment in deepening from 1985 to 1993. At the end of this period, the EC was transformed into a much more complex and potentially more influential creature.

The EC broadened its geographic vision in several stages from 1973 to 1986. Great Britain finally entered the EC on January 1, 1973, along with Ireland and fellow EFTA member Denmark. Britain took the leap only after two controversial referenda and a series of painful negotiations. By all accounts, Britain entered in 1973 on terms that were distinctly inferior to those offered in 1957. Britain's status as a European nation was determined, but its ambivalence about its relationship to Europe remained.

Greece entered the EC in 1981, followed by Spain and Portugal in 1986. In all three cases, EC membership was in part a reward for the triumph of democratic institutions over authoritarian governments. Free trade and closer economic ties were intended to solidify democracy and protect it from communist influences.

The broader market was not in all respects a stronger market, however. The entry of the poorer nations of Ireland, Greece, Spain, and Portugal magnified a variety of tensions within the EC. These less developed nations were less clearly a part of the pan-European market. Lower living standards limited the extent of

TABLE 11–1 Expansion of the European Union

YEAR	NATION	ORGANIZATION	YEAR	NATION	ORGANIZATION
1957	Belgium	EEC	1973	Great Britain	EEC
1957	France	EEC	1981	Greece	EEC
1957	Germany	EEC	1986	Portugal	European Community
1957	Italy	EEC	1986	Spain	European Community
1957	Luxembourg	EEC	1995	Austria	European Union
1957	Netherlands	EEC	1995	Finland	European Union
1973	Denmark	EEC	1995	Sweden	European Union
1973	Ireland	EEC			

their trade with richer member states. Lower wage structures threatened some jobs in EC industries. Finally, the entry of four largely agricultural nations to EC institutions, including the CAP, put severe fiscal strains on the other nations. The broader market was surely in the long-run interest of the EC, but it imposed great stress on cooperative relationships in the short run.

These economic and political stresses reached a peak in the mid-1980s. Higher and higher EC program costs, imposing a disproportionate burden on Great Britain, precipitated a split in the EC. Jacques Delors, the newly appointed president of the European Commission, traveled from capital to capital seeking ways to reunite the governments and peoples of the EC in some common enterprise. What could restore a measure of unity and cooperation? A common defense and foreign policy? A common monetary system? In the end, Delors concluded that international trade, which had brought the EC together in the first place, was the force most likely to reenergize Europe. In 1985, Delors produced a white paper proposing the creation of a single integrated market by 1992. The *Single Market Act* formalized this grand experiment in market deepening.

It might seem that the EC was already a single market—in theory no tariff barriers separated EC markets, and in practice goods flowed fairly freely across national borders. If, however, a single market is defined according to the principles observed in the United States (the world's single largest market and often its most dynamic one, too), then Europe was still a long way from its goal. Under Delors's leadership, the EC identified 200 general areas where agreement on "directives" was needed to achieve the goal of a unified market. The 1992 Single Market plan was off and running.

The goals of Europe 1992 might be characterized as "four freedoms": free movement of goods, of services, of capital, and of people. Each of these freedoms is much harder to achieve in practice than to imagine in theory. Free movement of goods, for example, requires much more than the absence of tariff and quota barriers if the freedom is to mean very much. There exist hundreds of nontariff barriers to the free production and sale of goods that must be addressed. Health, safety, and technical standards, each of which plays a constructive role, can all discourage imports from other countries (by raising the cost of selling) and encourage the purchase of domestically produced goods. These standards must be leveled (or *harmonized*, in the jargon of the trade) to allow, to the maximum possible extent, a good that can be sold anywhere in the group to be sold everywhere. (Some standards are difficult to harmonize because, for example, of the inevitable differences in such established factors as electrical voltage and automobile and road setups.) In many industries, the cost of satisfying these standards and proving regulatory compliance far exceeded in height any imaginable tariff barrier to trade.

Services represent an increasing proportion of world trade. Achieving free movement of services, such as financial and insurance services, is a tricky task, given the complex systems of financial regulations that each nation has in place. Free movement of money or capital requires the dismantling of capital controls and investment regulations, which affect flows of funds into and out of a nation. Finally, free movement of people requires agreement on many points, most especially the adoption of a common immigration policy. Once a person has entered one EU nation, he or she is free to enter any other.

Delors's Single Market initiative posed a real challenge to the EC member states. The year 1992 promised the creation of a larger, more dynamic market, with the wealth and political power that would flow therefrom. To achieve this big goal, however, required each nation to sacrifice its interests on hundreds of smaller issues, many of which had important domestic political impacts, before the four freedoms could be achieved.

National sovereignty and economic growth were often in conflict. Germany, for example, desired to see its own high environmental standards applied to all EC vehicles. Environmentalism is an important social value in Germany and the green party is a potent political force on some issues. These environmental regulations are costly, however, and were opposed on economic grounds by countries such as Greece and Portugal. To a certain extent, at least, the four freedoms for the EC as a whole actually required sacrifice of some domestic freedoms, such as the right to self-determination of environmental and safety standards.[8]

Although not all the goals of the Single Market were achieved by January 1, 1993, the basic thrust of the 1992 program succeeded. Europe, however, did not immediately experience the spurt of growth and efficiency that had been expected. Instead, 1993 and 1994 found Europe caught in a deep slump, with unemployment rates as high as 20 percent in Spain, for example. Europe's mid-1990s recession had many causes, including the burdens created by the collapse of communism in Eastern Europe and the stresses of rapid structural economic changes combined with long-term social and demographic changes.

Because the Single Market plan proved to be no panacea for Europe's economic problems, some writers have asked "so what?" Were the gains from 1992 worth the painful costs? The answer to this question is that it is too early to tell. It is especially too early to dismiss the Single Market as a failure. When economic integration works, it works by increasing somewhat the rate of economic growth over a long period of time. It takes time, for example, for new investments made in anticipation of the bigger market to come on-line and contribute to prosperity. Even then, however, the effects in any single year may be small. A 1.5 percent increase in the average rate of growth (an increase from, say, 2.0 to 3.5 percent) ends up doubling living standards over the course of a 50-year period, compared with the standard of living without this growth boost. If the Single Market were to be even half this effective in raising living standards in the next half century, it would be judged a clear success.

THE DEVELOPMENT OF POLITICAL INSTITUTIONS

The Treaty of Rome did more than commit six nations to economic integration; it also began the process of developing a set of political institutions to make policy, settle disputes, and provide leadership for Europe. The most important political institutions in the EU today are the European Commission (and its president), the Council of Ministers, the European Council, the European Parliament, and the European Court of Justice. Each of these institutions plays a specific role in setting the delicate balance between the national interests of member nations and the collective interest of the EU itself.

The European Commission acts as the EU's executive cabinet. Each commissioner has a special "portfolio" of responsibilities, such as competition or agriculture, making her or his responsibilities equivalent to cabinet ministers or secretaries in a typical nation-state. The president of the European Commission is the EU's chief executive officer, leading policy initiatives and representing the EU at international organizations such as the Group of Seven (G-7).[9] Romano Prodi, the former prime minister of Italy, began his term as president of the European Commission in 1999, replacing Jacques Santer of Luxembourg.

While the European Commission is designed to advance wide European interests, the Council of Ministers, the EU's main legislative body, is intended to provide a balancing forum for more narrow national interests. The Council of Ministers comprises one member from each member state. The Commission provides a forum for discussion and enactment of high-level policies. The voting rules of the EU allow a minority of member states to block action in the European Commission when they believe their national interests are threatened.

The European Parliament is a much larger body, with 567 members as of 1994, chosen through direct elections in each member state (thus voters in EU member nations elect both national and EU representatives). The Parliament is organized along political party lines, not according to national citizenship. Socialists from all EU nations act together, for example, as do conservatives and other party groups. The Parliament thus provides a forum for debate and discussion from the perspective of political ideology, not national interest (Council of Ministers) or European interest (European Commission). Interestingly, the Parliament is the only institution chosen directly by the citizens of the EU, not its constituent governments. The European Parliament is not a legislative body but can have important influence over EU policies.

The heads of government of EU members meet regularly as the European Council to consider high-level concerns. Leadership of the council rotates from nation to nation every six months, allowing each nation in turn a chance to shape the agenda of the body in important ways.

The European Court of Justice is made up of one representative from each of the EU member nations. The Court of Justice adjudicates conflicts between and among the EU and its member nations. The Court provides an independent agency to interpret and enforce EU agreements.

These EU institutions provide a comprehensive if somewhat unwieldy organization for setting policy and making decisions that affect the entire EU. In the early days of the EU, this political superstructure had more form than substance—its political powers were relatively limited and symbolic. As political and economic integration progressed, however, these political institutions have grown in importance. In a way, the broader and deeper EU has "grown into" its political clothing in the decades since the Treaty of Rome.

The broadening and deepening of the EU over the past 25 years has created real political problems which daily test the strength of the Union's political institutions. Deepening necessarily forced each member state to cede some economic and political powers to EU institutions, as more and more policies and regulations became EU-wide, not national, in scope. Widening has also posed

TABLE 11–2   Political Institutions of the European Union

POLITICAL INSTITUTION	FUNCTION
President of the European Commission	Head of state of the European Union. Leads the European Commission and represents the EU to other nations.
European Commission	The executive branch of the EU, serving much the same function as the cabinet in the United States or the UK. The Commission proposes legislation to the Council of Ministers, administers EU programs, and represents the EU in economic relations with other countries or international organizations.
Council of Ministers	The main lawmaking body of the EU, composed of a single representative from each member nation. The Council can accept or reject legislation proposed by the European Commission, but it cannot draft legislation itself.
European Council	Meetings of EU heads of state and government are called the European Council. Summit meetings of the Council are called at least once every six months by the country holding the presidency of the Council of Ministers.
European Parliament	The only body of the EU whose members are directly elected by the citizens of its member states. Formerly only a consultative body, the Parliament gained new influence under the Treaty on European Union. European Parliament committees review legislation proposed by the European Commission and may propose amendments to the legislation before submitting it to the Council of Ministers. The Parliament may veto a proposal after it reaches the Council of Ministers if it disagrees with the council's position.
European Court of Justice	The "Supreme Court" of EU law. Composed of 15 judges who are appointed to six-year terms. The court deals with disputes between member governments and EU institutions and among EU institutions, and with appeals against EC rulings or decisions.
European Central Bank	The EU's central bank (chief monetary authority), created after the decision to adopt the euro was made. There is an executive board, appointed for eight-year terms, and a government board, which includes the executive board and the heads of all EU member nation central banks.

political problems, because any increase in the size of the Union necessarily reduced the clout of existing members, who find their votes reduced in relative importance. These threats to nation-state sovereignty pose threats to EU unity. In 1994, Spain briefly threatened to try to block negotiations to admit Sweden to the EU, for example, because Spanish leaders feared their nation would lose political power and economic benefits from EU widening.[10]

THE 1990s: €URO, EUROPE, EUROPA?

John Newhouse began his book on the future of Europe with the ironic comment that "Western Europe had a good Cold War."[11] The Cold War was good for non-communist Europe, Newhouse argues, because the common enemy of the Soviet Union gave Western Europe a reason to set aside their disagreements and to unify. Economic integration provided the means to achieve the political goal of peaceful cooperation. Without the Cold War, this great achievement might never have occurred. In this sense, the Cold War *was* good for Western Europe.

The collapse of communism eliminated the threat of Soviet domination but not the need for peaceful cooperation. Europe at the millenium faced a number of important and divisive issues without a common enemy to bind nations together. Could Europe truly unify to address these problems? Could the promise of economic gain continue to convince European nations to set aside narrow national interests and work together?

Or is the title of Newhouse's book, *Europe Adrift*, prophetic? Will Europe drift back to its old pattern of conflict and disorder? This is the great open question of the twenty-first century for Europe and for much of the rest of the world, too. Is Europe just a geographical unit that lies north of Africa and west of Asia? Will it be united by money alone—its new common currency, the euro (€)? Or will it become more—*Europa*—a people with a common will?

Briefly, the European Union at the end of the Cold War was confronted by at least four issues that threatened to end whatever unity had previously existed:

1. *The Ever-Wider Union.* How to accommodate the new demands for membership in the EU without hopeless alienating current EU members.
2. *The Challenge of the Regions.* What to do about demands for greater regional autonomy within the EU.
3. *The Security Issue.* How to deal effectively with security issues other than the Soviet threat.
4. *The German Problem.* How to make sure that Germany remains committed to a united Europe.

The Ever-Wider Union

With the collapse of communism, the European Union was not only the richest and most prosperous club in town, it was also effectively the *only* club for nations with assurances of political stability, access to markets and capital, and—most important—a guarantee that they would not be left out or left behind in the future. Suddenly the EU found itself deluged with membership applications.

In all, 12 countries filed formal membership applications. Cyprus, the Czech Republic, Estonia, Hungary, Poland, and Slovenia were given priority and began the formal membership process in March 1998. They are on track to enter the EU early in the twenty-first century. Five more countries, Bulgaria, Latvia, Lithuania, Romania, and Slovakia, are scheduled to join a few years after the first wave. The twelfth country, Turkey, was not given a membership slot despite its persistence in seeking EU membership and the relatively large numbers of Turkish "guest workers" living within the EU today.

The EU will get larger in the future, growing from 15 to perhaps 25 or 30 countries in the next several years; there can be little doubt about this. EU widening will be very difficult, however, because the new members are much poorer than the current EU average and less developed both economically and politically. The new members will be net recipients of aid from the existing EU countries and will tend to shift the focus from Western to Central and Eastern Europe. Eastward expansion might not be very expensive in a relative sense, but it will cost something and paying for country B's aid is not always popular among the voting population of country A.

Popular or no, the EU has little choice but to open its doors to its Eastern neighbors. If these nations do not achieve some degree of economic success and democratic consolidation, they could revert to communism, elect radical nationalist leaders, or in some other way threaten Europe's new perpetual peace. It is better to embrace these nations and help them than risk what might happen if they are turned out into the cold.

The Challenge of the Regions

As nation-states secede power within the EU, regions have begun to assume more importance. Sometimes the regional focus is rooted in culture, as with the Catalan region in Spain. In other places the issue is money and the perceived need to be free of the shackles of the national government, as in Bavaria in Germany and in Northern Italy. (One Italian movement has gone so far as to propose that Northern Italy secede from the mother country and form a nation of its own—Padania.) Ironically, the EU needs to find a way to address the desires of some of its richest and most prosperous regions at the same time it tries to find a way to accommodate poorer new members. The EU is pulled at both extremes. Can the center hold?

The Security Issue

Europe is a dangerous place. With the one big threat of the Soviet Union gone, the EU has begun to recognize that it faces many smaller but often more serious threats that seem to require a unified security structure. The EU seems to be surrounded by conflicts (the Balkans, the Middle East, Northern Africa) and threats (terrorists, environmental dangers, organized crime, illegal immigration). The classic East-West confrontation of the Cold War has been replaced with a complex pattern of security issues that defy simple geographic orientation.

Europe needs to have a common defense policy, many people believe, or at least a far more effective system of cooperation and consultation on security issues. But a collective security policy would require a good deal more political unity than the EU has ever demonstrated in the past. The EU strategy, recall, has been to substitute economic cooperation for political consensus. So far, the EU has not found a way to deal effectively with security issues, although its coordinated actions in Kosovo in 1999 may reflect a change in this pattern. If the EU is the economic equivalent of Superman, in the past, however, it has politically been more like Homer Simpson.

The German Problem

Finally, Europe must find a way to deal with the German problem, the problem of how to keep Germany engaged in the project of European unity without dominating it. In fact, the German problem was one of the original problems that the EC was meant to address. Germany today, a decade after unification of its Eastern and Western sections, finds itself bound by the EU to the rest of Europe but faced with very serious economic, social, and political problems at home, both in the poorer Eastern provinces or *lander* and in rising tensions between East and West. Germany has so many problems of its own now that it would be natural for it to put domestic issues above those of European unity at least for a while. Given the problems noted above, however, and Germany's central place, with France, in the political and economic leadership of the EU, this cannot be allowed to happen.

POLITICAL UNION OR MONETARY UNION?

These problems were on the minds of EU leaders when they met in Maastricht in 1991. In fact, two ambitious plans were put on the table there, appropriately, by France and by Germany, the countries at the heart of united Europe.

France proposed monetary union—a single currency. In one respect, this was a continuance of the theme of this chapter. In theory, monetary union was thought to be able to solve all four of the problems outlined above in a single stroke. A single currency would make European markets more efficient and Europe's economies more dynamic. This would provide economic gains to offset the costs of enlargement and boost the prospects of the regions. The German problem would be solved because Germany would be chained to the rest of the EU with the strongest possible link—money. And, finally, political cooperation would be accomplished through an indirect mechanism. With a single currency, EU nations would need to cooperate more on political matters generally—especially those involving money, but eventually this would also require coordinated defense expenditures and pretty soon, voilá!—a common security policy would appear.

Germany did not have much interest in a common currency. With its own strong deutschemark, it saw more to lose than to gain in monetary union. But Germany did want political union. It wanted to be part of a united Europe, but not one that so lacked political power. So a deal was struck prior to the Maastricht meetings: Germany would get its political union and France would get its monetary union.

Except that is not how Maastricht turned out. When the meeting was over, monetary union had been adopted (albeit under harsh terms that were thought to exclude all but a few "core" countries) and political union was nowhere to be seen. In the end, the EU returned to its roots and picked an economic tool—the euro—to address its political problems.

Although the criteria for nations to be part of the single currency were thought to be very strict—low government debt, low inflation rates, low interest rates—in fact 12 of the 15 countries in the EU in 1998 were set to enter into monetary union. Greece failed to qualify on economic grounds, although it made great progress toward the goals, while Great Britain and Sweden elected to remain outside the euro zone, at least for the first few years. In most respects, then, going into the twenty-first century the European Union is, in fact, one market and one currency. But whether this will be enough to solve its political problems remains to be seen.

THE POLITICAL ECONOMY OF THE EURO

Although monetary union and the single currency, the euro, are superficially economic policy, it is important to understand that they are far more political than economic. Everything about the euro is political. Its name, for example, was chosen because it means nothing in any European language. For a time the name "ecu" (for European Currency Unit) was considered, but this was rejected as "too French" because a coin called the ecu once circulated in medieval France. When you look at euro currency, you will see what appear to be classic European images, but none of them are authentic. Putting any *real* European scene on the currency would cause political disagreements, so every euro image is fabricated by artists to look European without actually being European. Even the euro symbol (€) has been tested for political problems. The symbol looks like a C with an equal-sign running through it, perhaps to suggest common currency and the equality of all Europeans. But in fact it means nothing because if it meant something that could cause political divisions. Superficially at least, the symbols of monetary union reflect political division more than political unity.

Ironically, although the euro itself is politically correct, its implications are politically explosive. The political implications of the euro extend well beyond the logic of the French position at Maastricht that was explained above.

There are three levels of political issues that surround the euro. The first, and perhaps most important, is that monetary union has created a *reason* for nations to unify (or an excuse for them to do so) in the absence of a common security threat. It is not that having the euro makes, say, Italy, much more economically efficient and much richer. It is more that being left out of the euro would possibly doom Italy to peripheral status in the new Europe. The common enemy that unites Europe, then, is the threat of failure. This, apparently, is a strong force—not as strong as the threat of Soviet aggression, but strong enough to cause most EU members to do whatever was necessary to avoid being left out of the euro zone.

Secondly, and most obviously, qualifying for membership in the monetary union has forced European nations to make very difficult political decisions. They have had to cut government programs and increase taxes to meet the Maastricht criteria. European governments have necessarily become more laissez-faire as a consequence of the particular criteria required for membership in the monetary union. In a sense, Europe has changed its political stripes, or altered the pattern a bit anyway.

Third, once the single currency is fully implemented, the domestic political environment will be changed forever. The Spanish government will not be able to spend its way out of a recession, for example, or print money to pay unemployment benefits, because it will not have the full fiscal autonomy it had when the peseta was its sovereign currency. European politicians will be forced to consider other methods of satisfying the demands of their constituents including job creation through wage cuts and welfare state reform. This will indeed be a new world of politics in Europe.

In the end, however, the most important question remains unanswered and, at this writing, unanswerable. The biggest challenges that lie ahead for the EU are political, after all. Will monetary union create political union or foster an environment where political union can take root and grow? Or will it turn out to be only what it appears to be, just money?

The riddle that started this chapter still holds. If Europe can achieve political unity, it will be at most a real force to be reckoned with. Can it?

EURO-OPTIMISTS AND EURO-PESSIMISTS

There are optimists and pessimists about the future of the European Union. The so-called Euro-pessimists tend to focus on the deep historical divisions that separate the nations of Europe and keep them from cooperating. When faced with the problem of determining a unified policy regarding the violence within the former Yugoslavia, for example, the EU was paralyzed by ties of national interest dating from the nineteenth century and before.[12]

The point some Euro-pessimists make is that the universal pursuit of wealth is not strong enough to serve as a foundation for a true community of nations. The Italian journalist Luigi Barzini, in his 1983 book *The Europeans* put it like this:

> The reason why economic union is a dead-end street is that it is based on a limited, oversimplified, and inadequate philosophy that became predominant in Europe after the Second World War. It was believed to be the final solution of all problems. It holds these truths to be self-evident: one, that the economy is the principal motor of history; two, that an increasingly bigger GNP was the only and sufficient condition for progress. . . . There would be nothing wrong in this philosophy if man (single or en masse) were always a rational human being who knew what was best for him and his progeny and was always moved by the right economic choices. He is not. . . . The motivations of sudden and violent tempest in public opinion, revolts, revolutions, and wars have notoriously been many and irrational, religious, ideological, social, dynastic, patriotic, psychological, the hatred of a tyrant or neighbor, and the defense of national honor.[13]

Euro-optimists, on the other hand, see today's Union as far more than the economic enterprise formed by the Treaty of Rome. They genuinely believe in an authentic European spirit that can nurture a broader, deeper, better union.

Ironically, a political scandal in May 1999, which resulted in the resignation of all 20 members of the European Commission and its president, may have created an opportunity for greater European political unity.[14] Romano Prodi, an economics professor with such strong political skills and instincts that he rose to be prime minister of Italy, was appointed president of the European Commission and charged with the task of reestablishing the EU's political credibility, if it is possible to do so.

It might not happen, but it would be fitting, given the theme of this chapter, if Prodi, an *economist*, should lead Europe to achieve at last a fuller measure of *political* unity, because economic *means* have always been used to advance the EU's political *ends*.

INTEGRATION AND DISINTEGRATION

In 1992 Europe was caught in the clash between two opposing forces: The logic of economics and interdependence that spells community, and the logic of ethnicity and nationality that demands separation. . . . With [the Cold War's] demise Europe's nations and nationalities were liberated from past constraints and dependency. They are now freer to follow their own needs than at any time since 1945. Hence it is not a safe bet that the logic of unity and interdependence will prevail.[15]

Josef Joffe

The nineteenth century was a time of nation building in Europe. Europe achieved its modern form, a collection of unified nation-states, late in the 1800s. Germany and Italy, old nations, became unified states about a hundred years after the upstart United States.

What are the consequences of the modern nation-state? The twentieth century has been defined, to a considerable extent, by the process of answering this question, which began in World War I and is perhaps only now coming to an end. (Some commentators, cleverly, have framed this as the journey from Sarajevo/1914 to Sarajevo/1993.) The twenty-first century will, perhaps, be defined by the search for whatever replaces the nation-state. (Some might call this the search for postmodern IPE.)

The modern nation-state is being pulled by two opposing forces. In the nineteenth and twentieth centuries, the nation-state proved a stable and strong institution because of the existence of a national political interest that coincided, generally, with a national economic interest. The political interest was shaped by external threats that were best met by policies of national defense. The threat of the Cold War, for example, helped create a German national interest in security and a French national interest in security, and a reason for these two groups to put aside other factors to unite for their common defense. At the same time, the growth of economic activities created distinct national economies capable, to some degree, of macroeconomic management. In short, the nation-state had a valid political economy identity and purpose, even though it was seldom a unified body in other terms, such as culture, language, or history.

These two important defining forces of the nation-state—security and economics—have both changed dramatically in the last quarter of the twentieth century. The end of the Cold War's bipolar confrontation has not reduced security concerns around the world, but it has changed them. Organizations of nation-states such as NATO or the Warsaw Pact had a clear purpose in the Cold War but are less obviously relevant when the threat of nuclear arms is based in India or North Korea, not the Soviet Union.

Technological revolutions have also changed the way economies operate. Markets are increasingly either global or very local. Fewer and fewer products and jobs are tied to markets that fall principally within the nation-state. The ability of any nation to manage its own economy has been greatly weakened. The economic rationale for the nation-state still exists, but it is different now than before.

The nation-state is now simultaneously pulled in two directions. One force pulls toward international or global systems of organization of economics and politics. Many problems are now too large to be considered meaningfully by individual nations. At the same time, however, nations are also torn by increasingly local issues where subnational differences and concerns dominate.

It is easy to see both these trends in the world today. The North American Free Trade Agreement (NAFTA), for example, illustrates the way that global markets are creating supranational systems of political and economic organization. At the same time, however, NAFTA-member Canada is being pulled apart internally by forces of culture (English versus French ethnicity), history, and economics (West versus East).

Europe is also experiencing these forces. The growth of the European Union is an example of supranational forces at work, while the disintegration into multiple units of former nation-states such as Yugoslavia, Czechoslovakia, and the Soviet Union illustrates the force of local and regional differences. The nation-state is clearly caught in the middle in this squeeze, with its power and relevance weakened but still generally an important force.

These trends raise many questions in international political economy. Some observers foresee the deterioration of the nation-state, replaced for all intents and purposes by regional trading blocks (Lester Thurow). Others take this one step further, predicting a complete globalization of economics and politics, with the nation-state replaced by the multinational corporation (Paul Kennedy) or by a global class system (Robert Reich) as the organizing force of the IPE. Finally, others have a dual vision: global economics and local politics, bypassing the nation-state entirely.

These issues, which affect the entire IPE, are especially important in the European Union. Will the EU become a strong supranational structure, its politics mirroring its economics? Will it remain a body of autonomous nation-states? Or will it evolve into a geographic structure that encompasses various regions and localities?

One possibility is that none of these structures will dominate the EU, but rather they will all play a part in a federal system. Federalism is a system of overlapping layers of government, with different layers responding to different types of economic and social problems. Germany and the United States have two strong systems of federal-type governments as compared to the United Kingdom, whose government is far more unitary.

Nation-states would still have a role in a federal EU, but it would be different from the present one. Issues of pan-European importance or effect would be determined at one level, those of purely local or regional impact at another. The "little *s*" nation-states of Europe would become more like the "big *S*" states of the United States, completing, perhaps, Jean Monnet's vision of a United States of Europe. If the twentieth century has been a puzzle about the consequences of the nation-state, the twenty-first century may be the answer to the question "what happens next?"

DISCUSSION QUESTIONS

1. What is the European Union (EU)? How has it evolved over the last 50 years? Discuss both its broadening and its deepening. What is its importance today?

2. The theme of this chapter is the tension between the uniting force of markets versus the dividing force of the state. Discuss the ways that markets bring the citizens of different countries together and the economic benefits that integration creates. Discuss the political, cultural, and historical forces that bear on the state, keeping nations apart.

3. Explain the difference between static efficiency and dynamic efficiency. How is each important to the integration process? Explain.

4. The widening and deepening of the European Union has increased economic gains, but intensified political pressures. Discuss the political problems, citing specific examples where possible.

5. What is the Common Agricultural Policy (CAP)? Explain how and why the CAP illustrates the theme of this chapter and also how it creates tensions both among EU members and between the EU and its international trading partners.

6. Discuss the political economy of the euro. What are the likely economic effects of the euro? What are its likely political effects? How is the euro supposed to solve the EU's four political problems? Explain.

7. Do you think that Europe can be united? Explain what it would mean to be united and why you take your position.

INTERNET LINKS

The European Union:
   http://europa/eu/int/
The EuroTimes:
   http://www.irish-times.com/eurotimes/
This Week in Europe:
   http://www.cecorg.uk/pubs/we/
Welcome to the Euro:
   http://www.europa.eu.int/euro/
European Parliament:
   http://www.europarl.eu.it/
Financial Times Survey of the Euro:
   http://www.ft.com/emu

SUGGESTED READINGS

Paul De Grauwe. *The Economics of Monetary Integration*, 2d ed. New York: Oxford University Press, 1994.

"An Awfully Big Adventure: A Survey of EMU," *Economist*, 11 April 1998.

Michael Emerson, Michel Aujean, and Michel Catinat. *The Economics of 1992*. New York: Oxford University Press, 1988.

Clifford Hackett. *Cautious Revolution: The European Community Arrives*. New York: Praeger, 1990.

Paul Kennedy. *Preparing for the Twenty-first Century*. New York: Random House, 1993.

Charles P. Kindleberger. *A Financial History of Western Europe*, 2d ed. New York: Oxford University Press, 1993.

Kathleen R. McNamara. *The Currency of Ideas: Monetary Politics in the European Union*. Ithaca NY: Cornell University Press, 1998.

Larry Neal and Daniel Barbezat. *The Economics of the European Union and the Economies of Europe*. New York: Oxford University Press, 1998.

John Newhouse. *Europe Adrift*. New York: Pantheon, 1997.

John Pinder. *European Community: The Building of a Union*. New York: Oxford University Press, 1991.

Thomas Row, ed. *Reflections on the Identity of Europe: Global and Transatlantic Perspectives*. Bologna, Italy: Edizioni Baiesi, 1996.

NOTES

1. Samuel Huntington, "The US—Decline or Renewal?," *Foreign Affairs* 67 (Winter 1989–90), pp. 93–94.
2. Paul Kennedy, *Preparing for the Twenty-First Century* (New York: Random House, 1993), p. 286.
3. Immanuel Kant, "Perpetual Peace," *Kant's Political Writings* (1795), trans. H.B. Nisbet and ed. Hans Reiss (Cambridge: Cambridge University Press, 1970), p. 104. Quoted in Michael W. Doyle, *Ways of War and Peace* (New York: W.W. Norton, 1997) p. 251.
4. David Ricardo, *The Principles of Political Economy* (London: Dent, 1973), p. 81.
5. Monnet served as deputy director of the League of Nations in the 1920s, a position that no doubt taught him both the need for cooperation among European nations and the tremendous difficulty of achieving that cooperation.
6. They were not, of course, natural political allies, which has created many difficulties, but one of the aims of economic integration has been to overcome political divisions.
7. Not all could enter the EEC, however. Recall that one goal of economic integration was to create a capitalist democratic barrier to communism. EEC members were required, therefore, to be democratic members of the Western alliance. This kept neutral nations (Switzerland) or nations with authoritative government (Austria at this time) from achieving membership.
8. Some have termed this loss the *democracy deficit* of economic integration.
9. The Group of Seven nations are the United States, Japan, Germany, Canada, France, Italy, and the United Kingdom.
10. Spain feared that the expansion of the EU to include Sweden, Finland, and Austria would dilute its voting power in EU political institutions, thereby reducing its ability to veto policies that threatened its national interests. Spain was also concerned that Sweden's entry would harm its fisheries industries.
11. John Newhouse, *Europe Adrift* (New York: Pantheon, 1997), p. 3.
12. France has a long association with Serbia, while Germany's ties to the Austro-Hungarian empire tie it to Croatian interests.
13. Luigi Barzini, *The Europeans* (New York: Simon & Schuster, 1983), pp. 260–261.
14. A report found that members of the European Commission had ignored widespread financial irregularities and fraud.
15. Josef Joffe, "The New Europe: Yesterday's Ghosts," *Foreign Affairs* 72 (1992/93), p. 43.

12

Democracy and Markets: the IPE of NAFTA

by Professor David J. Sousa

OVERVIEW

This chapter examines the effort at the economic integration of the United States, Canada, and Mexico through the North American Free Trade Agreement (NAFTA), focusing especially on U.S.-Mexico relations. It reviews the reasons that Mexican and U.S. leaders entered into the agreement, and sketches NAFTA's basic goals and provisions. The chapter then turns to a discussion of the reasons that some groups in the United States resisted integration with Mexico despite the clear economic benefits of free trade.

The controversy over NAFTA illustrates a key issue in political economy: the tension between the "logics" of democracy and the market. NAFTA stoked U.S. citizens' fears about the impact of the emerging world economy on their jobs and communities and heightened their frustration at their inability to influence the international economic forces that increasingly shape their lives. The pressures of international economic competition and the global mobility of capital (which are increased by free trade agreements like NAFTA) may threaten the health, safety, labor, and environmental standards enjoyed by citizens in the advanced industrial democracies. Critics of free trade agreements like NAFTA see growing tensions between citizens' democratic claims to rights of clean air and water, safe working environments, healthy food, and decent wages and the prerogatives of business leaders seeking to maximize economic efficiency. The chapter shows that democratic claims can violate the logic of the free market and argues that the clash of democratic and market values is becoming increasingly important in debates over free trade.

The issue of free trade with Mexico stirred passions rarely seen in United States politics. For some, the *North American Free Trade Agreement (NAFTA)* symbolized the United States' acceptance of the globalization of the world economy and marked the beginning of an effort at hemispheric integration to meet the European and Asian challenges of the twenty-first century. Free trade with Mexico would be a boon for the United States, guaranteeing freer access to Mexican markets and creating thousands of export-based jobs. For others, however, NAFTA was a lightning rod for concerns about a lingering recession, and for deeper fears of a long-term erosion in the strength of the U.S. economy. Critics of NAFTA feared that Mexico's low wages and weak environmental, health, and safety regulations would lead U.S. companies to divert investment and production south of the border; these concerns resonated with pessimistic workers who had experienced declining incomes and seen mass layoffs and were deeply apprehensive about their economic futures. After a furious public debate, and in the face of sharply divided public opinion, NAFTA narrowly passed in Congress. The agreement now governs trade relations among the United States, Mexico, and Canada.

The public row over free trade with Mexico was in sharp contrast to the consensus among economists that the agreement was desirable, and that all parties would benefit from a lowering of barriers to trade. During the NAFTA debate some 300 economists, liberal and conservative alike, signed a letter to President Bill Clinton stating their support for the agreement. They argued that free trade with Mexico would have minimal but ultimately positive effects on incomes and employment in the United States.[1] U.S. trade barriers against Mexican products were low before NAFTA, and U.S. workers were much more productive than their Mexican counterparts; few economists believed that even completely eliminating barriers to trade would produce huge shifts in investment and employment from the United States to Mexico. NAFTA's advocates, steeped in a liberal tradition that holds that free trade yields maximum efficiency and welfare for all parties, saw the deal's benefits as self-evident. They dismissed their opponents as narrow-minded protectionists foolishly trying to hold back the tide of global economic change. MIT economist Paul Krugman called NAFTA "economically trivial" for the United States and denounced the "simplistic rhetoric" marshaled by its critics. He wrote,

> The hard core opposition . . . is rooted in a modern populism that desperately wants to defend industrial America against the forces that are transforming us into a service economy. . . . [C]linging to the four percent average tariff the United States currently levies on imports from Mexico might save a few low-wage industrial jobs for a while, but it would do almost nothing to stop or even slow the long-run trends that are the real concern of NAFTA's opponents.[2]

This chapter explores the contrast between the intense public struggle over NAFTA and the overwhelming agreement among economists and other members of the North American elite that free trade is desirable. The public debate over NAFTA was often superficial, but this chapter shows that it grew out of a fundamental tension in political economy. Robert Gilpin took a long step toward understanding this tension with his analysis of the conflict between the "logic of the state," which, he argues, is to locate economic activity where it will best serve state interests, and the "logic of the market," which is to locate economic activities where they can be carried on most efficiently.[3] Gilpin's discussion is a good beginning point, but it is not as useful as it might be because it fails to account for conflict *within* states, especially democratic ones, over exactly what "the logic of the state" should be. This chapter argues that the key to understanding the NAFTA fight lies in understanding the clash between the logic of the market and the expanding logic of democracy. Citizens' groups influenced the agreement in some ways, but the struggle over NAFTA grew out of the reality that, at a fundamental level, these logics could not be reconciled.

This chapter offers an overview of NAFTA and circles back to discuss the clash of values generated by the push for free trade. It will argue that while economists and others may be right to dismiss some protectionists as selfish and shortsighted, this is all too simple. The globalization of capital has thrown up powerful new challenges to democratic institutions, and in some areas the fight for protection is less about saving inefficient industries than about protecting democracy: guarding past gains made in the political arena, and expanding the spheres of life in which citizens exercise some control over forces that shape their lives. Free trade may maximize economic efficiency, but efficiency is not everywhere and always the highest value. Some opponents of NAFTA asserted alternative values—rights to clean air and water, healthy food, viable communities, decent wages and working conditions—and it is problematic to treat them as selfish, simple-minded protectionists. NAFTA was perhaps the first concrete target available to U.S. citizens concerned about the effects of the ongoing shift of employment and investment to the Third World on the domestic economy and on environmental, health, safety, and labor standards. These citizens feared that hard-won standards—these new rights—would be undermined by rules that facilitated the movement of capital to a country with weaker regulations and much lower wages. In this light, it is not surprising that there was a bitter public debate over free trade with Mexico.

WHAT IS NAFTA?

NAFTA was the culmination of a process set in motion by two Mexican presidents, Miguel de la Madrid Hurtado and Carlos Salinas de Gortari, in response to the Mexican economic crisis of the 1980s. The collapse of world oil prices and the failure of Mexico's long-standing efforts at import substitution had left the country facing a crushing foreign debt, staggering federal deficits, soaring inflation, high unemployment, and collapsing standards of living. Mexico was effectively bankrupt, and in 1982 announced that it could not pay its foreign debt. In response to this crisis, and in the face of powerful demands from the IMF, de la Madrid and his successor, Salinas, strove to liberalize the Mexican economy. The

Mexicans lowered tariff barriers on many products, sold off numerous government-owned enterprises, and signed the General Agreement on Tariffs and Trade, an international accord aimed at opening world markets. Salinas negotiated debt relief with the United States, cut public expenditures, relaxed laws that had inhibited foreign investment, and reprivatized the largest Mexican banks. He fervently embraced economic liberalism, attacking what he called the "outmoded view that confuses being progressive with being statist."[4]

The Salinas policies aimed at attracting foreign investment and promoting exports were quite successful. Foreign direct investment in Mexico nearly doubled, from $17.1 billion in 1986 to $34 billion in 1991. Mexico's manufacturing sector grew rapidly, and manufactures quickly displaced oil as the country's most important exports. Trade with the United States increased dramatically, doubling between 1987 and 1990 and growing another 50 percent between 1990 and 1991. Salinas was desperate to attract new foreign investment, and because 85 percent of Mexico's manufactured exports are shipped to the United States, stable access to the U.S. market became increasingly important to the Mexicans.[5]

In June 1990, President Salinas requested a free trade agreement with the United States. The decision to seek formal economic integration was controversial in Mexico, which has a long tradition of suspicion and hostility toward its powerful northern neighbor, but Salinas stressed his determination to push his country into the First World. He advanced an image of a "new Mexico" with its economic house largely in order, capable of meeting the challenges of global competition. NAFTA would be an instrument of economic change and a powerful symbol of the commitment to liberalism that is Salinas' most important legacy. Mexican writer Carlos Monsivais observed, "Salinas is NAFTA; his whole administration is NAFTA. He has bet so loudly, so heavily. It's like political theology; we will all go to heaven or we will all go to hell."[6]

If Salinas' "new Mexico" would be heaven, opponents of NAFTA in the United States had a very different vision of his country. NAFTA's critics saw Mexico as "Latin America's most authoritarian state except for Cuba and Peru," attempting to attract foreign investment by maintaining low wages, weak regulations, and a powerful apparatus for containing dissent and labor agitation.[7] Salinas' election victory in 1988 was widely reported to have been stolen from a candidate who left Salinas' party, the PRI, to oppose the liberal turn in economic policy; wages had long been held below the rate of inflation by agreement between the government and state-controlled unions, despite steady gains in productivity; dissident union leaders were jailed; Mexico's labor and environmental regulations were at best weakly enforced. The "new Mexico" was still an undemocratic country riven by poverty and extreme inequality, as the January 1994 peasant rebellion in the impoverished southern state of Chiapas (staged on the day that NAFTA took effect) reminded the world. NAFTA's critics worried deeply about the impact of economic integration on U.S. employment, wages, and labor and environmental standards.

How did U.S. officials view the call for a free trade agreement? The Bush administration was at first hesitant about free trade with Mexico, but a number of political and economic factors ultimately led it to pursue NAFTA. Bush was frustrated with the slow pace of GATT negotiations, wished to do something to address the growing problem of illegal immigration, and had an interest in buttressing liberalizing forces and a friendly president in Mexico. The health of the Mexican economy is extremely important to the United States. The countries are increasingly interdependent, as was evidenced in 1982 when Mexico's announcement that it could not repay its international debts put seven of the nine largest U.S. banks (which had loaned billions to Mexico) on the brink of bankruptcy. Bush hoped that the Salinas policy would strengthen the Mexican economy in ways that would avert future crises, and that economic vitality would buttress political order there. Finally, NAFTA offered substantial benefits to U.S. firms, which could team their capital and technological expertise with low-wage Mexican labor in joint production efforts, much like Japanese companies operating beyond Japan's borders in Asia—the United States could reap some of the advantages of participation in a trading bloc.[8] Mexico offered a young, literate pool of low-wage labor and a growing market for U.S. products (in an average year, approximately 70 percent of Mexico's merchandise imports come from the United States). U.S. firms have a substantial interest in the growth of the Mexican economy—a $1 increase in Mexican GDP yields a 15¢ increase in U.S. exports.[9]

In September 1990, President George Bush announced that he would begin talks with the Mexicans. The administration first won "fast-track authority" from Congress, which meant that legislators would have to vote yes or no on the deal as negotiated by the Bush administration and representatives of the Mexican and Canadian governments—members of Congress would not be allowed to offer amendments protecting constituency interests. The Bush administration claimed that without "fast track," it would have been impossible to negotiate NAFTA, because the Mexicans and Canadians would have feared that the deal would unravel in the legislative process in Washington. The three nations finalized the agreement in August 1992, laying the foundation for a trading bloc of 358 million citizens and economies with GDPs totaling $6.2 trillion.

"FROM THE YUKON TO THE YUCATAN": THE CORE OF THE DEAL

The North American Free Trade Agreement comes in five volumes and weighs nearly 15 pounds and is supplemented by accords on labor, the environment, and procedures for dealing with the problems of industries adversely affected by free trade. Despite its length and complexity, NAFTA's goal is very simple: to eliminate or lower barriers to trade in goods and many services, and create a limited common market "from the Yukon to the Yucatan."

The agreement has two major elements: It reduces or eliminates U.S., Mexican, and Canadian tariffs on many goods produced in North America and facilitates investment across borders on the continent. But it is important to note that NAFTA does not eliminate all trade barriers—the agreement contains provisions protecting economic interests in all three countries against free trade.[10]

First, NAFTA will eliminate tariffs on approximately nine thousand categories of goods sold in North America by the year 2008. On January 1, 1994, the volume of U.S. exports entering Mexico duty free jumped from 20 percent to 50 percent, and two-thirds of Mexican products entered the United States free of tariffs. The remaining tariffs will disappear over 5-, 10-, or 15-year periods mandated by the accord; these delays were negotiated to give some firms and economic sectors time to prepare for free trade. Before NAFTA, Mexico had much higher tariff and nontariff barriers in place than the United States, so the Mexicans have made far more significant tariff reductions.

Only goods adhering to NAFTA's "rules of origin" move across North American borders duty free: Goods must be produced in North America to qualify for duty-free treatment. Goods assembled in North America from components imported from elsewhere are eligible if the final product is substantially different from the imported materials—for example, timber imported by Mexico from Brazil could not then be shipped into the United States or Canada duty free, but paper made in Mexico from Brazilian wood pulp would qualify. NAFTA also requires that some products have substantial "North American content" to receive duty-free treatment: For example, automobiles, footwear, and chemicals must contain at least 50 percent North American components. The nationality of a factory's owners is irrelevant under the agreement—Nissan may ship automobiles from its modern Mexican facility to the United States duty free, as long as those cars meet NAFTA's requirements for North American content.

Second, NAFTA protects the property rights of those who invest across borders in North America and eliminates practices that had long discouraged foreign investment in Mexico. NAFTA requires each signatory country to treat foreign investors no differently than domestic investors and prohibits governments from imposing any special "performance requirements" on foreign investors. For example, before NAFTA, Mexico often required foreign-owned firms to buy certain inputs locally, or to export a specified percentage of their goods. Such requirements, which act as "nontariff barriers" to trade, violate the free trade agreement. Businesses confronting them may appeal to a three-nation panel for damages. Further, in another provision aimed directly at Mexico, NAFTA discourages the nationalization (or government seizure) of private enterprises by requiring governments to pay immediate and fair compensation to the nationalized firm's owners. Mexico is hungry for foreign investment, and the protections offered to investors by these provisions will undoubtedly increase investment there by "extending U.S. style property rights continent-wide. Investors can move as freely from the U.S. to Mexico as from Ohio to Kentucky."[11]

Again, while NAFTA lowers many trade barriers, it offers protectionist safeguards for certain domestic producers in all three countries. First, there are the so-called "snap-back" provisions, which allow governments to reimpose tariffs temporarily to protect specific economic sectors suffering substantial losses due to import surges. For example, if Mexican tomatoes flood the U.S. market and drive down prices, Washington can throw up tariff barriers against imported tomatoes while U.S. growers adjust to the new competitive environment. Second, each country insisted on protecting certain domestic industries, and the agreement contains many such arrangements. For example, Mexico protected its oil and gas drilling enterprises, and the United States its shipping industry. Third, many protectionist provisions emerged from the political process in the United States. President Clinton made many concessions to individual members of Congress, especially those representing agricultural interests, and the Mexicans agreed to reinterpret some of the original language of NAFTA to allow these concessions.

One such agreement empowered the United States to impose steep tariffs on orange concentrate if Mexican exports rise and the price drops to a specified level for a period of five days.[12] These provisions violate the spirit of free trade, but they were necessary to complete the "free trade" agreement—legislators withheld support for NAFTA until these arrangements were made.

While these are NAFTA's major elements, the deal has many other crucial components. There are provisions (aimed at Mexico) requiring each country to protect rights in "intellectual property" like copyrights and trademarks, and rules that will allow U.S. and Canadian banks to penetrate the Mexican market for financial services. The original text of NAFTA, later supplemented by "side agreements" negotiated by the Clinton administration (see below), contained important provisions on health and the environment. NAFTA does *not* require the three countries to adopt the same regulations protecting the food supply or the environment. The three countries made a nonbinding pledge to seek the "highest standard" of protection, but there is no way to force any country to raise its standards. The agreement requires each party to use international standards, set by a variety of international bodies, as the basis for their own regulations. Countries may set higher standards if they deem them necessary, but if those standards lack a "scientific basis"[13] they may be challenged as unfair barriers to trade. For example, the United States may insist on standards governing pesticide residues on produce that are stricter than the international standard, but if the scientific basis is in doubt, Mexico could challenge the U.S. law.

NAFTA supporters argued that U.S. regulations would not be threatened by free trade, but its critics were skeptical. They pointed out that under GATT, Mexico had challenged a U.S. law restricting the importation of tuna caught in ways that kill dolphins as an unreasonable barrier to trade. The fact that the GATT tribunal had sided with Mexico suggested that U.S. standards might well be in jeopardy.[14]

SUPPLEMENTAL AGREEMENTS ON THE ENVIRONMENT AND LABOR

As noted earlier, concerns about the effects of free trade on U.S. labor and environmental standards clouded NAFTA's prospects for acceptance by the Congress. Like all other poor countries, Mexico is an environmental laggard, with weak enforcement of its laws and virtually no infrastructure for dealing with environmental problems. NAFTA critics feared that (1) Mexico's weak environmental regulations would be a magnet for firms seeking to escape tougher laws in the United States and Canada; (2) the pressure of competition would force the United States to lower its own environmental standards; and (3) substantial, unregulated economic growth in Mexico would be environmentally disastrous. Tim Golden of the *New York Times* wrote:

> As officials evoke images of a vast consumer market with boundless opportunities for investment, Mexico's basic lack of environmental services is glaring: in the Valley of Mexico, home to the capital and some 16 million people, almost nine tenths of the waste water goes untreated, according to government figures. For some 60,000 industrial companies there is a single toxic waste landfill. There are no commercial incinerators for toxic wastes.[15]

A crucial source of concern for environmentalists was the condition of the border region, which had become an environmental disaster area as a result of the success of the so-called "maquiladora" program. This program, begun in the mid-1960s, offered companies operating on the Mexican side of the border tariff advantages to the extent that their material inputs came from the United States. The success of the maquiladoras led to a proliferation of virtually unregulated, labor-intensive factory operations in the border area, new concentrations of population without the infrastructure to support them, and a massive pollution problem.[16] Visitors to Big Bend National Park in southeast Texas can see the brown haze that is a product of the maquiladoras; in San Elizario, Texas, which draws water from an aquifer that extends under the border, 35 percent of children contract hepatitis by age 8, and 90 percent of adults have it by age 35.[17] The border mess was a substantial problem in and of itself, with estimated cleanup costs ranging from $5 billion to $15 billion. But more, it became a symbol of the environmental consequences of economic growth in Mexico, and the irresponsibility of firms operating south of the border.

There were also substantial fears about NAFTA's impact on U.S. employment. In 1992, average hourly compensation for Mexican manufacturing workers was $2.35 per hour, while average compensation for U.S. factory workers was $16.17.[18] NAFTA critics believed that Mexico's low-wage strategy for attracting investment and employment would eviscerate parts of the U.S. industrial base, causing massive job losses in high-wage, blue-collar sectors in the United States. Some economists explained that the productivity advantages of U.S. workers made them competitive with Mexican labor, even at a much higher wage; others argued that U.S. workers had already lost that advantage to some Mexican plants, and that in the long run it would disappear.[19] In any event, at a time of growing unemployment and slowing wage gains, many U.S. workers perceived a direct threat from NAFTA. They worried that they could not maintain their standards of living in the face of competition from workers being paid Third World wages just south of the border. Indeed, NAFTA became the focal point for concerns about the plight of unskilled and less-skilled workers in the United States.

During the 1992 presidential election campaign Bill Clinton endorsed NAFTA in general terms but argued that it would have to be supplemented by "side agreements" protecting the environment and U.S. labor before he could give it his full support. The "side agreements" eventually negotiated by the Clinton administration did not create any new labor or environmental regulations and required no harmonization of the three countries' labor or environmental standards.[20] Instead, they set up mechanisms to encourage the three countries to enforce existing environmental and labor laws, and to sanction those that try to use lax enforcement to attract investment and create competitive advantage for their firms. Further, the United States and Mexico created a North American Development Bank to help finance the costs of cleanup in the border area and the construction of sewage and water treatment facilities. The "side agreements" received mixed reviews from environmental groups and were dismissed as completely inadequate by organized labor in the United States.

NAFTA did not "take environmental standards out of competition" by forcing Mexico to conform to U.S. or Canadian laws, but some environmental groups (including the National Wildlife Federation and the Audubon Society) were pleased with the deal. Others were not so sanguine. In a full page ad in the *New York Times*, the Sierra Club ripped NAFTA as an "environmental catastrophe," complaining that it would undermine U.S. environmental laws and conservation efforts, and that companies moving to Mexico to evade the Environmental Protection Agency would create a "toxic hell" south of the border.[21] Union leaders were united in bitter opposition to NAFTA, arguing that they had gained even less from the side agreements than the environmentalists.[22] AFL-CIO President Lane Kirkland called NAFTA a "poison pill" and cried,

> Our people aren't sheltered in economic think tanks and they don't draw Laffer curves on cocktail napkins, but they didn't just fall off the back of a watermelon truck either. They know from bitter experience what will happen when a super-sunbelt opens for business south of the border. They are not interested in seeing Mexico turned into an economy for gringo bankers and flagless empire-building corporations, nor their brothers and sisters there indentured to their service.[23]

Obviously, the agreement was and remains quite controversial in some circles.

MARKETS, DEMOCRACY, AND PROTECTIONISM

The theory underlying NAFTA is well established. Most economic liberals insist that free trade yields the most efficient allocation of resources, greater incomes, and higher productivity for all partners. Obviously NAFTA will hurt some sectors in all three economies; it will hit hard at some U.S. agricultural interests and will cost some U.S. industrial workers their present jobs. But in theory free trade should raise all three countries' incomes, generating growth in relatively more efficient sectors. While protectionism may serve the interests of some industries, from a national perspective it is simply foolish. Nations pursuing protectionist policies are, in effect, choosing to be less efficient and, ultimately, poorer in the long run.

In this view, protectionist policies emerge when inefficient domestic industries lobby government for protection from foreign competition. Politicians are willing to grant protectionist policies because doing so may serve their short-term electoral interests—industries and unions lobbying for protection provide campaign contributions and other forms of political support. Consumers in the protectionist country pay higher prices for goods; protected industries lose the spur of foreign competition and grow ever more inefficient. The mainstream economists' most charitable view of protectionists is that they are short-sighted, irrationally opposing the best long-run policy. Less charitably, those demanding trade barriers are dismissed as selfish special interests, using state power to enrich themselves at a high cost to consumers and the society at large. Protectionism is a subsidy to the inefficient, and anathema to market values. It is seen as a blatant *political* interference with the natural and efficient workings of the market.

But in the NAFTA debate, different kinds of arguments—some that might be called democratic—were raised in opposition to those of the economic liberals. At one level, these democratic critics scored the process of negotiation and ratification for being insufficiently open to input from citizens' groups. They attacked the secrecy of the trade negotiations and argued that citizens' groups and workers should have been directly represented in the process. They questioned the "fast-track" procedure that was followed in Congress, and complained about the power of the unaccountable international commissions that set the health and environmental standards by which the validity of U.S. regulations would be judged. But their arguments sometimes went deeper than this, pointing to a basic conflict between the very logics of the market and democracy.

DEMOCRACY AND MARKETS

Political scientist Charles Lindblom provides insights into the nature of this conflict. He argues that the free market constrains democratic decision-making processes, and that at a fundamental level, democracy and the market are at odds.[24] Market economies are marked by private control of decisions about investment and production. Business leaders decide, on the basis of rational calculations of self-interest, whether to invest, and where, when, and how much to produce. These are *private* decisions, and business leaders have a right and a responsibility to maximize the return on their (and their stockholders') investments. As they do so, society sees the most efficient use of its productive resources.

Lindblom observes that business leaders' *private* decisions have enormous *public* consequences. That is, if the leaders of a local manufacturing enterprise decide that it will be profitable to invest in new production facilities and to expand output, local employment will rise and with it the economic health of the community. What is good for Boeing is, in important respects, good for the citizens of Seattle, Washington; when 3M Corporation thrives, the people of Saint Paul, Minnesota, reap substantial benefits in jobs and tax revenues. Conversely, if business leaders determine that it is economically rational to slow production or, worse, move their facilities to another state or country, unemployment will likely rise and the community may suffer. In extreme cases, like those in some of the old steel-producing areas of Ohio and Indiana, citizens may see a rapid deterioration in their communities, with fewer jobs, collapsing property values, deteriorating infrastructure, failing schools, and rising crime.

What is the relationship between capitalism and democracy? Lindblom contends that business leaders' control of investment and production decisions give them a "privileged position" in democratic political systems. Politicians considering raising taxes or increasing the regulatory burden on business, even for broadly popular purposes, must take into account the impact of their actions on the calculations of business leaders. When elected officials enact reforms that increase the cost of production and reduce profitability, society is "punished" as rational business managers reduce output and employment. In the worst case, managers will move their operations to a state or country with a "better business climate"—that is, a place with less intrusive regulations, a smaller public sector, and lower wages. Lindblom argues that in many cases the mere threat of disinvestment is enough to prevent citizens and their elected officials from attempting to build on existing reforms and may even cause them to back away from established reforms. The political and social consequences of disinvestment give business leaders substantial leverage over the policy-making process, and a kind of trump against political decisions that impinge upon their interests.

It is important to remember that Lindblom does not argue that business leaders are villains. He sees them as rational actors seeking to maximize the return on their investments, who respond to public policies that increase profitability (for example, tax incentives) by expanding output, and to public policies that reduce profitability (for example, higher taxes or stringent workplace safety rules) by cutting back. This points to the conflict between the *logics* of the market and democracy. The democratic impulse is to bring decisions on issues affecting the society at large under popular, or *public*, control. But in free market systems, a whole range of decisions with important public consequences are *private*, held in the hands of rational, profit-seeking business leaders. Citizens may prefer more government spending for universal health care, or tighter environmental and workplace safety regulations. They may organize to win higher wages and better working conditions, but these popular impulses may undermine profitability in ways that are unacceptable to business managers—democratic claims often violate the logic of the market.

DEMOCRACY, MARKETS, AND NAFTA

What does this have to do with NAFTA? Lindblom characterizes the market as a "prison," suggesting that while there is room for policy makers to increase taxes, redistribute wealth, or impose regulations, there are basic limits (the bars on the prison cell) set by the privileged position of business. Some argue that the globalization of the economy and the increasing mobility of capital have tightened the constraints that the market places on democratic decision-making processes by making the threat of disinvestment much more real; trade agreements like NAFTA facilitate disinvestment from countries with higher wages and stricter regulations to places like Mexico, where goods can be produced at lower cost. The social, political, and economic gains made by citizens and workers in the industrial democracies are increasingly difficult to sustain in the emerging world economy because they increase the cost of doing business for firms that can more and more easily move their operations to lower-cost environments. In Lindblom's terms, trade deals like NAFTA make the punishment that society suffers for efforts to reform the market swifter and surer in coming.

Obviously, production jobs have been moving from the industrialized nations to the Third World for decades, and many U.S. firms and low-skill jobs moved to Mexico long before NAFTA. Most economists think that NAFTA will barely accelerate this process; as noted earlier, Krugman argued that NAFTA will have negligible effects on the U.S. economy, and that the trade agreement should be understood as a "foreign policy" aimed at stabilizing Mexico and strengthening its economy.[25] While some criticisms of NAFTA may have been misplaced, the political attack on the agreement represented something much larger. How can U.S. citizens begin to assert themselves against the enormous, virtually uncontrollable changes in the world economy that are increasingly shaping their life prospects? NAFTA's critics made the agreement a symbol of the global economic changes whose consequences trouble many citizens. As was noted earlier, the agreement with Mexico was the first tangible target for citizens increasingly frustrated about the impact of the globalization of capital on the scope of democracy and the simple quality of life in the United States.

Journalist William Greider has characterized the global marketplace as a "closet dictator," pressuring not only firms but also political leaders to do whatever is necessary to make their economies more competitive. He quoted German social critic Wolfgang Sachs, who observed, "The fear of falling behind in international competition has become the predominant organizing principle of politics. Both enterprises and states see themselves as trapped in a situation of relentless competition, where each participant is dependent on the decisions of all other players. What falls by the wayside in this hurly-burly is the possibility for self-determination."[26] The pressures of global competition are forcing companies to streamline their operations (resulting in radical "downsizing," or mass layoffs) and the U.S. government to consider massive new investments in education and infrastructure to increase competitiveness. They are also bringing pressures on domestic labor, environmental, and health and safety standards, giving strength to arguments that we must "get government off the backs of business" to compete in the global economy. While it is easy to understand these arguments as aimed at inefficient and unnecessary government regulation of business, they also reflect the power of the market's logic—given the international economic pressures we confront, we may not be able to afford the environmental, labor, and health and safety laws that citizens have demanded and won through the democratic process over the last half century.

Dissatisfaction with free trade is likely to grow more intense with time, in part because new kinds of rights claimed by citizens increasingly bring them into conflict with the prerogatives of business leaders. Through history, rights claims have evolved from the purely *political* (rights to vote and speak), to claims to rights to basic *economic security* (unemployment compensation, welfare, old-age pensions), to what might be termed *social and political-economic* rights (a healthy environment, decent wages and safe working conditions, viable communities, consumer protections, health care). The language of rights is powerful in the West—it has torn down monarchies, established universal suffrage, and shattered legal segregation and apartheid.[27] In recent years, it has even made government benefits like Social Security nearly inviolable ("We have a *right* to that money!"). Citizen and labor groups opposing NAFTA made expansive claims to rights in jobs, good wages, viable communities, safe food, and clean air and water that, they maintained, should be respected by policy makers and even corporate interests. They raised bold, even radical, questions: Why should property rights and the mobility of capital supersede other social and political-economic rights claimed by citizens? When democratic claims and the logic of the market collide, how should the conflict be resolved? Why do we so often accord market values a higher priority than democratic ones?

It would be simplistic to characterize the NAFTA fight as a struggle between democratic forces and antidemocratic business groups, economists, and politicians. But the power of economic arguments for free trade should not distract us from the fact that NAFTA and other international trade agreements are part of a process—the emergence of a global economy marked by tremendous capital mobility—that challenges citizens' capacities to exercise control over fundamental decisions shaping their life prospects and those of their communities. Citizens in the United States, Canada, and Mexico may benefit greatly from NAFTA, but at some cost to their ability to preserve what they value from their pasts and to control their futures. Free trade may maximize economic efficiency and wealth, but it also restricts the scope of democratic decision making.

CONCLUSION: DEMOCRACY, NAFTA, AND THE FUTURE OF U.S. TRADE POLICY

From the perspective of groups interested in protecting U.S. environmental, labor, and health standards from the effects of globalization, the NAFTA vote in Congress appeared at best a mixed bag and at worst a stunning defeat. For these groups, perhaps the most positive thing to come out of NAFTA was the battle itself. Environmental, labor, and citizens' organizations managed to mobilize their members and to focus media attention on an international trade issue, and to increase public awareness of their concerns about free trade. Citizens could grasp the issue of free trade with Mexico, and the fight crystallized many citizens' concerns that the globalization of production was working against their interests. The opposition to NAFTA brought labor and environmental concerns with free trade principles into focus and pushed one of the great questions of our time onto the public agenda: How should the United States deal with the globalization of the economy, and the resulting pressures on labor, health and safety standards, and democracy itself?

NAFTA's defenders argue that the United States must embrace change in the global economy and protect democracy by finding ways to prosper in the new global order. The most familiar and powerful approach in this vein is the "investment" strategy championed by Clinton Labor Secretary Robert Reich.[28] Reich argues that the United States must accept the global nature of the market system and the incredible mobility of physical and financial capital—capital is *going* to move to Mexico and elsewhere—and adapt to these new facts of life. His prescription is simple: Leaders in the advanced, postindustrial democracies must invest in *human capital*, training their people to perform skilled jobs that add high value to products, and their *physical infrastructure* (roads, railroads, ports, communications and computer networks) to attract investment and the kinds of jobs that Americans want and expect, paying the kinds of wages to which they are accustomed. The United States cannot stop the forces that are moving low-skill production jobs to the Third World. Instead, it must prepare its labor force to perform the "brain work" that is ever more in demand in increasingly sophisticated global production processes. In Reich's vision, less-skilled workers in Mexico and Thailand and Malaysia will sew and rivet and hammer; U.S. workers will be "symbolic analysts," conceiving and designing new products and performing the complex, creative functions that bring the best wages in the new world economy.

The Reich model is attractive to Democratic party politicians, as well as to a good number of economists on the left and (many fewer) right, but it will be difficult to implement the program. The huge investments required are virtually inconceivable to many citizens, interest groups, and members of Congress, and the record of job training and retraining efforts in the United States has been mixed at best. Bill Clinton proposed a large investment package in his first year as president, but that program was cut to ribbons for budgetary and political reasons. While the United States does not lack the resources to pursue the "investment strategy" for dealing with the deleterious effects of globalization, it may lack the will to marshal those resources by severely cutting expenditures for current consumption, and the capacity to create effective and efficient programs.

Beyond this, even if it were vigorously pursued, the investment strategy would not address the problems of millions of U.S. workers still unable to compete in the global economy and would not mitigate the growing social and economic polarization that Reich sees as a product of the globalization of production. Even while the "symbolic analysts" prosper, many Americans will remain in competition with low-wage workers abroad, suffering the inevitable consequences of declining incomes and lowered living standards. The result is a sharp polarization in the income distribution. Reich fears a dark future marked by what he calls the "secession" of the symbolic analysts from the rest of the society. The better-off will be increasingly isolated from their fellow citizens economically, demographically, even psychologically. They will retreat into gated communities for themselves and private schools for their children and increasingly see that they have little in common with other Americans. Our normal political discourse will be as polarized as the NAFTA debate, with elites fervently embracing free trade and dismissing their opponents as simple-minded populists manipulated by demagogues, and apprehensive citizens and workers fearful that they are being sold down the river by their leaders. Reich hopes that massive investments in people and infrastructure will energize the American economy, mitigating these divisive trends and maintaining at least some threads of community and social comity in a polarizing political-economic order.

Democratic critics of NAFTA have argued for a different response to the challenge of globalization, one that would use one of the most significant inducements the United States has—access to its huge consumer market—to ratchet up labor and environmental standards abroad. Terry Collingsworth and colleagues argue that citizens and policy makers must take a stand against agreements like NAFTA, which encourage firms to shift production to make "use of highly productive workers kept cheap by the labor policies of a government more interested in keeping investors happy than in ensuring a decent wage for its citizens."[29] The mechanism, they argue, should be the imposition of global labor standards that would help to put an *absolute floor* under wages and working conditions worldwide. They point to the 1937 U.S. Fair Labor Standards Act, which outlawed child labor, and to Franklin Roosevelt's supporting declaration that, "goods produced under conditions which do not meet rudimentary standards of decency should be regarded as contraband and ought not to pollute the channels of interstate commerce." Collingsworth and his colleagues argue that global standards would slow the movement of capital to ever cheaper labor markets worldwide, and that higher wages for impoverished Third World workers would increase global demand for goods, raising global economic prosperity. Further, it would be a beginning toward protecting domestic labor standards. Greider wrote,

For ordinary Americans, traditionally independent and insular, the challenge requires them to think anew their place in the world. The only plausible way that citizens can defend themselves and their nation against the forces of globalization is to link their own interests cooperatively with the interests of other peoples in other nations—that is, with foreigners who are competitors for the jobs and production but who are also victimized by the system. Americans will have to create new democratic alliances across national borders with the less prosperous people caught in the same dilemma. Together they have to impose new political standards on the multinational enterprises and on their own governments.[30]

The United States has pursued a limited version of this strategy under a number of laws, the most prominent of which is the General System of Preferences Act (GSP). The GSP offers duty-free trade in some goods to some developing countries that meet certain labor and human rights standards: recognition of the rights of workers to unionize and bargain collectively, the prohibition of child labor and compulsory labor, reasonable standards for worker health and safety, and a mechanism for implementing a minimum wage. Presumably, the GSP encourages those countries to maintain at least these minimal standards; Collingsworth and colleagues would like to see the GSP standards significantly strengthened and extended to NAFTA and GATT.[31] Advocates of this approach argue that labor, environmental, and citizens' organizations should play a meaningful role in international trade negotiations, and that trade agreements must explicitly recognize and protect the fundamental rights of workers and citizens against the effects of globalization. This is asking for a great deal—for democratic values and human rights standards to play as powerful a role as the logic of the market in shaping the future of world economy.

This chapter began with the observation that much of the public debate over NAFTA was overheated, with both proponents and critics of the deal exaggerating its likely effects. Most economists argued that the United States would see marginal benefits from the deal, and that Mexico would enjoy significant economic growth as a result of NAFTA and its broader embrace of liberalism. There was little reason, they thought, for the sound and the fury. But the sound that they heard was the clash of great value systems, of the logic of the market with its incessant drive for lower costs and higher efficiency, and the logic of democracy, with citizens' claims to rights to control crucial decisions shaping their lives and the future of their communities. With NAFTA, we saw the language of rights enter the trade debate. Trade politics will never be the same.

AFTER NAFTA

Since its passage, the debate over NAFTA in the United States has focused on the actual economic, environmental, and social consequences of the agreement. Unsurprisingly, few scholars and commentators who opposed NAFTA have found positive results; few who favored the agreement have recanted and concluded that the free trade deal was a mistake. The result is a polarization in the policy analysis *following* NAFTA that mirrors the contentious political debate that preceded Congressional passage of the deal.

In May 1997 several groups critical of NAFTA published "The Failed Experiment: NAFTA at Three Years," which concluded that the deal had been responsible for (among other things) the bulk of the increase in U.S. trade deficits with low-wage countries; an increase in employers' threats to close their plants in the face of unionization drives and an increase in actual plant closings to avoid bargaining with unions; 420,000 lost jobs in the United States, the Mexican peso crisis and the resulting devastation of the Mexican economy; a recession in Canada and the unraveling of the Canadian welfare state; a weakening of food safety standards; increased environmental pollution, the opening of the U.S. border to trucks that do not meet the country's safety standards; increased drug traffic across the U.S.-Mexican border; and an increase in cases of Hepatitis-A reported in the border region. "The Failed Experiment" reported that the labor rights provisions of NAFTA were hopelessly flawed, that the environmental provisions were "utterly inadequate," and that the promised North American Development Bank aimed at cleaning up the border region had failed, generating only 1 percent of the promised funds.[a]

Contrast this dark picture with that drawn by Nora Claudia Lustig, a senior fellow at the Brookings Institution, in her policy brief entitled, "NAFTA: Setting the Record Straight."[b] Lustig acknowledged that no trade agreement can be evaluated effectively after just a few years, but contends that by 1996 the benefits promised by NAFTA's proponents had begun to materialize. In fact, she specifically rejected almost every argument advanced in "The Failed Experiment: NAFTA At Three Years"! She held that NAFTA has been a boon to Mexico in tough economic times, and that it has contributed to economic recovery in the country after the financial crisis of 1995. The peso crisis of 1995 makes it difficult to assess NAFTA's impact on U.S.-Mexican trade, but overall Lustig found NAFTA benefits: substantial increases in bilateral trade among the NAFTA partners and (at worst) tiny job losses in the United States despite the peso devaluation's impact on relative U.S. and Mexican wage rates.

So what are we left with? A qualified short-term success with guaranteed long-run benefits? Or a "failed experiment"? It is hard to imagine that we will ever be able to establish a definitive, consensual interpretation of NAFTA's effects. What can be said definitively about NAFTA—and the fight over the deal—is that it has profoundly shaped subsequent debates over trade in the Western hemisphere. In 1998 Clinton administration's effort to win fast-track authority to negotiate an expanded hemispheric trade deal (the so-called Free Trade Area of the Americas, or FTAA) was rebuffed by the Congress in an unprecedented legislative rejection of executive prerogatives in the trade policy field. Critics of NAFTA and the broader FTAA focused public attention on threats to environmental and labor standards in the United States, and, at least in the first round, managed to defeat the Clinton proposal. As evidence of the emergence of environmental and rights issues onto the political agenda, consider this: Between 1982 and 1990, about 25 percent of *New York Times* articles mentioning "free trade" also included some reference to the environment or generic rights. In the 1990s, the figure was 50 percent, and during the fight over the proposed Free Trade Area of the Americas (the expansion of NAFTA to much of Central and South America), over 60 percent of articles on free trade mentioned environmental or rights concerns. Concerns about "rights" have indeed entered the trade debate, and it is hard to see how this genie can be put back in the bottle.

---

[a] Economic Policy Institute, "The Failed Experiment, NAFTA at Three Years," June 26, 1997.
[b] Nora Claudia Lustig, "NAFTA: Setting the Record Straight,"
http://www.brook.edu/es/policy/polbrf20.htm.

DISCUSSION QUESTIONS

1. What is the North American Free Trade Agreement (NAFTA)? What nations are parties to this agreement? What have they agreed to do? What is the significance of NAFTA today?

2. The theme of this chapter is that markets can sometimes constrain the choices of the state, limiting the realm of democratic decision making. The market

can be a "prison." How does this theme apply to NAFTA? How do the supplemental agreements of NAFTA illustrate this theme? Explain.

3. Charles Lindblom contends that business leaders have a "privileged position" in democratic political systems, giving their interests undue weight in political decisions. Where does this power or influence come from? How can it be used?

4. Suppose that the voters of a nation decided to put domestic environmental concerns ahead of all other factors in making public policy. How would this affect the nature of their economic and political relations with other countries and with the global markets? How does this illustrate Lindblom's point? What, then, should citizens do if they value the environment? Explain.

INTERNET LINKS

The NAFTA Home Page: http://www.iep.doc.gov/nafta/nafta2.htm
The Economic Policy Institute: http://epinet.org

SUGGESTED READINGS

Mario Bognanno and Kathryn Ready. *The North American Free Trade Agreement: Labor, Industry, and Government Perspectives*. Westport, CT: Quantum Books, 1993.
Samuel Bowles and Herbert Gintis. *Democracy and Capitalism*. New York: Basic Books, 1982.
William Greider. "The Global Marketplace: A Closet Dictator." In *The Case Against Free Trade*. San Francisco: Earth Island Press, 1993.
Paul Krugman. "The Uncomfortable Truth about NAFTA: It's Foreign Policy, Stupid," *Foreign Affairs* 72 (1993).
Charles Lindblom. "The Market as Prison," *Journal of Politics* 44 (1982).
Peter A. Morici. "Free Trade with Mexico." *Foreign Policy* 87 (1992).
Robert A. Pastor. *Integration with Mexico*, New York: Twentieth Century Fund Press, 1993.
Sidney Weintraub. "US-Mexico Free Trade: Implications for the United States," *Journal of Interamerican Studies and World Affairs* 34 (1992).

NOTES

1. Before NAFTA, the average U.S. tariff on Mexican goods was only 3.4 percent. Sidney Weintraub, "US-Mexico Free Trade: Implications for the United States," *Journal of Interamerican Studies and World Affairs* 34 (1992); p. 34.

2. Paul Krugman, "The Uncomfortable Truth About NAFTA: It's Foreign Policy, Stupid," *Foreign Affairs* 72 (1993); pp. 13–14. For a critical view of NAFTA, see Jeff Faux, "The Crumbling Case for NAFTA," *Dissent* 40 (Summer 1993); pp. 309–315.

3. Robert Gilpin, *The Political Economy of International Relations* (Princeton, NJ: Princeton University Press, 1987); p. 11.

4. Robert A. Pastor, *Integration with Mexico* (New York: Twentieth Century Fund Press, 1993), pp. 17–20.

5. M. Delal Baer, "North American Free Trade," *Foreign Affairs* (Fall 1991); pp. 132–133.

6. Tim Golden, "U.S. Vote Crucial for Mexico's Chief and His Party," *New York Times*, 17 November 1993, p. A20.

7. Douglas Payne, "Mexico, Bound," *New York Times*, 20 November 1994, p. A21.

8. Pastor, *Integration with Mexico*, pp. 14–15; Peter Morici, "Free Trade With Mexico," *Foreign Policy* 87 (Summer 1992); p. 88.

9. Weintraub, "US-Mexico Free Trade," pp. 32–33.

10. This section draws on David S. Cloud, "The Nuts and Bolts of NAFTA," *Congressional Quarterly Weekly Report* 51, 20 November 1993; pp. 3174–3183; "What's in the Trade Pact?" *New York Times*, 14 November 1993, p. A14; and Anne M. Driscoll, "Embracing Change, Enhancing Competitiveness: NAFTA's Key Provisions," *Business America*, 18 October 1993, pp.14–25. See also *The NAFTA*, vol. 1 (Washington, DC: U.S. Government Printing Office, 1993).

11. Jonathan Schlefer, "History Counsels 'No' on Nafta . . ." *New York Times*, 14 November 1993, p. C11.

12. David E. Rosenbaum, "Administration Sweetens Trade Agreement," *New York Times*, 4 November 1993, p. A19; Keith E. Bradsher, "Clinton's Shopping List for Votes Has Ring of Grocery Buyer's List," *New York Times*, 17 November 1993, p. A21.

13. *The NAFTA*, vol. 1, pp. 7-30–7-31.

14. Lori Wallach, "Hidden Dangers of NAFTA and GATT," in *The Case Against Free Trade: GATT, NAFTA, and the Globalization of Corporate Power* (San Francisco: Earth Island Books, 1991), pp. 23–64. See also Marian Burros, "Eating Well," *New York Times*, 28 April 1993, p. C4. On the dolphin issue, see David Phillips, "Dolphins and GATT," in *The Case Against Free Trade*, pp. 133–138.

15. Tim Golden, "A History of Pollution in Mexico Casts Clouds over Trade Accord," *New York Times*, 16 August 1993, p. A1.

16. By 1994, the maquiladora program included 2,155 factories employing 544,500 workers; approximately 20 percent of Mexico's manufacturing workers are employed in the maquiladoras. NAFTA will probably end the maquiladoras' growth by eliminating the special trade advantages they enjoy. Joshua Cohen, *Business Mexico*, 4 (1994); pp. 52–55; see also Pastor, *Integration with Mexico*, pp. 13–14.

17. Pastor, *Integration with Mexico*, p. 55.

18. Sheldon Friedman, "NAFTA as Social Dumping," *Challenge* (September/October 1992): pp. 28–29.

19. Harley Shaiken, "Two Myths About Mexico," *The New York Times*, 22 August 1993, p. D15.

20. For example, the accord on the environment recognizes "the right of each Party to establish its own levels of domestic environmental protection . . . and to adopt or modify accordingly its environmental laws and regulations." See *NAFTA Supplemental Agreements* (Washington, DC: Government Printing Office, 1993), p. 3.

21. *The New York Times*, 15 November 1993, p. A5. See also David S. Cloud, "Environmental Groups Look for Ways to Ensure a 'Green' Trade Agreement," *Congressional Quarterly Weekly Report*, 28 November 1992, pp. 3712–3713.

22. Anthony DePalma, "Law Protects Mexico's Workers, But Its Enforcement Is Often Lax," *The New York Times*, 15 August 1993, p. A1; Keith Bradsher, "Side Agreements to Accord Vary in Ambition," *The New York Times*, 19 September 1993, p. A1.

23. Lane Kirkland, "Labor Unions and Change," *Vital Speeches* 60 (15 November 1993), pp. 81–84. See also Mark Anderson, "NAFTA's Impact on Labor," in Mario Bognanno and Kathryn Ready, *The North American Free Trade Agreement: Labor, Industry, and Government Perspectives* (Westport, CT: Quantum Books, 1993), pp. 55–60.

24. Charles E. Lindblom, "The Market as Prison," *Journal of Politics* 44 (1982), pp. 324–336.

25. Krugman, "It's Foreign Policy, Stupid."

26. William Greider, "The Global Marketplace: A Closet Dictator," in *The Case Against Free Trade*, p. 204.

27. Samuel Bowles and Herbert Gintis, *Democracy and Capitalism* (New York: Basic Books, 1982).

28. Robert B. Reich, *The Work of Nations* (New York: Vintage, 1991).

29. Terry Collingsworth, J. William Goold, and Pharis J. Harvey, "Time for a Global New Deal," *Foreign Affairs* (January/February 1994); pp. 8–13.

30. Greider, "The Global Marketplace," p. 196.

31. Collingsworth, Goold, and Harvey, "Global New Deal," pp. 12–13.

13

Japan and the Developmental State

OVERVIEW[1]

This chapter looks at Japan's dramatic rise and unexpected decline over the last half century and asks what lessons can be learned from this experience.

Rising from the ashes of World War II, Japan achieved an economic growth "miracle" that made it the envy of many other countries. One factor that contributed to Japan's dramatic rise was a particular set of close state-market relationships that is sometimes called "Japan, Inc." but may more appropriately be termed the "developmental state." Working as a team, Japan's state and market actors led their nation to become the second largest economy in the world.

In the first edition of this book, we asked what Japan would do with its great wealth and increasing power. Would it take a more active leadership role in international affairs, or would it continue its inward focus on national concerns? Events of the last decade now make these questions seem premature. During the 1990s Japan suffered a series of political upheavals and economic crises that have drained its wealth and sapped its power. Significantly, the developmental state that built Japan has seemed unable to guide it to a recovery. It is unclear at this writing when or even if Japan will regain vigor and return to the position it held at the end of the 1980s.

This chapter is therefore a discussion of the puzzle that Japan's postwar history presents. How did the developmental state contribute to Japan's economic miracle? How and why did Japan fall from the heights? Why has Japan been so slow to recover? And, most important of all, because of its potential implications for countries other than Japan, what is the future of the developmental state?

> Assessing the importance of the historical trends and events that have converged in these final years of the twentieth century, one scholar concluded simply: "The Cold War is over, and Japan has won."[2]

Like a phoenix from the ashes, within a single generation, Japan rose from military defeat and economic devastation to become a world-class producer, exporter, and financier. The Cold War was good for Japan, but the years since 1989 have witnessed a decline in Japan nearly as amazing as its dramatic rise. Taken together, Japan's rise and decline present a puzzle to students of IPE.

This chapter is about the factors that contributed both to Japan's amazing rise and to its surprising decline. In telling this story we hope both to gain some general insights into the nature of state-market relations and to learn more about the particular problems that Japan has faced.

Japan has employed a version of "developmental capitalism" that allows for a much greater government role in promoting Japan's international competitiveness than is typical in Anglo-American liberal capitalism. This different mixture of state intervention and market forces is not necessarily better or worse, but it comes with distinct trade-offs and creates different winners and losers. It was often given credit for Japan's dramatic rise. These days it is often blamed for Japan's sudden and prolonged fall. Does the developmental state deserve either the credit or the blame? This chapter looks at both sides of the issue and, in the end, asks you, the reader, to judge the future of the developmental state.

PATTERNS OF CONTINUITY AND CHANGE IN JAPANESE HISTORY

George Ball, former U.S. undersecretary of state, once remarked that Japan's history

> has never been charted by the same kind of wavering curve that has marked the progress of other countries; instead it resembles more a succession of straight lines, broken periodically by sharp angles as the whole nation, moving full speed, has suddenly wheeled like a well-drilled army corps to follow a new course. There is nothing in all human history to match it.[3]

These abrupt pivots took Japan from centuries of xenophobic isolation to open-armed emulation of the West in the last decades of the nineteenth century, from militarist imperialism to pacifist commercialism in the first half of this century, and from a position of economic straggler to one of the most important national economies in the world.

Despite these remarkable about-faces, Japan's association with the world has also been marked by several continuities. The first of these is Japan as *emulator*.

Throughout history, Japan has borrowed liberally from the ideas, institutions, and technologies of those cultures and societies seen as having something superior to Japan's own. The Japanese, however, have in no way felt compelled to maintain the purity of these borrowings from abroad, adapting them to fit their own needs and, in the course of this process, often improving or enhancing the original.

While we may be aware that VCRs and corporate "quality control circles" were both adopted from the United States and then adapted to Japan (and subsequently reintroduced to the United States), the same can also be said for Zen Buddhism and chopsticks, which were borrowed from China. Japan was introduced to Confucianism via Korea, and Western science and technology via the Dutch. It copied its first national constitution from the Prussians (postwar American occupation forces literally wrote Japan's current constitution) and also adopted the German school system. When a local Japanese militia was soundly defeated by British gunships in the 1860s, the militia leaders surrendered and immediately requested to come on board the British man-of-war to see (and learn from) what had defeated them.

Second, the Japanese have always viewed the world in terms of *hierarchy*. International entities (countries, empires, races) like internal entities (family members, classes, companies) are seen and ranked in stair-step fashion. For most of Japan's history, Japanese have viewed their nation as inferior to its powerful neighbors—China, Russia, Britain, and the United States. But as Japan has risen in stature and these neighboring countries have declined either relatively or absolutely, Japan has frequently shifted from idolizing to disdaining these countries.

A final continuity is Japan's national *corporatism*. Japan's island status and the relative homogeneity of the Japanese people have given them a very strong and sharply delineated sense of nationalism. This sense of tribe has often led the Japanese to adopt a mercantilist view of the world, with zero-sum gains and losses accruing either to Japan or its competitors. It has also inspired the Japanese to great sacrifice on behalf of their nation, often acting as Ball described—a "well-drilled army corps"—in both former military exploits and more recent economic campaigns. While there have been important voices of opposition to national marching orders of both the imperial and commercial variety, the Japanese have strong social and cultural incentives to comply and cooperate. We need to keep these continuities in mind as we trace the "sharp angles" of Japan's modern history.

HISTORY: FROM ISOLATIONIST TO IMPERIALIST

When European traders and missionaries first began arriving on Japan's shores in the mid-sixteenth century, they found a Japan that, for all its cultural differences, had a social and political economy strikingly similar to that of feudal Europe some 300 years earlier. At the end of the sixteenth century, one family emerged as the most powerful among these feudal lords and was able to name its successive patriarchs as the shogun, or dominant overlords, of Japan.

Over the next two and a half centuries, this dynasty led Japan from decentralized martial anarchy to increasing national unification under the guidance of a highly capable bureaucracy, staffed by members of the former warrior or samurai class. This legacy of a skilled, disciplined, and highly respected bureaucracy intensely loyal to its political leaders gave Japan a very valuable asset in its modernization drive during the last century and a resilient capacity for enduring rapid change.

This shogunal government also severed Japan's ties with the rest of the world through a "closed country" policy of almost total seclusion. During the first half of the seventeenth century, the government expelled all foreign missionaries, virtually cut off foreign trade, and made travel abroad punishable by death.

Two and a half centuries of seclusion were brought to an abrupt end with the arrival of U.S. Commodore Matthew Perry and his squadron of four American warships in 1853 with a presidential mandate to open trade negotiations with Japan. Well aware of China's failed efforts to resist Western gunboat diplomacy a decade earlier, the Japanese government acquiesced to a series of unequal treaties over the next few years, which opened certain Japanese ports to foreign trade.

This forced opening threw Japan into a quandary about how to react to this Western threat and the superior technology behind it. Although there was general consensus about the need to strengthen Japan's national defense, the role of foreigners and foreign learning was much debated. In the short run, xenophobic samurai terrorists succeeded in both angering the foreigners and weakening the government. In the long run, a group of forward-looking moderate reformer samurai prevailed, crushing the terrorists, ousting the crumbling feudal government in a near-bloodless coup, and establishing a new revolutionary government in 1868 in the name of the youthful Meiji emperor.

This group of young samurai-turned-bureaucrats presided over a revolutionary overhaul of the Japanese political economy and its foreign policy. These leaders were witnessing the literal carving up of neighboring China at the hands of Western colonial powers and realized quick action would be necessary to avoid a similar fate. As good mercantilists, Japan's leaders were convinced of the intimate relationship between economic development and industrialization on one hand, and military and political power in the international arena on the other. They promoted a mercantilist national policy of simultaneously building a "rich country and a strong army" (*fukoku kyoohei*).

Japan's "well-drilled army corps" of public bureaucrats, militarists, and private industrialists succeeded remarkably well on both counts of this national policy, establishing in the same broad stroke Japan as the first non-Western industrial capitalist economy and the first non-Western imperialist power. The state bureaucracy, staffed by able former samurai, played a crucial role in this Meiji industrialization working hand in hand with huge private conglomerates known as *zaibatsu*.

In less than 50 years, Japan went from a position of backwater isolation to that of the first non-Western world power in the international political economy. Over the next several decades, Japan industrialized at a frenetic pace, defeated both China and Russia in decisive military victories, and began a systematic imperial expansion throughout Asia. Inspired by both a perceived destiny to unite its Asian neighbors under its influence in a "Greater East Asian co-prosperity sphere" and the growing demands of a ravenous military-industrial complex, Japan saw its relations with both its Asian neighbors and the Western powers spiral downward during the 1930s as the Japanese empire expanded. Budding democracy within Japan during the 1920s gave way to rising militarism and ultranationalism, propelling Japan into war first with China and then the United States and its Western allies.

Like its nineteenth-century policy of seclusion, Japan's twentieth-century imperial expansion ended abruptly as the result of foreign pressure. In this case, it took the form of military defeat and U.S. military occupation of Japan for seven years. And like Commodore Perry before him, U.S. General Douglas MacArthur forced processes of change in Japan that ultimately proved beneficial and Japan would likely have been unable to make for itself. General MacArthur and his reform-minded administrators remained in Japan from the time of its surrender in 1945 until 1952, launching sweeping changes in the country's political, social, and economic institutions.

Initially planning to remake Japan as the Switzerland of Asia, MacArthur and his staff purged the military, ultranationalist societies, and most wartime political leaders and *zaibatsu* business leaders. This purge destroyed the military class, replaced entrenched politicians with technocrats, replaced *zaibatsu* families with professional managers, and most significantly, left the bureaucracy intact and in a position of overwhelming power relative to the other groups. MacArthur also presided over the rewriting of the Japanese constitution (including a clause renouncing forever the use of war or offensive military force), the breaking-up of the *zaibatsu*, extending the vote to all men and women, and guaranteeing to Japanese citizens civil rights similar to those in America.

But with the "loss of China" and the onset of the Cold War, MacArthur and the U.S. government began to fear that Japan too could fall to communism. This led to an about-face in occupation policy, beginning in 1947. The earlier emphasis on Japan as a Switzerland gave way to one of Japan as a full, albeit still unarmed, ally of the West with the full support and protection of the United States as patron. Conservative politicians supporting the alliance (many of whom had previously been purged) were rehabilitated and came to dominate Japanese politics. The broken-up *zaibatsu* reemerged as more loosely organized **keiretsu** and quickly regained their dominance of the Japanese economy. With the elite bureaucracy at the helm and as a favored client of the United States, Japan was ready for its remarkable postwar catch-up.

MULTIPLE EXPLANATIONS OF JAPAN'S ECONOMIC SUCCESS

Japan's extraordinary economic achievements during the post-World War II period inspired awe, and some trepidation, throughout the world. In the course of three decades, Japan transformed itself from a war-devastated country, whose industrial recovery centered on the production of "cheap gadgets" and light consumer goods, into an affluent and technologically sophisticated global industrial leader. In trade, Japanese export successes have contributed to expanding surpluses in the country's international accounts since the 1970s. These huge surpluses have been invested abroad, creating a huge stock of foreign assets for Japan. Indeed, by the mid-1980s, Japan had risen to prominence as the world's largest net creditor nation. Japanese economic growth following the American occupation was remarkable for its magnitude, speed, and downright relentlessness. Between 1957 and 1984, Japan's gross national product increased from $30.8 billion to $1.261 trillion, a 42-fold jump.[4] Moreover, Japan's economy grew at an annual rate of 9 percent per year during the high-growth years of the 1960s.[5]

Within a single generation, Japan rose from the ashes to become a world-class producer, exporter, and financier. How was this economic "miracle" achieved? This question has been the subject of a great deal of scholarly debate. Understanding what makes Japan "tick" is particularly important for Japan's trading partners that must compete with Japan in the international political economy.

Analysts have identified a wide range of reasons for Japan's economic success. The popular notion of "Japan, Inc." reflects the belief that the Japanese people are simply a more cooperative bunch than the rest of us. Unlike prototypical "individualistic" Americans who thrive amid dissent, the Japanese tend to favor group solidarity and consensus. As the argument runs, the government, corporate management, and workers in Japan all agree on the primacy of economic development as a societal goal and have worked together to achieve this end. In this, as well as in more specific ways, Japanese cultural traits have translated into high economic growth.

Others have discovered the roots of Japan's success in unique features of its domestic economy, notably the "three sacred treasures" of semilifetime employment, seniority wage scales, and company (as opposed to industrywide) unions. These institutions are said to contribute to employee loyalty, and to a high degree of harmony between workers and management.

Economists as a rule have focused on the primacy of market forces in Japan.[6] They highlight the role of individual and corporate initiative in a mostly open marketplace as the central drive behind economic development in Japan. According to this line of reasoning, there is nothing exceptional about Japanese-style capitalism, and noneconomic factors have played a negligible part in Japan's economic development. To the extent that the government has positively influenced economic growth, it has been through wise macroeconomic policies. For example, Japan's tax system has been historically conducive to high investment rates. The country's lack of antitrust regulations has also been a boon to business. Japanese companies are allowed to pool their resources in the pursuit of joint research and development.

Those who emphasize the role of private initiative in Japan's development are particularly critical of the view that government-promoted "industrial policy" is relevant to understanding Japan's remarkable economic performance. They are skeptical about the ability of economic bureaucrats to devise a coherent national economic plan that anticipates the "winner" and "loser" industries of the future, and see Japan's more recent downturn as vindication of their position.

A final argument about the roots of Japanese economic success after World War II nonetheless focuses on the role of the government or state in fostering Japan's economic development. Advocates of this "developmental state" argument take issue with both the cultural perspective (that Japanese behavior can be reduced to the society's "Japaneseness") and the economics perspective (that Japan operates according to free market principles). According to this perspective, the various "unique institutions" found in Japan are not isolated phenomena, but rather they are best understood as parts of a larger political and economic system. The government or state stands at the helm of this "GNP machine." During the postwar period, the Japanese government set its sights on catching up with the West industrially and pursued this goal with single-mindedness.

Because it challenges conventional "liberal" understandings of how capitalism functions, and because the view has been propounded as a potential model for development elsewhere, some care will be taken to delineate the "developmental state" argument. The following discussion elaborates on the nature of the Japanese state, and its methods of intervening in the Japanese economy to promote industrial development.[7]

MERCANTILISM MEETS CAPITALISM: THE DEVELOPMENTAL STATE

Those subscribing to this developmental-state explanation depict Japan as possessing a distinct variant of capitalism,[8] one that contrasts dramatically with the Anglo-American model. Three major factors distinguish *laissez-faire* capitalism from *developmental capitalism*. The role of the state, the general code of economic conduct, and underlying philosophical assumptions will be discussed in turn.

The Role of the State The factor that perhaps most distinguishes the two forms of capitalism is the function of the state in the economy. Where laissez-faire capitalism is practiced, such as in the United States, the state functions as a referee in the marketplace, making sure participants in the free enterprise system observe the rules of the game.

The government's major regulatory functions include maintaining an open and competitive market and protecting consumers. By contrast, in developmental capitalist systems such as Japan, the state exchanges referee garb for a player's jersey. An actual market player itself, the government does not obsess on rules and procedures but rather preoccupies itself with substantive social goals, most especially with promoting the international competitiveness of industry. The state's industrial policy is geared toward this end.

Codes of Economic Conduct Beyond the central role of the state in the economy, a general code of economic conduct throughout the entire political and economic system characterizes developmental capitalism. Lester Thurow's concepts of "consumer economics" and "producer economics" capture key differences in the guiding principles of laissez-faire and development capitalism, respectively.[9] Where principles of consumer economics reign, market participants are driven by the desire to maximize profits. Here, the overall measure of economic performance for the society is consumer welfare.

On the other hand, in producer-oriented countries, profit maximization is certainly desirable for capitalists, but hardly an end in itself. In countries such as Japan, managers aim rather for market share as an avenue to "strategic conquest" for their firms. The measures of performance in a production-oriented system are high savings and high investment, not increased consumption and leisure.

A frequently noted feature of the Japanese economy is the substantial size of its national savings. Japan's gross national savings (as a percent of gross national product) at its zenith, reached nearly 40 percent in the postwar period.[10] Japanese households account for a substantial share of the national savings. Between 1960 and 1980, the Japanese on average saved around 20 percent of their disposable personal income, which was at least three times the amount the average American saved during the same period.[11] Countries geared toward producer economics are organized to suppress consumption and encourage investment. During the latter half of the 1980s, Japan invested 35.6 percent of its gross national product, compared to a 17 percent investment ratio in the United States.[12]

Underlying Philosophical Assumptions Finally, distinct assumptions about the essential nature of economic activity undergird laissez-faire and developmental capitalism. From your knowledge of liberalism and mercantilism, you have probably already been able to identify the intellectual forebears of each of these strands of capitalism. While capitalism as we have come to know it in the West clearly possesses liberal roots, capitalism in Japan was built on mercantilist assumptions about the nature of economic production and exchange.

JAPANESE INDUSTRIAL POLICY

Japan's developmental state employs *industrial policy* to coordinate the nation's industrial adjustment in order to sustain long-run growth and global competitiveness. The concept of *dynamic comparative advantage* lies at the heart of industrial policy. This means that a government can actually work to create an enduring competitive advantage in industries where a country may have at one time had a comparative disadvantage. Industrial policies are used to influence the industrial structure of the entire economy, as well as to fashion developments within specific sectors and firms. The government's kit of policy tools will vary depending on the needs of the economy and the capacity of the government.

The Ministry of International Trade and Industry (MITI) and the other economic bureaucracies that carry out industrial policy in Japan do not seek to repress market forces when they intervene in the economy. Rather, the state aims to preserve competition and private enterprise so as to avoid some of the well known problems associated with centrally planned economies, such as endless bureaucratic red tape. On the other hand, under developmental capitalism, market forces are not allowed full reign in determining how resources are allocated. The market mechanism is considered inadequate for assuring a smooth and timely adjustment of the nation's industrial structure.

An important prerequisite for effective industrial policy is a "strong" state; that is, the government must not be captive to interest group pressures within society but rather must be invested with broad authority to formulate and implement economic policy. According to much empirical research on Japan, the economic bureaucracy has historically enjoyed a tremendous degree of latitude in policy making, especially given that Japan is supposed to be a "democratic" nation.

The period from 1949 to 1973 marks the heyday of Japanese industrial policy. After 1973, Japan's highly orchestrated "growth system" loosened somewhat in the face of heightened trade friction and internationalization of the Japanese economy. Since the 1970s, Japanese industrial policy has been specifically designed to target and promote new strategic "sunrise" industries, and to ease the transition of declining "sunset" industries.

In an article in the *Atlantic Monthly*, James Fallows examines the different premises operating behind "Anglo-American" and Japanese thinking about economics.[13] Here, he notes the great extent to which John Locke and Adam Smith have influenced British and American understanding of how society should function. From Locke, we have learned the supreme importance of individuals. From Smith, we have learned that free markets will maximize prosperity. Articles of faith in the West, these beliefs are not universally accepted in other parts of the world. In Japan, the welfare of the group takes precedence over individual rights. And in Japan, the ideas of German philosopher Friedrich List carry much more weight than do those of Adam Smith. As Fallows notes: "In Japan economics has in effect been considered a branch of geopolitics—that is, as the key to the nation's strength or vulnerability in dealing with other powers."[14]

The two economic visions divide dramatically over their perception of the degree of harmony and conflict in the international political economy. In outlining the two clashing worldviews of Adam Smith and Friedrich List, Fallows comments on the tremendous optimism among Americans and British that everyone can prosper at once from international economic exchange. World trade is viewed as a *positive-sum game*. But mercantilists in general, and the Japanese in particular, view business rather as war. Superior economic powers will inevitably vanquish those nations that fall behind. Trade is a *zero-sum game*. "Therefore nations must think about it strategically, not just as a matter of where they can buy the cheapest shirt this week."[15]

HOW JAPAN WON THE COLD WAR

The cultural explanation, the "free markets" explanation, and the "developmental state" explanation of Japanese economic development all share one common feature—they focus on the domestic determinants of Japanese economic success. An argument that we have not yet considered draws attention rather to the importance of the international context in which Japan's phenomenal economic growth occurred. Arguably, Japan's economic success can be explained largely by the Cold War, and the relationship between the United States and Japan that it produced.

Kenneth Pyle and Don Hellman are among those who have underscored the extent to which Japan benefited from the post-World War II international order. Pyle details the ways in which the Cold War rivalry between the United States and the Soviet Union led the United States to shelter Japan from the vagaries of international politics, permitting the Japanese to focus their attention and resources on achieving economic growth.[16] Likewise, Hellman refers to the "international greenhouse effect" of U.S. patronage, which permitted Japan to flourish "free from the costs and uncertainties of full participation in international political and security affairs."[17]

U.S. policy toward Japan in the post-World War II period logically followed from its preoccupation with the Soviet Union. In order to "contain" the Soviet spread of communism, the United States saw fit to establish allies around the world. As noted in the first section of this chapter, the mission of the U.S. occupation thus shifted from promoting democratic reforms to rehabilitating

Japan as America's chief Asian ally against the Soviet foe at the outset of the Cold War.

Advocates of the so-called "free rider" thesis have pointed to at least three specific ways in which the U.S.-Japanese relationship during the Cold War supported Japanese economic growth. First, the United States footed the bill for Japanese defense, thus freeing up Japanese resources for industrial production. By the terms of the U.S.-Japanese security treaty signed in 1951, the United States guaranteed Japan's security in exchange for extensive military prerogatives in Japan. Japan had essentially allowed itself to become a military satellite of the United States in order to focus single-mindedly on a mercantilist program of catching up with the West economically.

Second, the United States provided cheap technology transfers to Japan following World War II. The importation of technology from the more industrially advanced United States allowed Japanese producers to accelerate the development process. Japan was especially dependent on technology imports in the high-growth industries that were targeted for development.

Finally, the United States promoted the Japanese economic buildup through its international trade policy. Following the war, the United States worked to maintain a free trading order in the capitalist world. The United States opened wide its markets to Japanese exports and did not require the favor to be returned in kind during much of the Cold War period. However, the increasing global competitiveness of Japanese industry, and Japan's accompanying trade surplus with the United States, gave rise to expanding political friction between the trading partners. Since the late 1960s, trade tensions between the United States and Japan have gradually heightened in intensity and broadened in scope. But as long as Cold War security concerns prevailed in U.S. policy-making circles, the United States did not require Japan to maintain reciprocity in bilateral relations. Over time, however, growing U.S. protectionist sentiment has increasingly impinged on Japan's ability to take a "free ride" in the international trading arena.

Whether the source of Japan's economic growth was mainly domestic, as the theory of the developmental state asserts, or due in greater measure to the particular international political and economic environment in which the developmental state operated remains an open question. There is no ambiguity, however, about the outcome. Japan won the Cold War in the sense that it emerged from the long years of the U.S.-Soviet conflict with substantial economic wealth and growing political influence. In the first edition of this textbook we concluded that the main problem facing Japan in the international political economy would be to decide what to do with its wealth and power. The events of the 1990s showed that this question was, at the very least, considerably premature.

WINNING THE COLD WAR BUT LOSING THE PEACE

The first decade of the post-Cold War era was not kind to Japan. Its economy suffered several sharp reversals that shook the foundations of its unique economic institutions, such as lifetime employment. Japan's political system was also badly shaken by a series of corruption scandals and partisan realignments. Japan's political economy at the end of the 1990s, at least when viewed from the outside, has little in common with the strong state–strong market partnership that exist-ed before.

From an economic standpoint, the contrast between the 1990s and the Cold War years can be seen by looking at Japan's real Gross Domestic Product (real GDP), the most basic indicator of national economic conditions (see Table 13–1). Japan's economy continued to grow at historically high levels during the early 1990s (despite the collapse of its stock market, which is discussed in the next sec-tion). In 1992, however, it entered a period of stagnation, with economic growth rates much below the previous average. This situation is sometimes called a "growth recession." The economy was still growing, but at a very slow pace. Incomes rose and jobs were created, but at a rate much less than the expected rate. A growth recession can cause a crisis of expectations when business and person-al plans that were predicated on continuous high economic growth finally con-front the fact that the economy is not expanding fast enough to render a successful outcome. Certainly, as we will see below, this was part of Japan's problem.

Growth increased somewhat in 1996, suggesting a return to previous form, but then Japan instead plunged into a deep recession. Real GDP fell in both 1997 and 1998. Japan found itself in its most serious economic situation in the post-war period. Although a fractional decrease in real GDP may not seem like a very frightening statistic, it is a very frightening thing to experience in the real world. Each percentage change in real GDP represents literally billions of dollars of income and hundreds of thousands of jobs. When real GDP falls during a reces-sion, the impact is widespread and significant in economic, social, and political terms—all the more so in a nation like Japan, which had come to count on the developmental state's ability to keep the economy moving steadily ahead.

The economic crises in Japan were accompanied by proliferating political scandals and rampant party realignments. Although campaign finance scandals are certainly not new to Japan's political scene (or that of other electoral democ-racies), the number and nature of these scandals during the past decade have been particularly troubling (and scandalous). Generous and occasionally illicit contributions from the private business sector to the coffers of political parties (particularly the ruling Liberal Democratic Party) and individual politicians have been a fundamental aspect of Japanese politics.

TABLE 13–1: Japan's Economic Growth

YEAR	REAL GDP GROWTH RATE (%)	YEAR	REAL GDP GROWTH RATE (%)	YEAR	REAL GDP GROWTH RATE (%)
1979–88	3.8	1992	1.0	1997	-0.2
1989	4.8	1993	0.3	1998	-0.7
1990	5.1	1994	0.6		
1991	3.8	1995	1.4		
		1996	3.5		

Source: Economic Report of the President 1999 (Washington DC: President's Council of Economic Advisors, Table B-112) and OECD on-line statistics.

But up until the past decade, these payments, and certainly these scandals, had involved (or at least embroiled) only politicians, not the highly respected bureaucratic policy makers. These bureaucrats or civil servants were seen by the public as above the fray of back room political deals, acting in the national interest as they guided the nation's finely tuned economic machine. The winding down of this economic juggernaut in the early 1990s coincided with a proliferation of both campaign and bubble-related finance scandals and the unprecedented revelation that bureaucrats from the respected ministries of finance, health, and trade were also participating (and profiting) from the arrangements. This unfortunate convergence of events called into question not only the wisdom of bureaucratic policies (which, it was argued, had led to the bubble and its collapse), but also the legitimacy of Japan's system of stable bureaucratic governance that had been Japan's postwar hallmark.

These events (and the increasing unpopularity of government policies) in turn led in 1993 to the rapid and unprecedented fragmentation of the ruling Liberal Democratic Party (LDP), which had dominated the Japanese political scene for nearly four decades. Sensing the declining popularity of the LDP and increasingly frustrated at the conservative intransigence of its party elders, a number of reformers within the party jumped ship with their supporters, launching a rush to the exit which swept the LDP from office and threw Japanese parliamentary politics in disarray. During the subsequent three years, 11 separate political parties shared power and four different individuals (tenuously) held the office of prime minister. Although the LDP was able to reenter government, initially in an alliance with two other parties and then as the sole party of government by 1996, it would not return to its earlier position of sweeping dominance. Continued shuffling and realignments since then indicate that the political overhaul and its accompanying turmoil is not yet complete, compounding the challenge of generating a political solution to the economic crisis.

In short, Japan saw two bubbles burst in the 1990s: an economic bubble and a political bubble. When or how Japan will recover its economic growth and political efficacy remain unclear at this writing. The next two sections will look more deeply at the economic and political problems and speculate about how and when they might be resolved.

Japan's problems are striking. But what is striking is not that Japan has suffered political and economic crises—it seems no nation can avoid such problems indefinitely. What is striking is that these problems have persisted over a decade. Surprisingly perhaps, given our earlier characterization of its "well-drilled army corps," Japan has fundamentally been unable to reverse its direction and begin to move ahead again. Where is the leadership of the developmental state when it is needed the most? We will return to this question at the end of the chapter.

THE BUBBLE ECONOMY

In retrospect it is clear that the Japanese economy became dominated by a financial bubble in the 1980s and early 1990s. The bubble burst, although the pieces are still falling and it may be some time before the full impact of the bubble's explosion has been felt. The problem Japan faces today is how to reinvigorate its economy without reinflating the bubble.

"Bubbles" are a common problem in financial markets, as we saw when this concept was introduced in chapter 8. A financial bubble takes shape when economic activities are driven more by expectations of growth than by the fundamental factors that produce growth. Japan's dramatic economic successes in the postwar era set up expectations that high levels of growth would continue into the future. Slowly and subtly, investors began to act upon this expectation instead of a realistic assessment of current and future events.

The first bubble occurred in the market for land and real estate and was called the "property bubble." Japan has a very high population density and, as one would expect, land has long been an expensive item. Land-intensive products, such as golf course memberships, are startlingly costly in Japan, relative to their price in more land-abundant countries such as the United States and Canada. As the economy grew and more funds were available to spend on luxuries, the price of land shot up. As price increases continued, a bubble was formed. Investors bought land not because they wanted to use it, but only because they were convinced that someone else would soon be willing to pay even more for it.[18]

As the property bubble inflated, real estate prices soared in Japan, creating a mountain of financial wealth. Soon a form of contagion occurred as investors used the inflated value of their property as collateral for loans, which were invested in Japan's stock market. The property bubble thus fueled a stock market bubble. Soon investors were buying stocks based only upon the expectation of future price rises, not based upon the profitability of the underlying businesses. Table 13–2 shows how the bubble inflated. The Nikkei stock index[19] doubled between 1984 and 1987 and then nearly doubled again between 1987 and 1990—a growth of stock prices that exceeded the growth of the Japanese economy by an astronomical amount.

Financial bubbles can only sustain themselves as long as expectations continue to rise. A sudden shift in expectations can lead to a sell-off, where prices collapse suddenly as the force driving the market switches. This happened in the property market first. Japanese investors became concerned that real estate prices would not continue to rise and tried to sell off their property holdings before the price fell. A panic ensued and the Japanese land market collapsed.

Falling real estate prices were an even bigger problem than you might expect, however, because the stock market bubble was supported in part by loans based upon high property values. As real estate prices fell, investors were forced to sell off their stock holdings too. The result was the stock market crash seen in Table 13–2. Japanese stocks lost over 50 percent of their value during 1990–1993. To the extent that Japanese families and businesses had invested their wealth in property and stocks, they were now very much poorer. Stock prices fell even further in 1998 and 1999 as Japan entered a national recession. Overall the Nikkei stock index fell from 37,188 in January 1990 to 14,499 in January 1999.

Japan's banks were caught in the middle of the property and stock bubbles. They had accepted property as collateral and lent money to customers who bought stocks. As both real estate and stock bubbles burst, many banks were left

TABLE 13–2   Japan's Stock Market Bubble

YEAR	NIKKEI STOCK INDEX	YEAR	NIKKEI STOCK INDEX	YEAR	NIKKEI STOCK INDEX
1980	6,768	1987	20,023	1994	20,229
1981	7,284	1988	23,719	1995	18,694
1982	7,938	1989	31,581	1996	20,812
1983	8,103	1990	37,188	1997	18,330
1984	10,196	1991	23,293	1998	16,628
1985	11,992	1992	22,023	1999	14,499
1986	13,024	1993	17,023		

Source: Bank of Japan. Average Nikkei index for January of each year.

with huge liabilities and few assets of real value. Japan began to experience a banking crisis that got less publicity than the property and stock bubbles but has proved to be of even greater economic significance.

Banks were in many ways the key economic institutions of the Japanese postwar miracle. One of the unique characteristics of Japan's economic system was its dependence upon banks rather than markets as a form of financial organization. Most personal savings took the form of low-interest bank deposits, which the banking system funneled to government and business at a lower cost than in other countries, where financial markets rather than savings banks served this function.

The close ties that the developmental state forged between Japan's government (especially the powerful ministry of finance) and its financial community provided many benefits when the Japanese economy was growing rapidly, and during the period when the property and stock bubbles were building. But these relationships exacerbated problems during the collapse and its aftermath. Insolvent banks were propped up and kept going by sympathetic regulators, rather than being shut down or forced to merge with solvent banks. Some of these insolvent banks lent good money after bad, as they in turn extended credit to insolvent customers, in the hope that things would turn around, their loans could be repaid, and things would return to normal. As Tables 13–1 and 13–2 show, however, "normal" turned out to be persistently falling stock prices and slow growth that became a recession, not the hoped-for growth that would bail out everyone involved.

The debts just got bigger and bigger and the banks went further and further into the red. Japanese families rationally worried which banks would survive and which ones would eventually fail. When the government finally acted, the cost was very high, much higher than if arms-length regulators had acted quickly and decisively to enforce banking regulations. "Teamwork" between Japan's bankers and their government regulators made the financial system's problems worse, not better.

If Japan's "developmental state" was slow to respond to the recession, the famous *keiretsu* form of business organization only compounded the problem. During the boom years, the *keiretsu* were seen as a key to Japan's growth. These complex "teams" of businesses could support each other and take organized actions that were in their long-term collective interests (as opposed to U.S. firms which compete for short-term gain). At the heart of each of the *keiretsu* was a banking system that channeled funds to needy member businesses. As long as the economy was growing rapidly, there was plenty of money in the *keiretsu* to cover losses and to subsidize short-run problems with long-run investment strategies.

As Japan's economy slowed down and then eventually contracted, these banks found that their role within the *keiretsu* was in direct conflict with the fundamental principals of sound finance. During a recession, a bank should make loans only to the best-financed and most credit-worthy customers. But during a recession, a *keiretsu* bank is supposed to make loans to money-losing team members. As the economic slowdown persisted and intensified, the financial condition of *keiretsu* banks worsened dramatically until, finally, they represented a liability to the collective enterprise.

When the *keiretsu* were threatened, their banks kept them afloat. When, finally in the late 1990s, the banks themselves began to fail, the economic crash they produced was severe and widespread.

Critics of this Japanese economic system gave a new name to the developmental state in the wake of these economic woes. They began to call it *crony capitalism.* The Japanese political economy was not so much a "team" of able bureaucrats, loyal politicians, and efficient producers that sought the shared goals of national wealth and power, the critics said, but rather it was a set of tight personal and professional relationships that systematically exploited the public interest for the gain of a narrow group at the top.

JAPAN'S ECONOMIC DILEMMA

At this writing, Japan's recession continues and the question is asked frequently, who will lead Japan back into economic growth? On the face of it, this seems like a ridiculous question. Japan is a nation of well-educated, hard-working, technologically sophisticated people. How can any doubt their ability to recover from an economic recession? Still the question persists and some Japan scholars raise serious doubts about Japan's economic future. We can see why this is such a problem if we consider the four basic sources of economic stimulus: consumers, investors, exporters, and government.

Rising consumer expenditures often drive economic growth in the United States. This source of growth seems to be out of the question in Japan. One reason, of course, is Japan's traditionally high savings rates. Saving, not spending, was seen as a distinct advantage during the boom years, since the high saving rate made possible investments in Japan's economy. But this saving also served to inflate property and stock bubbles. Now that Japan needs consumers to spend more, they are naturally hesitant to do so. The future is uncertain. The stability of the banking system is uncertain, too. Worried people do not splurge on new luxury cars. They squirrel away their money in the safest place they can find in case it might be needed in hard times ahead. Consumer spending seems unlikely to power Japan's resurgence.

It doesn't seem likely that investment spending will provide the boost that Japan needs, either. Financial investors, of course, lost enormous sums in the property and stock crashes. *Keiretsu* investment was discouraged both by the stagnant economy and by their internal financial problems. In an attempt to stimulate domestic investment, the

Bank of Japan in 1998–1999 drove interest rates down to 1 percent, then to $1/2$ percent, and finally to 0 percent! But even at 0 percent interest no strong demand for investment loans appeared!

Perhaps the Japanese economy could be stimulated by an increase in exports. If exports were to rise dramatically, this would create jobs and incomes and perhaps alter expectations, shifting the economic momentum from recession back to growth. It makes sense that a large exporter like Japan might look to higher exports to solve its problems, but this has not happened for three reasons.

The first is that Japanese exports are not so large compared to the entire Japanese economy as you might think. Japan is like the United States in the sense that most of the goods that it produces are purchased domestically, not by foreign customers. Many of the "Japanese" products that U.S. consumers purchase these days, after all, are not exported from Japan but are made in Japanese-owned factories in North America and elsewhere. If you purchase a new Honda Accord, for example, you are buying a product built mainly in Marysville, Ohio, not Japan. From a simple mathematical point of view, if would be hard for Japan to export enough to shift its domestic economic momentum dramatically. But higher exports would help Japan's depressed economy, to be sure.

Unfortunately, Japan's financial crisis has made it more difficult for Japanese firms to export their products. As Japan's financial system weakened, firms began to shift foreign investments back home to shore up their accounts in Japan. As they did this, however, they had to purchase yen on foreign exchange markets, and the rising demand for the yen caused the currency to appreciate. As we saw in chapter 7, a strong yen makes Japan's products more expensive to foreign buyers. The Japanese have given a name to the problem of an overvalued yen, they call it *endaka*. And *endaka* frustrated Japan's attempts to export its way out of recession at several points in the 1990s.

The final reason why exports cannot be relied upon to lift Japan's economy is political. As Japanese incomes fell, so did their demand for imported goods and services. As economic growth actually increased in the United States, on the other hand, the demand for Japanese products rose. Ironically, it appeared possible that the U.S. market economy might do for Japan what it was unable to do for itself: revive the moribund economy.

But the combination of lower exports to Japan and higher imports from that country caused the U.S. trade deficit with Japan to soar. Concerned about this problem, many U.S. political leaders began to put pressure on Japan to reduce its trade surplus with the United States. Thus, just at the point when Japan would like to export more to create jobs, it faced stern international pressure to do just the opposite, or face a trade war with the United States.

Neither consumers, investors, nor exporters, therefore, seem to be the answer to Japan's economic problem. This leaves the government sector. Even the liberal economic tradition since the time of John Maynard Keynes has held that sometimes the government needs to do what the private sector, for whatever reason, cannot do. In Japan's case, this would means a series of spending increases, tax cuts, and financial reforms to stimulate consumer and investment spending. Japan has been unable to take decisive action so far, however, because of the political bubble that accompanied its economic bubble.

THE POLITICAL BUBBLE

The bubble that formed in Japan's political system during its years of growth and prosperity was distinctly different from the economic bubble. The economic bubble was like a balloon that grew bigger and bigger until it finally burst. The political bubble was more like a soap bubble—bright, shining, but fragile on the outside and essentially empty on the inside. The political turmoil that Japan experienced in the 1990s popped this illusory shell and revealed the vacuous contents of Japan's politics. Significantly, it may also have paved the way for a genuine political revolution.

The Japanese political bubble was the illusion that the Liberal Democratic Party, Japan's "ruling" party for nearly four decades, genuinely governed Japan, when in reality Japan's elected politicians have engaged in little more than soap-bubble politics. It has been observed that the LDP has been grossly misnamed: It has been neither liberal (L), democratic (D), nor even a party (P). As already discussed, the policies the LDP stood for have been neomercantilist, not liberal. Its politics have been decidedly elitist, not democratic. And organizationally, it has not been a party as much as a broad collection of factions or miniparties, divided more by personal loyalties and favors than policy differences. LDP politics in Japan was not so different from the picture of organized crime painted in the classic movie *The Godfather*—little more than wars between and among factions in the LDP for leadership and the spoils of political office.

Thus, a bubble facade of unity, democracy, and political effectiveness masked intramural divisions not over policy differences, but rather struggles for essential electoral resources—campaign funds and access to political pork barrels. This facade was perpetuated to please the American Cold War patrons (who desired both liberal policies and democratic politics) and to mollify the Japanese electorate. The underlying inefficacy that such a system entailed persisted because the politicians were never intended, expected, nor allowed to rule; rather, they reigned. Rather than being governed by elected politicians, Japan has been ruled by the bureaucratic mandarins who make up the powerful ministries responsible for Japan's developmental state.

In a frequently used Japanese metaphor, elected politicians have been the Kabuki puppets, whose strings have been pulled not by voters (or even special interest groups), but by the hidden bureaucratic puppet masters. These insulated architects of the developmental state were seldom questioned as long as the economy grew. Elected politicians, sustained in office by generous financial support from the keiretsu businesses, dutifully "rubber-stamped" policies that were formulated and ultimately implemented by the bureaucracy. But the implosion of the political bubble—which rent the curtain and revealed the manipulators—coincided with the bursting of the economic bubble, casting a particularly unfavorable light on the bureaucrats and the oftentime unseemly strings that connected them to both politicians and big business.

The collapse of these bubbles has likely ended the cozy division of labor between ensconced bureaucrats, compliant LDP politicians, and generous corporate contributors. Newly invigorated reformist politicians (both inside and outside the LDP) have recently passed reforms designed to strengthen the hand of the elected politicians at the expense of the bureaucrats and democratize the electoral system. New restrictions have also been placed on corporate campaign contributions in an effort to weaken the political influence of big business, but as we know from the American experience, "money politics," as the Japanese refer to it, is an endemic problem of electoral democracy in a capitalist system.

While these reforms will likely shift decision-making authority from non-elected bureaucrats to elected politicians, it is important to note that policies will not necessarily change just because they have become less elitist. Nor will these reforms magically bring about a solution to Japan's seemingly intractable economic challenges. In fact, some argue that the solution to Japan's economic problems still rests in the skilled and experienced hands of the bureaucrats.

If the developmental state has been a success, it is partly due to the skill, dedication, and influence of bureaucrats in agencies such as the Ministry of International Trade and Industry (MITI) and the Ministry of Finance (MoF). The essence of the developmental state was administrative influence not political control. While political factions plotted and warred over pork barrel programs, bureaucrats in the ministries implemented the long-term strategies that we associate with the developmental state. While the LDP factions frequently sought to further only their particular interests, the bureaucrats could look to larger concerns.[20] In short, Japan's bureaucracy was an island of stability in a stormy political sea.[21]

At the same time, the unwillingness or inability of Japan's government to take decisive action to reverse economic decline is more the result of decisions within the bureaucracy than policies adopted by elected leaders. In Japan the LDP "reigns" but the bureaucracy truly rules.

The idea that the government is controlled by nonelected government employees may strike many readers as undemocratic and undesirable. But the American management guru Peter F. Drucker has defended Japan's system, saying that it is both common and desirable.[22] Drucker asserts that elite bureaucracies are more the rule than the exception, even in market economies, and that Japan's system of bureaucratic rule is a good deal less authoritarian than some "liberal Western" nations, such as France. The key, Drucker says, is that a bureaucratic elite, elevated above political squabbles and insulated from economic pressures, is able to put society's interest above any narrow group's economic or political interest.

This, according to Drucker, is the reason why the Japanese government was so slow and unwilling to act during the growing economic crisis.

> In the end, the most important key to understanding how the Japanese bureaucracy thinks, works, and behaves is understanding Japan's priorities. Americans assume that the economy takes primacy in political decisions, unless national security is seriously threatened. The Japanese—and by no means the bureaucracy alone—accord primacy to society.[23]

In short, Drucker argues that Japan's bureaucracy acted wisely in the face of economic crisis. Rather than caving in to demands for politically expedient policies that would have torn apart important elements of Japan's social structure (for example, by forcing insolvent banks to close, thereby destroying some of the *keiretsu*), the bureaucrats confidently preserved Japanese society, sacrificing short-term wealth for long-run social stability.

If Drucker is right, then Japan should not reform its system and the crises of the 1990s should be viewed as bumps in the road, not a reversal of fortune. Not everyone agrees, however, with Drucker's optimistic analysis of the situation.

In his 1982 book *The Rise and Decline of Nations*, the political economist Mancur Olson provided an alternative view of Japan's dilemma. During long periods of stability and prosperity, Olson argued, it is possible for *distributive coalitions* to form. These are special interest groups, political or economic in nature, who use the state to get private gain. They seek regulations and policies that benefit themselves, even if they harm the nation overall. In a growing economy, the result of distributive coalitions is that some groups prosper far more than others and their policies slow economic growth but do not stop it, so the effect on the nation is somewhat disguised.

These distributive coalitions, Olson argued, eventually become large, powerful, and numerous and the regulations and policies that they seek become a set of *structural rigidities* that make the economy less dynamic and the state less responsive to changing needs. When a crisis occurs, this line of reasoning suggests, the state is unable to take decisive action because it is hamstrung by the distributive coalitions, all of whom demand protection from the changing environment. The crisis is thus magnified and the hardest hit are the members of the general public, who are not protected by any coalition of special interests.

This is not necessarily a bad image of Japan in the 1990s and the government's inaction in the face of economic crisis. In fact, writing in 1982, Olson used Japan as an example of his theory in two ways. First, he attributed much of the postwar Japanese economic "miracle" to the effect of that nation's defeat in World War II and its subsequent Allied occupation. Foreign occupation, Olson argued, effectively broke up the prewar distributive coalitions, such as the *zaibatsu* families, giving Japan a much more flexible political and economic system. Unhampered by special interests, Japan's developmental state could look to the national interest and achieve its amazing record of economic accomplishment.[24]

However, Olson wrote, "The theory predicts that the . . . Japanese will accumulate more distributive coalitions, which will have an adverse effect on their growth rates."[25] And this is what some observers suggest happened to Japan and to its bureaucracy. They became rigid and inflexible and, if not under the direct influence of distributive coalitions, they at least mistook the self-interested policies these groups advocated for the national interest.

If Olson's theory is correct with respect to Japan, then political problems lie at the heart of the decline of the developmental state. Political reform, not just market liberalization, is needed if Japan is to resume its place. Ironically, Japan needs a stronger democratic system of government to break the hold that distributive coalitions have on its bureaucracy.

THREE PERSPECTIVES ON JAPAN'S FUTURE

> So how can Japan set about charting a new course? Its old map had nothing on it about the end of the cold war, the globalization of markets, the rise of China, or the invention of the internet?[26]

There are, predictably, three distinctly different views of the future of Japan's developmental state, which we might call the liberal view, the nationalist view, and the skeptic's view.

The liberal view holds that Japan's political and economic problems in the 1990s show that the developmental state is a false model of economic growth. Even if the developmental state contributed to the boom years, it showed itself unable to adapt to the new political and economic environment. Essentially, the developmental state must be dismantled—only this time by the Japanese themselves, not by foreign invaders.

Economic reform is necessary. Japan's economy must be liberalized, made more market friendly and more market driven. This means it must become more open to competition from abroad (trade liberalization) and more open to competition internally (deregulation). No element of Japan's economic system is in more need of reform than its financial system. The Japanese must use their famous knack for borrowing from abroad to copy the West's more open economic system.

Economic reform, however, will be impossible without fundamental political reform. This means, most of all, breaking up the bureaucracy and dismantling the structural rigidities that they protect and defend. The world has become too complex, technological, and interdependent for a few handfuls of economic mandarins to manage, even if they aren't corrupt or narrow minded. The power must be returned to individuals and to their elected officials. In short, liberals argue, Japan must become not only liberal in economics, but in its democratic politics as well.

Such radical changes are both unwarranted and unwise, the nationalist view argues. One size does not fit all. In the end, Japan's political economy should and must remain essentially Japanese. The characteristics of the Japanese developmental state are, fundamentally, the characteristics of Japan. Liberal reformers want to transform Japan into California, which is as impossible as it would be unwise.

Clearly, the liberal critique of Japan's political economy begins from the wrong set of fundamental assumptions. Seeing Japan's great *economic* success in the postwar era, critics assume that the *goal* of the developmental state is wealth, as it would naturally be for the government of the United States, for example. But *economic success* was only a side effect, not the goal of the developmental state. The goal was the preservation and success of Japan's society—including the stability and sanctity of its social institutions, culture, and beliefs. You cannot preserve Japanese society by destroying it. Judge Japan's developmental state, therefore, by Japan's own standards, not your own.

The skeptics' viewpoint on this issue is the most cynical and in many ways the most convincing. Yes, it says, Japan must change, but it cannot. Paraphrasing Ogden Nash, "you just can't get there from here." To survive and thrive in a knowledge-based global capitalist political economy may require Japan to adopt free market economics and liberal democratic political values, which it cannot do. Japan tomorrow will be like Japan today, a wealthy nation helplessly adrift on uncertain seas.

The reason can be found in Japan's history and culture. This chapter began with a listing of Japan's three famous cultural characteristics: the ability to imitate and adapt, its emphasis on hierarchy, and its corporatist social structure. Liberals focus on the first of these characteristics, but they forget the other two. They think that Japan is a chameleon and can change its colors to suit any environment. The nationalists remember the last two but neglect the first one. They think that Japan's hierarchical elites (the bureaucrats) will look out for the nation. But they forget that Japan's corporatist structure can change as it has changed. Now each group looks out for itself, leaving the nation adrift, while the hierarchical structure keeps true political change from taking place.

The truth of the matter, according to the skeptic's view, is that Japan's ability to change and adapt is limited by its respect for hierarchies and its corporatist nature. Only a devastating crisis, like a foreign invasion, is likely to force Japan to change. Since nothing remotely so disruptive is on the horizon, Japan will remain as it is now, the nation that must change but cannot.

CONCLUSION

This chapter concludes, therefore, with questions. What is the future of Japan and its model of the developmental state? Can and should other nations engaged in "catch-up" development adopt or at least learn from this model? Or do Japan's political and economic problems in the 1990s reveal fatal flaws in the developmental state? Are liberal economic and political systems more effective after all? Or are we just looking at the wrong things, distracted by politics and economics to such an extent that we fail to see that social cohesion and cultural values are what really matter?

DISCUSSION QUESTIONS

1. Are Japan's mercantilist proclivities a product of its culture (and thus unlikely to change), or is Japan simply going through an economic nationalist stage common to many countries during their "catch-up" phase of development?
2. In what respects was the international environment different during the period of Japan's economic rise and during the period of its economic decline?
3. To what extent are the rise and decline of Japan due to domestic political and economic events versus the changing international environment?
4. Discuss Peter Drucker's theory of bureaucracy. What role does the bureaucracy play that is different from the role of elected political leaders? What trade-offs are associated with placing decision-making authority in the hands of insulated and unelected bureaucrats versus elected politicians who must be responsive to both voters and special interest groups?
5. How were Japan's economic and political bubbles related? Use the problems of Japan's banking system as a lens through which to view both bubbles.
6. Explan Mancur Olson's idea of distributive coalitions and structural rigidities. How can this model be applied to explain Japan's economic slowdown and its inability to restore economic growth.
7. Is Olson's model an economic theory or a political theory? Explain.
8. Must Japan change to regain its wealth and power? If so, can it change? Explain.

INTERNET LINKS

Japan-American Society:
    http://www.us-japan.org/resources.html
Ministry of Finance:
    http://www.mof.go.jp/english/index.htm
Japan Politics Central:
    http://www.people.virginia.edu/~ljs2k/webtext.html
Japan Policy Research Institute:
    http://www.nmjc.org/jpri/

SUGGESTED READINGS

Peter F. Drucker. "In Defense of Japanese Bureaucracy," *Foreign Affairs* 77:5 (September-October 1998), pp. 53–67.

James Fallows. *Looking at the Sun*. New York: Pantheon, 1994.

Yoichi Funabashi. "Tokyo's Depression Diplomacy," *Foreign Affairs* 77:6 (November-December 1998), pp. 26–36.

Frank Gibney. "Introduction," in *Unlocking the Bureaucrat's Kingdom: Deregulation and the Japanese Economy*, (Frank Gibney, ed.) Washington DC: Brookings Institution Press, 1998, pp. 1–15.

Chalmers Johnson. "The End of American Hegemony and the Future of US-Japan Relations," *Harvard International Review* (anniversary issue 1990), pp. 126–131.

Edward J. Lincoln. "Japan's Financial Mess," *Foreign Affairs* 77:3 (May-June 1998), pp. 57–66.

Mancur Olson. *The Rise and Decline of Nations*. New Haven, CT: Yale University Press, 1982.

Kenneth Pyle. *The Japanese Question: Power and Purpose in a New Era*. Washington, DC: American Enterprise Institute Press, 1992.

Lester Thurow. *Head to Head: The Coming Economic Battle Among Japan, Europe, and the United States*. New York: William Morrow, 1992.

Kozo Yamamura. "The Japanese Political Economy After the "Bubble": Plus Ça Change?" *Journal of Japanese Studies* 23:2 (1997), pp. 291–331.

Kozo Yamamura and Daniel Okimoto, eds. *The Political Economy of Japan: The Changing International Context*, vol. 2. Stanford, CA: Stanford University Press, 1987.

NOTES

1. Karl Fields and Elizabeth Norville were the authors of this chapter in the first edition of this book. This chapter has been extensively revised for the second edition by Michael Veseth and Karl Fields. Elizabeth Norville's contributions to the material presented here are noted with gratitude and respect.
2. Chalmers Johnson, quoted from video, "Losing the War with Japan," Front Line Series, 1991.
3. As cited by Kenneth Pyle, *The Japanese Question: Power and Purpose in a New Era* (Washington, DC: AEI Press, 1992), p. 12.
4. Kozo Yamamura and Daniel Okimoto, eds., *The Political Economy of Japan: The Changing International Context*, vol. 2 (Stanford, CA: Stanford University Press, 1987), p. 175.
5. Kozo Yamamura and Yasukichi Yasuba, eds., *The Political Economy of Japan: The Domestic Transformation*, vol. 1 (Stanford, CA: Stanford University Press, 1987), p. 95.
6. Some representative works include Gary Saxonhouse, "Industrial Restructuring in Japan," *Journal of Japanese Studies* (Summer 1979); Charles Schultze, "Industrial Policy: A Dissent," *Brookings Review* (Fall 1983), pp. 3–12; Philip H. Trezise, "Industrial Policy in Japan," in Margaret Dewar, ed., *Industrial Vitalization: Toward a National Industrial Policy* (New York: Pergamon Press, 1982); and Hugh Patrick, "The Future of the Japanese Economy," *Journal of Japanese Studies* (Summer 1977).

7. For an overview of alternative explanations of the Japanese miracle, see Chalmers Johnson, "The End of American Hegemony and the Future of U.S.-Japan Relations," *Harvard International Review* (anniversary issue 1990); pp. 126–131.

8. Adherents to this position have been labeled *revisionists* because they reject the orthodox view that capitalist democracies all look and act alike. Revisionists do not argue that Japan is evil or wrong, but rather that Japan is *different* from other advanced industrial democracies. See *Business Week*, 7 August 1989, pp. 444–451.

9. See Lester Thurow, *Head to Head: The Coming Economic Battle Among Japan, Europe, and America* (New York: William Morrow, 1992), pp. 113–151.

10. Yamamura and Yasuba, *The Political Economy of Japan*, vol. 1, p. 138.

11. Ibid., p. 100.

12. Thurow, *Head to Head*, p. 127.

13. See James Fallows, "How the World Works," *Atlantic Monthly* (December 1993).

14. Ibid., p. 64.

15. Ibid., p. 71.

16. Pyle, *The Japanese Question*, p. 43.

17. Donald Hellman, "Japanese Politics and Foreign Policy: Elitist Democracy within an American Greenhouse," in Yamamura and Okimoto, eds., *The Political Economy of Japan*, vol. 2, p. 345.

18. This is sometimes called the "greater fool theory." You buy land at foolishly high prices because you can be sure that an even greater fool will soon appear to buy it from you at an even higher price.

19. The Nikkei stock index is an indicator of stock prices in Japan, much like the Dow Jones index in the United States. The figures listed in the table are index numbers, not prices, designed to show relative changes in price, not any actual prices.

20. This is obviously a broad generalization offered as a stylized fact. Clearly there were many individual political actors who sacrificed self-interest for Japan's national interest.

21. Fans of old British TV shows may remember a series called "Yes, Minister" (and later, "Yes, Prime Minister") that told how wise career bureaucrats in British government were able to protect the true interests of the government from the politically driven short-term interests of apparently imbecilic elected officials. Each week's show would begin with some new moronic political policy and would end only when the bureaucracy had managed to stave it off and save the nation.

22. Peter F. Drucker, "In Defense of Japanese Bureaucracy," *Foreign Affairs* 77:5 (September-October 1998), pp. 53–67.

23. Ibid., p. 79.

24. Mancus Olson, *The Rise and Decline of Nations* (New Haven, CT: Yale University Press, 1982), p. 76.

25. Ibid.

26. "Hustling towards Paralysis," *Economist*, 21 March 1998, p. 24.

14

States and Markets in Transition

by Professor Patrick H. O'Neil

OVERVIEW

One of the greatest challenges that a nation can face is to change the entire nature of its political and economic system. Making such a dramatic change essentially redefines the ways that individuals relate to each other and to the state. The fundamental tension between states and markets is magnified as social institutions and individual responsibilities are altered.

This chapter examines the problems of states and markets in transition from one system of IPE to another. The goal of this chapter is to explore the nature of the transitions from communism to capitalism and the changing tensions these transitions produce.

This chapter begins with a general overview of the problems of states and markets in transition, and the global context within which their changes occur. We then focus first on what might be called the *classical socialist system*, commonly referred to as the *communist system*, and explore the economic, political, and social changes that formerly communist nations are experiencing. Russia, Eastern Europe, and China are singled out for special attention in this discussion because they represent three different approaches to the problems of economic and political transition.

Finally, we reflect on the problems and opportunities of the transition states and speculate about the future that awaits these nations. How to balance political and economic change is difficult, since change in one area is certain to affect the other.

Accounting and Control—these are the *chief* things necessary for the organizing and correct functioning of the *first phase* of communist society. *All* citizens are here transformed into hired employees of the state, which is made up of the armed workers. *All* citizens become employees and workers of *one* national state "syndicate." All that is required is that they should work equally, should regularly do their share of work, and should receive equal pay. The accounting and control necessary for this have *been simplified* by capitalism to the utmost, till they have become the extraordinarily simply operation of watching, recording and issuing receipts, within the reach of anybody who can read and write and knows the first four rules of arithmetic.[1]

V. I. Lenin (1918)

In chapter 4 we read how Marx envisioned the rise and fall of capitalism. Recall that according to his logic, the material world was driven primarily by economic forces, such that all aspects of society—politics, culture, history—were derived from the way in which the economy was structured. These structures would inevitably generate hostility between those with economic power and those without, until violent revolution would eventually destroy the existing order, creating in turn a new economic and social system which would in time succumb to its own internal flaws. History was thus not an incremental process, but one of sudden shifts and dramatic change resulting from underlying pressure—much like earthquakes. While capitalism was a necessary historical phase of human development, it too would eventually fall in the face of revolution, where the oppressed working class would rise up and seize control of the wealth of society for the good of all.

The theories of Marx attracted many committed followers—not just those who found such arguments convincing, but also those who sought to realize these ideas in practice. Lenin in Tsarist Russia and Mao in China turned Marx's ideas from *theory* into *practice* such that they could carry out revolution in their own home countries. Yet while communist theory became a powerful mobilizing force in many countries for revolution, upon seizing power communist leaders found themselves confronted with a problem: Once the revolution had overthrown capitalism and gained control over private property, how was the economy to be structured? Marx, after all, had provided no blueprints for what was to be done next. Many believed that the economy could easily be run by the government in a rational manner that would serve the public's best interest. As we see above, Lenin believed that the actual work of managing an economy would be no great task, which he likened to running a post office.

As history was to show, however, the challenge of replacing capitalism with a state-controlled system of economic production would prove to be much more difficult than expected. By the early 1990s Eastern Europe and the Soviet Union had rejected communism, while in China more evolutionary economic reforms had led to a unique fusion of state and market forces. This chapter focuses on the crucial issues of states and markets in transition from one system of state-market relations to another.

STATES AND MARKETS IN TRANSITION

Change is stressful. Change in something as complex and important as a nation's system of political economy causes stresses and strains at all levels: individual, market, class, nation, region, globe. It is significant, therefore, that perhaps half of the world's population is experiencing the stress of a change in their system of political economy at the beginning of the new millennium. These are stressful times for the IPE, with so many states and markets in transition. The nature of the strain, however, is different in each case.

One group of nations is engulfed in the problems of the dramatic transition from communism, or classical socialism, to some form of democratic capitalism—these are the "formers" as Czech leader Václav Havel has called them: the former members of the Warsaw Pact, including Hungary and Poland, and the former states of the Soviet Union, such as Russia and Ukraine.[2] These nations are trying to develop liberal economic institutions and democratic political institutions at the same time—a daunting task that requires a wholesale shift from a focus on collective interests to an emphasis on individual rights. Other nations, like China and Vietnam, are engaged in a somewhat less extreme but perhaps even more difficult transition, from communism (classical socialism) to *market socialism*, a hybrid system that retains central power in the state but encourages private economic activities.[3]

Fundamentally, the many tensions that these nations experience and the problems they must solve derive from a conflict between a political economy system based on individual economic and political choices (a "bottom-up" approach) versus the desire to make choices collectively for the greater public good (a "top-down" approach). No system of political economy is totally "bottom up" or completely "top down"—the problem of balancing individual and collective choices is universal. The problem of transition is to change dramatically the general direction of the flow of social choice without destroying valuable social institutions or undermining social stability. This, as you will see, is not an easy task.

This chapter cannot predict what will happen to these states and markets in transition. We can, however, explore the nature of the changes under way and examine briefly the recent history of economic and political reform. This survey will help us better understand the problems and stresses of today's world, and the prospects for tomorrow.

Every transition has three stages: the old order; the transition process itself, often characterized as *reform* of the old order or *revolt* against it; and the new order that finally emerges. We begin our discussion with an examination of the "old order" of communism. This is what the Hungarian political economist János Kornai calls *classical socialism*, which is the set of fundamental political economy relationships implemented by Joseph Stalin (1879–1953) in the Soviet Union and Mao Zedong (1893–1976) in China. This is the system of political economy that we commonly call *communism*.[4]

COMMUNISM AND THE CLASSICAL SOCIALIST SYSTEM

Socialism is a political economy system of communal ownership of production resources, with a strong emphasis on economic equality. There are various degrees of socialism, ranging from limited public ownership of resources in the United States, for example, to the opposite extreme, the classical socialist system, that we associate with communism in the Soviet Union and elsewhere. It is common to call these nations "communist" because of the importance of the Communist party in their political structures, and so it is tempting to label their form of political economy "communism." For Marx, however, and for the Communist parties in these countries, the term *communism* is reserved for the final stage in Marx's historical progression, when the state "withers away" and communal ownership becomes the natural order. Communism in this sense was never achieved and the state was always a dominant force in the communist nations.

To preserve this distinction, we generally will use the term *classical socialism* to refer to the social and political economy structure and use *communism* the way Marx did, in reference to the social goal and final stage of the historical progression. Hopefully this will not be too confusing. Table 14–1 shows the 14 countries that adopted "communist" or classical socialist systems, with the dates of transition.[5] With the exception of North Korea and Cuba, each of these countries had begun the transition from the "old order" of classical socialism to some "new order" by the early 1990s.

It is instructive to consider the general characteristics of the classical socialist system. Here are highly stylized and oversimplified descriptions of the principal political and economic aspects of classical socialism, which are useful background for us in considering the problems of transition.

The politics and economics of the classical socialist system are completely intertwined—the state *is* the market, for all practical purposes. It is a mistake, therefore, to discuss political and economic aspects of the system separately. Having made this point, it is still true that we must begin somewhere, and so we start with a discussion of the fundamental nature of politics in classical socialism, so that we can see more clearly, in the next section, the strong impact of politics on the economy.

TABLE 14–1 The Classical Socialist Countries

COUNTRY	YEAR	COUNTRY	YEAR
Soviet Union	1917	Poland	1948
Mongolia	1921	Romania	1948
Albania	1944	North Korea	1948
Yugoslavia	1945	China	1949
Bulgaria	1947	East Germany	1949
Czechoslovakia	1948	Vietnam	1954
Hungary	1948	Cuba	1959

THE POLITICS OF CLASSICAL SOCIALISM

It is convenient to break this analysis into four parts: power, ideology, government, and external political relations. Together, these elements define the political and economic basis of classical socialism.

Power

Power is rooted in one party, the Communist party, whose "leading role" was usually written directly into the nation's constitution, meaning that there was in effect no constitutional way to remove the party from power. Democracy as we define it, with limits on governmental power, individual rights, and open competition between different political viewpoints and groups did not exist. Membership in the Communist party was generally limited to about 5 to 10 percent of the population, although a much larger percentage participated in party-led programs and movements. Power in this system was thus *political* power; moreover, because economic resources are held by the state, political power also translates into *economic* power. This system of political divisions is commonly referred to as the *nomenklatura*, which refers to those positions which require party approval. For example, those with higher political standing could count on preferential treatment for better housing, the ability to travel abroad , or access to scarce consumer goods. In the last case, the most evident example was the existence of special stores, often stocked with Western goods or basic necessities in short supply, open only to the *Nomenklatura* or those with hard currency—usually one and the same, since possession of hard currency was highly restricted. While such stores were often explained as existing for tourists, anyone (like the author) who wandered into one of these stores quickly noted that most of the goods offered were of little interest to a foreign tourist—unless one was looking for a Japanese television set as a souvenir. The resulting irony of class divisions within a theoretically classless society are the source of a well-known Soviet joke: "Under capitalism, man exploits man. Under communism, it is the other way around." However, we should also keep in mind that although the economic differences did exist between ruler and ruled, by and large it was nothing like the economic divisions found in capitalist economies like the United States. Communist party leaders lived well, but few lived in a manner commonly seen in the West among the rich. This concentration of power in the Communist party is perhaps the most important distinguishing characteristic of "communism." Under democratic capitalism, power is separated into its political and economic components, though clearly there exists an overlap between the two. Those with economic power often seek to influence politics, and vice versa. Yet one does not automatically convert into another—just because Bill Gates is fabulously wealthy does not mean that he could necessarily become president. However, under the classical socialist system, the concentration of economic power into the hands of the state meant that economic and political power were one and the same.

This combination of economic and political power also meant that economic and political reform were tightly linked, as it would change the distribution of power between government and society, rulers and ruled. This made reform all the more difficult and helps explain why most of these countries did not so much reform as collapse. Reform assumes that the basic structure can be preserved. However, attempts to reform these systems threatened the economic and political resources of those in power. As a result, rejection, rather than reform, of communism eventually became the dominant path.

Ideology

The exercise of power in the classical socialist system was guided by a set of official beliefs, "the party line," concerning social, economic, and political relationships. Based fundamentally on Marx and Lenin, this ideology enshrines the achievements of communist revolution in terms of eliminating inequality and promoting economic development. Because the means of production are collectively owned, this argument holds, resources can be allocated to those industries that best serve the collective interest and achieve the highest levels of economic growth (compared to a capitalist system of private ownership, where resources go where the private benefits are highest). Indeed, in many countries under socialist rule the leadership could point to a rapid leap forward in economic development, typified by the growth of heavy industry, infrastructure, educational and health facilities, and urbanization. For many socialist countries, which had been in a stage of early capitalist or precapitalist development, these changes were indeed profound—though such progress eventually ground to a halt, for reasons we will explain below. "Personality cults," which use leaders and heroes to personify these official beliefs, were also often used to communicate ideology to the masses. Stalin and Mao were important both as real leaders and as ideological symbols, reminding citizens of the important beliefs that guided their country. Many observers have noted that classical socialist ideology, in keeping with Marx's view of communism as a utopia on earth, is in many ways a kind of secular religion, which asks for faith in a set of beliefs without question, sacrifice for a future reward, and which boasts its own set of saints, martyrs, and devils.

Government

One confusing element of politics in classical socialist systems is the distinction between the party and the state or government. In fact, when many referred to the "leader" of a socialist country they were usually referring to the General Secretary of the Communist party. However, this is not a government office—rather, is it the top leadership position of the Communist party. But because of the dominance of the Communist party over the state, the actual state positions have often been viewed as of secondary importance at best. Thus, the term *party-state* is often used in place of the term government. Power flows from the party, and the leadership rises and falls from power based not on public elections, but rather power struggles within the party. This lack of a clear set of mechanisms to make leaderships accountable proved to be dangerous. In the first decades of socialist rule in the Soviet Union, China, and Eastern Europe, terror was used as a means to eliminate opposition to the leadership or socialist rule. This in turn would often set the economy back by eliminating people the leaders mistrusted (such as intellectuals or other professionals). Millions perished in such campaigns, especially in the Soviet Union and China.

As for the actual structure of the party-state itself, the government by and large resembled political systems we see elsewhere in the world, typically with a prime minister or president (again, often a person of secondary importance), a parliament, judiciary, and local government—all positions which fell within the auspices of the *nomenklatura*. The Communist party mirrored the state to a large extent. The General Secretary and the Political Bureau (or Politburo) functioned as the party leader and his cabinet; a Central Committee acted as a kind of legislative body for the party, while below that committees existed at the regional and local level. These bodies extended all the way down to the place of work or residence, where party members were organized into basic party organizations or "cells." These cells were ostensibly intended to represent the interests of the people by transmitting their concerns to those higher-up, but they were also mechanisms by which the party could keep watch over the population. Traditionally the party as a whole would hold a party congress every few years where the party leadership would be elected, though these tended to be little more than confirmations of those already in power.

THE ECONOMICS OF CLASSICAL SOCIALISM

The economy of a classical socialist state was heavily conditioned by politics and ideology. It was convenient to examine the economy in terms of the role of property, the nature of economic coordinating mechanisms, the role of prices, and external economic relations.

Property

Communal ownership of the means of production was the hallmark of any form of socialism and this was especially true in classical socialism its extreme form. This is not to say that there was no private property. Private ownership of personal possessions unrelated to economic production was allowed, and in some countries limited forms of private property continued to exist—for example, agriculture remained largely private in Poland, and small private shops thrived in Hungary. However, most of the means of production—factories, land, property—were owned by the state on behalf of the people as a whole. Given what we have read about Marxism, this makes sense: If private property is a means by which one person can exploit another (an owner of a factory exploiting a worker, for example), then public ownership should eliminate any means by which one individual can exploit another. With the means of production held by the state, many of the typical aspects of capitalism that we take for granted—individual profit, unemployment, competition between firms, even bankruptcy—were eliminated. Individuals lost their right to control property, with the party-state making decisions instead on how resources should be used. A classical socialist economy functions in essence as a single large firm, with the public as employees of that firm. How well that firm does will directly affect the public—if resources are squandered, it is the public that will suffer as a result.

Economic Coordination Mechanisms

Along with the elimination of private property, socialist systems also eliminated the market mechanism. Like private property, markets were viewed in communist theory as an instrument of exploitation, leading to an ever-vicious cycle of competition that drove firms into bankruptcy, consolidated wealth among the successful few, and generated unemployment and misery for the working class. As a result, only in a few areas were free prices allowed, typically in small-scale agriculture where people were allowed to freely sell the produce from their gardens. Given their hostility to markets, socialist systems needed a different way to allocate resources, one that would be more just. What resulted was the creation of a large state bureaucracy in charge of deciding what should be produced, in what amounts, how it should be priced, and where it should be delivered. This system of state control over the market has led to classical socialist economies sometimes being referred to as *centrally planned economies*, because fundamental economic decisions flowed not from the market, but from plans issued by the state.

As one might imagine, planning an entire economy was an extremely difficult task. A market economy is not centralized, and so responds to demands spontaneously if they emerge; if there is a market for something, a producer will typically come along to fill it. In a centrally planned economy, however, planners must determine what needs to be produced. How much steel? How many women's size eight shoes? How many apartments? As one can imagine, this is an overwhelming task, as the needs of the public are hard to determine and always subject to change. Misjudgments in planning at this level led to many shortages in some areas and overproduction in others. A second problem involved the actual process of planning itself: determining what factories should be in charge of what production, from where they should get their resources, and how the final goods should be distributed. This is referred to as *material balancing*, because it requires that all of your inputs (what goes into production) and your outputs (what is being produced) match. If your inputs don't match your outputs, the plan will be thrown out of balance. And, as socialist planners found, perfect planning was impossible. There were simply too many things to plan—in the Soviet Union, some 40,000–50,000 items—and too many unforeseen outcomes, such as a factory failing to deliver its full output. Since most of these items were interdependent on one another, small problems could have a huge effect on the entire plan.

For example, say a factory making steel failed to meet its quota or plan. This would create a shortage of steel in the system for other factories. Let us speculate further that one of those factories which uses that steel makes turbines, necessary in the production of electricity. Now there will be a shortage of turbines needed for national electrical production, and so a shortage of electricity. Some factories will now get less electricity than they need for production (including the steel factory!), leading to further shortages. This is what is meant by the interdependence of many goods—one error in the plan can have a huge ripple effect on the plan as a whole. However, one place where the planners could shift resources without throwing the plan out of balance would be in the consumer sector, since these are not "intermediate inputs" that will go into the production of another good. Therefore, if there is not enough steel to make turbines, why not take it from the auto industry and simply produce fewer cars? The result is that consumer goods are shortchanged in the process.

Many believed that these problems were simply a result of processing large amounts of information, and that better computers or mathematical formulas would have solved these problems. Certainly, while information overload was a problem, a more critical issue was gathering the necessary information in the first place. Setting a fixed plan for the economy requires one to have perfect information about the present and the future—exactly what needs to be produced and what resources exist to produce it. Any mistakes or changes and the system begins to break down.

The Role of Prices

Prices are key elements of any system based on market coordination. Prices are signals that tell individual consumers and producers about the cost and benefits of different actions and thus coordinate their independent actions in the market. Prices also serve to ration scarce items. Scarcity drives prices up, which limits the quantities purchased in the market. In a capitalist system, therefore, prices rise and fall all the time. But under socialist systems, given the lack of a market to send price signals, central planners would set prices for goods themselves. Due to the lack of a market, prices could not accurately reflect the true value of any good, since a value is established by the interaction of supply and demand. Many resources were wasted as a result, since questions of cost were of no real concern.

In addition, prices did not change to reflect shifts in supply or demand over time. This contributed to what has been called *repressed inflation.* As opposed to inflation in market economies where prices rise as demand outstrips supply, under repressed inflation demand expresses itself in different ways. Let's take the example of consumer goods and services. For many people living in socialist countries, prices for goods were relatively low in relationship to their wages, but as noted earlier, the supply of consumer goods and services was often limited and of poor quality. Consumers found themselves with more money than they could spend. What did they do with it? In many cases a *black*, or illegal, market emerged in imported goods, hard currency, or products and services in short supply. In addition, a complex system of bribery also developed in such areas as health care to ensure access to better treatment. While the socialist system had outlawed the market, it continued to operate on the margins of the economy, allocating scarce resources and setting prices—albeit illegally.

The Role of Incentives

Just as prices for goods were set in ways that did not reflect their true value, this was also true for labor. As one might expect, classical socialist systems were hostile to large differences in wages, viewing this as the source of class inequality and exploitation. Highly trained workers could thus not expect to receive substantially greater pay for their work than, for example, manual laborers. This quest for equality in work also extended to the concept of unemployment, which was viewed as a core injustice of capitalism. Not only was unemployment ended, it was also made illegal—everyone who was able to work was required to do so.

Problems came to plague socialist economies as a result of this relationship between labor and the market. Because firms were evaluated largely on whether they had fulfilled their targets for the plan and because workers realized that there was little relationship between their salaries and how hard they worked, factories concentrated on the *quantity, not quality*, of their products. Firms would receive a bonus if they met their target in the plan, but whether those goods were substandard was of no concern. In a market system, a producer of shoddy goods would be run out of business by a competitor, but in a socialist system there were no such alternatives.

This led to an economy where many goods were of such low quality as to be virtually worthless, resulting in the waste of huge amounts of resources. This author recalls buying a new Soviet-made radio in Hungary in the late 1980s, where it took the store clerk four tries before he could actually find one which worked. A related problem could be found in the diversity of goods. Since planning targets were set using numerical indicators of some sort, firms would concentrate primarily on meeting this figure, even if production were distorted as a result. For example, Robert Campbell notes shortages in plumbing fixtures in the Soviet Union could be traced to the fact that the factories making pipe were evaluated on how many tons of pipe they produced—thus encouraging the production of large-scale and heavier diameters. This not only wasted metal, but also created shortages in small diameters needed for apartment construction.[6] Finally, the key element for economic development—innovation—was also undermined. Not only was there no reward for economic innovation (firms or their workers would see no profit from improved goods), most firms resisted change as a costly diversion from fulfilling the plan. The Soviet-made radio discussed above was not only of poor quality but was also very heavy and was decades out of date in comparison to Western models. Having been designed once, why improve it?

THE PROBLEMS OF TRANSITION

Hopefully our discussion should give you some idea of why classical socialism eventually fell apart. Rather than being a system based on the allocation of resources by the market, socialist economies attempted to use the state to make these decisions for both goods and labor. Yet in doing so, they eliminated the impact that the market has on economic performance. Under such conditions, economic production eroded as the quality of work declined and resources were wasted by an inefficient planning system. It is important that we keep in mind that socialism did not fail because the people in these societies were not as "smart" as we are. On the contrary, in many of these countries their educational systems ranked among the best in the world in many fields. Yet while socialist systems could still generate ideas, it could not harness them and in fact often turned against them. Stagnation and resignation reigned; economic performance ground to a halt, and in some countries even life expectancy began to decline, while in the West technological change grew exponentially.

It was this deepening problem that led leaders like Soviet General Secretary Mikhail Gorbachev to seek some reform of the system starting in the mid-1980s. Gorbachev's policy of *glasnost* (openness) and *perestroika* (restructuring) were meant to reform, not eliminate, socialism. Gorbachev, along with some leaders in Eastern Europe, hoped that a limited amount of political and economic liberalization would give the populace a greater stake in the system and help reinvigorate socialism. However, we should recall our earlier observation that under such conditions, reform is difficult, as it may threaten those in power; indeed, by admitting to the flawed nature of the system, the leadership only exposed its weakness. Allowed to speak openly for the first time in decades, the public quickly raced ahead of their leaders, demanding not just reform, but the complete transformation of the system. The public did not know exactly what capitalism or democracy would look like, but many were convinced that it had to be better than what they currently lived under. By 1989 Hungary and Poland initiated a series of economic and political changes that paved the way toward democracy and capitalism, which many of their socialist neighbors soon followed. Even the Soviet Union, more than seven decades after the Russian Revolution, saw not only socialism but the country itself collapse in 1991, as a failed coup against Gorbachev sparked its breakup into 15 separate countries.

Socialism had fallen; what would now take its place? Perhaps the biggest challenge to postsocialist countries was the fact that there was no blueprint for what to do; many countries had moved to socialism over the past 70 years, but not one had moved from socialism to capitalism. A second problem involved the fact that many of these countries were attempting to carry out economic and political transformation at the same time. Could a country carry out economic and political change without one undermining the other?

THE POLITICS OF TRANSITION

Since the late 1980s various kinds of political reform and transformation have been underway in socialist states. Some of these have proved quite successful (as in parts of Eastern Europe); others have experienced quite negative results (as in Russia), while still others have a path which remains unclear (as in China). These economic changes can rise from political reform, or be the source of it. Either way, power, ideology and government are inevitably affected.

Power

The transition away from the classical socialist system leads to a redistribution of power for several reasons. First, the move to freer markets requires that economic and political power be separated, at least to some extent. The party-state loses much of its ability to set prices or plan the economy, and the rise of private economic actors means that new sources of power apart from the state can and will emerge. Second, economic and political power tend to be decentralized to a greater extent than in the past. Ideally at the level of politics this means the creation of a multiparty system of government and democratic decision making. At the level of economics this means a movement to some form of private ownership, free markets, a system of flexible wages and prices, and individual "self-management" in buying and selling decisions.

Such changes can develop in two directions. Under *market socialism*, the ownership of key resources is retained by the state in the interest of equality, while a greater role for markets is allowed. Factories remain in state hands, but they are allowed to set prices freely, eliminating central planning. This is contrasted with a move to *capitalism*, where the role of the state is further reduced, and most publicly owned resources are *privatized*—either sold to private buyers or converted into privately held corporations.

These political and economic changes require an essential reorientation of power. Under classical socialism, power flows down from the top (the party-state). The move to a greater role for private actors and markets, however, ideally means that power is vested with the public, and flows *up*. However, as we shall discuss below, the move toward freer markets and private property does not mean automatically that power is dispersed. Rather, economic and political power may simply become reconcentrated in the hands of a few elites—as is seen in many developing countries.

Ideology

Economic transition means that to a great extent the ideology based on Marx or Lenin loses much or all of its power as a source of public mobilization or government legitimacy. Having failed in practice to deliver economic prosperity, socialist societies find themselves looking for new ideas that will help guide their countries in the future. The question is, what values and beliefs will replace communist ideology? For some countries, the Anglo-American model of liberalism is attractive, as it promotes a limited role for the state in the economy and a high degree of personal initiative and responsibility—a "cure" for the paternalistic and collective mind-set of communism. However, for others more nationalist or state-oriented ideas are appealing, including variants on mercantilist or even fascist ideology. All promise to "restore" the country to a position of wealth and international standing and compete for the hearts and minds of a public that has seen the justification for their way of life discredited. This vacuum of ideas can be dangerous in a transitional society.

Government

The change from classical socialism in many countries is also often accompanied by a transition from authoritarian government to a more democratic system. Economic failures under socialism are viewed by many as the product of a party-state system that was unaccountable to the public. Even many of those who did still support socialist ideals in the late 1980s believed that only democracy could save socialism. But of course, political change is not a simple task. In Eastern Europe and the former Soviet Union, democratization meant introducing a political system that either had not existed in the country for decades, or in many cases, never at all. While it is easy to take such practices for granted in the West, keep in mind that democracy is a complex system of institutions, rules, and norms, creating a system in which actors compete for power *and* accept defeat. In transitional societies, constructing a similar system requires the building of new constitutions, political parties, electoral rules, administrative and judicial structures, as well as educating all participants on "the rules of the game."

This is not an easy task. Various actors will seek to have their own preferences written into the constitution—for example, whether the country should have a strong, directly elected president, as in the United States, or a prime minister, who is chosen directly by the legislature. Political parties will find it difficult constructing a platform that appeals to voters, especially when voters still have only a fuzzy idea what their own political preferences are. How electoral rules are constructed will have a profound impact on how many parties make it into the legislature and how much power they have. Many sectors of the state will also have to undergo "housecleaning," while officials from the old *nomenklatura* are replaced with individuals whose position is based on their skill rather than party membership. Finally, all these changes must be accepted by the population as legitimate—even if their own desires have not been met.

Building these structures and having people agree to and abide by them is difficult. In some countries, economic reform has been carried out without accompanying democratic change, as in China, and demands for political reform have been met with force. This has also been true in some parts of the former Soviet Union and Eastern Europe. In fact, in some cases where new leaders have come to power, they have been quick to take up the old authoritarian policies of their predecessors, leading to repression and even civil war. Old habits die hard.

THE ECONOMICS OF TRANSITION

Economic transition also requires new institutions and ways of thinking, as well as a radical dismantling of the system of state ownership.

Property

The transition from communism to capitalism or a socialist market system requires a redefinition of property. Under the classical socialist system, the means of production are communal, rather than owned by any individual. In contrast, under capitalism private ownership is predominant. The process of privatization is not simply an economic task but also a political one—by disconnecting the relationship between the party-state and the economy, the goal is to *depoliticize* the economy and allow for private individuals to make decisions about the economy based on their own interests.

But this task is not easy. First, what are the means of production worth? In order to sell off the factories or land or apartments the state has to figure out what their value is—something difficult in a society where markets have played no role. Second, who should get these assets? One option would be to simply give the assets away—for example, transfer ownership of a factory to its workers, or a house to its occupants. But is it fair that one person winds up owning a nicer home simply because they were lucky enough to be living in it when the state privatized it? Or that some workers wind up owning a factory that turns out to be less profitable than others? Another option would be to sell assets to the highest bidder. But again, there is a problem. In a society where wages and profits have been restricted, who would have the money to buy a factory? Often only the old *nomenklatura* would be expected to have amassed any significant wealth, which would mean that the old party bosses would now become the new capitalist bosses. An alternative would be to allow foreign buyers, but this often generates public resistance to the idea that "the country is being sold to foreigners." Another complication involves those who had their land, homes, and factories seized by the previous socialist government. Are they (or their descendants) entitled to get them back? Finally, what about firms no one wants and which are not competitive—should the government let them go bankrupt? Marxist ideology stressed the fact that the means of production belonged to the people, but privatization involves convincing the public that they would be better off if these assets were now in private hands—not a easy argument to make.

Economic Coordination Mechanisms

Prices replace the bureaucracy as coordinating mechanisms during the transition from classical socialism. Although government coordination is still necessary in some parts of the economy, the rise of markets necessitates the increased use of prices to allocate and distribute resources. The logic of the market is that prices are critical bits of information that individual consumers, workers, and producers use in their decision making. Market prices contain information about the relative cost of producing goods and services, the relative value that buyers place on them, and the point at which the market clears without shortage or surplus.

The fundamental difficulty in moving to a decentralized system of coordination is the problem of responsibility. Under a decentralized system, individuals are responsible for gathering information, making decisions, and taking actions. This is totally different from the system of orders and reports that characterize classical socialism, and governments may still seek to control some aspects of economic production and allocation (such as in energy or food), motivated by considerations similar to those found under mercantilism.

The Role of Prices

For economies in transition, the problem is that the role of prices in a market economy, as stated above, are fundamentally at odds with their role in classical socialism, as stated earlier in this chapter. Under classical socialism, the bureaucratic apparatus sets prices to influence individual actions to further a social goal. It did not matter very much if the prices failed to reflect cost, or consumer valuation, or even the balance of demand and supply. With a market economy, the prices are set by the "invisible hand" of the market—and aim to achieve no social goal other than efficiency.

This transition is stressful. One area where this can be seen is in the area of inflation. As stated earlier, in socialist economies one of the major problems was repressed inflation. Given that prices were fixed and could not rise or fall, when demand outstripped supply (such as for consumer goods), this demand would spill over into other areas, such as black markets. Once a government eliminates its own control over prices and allows firms to charge what they will, this repressed demand for goods can now express itself as open inflation. Goods that had been in short supply appear in the shops, but at a high price. Many individuals who lived on small incomes in the past but found them sufficient to meet their needs, such as the elderly, find that under the new prices even basic goods are beyond their reach. High prices may in turn lead workers to demand higher wages from their places of work, which are often still owned by the state. The government may want to meet these demands to prevent unrest or to stay in power. However, the means to pay higher wages may be absent (for example, taxes did not exist in socialist economies since private sources of wealth had been eliminated). Governments may turn to simply printing money in order to meet such demands. This can spark hyperinflation and devastate the economy—as it did in Germany prior to Hitler's rise to power.

CASE STUDY: VARIETIES OF ECONOMIC TRANSFORMATION IN EASTERN EUROPE

If Gorbachev can be credited with the policies that created the first cracks in the edifice of socialism, then Eastern Europe is responsible for bringing the entire structure down. Already in the late 1980s, reform movements within Hungary, Poland, and Czechoslovakia were pushing leaders toward political change, which eventually turned into a full-fledged rout. Leaders lost power, to be replaced by democratically elected parliaments. But equally important was economic change: New political leaders came to power on anticommunist platforms and were now expected to lead their countries to Western European-style prosperity.

On the surface, these three Eastern European countries appeared to have much more going for them than many other socialist states. Historically, their proximity to Western Europe meant that their levels of economic development prior to socialism had been much higher than that experienced in Russia. Socialism had been in place for a much shorter period of time—only since the end of World War Two. Eastern Europe still remained strongly connected to the rest of Europe in a way which Russia or other socialist states were not, through such things as trade, tourism, and even foreign investment. Finally, in Hungary and Poland in particular, economic reforms had been permitted for a number of years, creating a prominent role for private agriculture and small businesses. Many Eastern Europeans thus understood and participated in markets to a much greater extent than in other socialist countries. However, it would be an exaggeration to say that these countries were able to undertake painless economic changes as a result. Poland and Hungary were burdened by foreign debts, which their governments had acquired in a desperate attempt to prop up their ailing economies. All three were confronted with an economy dominated by state-owned firms which were overstaffed, inefficient, and antiquated.

Hungary, Poland, and Czechoslovakia (which in 1993 peacefully separated into two countries, the Czech Republic and Slovakia) all made the move toward capitalism starting in 1990, but in very different ways. This variation reflects the central debate that emerged with regard to economic transformation. First, while many economists and political scientists agreed on exactly *what* needed to be achieved, *how fast* was another matter. Some argued that given the radical nature of economic transformation, changes should be gradual to minimize any social disruptions than might undermine these fledgling economies and democracies. Others, such as Harvard economist Jeffrey Sachs, argued for rapid market reforms that would be painful but shorter in their duration—what came to be known as "shock therapy." It was unclear which policy might be politically safer. Second, there was disagreement over *sequencing*—exactly what needed to be done, and in what order. What to do first? Third, observers were uncertain how privatization should take place.

With regard to privatization, one method favored by some was what was known as *voucher privatization*. Under voucher privatization, the public would be given or sold vouchers, which would in essence represent a piece of the total economic assets owned by the state. These vouchers could be sold, used to purchase shares in companies that were being privatized, or entrusted to investment funds—much as a mutual fund manages stocks for its clients. The main argument in favor of voucher privatization was that it would ensure a wide distribution of ownership among the population and hopefully boost public support for economic change by making them direct stakeholders in it. Others opposed voucher privatization, arguing instead for the direct sales of firms to the highest bidder, which would help generate revenue for cash-strapped governments and attract foreign investment. There also remained the lingering view that the government should retain some control over sectors of the economy seen as "vital," such as agriculture or certain ir.dustries. As with mercantilism, the idea that the market should drive the economic development of the country was hard for some to swallow.

In the end, Hungary, Poland, and the Czech Republic each pursued different paths to free markets and private property, making it difficult to say with any certainty which path is the "right" one. Rather, it appears that the kind of economic transition chosen depends to a great extent on the kinds of economic and political conditions that exist in a given country. Despite the similar experiences of socialism, Eastern European countries differ in their economic conditions, elected leaders, and political culture. What proves to be a suitable mix of economic policies for one country may not be suitable for another.[7]

Among the Eastern European countries, Poland stands out for its bold step to introduce "shock therapy" in 1990. One explanation for Poland's willingness to gamble with such radical changes was the country's already deep economic crisis, which resulted from mismanagement under the previous government. Following Sachs' recommendations, the government eliminated virtually all controls on prices, returning their control to the market. The local currency was sharply devalued and made freely convertible. Restrictions on international trade were also eliminated, allowing for the greater importation of foreign goods to compete with domestic ones that had in past monopolized the economy. With markets freed, prices initially rose but soon leveled off, and consumer goods that had long been absent from the stores reappeared. GDP also initially fell but soon recovered. Privatization, however, has been slower and more cautious, carried out through a mixture of vouchers and the direct sale of firms to the public or the employees of that business.

Hungary, in contrast, eschewed shock therapy, favoring instead a slower approach to market reforms. In part this reflected the fact that Hungary had already carried out some market reforms under the previous government starting as far back as the 1960s. In part it reflected the new government's own unease over carrying out such radical changes. However, by the mid-1990s disappointing economic results and a change in government as a result led to a more rapid pace. One notable aspect of the Hungarian economic transformation has been its policy of privatization, which relied primarily on direct sales to the highest bidder. A large proportion of firms sold in Hungary were purchased by foreign investors, unlike Czechoslovakia and Poland; in fact, a third of foreign direct investment in all of Eastern Europe and the former Soviet Union has been in Hungary alone. Vouchers have been limited to provide limited compensation for those who had private property seized by the regime.[8]

Finally, in the Czech Republic, economic transformation was similarly influenced by the legacies of the previous system. Much more politically rigid under communism than Hungary or Poland, Czechoslovakia made few reforms of its economic system; however, this also meant that it had avoided some of the severe problems that Hungary and Poland had to confront after socialism, such as a high foreign debt. Reforms in the Czech Republic have proceeded much more slowly as a result. This included the earliest introduction of a voucher privatization program in Eastern Europe; unlike other East European countries, the government sought to transfer property into private hands as quickly as possible and did not have to contend with significant public opposition to privatization. The vast majority of large businesses were privatized in this manner. Observers have been impressed with the Czech Republic's rapid privatization, but questions remain whether vouchers, by spreading ownership among too many people, have simply delayed tough decisions about reorganizing and closing unprofitable firms.[9]

In short, economic transformation in Eastern Europe has varied widely. In Hungary, Poland, and the Czech Republic, changes have been substantial. The private sector now accounts for the majority of GDP as state-owned businesses have been sold off, and all three have experienced economic growth. However, we should note that these three cases represent the brightest stars in Eastern Europe; many other countries have not moved as far toward economic transformation nor fared nearly as well.

CASE STUDY: ECONOMIC AND POLITICAL REFORM IN RUSSIA

In comparison to the three countries above, Russia's move to capitalism has been much more problematic for several reasons. First, historically Russia had little experience with capitalism prior to communist rule. Second, even limited markets were not tolerated to the extent found in Hungary or Poland. This meant that the country had less insight on its own transition to capitalism. Third, the country has traditionally been much less integrated into the world or European economy, relying on its own large internal market and its abundance of natural resources. The much smaller countries of Eastern Europe have long depended on international markets for imports and exports, even under socialism. Fourth,

Russia was a socialist country for a much longer period of time than Eastern Europe or China. Finally, the economic transformation of Russia emerged out of the disintegration of the Soviet Union itself and its decline from superpower status. Russia has thus had to cope with political changes much more dramatic than in Eastern Europe. As a result, building a working democracy and capitalism economic system has proved rather daunting.

While the Soviet Union had experimented off and on with limited economic reforms as far back as the 1920s, dramatic changes are best associated with Mikhail Gorbachev, who came to power in 1985. Gorbachev inherited a stagnant economy at a time when the costs of the Cold War were being keenly felt in the Soviet Union and Eastern Europe. Gorbachev also represented a new, younger generation of Soviet leaders who were not shaped by the rigidity of Stalinism or the horrors of World War II, and who were more willing to seek out compromise with the West and greater experimentation in politics and economic policy. He proposed a set of economic reforms and political reforms, based upon the concepts of *glasnost* and *perestroika*. Ideally, Gorbachev hoped that greater personal freedom and a reorganization of the economy could make socialism more dynamic and harness public initiative and support.

The perestroika reforms of the economy were clearly more ambitious than the glasnost reforms of the political sphere of Soviet life. But even perestroika was a half-measure. Factory managers were, in theory, given greater authority to make production decisions, but the state planning bureaucracy was still in place and maintained its power, making it unclear just where the balance of power stood. Private ownership and private enterprise were encouraged, but prices remained regulated. Eventually, glasnost and perestroika would be the Soviet Union's undoing. Both promised change and reform, but Gorbachev believed that power could still reside fundamentally with the party-state. As Marshall Goldman nicely put it, "like the bridegroom who can never quite bring himself to show up at his wedding, Gorbachev could never bring himself to accept the changes his proposals would inevitably set in motion."[10] The public was shown the failings of the system but were not given the power to change it. This contradiction eventually generated increasing conflicts within the party and state, public discontent, unrest, and eventually the end of the country itself, in 1991.

Since 1991 Russia's economic reforms have moved the country a long way from the system of central planning and one-party rule that dominated the country for so long. However, these reforms have been far from smooth, illustrating the difficulties involved in simultaneous economic and political reform. Part of the explanation for why these changes have been so difficult for Russia may lie in its historical experiences. As mentioned earlier, Russia cannot reach back to a presocialist history of capitalist development or democratic traditions. These are institutions largely unknown to the country, which in essence jumped from a largely agrarian and still feudal system directly to socialist industrialization and authoritarianism in 1917. As a result, democracy and the market must be built from scratch.

One of the first tasks of the Russian government under President Boris Yeltsin, was to check the high levels of inflation that had emerged during the final years of economic reform in the Soviet Union. To achieve this, Russia carried out its own version of "shock therapy," modeled after Poland, which cut many subsidies to firms and agriculture and eliminated fixed prices on most goods. This policy was expected to lead to temporary price increases, but this was to be mitigated by increased competition as new suppliers entered the market. In addition, starting in 1992 Russia began the process of selling off millions of apartments and over 100,000 small firms and over 15,000 large ones. Voucher privatization allowed workers and managers to buy shares in their firms and gave the public the ability to buy shares as well.[11] A second wave of privatization which took place in 1995 concentrated on many remaining large firms which had not yet been sold. However, rather than concentrating on vouchers, the government hoped to sell these firms to the highest bidder and earn desperately needed revenues in the process. However, the privatization process was badly managed and foreign investors discouraged from participating. In the end, a handful of private Russian banks wound up gaining control over many of the largest and most valuable firms in the country. This has helped discredit the privatization process in Russia and created a widespread public perception that the country is now owned by a few rich bankers—exactly what Marx had warned would take place under capitalism! Despite these problems, as of 1996 private firms accounted for around 60 percent of GDP—an impressive transformation from a system where just a few years before virtually no private sector existed.[12]

However, despite such dramatic changes, Russia still has a long way to go. The use of shock therapy has been criticized by some observers, who argued that Poland's preexisting conditions—a large role for private agriculture and small business and strong support for market reform—were nonexistent in Russia. As a result, prices rose dramatically in the wake of shock therapy in Russia, and GDP began to slide as consumption dropped. By 1996 the official economy had contracted by half of its 1989 size—a fall deeper than the Great Depression in the United States. While most firms are now in private hands, many of them have yet to be transformed into modern businesses that can truly compete in free markets. Many firms are not even able to pay their workers; by some estimates at least one-quarter of privatized firms will eventually go bankrupt.[13] The country is also still very weak in the development and enforcement of basic laws and practices necessary for a market economy. One result has been the rise of organized crime, which has sought to exploit weaknesses in the new political and economic system by "offering protection" to businesses or monopolizing certain markets. In one stark example, between 1991 and 1996 more than 100 bankers were assassinated. An estimated 20 percent or more of the population now live in poverty, and life expectancy for Russian men *fell five years* between 1990 and 1995.[14] The collapse of the Russian ruble in 1998 shows how fragile this economic system remains.

Finally, Russia still struggles to create a culture of capitalism. The public remains wary of the idea that there should be class distinctions between rich and poor and fears that private property could be renationalized by the state. As a result, long-term investment is replaced by short-term profit making, which does less good for the future development of the country as a whole. Overall, economic changes are far from complete, and the pain of transformation weakens an already fragile democracy.

CASE STUDY: CHINA'S TRANSITION TO MARKET SOCIALISM

The transition from planned economy to market economy has gone on the longest in the People's Republic of China and has achieved a great deal of success. This may inspire other nations engaged in political and economic reform, but China's case is unique and any attempt to distill lessons from China's experience must take into account its special features. The first and perhaps most important factor is that, unlike Russia and Poland, China's goal has been to introduce market forces to stimulate the economy but without giving up party power. While other countries in transition from socialism have introduced democracy and capitalism more or less at the same time, China has sought to carry out economic changes while limiting political change—even to the point of using force, as was seen in the Tiananmen Square crackdown in 1989. China, then, seems to be attempting a transition from classical socialism to market socialism.[15]

After the revolution in 1949, Chinese leader Mao Zedong (1893–1976) introduced a classical socialist system based on the Stalinist model, with state ownership of the means of production, collective farms, central planning, and other features described earlier in this chapter. However, in many ways China's conditions were unlike those found in the Soviet Union. Economically, China was even less agriculturally developed than the Soviet Union had been early in its socialist revolution. Ideologically, Mao, whose revolution had been primarily peasant-based, was hostile to the notion of bureaucracy and centralization common in Soviet-type systems, seeking instead a "continuous revolution" that would counter such tendencies. The first major step in this direction, the Great Leap Forward (1958–60) was a vigorous attempt to push industrial development by concentrating on the development of small local industries in the countryside. Top-down central planning was ended, and in the countryside people were organized into *communes,* which were intended to strengthen collective behavior by providing a common body for such things as employment, housing, and education. Even private meals were replaced by common dining halls.[16]

However, the Great Leap Forward did not produce rural development. Lacking technical skill, the communes' industrial production was of low quality, while agricultural production was neglected. Millions died of famine as a result. China then returned to a more centralized Soviet-type economic system. This, too, was disrupted by the Cultural Revolution, which saw its peak from 1966 to 1968 but continued on until Mao's death in 1976. During its first years, Mao encouraged the people to attack the party-state itself, which he saw as having grown too bureaucratic and opposed to revolutionary change. This struggle, which nearly came to civil war, also took the lives of tens, perhaps hundreds of thousands, and severely weakened the internal organization of the party and state. Central planning, for example, again declined in favor of greater decentralization and local self-reliance.

Ironically, China's tumultuous history under socialism helps explain how China was later able to make such radical moves toward market reform even while under Communist party leadership. Unlike the Soviet Union, economic and political power was much less centralized due to the effects of constant political turmoil, making the party-state in China a smaller obstacle to reform. Breaking with the past was less difficult as there was, in a sense, less to break with. After Mao's death, Deng Xiaoping (himself a victim of the Cultural Revolution) assumed leadership and introduced a plan for economic reform, which was adopted in 1978. Deng's described his program as "socialism with Chinese characteristics," combining elements of socialism with a greater role for markets and private property.

In agriculture, Deng allowed for the dissolution of the communal farms in favor of traditional family units, which were allowed to sell excess produce through free markets. Agricultural production increased dramatically as these reforms took root. The increasingly prosperous family farms stimulated growth of private rural enterprises as well. At the same time, Deng's plan created what was termed "the open door." Barriers to international trade and finance were lowered, opening China to global markets and foreign investment.[17] The new slogan which characterized these reforms, "to be rich is glorious," sounded anything but Marxist. Finally, private businesses were legalized. At first only small-scale firms with a few employees were permitted, but by the mid-1980s many large-scale private firms with hundreds or even thousands of workers had emerged with the tacit approval of the government.[18]

Taken together, these two reforms created an environment highly favorable to economic development. The agricultural reforms, which created a free market in food, brought immediate gains to the population and helped alleviate rural poverty. Food producers were more efficient and their efforts better rewarded, while food consumers benefited from increased production. International trade and foreign investment also created new markets for goods and increased access to resources and technology. Private businesses helped provide new sources of employment and goods for the population. Since reforms, Chinese economic growth has been dramatic, leading many to conclude that it will be a major economic center of the global economy in the next century.

But China has not completed its transition to capitalism, and many issues remain unresolved. Private enterprise and markets have flourished but still remain what the Chinese have called "the bird in the cage"—that is, held firmly within the cage of state control.[19] State-run companies suffer from the same problems as their Soviet and East European counterparts: inefficient, outdated, and kept afloat by government financial support that could be used elsewhere. Unemployment, inflation, declining growth, and economic turmoil elsewhere in Asia are serious threats to continued development. Similarly, political liberalization has moved forward since 1989, but the party-state appears willing to use force against any opposition, as was seen at Tiananmen in 1989, when the party-state used military force against public demands for political change. Yet at the same time as China modernizes, public pressure for political liberalization is likely to grow. Continued economic development could spur demands for accompanying political change, while an economic slowdown could undermine party legitimacy and authoritarian rule. Either path may prove dangerous for those now in power.

As opposed to the rapid collapse of socialism in Eastern Europe and the Soviet Union, during the 1980s and 1990s China has undergone cycles of *fang* and *shou*—relaxation and control, where liberalization leads to greater popular autonomy and assertiveness, to be followed by a backlash by the party-state and a return to more conservative policies.[20] Having witnessed the fall of socialism in Eastern Europe and the Soviet Union, party leaders see market reforms less as a step toward capitalism and democracy than as a means by which they can remain in power. How far reform will continue, and to what effect on the party's monopoly on power, remains to be seen, particularly given the death of Deng Xiaoping in 1996.

STATES AND MARKETS IN TRANSITION: TENSIONS, ISSUES, AND LESSONS

We began this chapter with a quote from Lenin that laid out how he envisioned the socialist economy. Capitalism had led to industrialization but also great injustices that would prove to be its downfall; socialism would build upon the strengths of capitalism while avoiding its injustices. But rather than being a simple affair, running an economy from the top down proved to a formidable task—there was too much to take into account and it was too hard to allocate resources efficiently without some way to measure their value. Moreover, people within these systems found little incentive for hard work and innovation.

For the Soviet Union and Eastern Europe, attempts to solve these problems eventually led to outright collapse; one might imagine the analogy of renovating a dilapidated house, only to find that the house is so run down that finally demolition is the only logical choice. The dual task of building both democracy and capitalism has now begun, with mixed results. China's path has been somewhat different, with its "house" in a nearly continuous process of renovation and change. While this ongoing change has helped stave off the kind of decay seen in Eastern Europe and the Soviet Union, its foundations are made up of an odd mixture of socialism and capitalism which in the end may prove no more stable. In all of these cases, the tension between states and markets is clear—in particular, the conflict between the right to individual economic and political choice (a "bottom-up" approach) versus the desire to make these choices collectively for a greater public good (a "top-down" approach). This conflict can be found in any society at any point in time, not just under socialism—it is one we struggle with every day.

Overall, the history of socialism in the IPE is a fascinating example of how a number of states sought to depart from the current path of global development and forge a new means of prosperity for their countries. And despite their failures, the idea behind such actions—providing a decent standard of living for all, at both the domestic and international level—remains as much a concern today as at the time of the Russian Revolution in 1917.

DISCUSSION QUESTIONS

1. What is the "classical socialist system" and how does it differ from "communism"? What nations have adopted the classical socialist system at different times during the twentieth century? Which nations currently employ this system? Explain.

2. What are the essential characteristics of the classical socialist system? How does this system differ from market socialism and from capitalism? How do the roles of state and market differ among these three systems of political economy? Explain.

3. Compare and contrast the economic and political reforms in Russia and in Eastern Europe. Suggest factors that have made Eastern Europe's reforms more successful, at this point, than those in Russia. Are there any general lessons to be derived from this experience? Explain.

4. How are China's reform experiences different from those of Russia and Eastern Europe? Focus on differences in both means and ends. China aims to reform its market without a radical alteration in its political system. Is it possible to change the market so dramatically without changing the state? Explain.

INTERNET LINKS

Harvard Institute for International Development:
    http://www.hiid.harvard.edu/index.html
Jeffrey Sachs's home page:
    http://www.hiid.harvard.edu/about/people/sachs/jsachs.html
Center for Civil Society International:
    http://www.friends-partners.org/~ccsi/
Russian and East European Network Information Center:
    http://reenic.utexas.edu/reenic.html
Open Society Institute (Moscow):
    http://www.osi.ru/VAD/english.nsf/pages/eng

SUGGESTED READINGS

Robert F. Ash and Y.Y. Kueh, eds. *The Chinese Economy Under Deng Xiaoping*. Oxford: Clarendon Press, 1996.

Joseph R. Blasi, Maya Kroumova, and Douglas Kruse. *Kremlin Capitalism: Privatizing the Russian Economy*. Ithaca, NY: Cornell University Press, 1997.

Maxim Boycko, Andrei Shleifer, and Robert Vishny. *Privatizing Russia*. Cambridge, MA: MIT Press, 1995.

Robert Campbell. *The Socialist Economies in Transition: A Primer on Semi-Reformed Systems*. Bloomington, IN: Indiana University Press, 1991.

"The Gate of Heavenly Peace" (videorecording; PBS *Frontline* series). Boston: WGBH, 1995.

Feng Chen. *Economic Transition and Political Legitimacy in Post-Mao China: Ideology and Reform*. Albany, NY: State University of New York Press, 1995.

Maurice Ernst, Michael Alexeev, and Paul Marer. *Transforming the Core:Restructuring Industrial Enterprises in Russia and Central Europe*. Boulder, CO: Westview Press, 1996.

Shangquan Gao. *China's Economic Reform*. New York: St. Martin's Press, 1996.

Marshall I. Goldman. *The USSR in Crisis: The Failure of an Economic System*. New York: W.W. Norton, 1983.

———. *Lost Opportunity: Why Economic Reforms in Russia Have Not Worked*. New York: W.W. Norton, 1994.

János Kornai. *The Socialist System: The Political Economy of Communism*. Princeton, NJ: Princeton University Press, 1992.

V.I. Lenin. *The State and Revolution*. New York: International Publishers, 1932.

Roderick MacFarquhar, ed. *The Politics of China, 1949–1989*. Cambridge: Cambridge University Press, 1993.

Barry Naughton. *Growing out of the Plan: Chinese Economic Reform, 1978–1993*. Cambridge: Cambridge University Press, 1996.

Adam Przeworski. *Democracy and the Market*. Cambridge: Cambridge University Press, 1991.

Carl Riskin. *China's Political Economy: The Quest for Development since 1949*. Oxford: Oxford University Press, 1988.

Jeffrey Sachs. *Poland's Jump to the Market Economy*. Cambridge, MA: MIT Press, 1993.

Salvatore Zecchini, ed. *Lessons from the Economic Transition: Central and Eastern Europe in the 1990s*. Dordrecht, the Netherlands: Kluwer Academic Publishers, 1997.

NOTES

1. V.I. Lenin, *The State and Revolution* (New York: International Publishers, 1932).
2. Václav Havel, "A Call for Sacrifice," *Foreign Affairs* 73 (March/April 1994), pp. 2–7.
3. Classical socialism is sometimes called *state socialism* to make clear its difference from *market socialism*.
4. See János Kornai, *The Socialist System: The Political Economy of Communism* (Princeton, NJ: Princeton University Press, 1992).
5. Excerpted from Table 1–1, of Kornai, *The Socialist System*, pp. 6–7. The reference date for this list is 1987, before the collapse of governments in Eastern Europe.
6. Robert Campbell, *The Socialist Economies in Transition: A Primer on Semi-Reformed Systems* (Bloomington, IN: Indiana University Press, 1991), p. 46.
7. Gabor Huyna, "Large Privatization, Restructuring and Foreign Direct Investment" in Salvatore Zecchini, ed. *Lessons from the Economic Transition: Central and Eastern Europe in the 1990s* (Dordrecht, the Netherlands: Kluwer Academic Publishers, 1997), pp. 275–300.
8. For details on Hungary, see *Transition Report 1996* (London: European Bank for Reconstruction and Development, 1996, p. 116; and Maurice Ernst, Michael Alexeev, and Paul Marer, *Transforming the Core: Restructuring Industrial Enterprises in Russia and Central Europe* (Boulder, CO: Westview Press, 1996), chap. 6.
9. For a discussion of the Czech Republic's economy, see Jiri Pehe, "The Disappointments of Democracy," *Transitions*, May 1999, <http://www.ijt.org/transitions/archmay.html>.
10. Marshall Goldman, *Lost Opportunity: Why Economic Reforms in Russia Have Not Worked* (New York: W.W. Norton, 1994), p. 9.
11. Joseph R. Blasi, Maya Kroumova, and Douglas Kruse, *Kremlin Capitalism: Privatizing the Russian Economy* (Ithaca, NY: Cornell University Press, 1997), pp. 39–49.
12. *Transition Report 1996*, p. 169.
13. Blasi, Kroumova, and Kruse, *Kremlin Capitalism*, p. 178.
14. *The Economist* (Survey of Russia), July 12, 1997, pp. 4-5.
15. See Shangguan Gao, *China's Economic Reform* (New York: St. Martin's Press, 1996).
16. Carl Riskin, *China's Political Economy: The Quest for Development since 1949* (Oxford: Oxford University Press, 1988), chaps. 12–13.
17. Ibid.
18. Feng Chen, *Economic Transition and Political Legitimacy in Post-Mao China: Idedology and Reform* (Albany, NY: State University of New York Press, 1995), pp. 130–36.
19. Barry Naughton, *Growing out of the Plan: Chinese Economic Reform, 1978–1993* (Cambridge: Cambridge University Press, 1996), p. 120.
20. Roderick MacFarquhar, ed. *The Politics of China, 1949–1989* (Cambridge: Cambridge University Press, 1993).

PART IV

IPE North and South

Many of the most interesting and important IPE problems revolve around what are termed "North-South" relations. The "North" is made up of the industrialized nations that were first to develop and have grown to be relatively rich. The "South" consists of the poorer, less industrialized nations of the world, many of which are former colonies of "North" states. North-South is therefore IPE shorthand for rich-poor, with differences in wealth creating further differences in power, status, and influence.

The three chapters in part IV look at three different aspects of North-South IPE that are especially relevant today. Chapter 15 examines the "two faces" of development, the elements of economic development that simultaneously attract and repel less developed countries.

Chapter 16 tackles a particularly controversial aspect of North-South IPE—that of Multinational Corporations (MNCs). MNCs are seen by some as engines of growth for LDCs, and by others as tools of exploitation. Chapter 16 lays out the arguments clearly and without bias, inviting you to make up your own mind.

The IPE of OPEC and oil is the topic of chapter 17, which stresses the complex interconnectedness of North and South through an extended case study of the political economy of petroleum since the 1970s.

15

The Two Faces of Development

by Professor Sunil Kukreja

OVERVIEW

For much of the twentieth century, the overwhelming majority of the world's population who live in developing nations did not experience the economic prosperity and affluence that the vast majority of people in developed countries did. An obvious question is: Given the great amount of wealth produced in the world each year, why have so many Less Developed Countries (LDCs) remained impoverished, "underdeveloped," or "undeveloped"? The issue of development has confronted most of the LDCs since the middle of the twentieth century, when many of them formally became independent nations. For the most part, economic development is an objective many LDCs are unlikely to achieve well into the next century.

This chapter examines theories about the causes of underdevelopment and what to do about it and provides a brief overview of the broad economic, political, and social disparities that distinguish the developed and the newly developing from the less developed LDCs. Discussion turns to the origin of these gaps—the historical context and circumstances that resulted in depressed circumstances that many LDCs find themselves in. Also examined is LDC use of international organizations as a mechanism for change in some of the institutions and processes of the international political economy.

While economic development does not appear to be forthcoming for many developing nations for a variety of reasons, the newly industrialized countries are the success stories of development in the postwar era. This chapter also explores the factors that account for the success of many of the NICs and some key obstacles for the LDCs in Africa, where development remains most elusive.

What the countries of the South have in common transcends their differences; it gives them a shared identity and a reason to work together for common objectives. . . . The primary bond that links the countries and peoples of the South is their desire to escape from poverty and underdevelopment.[1]

The South Commission (1990)

Development (or the lack thereof) is a global problem, not confined only to poor nations. Parts of developed industrialized nations remain underdeveloped. One need only travel through the old industrial sections or decaying regions of almost any industrialized nation to realize they have more in common with some of the developing nations than they do with their own. However, as the twentieth century came to a close, the great majority of the world's population was located in less developed regions of the world where the standard of living pales in comparison to that in the industrialized nations. The international political economy is marked by two significant income gaps. One is the widely recognized gap between the rich and poor nations, and the other is the growing differences between groups of LDCs.

The industrialized nations have, for the most part, achieved a certain level of development—a term generally associated with economic growth and that connotes a modern nation. *Economic development* is defined as the ability of a nation to produce economic wealth, which in turn transforms society from a subsistence- or agricultural-based economy to one where most of society's wealth is derived from the production of manufactured goods and services. In developed-industrialized societies, the majority of the population usually live in urban-industrial areas, are quite literate, and are well fed and housed. The annual average per capita GNP among the high income economies is approximately $25,800.[2]

The characteristics of LDCs usually contrast sharply with those of the developed nations.[3] Most LDCs exhibit very low income levels. Average yearly income varies from roughly $500 to $1,000, although several nations have per capita income of only about $300 and about 1.3 billion people (most in LDCs) survive on less than $1 a day. Starvation caused by war or drought may be present in some nations, while in many others as many as one-third of the population is seriously malnourished. One-half of all people in LDCs still lack adequate drinking water, basic shelter, and are illiterate. These conditions are all directly attributable to poverty, or the lack of income to demand products in the market. An estimated 80 percent of the world's wealth is possessed by a small minority of the world's population, most of whom live in the industrialized nations, while the vast majority of humanity living in LDCs must share the other 20 percent of the world's wealth.

The growing gap between rich and poor nations raises questions about equity and fairness related to the distribution of the world's resources.[4] Increasingly, though, another gap between nations is getting more attention, and that is the vast differences in levels of development among LDCs. Development efforts and other circumstances have produced gradations of success. In the 1950s and 1960s, LDCs had a great deal in common, especially their colonial history and potential for growth. More recently, a few have begun to realize some economic success. By 1990, the leading East and Southeast Asian economies like Singapore, Taiwan, South Korea, Malaysia, and Hong Kong were some of the fastest growing economies in the world although by 1997 this trend was severely disrupted by a financial crisis in the region. More critically, many low-income developing countries (especially in sub-Saharan Africa) continue to struggle with widespread poverty and a lower overall standard of living. Within the developing regions of the world, there appear to be at least four categories of nations: the richer oil-exporting nations; the economically dynamic NICs; the poorest countries, which include the sub-Saharan African nations; and the majority of other LDCs that are still thought of as Third World nations.

A few economic indicators demonstrate this trend. Between 1965 and 1996, for example, Niger's average per capita GNP growth rate was –2.8 percent, while oil-rich Oman experienced an annual average of 5 percent. Even more vivid has been the performance of economies like South Korea and Singapore averaging a per capita GNP growth of 7.3 and 6.3 percent, respectively, between 1965 and 1996. Disparities among LDCs are also reflected in regional growth trends. Over this same period, sub-Saharan Africa lagged behind in its economic performance, with an annual average GNP (per capita) growth rate of -0.2 percent, as East Asia/Pacific led the way with an average of 5.5 percent.[5]

These basic variations among regions are further complicated by severe disparities within regions and even within nations as well. In what was until recently the fast growing region of Southeast Asia, Singaporeans enjoy a per capita GNP of over $30,000, but nearby Indonesians approximately $1,080. Similarly, Uganda has a per capita GNP comparable to that of Haiti and Bangladesh, while its regional neighbor in sub-Saharan Africa, Mauritius has a GNP comparable to that of Mexico. Another noteworthy contrast among LDCs is presented in Table 15–1. The low rate of economic growth in sub-Saharan countries is associated with high adult illiteracy and low life expectancy. By contrast, these indicators in East Asia and Latin America are approaching those of the developed regions.

The distribution of income within LDCs is difficult to measure. In most cases income distribution is heavily skewed in favor of a wealthy minority or powerful elite. Income distribution remains one of the most controversial and urgent development problems. It drives to the heart of the matter—overcoming poverty and generating economic growth.

THE TWO FACES OF ECONOMIC DEVELOPMENT

To understand the development dilemma, we must understand some of the history of the LDCs—how they came to be in the position they are in and what problems must be overcome by those less successful in their efforts. By the 1950s,

TABLE 15–1　Selected Basic Indicators

	LIFE EXPECTANCY (YEARS)		ADULT ILLITERACY (%)		PER CAPITA ($)	GROSS NATIONAL PRODUCT
						AVE. ANNUAL PER CAPITA GROWTH (%)
REGION	1960	1996	1960	1995	1996	1965-96
Sub-Saharan Africa	40	52	72	43	490	-0.2
East Asia/Pacific	47	68	N/A	17	890	5.5
South Asia	44	62	67	51	380	2.2
Latin America and Caribbean	56	70	24	13	3710	1.1
N. Africa and Middle East	46	67	70	39	2070	-1.8

Source: Human Development Report, 1993, p. 213; *World Development Report,* 1997, p. 215; *World Development Indicators, 1998,* pp. 14, 26.

many of the former European colonial empires and territories began to disintegrate and new nation-states emerged in their place. The dismantling of the colonial empires unfolded differently in Asia, Africa, and Latin America. By the end of the 1950s, many of the former colonies became independent and many more were on the threshold of a new international order shaped by the Cold War between the United States and its industrial democracy allies (the so-called "First World") and the Soviet Union and its allies (the "Second World" in Cold War terminology).

As these new nation-states began to shape their respective national identities, it appeared that the long-standing colonial domination of the West had come to a close. Politically, the *Third World* had been born. Yet many of the newly formed nations of Asia, Latin America, and Africa confronted pressing and complex economic, political, and social problems that made it difficult to create truly sovereign national institutional structures.

Foremost on the agenda of many of the newcomers was the economic development dilemma—the lack of economic development and prosperity. The stark economic differences and disparities between the developed and less developed countries became the defining feature of what later became known as the *North-South dilemma.* The North consists of the developed, industrialized countries of Western Europe and North America and the LDCs of the world (regardless of whether they are geographically located in the Northern or Southern hemisphere) comprise the South. The North-South distinction is more than a label; in fact, as we shall see in the next section, it has also come to symbolize the often tense political and economic climate between the developed and less developed worlds. This inequality in wealth and prosperity became the centerpiece of the new problems and issues in the postwar international economic order.

For the LDCs, economic development has been crucial not just as an end in itself, but also as a means for ensuring sustained political development, independence, and a cultural identity. Much of the success of the newly independent states in the postwar international climate as well as in domestic politics has depended on the ability of leaders to deliver on the promises that helped propel nationalist and independence movements. As such, economic development—characterized by a growing and prosperous economy—has been crucial in order to establish a national identity and also ensure political stability domestically.

But LDCs approached economic development with mixed emotions. Development to them had two faces. One face promised an end to poverty and the start of true independence and was powerfully attractive to LDC leaders and citizens. But the other face of development was the face of exploitation, manipulation, and continued subjugation. This face repelled LDCs as much as the other face attracted them. We can see both faces of economic development by looking at the four major forces that shaped the development dilemma for LDCs in the early postwar period, with decolonization under way. First, colonial wounds were in many ways still fresh and deep. In this regard, political leaders often viewed former colonial powers with some suspicion. The social and economic impact and exploits of colonialism and capitalism were surely responsible for the economic "backwardness" of their new nation-states. Second, the way many LDCs dealt with their development problem was not merely a response to politically and economically exploitative colonial conditions but a resistance to cultural domination by the West as well.[6] In some parts of the developing world, these sentiments helped shape a cautious approach to adopting Western influence and methods of economic development. As we shall see, this view of the developed countries by Third World leaders remained quite strong and influential and became a central notion behind the solidarity of developing countries in the 1970s.

The third force to shape the economic development dilemma for many LDCs was the Cold War. Proximity to the United States or its allies or historical connections to former mother countries often shaped the kind of political and economic strategies LDCs chose when it came to economic development. Likewise, support for the Eastern bloc of nations by some LDCs blended with a preference for non-Western development strategies.

Finally, and paradoxically, the economic success of the developed countries also provided a strong rationale for some LDCs to follow in their footsteps, or at least adopt market-oriented prescriptions for economic development. The emergence of new international institutions like the IMF, the World Bank, and the General Agreement on Tariffs and Trade (GATT), whose role was to coordinate international trade, symbolized the expanding significance of the market in the world economy. To many observers (especially in less developed regions), these institutions were largely controlled by the developed countries. The political significance of pursuing a Western economic development strategy would also signal a tacit association with the West in the Cold War. Yet, in many cases, association with Western institutions offered real opportunities LDCs had to consider in their formula for pursuing a partnership with the industrialized nations and economic development. Hence, the participation of the LDCs in the postwar international economy with the developed countries remained a debatable option.

These forces combined to set the stage for the dynamics of the development process and North-South relations in the later stages of the Cold War. In the next section, we turn directly to the substance of the North-South dialogue that represented much of the framework for addressing development issues and problems.

THE NORTH-SOUTH DEBATE

Recognizing that individually, LDCs were unable to exert significant influence on the international system and its institutions, a number of countries, mainly from the Southern developing region of the world, attempted to promote a collective identity. The 1955 Afro-Asian Bandung Conference in Indonesia is widely regarded as the first major step to forging that identity and is the genesis of what came to be viewed as a Southern perspective. Led by Jawaharlal Nehru of India, Marshal Tito of Yugoslavia, Achmed Sukarno of Indonesia, and Gamal Abdel Nasser of Egypt, heads of state from the developing countries initiated a dialogue among themselves that subsequently led to the formation of the Non-Aligned Movement in 1961. As a political banner of many newly independent LDCs, the Non-Aligned Movement expanded to include a number of countries from Latin America. This movement served three purposes. First, it was to be the LDCs' political arm for addressing initiatives against the remaining remnants of colonialism (especially in Africa). Second, it was to be their vehicle for positioning themselves outside the sphere of the Cold War scenario, and lastly, it was to promote the interests of the LDCs.

One of the main priorities of what came to be referred to as the nations of the "South" was the issue of neocolonialism, or the continued economic domination of LDCs by the industrialized countries. A number of political leaders and intellectuals[7] argued that while the era of colonialism was largely over, former colonies were basically trapped in a capitalist international economic system dominated by institutions and mechanisms tilted in favor of the developed countries. In a "neocolonial" environment, multinational corporations and their subsidiaries, for instance, owned and controlled a substantial part of LDC economic resources. The wealth and political influence of multinationals, often backed by their home-based governments, gave them and the industrialized nations the ability to control international markets of commodities from LDCs.

One such scenario frequently noted was the case of oil companies. For much of the twentieth century, seven major (Western) oil companies controlled the exploration, processing, and supply of oil in a number of oil-rich regions. These "seven sisters," as they were known, often worked to divide the market share, regulate supply, and preserve their control over resources in developing countries. In varying degrees, these companies were seen to be supported by their respective home governments. With such political support, the major oil companies negotiated terms (involving some royalty for the host country) that ensured the companies control of oil exploration and distribution in the international market.[8]

Advocates of the neocolonial argument claimed that complementing the domination of multinational corporations was a restrictive system of trade, financial, and technological transfer that compounded the economic vulnerability of LDCs and weakened development prospects. In chapter 6, we discussed the LDC claim that the international terms of trade committed them to be producers of raw materials and primary goods. LDCs were disadvantaged by the head start the industrialized nations got in the production of value-added products and their extensive use of protectionist trade measures. Technological innovations and gains in productivity largely occurred in the developed countries, and the

LDCs found themselves lagging and unable to compete in the areas of new product development or production. Tight legal controls, copyrights, and licensing often curbed LDCs' access to such technology. The financial power of large multinationals, coupled with the developed countries' influence on the international financial system, also meant that developed countries and multinationals could influence the LDCs' access to funds for economic development.

CHANGING THE SYSTEM: UNCTAD AND THE NIEO

Frustrated by their meager success, increasing numbers of LDCs turned to their membership in international organizations to foster Third World solidarity and momentum for change in the international political economy. In 1964, the United Nations Conference on Trade and Development (UNCTAD) was established spearheaded by 77 LDCs that became known as the Group of 77 (G-77). UNCTAD meets roughly every four years in the capital city of an LDC. While its membership has increased over the years, G-77 has been the LDCs' representative organization at UNCTAD sessions. The G-77 sought to make UNCTAD a mechanism for dialogue and negotiation between the LDCs and the developed countries on trade, finance, and other development issues. At UNCTAD I, the G-77 proposed a new international trade organization to replace GATT. For the most part, the developed countries resisted UNCTAD initiatives when it came to trade and other economic activities. Nevertheless, through UNCTAD, LDCs were gradually able to secure some concessions and preferential treatment—a Generalized System of Preferences (GSP)—on tariffs for their exports to developed nations.

The Organization of Petroleum Exporting Countries (OPEC)[9] helped generate attention to Southern concerns in 1973 when this cartel made up of oil-producing LDCs embargoed oil shipments to some of the industrialized nations and significantly raised the price of oil (see chapter 17). A 400 percent increase in the price of oil jolted the developed economies and temporarily altered the global balance of political and economic power. By extension it also complicated the development dilemma.

Following World War II, the industrialized countries (in spite of the postwar reconstruction, or perhaps largely fueled by it) had experienced considerable economic growth. Western oil companies dominated the petroleum industry from exploration to marketing and had historically provided cheap and abundant access to the energy needs of the industrialized world. The cartel's pricing actions helped dampen economic growth and spurred an inflationary trend in the developed countries. From the standpoint of relations between the developed and less developed nations, the latter were to gain considerable leverage for the time being. The developed countries—being highly dependent on oil-exporting countries for their energy—could no longer ignore the considerable impact oil-producing countries from the South had on the economic well-being of the industrialized world.

OPEC political and economic leverage resulted in the sixth special session of the UN General Assembly in 1974, which called for the establishment of a *New International Economic Order (NIEO)*. This program for action was designed largely to facilitate the pace of development among LDCs and change the unequal economic balance between the LDCs and the industrialized nations. The development prospects of the LDCs were believed to be intimately tied to the larger functioning of the world economic order. Unlike previous efforts, the NIEO was seen by LDCs not so much as an attempt to fine-tune the existing international economic order but as an effort to elevate the issue of economic development to the top of the international agenda, changing respective institutional structures and making them more conducive to LDC development concerns. The NIEO included calls for

1. Creation of an Integrated Program for Commodities (IPC) to stockpile and control the price of commodities during periods of oversupply and scarcity
2. Extension and liberalization of GSP
3. Development of a debt-relief program
4. Increasing official development assistance from the rich, developed nations of the North to the less developed South
5. Changing the decision-making process in major international institutions such as the United Nations, IMF, and the World Bank to give more voice to Southern nations and reduce developed nations' control of these institutions
6. Increasing the economic sovereignty of LDCs. Several initiatives were stipulated under this umbrella. Key among them were ensuring LDCs' greater control over their natural resources; increased access to Western technology; the ability to regulate multinationals; and preferential trade policies that would stabilize prices for commodities from LDCs and ensure these countries greater access to developed countries' markets.

Despite the United Nations' adoption of these objectives, implementation in the years that followed remained incomplete. A number of factors coalesced to render the NIEO ineffective. Foremost among these was the general opposition of the industrialized countries to the NIEO initiatives, making implementation difficult. These countries, led by the United States, did not consider the initiatives central to the development concerns and dilemma of LDCs. Furthermore, many critics argued that the initiatives promoted an atmosphere of "micromanaging" the global economy, a task that, on the one hand, would be impractical, and on the other, restrictive of the free market. Many officials of the industrialized nations also saw demands for a NIEO as a political threat prompted by some radical LDCs to redistribute global wealth and power.

Further, while the OPEC oil crisis created momentum for cooperation among LDCs to seek substantive institutional reforms through the NIEO initiatives, the LDCs were plagued by competing and conflicting national interests, which often undermined their attempts at cooperation and unity. OPEC's economic strength and the prosperity of its member states added to the disparate economic conditions among the LDCs. Although OPEC made small loans and grants to poorer LDCs, its members were more inclined to pursue their own narrow political and economic interests rather than use their collective strength to promote the implementation of the NIEO initiatives.

Added to this, the international oil crisis also created devastating economic problems for the nonoil producing LDCs. For many LDCs, the markedly higher cost of energy simply compounded already acute economic problems. As a result, many of the poorer LDCs became increasingly dependent on the private banks of the developed countries and other multilateral institutions for financing their balance of payment deficits. The cumulative effect of the oil crisis was a global recession, which may well have hit the nonoil-producing LDCs harder than the more stable developed economies. This merely served to deflect attention from the NIEO and undermined the position of the LDCs.[10]

It is important to recognize that the unfolding of the North-South dialogue was shaped by fundamental theoretical debates, each presenting a different interpretation of the political economy of development and proposing different paths for development. In the following section, we survey three different perspectives on development.

THE LIBERAL MODEL AND ECONOMIC DEVELOPMENT

Much of the North's resistance to the efforts of the South to restructure the international political economy reflects the North's conviction about the functioning of the international market and the performance of the liberal model of economic development. Two general and interrelated points characterize the North's position on the economic development question in the South.

Advocating the liberal or Western model of development, the United States and other developed countries have insisted that with active participation and integration into the global market, LDCs would, in due course, experience economic growth. Trade is the primary stimulus—the "engine to growth" as it were—for increasing productivity and raising income levels in an LDC. Integration in the international economy through trade is supposed to stimulate growth, diffuse new technologies, generate investments, and transform traditional social-cultural practices that are incompatible with the market ethos. As "latecomers," LDCs undertaking efforts to use the market to develop and industrialize have a distinct opportunity and hindsight to benefit from the pitfalls and policy mistakes of the now developed North. Such hindsight translates into less waste of resources and inefficiency and also accelerates the development process for LDCs.

One of the critical features of the liberal model is that a major obstacle to economic development in LDCs stems from the anemic capital, productivity, and technological base of the economy. Added to these constraints are other institutional structures in many LDCs, such as a weak infrastructure and educational system, along with traditional cultural value systems that hinder the prospects for development. Following this line of reasoning, the liberal model largely deemphasizes the importance of international political and economic structural conditions in explaining the process of economic development (or lack thereof). Instead, it focuses on the internal conditions in LDCs that promote or stifle economic development.[11]

One of the most influential liberal assessments of the development dilemma to emerge was the work of W. W. Rostow.[12] According to Rostow, like the developed nations of the North, the less developed South must undergo a series of changes in their socioeconomic system in order to develop and industrialize. This "evolutionary" change is represented by a series of stages of economic growth that society passes through on its way to development. Traditional society experiences low levels of economic productivity due to the lack of technological development and a traditional social system of fatalistic values where individuals are constrained by rigid social goals. Increases in education and literacy, entrepreneurship, and investments in raw material and infrastructure expand the level of commercial activity. The seeds of economic growth are planted, even if new ideas that create a good deal of disharmony, even conflict, in society bring about changes that are compatible with the process of economic development.

In the critical "takeoff" stage, the pace of change accelerates. New industries increase rapidly as the entrepreneurial spirit becomes more dominant. The emergence of a capitalist class accelerates the change by initiating new economic activity, industrialization, and adopting new production processes. Conversely, the influence of traditional social values and goals diminishes. Existing economic activities such as extraction of raw materials and agriculture are also modernized. Later stages are characterized by the use of advanced technology and a relatively high level of savings and investment (approximately 15 to 20 percent of GNP) that sustains the drive to economic maturity. Countries with a higher level of savings and investments are, according to Rostow, more likely to grow and develop at a much faster rate than those with a lower savings rate. The final stage of mass consumption and self-sustaining growth follows when the major sectors of the economy are able to meet the consumer demands for goods and services for a large cross section of the population, which helps sustain the high level of economic activity.

Rostow's theory of economic development was based largely on the historical experience of Western nations, especially Britain and the United States. He perceived the stages of development as universal, arguing that in the long run, the North can model the development process for the South. The historical development and diffusion of technology will inevitably lead to changes that are necessary in the early stages of the economic development process.

DEPENDENCY: DEVELOPMENT OR UNDERDEVELOPMENT?

By the 1960s, liberal assumptions about the development prospects for many LDCs came under intense criticism from a number of scholars, especially in Latin America. These critics of the liberal model of development were primarily from the United Nations' Economic Commission for Latin America (ECLA). Among the earlier critiques was the work of Raul Prebisch,[13] which provided significant momentum for the dependency perspective and its interpretation of the development dilemma among LDCs.

A promoter of UNCTAD, Prebisch argued that the development dilemma in Latin America was inextricably linked to factors outside the region. Prebisch was especially critical of the existing international division of labor and free trade system. He and others argued that the international trade system reinforced the LDCs' role as producers of primary products and raw materials, while the developed countries continued to prosper as producers of industrial products. This international division of labor reinforced the dependence of the LDCs on the developed nations to be outlets for LDC primary products. In addition, production specialization also perpetuated LDC dependence on the developed countries for capital and technology, each of which were seen as essential for LDCs to generate economic development.

Dependence was considered particularly significant, as it contributed to the underdevelopment of the LDCs.[14] Early dependency theorists made a distinction between *under*development and *un*development. The latter was characterized by lack of development, the former by the outcome of a process that further regressed and undermined LDC economies while simultaneously contributing to the development of their counterparts in the industrial world. As such, underdevelopment in the LDCs was viewed as a product of the development process in industrialized regions. Underdevelopment and development were two facets of a singular global structure, much like the two sides of a coin.[15] Osvaldo Sunkel and Pedro Paz have noted that "both underdevelopment and development are aspects of the same phenomenon, both are historically simultaneous, both are linked functionally and, therefore, interact and condition each other mutually."[16]

This basic thesis represented the embryo of much of the analyses of dependency theorists during the 1960s and 1970s and was most forcefully articulated by Andre Gunder Frank in *Capitalism and Underdevelopment in Latin America*. According to this perspective, underdevelopment has its origins in the colonial order and European expansion prior to the twentieth century. Through political domination, the colonial powers successfully extracted raw materials and resources necessary for their development while impoverishing their colonies. Although decolonization removed the political dominance of European powers, the basic economic linkage and division of labor between the two remained largely intact, resulting in neocolonialism. Frank argued that the international capitalist economic order was organized along the lines of a metropolis-satellite system (regions) in which the metropolis state exploited and controlled the satellite by extracting economic surplus and wealth from the latter.

There are a number of mechanisms that reproduce this relationship and deepen the underdevelopment process in LDCs. Through multinational corporations, profits generated in LDCs are transferred out of LDCs. Investments in technology and other innovations are often dated or inappropriate and do not enhance the competitive edge of LDCs. The extensive resources of the multinationals also enable them to circumvent restrictive and regulatory measures in LDCs. Another widely cited mechanism is the unequal exchange relationship. The LDCs' "comparative advantage" in primary products and raw material is highly vulnerable to international market prices, which are generally well below those of manufactured goods that LDCs have to import from the developed countries. Over time, this creates a massive net outflow of revenue.

Some dependency theorists also find the international financial and foreign aid system to be exploitative. Foreign banks of the wealthier nations gain a stronghold on private lending. Critics charge that these banks are less interested in the development of a country than they are in acquiring lucrative terms for loans to LDCs. This results in a form of extended financial dependence for the indebted country and generous interest receipts for foreign banks. These theorists are also skeptical about foreign aid. They argue that the political and economic strings attached to such assistance reinforce a dominant-subordinate relationship between the developed and less developed nations.[17]

Within this framework, a number of differing interpretations about the approach to change emerged. For Andre Gunder Frank, the capitalist world economy posed the biggest obstacle for LDCs. Development for the poorer countries was inconsistent with their continued integration into the world economy. Instead, a socialist path was the only solution to this dilemma. In cases such as China from the early 1960s until 1972, through state ownership and control, a nation's economy is restructured primarily by severing economic ties with the developed capitalist world. In place of this, mutually beneficial ties with other socialist countries are supposed to eliminate the exploitative relations that govern the capitalist world economy and reverse the underdevelopment process.

Other approaches to the dependency dilemma have been less radical. The import substitution path to development has been one such alternative. This strategy, highly mercantilist and nationalistic (although not anticapitalist) in character, advocates constraints on adverse external influences (such as foreign manufactured goods and multinational corporations) in order to promote self-sufficiency and internal development. In place of importing manufactured goods, local manufacturing is prescribed. Promoting these enterprises requires strict controls on imported goods to reduce competition from abroad. The state plays a direct role in controlling strategic industries like utilities and energy, which are fundamental to the resource base of a manufacturing economy. As we see in the next section, the import substitution path was indeed a popular one, especially among some major Latin American economies.

Finally, after a good deal of dissatisfaction with these different models, many LDCs have adopted what essentially amounts to a combination of all of them. The "self-reliance" model emphasizes mixing economic growth with efforts to redistribute income over the largest number of people so as to establish a firm economic base in a nation with unique conditions. Basic human needs are targets of public policy and poverty eradication efforts. Linkages with external sources of income through trade, aid, and foreign direct investment are conditioned upon control over them and their impact on the national economy. As with all of these models, the state plays a major role in controlling investment in rural and industrial sectors of the economy, and making political, social, and economic adjustments when necessary. And finally, as in other models, the goal of development is an industrial society with sufficient production to meet the needs of society. Very few development experts have attempted to devise a model that did not seek to achieve this outcome.

UJAMAA: AN EXPERIMENT IN SELF-RELIANCE

Following independence in 1961, Tanzania—like other LDCs—sought development by promoting economic growth via the liberal development strategy. However, this effort was short lived, as Tanzania was unable to address its acute economic problems. Declining revenues from cash crop exports—something that Tanzania relied on heavily—worsened its financial stability.[a] Added to this, Tanzania had an anemic industrial base, and together, these circumstances created unemployment problems for an already impoverished nation. In 1967, the charismatic President Julius Nyerere ushered in an alternative approach to development known in Swahili as *Ujamaa na Kujitegamea* which generally translated means populist socialism and self-reliance.

The centerpiece of this approach took advantage of the country's highly rural and agrarian socioeconomic structure and the government organized thousands of agricultural collectives, known as *Ujamaa* villages, throughout the Tanzanian country-side. Contrary to the liberal development model, Nyerere's experiment emphasized, and perhaps idealized, the traditional, rural community-based African culture which was seen as a "natural" basis for instituting *Ujamaa* villages. These agrarian villages were seen as the vehicle for building a prosperous and equitable society.

However, when officials realized that there wasn't overwhelming enthusiasm among peasants to voluntarily migrate to these new villages, millions were forcibly uprooted and relocated. Each village had about 200 households, each with its own small plot of land, and a communal farm with a central distribution location linking the households together. The agricultural production of each village was sold to the government and production was monitored and managed by a local coordinator.[b]

By the end of the 1970s, much of rural life in Tanzania had been dramatically transformed. Over a third of the villages had medical clinics available, almost half had a clean water supply, and locally run schools in villages helped raise the literacy rate. However, productivity in these villages lagged behind expectations and like many other LDCs, Tanzania was heavily in debt. High oil prices during the 1970s were a tremendous drain on its revenue, while Tanzania's export earnings declined over the same period. The impact of the international market, coupled with low productivity, a poorly functioning state bureaucracy, and drought, created severe shortages in food supply and resources.

By the end of the 1980s, Julius Nyerere's vision of development through populist socialism had lost most of its steam. As a result, Tanzania has had to restructure its restrictive trade policies and has increasingly looked to the major international donors and lending institutions for assistance. Ironically, it had to turn back to the very international organizations and market it had sought to distance itself from through this experiment in self-reliance.

---

[a] Andrew Webster, *Introduction to the Sociology of Development* (Atlantic Highlands, NJ: Humanities Press, 1990), p. 177.
[b] Ibid., p. 178.

THE NEOLIBERAL CONSENSUS ON DEVELOPMENT

As the NIEO movement frizzled and efforts at self-sufficiency stalled, a renewed emphasis on liberal prescriptions for economic growth and development appeared in the 1980s. During this time, a number of LDCs (especially in Africa and Latin America) were excessively in debt, faced declining revenues from primary commodity exports, declining agriculture output, and overall economic stagnation. A consensus emerged that neoliberal policies might be the most effective path to economic development (although, obviously, not everyone agreed with this viewpoint). This notion was based in part on the success of liberal policies in some countries, but perhaps even more on the failure of other development strategies to either reform the international system or to generate economic self-sustaining economic growth. Given that LDCs could not change the international system substantially and given that self-sufficiency did not seem a viable strategy, neoliberal policies appeared to many to be the best of the remaining choices for LDCs seeking to grow.

The neoliberal consensus assumes that the domestic policies of the LDCs are the cause of their failure to grow. This is distinctly the opposite of the NIEO movement, which viewed problems in the international trade and finance structures as mainly responsible for continued LDC poverty. Neoliberal policies viewed excessive state spending and protectionist and antifree market policies among LDCs as the fundamental stumbling blocks to their economic growth. Neoliberalism, with its emphasis on privatization, deregulation, and free trade, served as a strong critique and response to the perceived shortcomings of the NIEO approach to development.

Multilateral development and financial institutions like the World Bank and the IMF which have typically relied on assumptions of the liberal model ushered in stringent requirements and conditions for aid recipients. Desperately in need of external help, many LDCs were prescribed the *Structural Adjustment Programs* **(SAPs)** by these international lending institutions. Foremost among the SAP requirements were to encourage privatization in place of direct government involvement in operating industries, creating incentives to attract foreign investors, easing regulations on the private sector, and currency devaluation to make local products competitive in the international market. Collectively, the IMF and World Bank—with strong support from the United States—saw these measures as essential to releasing LDCs from the bureaucratic and inefficient tentacles of state control and artificial manipulation of the economy.[18] Indeed, opening the troubled economy to international trade and competition was considered essential to stimulating growth. However, critics of the SAPs argue these policies were seen as draconian by many governments in Africa and Latin America and they symbolized an assault on the South's efforts at "seeking income redistribution at the global level" and greater economic independence from the North.[19] Further, it is important to note that as neoliberalism gained momentum the 1980s and 1990s, it symbolized a declining faith in the role of the state in dictating, if not guiding, development among LDCs.

THE NEWLY INDUSTRIALIZING COUNTRIES

Over the past three decades there have been significant changes in the economic development patterns for a number of countries, especially in Asia and Latin America. By the 1980s, South Korea, Taiwan, Hong Kong, and Singapore were widely being recognized as the economic "tigers" in East Asia/Pacific. The tremendous growth in these countries led many observers to increasingly group them as "newcomers" on the path to industrialization and development. Economic growth rates among the "cubs" of East Asia like Malaysia and Thailand during the 1980s and early 90s also fueled expectations for these two countries as potential NICs. Ironically, high expectations since the 1950s for the Third World to catch up with the industrial countries rested with the anticipated success of major Latin American countries like Argentina, Brazil, and Mexico. Although a financial crisis and slower growth in the latter half of the 1990s have taken some of the roar out of the region, the relative success of the East Asian NICs over the past three decades has amazed, puzzled, and intrigued many. As one source puts it:

The Asian NICs—Hong Kong, Singapore, South Korea, and Taiwan—have achieved growth rates virtually without historical precedent. . . . The speed with which the NICs have industrialized is astonishing. Nineteenth-century development in Europe and North America . . . pale in comparison with the record of the NICs.[20]

One illustrative comparison between the East Asian and Latin American NICs is presented in Table 15–2. By the end of the 1960s, the East Asian NICs were outperforming the major Latin American economies in growth rate. Although Brazil's growth rate in the 1970s was comparable to that of South Korea and Hong Kong, the overall pattern into the mid-1990s reflects the relative economic dynamism of the East Asian NICs vis-à-vis their Latin American counterparts.

Although some sharp economic and historical differences distinguish each of the NICs from one another, an understanding of the contrasting success of the East Asian and Latin American NICs can be found in the fundamentally different paths taken by these two groups of countries. South Korea and Taiwan, for example, adopted a strategy known as *export-oriented growth*; in Latin America, Mexico and Brazil are two cases that pursued the *import-substitution strategy*.

The export-oriented approach is based on a combination of liberal and mercantilist prescriptions for economic growth and development. For one, it calls for the state to strongly emphasize a country's comparative advantage in selected sectors of the economy and to promote exports from these sectors. However, instead of depending on a noninterventionist state and free-trade policies, the East Asian NICs aggressively pursued specific national and international policies that changed the basic structure and functioning of their economies. While there are specific differences between the East Asian NICs, certain common trends can be identified.

First, the export-oriented policies of East Asian NICs involved changing the fundamental composition of their production. Prior to the 1960s, like other developing countries, South Korea and Taiwan began promoting manufacturing with a particular emphasis on labor-intensive consumer goods. To accomplish this,

TABLE 15–2   Growth of Real GDP: Selected East Asian and Latin American NICs (compounded annual percentage change)

COUNTRY	1960–70	1970–80	1980–90	1990–95
S. Korea	9.5	8.2	9.4	7.2
Taiwan	9.6	9.7	6.8*	N/A
Hong Kong	9.3	8.7	6.9	5.6
Singapore	9.2	9.1	6.4	8.7
Argentina	3.0	2.5	−0.3	5.7
Brazil	N/A	8.6	2.7	2.7
Mexico	7.0	6.6	1.0	1.1
Venezuela	6.1	4.1	1.1	2.4

* 1980–86.

Source: Seiji Naya, Miguel Urrutia, Shelley Mark, Alfredo Fuentes, eds., *Lessons in Development* (San Francisco: International Center for Economic Growth, 1989), pp. 282–283; The World Bank, *World Development Report, 1997* (New York: Oxford University Press, 1997), p. 235.

the respective governments set up mercantilist-style restrictions to protect "infant" consumer manufacturing industries from foreign competition. This initial strategy had the added benefit of raising the level of employment, which theoretically also helped stabilize the political situation. The governments provided strong financial backing and incentives to promote manufacturing. (More on this point later.) The strategy used in this initial push to generate a viable manufacturing sector was not unlike the one pursued by Japan in the earlier part of this century and later after World War II (see chapter 13).

By the late 1960s, South Korea and Taiwan began to ease into the next phase of restructuring. Specifically, these countries increased their international market share by promoting the export of domestically manufactured durable goods. State intervention again played a strategic role in launching this initial export promotion effort. Selective barriers on imported goods remained in place, although raw material imports necessary for manufacturing were not suppressed, and selected domestic manufacturing industries were targeted with fiscal incentives to stimulate the level of exports. Another policy was to devalue the national currency, making exports from these East Asian countries more competitive in the international marketplace and imports less attractive to consumers domestically.[21] In a sense, the NICs created comparative advantages for their manufactured products through these measures.

During the 1970s, South Korea's manufacturing sector expanded into heavy (technologically intensive) industries including steel, petrochemicals, and automobiles. By 1980, these efforts in restructuring the economy were bearing fruit. Manufacturing's share of GDP in South Korea climbed from 14 percent in 1960 to 30 percent by 1980 and has remained stable since. Agriculture's share decreased from 37 percent to 15 percent over the same period and in 1995 dropped to 7 percent of GDP. In Taiwan, manufacturing's share of GDP increased from 26 percent (1960) to 40 percent (1993) after hovering at a high of about 47 percent in the mid-1980s. Correspondingly, agriculture's share of GDP declined from 29 percent to only 3.5 percent by 1993.[22]

A second major component of this export-led growth strategy—one that is also seen by advocates of the liberal model as a crucial ingredient for development—involved promoting a high level of savings and investment (including intense efforts in research and development). The liberal perspective suggests that without the necessary capital, basic investments in infrastructure, resource development, and equipment, growth would be quite impossible. Hence, capital formation is central to development. Generally, the East Asian NICs have been very successful at structuring specific institutional and policy measures to achieve this goal. As Table 15–3 shows, in 1960, the four major East Asian NICs all had a savings rate well below the three major Latin American economies, and by 1970, the picture had changed considerably as the East Asian economies essentially matched the savings rate in the major Latin American economies.

A combination of factors (in varying degrees) contributed to this process. In South Korea, for example, an increase in personal household savings was a major source of savings, largely stimulated by raising interest rates on bank deposits. The government also helped establish private banks and financial institutions, which began to overshadow traditional and informal money

TABLE 15–3   Gross Domestic Savings (expressed as percentage of GDP)

	1960	1970	1980	1986	1996
South Korea	1	15	25	35	34
Taiwan	13	26	N/A	36	N/A
Hong Kong	6	25	34	27	31
Singapore	−3	21	38	40	50
Brazil	21	20	21	24	18
Mexico	18	21	25	27*	23
Argentina	21	22	24	11	18

*1985.

Source: The World Bank, *World Development Report, 1981/1997* and *World Development Indicators,*
1998; Seiji Naya, Miguel Urrutia, Shelley Mark, Alfredo Fuentes, eds., *Lessons in Development* (San
Francisco: International Center for International Growth, 1989), pp. 289–290; Anis Chowdhury and
Iyanatul Islam, *The Newly Industrializing Economies of East Asia* (New York: Routledge, 1993), p.
128; The United Nations, *Human Development Report, 1994.*

markets widely used by small private customers. This financial policy allowed
the government to increase its oversight of financial stability and savings in the
economy.[23] The growth of financial institutions in Singapore and Hong Kong was
also crucial to the capital formation process in these countries. Interestingly, the
former developed an approach where government maintained a tight control and
oversight over financial institutions while the latter leaned in the opposite direction of minimal regulation of the financial sector.[24]

This high savings rate among the East Asian NICs was also generated by
maintaining strict controls on both public and private consumption. Strict fiscal
policies have helped keep budget deficits well under control. Results of this
deliberate fiscal approach were budget deficits that were among the lowest in
the developing world and a persistently low inflation rate in the East Asian
economies compared to their Latin American counterparts. In Hong Kong and
Singapore (historically free-market-based economies), public sector consumption
in 1960 was relatively low to begin with—7 percent and 8 percent of GDP, respectively. In South Korea, it declined from 15 to 11 percent by 1979 and has averaged about 10 during the 1990s.[25] This situation lent itself well to promoting
investment in the productive sectors of the economy—which is precisely what
the East Asian NICs have accomplished since the 1960s.

The influx of foreign capital and aid in East Asia is another crucial aspect of
the capital formation process there. Cold War tensions and the Korean War both
had a strong influence on the flow of Western aid into South Korea and Taiwan.
South Korea's dependence on foreign aid was especially crucial following the
Korean War in the 1950s. According to one estimate, approximately 70 percent of
South Korea's domestic capital formation came from foreign aid during much of
the 1950s.[26] Taiwan's domestic capital formation also depended heavily on foreign capital during the same period—about 40 percent was externally financed.
Recall that this was also the period when South Korea and Taiwan underwent
structural transformation in production, using protective measures to insulate its
newly emerging light manufacturing industries from foreign competition.

Throughout the literature on economic development, education and human resource development are recurrent features. It is no surprise that the success of the East Asian NICs have called even more attention to these issues. The combined impact of investment strategies in education and job training in the NICs have resulted in a quality labor force creating increased economic efficiency, industrial flexibility, and greater economic equality. Government initiatives in reducing the illiteracy rate and providing adequate access to job training are evident in comparatively high enrollment rates and government investment in creating an educated and skilled workforce. For example, government spending on education in 1972 was almost 16 percent of public expenditures in South Korea and Singapore. This commitment to education has continued in both nations as government spending in this area has averaged about 19 percent and 21 percent of total government spending (1991–95) in South Korea and Singapore, respectively. The Asian "cubs" like Malaysia and Thailand, which were also investing heavily in education, with 23 percent and 20 percent of government spending, respectively, have similarly not deviated from this governmental commitment to education.[27] The important point here is not that government expenditures in education have resulted in economic development. Rather, in a number of NICs, the emphasis on education has led to the growth of a literate and skilled workforce, which has been essential to the success of the industrial and investment policies and has promoted growth in productivity.

Finally, as we have seen, the state in these countries has been instrumental in setting and shaping development policies. South Korea presents a typical case in point. Following a coup in 1961 the military established the Economic Planning Board, which, among other things, acquired powers to control the nation's investment strategy. With the guidance of the military government, which dictated economic policy, the board became a coordinating body among the various governmental agencies. This centralization of power corresponded with the weakening of political parties and electoral politics in South Korea. Another significant unfolding was the systematic weakening of labor unions, which allowed the government greater control over enforcing its economic agenda. Hence, it should be noted that the East Asian "tigers" didn't simply "roll back the state" and let free competition reign as advocated by some neoliberals since the early 1980s.

This emphasis on a strong state apparatus to direct economic restructuring and export promotion is not exclusive to South Korea. Recall from the discussion in chapter 13 that Japan's phenomenal rise as a major global economic power is often attributed to its peculiar brand of capitalism. Of special importance has been the active role of the Japanese state in leading and guiding economic policy and the global competitiveness of its major industries. Some analysts see the "tigers" as following closely along the path of a mercantilist style "developmental capitalism" paved by Japan. Others go further and assert that the East Asian region has also been stimulated by Japanese investment, expertise, technology, and closer economic integration with Japan.[28]

Like South Korea, others in the region (e.g., Malaysia and Taiwan) have also developed strong central authority to manage their growth process. Having an influential state that supports capitalist development is often seen by some politicians and academics in the region as necessary. The state's role is considered especially crucial in the early and intermediary stages of the process (i.e., during the initial import-substitution stage and then during the transition to an export-led growth stage). As one prominent Malaysian politician noted:

> In most East Asian countries, politics is a means to an end. Leaders behave in a political manner they think will best achieve one objective: Filling the stomachs of their people. . . . The Western model has politics as an end in itself. The objective . . . is not about filling stomachs but about an ideal system. . . . The Asian countries that are doing well are those which, from the Western viewpoint, are not quite fully democratic. . . . There is a consensus in this region that economic development must precede political development. It is popularly felt that restrictions on politics are necessary, albeit temporary.[29]

The East Asia nations make no apologies for the suppression of Western-style democracy. In each of the above cases, the state has played a central role in guiding the transition of these economies from being exporters of primary products to being exporters of manufactured goods to the rest of the world.

The experience among the major Latin American economies has been quite different. But, as in the case of East Asia, the situation has been influenced by a complex set of forces. Recall that during the 1950s, Latin American scholars were increasingly skeptical of the "comparative advantage" road to development, and the dependency critique became an influential framework for development in that region. This critique fostered opposition to dependence on foreign capital and trade to promote development, which resulted in restrictive trade policies and stringent regulation and control of foreign investment. Instead, the inward-looking and nationalistic import substitution approach was implemented. This approach was supposed to reduce dependence on foreign capital, technology, and markets by promoting "home-grown" industries.

Government leaders and scholars alike were convinced that specializing in primary commodity products was an inherent disadvantage for developing countries in the region. The adverse terms of trade made manufactured imports a major foreign exchange drain that did not add to any tangible development. For this to change, countries like Brazil and Mexico, which had a relatively fragile industrial base, had to undertake significant steps to build a viable and sustaining manufacturing sector. After all, given the large internal consumer market in Brazil and Mexico, a shift in emphasis from importing manufactured consumer products to producing them locally would translate into new jobs across the economy, improve the adverse balance of payment situation, and promote economic development.

The import substitution path taken by countries like Brazil and Mexico can best be described as a series of stages during which these countries moved from being exporters of primary commodities to developing an indigenous industrial base. The first stage of the import substitution strategy was not unlike that followed by the East Asian NICs. By the 1950s, Brazil and Mexico were well into the process of promoting local manufacture of consumer goods (such as processed foods, textiles, and footwear) and curtailing foreign imports with protectionist measures. However, there were some significant differences affecting the import substitution strategies between the East Asian and Latin American cases. Historically, the resource and agriculture rich Latin American economies have been significantly more dependent on primary exports than their East Asian counterparts like Taiwan and South Korea.[30] Diversifying from this deeply entrenched primary-product economy was easier said than done.

Furthermore, protectionist policies were used more heavily in countries like Brazil to displace the foreign share of its consumer market, while in East Asia the focus of these measures was to enhance the international competitiveness of locally produced goods. Hence, by the late 1960s, as South Korea was moving into promoting its exports while maintaining some barriers, Brazil and Mexico were moving into the next stage of intensifying their import substitution strategy. Ironically, instead of reducing their dependence on foreign capital, borrowing from abroad to finance the deepening of their import substitution was necessary. This second stage of import substitution involved expanding the manufacture of labor-intensive consumer goods along with diversifying into capital-intensive goods as well.[31] In this stage, the role of the government also expanded; state-owned enterprises expanded. This increasing presence of the state was associated with increased concentration of production in the hands of a few firms (often state owned) that were not as productive as privately owned enterprises.[32]

Through this strategy, however, Brazil, Mexico, and others were able to generate sustained economic growth. Brazil had a 9 percent annual average growth in GDP between 1965 and 1980. Mexico and Venezuela lagged behind but still averaged a growth rate of 6.5 percent and 3.7 percent, respectively. The manufacturing sector in these countries also had a higher growth rate in relation to agriculture.[33] However, the performance of these economies has not been as strong as the export-oriented East Asian NICs. Brazil and Mexico had largely managed this growth by heavily depending on the domestic consumer market instead of the international market. In order to sustain growth, production reflected the consumption patterns of those with purchasing power. Ironically, this further aggravated income inequality as the gap between the "haves" and "have-nots" increased. By contrast, the income inequality gap among the East Asian NICs narrowed.[34]

Many highly protected industries remained uncompetitive and Latin NICs remained heavily dependent on the export of volatile primary goods. Conspicuous state-run enterprises and imprudent government spending were heavily financed through foreign borrowing (see Table 15–4), fueling an unprecedented fiscal crisis in these countries. By 1980, a number of Latin American economies were buried in debt. Excessive, and more important, inefficient government

TABLE 15–4 External Public Debt (US$ billions) (as percentage of GNP)

	1970	1979	1988	1991	1995
Argentina	1.8 (7.6)	8.7 (8.6)	48.1 (57.0)	63.7 (49.0)	89.7 (33.1)
Brazil	3.2 (7.2)	35.0 (17.7)	89.8 (26.3)	34.4 (65.0)	159.1 (24.0)
Mexico	3.2 (9.7)	28.8 (24.5)	81.2 (48.0)	101.7 (37.0)	165.7 (69.9)
Venezuela	0.7 (6.6)	9.8 (20.0)	25.4 (41.1)	116.5 (29 .0)	35.8 (49.0)

Source: The World Bank, *World Development Report, 1981, 1990 and 1997*; United Nations, *Human Development Report, 1994* (New York: Oxford University Press, 1994).

spending to implement import substitution policies was catching up with these countries. Indeed, this is reflected in a much lower (approximately 2.7 percent) annual average growth in GDP for Brazil since 1980. As their growth rates withered, the inflation rate in countries like Brazil hovered over 2,000 percent.

Under domestic and international pressure from lending institutions, Brazil began stripping away at the layers of import substitution policies. Privatization of the economy was a primary part of the prescribed solution, accompanied by reductions in tariffs. Meanwhile, Brazil's exports grew. In the early 1990s, foreign investment also increased. However, controlling inflation became the country's biggest challenge. The government's inability to curb spending and put its fiscal house in order put considerable pressure on the inflation spiral. To control inflation, Brazil underwent five currency changes over a dozen years, most recently in 1994. As one of the world's largest economies attempts to change course and move away from an inward-looking strategy to development, the process continues to be slow and costly.

LOSING GROUND: THE AFRICAN PREDICAMENT

The development problem is unquestionably most acute in Africa. Not surprisingly, Africa is also where we find the majority and the most dire of the LDCs. Directly related to the extent of the problem among these LDCs has been the sluggish performance of these economies. While each case is certainly unique, there are some clear threads running through the situations of many of these LDCs. In this section, we shall briefly outline some general but fundamental points that highlight the problem.

Like the NICs, the LDCs in Africa have also been keen about developing. Yet one expert notes: "It is quite hazardous to talk of development strategies in Africa . . . because it is not in the least clear that many African countries have a strategy which is identifiable."[35]

Although this may be an extreme characterization, the absence of consistency or an "identifiable" strategy can be traced to the absence of established and legitimate political institutions in many of these LDCs capable of promoting sustained policies. "Although the most pressing problems in Africa today are economic in nature, governments on the continent are more concerned about their political survival."[36] One basic indicator of this is the massive resources that have been diverted to arms expenditures and other repressive state efforts.[37] Hence, political survival has consistently competed with economic development priorities. In a region hard pressed to provide the basic amenities for its citizens, this diversion of resources indeed comes at a very high price.

The historical link that many African countries have had with the international economy continues to influence the fate of these LDCs. Since the early days of the colonial era, the African economies have been deeply entrenched in agriculture and primary commodity production (essentially directed for external consumption). Although this "comparative advantage" is not inherently detrimental, the almost exclusive reliance on primary commodity exports has left the LDCs consistently vulnerable to price volatility and unfavorable terms of trade for these commodities in the international market.

Most of the LDCs have been unable to markedly diversify their economies. In the aggregate, agriculture in Africa made up 47 percent of GDP in 1965 and had dropped to 38 percent by 1984. Industry's share of GDP during the same period increased from 15 to 16 percent. In Asia, agriculture declined from 42 to 36 percent of GDP as industry's share grew from 28 to 36 percent over the same period.[38] Hence, diversification remains a major priority for most African LDCs. Compounding this reliance on agriculture is the excessive dependence on limited products as the "bread and butter" of these economies. This phenomenon, known as commodity concentration, has been a conspicuous feature of most African LDCs. As a case in point, the level of commodity concentration in Zambia and Burundi has been over 90 percent during the 1970s and 1980s. Nigeria, which has been one of the few exceptions to move away from agriculture (and be classified as a middle-income country), has instead become excessively dependent on oil, which accounts for 90 percent of exports.[39]

Further, the economic crunch has been exacerbated by a systemic financial crisis. Since the oil crisis in the 1970s, the LDCs in Africa have seen their debt burden steadily and sharply increase from 25 percent in 1975 to 76 percent in 1987.[40] Of course, the debt crisis is not exclusive to Africa's LDCs, but the burden has been especially crippling, since many LDCs were experiencing reductions in export revenue. The IMF has attempted to steer these economies out of this situation by insisting that excessive government spending, agriculture subsidies, and artificial currency controls be eliminated. While there is some movement in this direction, skeptics insist that unless primary commodities prices in the international market rebound, the financial situation for these economies will not improve appreciably.

We also cannot ignore the complex ecological and physical impediments and conflicts that shape the history of the region. Obviously, development prospects in the region have been shaped by these factors. The Sudan is a typical case in point. With over 130 tribes, Sudan has historically been marred with ethnic, religious, and tribal tensions.[41] The Sudanese have also struggled to maintain a delicate balance between their largely subsistence agriculture system and the delicate ecology of the region. However, the inappropriate use of imported technology and intensification of commodity production for export have damaged the subsistence economy and the productive capacity of arable land. The devastation from ethnic conflicts for political control or survival has further compounded the ecological and productivity problem. In 1984, over 4 million people were displaced from their homes and the food shortage intensified. While the economic costs have been severe, the human costs remain immeasurable.

During the 1990s, ethnic violence between Hutus and Tutsis in Rwanda again brought to the world's attention some of the ugly perils of deeply entrenched ethnic divisions in many parts of Africa. Ethnic hostilities continue to represent a major impediment to stability and are often reignited by changes in economic or political conditions in parts of the continent. The experience of LDCs in Africa provides a poignant illustration of the collective interplay between IPE, local sociopolitical circumstances, economic survival strategies, and the environment.

WOMEN AND DEVELOPMENT IN LDCs

The controversy and complexity surrounding the process of development are partly captured by the concerns about the differential impact of development on women in the developing world. In recent years, much has been written about the role of female assembly-line workers in the *maquiladoras* of Mexico and other enterprise zones in many LDCs. As multinational corporations relocate their assembly operations in developing countries, they typically employ females as assembly workers at a fraction of the wage in developed countries. The pervasiveness of women in the informal economy (as servants, street vendors, cleaners, etc) in many Third World cities is also unmistakable.

The debates surrounding these recent trends are only the latest in a host of controversies related to the specific and general impact of development on women in LDCs. The literature is dotted with a range of interpretations and it is worth noting that most of them tend to fall into the following three major categories: integration, marginalization, and exploitation arguments.[a]

The integration argument sees economic development as inevitably expanding the opportunity structure and the level of participation of women not only in the economy but also in other societal institutions. For example, as capitalism and development expand, women are integrated into the workforce, making them wage earners which in turn increases their level of independence and autonomy. Accordingly, they become equipped not only to further strengthen their relative economic status but also to be more fully integrated into the social and political fabric. Through this, women in LDCs are also better able to influence reforms of traditional institutions that oppress them.

The marginalization argument posits an inverse association between the process of capitalist development and the position of women in LDCs. As development spreads, the formal sectors of the economy become more important. In turn, household production, the traditional domain of women in LDCs, is weakened as the emphasis shifts to production in factories and plants. Compounding this marginalization is the concern that men tend to benefit disproportionately from the employment opportunities created by this shift in emphasis from household production to the formal sectors. Thus, women in fact lose autonomy and economic resources and become more economically dependent on men. To supplement this diminished status, women in rural areas have to engage in subsistence agriculture. On the other hand, in the urban centers they are relegated to the informal service work (e.g., cleaning, selling food) or marginalized to the type of low-skill, poorly paying, and highly unstable employment in assembly plants operated by foreign multinationals.

Advocates of the exploitation argument note that because capitalist development in LDCs requires the exploitation of cheap labor, it ceaselessly "integrates" women into the labor force but this integration is persistently detrimental to women. For example, as multinationals establish their assembly and processing plants in LDCs, they "integrate" young, inexperienced female workers who are perceived as, among other things, docile and more amenable to the tedious nature of assembly work. This perception, and hence the ease at which they are exploitable, adds to the popularity of female workers in these industries. Often, by their mid-20s, these workers tend to be replaced by younger women at a lower wage rate. With little else to turn to, the former assembly workers often find themselves making ends meet through work in the informal service sector. Hence, their "integration" into the formal sector is rather shortlived. In this view, women serve as a pool of reserve labor that can conveniently be exploited for capital accumulation.

---

[a] This summary is based on Susan Tiano, "Gender, Work, and World Capitalism: Third World Women's Role in Development," in Beth B. Hess and Myra M. Ferree, eds., *Analyzing Gender* (Newbury Park, CA: Sage, 1987).

CONCLUSION

For over half a century the development process for Third World countries has been their foremost challenge. A complex mix of conditions both internal and external to these countries will continue to affect the outcome of development efforts.

Until recently, there was a growing consensus that neoliberal policies were the key to economic growth for LDCs and that the ongoing development dilemma might finally be resolved. Nations needed to streamline the state and introduce market reforms, it was argued, in order to tap the growth potential of global markets. As noted earlier, the East Asian NICs were often cited as evidence of the success of these neoliberal policies despite the fact that their actual policies often combined both liberal and mercantilist elements.

The Asian Financial crisis of 1997–98 (see chapter 8) has caused even the most strident proponents of neoliberal policies (including high officials at the IMF and the World Bank) to have some doubts about their unambiguous support for free market policies. The Asian countries that suffered the most from the Asian crisis and the contagion that followed were precisely those which were most thoroughly integrated into the global capital markets.

Economic development still has two faces, it seems, and the benefits of unregulated access to international financial markets in particular must be weighed against the inherent risk of financial crisis and instability that comes with it. Even the "Tigers" are held by the tail by the forces of global markets, it seems.

It is equally important to recognize that unique sociohistorical circumstances within each developing nation will continue to strongly influence not only the character of the state but also its relationship to the market and the larger international order. Recognizing the role of ethnic conflicts, class divisions, and other societal-specific conditions can provide much needed insight into the nature and role of the state in developing countries, and the development path taken. Countries like Iraq, The Sudan, Rwanda, Burundi, Algeria, and others are entangled in national and regional tensions and conflicts. These internal and regional conditions will certainly affect the character of the state and its role in the larger economy.

DISCUSSION QUESTIONS

1. The development dilemma has two distinct elements: the growing gap between rich and poor nations (North and South) and the increasing differences among less developed countries themselves (LDCs). Discuss these trends, citing evidence from this chapter.
2. What four forces have shaped the development process for LDCs? How do these forces create tensions within LDCs and between LDCs and industrial nations? Explain.
3. Compare and contrast the liberal ideas regarding economic development and export-led growth with the dependency perspective and the policy of import-substituting growth. How do market forces stimulate economic development? How do these same forces create dependency and underdevelopment? Explain.

4. What nations are included in the ranks of the Newly Industrialized Countries (NICs)? What specific factors seem to differentiate the NICs from the LDCs? What role does the state play in NIC development? Explain.

INTERNET LINKS

The World Bank: http://www.worldbank.org/

UNCTAD: http://www.unctad.org

World Bank quarterly magazine, *Finance & Development*:
      http://www.imf.org/external/pubs/ft/fandd/

The United Nations Development Programme: http://www.undp.org/

Third World Network: http://www.twnside.org.sg/

SUGGESTED READINGS

Kevin Danaher. *50 Years Is Enough*. Boston: South End Press, 1994.

Michael Fairbanks and Stace Lindsay. *Plowing the Sea: Nurturing the Hidden Sources of Growth in the Developing World*. Cambridge, MA: Harvard Business School Press, 1997.

Peter Lewis. *Africa: Dilemmas of Development and Change*. Boulder, CO: Westview Press, 1998.

Paul Craig Roberts and Karen Lafollette Araujo. *The Capitalist Revolution in Latin America*. New York: Oxford University Press, 1997.

Jon Woronoff. *Asia's "Miracle" Economies*. Armonk, NY: M.E. Sharpe, 1997.

NOTES

1. The South Commission, *The Challenge to the South* (New York: Oxford University Press, 1990), p. 1.
2. See World Bank, *World Development Indicators, 1998* (Washington, DC: World Bank, 1998).
3. There are numerous sources of comparison of the developed with the developing nations. These figures and trends are drawn from Joshua Goldstein, *International Relations* (New York: Harper Collins, 1994), pp. 467–469; World Bank, *Human Development Report, 1997* (New York, Oxford University Press, 1997).
4. For a sophisticated discussion of the political economy of development, see Charles K. Wilber and Kenneth P. Jameson, *The Political Economy of Development and Under-Development* (New York: McGraw-Hill, 1995). See also Ozay Mehmet, *Westernizing the Third World* (London: Routledge, 1995).
5. World Bank, *World Development Indicators 1998*, pp. 24–26.
6. See Daniel Chirot, *Social Change in the Twentieth Century* (New York: Harcourt Brace, 1977), p. 173.
7. One of the leading voices of the antineocolonial movement was the former president of Ghana, K. Nkrumah, who articulated this thesis in his book, *Neo-colonialism: The Last Stage of Imperialism* (London: Nelson, 1965).
8. Joan Edelman Spero, *The Politics of International Economic Relations* (New York: St. Martin's Press, 1981), pp. 246–247.
9. OPEC was formed in 1960 and its membership includes Iran, Iraq, Algeria, Nigeria, Gabon, Libya, Kuwait, Qatar, Saudi Arabia, United Arab Emirates, Ecuador, and Venezuela.
10. Robert Gilpin, *The Political Economy of International Relations* (Princeton, NJ: Princeton University Press, 1987), p. 300.
11. See Thomas Sowell, "Second Thoughts about the Third World," *Harper's* (November 1983); Douglas C. North, *Institutions, Institutional Change and Economic Performance* (New York: Cambridge University Press, 1990).
12. Walt W. Rostow, *The Stages of Economic Growth: A Non-Communist Manifesto* (London: Cambridge University Press, 1960).

13. Raul Prebisch, *The Economic Development of Latin America and Its Principal Problems* (New York: United Nations, 1950).
14. It is worth noting that many analyses of these early dependency theorists were based on the experiences of countries in Latin America.
15. Andre Gunder Frank, *Capitalism and Underdevelopment in Latin America* (New York: Monthly Review Press, 1967).
16. Osvaldo Sunkel and Pedro Paz, *El subdesarrollo latinoamericano y la teoría del desarrollo* (Mexico: Siglo Veintiuno de Espana 1970), p. 6, as quoted in J. Samuel Valenzuela and Arturo Valenzuela, "Modernization and Dependency," *Comparative Politics* 10 (1978) pp. 543–557.
17. For a good discussion of this position, see Teresa Hayter, *Aid as Imperialism* (Middlesex, England: Penguin, 1971).
18. In many respects the neoliberal consensus is a consensus among the IMF, World Bank, and the U.S. government concerning development policies, leading Paul Krugman among others to term it the "Washington Consensus" on development.
19. Walden Bello, "Global Economic Counterrevolution: How Northern Economic Warfare Devastates the South," in Kevin Danaher, ed., *50 Years Is Enough* (Boston: South End Press, 1994), p. 16. Also see Denny Braun, *The Rich Get Richer* (Chicago: Nelson-Hall, 1997).
20. William E. James, Seiji Naya, and Gerald M. Meier, *Asian Development: Economic Success and Policy Lessons* (Madison: University of Wisconsin Press, 1989), p. 10.
21. For example, see Wontack Hong, *Trade, Distortions, and Employment Growth in Korea* (Seoul: Korea Development Institute, 1979).
22. Seiji Naya, Miguel Urrutia, Shelley Mark, Alfredo Fuentes, eds., *Lessons in Development* (San Francisco: International Center for International Growth, 1989), p. 287; World Bank, *World Development Report 1997* (New York: Oxford University Press, 1997); C. J. Dahlman and O. Sananikone, "Taiwan, China: Policies and Institutions for Rapid Growth," in Danny M. Leipziger, ed., *Lessons From East Asia* (Ann Arbor: University of Michigan Press, 1997), p. 85.
23. James, Naya, and Meier, *Asian Development*, pp. 69–74.
24. Ibid., p. 81.
25. World Bank, *World Development Report 1981, 1997* (New York: Oxford University Press, 1981/1997).
26. Stephan Haggard, *Pathways from the Periphery: The Politics of Growth in the Newly Industrializing Countries.* (Ithaca, NY: Cornell University Press, 1990), p. 196.
27. World Bank, *World Development Report 1984, 1997* (New York: Oxford University Press, 1984/1997).
28. See James Fallows, *Looking at the Sun* (New York: Pantheon, 1994).
29. Musa Hitam, "How Politics Makes Asia Successful," *Asian Business* (December 1993), p. 39.
30. Jorge Ospina Sardi, "Trade Policy in Latin America," in Seiji Naya, Miguel Urrutia, Shelley Mark, Alfredo Fuentes, eds., *Lessons in Development*, p. 81.
31. Haggard, *Pathways from the Periphery*, p. 26.
32. Youngil Lim, "Comparing Brazil and Korea," in Seiji Naya et al., eds., *Lessons in Development*, pp. 102–103.
33. World Bank, *World Development Report, 1991.*
34. Nigel Harris, *The End of the Third World* (New York: Meredith Press, 1986), pp. 90–91.
35. See Claude Ake, *A Political Economy of Africa* (New York: Longman, 1981), pp. 141–144.
36. Julius E. Nyang'oro, *The State and Capitalist Development in Africa* (New York: Praeger, 1989), p. 147.
37. See Sunil Kukreja, "Militarization among Peripheral Nations," *Sociological Viewpoints* 8 (Fall 1992).
38. Adedotun O. Phillips, "Structural Change and Transformation of African Economies," in Adebayo Adedeji, Owodunni Teriba, and Patrick Bugembe, eds., *The Challenge of African Economic Recovery and Development* (Portland, OR: Frank Cass, 1991), p. 458.
39. Nyang'oro, *The State and Capitalist Development in Africa*, p. 40.
40. Figures from the World Bank, *World Development Report, 1988* (New York: Oxford University Press, 1988), p. 31.
41. This discussion of the Sudan is based on Mohamed Suliman, "Civil War in the Sudan: From Ethnic to Ecological Conflict," *Ecologist* 23 (May 1993).

16

The IPE of Multinational Corporations

by Professor Leon Grunberg

OVERVIEW

Multinational corporations are key agents transforming the international political and economic landscape. Because they are highly visible organizations, with great power and mobility, they inspire both awe and fear. It is the purpose of this chapter to lay out, dispassionately, what these organizations are, where they come from, and where they go, and to assess the impact they have on countries and workers around the globe.

Multinational corporations are firms engaged in productive activities in several countries. The vast majority originate in rich, developed countries and much of their foreign investment goes to other rich nations. Typically, they go overseas because they possess some special advantage they want to exploit fully and because there are benefits in locating their activities overseas. These benefits may result from avoiding barriers to imports to employing cheaper foreign labor.

While most political economists will agree with the above summary, there is far more debate as to the kinds of effects multinational corporations have. Economic liberals see them as forces for positive change, spreading good things like technology and efficiency around the world. Economic nationalists see them as threatening the sovereignty of nation-states. Marxists and structuralists worry that they are creating a world marked by inequality and dependency.

This chapter does not take sides. Rather, it presents each side's case so the reader can reach his or her own conclusion.

Although the multinational corporation spreads the production over the world, it concentrates coordination and planning in key cities, and preserves power and income for the privileged.[1]

Stephen Hymer (1972)

I have long dreamed of buying an island owned by no nation and of establishing the World Headquarters of the Dow company on the truly neutral ground of such an island, beholden to no nation or society.[2]

Carl A. Gerstacker, chairman of Dow Chemical Company

As these comments indicate, perhaps no other aspect of IPE has generated more controversy and grandiose claims than *Multinational Corporations (MNCs)*. There is, after all, something awe-inspiring and intimidating about huge, powerful economic organizations that span the globe. In the 1960s and 1970s, as the sudden explosion in their numbers and the expansion of their reach hit the public's and academic communities' consciousness, there was a flood of critical commentaries sounding alarm bells and warning of the dangers they posed to national sovereignty and to the security and stability of workers' lives around the globe.[3] Today, several decades later, as they have become an integral and established part of the international economic landscape, the criticisms have been muted. Multinational corporations have now become, in the words of the *Economist* magazine, "everybody's favorite monsters."[4] Rich, poor, former communist, and still communist nations all compete to attract MNCs to their shores. With the collapse of the Soviet economic model and with growing MNC control of a huge portion of the world's crucial economic resources (e.g., capital, technology, and management skills), it now appears as if there are few viable alternatives to a capitalist development strategy. For many countries, especially developing ones, attracting MNCs as part of that strategy becomes the only game around. Still, the underlying fears and criticisms have not disappeared. For even as they have become "everybody's favorites," they are still "monsters" bestriding the globe.

This chapter will try to cut through both the awe and the fear these economic organizations produce. It will be our purpose to examine MNCs dispassionately, and to answer a series of basic questions: What are MNCs? Where do they come from? Where do they go? Why do they exist at all? How do they operate? And how are the various groups and governments affected by MNC activities? Only then can we assess the nature of their role in the IPE of today and tomorrow.

THE NATURE OF MULTINATIONAL CORPORATIONS

Multinational Corporations (MNCs) are economic organizations engaged in productive activities in two or more countries. Typically, they have their headquarters in their country of origin (their home country) and expand overseas by building or acquiring affiliates or subsidiaries in other countries (the host). This kind of expansion is referred to as *Foreign Direct Investment (FDI)* because it involves engagement in directly productive activities overseas, such as Ford establishing a plant in Mexico to build cars, or Citibank setting up a branch office in London to provide financial services. Foreign direct investment has expanded at phenomenal rates since World War II. In the 1980s, for example, FDI grew at

28.9 percent per year, three times the rate of world trade, and it has been a key force integrating the world economy.[5] But FDI is not the only factor transforming economic relations around the globe. Trade and portfolio investments also connect national economies and have also grown rapidly. Indeed, portfolio investment flows, which refer to the international movement of money in search of high rates of return in currency and financial markets, dwarf the dollar value of the two other kinds of activities. We will not discuss portfolio investment in this chapter but restrict ourselves to FDI—or what amounts to the same thing, the productive activities of MNCs.

Although there are 45,000 MNCs with some 280,000 foreign affiliates worldwide, ownership and control of such assets are heavily concentrated. For example, just 1 percent of MNCs own half the total of all existing foreign assets.[6] The story of FDI is still primarily the story of large MNCs. Before World War II, many of the major multinational corporations were in extractive and natural resource sectors (for example, the oil producers Shell, Exxon, and BP). After World War II, manufacturing corporations like GM, Ford, Siemens, Sony, and Phillips Electronics dominated FDI. Increasingly, the newest and fastest growing wave of MNCs are in services, with companies like Citibank and Nomura Securities providing financial services around the globe. Some of these companies have sales revenues that exceed the gross domestic product of many countries in the world; and increasingly, the majority of these large MNCs have affiliates in many countries rather than just a handful. It is precisely such characteristics that give them such clout and attract labels like "leviathan" and "monster."

WHERE DO THEY COME FROM AND WHERE DO THEY GO?

One of the common yet understandable misconceptions about FDI is that most of it flows from rich, developed nations to poor, developing ones. Nothing could be further from the truth. FDI is in fact an activity conducted primarily between rich countries. The United Nations Center for Transnational Corporations, the leading monitor of MNC activity, estimates that for much of the postwar period developed economies were not only the home (source) of over 95 percent of recent foreign direct investment flows, but also the host (recipient) of over 80 percent of such flows. Even with the recent surge in FDI flows to developing countries, their total share of such inflows is only 37 percent, close to what it was at other periods of FDI booms.[7] Indeed, in the period since 1985, just five rich nations (the United States, the U.K., Germany, Japan, and France) were the home of almost 70 percent and the host of 57 percent of all FDI flows.[8] These facts should modify the popular notion that MNCs are solely or even mainly concerned with finding locations with the cheapest labor. While this might be true for some MNCs engaged in particularly simple and labor-intensive processes, for many others the more important concerns seem to be access and proximity to rich consumer markets and matching the locational moves of large rival MNCs.

However, we do not wish to imply by this that the activities of MNCs are unimportant to the development process in poor countries. A few large, powerful MNCs can significantly influence and possibly distort the political economy of a small, poor country. Rather, it reminds us that focusing all our attention on

MNCs in the developing world will create a narrow and misleading picture of the role of MNCs in the international political economy.

Looking more closely at the changes in the geographic origins and destinations of FDI reveals some dramatic trends that in a sense mirror the change in the relative economic power of the leading economies in the world. For much of the century, the powerful U.S. economy accounted for the lion's share of all outward FDI in the world. As late as the 1970s, the United States still accounted for more than 40 percent of total outward FDI. By the early 1990s, however, that figure had dropped to below 14 percent.[9] Although U.S. MNCs still dominate international economic activity because they have accumulated a large stock of foreign assets over many decades of FDI, it was Germany and, in particular, Japan that experienced the most rapid growth in outward FDI in the seventies and eighties. Japan's share of outward FDI jumped from less than 1 percent in 1960 to almost 12 percent in 1985, and by the late 1980s, Japan ranked first in terms of the annual flow of outward FDI.[10] The nineties gave us another reversal in fortunes, with the United States regaining its lead and Japan, suffering its most serious economic crisis since World War II, dropping to fifth place.[11]

Much of that outflow from Japan, Germany, and other rich European countries went to the United States, which remains the most popular destination for MNCs, receiving some 40 to 50 percent of all FDI flows in the mid-eighties and some 25 percent in 1996. By way of contrast, in the early 1970s, only 7.2 percent of such flows went to the United States. This sudden surge in MNC activity in the United States created quite an ironic public reaction. It was ironic because some Americans were voicing the very same fears and painting similar images that Europeans and Canadians had used decades earlier in response to the entry of U.S. MNCs into their countries.

At that time, the Europeans worried about the U.S. takeover of Europe, and Canada felt that it was becoming a dependent outpost of the U.S. economy.[12] In the 1990s, the tables were reversed and it was Americans who fretted about the Japanese invasion of the United States as famous institutions like Rockefeller Center and Columbia Pictures came under Japanese ownership. Even such a quintessentially American cultural pastime as baseball was penetrated by foreigners, as the Japanese video game producer, Nintendo, bought a majority share in the Seattle Mariners team.

But while these concerns are understandable, are they justified? The most forceful argument that such fears are exaggerated and misplaced has been made by the political economist Robert Reich. In a provocative book *The Work of Nations*, he argues that the nationality of corporations is becoming irrelevant. Japanese companies investing in the United States may do more to advance the standard of living of Americans than do American MNCs investing in Latin America or Asia. In one case, the factories, offices, machinery, and jobs are in the United States, and in the other they are located in foreign countries. The policy conclusion for Reich seems inescapable: "Nations can no longer substantially enhance the wealth of their citizens by subsidizing, protecting, or otherwise increasing the profitability of 'their corporations.'"[13]

If Reich is right, then the case of Japan seems to present a puzzle. Despite becoming a major source of outward FDI, Japan has virtually no inward FDI.

Unlike the United States, Britain, France, and Germany, where between 10 to 20 percent of total sales are accounted for by foreign-owned MNCs, in Japan it is less than 1 percent.[14] Indeed, to give you an idea of how little FDI there is in Japan, just two Japanese acquisitions of U.S. companies (Matsushita's of MCA and Sony's of Columbia Pictures) equal the entire value of the stock of inward FDI in Japan.[15] The primary reason for this minimal FDI has been the Japanese government's decades-long policy of setting up bureaucratic delays and barriers to frustrate inward FDI. Why Japan pursued such policies is a matter of debate but it probably has a lot to do with its history of economic nationalism and a desire to protect its growing companies. When Japanese companies became world-class competitors and went global in the 1970s and 1980s, other nations pressured Japan to open its borders to foreign MNCs. The government responded by removing most of the legal and bureaucratic barriers in 1980. But inward FDI still remains low, most probably because of the existence of *keiretsus* (corporations that are linked into a group by extensive cross-shareholdings) that make it extremely difficult for a foreign MNC to merge or acquire a Japanese corporation that is part of such a group.[16] This imbalance in the relationship between Japan and other countries—that Japan can buy foreign firms, but outsiders find it almost impossible to acquire major Japanese firms—is bound to be an additional source of tension in the IPE of the next few years.

Finally, before we leave this section, we need to note a couple of trends about FDI in the developing world. As we have pointed out, very little FDI originates in or goes to developing countries. The very poorest countries, many of them in Africa, are essentially bystanders in this global activity, attracting less than 1 percent of all FDI flows. Most of the FDI that goes to developing countries heads for just ten countries in Asia and Latin America (primarily China, Malaysia, Hong Kong, Singapore, Brazil, and Mexico).[17] These countries either have very large internal markets or have developed quite a sophisticated infrastructure (e.g., ports, banking, education).

It is also from among these countries that we see the development of a small but growing number of MNCs. These fast-growing industrializing economies are increasingly the home of FDI that flows to other developing countries. In particular, FDI flows from East Asia's newly industrialized countries (for example, Hong Kong, South Korea, and Singapore) have recently become larger sources of investment in countries like China, Indonesia, and Malaysia than those from Japan and the United States.[18]

WHY DO FIRMS INVEST ABROAD?

There exists no single elegant theory to account for foreign direct investment, as there is for international trade. Indeed, the existence and growth of international networks of subsidiaries controlled by the headquarters of large MNCs don't fit very comfortably into the perfectly competitive world of neoclassical economics, the dominant intellectual paradigm in economics. In this textbook world, firms would not grow beyond the size of a single efficient plant. Such plants would purchase necessary supplies from other independent firms (not from sister subsidiaries within the MNC) and would sell via exports what they produced at their single locations (rather than produce and sell their products in various locations around the globe). If they possessed a particularly unique technology, they might, for a fee, allow a foreign company to use that technology (often called a *licensing arrangement*). In such a world, multinational corporations would not exist. But as we have seen, such firms are pervasive and are beginning to dominate international economic activity. An understanding of this development, therefore, requires a less idealized and a more concrete *examination of the actual behavior of firms*. If we want to understand why MNCs exist, we have to look at what kinds of firms are multinational, and at their motives for investing overseas.

A comprehensive explanation of MNC decisions to invest overseas comprises several elements.[19] Perhaps the most important element is that the firm possess some *firm-specific competitive advantage*. This is important because the firm must be able to overcome the disadvantage of doing business a long way from home against foreign firms that will be more familiar with the local environment. There are several kinds of advantages that enable firms to go overseas and compete successfully against foreign producers. An important one is size. MNCs are usually large and have market power. They can, therefore, obtain finance capital relatively easily and at favorable terms. Furthermore, they are often technological or marketing leaders in their industry. They may, like Xerox Corporation, have pioneered a particular product, or like Toyota, developed an efficient system of production. Or they may have tremendous marketing power because of a brand name, like Coca-Cola, McDonald's, or Hilton Hotels. These advantages enable such firms to compete successfully in foreign countries.

Such firms could, of course, sell or license their technological or marketing advantages to foreign firms, thereby benefiting indirectly from their advantages. Some in fact do so via licensing agreements and partnerships or alliances. But many do not, insisting on complete ownership and control of their advantages. The primary reasons for this are twofold. First, when control of the advantage remains within the MNC, the MNC captures all the benefits that flow from the advantage. Since marketing and technological advantages often enable MNCs to earn high rates of return, they have a financial reason not to want to share these gains with others, especially firms that may be potential rivals. Secondly, supply or licensing agreements involve some degree of uncertainty. Will the licensee do as good a job as the licensing firm would at producing or marketing the product? For many firms, the uncertainties are sufficiently large to make full control attractive. Keeping the advantages in-house, as it were, is the second element in the explanation and is often referred to as *internalizing the firm-specific advantages*.

These two elements still do not satisfactorily answer why firms don't supply foreign markets by exports. A firm could maintain full control of its particular competitive advantage and export the product from its home country. Coca-Cola or Xerox copiers can obviously be shipped from the United States all over the world. One answer to the question has to do with what are sometimes called *location-specific advantages*. That is, there are advantages to producing at the foreign location itself, which the firm can only enjoy by being there. When the MNC locates overseas, it can obtain much better information about changes in customer tastes and can also respond more quickly to such changes. It avoids the transport costs involved with exporting across long distances and can enjoy the same labor costs as its rivals in that foreign market. Some governments, in an effort to assist domestic producers, raise barriers to imports. Getting under trade barriers becomes an additional, and often very important, reason for firms to locate inside the foreign country, thereby eliminating that particular disadvantage. One example among many is Nissan and Honda opening production facilities in Britain so they could get around Italian and French quotas placed on Japanese car imports. By producing in Britain, a member country of the European Union, these companies could circumvent the restrictions.

Raymond Vernon has married these location-specific advantages with the evolutionary life cycle of products to account for the timing and sequence of FDI by U.S. manufacturers.[20] The *product life-cycle theory,* as it is called, argues that at the birth of a new product, the firm faces few competitors and will tend to locate all its production close to its customers and research and development center. In this way it can more easily adapt the product to conditions in its primary market. Foreign markets are served by exports. As the product matures and the production process becomes routine and more easily imitated, foreign competitors begin to challenge the export markets of the pioneering firm. As we have seen, such foreign firms may be able to undercut the prices or services offered by the pioneering firm because they enjoy location-specific advantages. In order to preserve its market share, the pioneering firm may set up production facilities in the foreign country. As the product approaches old age and price competition becomes more severe, with perhaps the entry of low-cost rivals from developing countries, MNCs are again compelled to shift some of their production in search of even cheaper locations.

Another important element of the explanation for FDI concerns the strategies these large firms employ to remain competitive with their main rivals. Researchers have noticed that much U.S. FDI in the 1960s and 1970s occurred in "bunches," with several MNCs in an industry all locating in a foreign country or area at roughly the same time. Did all these companies have similar firm-specific advantages and did they all happen to discover the location-specific advantages by chance at the same time? This seems unlikely. A more plausible explanation is that many of the MNCs were matching the actions of their competitors lest one of them gain an edge by being the only one going overseas. By "following the leader" and acting in packs, these firms try to minimize their risks and maintain a certain market stability or competitive equilibrium in the industry.[21] This behavior pattern has continued. A current example of such packlike behavior can be seen in the European chemical industry. European MNCs like Ciba, BASF, Bayer, and ICI are all, at about the same time, in the process of shifting the production of bulk chemicals out of the stagnant markets of Europe to the faster-growing Asian markets.[22]

In sum, we can say that FDI is typically carried out by large firms possessing some particular competitive advantage that they do not want to share with rivals. These firms tend to become multinational so they can enjoy the advantages of locating in a foreign site. Such locational advantages include getting under trade barriers, operating close to large markets, and gaining access to inexpensive labor.

In the future, as the revolutions in communications and transportation shrink the globe and facilitate continued international economic activity, and as more and more firms become multinational, explanations of FDI will shift from a focus on why firms become multinational (many of them already are), to *how they behave as multinationals*. Also, as MNCs from different developed countries increasingly succeed in cross-penetrating each other's markets, the main competitive battles may revolve less on access to markets and more on who has the best technological innovations and the lowest production costs.

THE IMPACT OF MULTINATIONAL CORPORATIONS

We have now reached the heart of the controversy that swirls around MNCs. Should they be welcomed as forces for positive and progressive change in the international political economy, or do they help create a highly unequal and destructive global economy? Do they help the development of poor countries, or do they exploit and distort their economies? There are no simple or conclusive answers to these questions. How we assess the impact of MNCs depends on a variety of conditioning factors: on whether the host country is rich or poor; on whether the MNC investment is deep-rooted and long term, or shallow and short term; on the alternatives available to the host country; and on a variety of other factors we shall presently examine. A final assessment also depends on one's perspective and values. If one believes that economic growth overrides all other considerations, then one is likely to see MNCs as sources of progress in the world. However, if one believes that the pursuit of equitable and balanced (perhaps even slow) development is preferable, then MNCs may represent forces exacerbating inequality and exploitation. Rather than pick sides, we will provide you with a balanced account of the impact of MNCs by presenting the arguments made by each side in the controversy. It will be for you, the reader, to weigh the strengths of the contending positions, test them against actual cases and situations, and reach your own conclusions.

THE POSITIVE VIEW

Host Country Effects

Arguments in support of MNCs are usually made by liberal political economists and by the business community.[23] Since MNCs tend to be successful companies that possess a variety of competitive advantages, much of the positive case for them rests on the things they bring into host countries. MNCs, it is argued, transfer technology, products, finance capital, and sophisticated management techniques to countries that lack these. This infusion of resources into host nations would, for example, tend to create jobs and raise the skill level of the workforce as it learns to utilize the modern technology that MNCs transfer into the country.

These positive additions to a country's economy are greater if the MNC invest-ment is in a new or "greenfield" site than if the MNC simply acquires an existing local company.[24] In the first case, there is, presumably, a pure addition to the pro-ductive capacity of the nation, for without the foreign investment, that factory and its associated jobs would not have existed. While acquisitions may be less attractive to host countries, there is still some benefit, since the MNCs are likely to manage the operations more efficiently than the previous owners. As Robert Reich puts it, MNCs invest overseas because "they think they can utilize the other nation's assets and its workers better than that nation's investors and managers can [thus] rendering the assets and workers more productive than before."[25] A telling example is the case of Toyota, which took over the management of a Gen-eral Motors plant in California and managed to raise productivity by 50 percent and to reduce absenteeism substantially.

In addition to the direct positive effects of MNCs, there may also be spillover effects onto other companies and sectors in the economy of the host nation. For example, if Ford builds a car factory in Brazil, this *could* lead to the expansion of domestic supplier firms in the steel or rubber industries and to an increase in work for dealers and advertising agencies, *provided*, of course, that Ford buys its supplies in the host market and sells much of its production local-ly. In other words, the degree to which MNCs are linked with domestic firms is an important factor conditioning the extent of the spillover effects into the host economy. That is why many host governments insist that MNCs include a cer-tain proportion of domestically produced materials and supplies in their final products. Other indirect benefits include the increased competition MNCs pro-vide local firms, which may prod them to respond to the more efficient foreign rival by adopting the best practices of these MNCs. There can be little doubt that the U.S. "big three" automakers were shaken out of their complacency by the suc-cess of Japanese autos, both imported and manufactured in the United States by Japanese transplants.

Multinational corporations are also credited with helping to improve a nation's balance of payments (see chapter 8). On the capital side of the account, there is a flow of capital into the economy when the MNC builds a new sub-sidiary or acquires an existing one. Of course, the key question is the capital balance after one subtracts the subsequent outflow of capital in the form of repatriated profits, license fees, and royalties that the subsidiary sends home to its parent. While one may expect the capital balance to be negative over time, since MNCs expect not only to recoup their outlay but also to make a profit, it is the positive effect on trade that supporters of MNCs point to. MNCs can be expected to reduce a country's imports by substituting domestically produced products for those that were previously imported, and to increase a country's exports. MNCs, because of their international scope, have far better marketing and distribution systems than domestic firms and are, therefore, very success-ful exporters. Indeed, some MNC subsidiaries in developing countries serve primarily as export platforms, producing goods almost exclusively for sale in other countries. Again, however, one has to examine *the net effect* on trade, since many of these MNCs import much of their supplies from other subsidiaries of the MNC.

Home Country Effects

So far, we have focused on the positive effects on host countries. But do these gains for the host country come at the expense of home countries? Do capital, technology, and management skill that go overseas mean fewer jobs in, and less exports from, the home country? This is a very hard question to answer definitively because we cannot be sure what would have happened to the resources of the MNC if they had not gone overseas. Would, for example, the plant that was closed in the home country, so that the MNC could transfer its production to a cheaper labor site, have survived anyway? There is no way to be sure. Proponents of MNCs, however, argue that these companies make economically rational decisions. They transfer production overseas or open new factories in foreign countries as a defensive measure in response to competitive pressures. If they did not, they would jeopardize their access to foreign markets and perhaps the survival of the entire company—and with it the jobs of their workforce. Moreover, proponents argue that foreign direct investment can actually stimulate economic activity in the home country. U.S. MNCs, for example, export a great deal of their domestic output to their subsidiaries abroad. If these subsidiaries did not exist, there would be no guarantee that foreign markets for these exports would exist at all.

Finally, and at a more general, systemic level, proponents of MNCs make a series of political and cultural claims about the benefits of MNCs. At the systemic level, MNCs are viewed as forces integrating the world's economies, thereby reducing nationalism and international tensions. By increasing trade between nations, by connecting workers from different countries into one MNC network, and by spreading similar consumer products to all corners of the world, they undermine national differences and help create a world citizen with modern tastes and habits. Furthermore, by developing global rather than national horizons and by helping revolutionize the international flows of capital and communications, MNCs compel governments to collaborate politically so they can regulate and control these new international forces. In a similar vein, supporters of MNCs and of a more borderless economic world also claim that the economic growth that results from a more open world economy will foster a more liberal and democratic political order in countries that previously endured authoritarian regimes.

THE NEGATIVE VIEW

The case against MNCs has been spearheaded by radical-structuralists. At the most general level, they argue that MNCs integrate poor nations into an unequally structured world system, with poor countries languishing on the periphery, heavily dependent for their development on the decisions and actions of capitalists ensconced in MNC headquarters in rich core nations. The policy implications of the most radical of the dependency school arguments is for poor countries to cut their dependence by closing their doors to MNCs.[26] Whatever the merits of such a view, this is not a policy many countries are currently pursuing. Even communist countries like China and Cuba seek to attract MNCs to their shores. We shall, therefore, examine, at a lower level of analysis, some of the possible specific negative effects of MNC investment on, first, the host, and then the home countries.

Host Country Effects

Many of the less ideological arguments against MNCs rest on the particular conditions surrounding their investment. Take the issue of the supposed transfer of capital when FDI occurs. In several cases, MNCs may borrow the money for foreign investment in the local host market rather than transfer it from its home base. Since lenders believe it is safer to advance loans to large organizations, the MNCs may squeeze out young, potentially viable local firms from the local market and retard the *independent* development of indigenous businesses. Similarly, further capital investment may come from the profits of the subsidiary rather than from the parent company. When one adds the outflow of capital in the form of repatriated profits, the net infusion of capital into host nations may be much smaller than MNC supporters claim.

Doubts have also been raised about the benefits of the transferred technology, especially for poorer developing countries. First, the vast bulk of the research and development capability of MNCs remains at home in the parent company. Very little is carried out in developing countries.[27] Therefore, MNCs, it is argued, do not help develop an *independent* capacity to generate new technology in the host countries. Since locals receive little training and experience developing new products and processes, when the MNCs leave, little that was of lasting benefit remains. This would be particularly true for MNCs producing for export in low labor-cost locations, for they are likely to be short-term residents in these countries.

Second, there is the question of the appropriateness or suitability of the transferred technology for the host nation. Is a product or process developed in a rich country like the United States, to meet its particular circumstances, appropriate for poor countries? For example, is a manufacturing process that is highly automated best suited for a country like India, with a huge labor force, or would a labor-intensive technology be more appropriate for its needs? Similarly, is it appropriate for MNCs to introduce products primarily produced for sale in developed nations into poor countries that have massive unmet basic needs? Was Nestlé misguided or worse in marketing its infant powdered formula to African and Latin American women who had no access to safe water and who were breast-feeding their babies? Anyone who has visited developing countries will be struck by the ubiquity of American soft drinks and cigarettes. Should nutritionally empty drinks and cancer-causing products be so heavily promoted by MNCs? Questions such as these have no easy answers. How one responds depends on one's values and on an assessment of the alternatives developing countries face. For example, defenders of the MNCs might argue that the transfer of capital-intensive technology is better than no such technology if that is the alternative, and that providing consumers in poor countries with the same choices as those in rich nations assumes they are equally capable of making sensible choices.

Perhaps most important from the host countries' perspective is the *degree of linkage* between the MNCs subsidiaries and the local economy. The more the MNC employs local workers and managers and the more it contracts with local firms for supplies and services, the greater the beneficial spillover effects will be. MNCs that set up subsidiaries in host countries primarily to service the local market, as is often the case with FDI in developed nations, are likely to develop contractual linkages with local firms. Those primarily interested in *outsourcing*— that is, producing in overseas locations for export, usually back to the home market—tend not to develop extensive linkages with local firms. Indeed, several countries in Asia and Central and Latin America have set up special "export processing zones" explicitly to attract MNC investment.

The U.S.-Mexican border, with its two thousand or so maquiladoras, is perhaps the best-known example of such a zone. This zone provides U.S. MNCs with comparatively cheap, nonunion labor, in sites close to the large U.S. market. Taxes and tariffs are virtually eliminated, and environmental and labor laws are weakly enforced. U.S. MNCs in the garment, electronic, and auto industries have flocked to the zone, importing parts from the United States for assembly in Mexico and then shipping the finished products back to the United States. Similarly, in the field of semiconductors, U.S. MNCs pioneered the strategy of manufacturing wafers in the United States, air-freighting them to Asia for assembly into circuits, and then air-freighting them back to the United States for sale. The problem for some host countries is that such MNCs sink few deep roots into the economy, transferring little research and development and developing few linkages with local firms. This is particularly true of the maquiladoras in Mexico, which purchased only 2 percent of their total inputs in Mexico.[28]

There are several other specific criticisms that can be leveled at MNCs, and most of these focus on their impact on developing countries. Critics charge that MNCs tend to exploit workers in developing countries by paying them low wages and by providing them with inadequate benefits and unsafe working conditions. Some MNCs have also been accused of transferring environmentally unsafe production processes to poorer countries to escape strict U.S. or European environmental regulations. All these issues are highly controversial, and making a fair assessment depends to a considerable extent on one's frame of reference. If the actions of MNCs (whether it be on working conditions or environmental matters) are compared with those they pursue in developed countries like the United States, then there is no doubt that MNCs can be seen to be taking advantage of developing nations. However, if one compares MNC behavior to that of local firms in developing countries, then they are certainly no worse (and often are better) economic citizens.[29]

Finally, we need to consider briefly the effects of MNCs on the political conditions in host countries. MNCs are primarily concerned with a stable business climate wherein they can make uninterrupted profits. In developing countries that may translate into pressure on governments to "liberalize" their economies by frustrating the development of a strong labor movement or ignoring safety and environmental violations. What is certainly the case is that MNCs are not in the business of promoting democracy or any other human rights. MNCs have operated quite happily in countries ruled by left-wing and right-wing authoritarian regimes. Perhaps the most flagrant example of economic interests over-riding political differences was the case of the Gulf Oil Company in the socialist African country of Angola. Here was a case of Communist Cuban troops pro-tecting the oil refineries of a U.S. MNC, Gulf Oil Company, from guerrilla fight-ers supported by the United States and South African governments.[30]

Sometimes, when their interests were threatened, some MNCs have pressed their home governments to intervene in the internal political affairs of other nations. Most blatant was United Fruit's successful campaign to undermine the elected government of Guatemala in the 1950s. Angered by the expropriation of idle land it owned and what it considered inadequate compensation, even though the dollar amount was based on its own tax records, the company lob-bied the Eisenhower administration to orchestrate a military coup. The coup ush-ered in several decades of repressive rule in Guatemala.[31] Perhaps somewhat less blatantly, U.S. MNCs like ITT were also implicated in the overthrow of the elect-ed Allende government in Chile in 1973.[32] While these are extreme cases, they do show how the political independence of developing countries may be severely constrained by the presence of large MNCs from powerful rich nations.

It is only fair to point out that MNCs are also subject to political pressures. Government pressure or well-organized public campaigns can effect change in MNC behavior. A recent example is the success of a grassroots campaign to force many U.S. MNCs to disinvest from their operations in South Africa. Similarly, a consumer boycott of Nestlé and the subsequent involvement of the World Health Organization forced Nestlé and other infant formula manufacturers to change their marketing practices.[33]

Negative Effects on Home Countries

The central question raised by outward FDI for a home country is what such an outflow of capital, technology, and other goods does for that nation's standard of living. The claim made by trade unions and their academic supporters is that out-ward foreign direct investment means a loss of jobs in the home country and the gradual "deindustrialization" of the nation's economy.[34] There is little disagree-ment that jobs do disappear when MNCs locate productive activities overseas. Job losses have been especially heavy for routine production workers as MNCs find it relatively easy to transfer such routine work as assembly operations, key-punching, data processing, and even simple coding of computer software to cheaper overseas locations. The critical questions are, first, whether such job loss-es are balanced by the creation of new jobs stimulated by FDI, and, second, what would have happened to the lost jobs if no foreign investment had been made. Would foreign competition have eliminated these jobs anyway, albeit more slow-ly? While it is difficult to give definitive answers to questions subject to a host of varying assumptions, critics of MNCs nevertheless point out that even if there is a net positive effect on employment from FDI, those who lose their jobs are rarely the same people who get the newly created jobs. As several commentators have pointed out, many of the lost jobs are in routine production activities, while those created are in professional, clerical, and service fields.[35] It is these routine pro-duction workers, already reeling from the effects of technological change, who represent the greatest source of opposition to outward FDI and to free trade pacts like the North American Free Trade Agreement.

Governments of both home and host countries are also interested in the tax revenues MNCs generate. An MNC operating in several countries typically should pay taxes to each government on the profits it earns doing business in that country. Problems arise, however, because a sizeable portion of the business MNCs conduct is between their own subsidiaries or affiliates. A fairly typical case might involve a U.S. electronics manufacturer sending various parts to its subsidiary in Mexico for assembly and shipment back to the company in the United States. Similarly, management from the U.S. parent may be sent to the Mexican subsidiary to help local managers iron out production problems. The prices charged for these exchanges of goods and services are known as *transfer prices* because they don't occur between independent firms in the market. They are determined by the staff at parent headquarters.

Given that many countries have different tax rates, one can see why MNCs might be tempted to manipulate transfer prices so as to minimize their total tax burden. If Mexico had a higher tax rate than the United States, then MNCs can overprice the goods and services sent to Mexico and underprice the finished goods shipped back to the United States. In this way, little or no profit will be "earned" in Mexico and tax payments to the Mexican government will be minimized. The manipulation of transfer prices can get even more complex when MNCs use countries with very low taxes (known as tax havens) as invoicing offices. In these cases, the invoices (but not the actual goods and services) for all transactions between subsidiaries are routed through the tax havens and profits are "earned" there, thereby avoiding taxes in both the host and the home countries.[36] A particularly striking example of such practices was recently reported in the press. News Corp., a giant entertainment MNC that owns many newspapers and television stations around the world with an annual income of $1.3 billion in 1997, paid just $103 million in worldwide taxes. Throughout the nineties its effective tax rate has been 5.7 percent while those of more U.S.-based firms like Walt Disney, Time Warner, and Viacom have averaged in the 27 to 32 percent range. The report notes that News Corp., which operates 789 business units in 52 countries, reduces its tax bill by "channeling profits through dozens of subsidiaries in low-tax or no-tax places such as the Cayman Islands and Bermuda."[37] No one is sure how large the transfer pricing problem is, since it is very difficult for outsiders, including tax authorities, to prove that the transfer prices are different from market prices. What we can say is that the opportunity for such manipulation is vast—intracompany trade by some estimates, now accounts for one-third to one-half of total world trade.[38]

THE IMPACT OF MNCs: SUMMING UP

As we have seen, both the proponents and the critics of MNCs make good arguments in support of their positions. Proponents of MNCs have the advantage of being able to point to the successes of developing nations like Singapore, Taiwan, Mexico, and Brazil that have welcomed FDI. The recent success story of Malaysia seems to reinforce their case. Malaysia has seen its per capita income and GNP grow by over 6 percent a year, in part due to the large role foreign direct investment played in developing its manufacturing sector (since 1967, 60 percent of manufacturing investment has been based on foreign capital).[39] China seems to be rapidly following suit with a similar strategy. These are powerful real-life examples that bolster the position of advocates of open borders and foreign direct investment. Critics of MNCs have a harder time making their case because there are so few examples of countries succeeding in their economic development using alternative strategies. Japan is one country that comes to mind, but there may be unique conditions attached to its development that make it hard for poor developing countries to grow while emulating Japan's closed door policies toward inward FDI.

Lacking viable alternative development strategies, most governments and workers around the world have to be players in the global economy. Their best strategy, therefore, is to bargain with MNCs over the terms of FDI, seeking as best they can to get the most favorable terms they can. As we will see, while some countries and workforces are not completely helpless in their bargaining with MNCs, on the whole the relations tend to be asymmetric with much of the advantage in the hands of MNCs. This view is not shared by all political economists. Stephen Krasner argues, from an economic nationalist perspective, that nations have substantial bargaining power because they can deny MNCs access to their territory.[40] However, we believe that unless nations possess large quantities of resources, like raw materials, capital, technology, and the like, the tactic of closing off your territory to FDI, in today's world, is a little like shooting yourself in the foot.

WOOING MULTINATIONAL CORPORATIONS—THE CASE OF MERCEDES-BENZ[a]

Multinational corporations are in great demand around the globe. Whenever a large, well-known company announces that it is planning to establish a manufacturing facility, several countries engage in a fierce bidding war to attract the investment to their shores. The following example gives a fairly typical picture of the lengths to which governments (national and regional) will go to capture MNC investment. It also indicates the advantage in bargaining power MNCs possess relative to governments.

Mercedes-Benz is a quintessentially German manufacturer, well known for its excellent engineering and high-quality cars and trucks. In 1993, it made the decision to internationalize its production. Several factors combined to prompt the decision: Labor costs in Germany were extremely high; the German currency, the deutschemark, was highly valued against the dollar, raising the price of its cars in its main export market, the United States; and Japanese MNCs began challenging Mercedes' domination of the luxury car market with the Lexus, Infinity, and Acura models. Mercedes' decision to build a new Jeeplike sports-utility vehicle in a foreign location was part of its strategy to overcome these difficulties.

A team of Mercedes executives began a worldwide selection process in January 1993 and quickly narrowed the search to North America. Not only is the United States the main market for sports-utility vehicles, but also the combined costs of labor, parts, and transportation are lowest there. Transportation would be a substantial portion of the costs, since Mercedes planned to import engines and other components from Germany and to export over half of the finished vehicles to non-U.S. markets.

The Mercedes team, with the help of a consultant, then examined 100 sites in 35 states of the United States. The team visited 6 final sites and quickly narrowed the choice to South and North Carolina and Alabama. Each is a state with right-to-work laws and low unionization rates. North Carolina's package of incentives added up to $108 million. South Carolina offered about $130 million worth of incentives, in a package similar to one that had recently enticed BMW to locate its first U.S. plant there. But it was Alabama, with its $253 million incentive package that snared the $300 million plant.

Alabama, a state with a reputation as a backward place holding few attractions for MNCs, went all out to win the investment. The incentive package included $92 million to purchase and develop the site; $77 million for improvements to highways, utilities, and other infrastructure; tax abatement on machinery and equipment; and $60 million on education and training. The University of Alabama even agreed to run a special "Saturday School" to help the children of German Mercedes managers keep up with the higher standards in science and math back home in Germany. All this would be paid for by the taxpayers of Alabama. The governor of North Carolina was particularly upset by a tax break the Alabama legislature passed (labeled by some the "Benz Bill"), which allowed Mercedes to withhold 5 percent of employees' wages to pay off Mercedes debts.

The wooing of Mercedes went beyond financial incentives. It included an offer to name a section of an interstate highway "the Mercedes-Benz autobahn," airplane and helicopter tours, visits by the governor of Alabama and other state officials to Mercedes headquarters in Germany, a billboard in German near the site welcoming Mercedes, and the governor driving a Mercedes as the official state car. It is not surprising to read that a Mercedes executive claimed it was "Alabama's zeal" that was the deciding factor.

In return, 1,500 workers would get good-paying jobs, and several more thousand jobs would be created in supplier firms, restaurants, and the like.

ª This case study is based on the following sources: "Why Mercedes is Alabama Bound," *Business Week*, 11 October 1993; "The Invaders Are Welcome," *Economist*, 8 January 1994; "Alabama Steers Mercedes South," *ENR*, 11 October 1993.

BARGAINING RELATIONS BETWEEN MNCs AND GOVERNMENTS AND WORKERS

The MNCs' bargaining advantage is based on two factors. One is their control of scarce and crucial economic resources. The second flows from their mobility, allowing them to transfer resources around the globe. This global mobility means that MNCs often have the luxury of being able to choose where they will locate their resources and activities from a wide range of alternatives. Workers and governments, rooted as they are to certain locations, are thrown into competition with each other to attract MNCs. The business press is full of examples of MNCs being able to extract special benefits from governments, or concessions from workforces, because of their ability to play them off one against the other. Workers are particularly vulnerable to the actual or potential ability of MNCs to move around the globe. Low-skilled workers engaged in low-technology production have very little bargaining power because of the availability of a vast global pool of such workers. They are easily substituted. In the battle for FDI in these economic sectors, we can expect fairly frequent locational moves as MNCs move down the ladder of countries seeking lower-cost labor forces. Even some high-skill workforces in developed countries are vulnerable to locational shifts as more countries develop large pools of educated and well-trained workforces (e.g.,

India, South Korea, Singapore). In the future, pressure on workers' wages and working conditions from lower-cost locations can be expected to intensify as more productive activities become international. In these circumstances, workers' bargaining power will continue to erode, local and national unions will lose more power, and more workers from around the globe will be forced to compete with each other.

A fairly typical example of such MNC-inspired worker competition involved Hoover, a European appliance maker owned by the U.S. MNC Maytag. In 1992, Hoover decided to shut down its plant in Dijon, France, and to transfer production to a plant in Scotland. The transfer meant the loss of 600 jobs in France and the gain of 400 jobs in Scotland. To win the jobs, the Scottish workforce agreed to accept new working practices and limits on strike action. These concessions, coupled with the lower labor costs in Scotland, tipped the balance in favor of the Glasgow plant. The French government protested the decision and accused the British of "social dumping"—that is, of eroding workers' rights so as to attract foreign investment.[41]

Governments are also compelled to compete in "bidding wars" to attract MNCs. While it is clear that the primary factors determining where MNCs invest have to do with location-specific advantages of the country or the overall strategic plan of the MNC, it is also true that once an MNC has narrowed its choice of sites to two or three locations, then incentives do affect the final decision.[42] (See the case study box for an example of the "bidding war" between state governments in the United States to attract a Mercedes-Benz plant.)

Only international cooperation between national workforces and governments can reduce the bargaining advantages of MNCs. For example, in Europe, union representatives from several different subsidiaries of MNCs like Ford, GM, and Phillips have established company councils to facilitate the sharing of information and to coordinate bargaining with the parent company. Workers in Europe have also pushed hard for the adoption of a "social charter" by the European Union that would harmonize labor laws across the member states. Similarly, some small developing countries have sought to harmonize the rules and conditions governing FDI in their countries so as to strengthen their bargaining position. The Andean Pact, comprising Columbia, Chile, Peru, and Venezuela established a common set of regulations to govern FDI in the 1970s so as to minimize competitive bidding among themselves. Among the regulations were limits on profit repatriation and controls on technology transfers and increased requirements for local participation in the ownership of the subsidiary.[43]

These efforts rarely turn out to be very successful at redressing the balance of bargaining power. Take the attempt at international union cooperation. MNCs can often break union bonds of solidarity by making subsidiary workforces compete for investment resources. With large-scale unemployment in many European countries, it becomes hard for each workforce not to try and save its own skin when the issue boils down to "their jobs or ours," especially when "they" are of a different nationality.[44]

Still, the picture is not completely gloomy. Developed countries, with their large domestic markets, modern and well-developed infrastructures (roads, ports, and the like), large pools of educated workers, and stable political climates are attractive to MNCs and thus have considerable bargaining power. Ironically, these governments rarely seek to impose restrictions on the activities of MNCs. As both homes and hosts of MNCs, such governments are liable to retaliate against their home-based MNCs should they act too harshly against other countries' MNCs.

Some developing countries are also gaining leverage in their bargaining relations with MNCs. Singapore, for example, because of its superb transportation and communication infrastructure and its excellent science and technology research centers, is beginning to attract regional headquarters of MNCs, thereby winning for itself considerably more of the high-income-producing functions carried out by MNCs. Similarly, India, with its abundant supply of relatively inexpensive English-speaking engineers and scientists has attracted nearly every major computer and software producer in the United States to set up operations there. The companies include Texas Instruments, Motorola, Hewlett-Packard, Apple Computer, Sun Microsystems, Intel, Dell, and IBM.[45] Developing countries with such locational advantages will find several MNCs competing to locate there and can negotiate more favorable terms for inward foreign direct investment. (See the case study of China and Boeing for an example of how countries can extract favorable terms from MNCs.) It should be noted, of course, that other than the advantage of possessing scarce natural resources and cheap labor (which is really no advantage, since such labor is so widely available), most of the critical competitive advantages countries possess are man-made. They are, in fact, the result of the development efforts of the host country itself. While MNCs can assist the process of development, it is domestic factors that overwhelmingly determine the quality of the infrastructure, the level of education and training of the population, and the political situation.

WHEN COUNTRIES HAVE THE UPPER HAND: BOEING AND CHINA

While it is generally true that MNCs often hold the upper hand in bargaining with countries and states, there are exceptions. One such case is China, the country with the largest population and the fastest growing economy in the world. MNCs have been falling over themselves in the rush to get in on the action, and China now ranks as only second to the United States as a host to inward FDI flows.

Boeing, the largest manufacturer of airplanes in the world and America's leading exporter, is a huge multinational with considerable political and economic clout. Yet in its dealings with China, the Chinese government seems to have most of the leverage. The reasons are twofold. First, air travel in China is projected to grow at double the rate of growth in the United States and Europe,[a] with China poised to spend the massive sum of $124 billion on 1,900 planes over the next twenty years.[b] As a Boeing spokeswoman put it, "China is our ticket to the future. We have to get a majority of the Chinese market, our largest international market, to maintain our leadership in aerospace."[c] Second, there is a hungry, younger rival, eager and able to outbid and undercut Boeing out of its historic dominance in the Chinese market. Airbus, a consortium of four European airplane producers, in fact sent a scare into Boeing in the mid-nineties by winning a Chinese order for 60 planes as against only 14 for Boeing.[d] Very simply put, because China is such an attractive market, it can play these two MNCs off against each other.

China's bargaining position vis-à-vis Boeing has been quite clear: We'll buy your planes if you give us a share of your production, jobs and technical know-how. If you don't, we'll buy planes from Airbus. This negotiating position has produced a variety of tangible benefits for China. These include the production of various parts and sub-assemblies for Boeing planes; the recent transfer of the prodution of complete tails for the 737 from Wichita, Kansas to China;[e] the training of Chinese engineers and pilots by Boeing; the establishment of a major spare parts distribution center in Beijing; and Boeing investing in an aircraft maintenance joint venture.[f] Airbus, not to be outdone, also began to buy components from China and is considering a joint venture with a Chinese firm to build an entire airframe there.[g] These negotiated benefits are called *offsets* and are the cause of much controversy. Union leaders in the United States, in particular, worry that such deals with China not only mean lost jobs in the United States but may also create an Asian rival to Boeing that will eventually eat away its market share.[h] Boeing executives respond that agreeing to offsets that may reduce employment levels in the United States somewhat is better than "100 percent of nothing," as would be the case if all the orders went to Airbus.[i] Moreover, by developing a partnership relationship with China now, Boeing hopes that it can be involved in any Asian producer that might emerge.

This case also shows how China has manipulated its trading relationships with Boeing and other U.S. MNCs for political purposes. Despite the best efforts of left- and right-wing critics of China to impose economic sanctions against it for violations of human rights in its treatment of dissidents in the prodemocracy movement and in Tibet, China maintains its "most favored nation" trade status. Even the support of Microsoft for sanctions against China could not sufficiently counteract the powerful message China sent in 1996 when a large order for planes went to Airbus rather than Boeing.[j] As the threat of sanctions evaporated and the Chinese president was invited to Washington, China rewarded the United States and Boeing with a large order for airplanes. While such bargaining power is impressive, we should remember that there are few countries in the world with China's clout.

---

[a] Boeing, *1998 Current Market Outlook.*
[b] John Davies, "Bridging the Gap," *Journal of Commerce,* 27 October 1997, p. 67.
[c] Ibid.
[d] Ibid.
[e] William Greider, *One World Ready or Not: The Manic Logic of Global Capitalism* (New York: Simon & Schuster, 1997), p. 124.
[f] Robert Ropelewski, "Boeing Keeps Sharp Focus on China," *Interavia Business and Technology* (November 1995), p. 29.
[g] Stanley Holmes, "Boeing's Investment in China Increasing as Production Rises," *Seattle Times,* 17 October 1997, p. E1.
[h] Randy Barber and Robert E. Scott, *Jobs on the Wing: Trading Away the Future of the U.S. Aerospace Industry* (Washington, DC: Economic Policy Institute, 1995).
[i] Greider, *One World Ready or Not,* p. 131.
[j] Michael Veseth, *Selling Globalization: The Myth of the Global Economy* (Boulder, CO: Lynne Rienner, 1998), p. 60

CONCLUSION

We now come to the final and most speculative question about MNCs: What will be their impact on the IPE of tomorrow? Looking into the future is always a hazardous business. And in the case of MNCs and the international political economy, the prognostications are especially difficult since political and economic forces pull in opposite directions.

If we follow a strictly *economic logic,* we can foresee that international economic activity will continue to grow at a rapid pace. Technological advances in transportation and telecommunications will shrink the world, and the mobility of

MNCs and the fierce competitive battles among them will prompt them to spread their reach to all corners of the globe. This intensified economic competition will also entice many MNCs to seek shelter and respite from the rigors of these fierce economic battles by forming alliances and partnerships across borders. This is already happening in several industries. In telecommunications, Sprint, a U.S. company, has formed an alliance with the national providers in France (France Telecom) and Germany (Deutsche Telecom) so they can deliver a common set of telephone sevices.[46] In the airline industry, carriers from around the world are teaming up in cross-border partnerships to provide customers with truly international service. British Airways, for example, owns 22 percent of USAir and 25 percent of Australia's Quantas Airways. KLM Royal Dutch Airlines owns 20 percent of Northwest, and Delta has cross-shareholdings with Swissair and Singapore Airlines.[47] In electronics, IBM (U.S.), Siemens (Germany), and Toshiba (Japan) have joined together to develop a new computer chip. Not only are they collaborating in the research and development of the chip, but they also plan to produce the chip jointly.[48]

These trends have prompted Robert Reich to see a future where corporations do indeed lose their national identities, becoming global organizations that integrate the world according to their purposes. The big winners in this newly integrated world will not be particular nations and their citizens but highly skilled individuals ("symbolic analysts," Reich calls them) who can operate effectively in the high-tech world of the future. These individuals will form an international elite separated by income and lifestyle from their fellow citizens in each of their countries of origin. This scenario, if taken to its logical extreme, suggests a highly stratified world, with an international class of symbolic analysts and capitalists having significant power in the world and a weakening in the power and authority of national governments to regulate their economies.[49]

Of course, neither Reich nor any other thoughtful political economist goes so far as to suggest that the power of national governments will erode to the point that nation-states become irrelevant. While many agree that the task of governing and regulating national economies will be made more difficult by the presence of MNCs, few believe national governments will surrender their large numbers of prerogatives easily. As Raymond Vernon puts it: "With jobs, taxes, payment balances, and technological achievement seemingly at stake, governments are bound to act in an effort to defend national interests and respond to national pressures."[50]

In other words, there is also a countervailing and equally powerful *political logic* at work. Individuals remain deeply wedded to their national identities, and it is nation-states, not corporations, that enforce laws, levy taxes, and organize armies. Indeed, one scholar argues that economic integration and the globalizing trends it produces are often the *result* of the actions of nation-states intent on promoting the internationalization strategies of their MNCs. In this way, nation-states can increase their control over the external environment.[51] It is also possible that as people's economic lives become increasingly governed by large, distant international forces, ordinary citizens might start demanding greater political influence over their national governments. It is for these reasons that the historian Paul Kennedy concludes: "Even if the autonomy and functions of the state have been eroded by transnational trends, no adequate substitute has emerged to replace it as the key unit in responding to global change."[52] We are left, therefore, contemplating a future marked by continuing tension between political and economic forces.

DISCUSSION QUESTIONS

1. "Most multinational corporations are headquartered in the United States and take advantage of cheap labor in less developed countries to manufacture goods that are then sold in the United States." What is right and what is wrong with this statement as a general description of MNCs? Explain.
2. What is meant by "firm-specific competitive advantage"? How and why is this factor important in our understanding of the logic of foreign direct investment of MNCs? Explain.
3. What impacts do MNCs have on their home countries? On their host countries? Compare and contrast the different points of view on this question. What is your own opinion?
4. How does the growing importance of global markets and MNCs alter the role of the state in home and host countries? Explain.

INTERNET LINKS

Dictionary of International Trade and Business:
    http://pacific.commerce.ubc.ca/ditb/
Foreign Policy Index of MNCs:
    http://www.foreignpolicy.com/Resources/multinats.htm
"Nike: Tracks Across the Globe":
    http://www.oregonlive.com/series/nike11091.html

SUGGESTED READINGS

Richard J. Barnet and Ronald E. Müller. *Global Reach: The Power of the Multinational Corporations.* New York: Touchstone, 1974.
R. E. Caves. *Multinational Enterprise and Economic Analysis.* Cambridge: Cambridge University Press, 1982.
Peter Dicken. *Global Shift: The Internationalization of Economic Activity.* London: Paul Chapman Publishing, 1992.
John H. Dunning. *Explaining International Production.* London: Unwin Hyman, 1988.
Kenneth A. Froot, ed. *Foreign Direct Investment.* Chicago: University of Chicago Press, 1993.
Stephen H. Hymer. *The International Operations of National Firms: A Study of Direct Foreign Investment.* Cambridge, MA: MIT Press, 1976.
Robert B. Reich. *The Work of Nations: Preparing Ourselves for 21st Century Capitalism.* New York: Vintage Books, 1992.
United Nations Conference on Trade and Development (UNCTAD), *World Investment Reports,* various years. New York: United Nations.
Raymond Vernon. *Sovereignty at Bay: The Multinational Spread of U.S. Enterprises.* New York: Basic Books, 1971.

NOTES

1. Stephen Hymer, "The Internationalization of Capital," *Journal of Economic Issues* 6 (March 1972), p. 104.
2. Cited in Richard J. Barnet and Ronald Müller, *Global Reach: The Power of the Multinational Corporations* (New York: Touchstone, 1974), p. 16.
3. One of the most prominent critical works was Barnet and Müller's *Global Reach*.
4. "Everybody's Favorite Monsters: A Survey of Multinationals," *Economist*, 27 March 1993, p. 9.
5. Cited in Edward M. Graham and Paul R. Krugman, "The Surge in Foreign Direct Investment in the 1980s," in Kenneth A. Froot, ed., *Foreign Direct Investment* (Chicago: University of Chicago Press, 1993), p. 13.
6. United Nations Conference on Trade and Development (UNCTAD) Programme on Transnational Corporations, *World Investment Report 1993: Transnational Corporations and Integrated International Production* (New York: United Nations, 1993), p. 22 and *World Investment Report 1997: Transnational Corporations, Market Structure and Competition Policy* (New York: United Nations, 1997). These United Nations reports are excellent sources of data on MNCs.
7. UNCTAD, World Investment Report 1997, p. 11.
8. Cited in Graham and Krugman, *Foreign Direct Investment*, p. 14.
9. Robert E. Lipsey, "Foreign Direct Investment in the United States: Changes Over Three Decades," in Froot, *Foreign Direct Investment*, p. 115.
10. Peter Dicken, *Global Shift: The Internationalization of Economic Activity*, 2d ed. (London: Paul Chapman Publishing, 1992), pp. 52–53.
11. UNCTAD, World Investment Report 1997, p. 5.
12. See Jean-Jacques Servan Schreiber, *The American Challenge* (London: Hamish Hamilton, 1968) for a discussion of the perceived U.S. threat to Europe.
13. Robert B. Reich, *The Work of Nations: Preparing Ourselves for 21st Century Capitalism* (New York: Vintage, 1991), p. 153.
14. Cited in Froot, *Foreign Direct Investment*, p. 108.
15. Robert Lawrence, "Japan's Low Levels of Inward Investment," in Froot, *Foreign Direct Investment*, p. 86.
16. It should be noted that well over 50 percent of FDI involves acquisitions of existing corporations or assets. Because members of *keiretsus* own a sizable portion of each other's shares, they can collectively block any takeover attempt by a foreign competitor. For a fuller discussion of FDI in Japan, see Mark Mason, *American Multinationals and Japan: The Political Economy of Capital Controls, 1899–1980* (Cambridge, MA: Harvard University Press, 1992).
17. UNCTAD, *World Investment Report 1993*.
18. Froot, *Foreign Direct Investment*, p. 192.
19. For a fuller discussion of the ideas discussed in this section, see Stephen H. Hymer, *The International Operations of National Firms: A Study of Direct Foreign Investment* (Cambridge, MA: MIT Press, 1976); and John H. Dunning, *Explaining International Production* (London: Unwin Hyman, 1981).
20. Raymond Vernon, "International Investment and International Trade in the Product Cycle," *Quarterly Journal of Economics*, 80 (1966), pp. 190–207.
21. The original formulation of this idea was put forward in F. T. Knickerbocker, *Oligopolistic Reaction and Multinational Enterprises* (Boston: Harvard Business School, 1973).
22. "The Die is Cast by Growth and Costs," *Financial Times*, 31 May 1994, p. 14.
23. One of the most sophisticated and balanced arguments in support of MNCs is made by Raymond Vernon, *Storm over the Multinationals: The Real Issues* (Cambridge, MA: Harvard University Press, 1977).
24. See Dicken, *Global Shift*, p. 388. Acquisitions are the more common form of FDI in developed countries, partly because such countries have a larger pool of companies available for purchase.
25. Reich, *The Work of Nations*, p. 146.

26. Andre Gunder Frank, for example, has argued that Brazil grew very fast during World War II because it was isolated economically from Europe. See his *Capitalism and Underdevelopment in Latin America: Historical Studies of Chile and Brazil* (New York: Monthly Review Press, 1969).

27. Recent studies show that none of the largest U.S. firms with direct investments in Latin America carry out any basic research in these countries. Robert Grosse, "Competitive Advantages and Multinational Enterprises in Latin America," *Journal of Business Research* 25 (1992), pp. 27–42.

28. Leslie Sklair, *Assembling for Development: The Maquila Industry in Mexico and the United States* (San Diego, CA: Center for U.S.-Mexican Studies, University of California, 1993), p. 244.

29. Graham and Krugman conclude, "Studies basically find that foreign-owned firms behave very similarly to domestically owned firms in the same industry. They pay similar wages, engage in similar amounts of R & D, and so on," in Froot, *Foreign Direct Investment*, p. 32. See also Dickens, *Global Shift*, for a review of the evidence.

30. The case is cited in Robert Gilpin, *The Political Economy of International Relations* (Princeton, NJ: Princeton University Press, 1987), p. 250.

31. Stephen Kinzer, *Bitter Fruit: The Untold Story of the Bitter Coup in Guatemala* (New York: Doubleday, 1982).

32. James Petras and Morris Morley, *The United States and Chile: Imperialism and the Overthrow of the Allende Government* (New York: Monthly Review Press, 1975).

33. "The Formula Crisis Cools," *Fortune*, 27 December 1982, p. 106.

34. For the best argument in support of this thesis, see Barry Bluestone and Bennett Harrison, *The Deindustrialization of America: Plant Closings, Community Abandonment, and the Dismantling of Basic Industry* (New York: Basic Books, 1982).

35. See, for example, Reich, *The Work of Nations*, chap. 17, and Barnet and Müller, *Global Reach*, p. 302.

36. For an example, see Leon Grunberg, *Failed Multinational Ventures: The Political Economy of International Divestments* (Lexington, MA: D.C. Heath, 1981), chap. 4.

37. Paul Farhi, "Media Giant a Midget Taxpayer," *Washington Post*, reprinted in *The News Tribune*, 7 December 1997, p. A4.

38. "Everybody's Favorite Monsters," *Economist*.

39. "Malaysia Urged to Boost GATT Role," *Financial Times*, 21 July 1993, p. 3.

40. Stephen D. Krasner, "Multinational Corporations," in Jeffrey A. Frieden and David A. Lake, eds., *International Political Economy: Perspectives on Global Power and Wealth*, 2d ed. (New York: St. Martin's Press, 1991).

41. "Labour Pains," *Economist*, 6 February 1993, p. 71.

42. UNCTAD, *World Investment Report 1993*, p. 227.

43. Krasner, in *International Political Economy*, pp. 174–175.

44. See Grunberg, *Failed Multinational Ventures*, for examples.

45. UNCTAD, *World Investment Report 1993*, pp. 139 and 176.

46. UNCTAD, *World Investment Report 1997*, p. 165.

47. "Cross-Border Linkups Bring Airlines Range But Uncertain Benefits," *Wall Street Journal*, 7 June 1994, p. 1.

48. UNCTAD, *World Investment Report 1993*, p. 143.

49. Susan Strange has proposed that states have already lost considerable power and authority to markets and MNCs. See *The Retreat of the State: The Diffusion of Power in the World Economy* (Cambridge: Cambridge University Press, 1996).

50. Vernon, in *Foreign Direct Investment*, p. 73.

51. Linda Weiss, *The Myth of the Powerless State: Governing the Economy in a Global Era* (Cambridge: Polity Press, 1998).

52. Paul Kennedy, *Preparing for the Twenty-first Century* (New York: Random House, 1993), p. 134.

17

The IPE of OPEC and Oil

OVERVIEW[1]

Our survey of the history of the IPE of OPEC and oil reveals four tensions that are this chapter's themes. The first is that the world is increasingly *interdependent*. Events in one part of the globe affect people everywhere. It is no longer possible to ignore "outside" forces or actors in making political or economic choices. A second and related theme is that politics and economics have become so tightly *intertwined* in many areas that it is almost useless to try to distinguish between them. The economics of oil influence the politics of oil, and vice versa.

The third theme is that political economy is increasingly not just international but *global* in scope, involving all nations at once, not just relations between them. To an important extent, the two OPEC oil crises have been responsible for the acceleration of this trend along with a proliferation of actors involved in the IPE of oil. Multinational corporations and international organizations, not just large nation-states, are important actors in this global arena. Furthermore, and the final theme of this chapter, is that neither states nor markets *alone* can determine outcomes in this interdependent, intertwined global world. The case of oil demonstrates that IPE is a delicate balancing act, and that power often lies with those who have the potential to disturb that equilibrium. Thus a number of actors, including small oil producing nations, can greatly influence the IPE today.

Oil is a magnet for conflict.[2]

The year 1973 was a turning point for the international political economy. By 1973, students of politics and economics—and viewers of TV news—*should* already have realized that the world had changed from the early days of post-war U.S. hegemony. The Vietnam War's prolonged conclusion showed the weakened resolve of the United States to fight communism everywhere and anywhere. The collapse of the Bretton Woods monetary system, built on U.S. financial hegemony, was complete when President Richard Nixon took the United States off the gold standard in 1971. U.S. dominance in business was openly challenged by the flood of cheap but sturdy Volkswagen, Toyota, and Datsun cars from abroad. The balance of wealth and power was shifting.

Many people, however, did not realize that fundamental change was under way. The shift in the global patterns of IPE were invisible to them as they concentrated on the details of everyday life, which seemed hardly changed at all. Suddenly, however, their lives were disrupted at every level of personal, business, national, and global relations.

War in the Middle East in 1973 suddenly brought home consequences that until this day have not yet been fully resolved. United States support of Israel in the Yom Kippur War with Egypt caused the Arab members of the *Organization of Petroleum Exporting Countries (OPEC)* to ban exports of petroleum to the United States and the other allies of Israel. In short order, gasoline prices skyrocketed and gasoline shortages appeared; plans to ration gasoline were made. Because energy is so vital to every aspect of an industrial society, every element of daily life was altered.

By the time the dust settled a year later, the world had truly changed. The world oil market was dominated by the OPEC cartel. Oil prices continued to rise and the changing pattern of world payments caused sudden and dramatic shifts in the global distribution of wealth. Individuals, industries, and nations that were once rich were suddenly heavily burdened by oil payments. Trade, finance, and security structures were all changed.

The OPEC oil embargo of 1973–1974 was an earthquake that rocked the international political economy—a short, sharp shock that shook institutional structures and changed the landscape for years to come. Like an earthquake, however, the *causes* of the OPEC oil shock had built up over many years. The sudden and dramatic shocks released pent-up pressures but did not change them. The IPE of OPEC and oil traces a fault line; tensions build up over time, to be suddenly released. We must understand these continuing tensions as much as the quakes themselves.

As this chapter discusses the history of the IPE of OPEC and oil, four thematic tensions will be examined. The first is the tension that arises due to *interdependence*. The overlapping structures of IPE mean that states and markets are dependent on each other in ways that create tensions or pressures, giving perhaps one of the best illustrations of this condition. The second tension is created by the increasingly *intertwined nature of economics and politics* today. The tensions between states and markets that were highlighted in the first chapter of this book are magnified here as it becomes increasingly impossible to tell where politics leaves off and economic matters begin.

The third tension is created by the increasingly *global* nature of IPE structures. As problems and events become more global in scope, the role of the nation-state as the center of international relations is jeopardized. International organizations, including multinational corporations, seem to take on increasing importance. Finally, the IPE of energy and oil demonstrates that *neither states nor markets alone* can determine outcomes in this interdependent, intertwined world. IPE is a delicate balancing act, and power often lies with those that have the potential to disturb that equilibrium. Thus, even relatively small actors, such as small nations or even terrorist groups, can have great influence in IPE today. This creates added tensions of risk and uncertainty. The shock wave of the two oil crises of the 1970s could occur again, profoundly disturbing the IPE but also shifting wealth and power.

If oil generates conflict, as this chapter's epigraph suggests, it is because oil is centered in the nexus of these four tensions and is subject to the conflicting interests and motivations that result. To understand the IPE of OPEC and oil now and for the future we must appreciate the complex dynamics that characterize oil and its relationship to other areas of IPE.

OPEC AND THE POLITICS AND ECONOMICS OF OIL

The Organization of Petroleum Exporting Countries is an example of a *cartel*, or a producers' organization.[3] Cartels typically attempt to organize production in ways that increase commodity prices and their profits. Each cartel member agrees to an output quota that is less than the amount that would be produced under competitive market conditions. Simply put, the members of a cartel use quotas to create a collective monopoly in a given market, reducing total output so as to raise the market price. Profit are what cartels are all about.

OPEC is unlike other cartels, however, in that it is composed of sovereign nation-states, not ordinary business firms. OPEC's actions are therefore conditioned by not only by greed and the desire for wealth, but also the need for national security and political power. Politics (as well as profit, and sometimes instead of it) is thus the essence of OPEC. It is a serious error to think of OPEC in only economic terms or in only political terms. That is why the advent of OPEC is often associated with the modern renewal of the study of IPE.

The OPEC cartel was formed in 1960 when the major oil-exporting nations sought to gain more control over and profit from the oil located under their member nations. Up until then, the production, processing, and marketing of oil were dominated by seven major multinational oil corporations—the seven sisters—five U.S., one British, and one Anglo-Dutch company. The major oil companies blocked other companies from getting into the market and effectively controlled the price, processing, and marketing of oil. Host nations felt exploited and dominated by the oil companies and they sought in OPEC an organization that could advance their common interests.

OPEC's power derived from the developed world's economic reliance on petroleum imports. Before World War II, dependence on oil was something the United States and other industrialized nations had not experienced because the United States had been the world's largest oil producer and exporter. As industrialization gained a full head of steam after World War II, especially in the developed countries, their dependence on foreign oil increased as the demand for petroleum again accelerated. In the United States, Western Europe, and Japan, annual total oil consumption more than doubled: In Western Europe, consumption rose 270 percent; in Japan the figure was 500 percent. By 1973 generally rising demand plus increasing reliance on oil as a primary source of world energy[4] (coupled with specifically increasing demand for Middle East oil as the biggest, cheapest surplus pool of petroleum available) combined to make *countries* as vulnerable as *companies* to the growing assertiveness of Middle East statesmen.

Corporate control over oil gradually weakened in the face of a variety of political and economic conditions. The tone for a new relationship between host governments, the oil companies, and the industrialized nations was established in 1969, when Libya pressured Occidental Petroleum into new concessions. As it did, host countries were able to gradually wrangle bigger concessions from the oil companies. Libya demonstrated that revenue could be raised by increasing oil prices. OPEC as a whole, then, soon became more aggressive on questions of production and price levels and taxes.

THE OIL CRISES OF THE 1970s

The first oil shock occurred in late 1973, when an Arab-Israeli war was accompanied by a successful oil embargo imposed by the Arab states within OPEC against countries, including especially the United States, supporting Israel in the Yom Kippur War. Witnessing the potential of "the oil weapon," OPEC as a whole then quickly increased the price of a barrel of oil in the international marketplace from $2.90 per barrel to $11.65—a jump of over 400 percent.

The United States tried to form an oil-consumers "countercartel" at a conference held in Washington in early 1974, but the effort only demonstrated the inability of America, Japan, and Western Europe to respond collectively. Most of the industrialized states counted on bilateral agreements with OPEC producers to solve their oil import problems. The oil companies went along with the price hikes because they could easily pass higher gas prices on to consumers.

At the level of the international system, OPEC "unilaterally" controlled prices throughout the mid-1970s. Its members did so by collaboratively determining both the price of oil and the production reductions necessary to limit supply and maintain the agreed-upon price. Saudi Arabia was the key to this process. It has long had the highest level of proved crude oil reserves of any state in the world.[5] OPEC's ability after 1973 to fix prices was due, more than any other single factor, to Saudi Arabia's willingness to restrict its own national production.

Saudi Arabia, the largest oil producer and exporter, and with its vast financial reserves, influenced OPEC's policies the most. Basically pro-Western, the

Saudis were a steady, moderating voice, distinct from that of OPEC's more hawk-ish members. The Saudis made up for production cuts during times of recession and increased production enough to keep prices stable. Aside from their moder-ate political positions, Saudi Arabia and many of the richer OPEC members wanted to disrupt the international economy to some extent but not to the point of ruining their investment opportunities in the West. Other OPEC members, including Iran and Iraq, favored production cuts to drive up oil prices above the rate of inflation in the West.

Beyond Saudi moderation, conservation efforts and economic recession in the West led to a slackening of demand in world oil markets in the wake of the 1973 crisis. Newly discovered supplies of petroleum in the North Sea, Alaska, and Mexico were also finally coming on-line. The United States created a Strate-gic Petroleum Reserve that would release oil to the market in the case of anoth-er crisis. Ironically, then, the mid-1970s was a period of some stability in the international oil system.

A second global oil shock occurred at the end of the decade, when Iranian Jolanic fundamentalists finally succeeded in toppling the shah from his throne in Tehran. The ensuing panic in world oil markets pushed the price of a 42-gal-lon barrel of crude from $13 to $34 (by the early 1980s). In less than a decade, then, the oil-burning economies of the world saw their import bills for petroleum leap by almost 1,200 percent.[6] In real terms, the price of oil in 1981 was more than twice its price as recently as 1998. It is perhaps impossible to overstate the mag-nitude of the shock that rising oil prices dealt to the economies of both rich indus-trial nations and struggling less developed countries.

How was it that a full five years after the Arab embargo of 1973, one (non-Arab) country, accounting for less than 20 percent of all OPEC exports, could once again throw international economics—and politics—into such disarray? The answer in the short term has to do with the psychology of panic and the way in which the embargo of late 1978 revived unpleasant memories of 1973. A defining characteristic of any panic is a "look out for number one," "devil take the hind-most" inability to consider common benefits in the face of imminent threat to oneself. Panic, or at least the inability to cooperate in the short term, *had* charac-terized "the Western response" to the crisis of 1973.

Now a similar inability began to infect OPEC in general and Persian Gulf producers in particular. Oil producers sell their product to the world by way of two different (but related) markets. A long-term contract market accounted for most sales in the late 1970s: The contract, between oil company and producer, reflected the price set by OPEC. Oil not sold on this market is traded on spot mar-kets, and such markets reacted swiftly to the withdrawal of Iranian oil in late 1978.

As spot market prices shot up, the gap between these prices and long-term market prices widened. The primary beneficiary of such a gap was clear—the oil companies, whose long-term contracts gave them a supply of oil at a relatively cheap, stable price, which they could then sell at prices reflecting the spot market frenzy. OPEC states, remembering long years of perceived exploitation at the hands of the oil MNCs, now began to place their own surcharges on top of prices previously determined by OPEC. And many began to break long-term contracts in order to sell their oil on the more lucrative spot market. The Saudis tried to hold the line, but the momentum was inexorable.

In 1980, the Saudis and other moderate states regained control over the situation. But the outbreak of the Iran-Iraq war again destabilized oil markets. World production decreased by roughly 10 percent, driving up the spot market price of oil to $41 a barrel. The West responded by cutting consumption and trying to improve political relations with the oil producers.

REACTIONS TO THE OPEC OIL CRISES

The two OPEC oil crises changed and shaped the views of officials, experts, and the public about national security in several ways. The economics of oil blended with efforts to use it as a political weapon to change the distribution of wealth and power in the international political economy. The bipolar East-West conflict gave way in many respects to a multipolar struggle, one component of which was development problems between the rich and poor nations. Sandwiched in between these nations were the Newly Industrialized Countries (NICs) that had successfully developed to some extent, but many of whom, like the West, were dependent on external sources of energy.

The oil crises also made it difficult to undo political and economic interdependence in the international political economy. States could no longer insulate or isolate themselves as easily from the international political economy in ways they could earlier. Trade has always made states interdependent with one another to some extent. Now most states needed energy and other resources if industrial development and economic growth were to continue. LDCs had been important to the United States as allies in its battle to contain international communism. LDCs were now important for their markets and also for their resources. A nation's military power was now dependent on access to natural resources and raw materials to feed the economy's industrial base. The oil-producing nations were also affected by interdependence, as demonstrated by their efforts to charge more for oil but not at the expense of bankrupting the West.

Many states found themselves caught between a rock and a hard place—between mercantilist and liberal forces. The economic health of a society became a matter of national security concern in a domestic and international environment where resources—natural or man-made—were increasingly viewed as scarce or becoming finite and were in any case difficult securely to obtain.

Another result of the changing IPE of OPEC and oil in the 1970s was a dramatic shift in the patterns of world finance (see chapter 8 for a broader discussion of this). During most of the Bretton Woods period international finance was more state-to-state than market-to-market. Suddenly in 1973–74, however, a massive flow of funds was redirected first to the Middle East oil exporters, then to world financial markets, and then, ultimately, to the rich and poor oil importing countries. This process was called "petrodollar recycling" and it was based on the need of oil-rich countries to lend money to their oil-poor customers.

This was the first step in the creation of the global financial markets of today. The oil crises of the 1970s, by creating a need for global financial markets, added a new level of complex interdependence to the rapidly changing world of IPE.

OIL AND OPEC IN THE 1980s

The start of the Iran-Iraq War in August 1980 removed a little less than 10 percent of world oil exports from international markets, and OPEC and spot market prices soon reflected the diminished supply. But as the war dragged on and on, the long-term impact of changes in market conditions from 1973 to 1979 became dramatically apparent. When the war moved into the Gulf itself in the mid-1980s, and tankers and production and shipping platforms became the objects of each side's attacks, no further run-up in oil prices occurred. In fact, as the war struggled on for eight long years, OPEC's ability to control world energy prices and markets all but collapsed. According to Joan Spero,

> OPEC's problems in the 1980s stemmed from its successes. The cartel's ability to increase the price of oil eventually transformed the world oil market. The demand for oil fell, non-OPEC production grew, and as a result, a long-term surplus emerged, putting sustained downward pressure on prices. Moreover, the excess supply made it more difficult, if not impossible, for OPEC to manage prices, as it had in the previous decade.[7]

In fact, in 1983, for the first time in OPEC history, the organization actually *reduced* the price of its "benchmark crude"—but still failed to halt OPEC's erosion as an effective, cooperative price-setting cartel. At the end of the Iran-Iraq War in 1988, oil prices in "real terms" were below their 1974 level.

There are several reasons for the collapse of oil prices in the 1980s. The first, ironically, is the delayed impact of oil price increases in the 1970s. One reason why the demand for oil is *inelastic* or relatively unresponsive to price changes *in the short run* is that the consumption of oil is tied to relatively large capital expenditures, such as automobiles, factories, and heating plants. In the short run, it is uneconomic to replace all of these items when the price of oil rises, even if they are wasteful of oil, with more fuel-efficient facilities. In the longer run, however, sustained high oil prices provide a strong incentive for new investments that conserve oil and the demand for oil becomes more *elastic* or responsive to price changes. By the 1980s many of these investments had been made, reducing the world oil demand. To a certain extent, then, the high oil prices of the 1970s were partly responsible, through this delayed investment effect, for the changes in demand that contributed to the much lower oil prices in the decade of the 1980s.

Oil prices were also driven down by increasing production by non-OPEC nations. As noted earlier, high oil prices in the 1970s provided all the incentive necessary for Mexico, Norway, Britain, and the United States to develop new oil fields. Although finding and producing oil in the stormy North Sea and the frozen Alaskan North Slope were technically and physically challenging (and enormously expensive), the high price and uncertain supply of oil made these expenditures economically (as well as politically) attractive. As OPEC cut production to raise prices in the late 1970s, non-OPEC nations expanded investment and production, pressuring prices to fall back somewhat. OPEC was forced to cut its own output more and more to offset the non-OPEC production increases.

To a certain extent, the true beneficiaries of OPEC's action, in the short run at least, were the non-OPEC producers and the multinational oil firms that sold increasingly large amounts of oil at the high OPEC-influenced prices. Although OPEC nations also benefited from price increases, their gains were strictly limited by the output cuts to which they had agreed. Selling less for more (which is what the OPEC members did) is not as profitable as selling more for more, as the non-OPEC nations were able to do.

Before long, some OPEC members were questioning the wisdom of their decisions to restrict sales. The cartel fell into a *prisoners' dilemma* problem that in theory characterizes all cartels. While it is the cartel members' collective interest to cut production to raise price, once price has increased it is in each individual member's interests to expand output to get more revenue. This conflict between the group's collective interests and the individual interests of its members was long predicted to be the cause of OPEC's demise. But it is important to remember that OPEC was always as much a political organization as an economic one. OPEC hung together tightly, in spite of the incentive each nation had to "defect" and increase output, as long as oil prices were rising. But when prices began to fall and non-OPEC members got the benefits of the cartel's self-restraint, it was too much for many OPEC members to bear.

For a time Saudi Arabia kept the cartel pricing policies in force through a policy of self-sacrifice. When non-OPEC nations expanded production and some OPEC members surreptitiously followed suit, driving prices down, Saudi Arabia cut its own production back drastically to counter. The Saudis sacrificed their own short-term economic interests to the preserve the long-term political and economic benefits of a strong OPEC organization.

Finally, however, Saudi Arabia concluded that this strategy was flawed and changed course, vastly expanding production instead of restricting it. The world price of oil fell from almost $30 in 1998 dollars to little more than $10 over the course of a few months. This rapid and dramatic price drop was a boon to oil consumers, of course, but its negative effects were perhaps more important. Lower prices punished nations like Mexico that had invested in high-cost oil production on the assumption that high prices were here to stay. The vast investments in oil conservation that had been made in the 1970s were also, at a single stroke, made uneconomic. Ironically, the impacts of lower oil prices, although different from them, were nearly as disruptive as the effects of the price surge of the 1970s.

The lesson of the 1980s was very different from what world leaders thought they had learned from the 1970s. The decade of the 70s showed how much economic *and* political power a small group of nations could have when they were able to exercise control over a scarce resource. The 1980s, on the other hand, taught the lesson that the growing and increasingly complex interdependency among nations and between states and markets made it difficult for *any* nation (even the powerful Saudis) really to control world oil. The unified efforts of OPEC in the 1970s gave way to (and helped produce) the chaotic oil regime of the 1980s and the falling prices that were its hallmark.

And, needless to say, the prospect of a new era of falling oil prices created a surge in oil consumption and a growing dependency on petroleum imports. By the end of the 1980s the *market* conditions that had made OPEC so powerful in the 1970s were in place once again, to a certain extent at least.

OIL AND THE GULF WAR OF 1990

One might have been excused, therefore, for a feeling of dejá vu when oil prices shot up once again in August 1990 due to military conflict in the Middle East. The conflict this time was between two Arab nations, Iraq and Kuwait, and oil was this time both a tool in the conflict and the source of the conflict itself.

The feud between Iraq and Kuwait had a long political history, of course (though not as long a history as the Iran-Iraq disagreement). Unsurprisingly, it was stirred into open warfare by events squarely within the changed IPE of oil. Iraqi President Saddam Hussein was particularly incensed by what he took to be Kuwaiti cheating on its oil production quotas as set by OPEC. Any such cheating, of course, would only further depress the price of petroleum, and Baghdad figured that Kuwaiti deceit had, by 1990, cost the Iraqi state treasury billions in lost oil revenues. Kuwait was also accused of duplicitously taking more than its share of oil from the neutral zone between the two countries and with pushing too hard for repayment of loans made to Iraq during the Iran-Iraq War.

For all the sympathy Iraq's accusations provoked before the invasion, the act of sending in the tanks quickly cost Baghdad all but a handful of supporters. To oil consumers, the move was too reminiscent of 1980, when Iraqi troops had pushed toward the Iranian oil fields in the early days of that war. Had Iraq gained control of either the Iranian or the Kuwaiti oil fields, Iraq's influence as a regional—and global —power would have grown immensely. The addition of either neighbor's oil reserves to Iraq's own would have made Iraq a strong second to Saudi Arabia as the world's premier oil producer—and Saudi Arabia, of course, shares every bit as much of a border with Iraq as does Iran or Kuwait. This was a threat that consumer states, having grown used to a world of diminished "oil power" (and prices!) in the 1980s, could quickly come together to turn back, as they did through the military response of "Operation Desert Storm."

The economic impact of the Gulf War on oil prices was short lived. Oil prices doubled in the wake of the Iraqi invasion of Kuwait but dropped back to their previous low level upon the successful completion of the allied military response. The political impacts, however, were considerably greater.

Upon invading Kuwait, Saddam Hussein had very few supporters in the Arab world, but one of the most vociferous was the Palestine Liberation Organization (PLO). With Iraq defeated, the PLO found itself with so few friends in the international system that it finally began to move in the direction of peace with Israel.

OPEC'S OBITUARY?

For most of the 1990s an eerie stability characterized the international political economy of oil. Demand for petroleum was up and heading higher, as was the demand for energy generally. While oil is not a renewable resource, ongoing discoveries of new pools of oil nonetheless for the present appear adequate to replenish current production. And in the Middle East, the source of so much of the international political and economic systems' turmoil over the last 50 years, an atypical peacefulness seemed to reign (broken sporadically by military actions between Iraq and United Nations forces on the scene for enforce Gulf War agreements).

So different was the IPE environment as it related to oil that Fadhil J. Chalabi, acting secretary general of OPEC during 1983–1988, published an article proclaiming the organization's forthcoming demise, "OPEC: An Obituary."[8] Chalabi contrasted OPEC's strong influence in the 1970s with its seemingly weak economic and political clout at the end of the 1990s. Then, he wrote, OPEC was a force to be reckoned with, but

> Today, OPEC meetings barely register as more than blips in anything other than trade publications and the inside pages of the *Wall Street Journal*. The news is typically not what OPEC's oil ministers have agreed upon but what they have failed to agree upon. ... Put bluntly, its decisions are no longer taken seriously.[9]

There are a number of reasons for the apparent decline of OPEC's influence and power. The "defection" of many OPEC members is one obvious problem— it is hard to take pledges of output cuts seriously when there is such a long history of cheating on these pledges (and such large economic payoffs for defection). The Gulf War also reduced the solidarity of the group by driving a wedge between Saudi Arabia (still the key member of the cartel) and Iraq, a major producer. According to Chalabi, however, four economic factors have perhaps contributed as much as anything else to reduce OPEC's power and influence.

Increased reliance on nonoil energy sources. There has been a fairly dramatic shift away from oil as an energy source. This change may not be readily apparent to readers who equate oil with gasoline and think of the rising traffic levels on local highways. It is true that, despite many attempts to develop alternatives, petroleum still rules on the roads. There have been, however, significant shifts in other areas, especially in the production of electricity, where the use of oil has declined. Nuclear power and natural gas have replaced oil to a considerable extent, reducing the global oil demand.

Biotechnological research promises to expand nonoil energy supplies even more in the future by unlocking the market potential of renewable energy sources.[10] There are also strong concerns about the impact of the use of hydrocarbons on the environment, which may restrain energy use generally in the future. The search is on for energy sources that are cheaper than oil, renewable (not finite in total supply, like oil), and less harmful to the environment.

Some of the efforts to generate non-OPEC energy supplies are driven by simple economics— the potential for profit— but there are other factors at work, too. U.S. Senator Richard Lugar and former CIA Director R. James Woolsey argue that both national security and environmental security are at stake.

> Our growing dependence on increasingly scarce Middle Eastern oil is a fool's game—there is no way for the rest of the world to win. Our losses may come suddenly through war, steadily through price increases, agonizingly through developing-nation poverty, relentlessly through climate change, or through all of the above. It would be extremely short-sighted not to take advantage of the scientific breakthroughs that have occurred and that are in the offing, . . . If we do, we will make life far less dangerous and far more prosperous for future generations. If we do not,

those generations will look back in angry wonder at the remarkable opportunity that we missed.[11]

Rising oil supply. The world's oil corporations have not been idle in the period since OPEC took over their facilities in the 1970s. Unable to invest in OPEC nations, these companies have instead made large investments to develop new oil reserves in non-OPEC nations. Their huge investments have begun to generate increased oil supplies that dramatically affect OPEC's price-setting ability. Non-OPEC production (not counting oil from Russia and the United States) has risen from 9 million barrels per day (mbpd) in 1976 to 26 mbpd in 1995. Any attempt by OPEC to raise world market prices today would be terribly costly (and therefore politically difficult for the cartel) because OPEC would need to cut output among its members to make up for the rising production of non-member countries. OPEC's leverage against the world oil market is much reduced by the growth of production in other countries.

Changing oil technology. Oil has long been an industry with high natural barriers to entry. The search for oil is full of risks and the development of oil assets enormously expensive. High risk and high cost have limited the ability of new firms and new nations to enter oil markets. Recently, however, technological changes have reduced both risk and cost. Computer technology makes the search for oil more scientific and reliable. New drilling techniques have reduced the investment needed to exploit oil reserves once they are located. As a result, oil supplies are both greater and more flexible than in the past, reducing OPEC's market power.

Changing market structures for oil. OPEC's power was greatest when much of the world's oil was traded on the "spot" market— the market where oil is exchanged here and now for money. Because of the volatility of prices in this market, buyers and sellers have increasingly sought to protect themselves in several ways. Many have signed long-term contracts, which guarantee prices well into the future. This protects both buyers and sellers from sudden and disruptive twists and turns in the market. Others have taken advantage of the growth of a futures market for oil, where traders exchange the right to buy or sell oil at a certain price at a fixed date in the future. Using long-term contracts and the futures market, large users of oil can effectively protect themselves from sudden spikes in the price of petroleum while still allowing themselves to take limited advantage of falling prices should they appear. One of the consequences of this change in market structure is that a rising oil price does not necessarily benefit the actual producers of oil, at least not immediately. In the short run, they may find themselves forced by contractual commitments to supply oil at low cost to non-OPEC firms that then reap windfall gains by reselling it on higher-priced spot markets.

The argument against OPEC's continued viability, then, is as simple as supply and demand. The demand for oil is lower now than in the past. The supply is greater and there are fewer barriers to the development of even more oil resources, if rising market prices should create an incentive to do so. Oil prices are therefore low, OPEC has less power to raise them, and if it did do so it would not necessarily capture all the short-term profits. From a supply and demand standpoint, OPEC clout is pretty much gone.

This does not mean that oil prices will always be low, the authors of OPEC's obituary warn. But now they will rise and fall according to changes in demand and supply, *not* votes of OPEC oil ministers. As East Asia recovers from its economic crises, the demand for oil is sure to rise as will its price.[12] Looking deeper into the future, the economic development of China, the growth of a market economy in India, and the stabilization and recovery of industrial production in Russia are all forces that will increase oil demand more than they are likely to raise its supply and thus tend to drive up the cost of a barrel of oil. The death of OPEC as a market force does not mean an endless future of cheap oil.

> But while Asia might provide a short-term windfall for the oil-producing countries of the Gulf, it is unlikely to solve OPEC's myriad problems in the long run. Gone are the days of "oil nationalism" and the "oil weapon." The catchwords of today's global marketplace are "integration" and "interdependence." The exclusive club of oil companies has been replaced by a hypercompetititve market that relies upon the free flow of information and high technology to remain viable. . . . If OPEC is to remain viable, it must once and for all forsake old habits in the face of new realities.[13]

EXAGGERATED RUMORS

Mark Twain was lecturing in Australia when he was shown a copy of his own obituary in a U.S. newspaper. "The rumors of my death," he telegraphed the newspaper's mistaken editor, "are exaggerated." Many authors and editors have written OPEC's obituary already, but is the organization *really* finished? Or are its death notices just a bit exaggerated?

There are at least three good reasons to believe that OPEC lives on as a potent force in the international political economy. The first reason is that, like Mark Twain, OPEC seems alive in reality, even if it is doornail-dead in print. In the spring of 1999, for example, the OPEC ministers met and set production quotas aimed at reducing global oil supply and driving up prices. The plan went into effect on April 1, 1999, and, sure enough, the price of a barrel of oil rose from about $12 to a bit more than $20 over the next few months. Certainly there were other factors at work beside the OPEC agreement, but it is hard *not* to conclude that OPEC's actions were at least part of the reason for the price rise.

If OPEC is dead, then its ghost has inherited its old power to levitate oil prices. Of course, the fact that OPEC was able to push up oil prices in 1999 does not completely refute the arguments made above that market forces, not OPEC actions, will dictate the price of oil in the future. But it does make you question the theory that OPEC is already finished.

The second reason to believe that OPEC has retained its power is to consider that oil prices are a double-edged sword and that OPEC, in the past, has relied upon only one edge of this weapon. When we think about OPEC power we think about its ability in the 1970s to cut output and push up global oil prices. Certainly this is one edge of OPEC's sword and it was a sharp cutting edge 25 years ago. As noted in the previous section, OPEC is a good deal less able to reduce global supply now than it was then.

But consider the other edge of the oil price weapon. OPEC remains able to increase production and drive price *down*. No one comes close to having the same power to drive *down* oil prices. The OPEC nations have vast reserves of oil, efficient production facilities, and very low production prices. What if OPEC opened its spigots and let the oil gush into world markets?

Ironically, low oil prices are as much or more of a problem to much of the world as were high oil prices in the 1970s. According to a study reported in the *Economist*, OPEC producers in the Middle East can sell oil profitably for prices as low as $2. The cost of producing oil in the rest of the world is far higher: $10 in the United States, $11 in Canada and Western Europe, and $14 in Russia.[14]

Cutting the price of oil to very low levels would be a boon to consumers, but it would strike a devastating blow to the states and the firms that depend upon oil revenues. OPEC could crush its competitors if it drove prices down to $5, as it easily could, and kept them there for a sustained period. The result would be economically disastrous for non-OPEC oil producing nations and, perhaps, ecologically devastating for the entire earth (due to the impact of much higher use of oil products around the world). But OPEC would make a lot of money. If that isn't power, what is? Oil is power, there is no doubt about it. OPEC retains the power that comes with its vast oil reserves. The issue, according to many observers, is not whether OPEC has power but if it has a reason to use its power. It does—political reasons.

Politics is thus the third reason to believe that the rumors of OPEC's death are exaggerated. One of the weaknesses of the case against OPEC is that it is based on economics, pure and simple, and assumes implicitly that economic forces always rule. But the lesson we should perhaps have learned from OPEC's activities in the 1970s is that oil is an economic *means* to social and political *ends* as far as OPEC is concerned. OPEC is likely to remain a potent political force as long as there are social and political reasons for it to play the "oil card" in international relations.

The political importance of oil is perhaps nowhere as important as in Saudi Arabia. The Saudi royal family has used that nation's oil revenues to raise the living standards of the large and growing population while preserving many aspects of a traditional Islamic state (including, of course, royal family rule). It is very expensive for a nation to try to achieve high living standards while preserving traditional culture and gender roles and in recent years Saudi Arabia's declining oil revenues have been insufficient to finance fully these programs. This has created social tensions within Saudi Arabia, which have put political pressures on the Saudi government.

New York Times columnist (and Middle East expert) Thomas Friedman reported on how oil and domestic politics are related in Saudi Arabia in his 1999 book *The Lexus and the Olive Tree*.[15] As falling oil revenues and rising social program costs have squeezed budgets, Saudi citizens have had to cut back on foreign goods and services. One cutback area was foreign chauffeurs. To save money, foreign chauffeurs were replaced with Saudi drivers including, for the first time, the prospect of *female* Saudi drivers. Up until now, women have been forbidden to drive in Saudi Arabia, so this would be a major change in Saudi society. But Friedman reports, the Saudi's cannot afford to continue to pay all of the half-million foreign workers they currently employ *and* provide social welfare benefits to Saudi citizens *and* preserve their traditional Islamic culture, with which the royal family is closely identified.[16] So the Saudis will have to make choices.

> The choice is simple. Either the Saudis must cut back their welfare state, by slashing benefits and raising taxes, or they must find a way of increasing oil revenues. But the ruling family's delicate domestic situation makes the first option difficult. So instead the Saudis may now do what once would have been unthinkable: throw open the taps.[17]

Falling oil prices would perhaps solve the domestic political and social problems of Saudi Arabia, by providing sufficient revenue to maintain its traditional society. In today's world one must be very rich to be insulated from the forces of global markets, media, and culture, and many of the Arab and Iranian members of OPEC put high value on domestic social and political autonomy. If the Saudi royal family is sufficiently threatened by the forces of cultural and political change, then they may push down the world price of oil for reasons that are not primarily economic in nature.

This might solve Saudi Arabia's domestic political problems, but this would create new and very serious problems for other countries, particularly Russia. Russia depends upon oil exports for almost half of its hard-currency export earnings.[18] If low oil prices cause Russia's oil industry to collapse, the impact would be felt around the world in ways that cannot be predicted with confidence. How would Russia make up the short fall? Perhaps by dumping other products on world markets, driving down those prices? Perhaps by cutting back sharply on imported goods? Maybe Russia would try to get funds by exporting arms and nuclear weapons instead of oil? Perhaps, if none of these options are available, Russia will enter an even deeper economic recession. Is it likely that the Russian bear would emerge from this cold winter with its democratic institutions still in tact? Or would Russia slip back into some form of authoritarian state—communist, ultranationalist, or both?

Ironically, the political fate of Russia (and other oil revenue-dependent states such as Venezuela, Nigeria, and Algeria) depends on Saudi Arabia and on the political pressures that shape OPEC decisions in the future. Russian oil exports account for almost half of that nation's hard-currency earnings.

Falling oil prices would create real economic hardship for Russia. How would it react? By dumping more oil on the markets to make up revenue? By dumping other natural resources on world markets, perhaps causing a global recession among primary product exporting nations? By selling Cold War weapons or technology to less developed nations or international terrorist groups? By shutting itself behind mercantilist trade barriers? Would its government remain democratic, turn violently nationalistic, or revert to communism? These questions are so frightening that no one would want to know their answers. The way to prevent more economic hardship for Russia is to keep oil prices from falling too far.

There are good political reasons for wanting to keep the price of oil within a range that allows Russia and other petroleum exporting nations to participate in the international system. In the long run, therefore, the political aspects of oil, intertwined as they are with the economic and environmental, are perhaps the most serious ones for us to consider.

In fact, according to at least one observer, OPEC's political concern for its relations with non-OPEC nations may account for the fact that it has not *yet* driven oil prices down to rock bottom levels that only Middle Eastern producers could profit from. "If it weren't for politics every barrel of oil would be pumped out of the Gulf— especially Saudi Arabia."[19]

CONCLUSION

This chapter began by citing four themes that apply with particular force to the study of OPEC and oil and are also part and parcel of IPE today. If this chapter has been successful, then the relevance of these themes with respect to oil and OPEC should be clear.

- *The fundamental interdependence of states and markets in today's IPE.* The IPE of OPEC and oil demonstrates perhaps better than any other example how much state actions can affect market outcomes and how changing market outcomes condition state behavior.
- *The intertwined nature of economics and politics.* For OPEC, economics is a means to a political end— it is impossible to separate the two in practice. For non-OPEC nations, the line between political security and economic security is now totally blurred. What is more, the complex dynamics of interdependent states and markets combined with intertwined politics and economics places us on a stark new international relations landscape with few historical landmarks to guide us. How else can we explain the conclusion, which seems to follow from this chapter, that the best policy for the United States to adopt if it wants to keep Russian nuclear weapons out of (say) Japanese terrorist hands may be to persuade Saudi Arabia to raise the price of oil?
- *The increasing global scope of IPE.* To understand the oil market we need to understand a very broad range of forces, interests, and events. As this chapter has shown, the price of oil is affected by technology, the desire for profits, the quest for social and cultural autonomy, international politics, domestic politics, environmental concerns, and a whole lot more. Although OPEC and Saudi Arabia are perhaps at the center of the IPE of oil today, it is not an understatement to say that the influences and effects, direct and circuitous, extend globally. Truly, everyone everywhere has a stake in the IPE of oil.
- *The inability of either states or market* alone *to determine outcomes.* The example of oil proves this point. Actions by states produce waves of reaction in markets and by other states. International organizations and nongovernmental organizations enter the mix as well. Even Saudi Arabia cannot determine outcomes, it can only influence them and then wait for the dust to settle.

The famous British economist Alfred Marshall was once asked which side of the market determines price—supply or demand? He replied by asking which blade of a scissors cuts a ribbon? The correct answer, of course, is *both*. If Marshall were alive today, we might ask him which force determines the price of oil—states or markets? What would his answer be to *that* question? Both? Or neither? So complex and interconnected is the world today that it is hard to know the answer to this most basic question of IPE.

DISCUSSION QUESTIONS

1. List and discuss the four themes of this chapter, providing specific examples to illustrate each.
2. One weakness of a cartel such as OPEC is that it is subject to the prisoners' dilemma problem. State the prisoners' dilemma problem in general and explain how it applies to the specific case of OPEC.
3. What four economic factors have changed in the world oil market that make it more difficult or more costly for OPEC to raise oil prices? Explain how each contributes to OPEC's weakened economic influence.
4. One of the points of this chapter is that OPEC has two ways to exercise its economic power: by raising prices (as in the 1970s) and by lowering them. Explain who would gain and who would lose in each case (higher prices and lower prices).
5. "In today's world one must be very rich to be insulated from the forces of global markets, media, and culture," Explain what this quote is saying and its relevance to IPE today.
6. "The best policy for the United States to adopt if it wants to keep Russian nuclear weapons out of (say) Japanese terrorist hands may be to persuade Saudi Arabia to raise the price of oil?" What is the logic behind this statement?

INTERNET LINKS

A Chronology of Oil Prices:
    http://www.eia.doe.gov/emeu/cabs/chron.html
OPEC Home Page:
    http://www.opec.org/
Energy Information Agency (U.S. Department of Energy):
    http://www.eia.doe.gov/

SUGGESTED READINGS

Fahid J. Chalabi. "OPEC: An Obituary," *Foreign Policy* 109 (Winter 1997–98), pp. 126–140.
Thomas L. Friedman. *The Lexus and the Olive Tree.* New York: Farrar Straus Giroux, 1999.
"Cheap Oil: The next shock?" *Economist* 350:8109 (March 6–12, 1999), pp. 23–25.
George Horwich and David Leo Weimer. *Responding to International Oil Crises.* Washington, DC: American Enterprise Institute 1991.
Neil H. Jacoby. *Multinational Oil.* New York: Macmillan 1974.
Richard G. Lugar and R. James Woolsey, "The New Petroleum," *Foreign Affairs* 78:1 (January/February 1999), pp. 88–102.
R. K. Pachauri. *The Political Economy of Global Energy.* Baltimore, MD: Johns Hopkins University Press, 1985.
Ian Skeet. *OPEC: Twenty-five Years of Prices and Politics.* New York: Cambridge University Press, 1988.

Joan Edelman Spero. *The Politics of International Economic Relations*, 4th ed. New York: St. Martin's Press, 1990.

"World Energy Survey," *Financial Times* (special section), 15 April 1999.

Daniel Yergin. *The Prize; The Epic Conquest for Oil, Money, and Power*. New York: Simon & Schuster, 1991.

Daniel Yergin, Dennis Eklof, and Jefferson Edwards. "Fueling Asia's Recovery," *Foreign Affairs* 77:2 (March/April 1998), pp. 34–50.

NOTES

1. This chapter is a revision of "The IPE of Energy and Oil," which appeared in the first edition of this textbook. That chapter was written by Dr.Timothy Amen, to whom we give both credit and thanks. For this revision, the focus of the chapter was narrowed to oil and OPEC (not energy and oil) and a substantial amount of updating was done. Michael Veseth is the principal author of these revisions.
2. Richard G. Lugar and R. James Woolsey, "The New Petroleum," *Foreign Affairs* 78:1 (January/February 1999), p. 88.
3. Not all oil-exporting countries are members of OPEC. Mexico and Great Britain, for example, are non-OPEC oil exporters, and the United States, although it is not a net exporter of oil, is currently the world's largest oil producing nation. The members of OPEC in 1973 were Iran, Iraq, Kuwait, Saudi Arabia, Venezuela, Abu Dhabi, Algeria, Libya, Qatar, the United Arab Emirates, Nigeria, Ecuador, Indonesia, and Gabon. Ecuador and Gabon left OPEC in the 1990s.
4. In the early 1960s, coal still accounted for roughly 40 percent *more* of the world's *total* energy consumption than oil. That is, coal represented 41 percent, and oil 29 percent, of total world energy consumption. "Energy Survey," *The Economist,* 18 June 1994, p.4,
5. To put numbers one and two (and three and four) in perspective, Saudi Arabia (number one) in the mid-1970s had proved reserves two and one-half times greater than Kuwait's (number two). Number three, just slightly behind Kuwait, was Iran, and number four, Iraq, had reserves less than half of Kuwait's.
6. Assessing the transformation of the IPE which resulted, Robert Gilpin asserts that "world history records few equivalent redistributions of wealth and power in such a short period." Robert Gilpin, *The Political Economy of International Relations* (Princeton, NJ: Princeton University Press, 1987), p. 232.
7. Spero, *The Politics of International Economic Relations*, (New York: St. Martin's Press, 1989) 4th ed., p. 277.
8. Fadhil J. Chalabi, "OPEC: An Obituary," *Foreign Policy* 109 (Winter 1997–98), pp. 126–140.
9. Ibid., p. 126.
10. See Lugar and Woolsey, "The New Petroleum," pp. 88–102.
11. Ibid., p. 102
12. See Daniel Yergin, Dennis Ekloff, and Jefferson Edwards, "Fueling Asia's Recovery," *Foreign Affairs* (March/April 1998), pp. 34–50.
13. Chalabi, "OPEC: An Obituary," p. 139.
14. "Cheap Oil: The Next Shock?" *Economist,* 6–12 March 1999, p. 25.
15. Thomas L. Friedman, *The Lexus and the Olive Tree*. New York: Farrar Straus Giroux, 1999.
16. Ibid., pp. 208–210.
17. "Cheap Oil," *Economist,* p. 24.
18. According to "Cheap Oil," *Economist,* p. 24, this figure is 80 percent for Venezuela and 95 percent for Nigeria and Algeria. So what is said about Russia here applies even more to these countries.
19. Ibid.

PART V

Global Problems

It is increasingly clear that many IPE problems are more than international; they are *global* in nature. That is, these problems are not just conflicts or tensions between and among nation-states. They transcend the boundaries of nation-states and have become truly global in their impacts. The final part of this book looks at three aspects of these global problems. Chapter 18 examines the IPE of food and hunger, with special emphasis on the roles of states and markets as sources of the food and hunger problem. Chapter 19 presents an analysis of the IPE of the global environment, perhaps today's most serious global problem. Three case studies explore the IPE of the greenhouse effect, deforestation, and ocean nuclear waste dumping. Finally, chapter 20 is a conclusion that explores a number of issues related to the use of the IPE method, the three perspectives, and four structures. We also discuss a number of dominant sources of tension and four scenarios for the future of the IPE. A glossary of IPE terms follows chapter 20 on page 455.

18

The International Political Economy of Food and Hunger

OVERVIEW

The title of this chapter is purposely missing the word *world* because, technically speaking, the whole world is not hungry. Paradoxically, some countries are awash in a "sea of grain," while people in other parts of the world do not receive the daily required amounts of protein and calories necessary to fight off diseases usually associated with malnutrition and hunger, such as kwashiorkor and marasmus. One authority on the subject estimates that every day over one hundred million people on the earth are hungry or malnourished.[1]

Since World War II, media coverage and public attention to hunger in different places in the world have seemed greatest during or shortly after episodes of localized mass starvation brought on by drought or war. Yet malnutrition and even starvation remain permanent features of many countries, especially those designated by the United Nations as *Most Seriously Affected* (MSA) countries. Why is this so? Can international political economy teach us anything about the causes of hunger and how it might be overcome?

This chapter makes two arguments. First, that an IPE of hunger incorporating the three traditional political economic perspectives of mercantilism, liberalism, and structuralism better explains hunger than the accepted dictum that hunger is chiefly the result of overpopulation and/or a lack of food production. Second, an IPE of hunger points to many of the conflicting interests and values of some of the many food actors who do not also share a consensus about the causes or solutions to hunger. This makes it difficult in the near future to solve the hunger problem.

It is observed by Dr. [Benjamin] Franklin, that there is no bound to the prolific nature of plants or animals but what is made of their crowding and interfering with each other's means of subsistence. . . . Necessity, that imperious, all-pervading law of nature, restrains them within the prescribed bounds. The race of plants and the race of animals shrink under this great restrictive law; and man cannot by any efforts of reason escape from it. . . . When population has increased nearly to the utmost limits of the food . . . [v]icious habits with respect to the sex will be more general . . . [and] the probability and fatality of wars and epidemics will be considerably greater; and these causes will probably continue their operation till the population is sunk below the level of the food; and then the return to comparative plenty will again produce an increase, and, after a certain period, its further progress will again be checked by the same causes.[2]

Thomas Malthus (1798)

Until the 1970s, the dominant approach many scientists (especially biologists), commentators, and popular journalists used to explain *world hunger* was in terms of an imbalance between the amount of food produced in a particular geographic area in relation to the people who consumed it. In the eighteenth century, Thomas Malthus made popular the idea that food production increased arithmetically while human population grew exponentially, and so "man cannot by any efforts of reason escape" from hunger and famine. Malthus argued that because labor-intensive food production techniques did not lend themselves to producing surplus quantities of agricultural commodities, war, famine, and disease were left to check population growth rates.

In the 1930s and 1940s, the application of new technology such as tractors and other labor-saving devices, along with chemical fertilizers, eventually helped spur agricultural production to the point of huge surplus capacity in the United States, Canada, Western Europe, and Australia. Farm policies in these countries after World War II subsidized crop production, which led to huge surpluses of wheat, corn, and pork. In an effort to increase farm prices and income, many farmers in the United States, for instance, were even paid not to grow certain commodities.[3]

Before World War II was over, hunger became of major concern to the United States and its European allies that had incurred a good deal of damage to their economies during the war. President Franklin Roosevelt called a meeting in Hot Springs, Virginia, in 1943 to discuss hunger and the possibility of increasing world food supplies. This meeting produced the United Nations' first specialized agency, the Food and Agriculture Organization (FAO). The FAO studied the food situation in Europe and in the rest of the world, including the newly independent nations and colonies of the Western European nations, countries that collectively came to be known as the Third World.

Many experts questioned whether food production in the developing areas of the world would be able to keep up with expected global population growth rates. The solution to the problem looked fairly simple: Help Less Developed Countries (LDCs) produce more food while encouraging them to lower their population growth rates. The tendency to view hunger as a lack of food production coupled with an overpopulation problem endemic to developing nations continued in the 1950s and 1960s. Some experts believed that assistance from an assortment of international organizations and individual countries, in particular the United States, was necessary if LDCs were to eventually overcome their hunger problems. During the 1950s and 1960s, food shortages in some developing nations were temporarily overcome when surpluses of U.S. commodities were distributed or "dumped" overseas in trade and aid channels. Public Law (PL) 480 and the U.S. "Food for Peace" program made food aid easily available to nations whose governments were also anticommunist and whose economies looked to be good markets for future sales of U.S. commodities and commercial products.

Many government officials and academics felt that hunger was likely to prevail in developing nations as long as "traditional" societies remained underdeveloped or "backward." LDCs were expected to eventually overcome their hunger problems as their economies developed and their governments and societies modernized. The World Bank and other financial institutions funded development projects that promoted the industrialization of underdeveloped economies along the lines of Western nations (see chapter 15).

None of these measures overcame the malnutrition and starvation that routinely occurred in India, parts of Southeast and East Asia, and in Africa. In many Third World Asian and African nations, hunger continued to be attributed to either poor growing conditions, traditional farming techniques, and/or a lack of capital and economic infrastructure. Once again, overpopulation and rising birth rates were expected to wreak havoc on countries like India and China. Assistance from international relief agencies and financial institutions seemed to be too little, too late.

In the 1960s, a number of well-intentioned private foundations and nations financially supported the research and development of new varieties of wheat in Mexico and rice in the Philippines. The so-called *green revolution* produced grains that supposedly could be adapted and grown in LDCs that faced hostile growing conditions. Another technological solution to the hunger problem that gained popularity about the same time was the proposal to educate people in the Third World about birth control. Stanford University Professor Paul Erhlich persuasively argued that the world's growing population was a time bomb waiting to explode.[4]

LIFEBOAT ETHICS

Other food and population experts were not so optimistic. Many of them painted a picture of a world fated to experience global starvation and wars if more commodities were not produced in time to feed growing numbers of hungry people in developing regions of the world. In the late 1960s, this view was made popular by biology professor Dr. Garrett Hardin. Hardin's views were well received in some official circles and by many food experts, religious groups, and well-intentioned concerned citizens.

Hardin used the analogy of overgrazing a commons to explain the relationship of population to the availability of food.[5] He argued that the world was much like a commons whereupon only so many animals could graze without eventually destroying it. The *tragedy of the commons* was that people acted in their short-term, rational interests by continually producing more livestock, which eventually used up the commons, dooming both them and society. For Hardin, freedoms and liberties must be restricted or people would have too many children and destroy the global commons.

Based on this analogy, Hardin made popular a proposal to deal with overpopulation and the lack of food in Third World nations. Given that the industrialized nations were not likely to transfer a sufficient amount of food and other resources to Third World countries to stave off their hunger (because it was not in their political or economic interest to do so), it would be merciful if the donors instead practiced triage or "lifeboat ethics."[6] *Triage* is the medical practice of separating patients into three groups in an emergency situation when resources are limited. Some injured need only minimal assistance, some require attention and even surgery to survive, and some would die anyway, in which case it would be wasteful to use precious resources on them.

For Hardin, the world was like a lifeboat overcrowded with people and about to be pulled under as more and more survivors clung to the lifeboat. If the industrialized nations do not want to be swamped by the growing masses of people in the Third World, they should cut them off and let those who were not going to make it on their own simply perish. Furthermore, Hardin argued that food aid was an unethical disservice to those whose life would end anyway after aid was discontinued.

In the early 1970s, this argument was well received by many U.S. aid administrators and other government officials who felt that assistance to Third World countries was equivalent to pouring money down a rat hole.[7] These officials were already under attack from critics of U.S. aid programs and those who wanted to limit food aid because of the political strings attached to it. Coinciding with this development, in the late 1960s, U.S. foreign aid laws were changed as part of an effort to market grain to industrialized nations, or to at least earn some income from developing nations for the commodities they received.

LIFEBOAT ETHICS CRITIQUED

Some critics charge that Hardin's analogies of the world as either a commons or a lifeboat with limited resources are flawed. Even if the world does have a finite amount of resources, he is wrong to suggest that the earth has reached the point where there are just enough resources available for a certain number of people to live comfortably while others should perish. A question some critics often ask is: Must those in the industrialized nations live as lavishly as they do compared to people in developing nations? Might the rich still live relatively comfortably at a lower level of existence if it meant that more people could survive by consuming what the "haves" do not want to share with the "have-nots"? Is it fair for instance, that the United States, with 6 percent of the world's population, consumes 35 percent of the world's resources? How can the United States and other major commodity producers such as Canada and the European Union (EU), for instance, justify "mountains" of surplus wheat, butter, and cheese stored in the major food-producing nations, while so many people in the developing regions of the world are malnourished, hungry, and starving?

Critics such as Colin Tudge argue that the poor do need the world's rich given the wealth the rich produce, and that the rich cannot be expected to change their political and economic interests or their consumption habits enough to solve hunger problems.[8] More importantly, Tudge and a large number of others also challenge Hardin's assumption that overpopulation is the root of the hunger problem and that LDCs are overpopulating the earth. Many demographers point out that Hardin's assumptions about population growth rates do not adequately reflect the history of population growth in the industrialized countries. Population growth rates went up in the Western developed nations when their economies were transformed from primarily an agricultural to an industrial base. Death rates gradually decreased due to improved hygiene and life-saving medical care. As people lived longer and per capita incomes increased, population growth rates naturally slowed. There is evidence that the Newly Industrialized Countries (NICs) are in or have already passed through the *demographic transition*. Family financial security takes away the incentive to have more children who serve as laborers or secondary sources of income.

The debate about how fast developing nations were overpopulating themselves has been hotly contested for years. In 1997, the United Nations Population Division used a new formula to estimate population growth rates and reported that instead of LDC's contributing to an estimated 11 billion people by 2050, the world population will reach about 7.7 billion in 2040, and then sink. According to this study fertility replacement rates are dropping faster than expected in developing regions. Some 27 LDCs have already reached the below-replacement population level.[9] Tudge and others point out that people in LDCs often adopt a variety of positive measures to control their population during times of drought or severe food shortage. Furthermore, with maybe the exception of China, massive social intervention programs to control population growth have not worked. In cases like India and elsewhere these programs are often viewed as another example of Western imperialism over the developing nations—blaming the LDCs instead of focusing on Western (over)consumption habits.

The point here is not to claim that (over)population is not a national problem—of even global proportions—related to the number of stresses put on the earth's carrying capacity. In many societies, especially in developing regions, the amount of food and other resources are often inadequate to meet the needs and demands of the local population. And of course, it may be the case that at some point in the future food production may not be able to keep up with demand given the earth's population and its income levels. Yet, as so many now recognize, overpopulation is not a problem for all societies. Rather, in some of the developed industrialized nations such as Austria for example, sustaining the current population is a problem and worry for many people.

While it *is* important to look at demand and production levels, Hardin was also criticized for overlooking the distribution of the world's resources, including food. By some estimates, enough food is produced in the world to feed each person more than 2,700 calories a day. However, developing societies that need it the most lack the financial resources to purchase what they need. Many of them also lack the mechanisms and distribution channels necessary to ensure that individuals receive the daily minimum requirements of nutrients and calories. Hardin also overlooks the "pockets of hunger" in developed regions of the world. Living in an industrialized nation does not guarantee one an adequate diet. Furthermore, many of his critics complain that even if population growth rates were to come under control, more food would *not* necessarily be available to poorer members of society. Society's elites or the rich quite often control the nation's food distribution channels.

Thus, some critics of lifeboat ethics raise the issue of how much the relationship of the rich Northern industrialized nations to the poor Southern developing nations is responsible for poverty and, ultimately, hunger. The developing nations were relatively food self-sufficient before they were colonized by the West. A number of structuralists (see chapter 4 and below) point out that colonization or interaction with the industrialized nations via trade, aid, and investment in LDCs by Western banks and industries "immiserized" local economies. Those developing nations that overcame poverty and hunger, such as South Korea and Taiwan after World War II, were given huge amounts of aid because of their strategic (military) interest to the Western powers.

In the 1970s a number of critical works appeared with the theme that overpopulation alone was not responsible for hunger. Lappé and Collins, George, and Tudge, among others,[10] made popular the "food first" thesis that hunger is more a matter of wealth and income distribution than it is food production and distribution. In direct contrast to Hardin's views, they argue that hunger is a product of inadequate distribution mechanisms, but more important, a direct consequence of poverty. Poorer people anywhere in the world are likely to be malnourished or face starvation. Only a small sector of a poorer economy profited from political and economic relations with industrialized nations. The great masses of people in large "underdeveloped" sectors of these economies become less capable of either producing the food they need themselves or purchasing it through trade channels. The relationship between the North and the South is defined by international *interdependence*, albeit one that is asymmetrical (unequal).

Hunger then is *not endemic* to LDCs, but is a *byproduct* of their political and economic relationship to the industrialized nations. Many poorer nations have no choice but to become dependent on food and financial aid handouts to sustain their already low food-per-capita consumption levels. According to Lappé and others, what officials and international organizations should aim for in developing nations is producing food first for themselves before growing it for exports markets or becoming dependent on food aid.

What Hardin and the food first people did was to draw necessary attention to the hunger issue from a global IPE perspective. Together they outlined some of the multidimensional political, economic, and social factors and conditions that have made it difficult if not impossible to solve this problem. In the early 1970s a "world food crisis" drew even more attention to the multidimensional IPE character of hunger when people in developing nations and also all over the world were faced with the prospect of the declining availability of food supplies related to poor growing conditions and other factors that disrupted food trade and aid channels.

THE WORLD FOOD CRISIS

In 1972, the FAO proclaimed a world food crisis[11] because the supply of world grain reserves reached record low levels and commodities of grain and feed grains usually available to food-import-dependent nations in the Third World were no longer available to them. During this crisis, several events occurred almost simultaneously that resulted in a good deal of hunger and starvation in some of the poorer regions of the world.

The crisis began when the United States and Soviet Union experienced two consecutive years of drought in the major grain-producing regions of their countries. Before the Soviet shortfall became public information, the U.S. government purchased huge quantities of wheat from its producers and subsidized wheat and other grain sales to the Soviet Union. U.S. foreign policy officials used these grain sales, among other things, to promote détente (relaxation of tension) with the Soviet Union after the two countries signed the Strategic Arms Limitations Talks (SALT I) agreement in 1972. At first, U.S. farmers praised the deal because it would clear away surpluses that were holding down commodity prices. Soon, however, they felt cheated when the Soviet shortfall was made public and the price of grain shot up.

One consequence of the U.S. and Soviet shortfall and their grain deal was to reinforce the shift that had been occurring in the pattern of international grain trade since the late 1960s. Changes in the international production and finance structures, especially after the United States devalued its dollar in 1971, made U.S. grain exports more attractive to nations such as Japan and EU countries that wanted to "upgrade" their diets to include more wheat and meat products. Poorer nations that had relied on food imports to meet basic needs could no longer afford higher-priced commodities of the major food exporters. Thus, many LDCs became even more dependent on food aid at a time when aid channels were drying up or grain corporations were more interested in selling grain than in getting rid of it through aid channels.

As grain stocks in the United States declined to record low levels, commodity prices shot up, resulting in food price inflation, which generated more demand by U.S. consumers to limit commodity exports and food aid. Commodities such as wheat and feed grains were rerouted away from LDCs to the industrialized nations that could more easily afford them at a time when poorer countries found themselves in great need of them.

Many developing nations also found themselves hostage to another political economic development that drained them of resources and limited their ability to pay for food imports. In 1973, the OPEC oil cartel embargoed shipments of oil to the United States and then dramatically raised the price of oil (see chapter 17). Many LDCs found it necessary to limit imports of food commodities and food products in order to pay their higher oil bills. Rather than remain dependent on food exporters for needed supplies, many LDCs reluctantly adopted food self-sufficiency policies.

On top of these political and economic conditions during the world food crisis, many LDCs were crippled by other routinely occurring natural events such as monsoons in Asia and drought in the Sahel region of Africa. Across the Sahel, almost a million people starved to death when food relief efforts were intentionally blocked.[12] Fertilizer production for many Third World countries was also hurt by an unexpected shortfall in the anchovy catch off the coast of Peru.

After the world food crisis, hunger conditions did not improve that much for many people living in the poorer areas of many Third World countries. Later in the 1970s, instances of mass starvation mounted because of civil war in Bangladesh and in many African nations; a drought in the Sahel region of Africa only served to make matters worse. Food was also intentionally used as a weapon in many wars, including Ethiopia and the "killing fields" of Cambodia.

HUNGER AMONGST PLENTY

Throughout most of the 1980s, the entire Sahel region of Africa experienced several more rounds of mass starvation and hunger. Ethiopia and Sudan, in particular, seemed beyond help. Efforts by international food relief organizations such as the UN's Food and Agriculture Organization (FAO)[13] and Office of the UN High Commissioner for Refugees (UNHCR) for instance, resulted in few victories when it came to dealing with hunger in these and other countries. At the same time the major grain producers were cutting back on and shifting much of what had been food aid into concessional (trade) channels. Likewise, many of a growing number of private organizations and agencies such as World Vision, Doctors Without Borders, and Oxfam, to name only a few, were also unable to do much more to halt the spread of hunger and starvation that seemed to be occurring more often on the African continent.

Interestingly, in the 1970s and 80s hunger gained some attention as a public policy issue in some of the industrialized nations that experienced two economic recessions.[14] Even as they took as much as 20 percent of their land out of production, most major food-producing countries—especially the United States and EU nations—continued to accumulate surpluses of agricultural commodities after farmers put pressure on their national legislatures for export subsidies and other income support measures.

The occasion of the Persian Gulf War in 1991 once again demonstrated the connection between war and hunger when millions of Kurds were left stranded in a desolate region between Iran, Turkey, and the Soviet Union. The United States set a new precedent in 1992 by sending its forces (backed by a United Nations resolution) into Somalia to feed millions of starving people besieged by civil war and political strife.

THE IPE OF FAMINE IN SOMALIA

Hunger, in its deadliest form, is often the result of political strife and war. Market forces in Somalia were disrupted by civil war and efforts to gain political control of the country. Nations that try to use food as a military weapon usually do so by withholding food from an enemy in order to extract concessions from them. In Somalia, however, food has been used as a peace-keeping tool to overcome famine and starvation brought on by war as much as anything else.

In 1992, the United Nations peacekeeping operation in Somalia marked the first time UN or U.S. forces have intervened in a nation for the express purpose of humanitarian relief. The United States headed a United Nations multinational military contingency and rescue operation, used 12,000 of its own troops, and 13,000 troops from 20 other nations to distribute 100,000 tons of food supplies to millions of starving Somalis. The operation was also intended to settle political conflicts among a variety of clan leaders who controlled food supplies and distribution networks in Somalia.

Another objective of these combined forces was to reestablish some kind of national government in Somalia. Located on the "horn" of Africa's East coast, Somalia had recently been besieged by famine and civil war. Intense rivalry among six major clan families and, to a lesser extent, drought resulted in 300,000 people dead and another estimated 2 million facing starvation.

In 1992, the government of President Mohammed Siad Barre quit and went into exile, leaving local clan leaders to fight it out for control of the country. Refugees streamed into cities in search of aid and medical assistance. Clan members ambushed truck convoys and confiscated food supplies. Clans blocked and disrupted food distribution efforts in parts of the country they controlled and in many cities. They also blocked port facilities from receiving Red Cross and World Food Program food relief supplies. Many of the clans attacked officials and workers of the international food relief agencies who were conducting relief operations in cities and in rural areas.

Ironically, the roots of this internal strife and starvation can be traced to the geopolitics of the Cold War international security structure, namely the superpower conflict between the United States and the Soviet Union. Many of the clans acquired their weapons from both the Soviet Union and from the United States and its allies in the 1970s and 1980s, when the two superpowers competed for political influence in Somalia. The Soviets supplied the Somalis with AK-47 assault rifles and small weapons in the 1970s as part of a program to expand communist influence within Africa. After Somalia invaded Ethiopia, a Soviet ally, in 1977, the USSR withdrew support. The shah of Iran, along with Egypt and other Arab nations, then supplied Somalia with weapons. From 1981 to 1989, the United States supplied the government of President Barre with $35 million worth of "lethal assistance" that included TOW antitank missiles and armored personnel carriers.

During the famine rescue operation, the United States and allied military forces tried to stay neutral among local clan leaders. Contrary to accepted military practice, the weapons of these groups were not quickly confiscated. After an ambush resulted in 22 dead Pakistani soldiers, however, efforts were made to round up the larger weapons and to control the use of small rifles and other weapons.

In March 1993, a peace accord was signed by 15 Somali chiefs, establishing a three-tiered, federal-style administration that would guide the country for two years, until elections could be held. Most of the U.S. and other forces were subsequently withdrawn from the country. The UN Security Council established a multinational force of 20,000 peacekeeping troops to replace U.S. forces. When a number of the clan leaders rejected the peace plan, military conflict returned.

During the rest of the 1990s, war, especially civil war, once again contributed to the deaths of millions due to hunger and even starvation in Rwanda,[15] Sudan, and Angola, among a large number of African countries.[16] Once again aid agencies were at a loss to make a significant impact on hunger in Tanzania, Namibia, Botswana, Malawi, and Zambia which were stricken by drought at one time or another. In most cases they have been able to do little to overcome the hunger problem.

Against a backdrop of these dramatic conditions, production conditions in the 1990s went on a roller coaster ride from worry in the mid-1990s about depleted food reserves and predictions of an outbreak of global famine[17] to concerns that oversupply conditions in the late 1990s were clogging trade markets and lowering farm incomes to the point where legislatures had to find new measures to deal with these surpluses.[18] Oversupply conditions made it still more difficult for the WTO to negotiate away export subsidies and other assistance measures national governments use to financially assist their farmers (see chapter 6). In 1996 the FAO once again sponsored another world food conference—in Rome. The 187 states represented at the meeting produced a World Food Summit Plan of Action that pledged to halve the number of hungry people in the world (about 800 million) within 20 years. The Plan of Action also included a Declaration on World Food Security whereby food was recognized as a human right. Despite pledges to increase food reserves and to use stocks for more humanitarian assistance, little has been accomplished by way of accomplishing these objectives since then. If anything, the conference returned to emphasizing population control as a means of dealing with hunger in Third World countries. These efforts met with opposition from the Holy See as well as from states that view population arguments as distracting from bigger issues of poverty and inequality.[19]

If anything, food surpluses continue to be channeled into trade markets and away from international and bilateral food aid programs. The United States in particular has recently linked food aid to its strategic security interests in Russia, Indonesia, and North Korea.[20] An estimated 2 million people have died of starvation in North Korea, and the United States has linked food assistance to North Korean cooperation over development of its nuclear weapons system, among other things.[21]

The events of the world food crisis, along with numerous events and conditions that came after it, highlight the extent to which factors that routinely contribute to hunger and starvation in some of the poorest countries of the world do include an immediate supply and demand problem. At the same time however, they are also part of a much broader political-economic set of issues.

AN IPE OF FOOD AND HUNGER

What specifically does IPE teach us about world hunger? Broadly speaking, an IPE of hunger accounts for the ways in which a combination of political and economic forces and factors generate hunger in different geographical areas of the world. Two important questions are: What is the connection between the acquisition of power and wealth and poverty and hunger? What role does the international political economy play in preventing people from acquiring the food necessary to sustain themselves?

We can begin to answer these questions by outlining some basic features of the international political economy, especially the relationship of states to markets. The state (a collective set of each nation-state's governing institutions; see chapter 1) plays an important, if not the central, role in the international system today. International organizations such as the FAO exist at the behest of nation-states that regulate both public and private international affairs. International organizations do not, as yet, have the authority to unilaterally impose solutions to hunger on states or subnational actors. Officials of both nation-states and private nongovernmental organizations usually identify themselves as nationals from one country or another. Multinational Corporations (MNCs) are not sovereign political entities either. That status still belongs to the nation-state, which regulates the money supply and establishes the political conditions in which international corporate agribusinesses must operate.

Subnational groups may contend with the state for authority to govern a distinct territory or nation of people. These groups also play key roles when it comes to producing commodities or making any national or local food distribution system work. However, in most cases national governments adopt policies that, for good or bad, influence hunger and/or provide the resources necessary to overcome a myriad of hunger-related problems.

Interacting with states are markets (i.e., exchanges), which also take place within and among all nation-states at various levels of analysis. Markets, together with developments in the international production and finance structures, directly influence hunger in a number of important ways. First, some agricultural commodities are routinely sold by the United States and other major commodity exporters to earn foreign exchange. Commodities are also purchased by nations unable to produce them for themselves or whose consumers desire to purchase items that cannot be grown locally. Actually, only about 10 percent of all agricultural commodities are exchanged via international commercial transactions. The rest are produced for domestic consumption and exchanged in local markets. However, for some groups and even entire nations, accessibility to that 10 percent of exchanged commodities can mean the difference between maintaining a healthy diet and slipping into a state of malnutrition and hunger.

Second, markets play a role in establishing agricultural commodity prices. In most societies, prices reflect the demand for goods related to their supply or availability. In cases of communist, socialist, or otherwise highly regulated societies, prices may be fixed according to some ideological principal. Prices can either deter or act as an incentive for farmers to produce and market their commodities. Furthermore, the price of commodities makes them relatively more or less available to certain individuals or income groups, thereby influencing the amount of hunger present in a society.

The third way that markets influence hunger is more generally in the way they condition the economic vitality of a particular nation-state or group of its people. Tension often occurs between states and markets when states attempt to regulate markets in order to accomplish a variety of national, political, social, and economic objectives. Both domestic and international markets—the latter more often—are looked to by groups and nation-states as sources of economic growth. The extent to which goods are successfully produced and marketed, either at home or in trade channels, can significantly influence the hunger problem. Those who profit from market transactions are less likely to go hungry, while those who do not are more likely to feel the effects of poverty, malnourishment, and even starvation.

Aside from international trade, agricultural commodities and food products are impacted by at least two other types of international economic transactions characteristic of the international finance structure. A good deal of controversy surrounds the issue of food aid or money that is donated or loaned to a group of people on a short- or long-term basis. Finally, international food production and distribution are affected by the international investment practices of different nations and MNCs. These businesses provide jobs for people, and in the case of agribusinesses, produce crops that are often sold abroad to earn foreign exchange. In many cases, crops grown specifically for export substitute for commodities that would be grown and consumed locally.

Each of the three traditional IPE perspectives—mercantilism, liberalism, and structuralism—locates the causes of hunger and solutions to the problem in a variety of relationships of states and other actors to the market. What follows is a brief discussion of how each ideological school of thought looks at agricultural trade, food aid, and agribusiness activity as specific causes and/or solutions to the hunger problem.

AMARTYA SEN AND THE CAUSES OF FAMINES

The 1998 Nobel Prize in Economic Science was awarded to Amartya Sen, a specialist in the theory of economic welfare and the practical problems of starvation and famines. Sen was born in Bengal, India in 1933 and teaches at Trinity College, Cambridge University, in the United Kingdom.

Sen is the author of many scientific works, including *Poverty and Famine* (Oxford University Press, 1983), a study of the causes of famines that debunks much of the conventional wisdom about food and hunger. Sen found, for example, that famines often occur even when there is no overall shortage of food. When famines do occur, their impact is not at all uniform: Some population groups experience starvation while others have adequate food supplies. In some cases regions experiencing famine and starvation have actually exported food to other (nonfamine) areas.

The problem, Sen concluded, is not a simple matter of too much population or not enough food. The problem is an imbalance between what food costs and what hungry people can afford to pay. The Bangladesh famine of 1974, for example, occurred because the incomes of rural workers fell at the same time that food prices shot up. Flooding in Bangladesh depressed farm yields and eliminated the jobs of many rural peasants.

Families had less income to spend, but that alone would not have caused a real famine if the price of food had remained at normal levels. There are many ways that a family can economize without starving when its income falls.

The price of scarce food went up, but that alone was not enough to produce a famine if people had had their normal incomes. Indeed, urban workers who did not experience falling incomes due to the floods were able to feed themselves adequately despite higher prices. It wasn't the high price of food, nor was it the low incomes of farm workers. It was the combination of lower incomes and higher food prices that created the human disaster of famine in Bangladesh in 1974.

There are many important implications of Sen's analysis. One insight is that famines can be prevented not just by keeping food prices down but also by paying attention to the distribution of income among rural poor groups.

THE MERCANTILIST PERSPECTIVE

For mercantilists, food and hunger issues are tied up in considerations of national wealth and power. Mercantilists, or economic nationalists, view the world in ways similar to political realists (see chapter 9). Nation-states compete with each other for power and wealth in order to improve their relative position in a self-help international system where there is no sovereign political authority above the nation-state. Mercantilists emphasize how a nation's wealth and money ultimately contribute to its security.

For mercantilists, hunger is a regularly occurring condition related to a combination of physical and political-economic situations. Some countries are simply better endowed with a variety of natural resources, raw materials, and growing conditions that enhance food production. Mercantilists and realists consider food to be an essential ingredient of power.[22] Those states that are relatively food self-sufficient or that have the capacity to feed their population are less likely to be dependent on other states for food. Thus, they are less vulnerable to those that during a time of crisis or war would be likely to cut off their food supply. Many nations will go out of their way to enhance their food security. Japan, for instance, has always been very self-conscious about its dependency on other nations for raw materials and food supplies. Its desire to achieve food security in part explains its willingness up until recently, to assist rice farmers with price and income support measures that at one time pushed the price of rice in Japan to as much as ten times higher than world market rice prices.

Nations with the capacity to produce large surpluses of commodities, such as the United States, Canada, EU members, Australia, and a few others, quite often benefit from the dependency of other nations on their agricultural commodities and food products. Agricultural commodities sold abroad earned the United States a good deal of foreign currency after World War II. Agricultural trade accounted for as much as 26 percent of all U.S. exports in the 1980s and still did in the 1990s. Many governments have also resorted to neomercantilist protectionist trade policies to insulate their farm support programs from international market forces and the protectionist policies of other countries. The major grain-trading countries also use export subsidies and a variety of other measures to compete with one another for what have been declining shares of commodity export markets. For instance, recently, the U.S. Department of Agriculture set its sights on markets in East and Southeast Asia as a chance to help U.S. firms and farms boost sales in the region. According to a recent report, the region has 1.9 billion people and a rapidly growing population.[23] However, Australia and some Third World countries have adopted a variety of economic liberal measures to make their commodities more competitive with U.S. commodities. China now competes with the United States as the world's biggest grain producer. The existence of large stockpiles of agricultural commodities puts pressure on major producers to clear markets of surplus commodities and also to attract new buyers and markets. Nor are states eager to pay the costs of domestic economic and social adjustments after reducing protection for their farmers and making them more internationally competitive.

Agricultural trade enhanced U.S. power and its positions in the international security structure after World War II in other ways. A case in point are the power and influence the United States derived from supplying many of its allies with commodities through trade and aid channels. Along with loans and technical assistance, PL 480 food aid helped shore up prodemocratic-capitalist economies in the Third World and helped the United States contain Soviet influence in those regions. Many recipients of U.S. food aid, such as South Korea, Taiwan, and Egypt, later "graduated" from U. S. assistance and became major purchasers of U.S. commodities and food products.

At times, the United States has intentionally tried to use "food as a weapon." One case in point was in 1972, when the United States used a grain deal with the Soviet Union as a "carrot" to reward its arch rival for entering into an arms control agreement (SALT I) and pursuing détente with the United States. In 1980, the United States embargoed shipments of grain to the Soviet Union because it had invaded Afghanistan. In this case, the United States used its commodities as a "stick," not so much to change Soviet behavior as to embarrass it and force the Soviet people to reduce their consumption of meat—an unpopular policy, given that the government had recently promised Soviet citizens more meat.

Robert Paarlberg argues quite convincingly that food does not have a lot of political utility unless the supplier has a monopoly over food supplies.[24] In this case, the Soviet Union sought out other suppliers—and Argentina responded to the call. Argentina became a major grain producer and exporter and also an export competitor of the United States. To some extent the use of food as a weapon backfired on the United States. U.S. farmers complained that the government played politics with U.S. trade policy. President Carter responded by raising government deficiency payments to farmers. President Reagan later rescinded the embargo, in part because U.S. officials feared that other importers of U.S. grains and foodstuffs would consider the United States an "unreliable supplier" in international grain markets. Many LDCs that formerly were willing to purchase agricultural commodities from abroad were no longer willing to do so and turned to self-sufficiency policies encouraging local farmers to meet consumer demand.

If anything, the case of the Soviet grain embargo demonstrates that the United States was discomforted as much as the Soviet Union: U.S. officials realized the extent of U.S. dependency on agricultural exports. More important, however, the embargo demonstrated that regardless of whom was most inconvenienced, nations are always *tempted* to use food as a weapon, even if only symbolically, if their political and military arsenals lack appropriate instruments.

As suggested above, mercantilists and realists consider foreign aid to be another tool of foreign policy. The United States employed PL 480 food aid quite effectively in its effort to contain the USSR. Grain shipments also benefited U.S. farmers and shippers and helped hold down costs of government price and income support programs. Few experts would disagree with the argument that food aid provided to countries to deal with short-term emergencies benefited the aid recipient as much as it did the donor.

For mercantilists, agribusinesses operate at the behest of nation-states, which benefit from their investment and production of commodities. Most of the

Western industrialized countries, along with international organizations, have chosen not to seriously restrict agribusiness practices in other countries. What regulations of agribusinesses and other transnational corporations there are originate with host governments.

Agribusinesses and other MNCs add to the wealth and power of both the host and country of origin. Aside from providing investment opportunities, from a mercantilist perspective they help transform the traditional agriculture sector of the economy from primarily labor to modern capital-intensive production techniques. They provide employment opportunities and infrastructure for people. They also benefit many of the LDCs in which they are located by transferring to them technology, managerial skills, and marketing and production techniques. MNCs also help LDCs earn foreign exchange, which, in turn, they can use to purchase needed commodities or consumer items (see chapter 16).

According to mercantilists, agribusinesses and other MNCs, then, earn income for the country in which they originate and help eradicate poverty in host nations. Higher income levels mean that locals generally eat more nutritious and larger quantities of food. Development also means that revolution is less likely and that governments that support MNC investment efforts in their country are likely to support the political and economic policies of the countries in which the enterprise originated.

In sum, to mercantilists, states regulate markets—employ trade, aid, and investment policies—in such a way as to attain state goals and objectives, which ultimately affect a state's ability to secure itself. Hunger is not likely to be overcome in any great measure unless it is in the national interest of states to overcome the problem, and even then more on a local or national as opposed to global basis. In the 1970s, it became clearer all the time that the distribution of financial resources and food was as much the result of how much power a nation had as it was a nation's ability to produce needed commodities. People in the industrialized-developed Western nations were less likely to go hungry than their counterparts in developing nations. Mass starvation was more likely to occur in the politically weaker nations than in the more powerful countries.

In the past, the rule of thumb has been that, more often than not, food insecurity weakens some states and works to the advantage of food suppliers. On the other hand, economic interdependence among nations has made suppliers quite dependent on foreign markets to absorb excess commodity surpluses and food products. However, as long as nation-states compete with one another for limited resources, food is likely to remain a symbolic, if not a real, weapon in national arsenals.

THE LIBERAL PERSPECTIVE

Liberals look on the food problem in ways that mercantilists find politically naive, if not wishful thinking. For liberals, hunger is a problem that could easily be overcome if nation-states followed some basic economic principles and, for the most part, kept politics out of the hunger issue. For liberals, individuals or households *should* be the major actors who make economic and political decisions. Liberals prize efficiency, economic growth, and productivity beyond other values. When it comes to the relationship of food production to hunger, their outlook is simple: Market forces should be allowed to set food prices, which—if governments did not interfere in markets—would result in enough food produced to meet even the tremendous demand in developing regions of the world.

States that cannot produce enough food locally usually import needed commodities from abroad. Liberals do not view imports as inherently bad, in and of themselves. If nations specialize in producing items for which they have a comparative advantage and trade with other nations for what they need, both countries gain and increase the wealth of both nations. Imports, then, are justified if they comprise products that can't be efficiently grown domestically.

What bothers liberals more than anything else are trade problems that originate in national farm income and price support programs. When large surpluses develop, governments in the major grain-producing regions of the world have distorted market forces by paying farmers not to grow food. Governments may also pay farmers a deficiency payment to bring farm prices or farm income up to the level of nonfarm workers. Inflated or artificial prices merely generate more production, compelling governments to adopt an array of agricultural export enhancement and/or food aid measures to get rid of these surpluses. States will also often employ a variety of measures to limit agricultural imports to protect their farmers.

Implied in a liberal argument about food and hunger is the assumption that many grain-exporting countries support their farmers because farm organizations are still quite politically influential despite the declining numbers of farms and farmers. In effect, state agencies are "captured" by farm groups and organizations when it comes to designing and implementing government farm policies and programs—extending the life of the farming vocation beyond its economic worth.

Recently, liberals gave a good deal of attention to the Uruguay round of GATT negotiations (1986–94) held in Geneva, Switzerland, and to impact the new WTO is likely to have on food trade conditions. Agricultural import barriers and export subsidies were a major stumbling block to liberalizing the international trade system in the Uruguay round (see chapter 6). Liberal trade experts blamed national government farm support, self-sufficiency, and food security policies for failure to significantly reduce the level of trade protection for agricultural products and for failure to realize the goal of making the food production process more efficient.[25] Further reductions in domestic assistance and agricultural trade measures are scheduled to be dealt with again in upcoming WTO meetings.

Liberals also have strong feelings about both trade and aid policies when it comes to LDCs and their efforts to overcome hunger. Hunger is not only the result of government intervention in markets in industrialized regions of the world, but also LDC mismanagement of their own economies. In the past, liberals have generally believed that the Western development model, emphasizing industrial productivity and economic growth, was applicable to developing nations. LDCs could grow out of and overcome their poverty and hunger problems if they imitated the West's approach to development. Trade was viewed as an "engine to growth." LDCs were to specialize in producing a few commodities, such as bananas, coffee, sugar, or tea, that could be exported abroad to earn foreign exchange. Food deficits would be made up by imports. This strategy required government to at first play a relatively strong role in the economy to ensure that market forces determined prices and that the growth of industry would be carefully coordinated and balanced with the extraction of resources from the agricultural sector of the economy.

Food aid was to help a government overcome the lack of infrastructure or a short-term capital deficit. Aid of all types would allow the government the opportunity to invest in industry and manufacturing. Food aid was supposed to give LDC governments some breathing room. Food aid would make up for agricultural production deficits and help governments overcome immediate hunger problems.

Liberals view dependency on long-term aid, and food aid in particular, as likely to distort local food production and distribution. Corrupt officials can always be counted on to misuse funds or sell food aid on the black market. Liberals continue to fault many governments for keeping food prices artificially low for financially better-off consumers in urban areas; this acts as a disincentive for farmers to produce more commodities. Food aid is to be used only in short-term emergency situations and/or in consideration of efforts to correct market deficiencies.

Liberals generally view MNCs and agribusinesses as an asset to LDCs because of their economic effect on local economies. The positive economic effects of agribusinesses "spill over" and "trickle down" from the top to lower levels of the economy. What bothers liberals is when, for largely political reasons, agribusinesses do not realize their full potential. Local officials are either suspicious of them or tax them to the point of discouraging them from investing further in the local economy.

Liberals also seem to have an implicit faith in the ability of technology to help solve the hunger problem. Recently a good deal of attention has been given to a second green revolution, furthered in part by MNCs and agribusinesses. One of the most important figures associated with the green revolution is plant pathologist Dr. Norman Borlaug, who started the revolution in Mexico and the Philippines in 1944 with his work for the Rockefeller Foundation. Fifty years later, he was still working to apply the practical and scientific principles of the green revolution to 150,000 farms in Ghana, the Sudan, Tanzania, Togo, Nigeria, and Ethiopia. Dr. Borlaug cites China and other Asian nations as major success stories in the green revolution.[26]

More recently still another revolution in plant production is linked to the information and knowledge structure and centers around the use of newer varieties of bioengineered—"genetically modified"—plants and animals.[27] Growth hormones are soon to be used in cattle to produce more milk, while genetic alterations to the reproductive cells of pigs, sheep, poultry, and other animals are expected to dramatically increase food production in both the developed nations and LDCs. Once again, new crops and virus- and insect-resistant plants are also expected to revolutionize and increase crop production. Liberals argue that through commercial markets and trade many of these technologies will be developed and their benefits diffused throughout the world via MNCs. Furthermore, MNCs are expected to work closely with national and local governments to implement the technology and spread its benefits.

In sum, liberals emphasize that hunger results when governments intervene in markets and distort food production and distribution processes. The result is a glut of food in the major grain-producing countries of the world, most of them the Western industrialized nations. Meanwhile, demand for food in much of the developing and overpopulated regions of the world goes unmet. Abundance coexists with hunger and starvation. Economic growth achieved through trade investment in production promises to help nations move through the demographic transition, bringing down birth rates, but also helping these countries overcome their hunger problems.

THE STRUCTURALIST PERSPECTIVE

For structuralists, the dominant actors are classes within a nation-state and classes of rich and poor whose interests cut across national boundaries. The nature of the relationship of rich classes and nations to poor ones is *exploitation*. Exploitation is a feature of the international production and finance structures that links rich with poor nations. While formal colonialism is supposedly a thing of the past, rich nations continue to subjugate dependent countries by practicing *neoimperialism*, that is, penetrating Southern economies via trade, aid, and investment policies and practices.

Similar to liberals, structuralists argue that markets fail due to government intervention in the economy. However, where the two perspectives differ is in the rationale for that interference. For structuralists, state policies reflect not so much protection of private (group) interests but the interests of a wealthy class of financiers, manufacturers, and businessmen. The rich became wealthy at the expense of the poor, both nationally and internationally. Rich nations continue to dominate poor ones, intentionally making them dependent on the rich for a variety of goods and services to develop their economies.

Hunger is the result of this exploitative relationship. Structuralists criticize mercantilists and liberals for not giving enough attention to factors and conditions that prevent food from being distributed more equitably in local, national, and international distribution systems.[28] Rich nations usually produce more food than their consumers can eat, yet millions of people in poor countries go hungry simply because surplus food is not redistributed to those who need it most.

Dependency theorists emphasize the negative consequences of the transfer of wealth and resources from Southern LDCs to Northern industrialized nations. Linkages between rich and poor nations "immiserize" the poor, who become worse off as a result of various transactions with the North. Most LDCs were relatively self-sufficient food producers until they were colonized by imperial powers. Exposure to the West brought about development of only a small sector of the economy, while in the larger poor enclave of the economy, the masses became impoverished and were more likely to be malnourished or even starve to death.

From the perspective of dependency theorists, trade is a weapon used by the rich to penetrate and make dependent poor countries. The *terms of trade* (value of trade exchanges) favor rich nations. Free trade policies benefit advanced industrial economies at the expense of the development of poorer economies. In the past, LDCs have produced mainly primary commodities that earned less income than the value-added products of a rich nation. Elites within developing nations joined with their counterparts in rich nations to establish and benefit from a local power structure that exploited the masses.

Instead of focusing on meeting the needs of its people, these governments adopted an array of policies that continued to benefit rich nations. Many LDCs specialized in producing one or two major export crops to earn foreign exchange. Quite often these crops are still financed and grown by large agribusinesses that were encouraged to invest in the country by the national power structure. These enterprises grow soyabeans (Brazil), vegetables (Mexico), beef (Costa Rica), or peanuts (Senegal), while the masses of people subsist on substandard diets and local staple crops.

There are two consequences of playing the development game. First, most of the masses never share in the income earned from trade. Trickle down does not work. Instead, the rich get richer and the poor get poorer. Second, governments of these countries are forced to import food they need to make up for food deficits created by an inappropriate development strategy that relies on trade.

In many cases, people and governments are simply too poor to purchase the commodities grown in their own country and instead become even more dependent on donations for food aid to make up the difference. Foreign aid usually has strings attached to it, such as requiring that payment be made in certain currencies. Governments are also known to resell aid to earn foreign exchange or to distribute aid to the middle class or to those groups, such as the police, they feel are likely to make a significant contribution to the economic development of society.[29] Foreign aid, then, merely further entrenches poor countries in a vicious cycle of dependency, poverty, and hunger.

Agribusinesses and other MNCs also negatively impact LDCs in many ways. Their high-tech production methods displace local labor and small farmers, destroying the traditional agriculture or farm sector of local economies. Masses of people leave agriculture to find work in cities, putting pressure on urban centers for social services. Aside from producing inappropriate crops for export, agribusinesses use pesticides and insecticides that are outlawed in their home country. Many of them bribe local or national officials, complicate land ownership and reform programs, and disturb local food distribution programs. Structuralists are just as pessimistic about the benefits of biotechnology today as they were about the first green revolution. They worry that attempts to diffuse biotechnology throughout the Third World will contribute to environmental damage and widen the income gap between rich and poor within developing nations as well as between the North and South. Critics charge that the use of genetically modified foods will result in a monoculture crop production system, there will be fewer types of plant and animal varieties, more reliance on herbicides, and because of its close relationship to business, lack of state regulation of the technology itself.[30] Structuralists also worry that those who support the green revolution or biotechnology in the Third World overlook the food distribution system, land tenure system, and the fact that many LDCs continue to grow cash crops for export instead of producing food for domestic needs.

Many dependency theorists would have LDCs cut themselves off from the industrialized nations and adopt either self-sufficiency or import substitution policies.[31] The development strategy China practiced before 1978 was often recommended by them as a way for LDCs to eradicate poverty and hunger first before exposing the economy to outside political and economic influences. Poverty and hunger are wasteful and inefficient. Development experts should find ways to build an economy from the inside out rather than the outside in.

Other critics of industrial nation practices believe that the North and South can accommodate each other provided a New International Economic Order (NIEO) is worked out between them. So far, however, the NIEO movement that began in the 1970s has ground to a halt. The South simply does not have the political clout to demand and bring about major reform of the entire international political economy.

The modern world systems approach focuses more directly on international structures of wealth and power that cause hunger in LDCs. Core rich states have dominated world trade networks since the sixteenth century. Peripheral regions were first colonized and then exploited for their resources and labor. Only semiperipheral countries like the NICs have been able to develop successfully to any great extent. However, they did so because it was in the strategic and foreign economic interests of the United States to flood them with technical assistance, loans, food aid, and military security. As clients of the United States that bordered the Soviet Union, many of the NICs played a major role in helping the United States contain the USSR. From the perspective of modern-world-system scholars, conditions for the poorest countries are not likely to improve until or unless the international division of labor changes.

Finally, a number of antiglobalization scholars have recently taken up the cause of the effects globalization has on agriculture and food production and distribution systems.[32] Structuralist in tone because they focus on how the underlying economy shapes political and economic behavior, some of the antiglobalists have examined the connection between trade and aid policy and also the role of agribusiness and international conglomerates. Much of the antiglobalist campaign is directed at international organizations, especially the IMF and World Bank, for the way their policies perpetuate poverty, hunger, and malnutrition in poorer nations by supporting local tenure systems and encouraging these countries to become dependent on foreign aid and investment.

CONCLUSION

Currently, record numbers of people are malnourished and starving in different parts of the world. Since the early 1970s, studies of hunger have decidedly moved away from almost an exclusive focus on the lack of food accompanied by overpopulation in developing areas of the world, to more attention to international political-economic explanations of the issue. Now hunger is more often seen as a multidimensional problem that affects different locales, nations, and regions of the world differently. An IPE of food and hunger accounts for how both food production and distribution are influenced specifically by international trade, aid, and investment practices and also how they interact with the international production, finance, knowledge, and national security structures. Each traditional IPE perspective accounts for a piece of the hunger puzzle.

An IPE of hunger also teaches us that solving the problem is nothing short of a Herculean task. This chapter has outlined just some of the conflicting interests of the many actors—nation-states, international organizations, and international businesses, among others—as well as their different values and what they see as causes and possible solutions to the hunger problem. However, reconciling the conflicting political and economic interests of these actors seems unlikely given their lack of consensus about the causes of hunger, let alone what to do about it.

For instance many people find Hardin's suggestions about triage and lifeboat ethics unethical; likewise his suggestions about population control either politically unacceptable or unnecessary at this time. In the meantime however, what to do about immediate hunger problems in some of the poorer regions of the world? The food first people would have national and international leaders and officials develop economic growth and food production strategies that promote self-sufficiency, or that at least attempt to limit the exploitative connections between rich and poor nations. Others believe that to permanently solve the hunger problem requires attention to promoting *food security*[33] for each and every individual and how that security is linked to national and international political and economic structures of wealth and power. Still others argue that there is no truly global solution to hunger because these problems vary so much from place to place or region to region of the world. They want to solve hunger problems by promoting "food security" on both a national and regional basis. [34]

While worthy of consideration, these recommendations cannot overcome the fact that local and national elites profit a great deal from trade and foreign investment, from local land tenure systems, and from domestic public policies that often favor the rich over the poor. In essence, to significantly improve hunger conditions in many of the poorer countries requires nothing short of a complete political and economic transformation of both the international and domestic political economic orders. In part, this explains why some of the food first people are now promoting democracy and human rights as partial solutions to hunger problems.

At the level of international organizations, food and hunger issues have become more difficult to separate from other issues such as economic growth and development strategies, the environment, and human political and economic rights. In this chapter we regret to report that an IPE of hunger compels us to expect continued incidents of malnutrition and even starvation given the relationship of states and other actors to market conditions and the distribution of wealth and power in the world. For the moment, however, at least we have a better understanding of why this is the case.

DISCUSSION QUESTIONS

1. Outline the overpopulation/lack of production thesis about world hunger and discuss some of the consequences of this argument for dealing with the hunger problem. Whose problem is it? What is being done about it? What should be done about it?
2. Do the same as in question 1 for the political economic food first thesis about hunger.

3. Outline the dominant themes and concepts applied to the hunger problem from the perspective of each of the major approaches to IPE: mercantilism, liberalism, and structuralism.

4. After reading the entire chapter, discuss the extent to which you feel that the hunger problem can be overcome. What are the major political economic fault lines or dilemmas one has to consider if the problem is to be solved?

5. Discuss some of the proposed solutions to the hunger problem. Which do you favor, or not favor? Explain.

INTERNET LINKS

FAO: http://www.fao.org/

Gender and Food Security: http://www.fao.org/Gender/gender.htm

CGIAR (Consultative Group on International Agricultural Research) :
 http://www.cgiar.org/

SUGGESTED READINGS

J. I. Hans Bakker, ed. *The World Food Crisis: Food Security in Comparative Perspective*. Toronto: Canadian Scholars' Press, 1990.

Joseph Belden, ed. *Dirt Rich, Dirt Poor: America's Food and Farm Crisis*, Washington, DC: Institute for Policy Studies, 1986.

Alessandro Bonano, Lawrence Busch, William Friedland, Lourdes Gouveia, and Enzo Mingione, eds. *From Columbus to Conagra: The Globalization of Agriculture and Food*, Lawrence: University of Kansas Press, 1994.

Joseph Collins. *What Difference Could a Revolution Make*? San Francisco: Institute for Food and Development Policy, 1982.

Susan George. *How the Other Half Dies*. Montclair, NJ: Allanheld, Osmun, 1977.

———. *Ill Fares the Land*. Washington, D C: Institute for Policy Studies, 1984.

David Grigg. *The World Food Problem: 1950–1980*. New York: Basil Blackwell, 1985.

Betsy Hartman and James Boyce. *Needless Hunger*. San Francisco: Institute for Food and Development Policy, 1979.

Ray Hopkins and Donald Puchala. *Global Food Interdependence*. New York: Columbia University Press, 1980.

Marc Lappe and Britt Bailey. *Against the Grain*. Monroe, ME: Common Courage Press, 1998.

Frances Moore Lappe, Joseph Collins, and Peter Rosset. *World Hunger: Twelve Myths*. New York: Grove Press, 1998.

Philip McMichael. "Rethinking Globalization: The Agrarian Question Revisited," *Review of International Political Economy* 4 (Winter 1997).

Physicians Task Force on Hunger in America. *Hunger in America*. New York: Harper & Row, 1985.

Ross Talbot. *The Four World Food Agencies in Rome*. Ames: Iowa State University Press, 1990.

Mitchell B. Wallerstein. *Food for War—Food for Peace*. Cambridge, MA: MIT Press, 1980.

NOTES

1. Thomas Poleman, "World Hunger, Extent, Causes, and Cures," in *Cornell International Agricultural Economics Study* (Ithaca, NY: Cornell University, A.E. Res. 82-17, 1984).

2. Thomas Malthus, *An Essay on the Principle of Population*, excerpted in Charles W. Needy, ed., *Classics of Economics* (Oak Park, IL: Moore Publishing, 1980), pp. 48, 55.

3. See, for example, Joseph Belden, ed., *Dirt Rich, Dirt Poor: America's Food and Farm Crisis* (Washington, DC: Institute for Policy Studies, 1986).

4. Paul Ehrlich, *The Population Bomb* (New York: Ballantine Books, 1971).

5. Garrett Hardin, "The Tragedy of the Commons," *Science*, 13 December 1968. A commons is an unfenced, communal grazing area.

6. Garrett Hardin, "Lifeboat Ethics: The Case Against Helping the Poor," *Psychology Today* (September 1974).

7. See, for example, William and Paul Paddock, *Famine—1975* (Boston: Little, Brown and Co, 1967).

8. See, for example Colin Tudge, *The Famine Business* (New York: St. Martin's Press, 1977) p. 9.

9. See "Diminishing population takes wind out of alarmist sails," *Tacoma News Tribune*, 24 January 1997, p. A13.

10. See for example, Tudge, *The Famine Business*; Susan George, *How the Other Half Dies: The Real Reasons for World Hunger* (Montclair, NJ: Allanheld, Osmun, 1977; and especially Frances Moore Lappé and Joseph Collins, *Food First: Beyond the Myth of Scarcity* (Boston: Houghton Mifflin, 1977).

11. For a more detailed discussion of the world food crisis, see Sartaj Aziz, ed., *Hunger, Politics and Markets: The Real Issues in the Food Crisis* (New York: New York University Press, 1975).

12. See Jack Shepherd, *The Politics of Starvation* (New York: The Carnegie Endowment for International Peace, 1975).

13. For an interesting and yet devastating critique of the four major world food agencies see Ross Talbot, *The Four World Food Agencies in Rome* (Ames: Iowa State University, 1990).

14. See, for example, the Physicians Task Force on Hunger in America, *Hunger in America* (New York: Harper & Row, 1985).

15. See, for example, the excellent account of the Rwandan civil war in 1994 in Fergal Keane, *Season of Blood* (New York: Viking Press, 1998).

16. See, for example "A Holocaust of Hunger," *Tacoma New Tribune*, 10 January 1999, p. C6.

17. Some of the most pessimistic outlooks about hunger come out annually from Lester Brown, head of the Worldwatch Institute in Washington, DC. See Lester Brown, Christopher Flavin, Hilary French, Linda Starke, *State of the World 1999: The Millenium Edition* (New York: W.W. Norton).

18. See for example "The New Economics of Food," *Business Week*, 20 May 1996, pp. 78-87.

19. John Tessitore and Susan Woolfson, eds, A Global Agenda: *Issues Before the 52nd General Assembly of the United Nations* (New York: Rowman and Littlefield Publishers, 1997), p. 165.

20. See "Latest US diplomatic tool: corn and grain," *Christian Science Monitor*, 9 February 1999, p. 15.

21. See "North Koreans Flee a 'Creeping Famine,'" *Tacoma New Tribune*, 31 March 1999, p. A9.

22. The classic statement to this effect is by the realist Hans Morgenthau, *Politics Among Nations* (New York: Knopf, 1948).

23. See Steven A. Breth, James A. Auerbach, and Martha Lee Benz, *The Future Stakes for U.S. Food and Agriculture in East and Southeast Asia*, NPA Report No. 291 (Washington, DC: National Policy Association, 1999).

24. Robert Paarlberg, "Lessons of the Grain Embargo," *Foreign Affairs* 59:1 (Fall 1980).

25. See, for example, Robert Paarlberg, "Agricultural Policy Reform and the Uruguay Round: Synergistic Linkage in a Two-Level Game?" International Organization 51 (Summer 1997), pp. 413–444.

26. See "Bringing the Green Revolution to Africa," *New York Times*, 14 September 1992, p. A13.

27. George Moffatt, "'Super Rice' May Ease World Food Crisis," *Christian Science Monitor*, 26 October 1994, p. 3.

28. See, for example, Betsy Hartman and James Boyce, *Needless Hunger: Voices from a Bangladesh Village* (San Francisco: Institute for Food and Development Policy, 1979).

29. See Hartman and Boyce, *Needless Hunger.*

30. See, for example, Marc Lappé and Britt Bailey, *Against the Grain* (Monroe, ME: Common Courage Press, 1998).

31. Andre Gunder Frank, *Latin America: Underdevelopment or Revolution* (New York: Monthly Review Press, 1970).

32. The literature on the effects of globalization on agriculture has proliferated recently. See, for example, Karen Lehman and Al Krebs, "Control Over the World's Food Supply," in Jerry Mander and Edward Goldsmith, eds., *The Case Against the Global Economy and For a Turn Toward the Local* (San Francisco, CA: Sierra Club Book, 1996), pp. 122–130; Philip McMichael "Rethinking Globalization: The Agrarian Question Revisited," in *Review of International Political Economy* 4 (Winter 1997); and Alessandro Bonanno, Lawrence Busch, William Friedland, Lourdes Gouveia, and Enzo Mingione, *From Columbus to Conagra: The Globalization of Agriculture and Food* (Lawrence: University of Kansas Press, 1994).

33. The issue of food security is discussed and applied in J. I. Hans Bakker, ed., *The World Food Crisis: Food Security in Comparative Perspective* (Toronto: Canadian Scholars' Press, 1990).

34. This is the central thesis of David N. Balaam and Michael J. Carey, *Food Politics: The Regional Conflict* (Totowa, NJ: Allenheld, Osmun Publishers, 1981).

19

The Environment:
The Green Side of IPE

OVERVIEW¹

Environmental issues have become increasingly important in recent years, as the pace of economic development, industrialization, and population growth have quickened, testing the limits of nature. Environmental problems have always existed in different nations; however, today's ecological and environmental problems are increasingly *global* in nature. The problems of deforestation and global warming, for example, are much broader in scope and difficult to deal with than any single nation's ability to solve them.

The problems of the environment involve states, international organizations, and increasingly nongovernmental organizations along with markets throughout the globe. International political economy, therefore, must expand to accommodate the "green" issues of today and tomorrow. This chapter probes the frontiers of the green side of IPE.

In this chapter, we examine three cases of global environmental problems and discuss several international political and economic dimensions of these problems. We also examine a number of proposed global solutions to environmental problems. A conundrum has developed around the goal of "sustainable development." The primary question for an international political economy of the environment has become: How do nations and other political actors create wealth for today's generations without at the same time leaving a despoiled and depleted environment for future generations? So far there are indications that most political actors are in agreement that this *is,* in fact, the most important question to ask about economic growth and the environment. As yet however, the international system has not witnessed much progress in reconciling these two goals.

I wander thro' each charter'd street,
Near where the charter'd Thames does flow,
And mark in every face I meet
Marks of weakness, marks of woe.

In every cry of every Man,
In every Infant's cry of fear,
In every voice, in every ban,
The mind-forg'd manacles I hear:

How the Chimney-sweeper's cry
Every black'ning Church appalls;
And the hapless Soldier's sigh
Runs in blood down Palace walls.

But most thro' midnight streets I hear
How the youthful Harlot's curse
Blasts the new-born Infant's tear,
And blights with plagues the Marriage hearse.

"London," by William Blake

Prophets proclaiming imminent catastrophe are nothing new in the history of Western culture. However, at no time in the past have predictions of global disaster achieved such wide currency and been given so much respectful attention by policymakers and the general public. The approach of inevitable doom has become the conventional wisdom of the late twentieth century.[2]

Ronald Bailey

The relationship between the environment and the international political economy is a two-way street with many twists and turns. Tensions among markets and political and economic actors impact the environment locally and, increasingly, globally. Likewise, environmental problems routinely influence the international political economy, yet increasingly more often in unexpected ways.

For instance, the two-way street between the international political economy and the environment was illustrated in chapter 12's discussion of the NAFTA agreement among Canada, the United States, and Mexico. Differences in domestic political economy concerns in these countries produced dramatically different environmental regulation regimes. The free trade agreement among them was possible only after a series of environmental side agreements were reached that would minimize the impact of free trade on the environment.

This chapter focuses on the international political economy of the global environment. In it we discuss four aspects of environmental problems in general: the environment as a communal good, the increasing global scope of environmental problems, the proliferation of actors involved in these issues, and the multidimensional makeup and linkage between the immediate causes and effects of environmental issues. We then apply this general analysis to three cases of global air, land, and sea problems: the greenhouse effect, deforestation, and ocean disposal of nuclear waste. Finally, we explore a variety of proposed global solutions to environmental problems focusing on the role states and other actors, markets, technology, and even social and ethical values play in these solutions.

OUTLINING THE PROBLEM: THE ENVIRONMENT AS A COMMUNAL GOOD

The fundamental dilemma that any IPE of the environment confronts is *the tragedy of the commons*[3] (introduced in a different context in chapter 18). The earth's stock of resources is limited—finite resources such as oil can be used up, living resources such as forests and fish runs can be overused and depleted. For the most part, the environment is a ***collective good***, one that is shared by everyone but owned by no one. As the tragedy of the commons explains, such goods are prone to abuse because of the selfish character of human nature. Actions such as industrial production and the overconsumption of manufactured goods and services that abuse the environment benefit the individual but may harm the community. Human nature, alas, drives us to seek individual benefit, even at the expense of the environment, if the costs are borne principally by others.

This tragedy can easily be seen in the current concern over the depletion of the atmospheric layer of ozone that protects the earth from harmful solar radiation (discussed in more detail below). Each time someone uses the chemicals that are responsible for ozone depletion—in a refrigerator,[4] for example, or in an aerosol spray—that person gets a direct and immediate benefit. Yet the harm to the environment is shared by all the inhabitants of earth and may not become apparent for years to come. In weighing costs and benefits, we find that the benefits are clear and immediate while the direct costs (to the person making the choice) are negligible, diffused, and hard to evaluate. In effect, consumers get a "free ride" because there is no incentive for them to pay the costs associated with helping overcome the problem. So environmentally damaging activity takes place.

Many argue that the state *should* play a role in preventing or correcting the environmental tragedy of the commons. If society values the environment, but individuals abuse it, the state is left to take corrective action. State environmental regulations are, in fact, prevalent in many nations. In some nations, political green parties have formed to influence state environmental policy in this direction. When environmental problems become *global*, however, the state's ability to deal with them breaks down. Even environmentally concerned governments fall victim to a *prisoners' dilemma* when it comes to global environmental problems.

The prisoners' dilemma occurs when self-interest becomes a barrier to the cooperation that is necessary to achieve collective benefits. (In chapter 8, we saw that the prisoners' dilemma prevented international banks from cooperating to provide LDCs with the debt relief that was necessary for their mutual success.) The environmental prisoners' dilemma is created by the nature of the costs of environmental improvements relative to the benefits.

Consider once again the example of global ozone depletion. Scientists are fairly clear about what is necessary to reduce or reverse ozone depletion: an expensive change in how some goods and services are produced. If *all* nations were to adopt policies to regulate ozone-depleting industry, the problem could be significantly reduced. Cooperation, with everyone sharing the costs, is necessary here.

Suppose that all nations have adopted the necessary regulation. What would happen if a single nation, say South Korea, were to "defect" from the group and begin once again to use cheaper industrial processes that harm the ozone layer? The effect on the global ozone problem would be small—no single country has that much impact on a global problem. The benefit to South Korea, however, would be relatively large and quite positive. South Korea would suddenly be relieved of a costly burden; its products, because they would be cheaper, would have a competitive advantage on world markets. South Korea, the environmentally unfriendly defector, would gain wealth and perhaps power at the expense of other countries, while hardly harming the ozone layer at all.

If a nation can achieve competitive benefits with little cost from "defecting" from an environmental agreement, then some nations will be tempted to do so. If one nation defects, others may follow. The prisoners' dilemma explains why it is so much harder to address global environmental problems than those problems that are confined to a single nation or locality. This insight is critical because of the changing nature of environmental problems today. Because states are usually more interested in generating wealth and power than they are in saving the planet, many look past the nation-state for solutions to global environmental problems that are becoming more severe every day.

THE GLOBAL SCOPE OF PROBLEMS

Environmental and ecological problems have been around for centuries. Beginning in the seventeenth century during the industrial revolution, science and technology were harnessed to produce new labor-saving devices, industrial machines, and goods for mass consumption. Manufacturing industries were fueled by great quantities of inexpensive natural resources and raw materials, many of which were located nearby but the preponderance of which were located in colonial regions of the world. During the period of classic imperialism, the Europeans conquered and colonized "underdeveloped" territories, exploiting them for, among other things, their resources and raw materials. Meanwhile, on the European continent, air, water, and soil pollution spread beyond local areas. The development of the gasoline-driven engine at the end of the nineteenth cen-

tury shifted demand away from coal and steam to oil and petroleum-based energy resources. Resources remained plentiful in supply and relatively inexpensive
in cost—transportation being the biggest expense.

As industrialization spread throughout Western Europe and the United
States, industrial pollution gradually became a bigger problem. Local authorities
were primarily responsible for cleanup efforts. Many problems became transnational in scope, that is, problems spread over several nation-states. For instance,
in the 1920s, the United States and Canada argued about the effects of lead and
zinc smelting in British Columbia that carried down the Columbia River into the
United States.

The global magnitude of environmental problems was not fully realized
until the 1960s. In the United States, global resource depletion became one of the
issues of the student movement and the environmental movement that grew
alongside of it. As the absolute amount of pollution discharged worldwide grew,
so did scientific knowledge and public awareness.[5] In 1972, a Conference on the
Human Environment was held in Stockholm, Sweden, at which the United
Nations instituted its Environment Program (UNEP). The conference also produced an Action Plan for the Human Environment with 109 recommendations
for governmental and international action covering a wide variety of environmental issues.

The OPEC oil embargo of 1973 and resultant high prices pushed the issue of
energy resource scarcity onto the agenda of many nation-states but also further
up the global agenda. Yet many LDCs viewed the attention the developed
nations gave to the environment as an attempt on their part to sidetrack discussion of LDC reliance on energy resources for the purpose of industrial and economic development. This fundamental difference between the way developed
and developing states tend to view the relationship of the environment to economic growth still exists today.

The critical importance of the environment was further stressed in a shocking study done by the Club of Rome and released to worldwide attention in 1972.
The Limits to Growth[6] provided a set of projections for the world based on postwar
economic and environmental trends. The study argued that if previous patterns
of economic activity and environmental abuse continued, it would be the *environment*, not land, food, or other factors, that would limit global progress. A rich
future on an uninhabitable planet was the report's shocking prediction. Policy
makers and experts alike continued to debate how serious environmental problems were. In 1980 U.S. President Jimmy Carter commissioned *The Global 2000
Report to the President*[7] that predicted continued population growth, depletion of
natural resources, deforestation, air and water pollution, and species extinction.
A less pessimistic outlook was issued two years later by Julian Simon and Herman Kahn in their *The Resourceful Earth: A Response to Global 2000.*[8] Kahn went
on to refer to the fatalistic outlook of the *ecopessimists* as "globaloney."

In the 1980s oil supplies gradually increased and oil prices declined or held
steady, weakening interest in resource scarcity and environmental problems.
Yet national and international attention to environmental problems reached new
heights of intensity and worry in responses to a number of problems and
events shifted attention away from pollution to broader issues of ecological

(mis)management. Just some of these events included a major chemical spill at a Union Carbide plant in Bhopal, India; the acid rain debate between the United States and Canada; the Chernobyl nuclear reactor incident in the Soviet Union; discovery of a hole in the ozone layer over Antarctica; major drought and famine in Africa accompanied by drought in the United States; a chemical spill in the Rhine River; accelerated rates of deforestation in Brazil, the Ivory Coast, Haiti, Thailand, and other nations; the closing of many U.S. beaches due to toxic waste or spills; the Exxon tanker *Valdez* oil spill in Alaska; and the possibility of greenhouse warming effects on the Earth.

In 1987, UNEP published a report entitled *Our Common Future* that shifted more attention to the connection between the environment and the survival of developing nations.[9] Sometimes referred to as the Bruntland Report because the chair of the UN commission was Gro Harlem Bruntland (who later became the prime minister of Norway), the report was a best-seller outside of the United States. The report linked hunger, debt, economic growth, and other issues to environmental problems.[10] The environment was gradually becoming an issue often linked to national security when in 1988 British Prime Minister Margaret Thatcher and Soviet Foreign Minister Eduard Shevardnadze gave speeches that connected the environment to concerns about global security. According to Shevardnadze, the environment is a "second front" that is "gaining an urgency equal to that of the nuclear-and-space threat."

Not all leaders and nations felt the way these leaders did.[11] For instance, the Reagan and Bush administrations aligned themselves with many optimists who downplayed threats to the environment and argued that more study needed to be done. Furthermore, they claimed, many of the measures proposed to protect the environment were too costly, and unfairly penalized U.S. businesses. While the Western Europeans generally tended to be more willing to adopt new environmental policies, U.S. government officials argued that technology and markets could better solve these problems than coordinated efforts by nation-states in international forums.

Multilateral efforts to deal with the environment occurred once again at the 1992 "Earth Summit" in Rio de Janeiro. At the UN Conference on the Environment and Development (UNCED)178 national delegates, 115 heads of state, and more than 15,000 environmental NGO representatives primarily focused on *sustainable development* or ways to generate wealth and development while preserving the environment. Agenda 21 laid out plans for states, IOs, NGOs, and private sector groups to achieve new goals in a variety of different issue areas connected to the environment. The Rio summit also produced a treaty on climate that seeks to reduce greenhouse emissions (discussed in more detail below) and a treaty on biological diversity. As a result of the conference, the UN General Assembly also created a 53-nation Commission on Sustainable Development (CSD) to translate the Rio accords into action (discussed in more detail below).

Shortly before and at Rio, many nations became upset that the United States wanted to play only a minor role in managing the planet's environment and ecological system. By signing the Biological Diversity Treaty in 1993 the Clinton administration claimed that it hoped to once again make the United States a major player in international negotiations to design and implement global environmental rules and regulations. In 1994 it also reversed the course of the Reagan and Bush administrations and signed the Law of the Sea Treaty.[12] Outside of these and a few other important but little talked about agreements such as the Montreal and Kyoto Protocols (discussed below), most experts agree that these coordinated efforts and activities have resulted in limited progress toward the objective of sustainable development.

THE PROLIFERATION OF ACTORS

In the 300 years since the start of the industrial revolution, the problems of the environment have gone from being local and often temporary to global and possibly permanent. As these problems have expanded in scale and scope, they have encompassed an increasingly large number of *actors*, namely governments, business firms, international organizations, NGOs, and even individuals. This has complicated both the analysis of environmental problems and the efforts to solve them.

Membership in different national environmental groups increased dramatically in the 1980s. Groups in the United States include the National Wildlife Federation, the Environmental Defense Fund, the Sierra Club, Friends of the Earth, the Public Interest Research Group, the Rainforest Action Network, and Public Citizen. The number of environmental NGOs with cross-national connections has also increased tremendously. Also known as Transnational Environmental Advocacy Groups (TEAGs),[13] these groups are increasingly known for their ability to shape environmental issues while also playing a role in helping enforce national compliance with international treaties. The World Wildlife Fund (WWF) for instance, was established in 1961 to protect endangered specials and habitats. It is the largest private NGO devoted to conservation with a $40 million annual budget and over 5 million members in 28 different countries. The WWF has over 800 projects underway and works with 7,000 NGO's in developing countries to help preserve wildlife and educate people. Likewise, Friends of the Earth has political or other connections with public interest and pressure groups in other nations. And of course Greenpeace is notorious for generating public awareness and promoting environmental campaigns. Greenpeace's goal is to influence national and international environmental legislation the world over even if it means practicing civil disobedience on the high seas for instance.

The size, cohesion, and effectiveness of all these groups vary within different nations, depending on the extent to which environmental causes permeate not only politics but also popular culture, music, and even esthetics and religion. For many environmentalists, especially in developed regions of the world, the cause has become another basis upon which to attack the alienated individualism of a consumption-oriented capitalist society. Some environmental pressure groups, such as Poland's Ecological Club and Bulgaria's *Ecoglasnost*, have become political (Green) parties. Many European Green parties have their roots in the environment-feminist-antinuclear movement of the late 1960s. Aside from winning as many as 2,000 seats in national European elections, the Greens won 11 percent of the seats in the 1993 European Parliament election.

Nation-states have responded to environmental problems in different ways. In many LDCs, environmental issues often produce tension between the supporters of economic development and industrialization, and supporters of income redistribution, conservation, and sustainable development. In developed countries, this tension usually appears alongside such issues as public health, conservation, and even social engineering. One expert reports that in the mid-1980s, 110 LDCs and 30 developed nations had created environmental ministries or agencies to deal with an array of problems.[14]

Within the UN, the issue of the environment cuts across many different agencies and commissions. A few of the many are the Food and Agriculture Organization (FAO) and its subsidiary agencies, which monitor global hunger but also poverty and resource levels, especially in LDCs; the UN Population Fund, which supports population control programs in South Korea, China, Sri Lanka, and Cuba; and UN regional and global population conferences, which have been held in Rome, Belgrade, Bucharest, Mexico City, and most recently in Cairo in 1994. UNEP's job is to focus specifically on environmental problems (see UNEP box).

UNEP: SOLUTION OR PROBLEM?[a]

UNEP was established in 1972 as a result of the UN Conference on the Human Environment in Stockholm, Sweden. It's the first UN agency to be headquartered in a Third World country—Nairobi, Kenya—and the first UN agency whose main function is to focus solely on the environment. Since its inception it has built a rather extensive network of smaller organizations around itself while attempting to coordinate action within the UN on environmental problems.

UNEP's functions include drafting treaties, providing forums for cooperation, and creating databases and references for scientific assessments of the environment. It has jurisdiction over national environmental situations, transnational pollution issues, and global and regional issues like waterways in its Regional Seas Program. UNEP has also focused a great deal on the issue of global warming. Working with the World Meteorological Organization, UNEP's "Earthwatch" network monitors atmospheric and marine pollution conditions all over the world. An International Referral System connects national information centers to a central data bank in Geneva. Two other major UNEP environmental projects are water pollution and desertification. In an attempt to solve some of these and other problems related to human settlements and refugees, conferences and conventions have been organized to produce studies, resulting in a number of treaties and protocols applicable to nation-states and businesses.

UNEP routinely spends millions of dollars a year on cleanup and management projects. Often it assembles scientists to study and discuss problems and it is often instrumental in getting issues onto the international agenda. UNEP was the first agency to publicize the idea of sustainable development. Quite often UNEP brokers agreements and pulls together drafts of treaties by other agencies to make sure the environment is considered in them.

UNEP has always had a funding problem, receiving significantly less than other UN agencies. It usually works on joint ventures with other agencies and organizations, including NGOs, often providing them with administrative assistance. According to one expert, "UNEP seeks to involve both NGOs and the public in its activities, for which it has sought worldwide grassroots support."[b] Its publications and television programs are meant to be easily accessible while promoting environmentally sustainable development.

Despite some success promoting environmental treaties, UNEP has endured serious criticism, especially in the 1990s. UNEP is often accused of not doing enough to coordinate environmentally sensitive resolutions through the UN. With a staff of only 300, it cannot seem to muster the authority to coordinate agencies that are larger than it. Given its location in Africa, UNEP is sometimes criticized for being too far away from other organizations. Like other agencies UNEP is sometimes the victim of huge delays in drafting agreements and setting up global monitoring networks. Finally, like other agencies UNEP has to rely on national and regional governments to implement its policies. Some developing countries do not see themselves as being adequately represented on UNEP's Governing Council and prefer not to use UNEP. Likewise some of the developed nations see UNEP as merely another voice for frustrated ex-colonial states. These and other problems were some of the reasons the UN bypassed UNEP in 1992 in Rio and created the Commission on Sustainable Development to implement Agenda 21. As criticism of UNEP has mounted, so other UN agencies have often left it out of negotiations.

Most experts agree that UNEP has already catalyzed a good deal of environmental awareness, nationally and internationally. But because it suffers from somewhat of a cloudy role, has lost some respect of other agencies and organizations, and its functions have recently been challenged by those of the UNCED and other agencies, UNEP's future prospects are unclear.

---

[a]Our thanks to Erin Speck for research assistance on UNEP.
[b]Peter M. Haas, "United Nations Environment Programme," *Environment* 36 (1994), p. 43.

International businesses have become increasingly more concerned about the environment. Until recently, the attitude of many of them has been that environmental rules and regulations were annoying and inefficient, to say the least. However, as environmental issues have become more pronounced, the definition of efficiency has come under attack for not including the cost of environmental damage. Deforestation (discussed below) is one such case. Many businesses have taken into account public interest and support for the environment. Many have changed the ingredients of some of their products, or in some cases eliminated the product altogether. Green products have become big business. Likewise, businesses that specialize in the production of environmentally friendly items have become big investment opportunities.

LINKAGES TO OTHER ISSUES

Despite these positive trends, nation-states continue to be pressed to deal with environmental problems. In the past, environmental issues were viewed as secondary to national security and economic growth objectives. Yet it has become clear that costs associated with a lack of resources and damage to the ecosystem add to the tension between nations when it comes to developments in the international security, production, and finance structures. Dependency on oil is a good case in point (see chapter 17 for more detail). Not only has the price of oil been raised and distorted, causing inflation, recession, and various other economic maladies, but nations have gone to war to preserve access to it. In 1991, the Persian Gulf War incalculably damaged Kuwaiti oilfields, as well as the region's water and air supply, climate, wildlife, and sea (see chapter 9).[15]

The economic growth, industrialization, trade, and investment policies of the industrialized nations have proved to be very costly to the environment. Growing international trade and investment means more industrially manufactured products and services that require vast amounts of energy resources. Trade protection in the case of production subsidies, which lead to the overproduction of agricultural and industrial goods, has been just as damaging as free trade to the environment. International economic interdependence, integration, and competitiveness have also compelled states to redefine national security in ways that better account for the environment (see chapter 9). Likewise, many LDCs have not been as environmentally conscious as they could be, given their economic growth and development objectives and strategies. Countries like Brazil, Mexico, the Philippines, and others sometimes have large debts to pay and must generate growth via trade or provide foreign direct investment opportunities to international businesses (see chapter 8). Many of the Newly Industrialized Countries (NICs), such as China, Taiwan, Indonesia, Thailand, and India among others, have also been criticized for their failure to take into account the environment. These criticisms have applied equally if not more so to the former socialist developing countries such as Poland and other East European countries because the socialist development model was as industrial-oriented as the Western liberal economic industrial-based growth model.

The environment, and its connection to investment and trade policies in particular, became a topic for negotiation in the Uruguay round of the General Agreement on Tariffs and Trade (GATT)[16] (see chapter 6). As a result of those negotiations, the new World Trade Organization (WTO) has set about implementing a series of provisions referred to as Multilateral Environmental Agreements (MEAs) that supposedly accommodate the use of trade-related measures and the environment. In some cases LDCs are exempted from GATT articles and WTO agreements so they can place their public health and safety and national environmental goals ahead of their obligation not to raise trade restrictions or use other protective measures.[17] While many LDCs see these exceptions as necessary to overcome other advantages the developed countries have over them, trade officials in the developed nations often see them as LDC excuses for continued trade protection.

The knowledge and information structure is also part of the global environmental balance. A nation's access to modern technology affects its environment in many ways. While high technology often involves the use of dangerous chemicals and potentially damaging processes, it has also helped cut down on pollution or solve any number of other problems.

CASE STUDY: THE GREENHOUSE EFFECT

Global warming and depletion of the stratospheric ozone layer are two interconnected problems that generate a great deal of controversy. Carbon dioxide, nitrous oxide, methane, chlorofluorocarbon ozone, and other infrared-absorbing gases are released by industrial, agricultural, and forestry activities. Greenhouse gases trap the sun's rays, contributing to a gradual warming of the earth's lower atmosphere. In theory, the earth's temperature has gradually been rising since recorded history, if only an average of a few degrees. The heavy concentration of industrial gases released into the atmosphere since the industrial revolution, and especially since the mid-1970s, has rapidly accelerated the rate of the earth's warming. Carbon dioxide makes up the largest concentration of these greenhouse gases, produced by the burning of fossil fuels (e.g., coal, oil, and natural gas), cement manufacturing, land deforestation, and the burning and clearing of land for agricultural purposes. Carbon dioxide emissions from fossil-fuel consumption between 1950 and 1987 alone totaled an estimated 130 billion metric tons.[18]

For almost the past 30 years scientists have disputed the magnitude of the global warming trend and its consequences for the earth's natural and societal systems. A majority of scientific experts seem to be of the view that there is a "compelling basis for legitimate public concern" about human-induced climate change.[19] Also for a good many politicians, global warming is real and has dire consequences for the Earth. Together they believe that the average surface temperature of the Earth has risen by about 1 degree over the last century, compared with a difference of 5- to 9-degree increase over the last 20,000 years.[20] The atmospheric concentration of gases is expected to double the 1900 level between the years 2030 and 2080,[21] increasing the earth's temperature anywhere from 3.5 to 5 degrees Fahrenheit. The Earth's warming is a global phenomenon that threatens natural ecosystems such as spruce and fir groves in Canada. The 1980s and 1990s have seen some of the hottest years on record. The decline in rainfall from time to time has threatened U.S. agricultural production in the Western states and Great Plains region, all the while impinging on international food security. Some scientists also expect global warming to produce a rise in sea level of 0.2 to 1.5 meters on all coasts, damaging groundwater supplies, covering many island nations, and producing large numbers of refugees, especially from Bangladesh, China, and Egypt.

A number of scientists however, are more skeptical of the extent of global warming and the methods used to test the Earth's temperature. For example, S. Fred Singer, a prominent scientist, argues that surface level measurements overstate temperatures related to the "heat-island effect" that results from heat radiation off concrete and asphalt in cities, while satellite measurements are more globally uniform.[22] Also, computer models cannot accurately account for such things as the interaction of oceans with atmosphere, cloud behavior, and the role of water vapor.

In early 1998 representatives from 150 countries established the ***Kyoto Protocol*** which requires that industrial countries reduce their greenhouse emissions by more than a third, or 7 percent below the 1990 level by 2012. The protocol strengthens the treaty on global warming negotiated in Rio in 1992. A unique feature of the treaty is *emission credits* whereby countries can buy and sell or swap emission production quotas with one another. The United States accounts for 60 percent of industrial greenhouse gases. By 2050 LDCs are expected to account for most of long-term buildup of gases and yet they are largely exempted from required cuts. China and India are expected to catch up to the United States in greenhouse gas production in about 15 years. Both have resisted calls for cuts in pollutant emissions. African and Latin American countries are more supportive of the treaty but want guarantees they will get their share of aid from the developed nations to help them cut emissions.

The United States signed the Kyoto Protocol in November of 1998 in Buenos Aires, Argentina. At that meeting signators of the treaty gave themselves two more years to develop operational rules for the treaty and to solve a number of problems associated with it. Given that many other countries look to the United

States to support the treaty, some worry that if a number of issues are not settled soon, the treaty will not go into effect in 2008. [23] First, the treaty must be ratified by the U.S. Senate, which a year earlier passed a resolution 95–0 telling the president not to sign any treaty unless the same limitations are put on developing countries or LDCs commit to a complex scheme for trading emission permits and credits. Currently, LDCs are not bound by the treaty's targets, but they are encouraged to set voluntary reduction targets. Second, U.S. groups representing fossil-fuel producers and users such as the coal and auto industries are also skeptical of the treaty related to the costs associated with implementing it. However, many businesses are already lobbying for credits in case the treaty goes into effect. Finally, the European nations are the biggest opponents of trading emission credits because the United States can buy its way into compliance with the treaty by paying Russia and other countries to cut their emissions more than the treaty requires.[24]

Another major global atmospheric problem is that some greenhouse gases—especially chlorofluorocarbons (CFCs)—have also eaten away at the earth's stratospheric ozone layer, which acts as a natural shield against the sun's ultraviolet rays. There is less controversy about the problem of ozone depletion than there is global warming. In 1975, scientists discovered a hole in the stratospheric ozone layer over Antarctica, and for a good part of the year over nations in the region such as Australia, New Zealand, and southern Chile. Many scientists believe that in the past 25 years, 2 to 10 percent of the stratospheric ozone layer over the Northern hemisphere has disappeared. CFCs have contributed the most to the ozone layer problem. Used as refrigerants, aerosol propellants, cleaning solvents, and blowing agents for foam production, CFCs contain chlorine atoms that destroy ozone.

The effects of a depleted ozone layer around the earth are global in scope. They include a dramatic increase in the incidences of skin cancer, particularly melanoma, one of the most deadly varieties; more cataracts; damage to the body's immune system; as well as damage to crops and ocean phytoplankton. Scientists estimate that even if CFCs were to be completely banned, the ozone layer problem would last at least another 100 years given the present level of atmospheric CFC concentration.

What has been done about the interrelated problems of global warming and depletion of the earth's ozone shield? In most instances, efforts to slow the production of greenhouse gases usually run up against the issues of industrialization and economic growth. In 1987 diplomats signed the UN-sponsored Montreal Protocol which requires states to reduce CFC production by one-half by the year 2000. After discovery of more serious damage to the earth's ozone layer, the treaty was amended to call a complete halt to CFC production by the same year.

The regions of the world that produce the most greenhouse gases are Asia (minus Russia), North and Central America, and Europe, in that order—regions where large amounts of industrial activity have recently occurred.[25] In the industrialized nations a number of approaches and policies have been adopted to deal with these problems. Most of them have been preventive in nature, such as efforts to cut auto and industrial plant emissions. Shifting from one type of fuel to another has been tried in some cases. New technologies have also helped local governments better monitor pollution levels and pinpoint polluters that can be held responsible for damages.

On the other hand, low oil prices have stifled interest in the development of alternative energy resources. In many cases, officials have had to trade off the effects of pollution for the benefits of the activity. A great deal of global warming is caused by forestry and agricultural practices. Cows, for instance, are a major source of methane gas. The point here is that cutting back on the production of greenhouse gases would mean major changes in the lifestyles of the industrialized nations. Estimated costs are $95 billion a year by the year 2000 to achieve a 20 percent reduction in U.S. emissions. Given these conflicting interests, it is easy to see why the policy approach of solving atmospheric problems at the local and national government levels has been incremental.

For LDCs, the situation is quite different. The issue primarily comes down to conserving energy resources, which translates into slowing down economic development and industrial activity. Yet most LDCs have not realized their development objectives and in many cases have a great deal of debt to erase. For many LDCs, solving environmental problems must be subordinated to more immediate development objectives. When it is convenient, the industrialized nations blame the LDCs for atmospheric problems the industrialized nations have contributed the most to so far.

Some LDCs have come around to the perspective enunciated in the Bruntland Report that the problems of development and the environment are interconnected. Damage to the environment only worsens local economic conditions and frustrates growth strategies. In 1987, many countries signed the Montreal Protocol to Control Substances that Deplete the Ozone Layer. The industrialized nations agreed to cut ozone-depleting gases by 50 percent from the 1986 level, while LDCs are permitted to increase their output of gases for the time being. Measures such as phasing out old refrigerators and aerosol spray cans have been enacted in a number of countries. A number of nations have recently called for a change in the treaty to completely phase out CFCs by the year 2000.

A good many LDCs have begun to rethink their deforestation policies, as well as some of their agricultural practices. For the most part, however, these issues exhibit the same tendencies of most collective goods problems, namely free riders. It is not in the immediate interest of nations to pay the cost of trying to limit damage to the atmosphere. Those who do not pay are just as likely to enjoy the benefits of conservation and cleanup efforts should they decide not to pay. Yet in the last decade, as these problems have become more global in scope, they are being redefined as immediate threats to all levels of the international political economy, from nation-states all the way down to each citizen of the planet.

CASE STUDY: DEFORESTATION

Deforestation is such a case, the scope of which has until quite recently been viewed largely as a local problem. Physically, deforestation threatens the earth's land, water, and air, making it a truly global problem in scope. In many cases, forest material is burned, releasing greenhouse gases that contribute to global warming. Rainforests are also the home of thousands of species of mammals, birds, fishes, snakes, lizards, frogs, and insects as well as plant varieties. The financial loss attributed to deforestation is incalculable because prices cannot be fixed for the losses of the many genetic codes in plants and insects, diversity that comes with organism mutation, and the 99 percent of naturally occurring species not exploited by man for food and medicines. Many of the tropical rain forests also contain plants that have proven to be effective in the fight against some forms of cancer and other diseases. The cases of Haiti, Brazil, and the Ivory Coast demonstrate that deforestation creates as many refugees as it resettles on land that has been stripped.

Ecologically, the negative effects of deforestation also include an increase in watershed runoff, which can result in either desertifying countries such as the Sudan or worsening flood conditions downstream in regions or countries such as Bangladesh, India, and Thailand. Tropical rain forests now represent roughly 6 percent of the land surface of the earth, half of what they did 50 years ago. Since preagricultural times, they have shrunk by one-third. Some 30 million acres of forest are cut down each year. Large tracts in the Ivory Coast, the Philippines, Thailand, and over 30 other developing and industrialized nations have been cleared for farmland, grazing, mining, and for fuel.

Scientists, national and international officials, and environmentalists seemed to realize the severity of the problem almost overnight. Many feel that the damage done to the earth by logging and cutting down the tropical rain forests might even be too late to overcome. Less controversy surrounds the causes of deforestation, compared with other environmental issues. Where most of the tension remains is between international organizations, governments and business practices, and proposed political and economic solutions to the problem.

In nations such as Brazil, deforestation results, in part, from a government effort to resettle people away from urban areas into undeveloped jungle areas. Quite often huge quantities of wood are shipped overseas to earn foreign exchange. As many as 33 LDCs have been net exporters of wood, yet the 1990s have seen many of them actually become net importers of wood. Japan uses much of this wood to make cement foundation forms for its office buildings. After several uses, the wood is usually discarded, ending up in landfills. The United States also supplies Japan and a number of other Pacific Rim nations with logs and lumber from its ancient forests in the Pacific Northwest and Alaska.

What has been done about the problem of deforestation so far amounts to a resounding "not much" in relation to the severity of the problem. One estimate is that it would take 320 million acres (roughly twice the size of Texas) to begin to replace the rain forests that play such an important role in absorbing carbon dioxide[26] and perpetuating biodiversity. In many industrialized nations, conservation has a history of political support backed by national legislation. Even so, economic pressure to log timber continues in many regions within these nations. In some cases, environmentalists have successfully used legal tactics to slow up or even halt timber cutting and logging. Timber cutting remains a major public policy issue in places like the United States and Canada, where the economics of forestry come face to face with the conservation and environmental values and ethics of so-called "tree huggers." For the most part, the timber industry has found it economically and also politically profitable to invest in tree replacement and to employ a variety of new technologies and management techniques to stabilize the relationship between economic and ecological forces.

Forest replacement is not the objective of many environmental groups whose focus is the preservation of the tropical rain forests in developing nations. Until recently, LDCs have resisted the arguments of environmental groups, international organizations, NGOs, and others that campaign for slowing down or even halting deforestation. From an LDC perspective, deforestation is not a cardinal sin; rather, it is a political and economic necessity. The forest helps pay off national debt and provides badly needed jobs. Many LDCs complain that the industrialized nations and international organizations are practicing "ecocolonialism" or "ecoimperialism" to the extent that they demand that LDCs shift their development objectives and strategies away from an emphasis on the extensive use of tropical rain forests and industrial activities.

A number of LDCs such as Costa Rica have adopted forest conservation programs of their own. In an effort to pay off their bank loans, some LDCs have been willing to swap part of their debt for preserving a part of the rain forest. A number of NGOs, multilateral lending institutions such as the World Bank, and international organizations have helped make these agreements. The U.S. Agency for International Development (USAID) joined with a number of NGOs and public interest groups to sponsor a reforestation project in Haiti. Still many LDCs want more aid from the industrialized nations to replace what they would have earned through use of the forest. The United Nations reports that "tropical timber is worth $7.5 billion a year in an $85 billion-a-year global industry."[27] Many LDCs also complain that the industrialized nations have not done their fair share when it comes to slowing down timber cutting in their own countries.

At the Earth Summit in Rio 160 states signed the Convention on Biological Diversity—more commonly known as the Biodiversity Treaty. In 1993 when Bill Clinton became president of the United States the United States became a party to the convention. The treaty seeks to protect the habitats of endangered species by promoting national conservation programs that attempt to sustain biological diversity. A number of other treaties were agreed to earlier that deal with endangered species. One of the most well known is the Convention on the International Trade in Endangered Species (CITES) 1989 ban on ivory for instance. In many cases of items that are covered by different CITES, export and import permits are required or complete trade bans exist. Since the Earth Summit in 1992 there also have been a number of public campaigns to protect the rainforests. These campaigns included boycotts of imports from certain countries along with demand that wood imports come from sustainably managed forests. In 1995 the CSD established an Intergovernmental Panel on Forests to promote forest sustainability. However, since 1997 the panel's recommendations about sustainability have encountered stiff opposition from those concerned about sovereignty and trade.[28]

CASE STUDY: OCEAN NUCLEAR WASTE DUMPING

Along with deforestation, the problem of ocean waste dumping has also climbed high on the international environmental agenda. Like the other two cases, politics and economics play important roles as both causes and solutions to what many increasingly perceive as a severe global problem linked to many other issues. Aside from accidental oil spills that have become quite common these days, the United States, Great Britain, France, and the ex-Soviet Union have dumped large amounts of nuclear waste into different areas of the ocean since the mid-1940s.

In 1946, the United States began dumping low-level radioactive waste near the Farallon Islands west of San Francisco. Since then, the barrels have corroded and leaked. The International Atomic Energy Agency (IAEA) banned the dumping of high-level radioactive waste in the late 1950s. For the next 20 years, Belgium, France, Germany, Italy, Japan, South Korea, the Netherlands, New Zealand, Sweden, Switzerland, and Great Britain admitted to having dumped nuclear waste into the ocean. Up until 1970, the United States allowed dumping of radioactive waste at sites in the Pacific, Atlantic, and Gulf of Mexico. The practice was later abandoned, and in 1988, Congress enacted the Ocean Dumping Ban Act in an effort to end the dumping of industrial waste and sewage sludge at sea. The Soviet Union claimed to have never dumped radioactive waste at sea, but after the Soviet Union broke up, Russian officials admitted having done so. By some estimates, the Soviet Union dumped more nuclear waste into the ocean than the total of all other nations combined.[29]

As in the cases of greenhouse gases and deforestation, the issue of nuclear waste dumping is part of a broader set of environmental issues. Chemicals, solids, and nutrients from agricultural runoff, oil and gas development, logging, dredging, filling, and mining are routinely dumped directly into the ocean or otherwise end up in rivers and streams and make their way to the world's oceans.[30] Some of the effects of ocean pollution include destruction of the world's fisheries, climate and sea level change brought on by changes in ocean temperature, and the destruction of salt marshes, mangrove swamps, coral reefs, and beaches, which means the loss of habitat and biological diversity.

The case of radioactive waste dumping in the ocean is as much, if not an even greater threat to these ecosystems. Many assume that because oceans are so vast, they can absorb any amount of pollution. Radioactive waste tends to be absorbed by clay on the ocean floor and spreads easily through "ocean storms." Even if the effects on humans of radioactive waste in the ocean are not completely understood, the possibility always exists that localized concentrations of nuclear waste could cause cancers in humans and damage ecosystems in as yet unpredicted ways.

In 1972, the London Dumping Convention was formed with a membership of 71 nations. In 1983, its members agreed to stop putting even low-level radioactive waste into the world's oceans. In November 1993, a new international convention was agreed to in London that permanently bans the dumping of radioactive waste at sea. Japan and the United States originally opposed the ban because they wanted to leave open the possibility of dumping low-level nuclear waste. Greenpeace and other environmental groups mounted a major campaign to support the ban. In October 1993, Greenpeace observed a Russian navy ship dumping radioactive waste into the Sea of Japan. Since then, both Japan and the United States have reversed their positions. The Clinton administration declared that "the nuclear powers have a special responsibility to display leadership on sensitive ocean environmental issues."[31] Meanwhile Britain, France, and Belgium reserved the right to opt out of the agreement after 15 years.

Britain, France, and China have no secure method of waste disposal. The United States has been forced to bury its contaminated submarine reactors in the sand at a site in Hanford, Washington, after moving the reactors by barge up the Columbia River. Many suspect that China dumps its waste down wells and mines or buries it in Tibet. Meanwhile, the Russians still have a total of 407 reactors that produce 26,000 cubic meters of liquid and solid reactor waste each year. Russia has asked the international community for aid in disposing of its nuclear waste, threatening to continue dumping in the ocean if it is not forthcoming. The United States has offered Russia $800 million to help deactivate its nuclear weapons as part of the Strategic Arms Reduction Treaty but is cool about helping with the problem of naval waste.

SOLUTIONS: A GREEN IPE?

Global warming, deforestation, and nuclear waste dumping in the ocean all exhibit the tendencies of increasing severity, global scope, proliferation of actors, and linkages to other problems. Like so many other environmental problems, these three have been very difficult to solve. Yet the four characteristics of each problem we have discussed may actually force nation-states and other actors, with the assistance of international organizations, to compromise or otherwise find real solutions to them.

In considering solutions to these and other related issues, experts, officials, and activists must consider a number of questions. Who is most likely to pay the political and economic costs associated with solving these problems? Will new technologies help solve environmental problems or simply make them worse? Because issues are becoming more global in character, will solutions necessarily be most effective at the global or local level? Do international organizations have enough political authority and clout to design and implement global solutions? Or is attention on international organizations misplaced and better directed at nation-states—the basis of real political authority? And what about markets? Is there a positive role for the economy in solving environmental problems?

In an economic environment where pressure on the earth's resources is likely to continue to grow, will nation-states be willing to pursue objectives that do not require excessive amounts of natural resource consumption? This raises yet a more fundamental question: Can social values that emphasize economic growth and the consumption of industrially manufactured goods and services be reconciled with values that are more environmentally friendly? We will try to briefly answer some of these questions, focusing on the most-often proposed solutions to environmental problems and on the role the international political economy plays in them.

Limit Population Growth

Population certainly plays a role in making demands on the environment. However, there is still no conclusive evidence that overpopulation itself is a *global* problem at this point (see chapter 18). Population growth patterns and forecasts are an aggregation of population growth trends in different nations and regions of the world. The claim that environmental problems result primarily from increased industrial activity that stems from population growth assumes that the growing number of people in the future will have the income to make demands on their economy for more energy and food resource products.

Most of the world's poor live in developing regions of the world and do not have that much economic influence. Reduced population in a society does not necessarily mean that people will consume fewer resources. In many cases increased industrial activity is a result of increased demand and consumption by a relatively wealthy minority. As a result of increased income and living standards, people in the newly industrialized countries have been able to demand more industrial goods and products associated with the developed countries. And of course, as economic development continues to spread, so will the ability of more people to consume the earth's resources.

The *demographic transition* promises that population growth rates will slow down naturally as people's income and standard of living increase (see chapter 18). From this perspective the population problem is actually a political economic problem of an unequal distribution of wealth between the have and have-not nations of the world accompanied by an unequal distribution of income within many developing societies. Many states in developing nations are quite authoritarian in nature and pursue development strategies that emphasize economic growth and the postponement of meeting people's basic needs (see chapter 15).

Ironically, it was the industrialized democratic Western nations that promoted that model of development after World War II, for a variety of reasons related to national security and the preservation of capitalism (see chapter 9). Yet these objectives have been attractive to many LDCs, not so much because officials had to deal with an overpopulated society, but because in many cases such as the Philippines and Indonesia for example, they matched the political and economic interests of society's elite.

Does that mean that nothing should be done about current overpopulation problems in different nations? Not surprisingly, officials in some countries have tried to increase their population due to a lack of men for military service. Yet a good many nations still feel compelled to slow their population growth rate because of the economic burden more mouths make for society. Most have done this through education and providing people with birth control devices. In extreme cases such as China and India, however, officials in the past have resorted to forcing some women to have abortions, be sterilized, use contraceptives, or inserted birth control devices into them without their knowledge.[32] For many humanists and culture experts, the empowerment of women and society's guarantee of political rights based on democratic principles are the best solution to the poverty and overpopulation problems.

Move Beyond the Nation-State:
International Organizations and Regimes

A popular recommendation is to shift political authority to bigger and more comprehensive units such as international organizations. The presumption is that these agencies will put cooperation and the interests of the globe ahead of national interests. The cases discussed above demonstrate that a number of international organizations have indeed been quite busy when it comes to the environment. As yet, however, there is little evidence that they have been effective outside of the desire of their members to solve common problems. Most of the time, agencies like UNEP lack funds and have served more as a forum for discussion than as an agent with real authority to assign costs or impose sanctions on those that damage the environment. This is not to say that international organizations are not important. Rather, they are as yet at the mercy of their nation-state creators. This situation stands to change as problems become more severe and states are unable to solve them. Necessity being the mother of invention, international organizations are likely to continue to be looked to as cooperative ventures in the solution to many environmental issues.

There are variations on this theme. One is that the agents most likely to help solve environmental problems are *regimes:* norms, principles, values, and decision-making procedures that surround an issue.[33] Some believe that a number of regimes have already formed around a number of different environmental issues.[34] What is not clear, though, is how much regimes matter apart from the activity of nation-states that comprise them. Some believe that hegemons (see chapter 9) are necessary to promote cooperation and maintain regime institutions and procedures. Another problem is the extent to which linkages between issue areas make it difficult to separate one regime from another. For instance, should nuclear waste dumping be considered its own regime or part of the Law of the Sea regime? It is likely that the term *regime* will continue to be used in recognition of the many principles, norms, values, and political institutions that already deal with such problems as global warming or deforestation. The existence and analytical utility of regimes have yet to be firmly established.

It seems most likely that future solutions to environmental issues must account for political and economic structures of the international system as conditioned largely by the distribution of wealth and power in the world or by a hegemon. At present, it appears that the international system is shifting away from a Cold War structure toward some type of, for lack of a better term, "new world order." As with the case of so many environmental issues and its behavior at the UN Rio Conference in 1992, it appears that the United States does not want to be a hegemon, given the costs involved with that responsibility. On the other hand, President Clinton and his administration have made some effort to place the United States in a more active leadership role when it comes to dealing with global environmental problems. This does not mean that the United States will not put some of its own economic interests before environmental interests, as it did in the NAFTA (see chapter 12) and Uruguary round trade talks (see chapter 6).

Ironically, the fact that there is presently no firm international security structure in place may be good for the environment. At this time, environmental issues are more than likely to be high on the international agenda given that that agenda is not at present completely dominated by security issues as it was during the Cold War. The increasing severity and scope of environmental issues compel many states to redefine national security and economic growth. These older objectives will not be cast aside but must be balanced with environmental considerations.

Markets for the Environment

Another solution to environmental problems is the market. Its supposed benefits are its flexibility over more rigid command and control policies of states. Many economists argue that some environmental problems should be "privatized" or assigned "property rights," which would help overcome the *free rider problem*. Many economists have argued that government regulations do not work and that the market could be used as a mechanism to curb pollution by assigning permits to polluters. The Kyoto Protocol is to include the use of these permits thereby allowing states to sell or exchange with one another certain allowable amounts of pollution, hopefully lowering the overall level of pollution. Still another argument is that some problems are more costly to solve than others and that it would be more efficient to spend money on problems where the chances of achieving real success are greatest. Why spend billions on curbing greenhouse gases when it might be more efficient to purchase tropical forest reserves?

The market is usually not viewed as the best solution to environmental problems because economic costs of pollution are hard to calculate. Someone has to impose sanctions on violators or assign property rights, and that is usually the state. Once again, the economy does not operate in a political vacuum. Governments must balance the costs and benefits of any environmental problem. Despite the limits of the market, any realistic solution to the problem must include considerations about who pays and how far the money is likely to go to do what. Most experts want to use the market to stimulate people and nations to conserve resources or cut down on pollution.

A New Vision

This argument has received quite a bit of attention lately, and it takes many forms. Dennis Pirages made popular the idea of *ecopolitics*.[35] He argues that values associated with economic growth and technological fixes will not sustain the planet in the twenty-first century. Although not explicit as to exactly what objective should be pursued, Pirages argues that, along with literacy and democracy, the dominant social paradigm of the next century must reconcile limited energy resources with increasing demand for economic growth.

A number of critics have always been cynical about capitalism and its impact on the environment. Yet no comprehensive political economic systems have been developed so far as an alternative to what remains the most attractive economic system in the world. Others move further beyond discussions of the immediate political economy into the realm of religion and philosophy. A growing number of Christian communities emphasize the value of stewardship and trusteeship over the earth and its resources. Increasingly, more emphasis is put on sustaining the quality of life and replacing consumerism with an appreciation for respect and community with nature, instead of control over it.[36]

Sustainable Development

A general consensus has emerged that one of the most important goals of nation-states and international organizations must be the pursuit of sustainable development. As we enter the next century, the most often asked and pressing environmental question is: How do nation-states and other political actors create wealth for today's generations without at the same time leaving a despoiled and depleted environment for future generations?

The latest effort to answer this question was made at the UN Conference on Environment and Development that met in Rio de Janeiro in June 1992. There the members present at the "Earth Summit" created the Commission on Sustainable Development to oversee provisions of Agenda 21, a 500-page blueprint for sustainable development. Some of the measures of Agenda 21 read like updated versions of the New International Economic Order (NIEO) provisions of the mid-1970s (see chapter 15) including efforts to accelerate sustainable development through international economic policies that include LDC access of their exports to the industrialized nations and debt relief measures; and meeting basic human needs in the provision of food, clean drinking water, sanitation, and waste management. Agenda 21 though blends these economic development measures with many provisions for protecting the environment including promoting consumption and production patterns and the education of people in order to reduce environmental stress in national policies and strategies.[37] The Agenda seeks to accomplish these objectives through a combination of government-designed and -implemented programs complemented by market activities. Clearly, Agenda 21 reflects an attempt to accommodate the interests of the Northern industrialized nations to the Southern developing nations.

Agenda 21 makes a decided effort to involve a wide range of actors in achieving sustainable development. These actors include the appropriate international organizations and nation-states, and also a large number of NGOs represented by some 20,000 delegates at Rio. Some experts have come to believe that many environmental problems are best solved "at the most decentralized level of governance that is consistent with efficient performance of the task."[38] The intention is to involve as many people and grassroots groups as possible in solving environmental problems. Many international businesses have also made some commitment to sustainable development. Fifty chief executives of the world's largest corporations were active in the meetings preceding the Earth Summit. Although the Business Council for Sustainable Development opposed language in Agenda 21, it has advocated its own new standards to regulate international business and encourage the view that business practices should go hand-in-hand with environmental policies. Some lumber companies have made an effort to include environmental considerations and even the objective of sustainable development in their criteria for logging and other potentially damaging activities.[39]

Despite broad agreement as to the worthiness of sustainable development, actually achieving the objective is another matter. While a number of governments have adopted sustainable development as a national objective, Lester Brown and his associates at the Worldwatch Institute in Washington, D.C., continue to argue that the world lacks the political will to formulate and follow through on the measures enunciated in Agenda 21.[40] Others believe that the Earth Summit might end up on the rocks of history if the political and economic relationships of the North to the South are not fundamentally transformed into a more cooperative and less polarized, confrontational relationship.[41]

And finally, three skeptical scientists argue that not enough is currently known to account for the normal fluctuations in nature to specify what a sustainable condition looks like. They suggest that science is probably incapable of predicting safe levels of resource exploitation. And even if accurate predictions were possible, history shows that human shortsightedness and greed almost always lead to overexploitation, often to the point of collapse of the resource.[42]

CONCLUSION

Many environmental problems are becoming more global and more severe all the time, compelling nations and other political-economic actors to deal with them.[43] The international system is going through fundamental changes that require actors to broaden the conception of their interests to include those that are environmental in nature and scope. Despite the interest in new political, economic, and social values, there has yet to develop an alternative set of ideas that comfortably wed modern industrial society with the idea of preserving the environment. Efforts to deal with environmental threats to both nature and mankind are helping transform the international production, finance, security, and knowledge structures. Even if all the facts are not in, or there is no consensus as to the significance of those facts, for the time being it would probably not hurt us to do as much as we can to limit damage to the environment—adopting a "no regrets" policy outlook.[44] Likewise, even if we cannot as yet determine how efficient or effective some environmental policies and programs are, their implementation will help limit damage to the environment.

The international political economy remains a source of many global environmental problems. It is also an integral part of any solution to those problems. While scientists and officials have yet to completely understand and explain many of these problems, it is painfully clear that in the future the study of international political economy cannot ignore its green dimensions.

DISCUSSION QUESTIONS

1. Outline and discuss the tragedy of the commons and the prisoners' dilemma. In what ways do these concepts contribute to our understanding of environmental problems?

2. The authors assert that environmental problems have become increasingly global in scope. What factors—political, economic, social—contributed most to this trend? Explain. *(Note:* The category economic includes such items as trade and finance and also the role of knowledge and technology.)

3. Examine each of the three case studies (global warming, deforestation, and ocean dumping) in terms of:
   a. the source of the problem—political, economic, social?
   b. the major actors and their interests in the problem.
   c. potential solutions to the problem, noting the tension between issues related to economic growth and the goal of sustainable development.

4. Review the box on UNEP. Discuss the factors and conditions that have compelled international organizations to increasingly play a larger role in dealing with environmental problems, and also what conditions and factors limit their effectiveness.

5. After reading the entire chapter, discuss the assertion by Lester Brown that we lack the political will to solve environmental problems. Do you agree or disagree? Explain. What other things would you say that we lack or need in order to solve these problems?

INTERNET LINKS

UNEP: http://www.unep.org

A Guide to the Kyoto Summit: http://www.oneworld.org/guides/kyoto/front.html

Worldwatch Institute: http://www.worldwatch.org

Center for Sustainable Development in the Americas: http://www.csdanet.org/home.html

Worldwide Web Virtual Library Sustainable Development Index:
   http://www.ulb.ac.be/ceese/meta/sustvl.html

SUGGESTED READINGS

Robin Brand and John Cavanagh. "Beyond the Myths of Rio: A New American Agenda for the Environment," *World Policy Journal* 10 (Spring 1993), pp. 65-72.

Frances Caircross. *Costing the Earth.* Cambridge, MA: Harvard Business School Press, 1992.

Lynton Caldwell. *International Environmental Policy: Emergence and Dimensions.* Durham, NC: Duke University Press, 1984.

Alfred Crosby. *Ecological Imperialism and the Biological Expansion of Europe, 900–1900.* New York: Cambridge University Press, 1986.

Thomas Homer-Dixon. "On the Threshold: Environmental Changes As Causes of Acute Conflict," *International Security* 16 (Fall 1991), pp. 76–116.

Jessica Tuchman Mathews. "Environmental Policy." In Robert J. Art and Seyom Brown, *U.S. Foreign Policy: The Search for a New Role.* New York: Macmillan, 1993.

Dorella H. Meadows, Dennis L. Meadows, Jorgen Randers, and William W. Brehens III. *The Limits to Growth: A Report for the Club of Rome Project on the Predicament of Mankind.* New York: Universe Books, 1974.

Mirian A. L. Miller. *The Third World in Global Environmental Politics.* Boulder, Co: Lynne Rienner, 1995.

William Ophuls. *Ecology and the Politics of Scarcity.* San Francisco: W. H. Freeman, 1977.

Dennis Pirages. *The New Context for International Relations: Global Ecopolitics.* North Scituate, MA: Duxbury Press, 1978.

———. *Global Technopolitics: The International Politics of Technology and Resources.* Pacific Grove, CA: Brooks/Cole, 1989.

Gareth Porter and Janet Welsh Brown. *Global Environmental Politics*. 2d ed. Boulder, CO: West-view Press, 1996.

Michael Redclift. *Sustainable Development: Exploring the Contradiction*. New York: Methuen, 1987.

Scientific American. *Managing Planet Earth*. New York: W. H. Freeman, 1990.

Marc Williams. "International political economy and global environmental change," in John Vogler and Mark F. Imber (eds.) *The Environment of International Relations* (London: Routledge, 1996) pp. 41–58.

NOTES

1. Our thanks to Kristine Kalanges and Sarah Garfunkel for research assistance on this chapter.
2. Ronald Bailey, *Eco-Scam: The False Prophets of Ecological Apocalypse* (New York: St. Martin's Press, 1993), p. 2.
3. See Garrett Hardin, "The Tragedy of the Commons," *Science*, 13 December 1968, pp. 1243–1248.
4. See John Holusha, "The Next Refrigerator May Take a Step Back," *New York Times*, 4 March 1989, p. A37.
5. See, for example, Rachael Carson, *Silent Spring* (Boston: Houghton-Mifflin, 1962).
6. Donella H. Meadows, Dennis L. Meadows, Jorgen Randers, and William W. Brohens III, *The Limits to Growth: A Report for the Club of Rome Project on the Predicament of Mankind* (New York: Universe Books, 1974).
7. See the Council on Environment Quality and Department of State, *The Global 2000 Report to the President: Entering the Twenty-First Century* (New York: Penguin Books, 1982).
8. Julian Simon and Herman Kahn, eds., *The Resourceful Earth: A Response to Global 2000* (Oxford: Basic Blackwell, 1982).
9. For more discussion of this report, see Jim MacNeill, "Strategies for Sustainable Economic Development," in Scientific American, *Managing the Planet Earth* (New York: W. H. Freeman, 1990), pp. 109–124.
10. Cited in Jessica Tuchman Mathews, "Environmental Policy," in Robert J. Art and Seyom Brown, eds., *U.S. Foreign Policy: The Search for a New Role* (New York: Macmillan, 1993), p. 234.
11. For a critical examination of how states differ in their outlook about environmental problems see Detlef Sprinz and Tapani Vaahtoranta, "International Environmental Policy" *International Organizations* 48 (Winter 1994), pp. 77–106.
12. See "U.S. Having Won Changes, Is Set to Sign Law of the Sea," *New York Times*, 1 July 1994, p. A1.
13. See Paul Wapner, "Politics Beyond the State: Environmental Activism and World Civil Politics," *World Politics* (April 1995), p. 311.
14. Jessica Tuchman Mathews, "Environmental Policy," p. 239.
15. See Michael G. Renner, "Military Victory, Ecological Defeat," *World Watch* (July/August 1991), pp. 27–33.
16. For a detailed discussion of efforts to reconcile trade and environmental issues in the GATT, see Daniel C. Esty, *Greening the GATT: Trade, Environment, and the Future* (Washington, DC: Institute for International Economics, 1994).
17. See www.wto.org/wto/environ/relation.htm.
18. See World Resources Institute, "Climate Change: A Global Concern" *World Resources 1990–91* (Washington, DC, 1990), p.14.
19. See "Scientists Warn Against Ignoring Climate Change," *New York Times*, 29 January 1999, p. A14.
20. Ibid.
21. Stephen H. Schneider, "The Changing Climate," in Scientific American, *Managing Planet Earth*, p. 30.
22. See Kim A. McDonald, "Debate Over How to Gauge Global Warming Heats Up Meeting of Climatolgists," *The Chronicle of Higher Education*, 5 February 1999, p. A17.

23. See "U.S. Signs A Pact To Reduce Gases Tied to Warming," *New York Times*, 13 November 1998, p. A1.

24. See "Big Problem, Big Problems: Getting to Work on Global Warming," *The New York Times*, 1 August 1998, p. E4.

25. World Resources Institute, "Climate Change," p. 15, Table 2.2. According to this report, the biggest contributors to the global greenhouse effect in 1987 were the United States, the former Soviet Union, Brazil, China, India, Japan, West Germany, and the United Kingdom.

26. Some Harvard University researchers have found that "temperate-zone forests may play a more important role in absorbing atmospheric carbon dioxide . . . than was previously believed." For a more detailed discussion of this finding, see "A Forest Absorbs More Carbon Dioxide Than Was Predicted," *New York Times*, 8 June 1993, p. C4.

27. "Rich and Poor Nations Close to Agreement on Forest-Preservation Pact," *Seattle Times*, 23 January 1994, p. A19.

28. See John Tessitor and Susan Woolfson, eds., *A Global Agenda: Issues Before the 52nd General Assembly of the United Nations* (New York: Rowman & Littlefield Publishers, 1997), p. 144.

29. "Extensive Dumping of Nuclear Waste," *New York Times*, 27 April 1993, p. A1.

30. "Most Ocean Pollution Starts on Land," *Christian Science Monitor*, 29 November 1993, p. 17.

31. "Ban on Dumping Nuclear Waste at Sea," *Christian Science Monitor*, 15 November 1993, p. 15.

32. "Third World Women Forced into Abortions, Sterilizations," *Seattle Times*, 10 July 1994, p. A9.

33. See Stephen Krasner, ed., *International Regimes* (Ithaca, NY: Cornell University Press, 1983).

34. See, for example, Oran Young, *International Cooperation: Building Regimes for Natural Resources and the Environment* (Ithaca, NY: Cornell University Press, 1989).

35. Dennis Pirages, *The New Context for International Relations: Global Ecopolitics* (North Scituate, MA: Duxbury Press, 1978).

36. See "Environmental Legacy," *Christian Science Monitor*, 1 December 1993, p. 22.

37. For a more detailed list of the items on Agenda 21, see "Agenda 21: The Cross-Cutting Edge of Sustainable Development," *United Nations Chronicle* (June 1992), p. 49.

38. Hilary F. French, "Forging a New Global Partnership," in Worldwatch Institute, *State of the World 1995* (New York: W. W. Norton, 1995), p. 171.

39. See "Rio Condor, An Experiment in Ecology," *Seattle Times*, 10 April 1994, p. B5.

40. French, "Forging a New Global Partnership," p. 171.

41. Robin Broad and John Cavanagh, "Beyond the Myths of Rio: A New American Agenda for the Environment," *World Policy Journal* 10 (Spring 1993), p. 72.

42. William K. Stevens, "Biologists Fear Sustainable Yield Is Unsustainable Idea," *New York Times*, 20 April 1993, p. B10.

43. See, for example, the yearly publication, *State of the World*, by the Worldwatch Institute in Washington, DC.

44. For a more detailed discussion of this policy, see C. Boyden Gray and David B. Rivkin, "A 'No Regrets' Environmental Policy," *Foreign Policy* 83 (Summer 1991), pp. 47–65.

20

Conclusion:
Where Do We Go
from Here?

OVERVIEW

This chapter looks back on some of the most important concepts and ideas we have studied in this text and discusses how the understanding of IPE you now have can help you make sense of the past, the present, and the future. The first section of the chapter reviews briefly the IPE approach and especially the mercantilist, economic liberal, and structuralist analytical perspectives. We then review and comment on the increasing connections between the four structures of IPE, namely the production, finance, knowledge and technology, and security structures that were developed in the first ten chapters of this text.

The second section of the chapter considers four important IPE issues or problems that are likely to shape and influence developments early in the next century. Finally, drawing on this discussion, in the last section of the chapter we examine four possible scenarios for how the international political economy could develop early in the next century that have some bearing on possible IPE scenarios that may develop in the near future.

> [IPE is] . . . a vast, wide open range where anyone interested in the behavior of men and women in society [can] roam just as freely as the deer and the antelope. There [are] no fences or boundary-posts to confine the historians to history, the economists to economics. Political scientists [have] no exclusive rights to write about politics, nor sociologists to write about social relations.
>
> Susan Strange[1]

This chapter is intended to help you in the transition from student of IPE to informed world citizen. You will be leaving the fenced-in territory of the academic world and entering the wide-open spaces of the real world. It is a big step. This chapter makes the transition in three steps. First, we look back at the basic method of IPE analysis that you have studied in this book. This is to remind you of the breadth and power of the IPE approach to the study of world problems and to caution you about some weaknesses, too.

Second, we consider briefly a few essential issues in IPE that shape or condition many of the issues and policies of today. This is to remind you of the fundamental tensions and complex interconnectedness that define IPE and the ways these tensions and connections reveal themselves in many parts of today's IPE. Finally, we will turn to a discussion of the future and examine four alternative scenarios of how these tensions could resolve themselves in the years ahead of us. This is to stimulate your thinking about what you have learned and how it can help you understand what sort of future you may experience.

THE IPE APPROACH: SOME CONCLUDING THOUGHTS

IPE gives the student great freedom to select an analytical approach that best suits a particular issue or answer a specific question about an actor or set of values. It is useful to do the following when studying any IPE issue: Look at that issue from several different angles or perspectives; consider how it is connected to other issues and how other matters are connected to it, examine the nature of the power relationships at play; and finally, ask who benefits from these relations as a way to stimulate analysis and prevent our work from becoming purely descriptive.

Theoretical Perspectives

The IPE approach begins by looking at problems and issues from several different points of view, trying to take into account all three levels of analysis (i.e., the individual, state, and international system). The three main theoretical perspectives discussed in this text were economic *liberalism, mercantilism* (and political realism), and *structuralism*. Each perspective focuses on different political actors and their unique relationship to the market and other economic activities. Each emphasizes different values and usually a preference of the political over the economic or vice versa. Each also has a unique outlook about how to solve problems today and what the future holds for individuals and society. On the other hand, each also obscures some important elements.

We propose that you consider the features of each of these perspectives, along with the traits of the other IPE perspectives outlined in chapter 5 before studying the problem at hand. In many cases it may be the elements of the issue at hand that fit one perspective better than another may. In other cases, the question(s) that interests you most will help determine which perspective(s) you employ in your analysis.

Structures and Arrangements

As we noted in chapter 1 and elsewhere in the text, the world of IPE is tightly interconnected, although it might be wrong to say that it is a "small world." States and markets are tied together through multiple overlapping sets of arrangements and relationships. The United States and China, for example, are connected simultaneously by a variety of production, finance, security, and knowledge relationships or arrangements. Some of these relationships reflect bargains and agreements strictly between these two nations (e.g., the United States and China), while others are bargains that affect or are affected by some of the many other actors in the IPE (e.g., multinational corporations, international banks, or any number of international organizations such as the United Nations). To truly understand any single aspect of U.S.-China relations, for example (see chapter 1), it is necessary to gain an appreciation of how the several structural layers are connected and the nature of their interaction.

The fundamental contribution of IPE to the study of the modern world has been its success in tearing down the fences that keep serious students from looking at the interconnectedness of the multiple overlapping structures that connect states, markets, and people. This helps us understand more clearly how an event that happens to someone or in someplace, that is seemingly unconnected to us, can have profound impact on us and on the world.

Types of Power

Once we understand that individuals and states are connected through structural systems, we can appreciate that there are two types of power that can be exercised. The first is called *relational power,* which is more or less what people think about as power in daily life: the ability to get someone to do something that you want them to do. Relational power is one-to-one power: your ability (or inability as the case may be) to get your boss to give you a raise, for example.

Once we understand how political, economic, and social structures work, however, we can also understand how *structural power* works. Structural power is the ability of actors like states and international organizations to cause something to happen because one's position within the structure allows an actor to either control or effectively condition the behavior of states and markets. The bourgeoisie are assumed to have power over the proletariat in Marxian analysis, for example, but it is not because they have guns and soldiers, but because of their place within the structure of capitalist production, upon which the proletariat depend for wages.

Cui Bono?

Finally, after we have examined an issue from the three perspectives, sought to understand the interconnectedness of the four structures, and determined the nature of the power systems at work, we are ready for the $64 question: Who benefits? This is the question that Susan Strange pointedly asked her students. *Cui Bono?*—Who ends up better off because the world is arranged in this particular way?

Cui Bono? is a question with an edge. It forces us out of a descriptive mode and into an analytical one. We are forced to make some judgments and to have some opinions. We are driven, in short, to think. For example, in the case of multinational corporations, it is often assumed that they benefit LDCs a great deal and can help them develop. In many cases however, the *Cui Bono* questions help us understand some of the complex issues surrounding the issue of MNC-LDC relations. In some cases MNCs do benefit some LDCs, but not in all cases. Yet, our analysis also reveals that it would be too simple to say that LDCs do not benefit from their relationship to MNCs. Furthermore, the answer we eventually arrive at might or might not be an intellectually satisfying one depending on which perspective or combination of perspectives we chose to analyze the issue. For reasons related to their values, liberals, for instance, are more prone to accept MNCs as beneficial to LDCs while structuralists are not. Liberals of course would focus on the economic gains to all the actors in the relationship, while structuralists would focus on resultant inequalities—who gained more at whose expense.

Strengths and Weaknesses of the IPE Approach

Let us consider briefly the strengths and weaknesses of the entire IPE approach just outlined. The strengths, which need little restatement at this point, are that IPE encourages us to consider different points of view, to draw on the tools and methods of different academic disciplines, to seek out the complex interconnections that characterize modern life, and define today's most interesting problem. Essentially, in our quest for understanding, our motto should be "don't fence me in."

We should beware of the weaknesses of the IPE approach however. There are more than just three valid perspectives to consider and we should avoid narrow-mindedly limiting ourselves in this regard. We have chosen in this textbook to focus on mercantilism, liberalism, and structuralism because they have been very important theoretical perspectives in the past—their interaction has shaped IPE and shaped human history, particularly in the twentieth century. The future is an open book, however, and there is nothing to say that these three perspectives will shape the future as much as they have the past. Thus we especially draw your attention to the four other IPE perspectives presented in chapter 5: the rational choice, feminist, green, and postmodern critiques of mainstream IPE thought. We can all use an open mind to see the world around us in new ways.

Another potential weakness of IPE is that we may fail to see the emergence of other IPE structures that are important. For example, personal linkages are becoming increasingly common and important as the world gets stronger. The media, through electronic communication, helps generate these linkages, but so do tourists or international business travelers, or immigrants on the move from village to city or from poorer nation to richer one.

Finally, and this is very serious, one weakness that international political economists must take seriously is that the flipside of breadth is depth. In IPE we are let loose on the fenceless prairie where we can take the long and broad view of world events. In doing so, however, we risk the natural tendency to sacrifice depth and rigor of analysis—and this we must avoid. This is the responsibility that comes with the freedom of IPE. Some details and descriptions of intricacies are needed if we are to explain, understand, and appreciate the relationship of different actors to one another and the impact the market and economy have on their behavior.

IPE TODAY: FOUR FUNDAMENTAL TENSIONS

There are many persistent problems, issues, and controversies in IPE today. Many of these have been discussed elsewhere in this book. For this concluding chapter, we have selected four fundamental and interrelated IPE tensions that are worthy of restatement and reconsideration in light of our discussion above about *how* to study IPE. The issues that we have chosen to highlight are as follows:

- First is fundamental tension between a state's domestic needs and its international obligations. How can states balance domestic needs and international obligations and what can they do when they conflict?
- Second is the continued tension between and among various elements of security, namely military, economic, and technological security. How secure can nations and other actors be within the complex framework of today's multilayered global security structure?
- Third is the question of the status of the nation-state in a world of economic *globalization*. Has the tension between state and market shifted decisively in the direction of the market? Is the state still relevant? Has the importance of the state's role increased, decreased, or changed?
- Fourth and finally, we want to examine the issue of *hegemony*. Can the international political economy manage itself or is leadership needed to provide stability and direction for states and markets? If a *hegemon is* needed, then which state or group of states has the wealth, power, and will to organize the IPE and provide international public goods such as security, a stable monetary system, and a workable system of international trade?

Domestic Needs versus International Responsibilities

One of the most difficult problems in IPE is how states are to achieve a stable balance between their domestic needs and international obligations. States need both to address the needs of their citizens for political and economic security and to live up to their responsibilities as participants in international agreements and organizations and members of the world community of nations. This tension that twists and pulls the nation-state mirrors the fundamental tension that all of us experience as we try to satisfy both our own needs and those of our families and friends as well as our responsibilities as members of a larger society.

The tension between domestic and international priorities is especially strong today. During the Cold War nations were driven by threats to their national security to place a high priority on their international obligations and good relations with their allies and other powerful nations. When the Berlin Wall fell in 1989, many people wrongly assumed that many international obligations would disappear, or at least be noticeably reduced, making room for increased attention to their domestic agendas. There was talk of a "peace dividend" in the Western industrialized nations because of reduced expenditures for national security.

The tension between domestic needs and international obligations has, if anything, increased since 1989. Without the threat of a common enemy to cause nations to be good citizens and to live up to their international obligations, the pull of serving domestic needs has seemingly increased, threatening the stability of the IPE.

The apparent conflict between international obligations and domestic needs is perhaps nowhere clearer than in the area of international trade. The GATT was established in the early postwar years to be a strong advocate of free trade and open markets. Membership in GATT gave countries access to foreign markets but imposed upon them the obligation to keep their own markets open and to reduce trade barriers through the multilateral GATT negotiation "rounds." This system was based partly on liberal ideas of free trade and partly on U.S. self-interest. In the early postwar years the United States stood to benefit from open global markets because of its unrivaled industrial economy. In a sense, the United States was able to advocate the free trade principles of the GATT at this time because there was no conflict between international obligations and domestic economic needs—both were served by free trade policies.

Tensions between domestic and international interests slowly built, however, as the U.S.-centered "workshop of the world" was gradually replaced with a more "global production line." Increased world trade no longer necessarily meant clear economic gains for the United States.[2] For other nations, which had always felt this problem, tensions intensified as the production process globalized and international competition increased.

There have been many reactions as nations have tried to balance an international commitment to free trade with the need to protect domestic jobs and industries. Regional trade groups such as the European Union and NAFTA, for example, can be seen as attempts to expand free trade on a regional basis without throwing open markets to the threat of global competition. Some nations—the United States and Japan are the most noteworthy examples—have supplemented the multilateral negotiations of the GATT with bilateral trade discussions. We have also seen an expansion of restrictive trade policies and neomercantilism.

The World Trade Organization (WTO) was created in part to be a stronger voice for free trade and open markets and as a way to make nations renew their commitment to this international goal. It remains to be seen, however, whether the WTO is a strong enough international force to offset the increasing demand for protectionism.

There are many views about how the tension between trade and jobs should be resolved. One view holds that free trade and domestic jobs are irreconcilable: That the tradition of advocating free trade must be abandoned in the interests of domestic prosperity. The state must step in to "manage trade" to keep jobs secure and also to help structure international political economic conditions in ways that are favorable to the nation.

An alternative view holds that free trade and jobs *can* be reconciled, but only if nations are willing to make the many changes and investments necessary to make the economy more productive. The United States for instance, would need to reduce its debts (especially the government budget deficit) and cut consumer spending to provide resources to invest in workers, factories, and technology. Proponents of this view call for an emphasis on "productivity" through investment rather than "competitiveness" through trade barriers.[3] Others, however, promote trade competitiveness through such efforts as breaking down regional trade barriers and extending free trade to the entire globe in multilateral forums like the WTO.[4]

Until the tension between free trade and domestic jobs is resolved one way or another, many nations face a difficult dilemma. Both domestic *and* international policies are bound to lack unassailable credibility when their foundations are weakened by such fundamental fissures as these.

Guns and Butter: Military Security versus Economic Security

The rise of economic globalization and the increasing stress on economic objectives have raised the tension between political or military security and economic security.[5] The focus of the Cold War was mainly on *hard power*. In the Cold War era ideas about national security were dominated by realists who usually thought of security as an objective a nation achieved by converting its population, territory, natural resources, economic size, and military force into tools that helped it secure its borders or control others. These "hard" elements produced "command" power in that results were achieved by punishing or rewarding other states.[6]

Since the end of the Cold War many experts have focused on *soft power*, which is composed of such things as technology, finance, a nation's position in the trade system, and even education and media influence. In a sense, the discussion has shifted (although incompletely) from an emphasis on the strategic use of hard **relational power** to the systematic use of soft *structural power*. In the words of Joseph Nye:

> If a state can make its power legitimate in the eyes of others, it will encounter less resistance to its wishes. If its culture and ideology are attractive, others will more willingly follow. If it can establish international norms that are consistent with its society, it will be less likely to have to change. If it can help support institutions that encourage other states to channel or limit their activities in ways the dominant state prefers, it may not need as many costly exercises of coercive or hard power in bargaining situations.[7]

The United States, according to this line of reasoning, gains structural power from its place within the international political, economic, technological, and cultural spheres. This structural power enhances U.S. security and furthers its interests. This point is obviously true, but how far can it be pushed? Does the fact that the people of the world use U.S.-based software, eat U.S.-based fast foods, and watch U.S.-based movies give the United States *much* greater power, influence, and security than it already has?

Perhaps it is true that guns (political and military security) are in the process of being replaced by butter (economic security) in the hierarchy of national priorities. But it would be a mistake to argue that military considerations in the twenty-first century will become wholly subordinate to economic concerns. If anything, the twenty-first century promises to further intertwine military and economic security issues with technological and other issues, making it even more difficult for nations to sort out one set of problems from another.

Globalization and the Nation-State Today

The third issue we want you to consider is the status of the nation-state in the global economy. In the past decade it has become a cliché to say that we live in the age of globalization. Certainly it is true that each of the IPE perspectives has become less distinctly national and more fundamentally global in your lifetime. The production structure has become more global. Multinational corporations (like McDonald's) and global commodity chains (like the market linkages that give us Nike products) are increasingly common, even if they do not yet dominate markets to the extent that some fear they eventually will. There is, increasingly, a global division of labor in the production of some goods and services.

The global web of the finance structure was established ahead of the production structure. Financial interdependence has reached a remarkable level, bringing with it riches and risks. Global finance exposes everyone to the potential of global economic crises and financial instability. The security structure has become global, too. Many issues of national security are, by their nature, beyond the scope of any individual state to resolve. In any case, states must play alongside a variety of other actors in matters of security. Finally, knowledge and technology both accelerate globalization of the other IPE structures and are increasingly becoming global themselves. Advances in computer science and telecommunications technology simultaneously increase the incentives of states to try to control access to knowledge, while making it seemingly impossible to do so.

Globalization also extends to other influences that are important even if they do not fit easily into the framework of four structures we have adopted here. The media, including entertainment and advertising, are more global than before, creating the first uncertain elements of global culture. (Certainly there are a few corporate logos, movie stars, and sports heroes—you can name them—that would be recognized in most places on the globe.) We are also beginning to realize that environmental problems are global in scope and that certain important environmental problems cannot be solved by either individuals or by nation-states alone.

Where does the nation-state fit into a world increasingly characterized by the forces and effects of economic globalization? As the market's domain grows beyond the borders of state authority, the state's ability to protect its interests and assure its economic security is seemingly diminished. In the extreme case, globalization could create a "borderless" economic world. What would be the relevance of a territorial state, whose authority is limited by its borders in such a world?

At one extreme, it has been argued that the state is becoming irrelevant, a slave to global market forces. If a nation tries to increase labor safety standards, for example, it risks a flight of jobs to foreign factories that do not regulate the workplace as tightly. If a nation tries to regulate industry to protect the environment, it faces the same dilemma. Business will take factories and jobs abroad to countries that do not impose high environmental standards. There are natural market forces at work that individual nations ignore at their peril. Markets rule and states must evolve and adapt to accommodate global market forces, it is argued. Since the 1980s the number of states that have adopted liberal, free-market policies is often cited as evidence of the "borderless world" theory of the decline of the nation-state.

Not everyone thinks that the nation-state is dead, however, and there are many reasons to think that the state is alive and well, albeit somewhat changed.[8] We will consider just three of them here. Certainly states retain a virtual monopoly on hard power and hard power still matters—conflict, war, and security remain very important concerns in the twenty-first century.

A second reason to believe in the relevance of the nation-state is that strong markets (even global ones) require strong states. Markets need states to provide security, to enforce laws, contracts, and property rights, and to regulate competitive market failures, which result in pollution or monopoly, for example. The discussion of intellectual property rights in chapter 10, for example, noted that global markets in high-technology products could exist only if states were strong enough to enforce property rights and prevent illegal patent, copyright, and trademark infringement.

Finally, it is a mistake to think that markets can change and shape the environment and that states simply and passively react to these changes. States can extend their authority in many ways, especially through their participation in international organizations and regional initiatives. The labor and environmental agreements that were part of the NAFTA treaty, for example, are examples of how state authority in North America was expanded to match the requirements of the growing regional economy.

Globalization doesn't affect the state the way that kryptonite affects superman, so it is too soon to write it off as a force in IPE. The state hasn't become powerless—it is, indeed, in many respects still the dominant player in IPE today—but the nature of state power *has* changed and the means by which its authority can be exercised is evolving. This forces us to consider the issue of state leadership.

The Leadership Problem: What about Hegemony?

A hegemon is a rich and powerful state that undertakes to organize the IPE by providing security and by setting and enforcing the "rules of the game" under which states and markets interact. The motives of the hegemon are its most controversial aspects. Does the hegemon act in enlightened self-interest—helping other countries because it knows that this is the best way to help itself? Or does it manipulate the system in order to increase its own wealth and power, to make other countries dependent upon it? Or is the hegemon just a tool of the global bourgeoisie class in the capitalist struggle against the proletariat? Scholars of the three perspectives will probably never agree about how and why a hegemon behaves the way it does.

There is greater agreement, however, about the importance of a hegemon. Periods of strong hegemony are often (but not always) associated with peace and prosperity. In those periods when no country has taken the international obligations of hegemony, chaos has sometimes (but not always) reigned. Compare the peace and prosperity of the years of British hegemony in the nineteenth century, for example, with the war and depression that followed in the period 1914–1945, when no international leader played the hegemon's part. Peace and prosperity returned, although not everywhere and not evenly, during the Cold War period.

Many wonder if the United States either wants or has the resources to lead the international political economy? This question has generated active debate among scholars and public officials during the last 25 years. To a great extent, the debate has focused on two related questions. Is the United States strong enough to lead? And who will act as hegemon if the United States lacks either the strength or the will to set the rules of the international political economy of the future? Clearly, Japan has no intention of assuming that role.

There are at least three sides to this debate over decline. Some scholars believe that the United States has entered a period of *absolute decline*, by which they mean that the United States is absolutely weaker than it was 20 or 30 years ago, and therefore too weak to be a global hegemon. Advocates of this viewpoint point to a variety of domestic public policies that would be better served than using those resources to provide leadership of the international political economy. They see the United States today as similar to Great Britain 100 years ago: well past its zenith, burdened by outdated roles and institutions, still influential, but not really very powerful.[9] This viewpoint was particularly prominent in the late 1980s and early 1990s when the U.S. economy was stagnant. Support for the absolute decline argument faded, however, when the United States entered a prolonged period of economic expansion during the Clinton administration.

A second and larger group of scholars believes that the United States is a victim of *relative decline*, not absolute decline. This is the notion that even if the United States has not lost wealth or power, other countries have caught up with it, creating a pluralist or multipolar international environment. The European Union and eventually perhaps China could stand alongside the United States. The United States is still one of many major powers in this environment, but its role is necessarily different from that of a hegemon.

Evidence in support of the relative decline hypothesis is easy to find. Other countries now have incomes that equal or exceed the U.S. average. More important, perhaps, is evidence that the United States is no longer the dominant force in international trade and finance. Japan and the EU seem able to compete with the United States head to head in these areas. Other countries have clearly caught up with the United States in some areas, if not all of them.

In his important book *The Rise and Fall of the Great Powers* historian Paul Kennedy argues that relative decline is perhaps inevitable. Hegemony is costly, and other nations take the benefits of a secure and prosperous world without necessarily paying their fair share of the costs. These other nations rise up and overtake the weary Titan. A more pluralist system necessarily emerges. What is important, then, is not that the hegemon withers away, which is nearly inevitable, but what sort of international structure replaces hegemony.[10]

Finally, a third group of scholars and policy makers insist that the United States is still the dominant force in the IPE today.[11] They make several good arguments. The first is that power in the IPE is both soft power (economics) and hard power (military power). No nation approaches the United States in its ability to mobilize hard power resources. If hard power counts, then no country comes even close to the United States in overall strength.[12] The antideclinists point to the 1991 Persian Gulf war and other military and humanitarian actions as evidence of continued U.S. hegemony. When real economic and political strength is needed, as in Kuwait or Kosovo, everyone looks to the United States. Finally, opponents of decline theories ask the question: If the United States is not the hegemon, who is? No nation seems to possess greater strength than the United States, making it, perhaps, hegemon by default because of, more than anything else, its great military power.

The decline debate is more than a battle of statistics and footnote references. Some worry therefore, that if the United States chooses not to remain a strong international force, the liberal international regime that emerged from Bretton Woods may be difficult to sustain much longer. Yet, if the United States were to choose to be a hegemon, a liberal world order would still be possible, provided the other major powers agree to comply with the U.S. version of that world order. However, hegemony is no guarantee of peace and prosperity. These questions force us to come to grips with the even deeper issue of choice. Are hegemons the result of conscious choices on the part of national leaders and their states? Or are they the result of systemic forces that compel one state or another to come forward and assume that role? David Calleo has dealt with this issue and argues that the major powers could choose to collectively manage the international political economy without a hegemon.[13] We shall see!

THE FUTURE? FOUR SCENARIOS

How will these and other fundamental IPE tensions play themselves out in the future? There is no way that we can predict the future, but it can be both fun and informative to brainstorm about where IPE will go in the future. Here we present four scenarios for you to ponder and critique.

Scenario 1: The Triumph of Global Liberalism

Many people believe that globalization is one of the dominant features of the post-Cold War world. The argument goes like this. Liberalism and globalization were the dominant forces in the IPE a century ago, but the forces of nationalism (the two world wars) and the conflict between liberalism and structuralism (the Cold War) drove the nations of the world apart. It took almost 100 years for us to learn that nationalistic mercantilism is destructive and that socialism, however useful as a philosophy or method of analysis, is not a practical system of political economy. We have learned that liberalism and globalization are the keys to freedom and economic prosperity.

Whether you believe in it or not, this idea is a powerful force in today's world. Let us suppose that globalization continues unabated for the next 25 years. What sort of world would result? It might well be a richer world. It would certainly be a less equal world—markets produce wealth, but they do not see to it that wealth is evenly distributed —that is the job of the state.[14] Would people be satisfied with higher absolute living standards, or would they be more concerned about the widening gap between rich and poor?

It might also be an economically less stable world. No nation-state can hope to even out the ups and downs in the global economy as Keynes proposed that they do with their own national economies.[15] Booms and busts could be more severe, unless some sort of global hegemon emerges to stabilize the world economy.

Would we be more secure? It depends upon what type of security you are talking about. In this scenario, the nations of the world would be so tightly intertwined economically that war would never pay—the economic consequences of enforcing national borders would be too great. So the nations of the world would avoid conflict, diffusing their differences over the multiple overlapping structures that unite them. Given the fundamental inequality of globalization, a different type of security may be sacrificed. Crime, terrorism, and internal revolt may replace international conflict as the principal security problem we face.

The triumph of globalization is thus an ambiguous condition. As individuals we might be richer but unable to enjoy fully our wealth because of personal and economic security concerns—crime and depression would haunt us. Call this the Age of Anxiety.

Scenario 2: Workers of the World Unite!

William Greider described another globalization scenario in his 1997 best-selling book *One World, Ready or Not: The Manic Logic of Global Capitalism*.[16] Greider provides a structuralist scenario for us to consider. Global capitalism makes the rich richer and the poor poorer. Footloose capital has the advantage over place-bound labor, however. Multinational firms set nations against one another in a bid for capital, technology, and jobs that global firms can provide. In a "race to the bottom," states will offer lower taxes, lower wages, lower benefits, lower labor standards, and lower environmental regulations in an attempt to attract foreign investment. Welcome to the world of the least common denominator—the lowest bidder gets the job.

Welcome once again to the world of Karl Marx! Would the workers of the world finally unite? Is a global revolution inevitable? Possible? Imminent? Reading Greider's book, it is easy to arrive at the conclusion that conditions for revolution are riper today than they were when Marx and Engels wrote the *Communist Manifesto*. Certainly capitalism has become a more potent global force today than it was in Marx's day, with all the costs and benefits that go along with it.[17]

Greider seems to advocate the rise of global labor unions as a countervailing force to the global corporations. Global power against global power—a whole new framework on which to negotiate the arrangements of production, finance, knowledge, and security. Even if Greider does not imagine revolution and the overthrow of capitalism, he does apparently envision a revolutionary change in the fundamental fabric of IPE. It is dialectical materialism on a global scale. This is the Age of Discontinuity.

Scenario 3: The Return of Nationalism

Does advancing globalization necessarily mean constantly increasing wealth? Many people seem automatically to assume this, perhaps taking for granted that globalization and the rise in U.S. stock prices during much of the 1990s are linked by some natural law. No one in Asia or Latin American would think this, however, as in the 1990s they experienced just how quickly globalized markets can cause both boom and bust. What would happen if a major global recession were to occur? How would that change our scenario?

MIT Professor Paul Krugman raised this question in his provocative 1999 book *The Return of Depression Economics*.[18] Much of the world's population, in fact, experienced economic collapse or stagnation during the "boom" years of the 1990s. How can we continue to believe in unending prosperity when we consider the harsh economic impact of the Asian Crisis on Japan and the Asian Tigers, for example, or if we ponder the continuing economic meltdown in Russia?

What do people do when a severe recession hits them—when they are forced to tighten their belts because of market forces beyond their control? What do they do when they are asked to sacrifice their children's futures to pay yesterday's bad debts?

The answer to this question in the 1930s was simple: They turned inward and became isolationist. Nationalism, either benign or corrosive, was the flavor of the decade and zero-sum mercantilism dominated every structure of IPE. Nations sacrificed their international responsibilities so they could look after the needs of domestic citizens and interests.

The return of nationalistic mercantilism would not be an unexpected outcome of a global recession. It would change everything, however. It would spell the end of liberal globalization and the beginning of an even more divided, even more conflict-prone IPE. This scenario is no more comforting than the first. In fact, given the wide proliferation of nuclear weapons today, this scenario is positively scary. The Age of Anxiety becomes the Era of Paranoia.

MAD MONEY

"There are now two serious threats that jeopardize civilization and the life chances of our children and grandchildren—both "threats without enemies."[a] The biggest threat—a long-term threat, wrote Susan Strange shortly before her death in 1998, was environmental.[b] In the long term, the innocent actions that we each take individually could collectively alter the global environment and put life as we know it on earth at risk (see chapter 19). One of the great challenges of IPE today is to consider how risks to our security that threaten us at the *global* level, but that arise, fundamentally, from acts that we take at the *individual* level can adequately be addressed by *states*, which lie in the uncertain territory between the two. Because, despite the rise of international organizations and transnational nongovernmental organizations, states remain the fundamental institutions of governance in the world today.

The environment is clearly a global threat that is not matched by any sort of organized global response. But not the only one.

The second threat to civilization and to future generations, Strange wrote, is a short-term threat: the threat of global financial collapse. In her 1986 book on this subject, Susan Strange has proposed that the increasingly deregulated financial markets had been transformed from what we might call (following Lenin) financial capitalism to what Strange called *Casino Capitalism*.[c] The financial system had become a great casino, where people bet on the red (market up) or the black (market down), not on the investment decisions of real people. In becoming a casino, she worried, the financial markets had ceased to play their critical role in the capitalist system, the efficient use of scarce resources to make investments today that will benefit society in the future.

Writing 12 years later in 1998, Strange was even more pessimistic. Financial markets have deteriorated. They are no longer casinos, according to Strange, because even casinos are rational institutions that can be understood abstractly according to the laws of chance and outcome. We have entered the age of *Mad Money*, she argued. Finance is global, beyond the ability of individual nation-states to stabilize or control. Indeed, as Benjamin Cohen has argued, the "geography" of money has changed—no nation can really control money's power any more, not even its own money.[d]

Global financial markets have become more and more unstable. Financial crises, like the Asian Crisis, of 1997–98, seem inevitable in this chaotic environment. (See chapter 8 for a discussion of global finance and financial crises.)

It would not matter very much that global money is mad if financial markets were isolated institutions—like riverboat casinos—and affected only those who choose to get on board. But financial markets are at the heart of the capitalist system. The finance structure is interwoven with the security, production, and knowledge structures. The finance structure cannot collapse without pulling down elements of the other structures and changing in very significant ways the very nature of the IPE as we know it. Maybe Strange exaggerates when she says that global financial collapse is a threat to "civilization," but maybe not.

Like the environment, mad money is a global problem caused by the actions of individuals. The responsibility for regulating financial markets to prevent panic and crisis, according to such IPE notables as Walter Bagehot and John Maynard Keynes, falls on the state. But, Strange argues, states have systematically backed away from this responsibility in recent years as they embrace free market ideology in an attempt to reap the benefits of globalization.

Can states reverse direction and impose a governance structure on financial markets to reduce the risk of global collapse? Perhaps they cannot, Strange writes; states may not any longer have enough power to regulate financial markets. Or perhaps they will not, she argues, because their political leaders are unwilling to do so.

She ends her book, then, on an uncharacteristically pessimistic note:

Our problem in the next century is that the traditional authority of the nation state is not up to the job of managing mad international money, yet its leaders are instinctively reluctant to entrust that job to unelected, unaccountable (and often arrogant and myopic) bureaucrats. We have to invest a new kind of policy but we cannot yet imagine how it might work. Perhaps, therefore, money has to become really very much more mad and bad before the experience changed preferences and policies.[e]

At the beginning of this chapter we quoted Susan Strange on the benefits of an intellectual frontier free of fences. We have discussed why IPE is and needs to be a fence-free zone of thoughtful inquiry. But fences, which represent the negotiated boundaries of political control, still have their place. Ironically, in *Mad Money* we perceive Strange's fear—that because you cannot fence either the global environment or global financial markets, they will fall victim to some variation on the tragedy of the commons theme, with dire consequences for society.

---

[a] Susan Strange, *Mad Money: When Markets Outgrow Governments.* (Ann Arbor: University of Michigan Press, 1998), p. 2.
[b] Susan Strange (1923–1998) was a founder of contemporary IPE. She was at her death professor of international political economy at the University of Warwick. Many of today's IPE scholars benefited from her warm heart and sharp critical eye.
[c] Susan Strange, *Casino Capitalism* (Oxford: Blackwell, 1986). This is probably her best-known and most influential book.
[d] See Benjamin J. Cohen, *The Geography of Money* (Ithaca, NY: Cornell University Press, 1998).
[e] Susan Strange, *Mad Money*, p. 190.

Scenario 4: Surprise!

We cannot go to the library and find a book that tells the future, but we *can* look up the history of futures past. Reading history, we can discover what people at different times expected of the future and then see if they got what they expected. The modern era has been filled with writers' dreams of what's to come, from Jules Verne to John Maynard Keynes.[19] What we learn from this study of the history of the future is that, when the future finally appeared, people were surprised by it. The future that appeared was different than the one they expected. As Kenneth Boulding wrote, "The safest way to prepare for the future is to prepare to be surprised, as you surely will be."[20]

Any number of unexpected events could change the course of history and turn the first three scenarios discussed here into just so much recyclable paper. Without going into too much detail, let us consider the possibility of a Surprise Scenario. One surprise, for example, would be the reemergence of a bipolar security structure such as the one that characterized the Cold War years. Contemporary writers frequently preface their remarks by saying, "Now that the Cold War is over . . ."—but what if it got started again? The Soviet Union is gone, but Russia remains a potent force, with a large population, vast geography, and large quantities of natural and human resources. It is also still equipped with a large number of nuclear weapons. If not the Russian surprise, then perhaps a Chinese surprise awaits us.[21] If China's political and economic relations with the West deteriorated, then another Cold War standoff could result.

The reemergence of OPEC or the rise of another resource-based cartel is another Surprise Scenario. OPEC's power has waned since the 1970s, but dependence on oil imports is such today that just a few unexpected economic or political events could once again put OPEC in the driver's seat of IPE. Who knows what group might set OPEC policy, and to what end?

Not all surprises are unhappy ones, however. Thomas Malthus, writing at the end of the eighteenth century, foresaw a world of overpopulation, starvation, and unrelenting violence. When it came around, however, the future was much different. The rising population, which Malthus saw as the main problem, was accompanied by technological improvements in farming, industry, and transportation. A number of relatively small improvements in science and industry combined could create something of a golden age. If peace and prosperity were not always and everywhere present, they were certainly far more prevalent than Malthus expected.

CONCLUSION: DAYS OF FUTURES PAST

At the Great Depression's darkest hour, John Maynard Keynes penned an essay called "Economic Possibilities for our Grandchildren," in which he speculated about the future of you who now read this book. Keynes wrote that the problem that preoccupied his times—the *economic* problem of unemployment—was temporary. Looking 100 years ahead, he saw economic growth sufficient to meet the material needs of humans. With material want cured, he believed, we could turn our attention to more serious concerns about human existence.

For Keynes, the *pace* at which we can reach our destination of economic bliss will be governed by four things—our power to control population, our determination to avoid wars and civil dissensions, our willingness to entrust to science the direction of those things which are properly the concern of science, and the rate of accumulation [saving]. Meanwhile, there will be no harm in making mild preparations for our destiny, in encouraging and experimenting in the arts of life as well as the activities of purpose.[22]

Keynes was an optimist. If he could look back today on this 1930 essay, he might well be surprised. The advance of science and technology has been impressive and is more important today than ever before. Hunger and population, war and revolt, and the problems of saving and debt remain however, limiting progress toward "economic bliss." Even so, Keynes might remain a confident optimist, knowing that the enemies of progress are fear, uncertainty, and doubt.[23]

The future *is* uncertain. Fear and doubt are justified. The best way to prepare for an unknowable fate is with knowledge, and that has been the goal of this text and chapter. We hope that this book has given you some tools you can use to grasp and understand some of the most important and vital issues of international political economy. The twentieth century was a century of great change. One thing we are sure of is that change will continue, even at accelerated rates.

The readers of this book have a personal stake in what happens in the IPE of the future. It is important that we continue to study the events, issues, and forces that shape the environment of our daily lives. It is critical to appreciate change and to be able to interpret its effects. It is also important that we have opinions—informed opinions—about these things. Armed with understanding, the future is yours—go for it!

DISCUSSION QUESTIONS

1. Review the basic elements and features of the IPE approach: the three main theoretical perspectives, four structures, and types of power. Which ones do you feel most comfortable and uncomfortable with? Discuss the connection between how comfortable you are and your own values related to IPE.
2. Briefly outline the four fundamental tensions states are likely to encounter in the near future. Which do you feel are most important? Explain. Discuss the connections between all four of these tensions.
3. Is globalization a positive or a negative force in the world today? Explain, citing both theoretical arguments and personal observations.
4. This chapter ends with four scenarios for the future. Compare and contrast these different visions of the future. Which do you think is the most likely? Explain. Why does it matter which of these scenarios (or other set of conditions) actually occurs? How does what happens in the IPE affect you? Explain.

INTERNET LINKS

The Center for the Study of Alternative Futures:
    http://www.csaf.org/csafpage.htm
SPACECAST 2020 Alternative Futures page:
    http://www.au.af.mil/Spacecast/alt-futr/alt-futr.html
The Globalization Forum:
    http://www.lexusandtheolivetree.com/disc1_frm.htm

SUGGESTED READINGS

Benjamin J. Cohen. *The Geography of Money.* Ithaca NY: Cornell University Press, 1998.
William Greider. *One World, Ready or Not: The Manic Logic of Global Capitalism.* New York: Simon & Schuster, 1997.
Paul Hirst and Grahame Thompson. *Globalization in Question.* Oxford: Polity Press, 1996.
Paul Krugman. *The Return of Depression Economics.* Cambridge MA: MIT Press, 1999.
Richard C. Longworth. *Global Squeeze: The Coming Crisis for First-World Nations.* Chicago IL: Contemporary Books, 1998.
P.J. O'Rourke. *Eat the Rich: A Treatise on Economics.* New York: Atlantic Monthly Press, 1998.
Dani Rodrik. *Has Globalization Gone Too Far?* Washington DC: Institute for International Economics, 1997.
Susan Strange. *Mad Money: When Markets Outgrow Governments.* Ann Arbor: University of Michigan Press, 1998.

NOTES

1. Susan Strange, ed., *Paths to International Political Economy* (London: George Allen & Unwin, 1984), p. ix.
2. For example, some ships today arrive at west coast U.S. ports to unload manufactured goods from Asia; they return with their cargo holds full of waste cardboard, to be recycled

into new boxes abroad. This uncharacteristic "trash for cash" trade, whatever its origins or logic, seems an unlikely source of high-paying jobs for U.S. college graduates.

3. Paul Krugman is a leading advocate of this viewpoint. In his *Peddling Prosperity* (New York: Norton, 1994), he criticizes political entrepreneurs who "sell" trade policy as a patent medicine cure for economic woes.

4. See, for example, C. Fred Bergsten "Globalizing Free Trade," *Foreign Affairs* 75 (May/June 1996), pp. 16-37.

5. For a more detailed discussion of this subject, see Peter F. Drucker, "The Global Economy and the Nation-State," *Foreign Affairs* 76 (September/October 1997), pp. 159–171.

6. Joseph S. Nye, Jr., "The Changing Nature of World Power," *Political Science Quarterly* 105 (Summer 1990), pp. 177–192.

7. Ibid., p. 182.

8. See, for example, Linda Weiss, *The Myth of the Powerless State* (Ithaca, NY: Cornell University Press, 1998).

9. See David Calleo, *The Bankrupting of America: How the Federal Budget Is Impoverishing the Nation* (New York: William Morrow and Company, 1992). Calleo is more an advocate of the relative decline hypothesis, but in this notable study, he provides a good deal of evidence of decline.

10. Paul Kennedy, *The Rise and Fall of the Great Powers* (New York: Random House, 1987).

11. See, for example, Susan Strange, "The Persistent Myth of Lost Hegemony," *International Organization* 41 (August 1987), pp. 551–574.

12. See Henry R. Nau, *The Myth of America's Decline* (New York: Oxford University Press, 1990).

13. See David Calleo, "Can the U.S. Afford the New World Order," *SAIS Review* 12 (Summer/Fall 1992), pp. 23–33.

14. See Dani Roderick, *Has Globalization Gone Too Far?* (Washington, DC: Institute for International Economics, 1997).

15. See, for example, Richard C. Longworth, *Global Squeeze: The Coming Crisis for First-World Nations* (Chicago, IL: Contemporary Books, 1998).

16. William Greider, *One World, Ready Or Not: The Manic Logic Of Global Capitalism* (New York: Simon & Schuster, 1997).

17. For another provocative piece on this subject, see Ethan B. Kapstein, "Workers and the World Economy" *Foreign Affairs* 75 (May/June 1996), pp. 16–37.

18. Paul Krugman, *The Return Of Depression Economics* (Cambridge, MA: MIT Press, 1999).

19. Indeed, thinking about the future is the essential aspect of the modern era. Premodern humans lived in a world of fundamental changelessness. For them, the future was the past, so they seldom imagined a different world.

20. Kenneth E. Boulding, *Beasts, Ballads, and Bouldingisms: A Collection of Writings by Kenneth E. Boulding*, ed. Richard P. Beilock (New Brunswick, NJ: Transaction, 1980), p. 175.

21. See, for example, Richard Bernstein and Ross Munro, *The Coming Conflict with China* (New York: Alfred Knopf, 1997).

22. John Maynard Keynes, "Economic Possibilities for our Grandchildren," in *Essays in Persuasion* (New York: W. W. Norton, 1963), p. 373.

23. Keynes wrote about fear, uncertainty, and doubt as limits on self-interested action in his *General Theory of Employment, Interest, and Money* (New York: Harcourt Brace Jovanovich, 1964).

Glossary

Absolute decline The idea that a nation's wealth and power have fallen in absolute terms, measured by factors such as falling GDP, for example.

Appreciate A term used in foreign exchange markets when one currency rises in value relative to another currency. See *Depreciate.*

Asia-Pacific Economic Cooperation Forum (APEC) A forum for discussion and negotiation of trade and other issues among Asia-Pacific nations, including the United States, Japan, and China, and many other countries in this region. At the 1994 APEC meetings in Bogor, Indonesia, the group pledged to create a regional free-trade zone.

Autocracy Government by a single person who has ultimate power. Generally, autocracy refers to a system of highly centralized power in government.

Autonomous state A state that is independent, not controlled by outside forces. Autonomous states have *sovereignty.*

Baker Plan A plan to deal with Third World debt problems proposed by U.S. Treasury Secretary James Baker.

Balance of Payments (BOP) A tabulation of all international transactions involving a nation in a given year, the BOP is the best indicator of a nation's international economic status. The most important parts of the BOP are the *current account* and the *capital account.*

Balance of payments deficit This term usually refers to a *current account deficit* (see *Current account*).

Balance of power A concept that describes how states deal with the problems of national security in a context of shifting alliances and alignments. The balance system is produced by the clustering of individual national interests in opposition to those of other states. Peace among nations is usually associated with an approximate equilibrium in the distribution of power between nations in this system. Others argue that peace is enforced by a hegemon, not an equilibrium. See *Hegemony.*

Bipolar system An international security structure with two centers of power. The Cold War was a bipolar security structure, with hegemonic military power distributed between the United States and the Soviet Union.

Bipolycentrism A configuration of power whereby global political, military, and economic power is distributed among two (bi) hegemons and any number of other major or rising powers. In the 1970s, the international security structure was said to be bipolycentric as a reflection of the continued superpower status of the United States and Soviet Union but also the growing influence of Japan, the EU, and the NICs.

Black markets Illegal markets; markets that trade forbidden items, or legal items at forbidden prices. Many soft currency countries have black markets in currency, where exchanges are made at rates different from the official exchange rate.

Blocs Groups of nation-states that are united or associated for some purpose. Examples of blocs are defense blocs, such as *NATO* and the *Warsaw Pact* and trade blocs such the *European Union* and *NAFTA.*

Bourgeoisie In Marxian analysis, the bourgeoisie is the capitalist class comprised of those who own the means of production. In everyday language, this term often refers to the middle class. See *Proletariat*.

Brady Plan A plan to deal with Third World debt problems proposed by U.S. Treasury Secretary Nicholas Brady.

Bretton Woods Conference Bretton Woods is a place, a meeting, and a set of institutions and practices. Bretton Woods, New Hampshire, was the site of a series of meetings that took place in July 1944 among representatives of the Allied Powers of World War II (including the United States, Britain, France, Canada, and the Soviet Union, and also involving many smaller states). The Bretton Woods agreements created the International Monetary Fund, the World Bank, and the system of fixed exchange rates that prevailed in international finance until 1973.

Capital "Stuff that is used to make stuff." Broadly speaking, capital is any long-lasting productive resource. Types of capital include physical capital, such as machines and factories; human capital, such as knowledge and learned skills; and financial capital, which is another term for money available for investment. The term *capital* is used in Marxist analysis to identify the owners of physical capital (capital versus labor).

Capital account The part of the *balance of payments* that records international borrowing, lending, and investment. If a nation has a capital account surplus, it means that it is a net debtor during a particular period.

Capital controls Capital controls are government rules and regulations that seek to limit or control inflows and outflows of international investment funds. The goal of capital controls is to maintain orderly international capital movements and prevent financial and foreign exchange instability.

Capital mobility The ability of investment funds to move from one nation to another. The degree of capital mobility depends on the domestic financial regulations of the nations involved, which can either encourage, permit, or restrict international investment flows, and on market forces seeking to profit from differences in returns between countries.

Capitalism Originally, the term described a political ideology that was identified with the capitalists, the owners of capital. Today, however, it usually refers to a market-dominated system of economic organization based on private property and free markets.

Cartel A group of firms or nations that form a *bloc* to restrict supply of and increase profits from a particular product. OPEC is an example of an oil *cartel*.

Central bank The chief monetary institution of a nation. Central banks regulate domestic financial institutions and influence domestic interest rates and foreign exchange rates. The central bank of the United States is the Federal Reserve System, which issues U.S. currency.

CFA franc zone A group of African nations that are former colonies of France and that fix their exchange rate to the French franc.

Class A collection of individuals that share certain socioeconomic attributes. Marx defined classes based upon their relation to the means of production. See *Bourgeoisie* and *Proletariat*.

Classical imperialism State-based imperialism as practiced, for example, through colonial systems.

Classical socialism The economic system usually associated with communism. Classical socialism is a highly centralized system of production and distribution. The Soviet Union typified the classical socialist system prior to 1989.

CNN effect The pressure put on nation-states or the United Nations to "do something" in cases where the news media generates a good deal of interest in stories such as massive starvation in Somalia (1992) or fleeing refuges in Rwanda (1994).

Cold War A phrase first used by Bernard Baruch in 1948 to describe the bipolar security structure that existed until 1989. The Cold War refers to the military and political confrontation between the United States and the Soviet Union and their allies.

Collective good A tangible or intangible good that, once created, is available to all members of a group. The issue of collective goods raises questions about whom should pay for these goods when they are to be provided to the entire group. No single person or entity has an incentive to pay for something everyone derives a benefit from, for example, cleaning up air pollution.

Common Agricultural Policy (CAP) The system of agricultural subsidies employed by the *European Union*.

Communism The system of political economy where control over state and market is centralized in a single, authoritarian party.

Comparative advantage A nation has a *comparative advantage* in production of a good or service if it can produce it at a lower cost, or *opportunity cost*, than other nations. The theory of comparative advantage holds that nations should produce and export those goods and services in which they hold a comparative advantage and import those items that other nations can produce at lower cost.

Consumer economics An economic system organized primarily to satisfy consumer demands. See *Producer economics*.

Coordination mechanisms Private and public institutions that organize the production and distribution of goods and services.

Core A term used in the modern world system analysis (core versus periphery) in reference to the more-developed capitalist part of the economic system, which interacts with the *periphery*, or less developed part of the system. These terms can refer to international geographic regions (e.g., *North-South*) or to sectors within a particular economy. See *Modern world system*.

Corporatism A system of political economy built upon collective organizations within society such as labor and business organizations, and so forth (rather than focusing on individuals or classes, for example).

Corn Laws Trade barriers that restricted agricultural imports into Great Britain from 1815 to 1846.

Counter trade A form of barter in international trade, where goods are paid for with other goods instead of money. *Counter trade* is most common in trade with *soft currency* nations, which often experience a shortage of *hard currency* funds with which to pay for imports.

Countervailing trade practices Defensive measures taken on the part of the state to counter the advantage gained by another state when it adopts protectionist measures. Such practices include antidumping measures and the imposition of countervailing tariffs or quotas.

Cui bono? (kwē bōnō) Who benefits? This term suggests that benefits drive actions, so we should "follow the money" to see in whose interest are the actions and institutions we perceive.

Currency Board Currency boards are government institutions that regulate a nation's domestic money supply and its foreign exchange rate. The goal of a currency board is to use the commitment to a fixed foreign exchange rate as a tool to stabilize the domestic economy.

Currency devaluation (or depreciation) By devaluing one's currency, exports become cheaper to other countries, while imports from abroad become more expensive. Currency depreciation thus tends to achieve the effects, temporarily at least, of both a tariff (raising import prices) and an export subsidy (lowering the costs of exports). Currency changes affect the prices of all traded goods, however, while tariffs and subsidies generally apply to one good at a time.

Current account A part of a nation's balance of payments that records financial flows due to international trade in goods and services and unilateral transfers (aid or gifts) between nations. A *current account deficit* means that a nation is paying out more for goods and services than it receives for the goods and services that it sells on international markets; this leads to rising international indebtedness.

Customs union A group of nations that agree to eliminate trade barriers among themselves and adopt a unified system of external trade barriers. The *Treaty of Rome* created a *customs union* in the form of the *European Community*.

Deflation A condition where the general level of prices falls over a period of time. Deflation (falling prices) is commonly associated with falling incomes, as during a *depression*.

Deforestation The destruction of forests, usually through excessive tree cutting by humans.

Demographic transition The point where income growth exceeds population growth, making possible rising per capita income levels.

Dependency theory A theory of the relationship between industrialized (core) nations and less developed (periphery) nations that stresses the many linkages that exist to make LDCs dependent on richer nations. These linkages include trade, finance, and technology.

Depreciate A term used in foreign exchange markets when one currency falls in value relative to another currency. See *Appreciate*.

Depression A period of very significant decreases in incomes and employment in a nation as indicated by substantial decreases in gross national product and a high level of unemployment. A *depression* is more severe than a *recession*.

Devaluation Also termed *currency depreciation*. A situation where the value of the domestic currency is reduced relative to foreign currencies. *Devaluation* increases the prices of imported goods, while making exports relatively less costly to foreign buyers.

Developmental capitalism Term used to describe the system of political economy of postwar Japan, where state policies are used to encourage industrial growth.

Direct Foreign Investment (DFI) Investments made by a company (often a *multinational corporation*) in production, distribution, or sales facilities in another country. The term *direct* implies a measure of control exercised by the parent company (U.S.-based IBM, for example) on resources in the host nation (e.g., Mexico).

Dual economy The theory of the *dual economy* is a liberal theory of economic development that views the world as having two sectors: a modern progressive sector and a traditional sector. Economic development and structural change take place as the progressive, market-driven sector interacts with and transforms the tradition-based less developed sector. Although the theory of the *dual economy* appears similar to the *core–periphery* interaction of the *modern world system*, the nature of the interaction between sectors is distinctly different.

Dumping The practice of selling an item for less abroad than at home. *Dumping* is an unfair trade practice when it is used to drive out competitors from an export market with the goal of creating monopoly power.

Dynamic efficiency An economic structure that produces high rates of economic growth.

Economic development Increase in the level of economic activity in a nation, often measured by growth in GDP or per capital GDP. Generally, *economic development* involves structural changes, with populations moving from agricultural (primary sector) to manufacturing (secondary sector) to services (tertiary sector). The concept of *economic development* is rooted in the experiences of Western nations, especially Britain, the United States, and Germany.

Economic globalization The expansion of market activity, including especially finance and production, from a national to a truly global scale.

Economic liberalism The ideology of the free market. *Economic liberalism* holds that nations are best off when the role of the state is minimized. See *Laissez-faire*. *Economic liberalism* derives in part from fear of state abuse of power and the philosophy of individualism and liberty of the eighteenth-century Enlightenment.

Economic nationalism The ideology of *mercantilism*. *Economic nationalism* holds that nations are best off when state and market are joined in a partnership. The state protects domestic business firms, which become richer and more powerful, which in turn increases the power of the state. Alexander Hamilton and Friedrich List are two famous proponents of economic nationalism.

Economic structuralism The idea that the economic structures of society, in particular, condition the outcomes for actors in society. See *Structuralism*.

Economic union A degree of economic integration that goes beyond that found in a customs union. An economic union eliminates both tariff and non-tariff barriers to trade and finance among a group of countries.

Ecosystem An ecological community and its environment considered as a single unit.

Elastic demand The demand for a product is said to be elastic if a given change in price produces a relatively larger proportionate change in the quantity that is demanded. If a 10 percent price cut results in an increase in the quantity demanded of more than 10 percent (say, 15 percent), then the demand is elastic. See *Inelastic demand*.

Embargo A government prohibition of a certain activity. A trade embargo is a prohibition of trade with a nation.

Emerging market economies Nations making a transition from heavily state-controlled systems of political economy to more market-oriented policies. In 1999 the Institute of International Finance included the following countries in the list of "emerging market economies": China, India, Indonesia, Malaysia, Philippines, South Korea, Thailand, Argentina, Brazil, Chile, Colombia, Ecuador, Mexico, Peru, Uruguay, Venezuela, Bulgaria, Czech Republic, Hungary, Poland, Romania, Russian Federation, Slovakia, Turkey, Algeria, Egypt, Morocco, South Africa, Tunisia.

Endaka Japanese term for the problems associated with an over-valued yen.

Ethnic cleansing The harassment, removal, or murder of citizens based solely on their ethnic or racial attributes, a term that emerged in the conflict following the breakup of the former Yugoslavia.

European Coal and Steel Community (ECSC) Organization established in 1952 to integrate the coal and steel resources of six European nations. Eventually evolved into the European Economic Community.

European Community (EC) A creation of the *Treaty of Rome*, the *EC* was a group that eventually numbered 12 nations engaged in economic (and to a lesser extent, political) integration. Taken together, the EC member states formed the largest single market in the world. EC members were France, Germany, Italy, Belgium, the Netherlands, and Luxembourg (the charter members), plus Great Britain, Ireland, Denmark, Greece, Spain, and Portugal. See *European Union*.

European Economic Community (EEC) The original European "Common Market" of seven countries created in 1957 by the Treaty of Rome.

European Economic Space (EES) Group of nations that are not members of the *European Union* but that have negotiated free-trade or preferential trade agreements with the EU.

European Union (EU) Successor organization to the *European Community* as defined by the *Maastricht Treaty*. As of 1995, the following countries were members of the EU: France, Germany, Italy, Belgium, the Netherlands, Luxembourg, Great Britain, Ireland, Denmark, Greece, Spain, Portugal, Austria, Finland, and Sweden.

Exchange rate The ratio of exchange between the currencies of different countries (e.g., between the dollar and the yen). Changes in the *exchange rate* affect the prices of goods in international trade and, therefore, have important internal affects in nations. (See *Devaluation*.) The international system of *exchange rates* can be based on *Fixed (pegged) exchange rates*, as during the Bretton Woods period (1946–1973) and the period of the *gold standard* in the late nineteenth century, or *flexible (floating) exchange rate*, as during the period since 1946. *Fixed exchange rates* are determined by international agreements among states; *flexible exchange rates* are determined by market forces.

Exploitation An economic relationship where one side of a transaction selfishly attempts to achieve the maximum possible gain, generally at the expense of the well-being of others.

Export A good or service that is sold to the citizens of another nation.

Export-oriented growth A strategy for economic growth that focuses on exports and integration into global markets. Contrast this strategy with *Import-substituting industrialization*.

Export quotas These international agreements limit the quantity of an item that a nation can export. The effect is to limit the number of goods imported into a country. Examples include Orderly Marketing Arrangements (OMAs), Voluntary Export Restraints (VERs), or Voluntary Restraint Agreements (VRAs). The Multifibre Agreement establishes a system of *export quotas* for less developed countries, for example.

Export subsidies Any measure that effectively reduces the price of an exported product, making it more attractive to potential foreign buyers.

External cost A cost that is not factored into market decisions. An external cost is created when an individual makes decisions that impose costs on others, such as when a factory pollutes.

Feudal system Medieval system of political economy organized around land holdings, or fiefs.

Finance structure The system of institutions, practices, and arrangements that condition the use and exchange of financial resources. The international monetary system and the institutions that condition the distribution and payment of international debts are parts of the finance structure.

Fiscal austerity Attempts to reduce current account deficits through measures including higher taxes, reduced expenditures and subsidies, privatization of state-owned enterprises, and monetary restriction.

Fixed (pegged) exchange rates *Exchange rates* that are determined principally by state actions, not market forces.

Flexible (floating) exchange rates *Exchange rates* that are determined principally by market forces, not state actions

Food security An element of nation security; concerns about the security of a nation's food supply.

Foreign Direct Investment (FDI) Purchase of business assets such as factories, stores, warehouses, and the like, by a foreign firm. Investment that gives a foreign firm a tangible business presence in a country.

Foreign Exchange (FX) Foreign currencies and foreign currency markets.

Free rider problem Difficulty associated with *public goods*, where an individual is able to enjoy the benefits of a good or service without paying for them.

Free trade area A group of nations that agrees to eliminate tariff barriers for trade among themselves, but which retains the right of individual nations to set their own tariffs for trade with nonmember nations.

GATT (General Agreement on Tariffs and Trade) An international organization, based in Geneva, that negotiates reductions in trade barriers among its many member nations. GATT negotiations take place over a period of years and are termed "rounds," as in the Kennedy round and the Tokyo round, which reduced trade barriers for manufactured goods, and the recent *Uruguay round*, which aims to create freer trade in services and in agricultural goods.

Generalized System of Preferences (GSP) Regulations regarding tariffs set as part of the GATT.

Geopolitics The combination of political and geographical factors that influence a nation within an IPE structure, especially the *security structure*.

Glasnost A policy of openness, especially regarding public information.

Globalization The process by which all of the structures of IPE have become less strictly associated with the boundaries of the nation-state. See *Economic globalization.*

Global warming The increase in the temperature of the earth's atmosphere that results from the greenhouse effect.

Gold standard A monetary system of *fixed exchange rates* where currency values are defined in terms of a fixed quantity of gold.

Great Leap Forward A 1958 economic and social development program in China that organized a half-billion peasants into 24,000 "people's communes."

Green The adjective *green* often indicates an emphasis on environmental issues. The *green* party in Germany, for example, is a political party devoted to furthering environmental and related positions.

Green revolution Various scientific, technological, and economic programs that attempt to increase food production through introduction of advanced plant strains and farming techniques.

Gross Domestic Product (GDP) Like GNP, GDP is a measure of a nation's economic production in a year. Unlike GNP, however, GDP measures only production that takes place within a nation. GDP is the accepted international measure of national economic performance. "Real" GDP adjusts GDP for changes in inflation. "Per capita" GDP is a measure of average income per person in a country.

Gross National Product (GNP) The total value of all goods and services produced in a country in a year. GNP is a measure of a nation's overall economic activity. "Real" GNP, which adjusts GNP for the effects of inflation, is a more reliable indicator of changes in a nation's production. GNP was the main measure of economic performance in the United States until 1991. Now the United States and most other nations rely on *gross domestic product* measurements.

Group of Seven (G-7) The seven largest industrial democracies: the United States, Japan, Germany, France, Canada, Italy, and Great Britain. The leaders of the G-7 nations meet regularly to discuss common economic and political problems and to attempt to coordinate policies in some areas.

Hard currency A currency of known value that can readily be exchanged on foreign exchange markets and is therefore generally accepted in international transactions. Examples of hard currencies today include the U.S. dollar, the Japanese yen, the German deutschemark, and the Swiss franc. See *Soft currency.*

Hard power Military power. See *Soft power.*

Hegemonic stability The theory that the international system is more stable in the presence of a *hegemon.*

Hegemony Dominance or leadership, especially by one nation over other nations. The theory of hegemonic stability holds that the international system achieves growth and stability only when one state acts as the hegemon, dominating the others but also paying the costs associated with counteracting problems in the international system.

Hierarchy A social or organizational system using a clear ordering of rank, authority, and priorities.

Historical materialism The idea, central to Marx, that social and political institutions are built upon a foundation of economics.

Hot money Highly interest-sensitive short-term international capital movements.

Imperialism Idea associated with the works of J. A. Hobson, V. I. Lenin, and R. Luxemburg. A superior-inferior relationship in which an area and its people have been subordinated to the will or interests of a foreign state. *Imperialism* is often associated with historical periods that correspond to conquest and colonization of developing territories by developed "modern" industrialized nations. Economic *imperialism* may result from a conscious policy or from the capital flows of private foreign investment. See *Direct foreign investment.*

Import A good or service purchased from citizens of a foreign country.

Import quotas A limit on the quantity of an item that can be imported into a nation. By limiting the quantity of imports, the quota tends to drive up the price of a good, while at the same time restricting competition.

Import substituting-industrialization An economic development strategy that attempts to encourage industrial development, often by restricting imports of industrial productions or encouraging exports of these items. Contrast this strategy with *Export-oriented growth.*

Industrial policy Economic policies designed to guide or direct business investment and development.

Industrial revolution The period from approximately 1780 to 1840, when an industrial sector developed in Europe, especially in Great Britain. This period is sometimes called the "first industrial revolution" to distinguish it from the "second industrial revolution" (approximately 1880 to 1910). The first revolution relied on mechanical innovations, while the second revolution was based on chemical and electrical innovations.

Inelastic demand The demand for a product is said to be inelastic if a given change in price produces a relatively smaller proportionate change in the quantity that is demanded. If a 10 percent price cut results in an increase in the quantity demanded of less than 10 percent (say, 5 percent), then the demand is inelastic. See *Elastic demand.*

Inflation A rise in the general level of prices in a country (as opposed to a rise in the price of a particular good). Hyperinflation is a condition where very high rates of inflation (1,000 percent per year price increases and more) are experienced.

Integration In IPE, *integration* occurs when nation-states agree to unify or coordinate some political and economic activities.

Intellectual property rights Patents, copyrights, and other rights to ownership or control of ideas, innovation, and creations.

Interdependence Usually thought of as interconnectedness between nations and other actors in the international political economy conditioned by trade, aid, finance, and investment. Reactions to interdependence include the need to cooperate but also negative reactions related to the vulnerability and sensitivity it engenders.

International division of labor The organization of global economic activity, often with special emphasis on the activities of *core* and *periphery.*

International Monetary Fund (IMF) Created as part of the *Bretton Woods* system, the *IMF* is an organization of over 150 member states charged with stabilizing the international monetary system. The *IMF* makes loans to member states when they experience severe *current account deficits.* These loans are made subject to enactment of economic reforms, a practice called "conditionality."

International Organizations (IOs) Voluntary associations such as the United Nations that draw their members from the ranks of nation-states. See *Nongovernmental organizations.*

International Political Economy (IPE) The study of international problems and issues with special attention to social, political, and economic arrangements.

International Trade Organization (ITO) An original element of the Bretton Woods system that was not successfully implemented. A weaker institution, the GATT, was eventually created to take the place of the ITO alongside the World Bank and the IMF. See *General Agreement on Tariffs and Trade* and *World Trade Organization.*

Intervene (in foreign exchange markets) The action by a government agency or central bank to alter the foreign exchange value of a currency, especially by buying or selling that currency.

Isolationism The policy of withdrawing from world affairs, especially to prevent disruption or exploitation from external sources.

Keiretsu Japanese "business families"; groups of businesses in different economic sectors that engage in cooperative strategic behavior—buying and selling goods within the group whenever possible, for example.

Keynesian compromise The Keynesian compromise is one aspect of the Bretton Woods system. Nations retain the ability to intervene in their domestic economies but are limited in this by their agreement to leave international economic markets

Keynesian theory To be *Keynesian* is to be in agreement with the general thrust of the political economy of John Maynard Keynes (pronounced "Canes") (1883–1946). Because Keynes's views were complex, original, and constantly changing, there is no precise definition of what it means to be *Keynesian*. A general definition is to believe that there is a positive role for the state to play in domestic affairs (fighting unemployment and poverty, for example) and in international affairs (the kind of role conceived for the *IMF* and the *World Bank*). Keynes's views were influenced by the catastrophe of World War I and the chaos of the interwar period.

Knowledge structure The set of institutions and practices that condition the production, exchange, and distribution of intellectual and technological goods and services, property rights, and their associated benefits.

Kyoto Protocol Environmental rules that derive from the 1997 Kyoto, Japan , summit on global warming.

Laissez-faire A French term ("let be" or "leave alone") commonly associated with Adam Smith, the eighteenth-century Scottish economist who advocated free market solutions to economic and social problems. Today, it refers to a view that individuals are best left to solve problems themselves through the "invisible hand" of market interactions, rather than through government policies.

Lender of last resort An institution that pledges to provide liquidity to financial markets during a panic in order to prevent the collapse of a financial bubble.

Less Developed Country (LDC) A nation with relatively low levels of income and industrialization.

Levels of analysis The three levels of analysis are the individual, the state, and the international system. The levels of analysis approach was originally developed by the political scientist Kenneth Waltz to help understand differences of opinion regarding the fundamental sources of international conflict and war.

Liberalism The IPE perspective that focuses on the individual and the primacy of freedom or liberty. There are many varieties of liberalism today that reflect different points of view regarding the proper role of the state in private activities.

Maastricht Treaty This treaty creating the *European Union* was ratified by members of the *European Community* in 1993.

Managed exchange rates *Exchange rate* system where day-to-day FX (Foreign Exchange) changes are determined by market forces, but long-run changes are conditioned by state actions. Sometimes termed a "dirty float." See *Flexible exchange rate*.

Maquiladora Assembly plants in Mexico that use foreign parts and semifinished products to produce final goods for export.

Market A form of social organization based on individual action and self-interest. Individuals exchange goods and services through market institutions. Markets are sometimes distinct physical places (such as the New York Stock Exchange or Pike Place Market in Seattle), but the term *market* generally refers to the broader market forces of profit and self-interest.

Market Leninism See *Market socialism*.

Market socialism A system of political economy that combines state ownership and control of some sectors of the economy with private ownership and market allocations in other sectors. See *Classical socialism*.

Marshall Plan Named for U.S. Secretary of State George C. Marshall, who proposed the program in 1947. A 1948–1951 U.S. postwar assistance program that provided $12 billion in aid to European countries. Also called the "European Recovery Program."

Marxism An ideology that originated in the works of the German sociologist Karl Marx. There are many strains of *Marxism* that have evolved from Marx's works. Generally,

Marxism is a critique of *capitalism* (as distinct from *economic liberalism*). *Marxism* holds that *capitalism* is subject to several distinctive flaws. *Marxism* tends to view economic relations from a power perspective (capital versus labor) as opposed to the cooperative relationship implicit in *economic liberalism*. See *Structuralism*.

Mercantilism A seventeenth-century idea that won't go away, *mercantilism* was an ideology that put accumulation of national treasury as the main goal of society. Today, it is an economic philosophy and practice of government regulation of a nation's economic life to increase state power and security. Policies of import restriction and export promotion (to accumulate treasure at the expense of other countries) follow from this goal. See *Economic nationalism* and *statism*.

Ministry of International Trade and Industry (MITI) Japanese government ministry that deals most directly with trade issues. *MITI* has been credited by some for Japan's rapid industrialization in the 1960s and 1970s.

Mixed economy An economy that combines important elements of *state* and *market* (although relative importance of these two elements may vary). Britain and France are both mixed economies, for example, although the state is relatively larger in France and the market relatively more important in Britain.

Miyazawa Plan Third World debt plan proposed by Japanese Prime Minister Kiichi Miyazawa.

Modern World System (MWS) A theory of economic development based on Marxist-Leninist ideologies. The *MWS* views economic development as conditioned by the relationship between the capitalist *core* and the less developed *periphery* nations. The historic mission of the *core* is to develop the *periphery* (often through the *semi-periphery*), but this development is exploitive in nature. The *MWS* therefore presents a theory that runs counter to liberal theories such as "hegemonic stability." See *Core*.

Monetarism A school of thought that focuses on the money supply as a key determinant of the level of economic activity in a nation. Monetarists tend to view state economic actions as likely to disrupt domestic and international affairs. Monetarists tend, therefore, to be closely associated with *economic liberals* in their dislike of state influences.

Monetary autonomy The ability of a nation, through its central bank, to determine domestic monetary policy without regard for international agreements or restraints.

Monetary union A group of nations that actively coordinate their monetary policies. Members of a *monetary union* might adopt a common currency, for example.

Most Favored Nation (MFN) Trade status under GATT where imports from a nation are granted the same degree of preference as those from the most preferred nations.

Multinational Corporation (MNC) A business firm that engages in production, distribution, and marketing activities that cross national boundaries (see *Direct foreign investment*). The critical factor is that the firm have a tangible productive presence in several countries. This factor distinguishes a *MNC* from an international firm, which produces in one country and exports to other countries. *MNCs* are sometimes called Multinational Enterprises (MNEs) or Transnational Enterprises (TNEs).

Multipolar system A security structure with more than two centers of power.

Mutual-Assured Destruction (MAD) The Cold War strategy of the United States and the USSR where each had sufficient military power to destroy the other even if destroyed itself, thus assuring that neither nation could realistically "win" a nuclear war.

Nation A social group that shares a common identity, history, language, set of values and beliefs, institutions, and a sense of territory. Nations do not have to have a homogeneous ethnic culture but usually exhibit a sense of homogeneity. Nations may extend beyond states, be circumscribed by states or be coterminus with states. Since the seventeenth century, the nation-state has been the major political (sovereign) unit of the international system.

Nation-state Synonymous with the term "country," since the seventeenth century the nation-state has been the major political (sovereign) unit of the international system.

The nation-state joins the nation—a group of people with a shared sense of cultural identity and territoriality—with the state—a legal concept describing a social group that occupies a territory—and is organized under common political institutions and an effective government. As sovereign entities, nation-states have the right to determine their own national objectives and to decide how they will achieve them.

Neoconservatism A term used in the United States to describe a movement that is liberal in fundamental nature that arose in reaction to the growth of the state in the 1960s.

Neoimperialism An element of the structuralist interpretation of capitalism. Core nations exploit the periphery and create dependency through financial and production structures in neoimperialism. See *Classical imperialism.*

Neoliberal A late twentieth-century term used by persons who do not subscribe to the liberal perspective to describe the ideas of those who do. More generally, policies that seek to promote market-oriented policies, such as free trade and deregulation, by reducing the state's role in society.

Neoliberal policies. Economic policies that stress reductions in the size and influence of the state combined with free market reforms. See *Structural adjustment policies.*

Neomercantilism A version of mercantilism that evolved in the post-World War II period. Neomercantilism is basically mercantilist policy enacted with a liberal system of interantional trade.

New International Economic Order (NIEO) A set of proposals made by less developed nations to reform international trade and financial structures.

Newly industrialized countries (NICs) Nations that have achieved a large measure of industrialization in the second half of the twentieth century. Most lists of the *NICs* include South Korea, Taiwan, and Brazil, and sometimes Singapore and Hong Kong.

Nichibei economy The economies of the United States and Japan considered as a single entity, not two separate units.

Nominal interest rate The interest rate unadjusted for changes in the purchasing power of money over the period of a financial transaction. See *Real interest rate.*

Nongovernmental Organizations (NGOs) National and international voluntary organizations that exist at a level between the individual and the state. Examples of NGOs include Greenpeace and the Red Cross. See *International organizations.*

Nondiscrimination A principal of the GATT trade system whereby products of different nations are treated equally (and equal with domestic products once imported). The products of a specific nation cannot be discriminated against under this rule. See *Most favored nation.*

Nontariff Barriers (NTBS) Other ways of limiting imports include government health and safety standards, domestic content legislation, licensing requirements, and labeling requirements. Such measures make it difficult for imported goods to be marketed or significantly raise the price of imported goods.

North American Free Trade Agreement (NAFTA) A free trade area among the United States, Canada, and Mexico, to be fully implemented by 2005. The NAFTA treaty was signed in 1992 and took force in 1994.

North Atlantic Treaty Organization (NATO) International security organization founded in 1949 and based in Washington, D.C. NATO served as the main western alliance during the Cold War. See *Warsaw Pact.*

North-South The relationship between developed, industrialized countries (the North) and less developed countries (the South). This concept is often associated with *core-periphery* analysis but can also be simply a descriptive device.

North-South dilemma. The continuing problem of the uneven distribution of income and wealth between the richer and poorer nations of the world.

Oligarchy System of government where control is held by a small group.

Opportunity cost The value of the best foregone opportunity when a choice is made. See *Comparative advantage.*

Organization of Petroleum Exporting Countries (OPEC) Organization of nations formed in 1960 to advance interests of Third World oil exporters. OPEC members include Saudi Arabia, Iran, Iraq, Kuwait, Qatar, Abu Dhabi, Algeria, Gabon, Libya, Nigeria, Indonesia, Ecuador, and Venezuela.

Overvalued currency A condition where a currency's purchasing power abroad (converted at the going exchange rate) is greater than its purchasing power in the home country. The exchange rate thus biases economic activity in favor of foreign goods over domestically produced items. See *Undervalued currency*.

Paradox of thrift The paradox of thrift is an example of the potential problems of an unregulated economy. If one individual saves much more income, that individual may be more secure economically. If everyone does this, however, the combined actions can cause a recession and everyone is less secure economically.

Pax Americana The period of U.S. hegemony following World War II. "Pax" means "peace."

Pax Britannia The period of British hegemony following the Napoleonic wars. "Pax" means "peace."

Pax Consortis A period of "universal peace" provided by a collective hegemon in a multipolar system.

Peace dividend Resources that become available for other uses during peacetime due to decreased expenditures on national defense.

Perestroika Restructuring or reformation, especially the programs of governmental restructuring implemented in the Soviet Union in the mid-1980s.

Periphery Nonindustrialized sector of the *modern world system* that produces agricultural goods and natural resources. See *Core* and *Modern world system*.

Pluralism Existence of many different ethnic, social, and political groups within society.

Political economy The social science that examines the dynamic interaction between the forces of *market* and *state*, and how the tension and conflict between these aspects of society affect the world. The term *political economy*, in certain contexts, has different meanings. In economics, for example, *political economy* is the name sometimes applied to Marxist analysis and sometimes applied to economic tools used to analyze political behavior.

Portfolio investment Pattern of international investment where firms seek to acquire ownership in many industries or world regions in order to hedge investment risk.

Positive-sum game Any human interaction that makes all participants simultaneously better off. See *Zero-sum game*.

Postmodern A school of thought that reacts against "modern" institutions and ideas, such as the primacy of the nation-state.

Prisoners' dilemma Term coined by Princeton mathematics professor A. W. Tucker to describe a situation where the best interests of persons in society taken individually are opposite from those of the same individuals taken as a group. A group may benefit the most if everyone cooperates on an issue, for example, but each individual member may face an incentive to "defect" and eschew cooperation.

Process innovation Inventions and improvements on producing existing goods, services, and techniques, but which do not result in new items. See *Product innovation*.

Producer economics An economic system organized primarily to generate sustained increases in production. See *Consumer economics*.

Product cycle or **Product life cycle** Terms coined by Harvard political economist Raymond Vernon to describe production and trade patterns stemming from product innovation and technological diffusion.

Product innovation Pattern of inventions that focuses on creation of new goods and services, not refinements of existing items. See *Process innovation*.

Production structure   The institutions and practices that condition the production, exchange, and distribution of goods and services in the IPE. International trade is a key component of the *production structure*. Essentially, the factors that determine what is produced, where, how, by whom, for whom, and on what terms. See *International division of labor*.

Productive power   Term used by Friedrich List to describe technology, education, and training, especially with respect to the industrial sector of the economy.

Proletariat   In Marxian analysis, the class of workers who do not own capital.

Property rights   A bundle of rights associated with ownership of a resource. Property rights include the right to use a resource and exclude others from its use, to gain from or control its use by others, and dispose of it. *Property rights* are defined by the state.

Protectionism   Theory of or belief in the advantages of restricting trade so as to encourage or benefit domestic producers.

Public goods   Goods or services that, once provided, generate benefits that can be enjoyed by all simultaneously. A lighthouse is the classic example of a *public good*.

Purchasing Power Parity (PPP)   An *exchange rate* such that a given amount of a currency will purchase the same amounts of goods and services at home as abroad.

Rational choice theory   A theory of *political economy* that focuses on the incentives facing individuals and states and how those incentives affect their behavior. The structure of incentives (costs and benefits) of the international system is seen as an important determinant of state behavior by *rational choice* theorists.

Realism   A theory of state behavior that focuses on national interest as a determinant of state behavior. States, like individuals, tend to act in their own self-interest, in the view of *realists*.

Real interest rate   The *nominal interest rate* adjusted for expected changes in the purchasing power of money over the relevant time period.

Recession   A decline in the overall level of economic activity in a nation as indicated by a decrease in real *gross national product*.

Reciprocity   A principal of the GATT trade system whereby trading partners simultaneously reduce trade barriers, providing each greater access to foreign markets.

Regime   The environment in which a particular type of IPE activity takes place, including the various actors, institutions, and practices that exist to deal with a specific problem. The oil *regime*, for example, includes the nation-states, international organizations, private-sector firms, markets, agreements, and so on, that condition oil production, exchange and distribution, and related activities.

Relational power   Power of one actor vis-à-vis another based upon the hard and soft power that each possesses. See *Structural power*.

Relative decline   The idea that a nation's wealth and power have fallen compared to other nations as these nations have grown at a faster rate.

Rent-seeking behavior   Efforts to achieve personal gain by creating an artificial scarcity rather than through efficient production. Many corrupt activities can be viewed as examples of rent-seeking behavior.

Rio Earth Summit   International conference held in Rio de Janeiro, Brazil, in 1992 to discuss global environmental problems.

Rogue state   States that are regarded as hostile to or who refuse to cooperate with the Western industrialized nations: Iran, Iraq, Syria, and North Korea, among others. Often these states are cited as potential sources of arms sales and terrorism.

Security structure   The sets of institutions, practices, and beliefs that condition international behavior as it relates to national security issues.

Semiperiphery   An intermediate zone between *core* and *periphery*. Korea and Taiwan might be considered part of the *semiperiphery* today in the *modern world system* theory. See *Core*.

Socialism A system of political economy that gives high priority to equity and economic equality. Socialist systems often feature the communal or public ownership of some of the means of production.

Social safety net Social programs, such as old-age pensions and unemployment insurance, that provide for economically disadvantaged groups in society.

Soft currency Currencies of uncertain value (due, perhaps, to high inflation rates) that are not generally accepted in international transactions. *Soft currencies* can usually be spent only within the nation that issues it, whereas a *hard currency* can be exchanged and spent in most nations. Some *soft currencies*, such as the ruble in the former Soviet Union, are called "inconvertible currencies" because it is illegal to convert them into *hard currencies*.

Soft power Wealth, as used to influence the actions of foreign states. See *Hard power*.

Solidarity Polish labor union (and political party) founded in 1980 by Lech Walesa.

Sovereignty Independence from foreign control. See *Autonomous state*.

Special economic zones Regions of China where private ownership is permitted and market forces are used to encourage rapid economic growth. See *Market socialism*.

Speculative attack A form of currency speculation where speculators sell large quantities of a currency in the hope that they will be able to buy it back later at a lower price.

Sphere of influence The area or territory in which a hegemon or major state has interest and sustains either political, military, or economic influence. During the Vietnam war, it was common practice to refer to Southeast Asia as being in the United States' sphere of influence.

State A legal concept describing a social group that occupies a defined territory and is organized under common political institutions and an effective government. A *state* has some degree of independence and autonomy. *States* are the primary units of the international political and legal community. As sovereign entities, *states* have the right to determine their own national objectives and the techniques (including the use of force) for their achievement.

Static efficiency An efficient use of current resources, especially specialization according to the *comparative advantage*. See *Dynamic efficiency*.

Statism A trend whereby states subordinate economic policies to national and state political objectives. In more authoritarian or communist states, the state may restrict or otherwise heavily regulate market activities in favor of some ideological or nationalist objective.

Strategic Arms Limitation Treaty (SALT) Arms control and reduction agreement between the United States and the Soviet Union, signed in 1972.

Strategic resources Resources, such as oil and rubber, that have national security value to a nation.

Strategic trade policies Efforts on the part of the *state* to create *comparative advantages* in trade by methods such as subsidizing research and development of a product, or providing subsidies to help an industry increase production to the point where it can move down the "learning curve" to achieve greater production efficiency than foreign competitors. *Strategic trade practices* are often associated with state industrial policies, that is, intervention in the economy to promote specific patterns of industrial development.

Structural Adjustment Policies (SAPs) Economic policies that seek to reduce state power and introduce free market reforms to help LDCs establish a foundation for economic growth. The IMF often makes the adoption of structural adjustment policies a condition for financial assistance.

Structural power The power that an actor possesses due to its position in the international system and its ability to shape the "rules of the game." See *Relational power*.

Structural rigidities Inflexible elements of the structure of an organization that resist the forces of change.

Structuralism This theory accounts for the political-economic interconnectedness (structural relationship) between any number of entities: the *bourgeoisie* and *proletariat*, the *core* and *periphery*, the *North* and *South*. A number of ties bind these entities to one another, including trade, foreign aid, and direct investment. Much debate exists as to whether and how structural conditions can be changed or reformed. See *Marxism*.

Structures of IPE Sets of institutions, practices, and beliefs that condition the international production, exchange, and distribution of production, finance, security, and knowledge.

Subsidy Government payment to encourage some activity or benefit some group. See *Common agricultural policy*.

Sustainable development A pattern of economic development that is consistent with the goal of nondegradation of the environment.

Symbolic analysts A term coined by U.S. political economist Robert Reich to describe a class of highly trained persons. To use the language of *modern world systems* analysis, *symbolic analysts* form the *core* of a knowledge-based global division of labor.

Tariff A tax placed on imported goods to raise the price of those goods, making them less attractive to consumers. Though *tariffs* are used at times to raise government revenue (particularly in *LDCs*), they are more commonly a means to protect domestic industry from foreign competition.

Terms of trade The value of a nation's exported goods relative to the value of the goods that are imported. A measure of the prices paid for imports relative to the prices received for imports.

Third World A Cold War term that is still in use. During the Cold War, the term "Third World" applied to LDCs that were not part of either the "First World" (the United States and its allies) or the "Second World" (the Soviet Union and its allies). In the post-Cold War era, this term refers to LDCs generally.

Tragedy of the commons Term coined by Garrett Hardin to describe situations where human nature drives individuals to overuse communal resources.

Treaty of Rome A 1957 treaty among France, Britain, West Germany, Belgium, Luxembourg, and the Netherlands that established the European Economic Community in 1958.

Undervalued currency A condition where a currency's purchasing power within its home country is greater than its purchasing power abroad when converted at the going exchange rate. The exchange rate thus biases economic activity in favor of domestic goods over foreign goods. See *Overvalued currency*.

Unholy trinity A property of international monetary systems. It is impossible for such systems to provide stability, capital mobility, and national monetary autonomy. One of these goals must be sacrificed to achieve the other two.

Uruguay round Set of negotiations of the members of the *General Agreement on Tariffs and Trade* (1986–1994) that focused on reducing trade barriers, especially regarding services and agricultural goods.

Vietnam syndrome Essentially a lesson the United States supposedly learned from having lost the Vietnam war: Essentially, don't intervene in other Third World nations unless U.S. vital interests are at stake, the United States is assured of a quick and relatively inexpensive victory, and the U.S. public will support the operation.

Voluntary Export Restraint (VER) or **Voluntary Export Agreement (VEA)** Agreements that limit the quantity of an item a nation can export. Importers ask exporters to "voluntarily" set limits on the numbers of exports, backed by an implied threat of economic sanctions or some form of retaliation if the exporter does not comply with the importer's request.

Warsaw Pact The Warsaw Treaty Organization (1955–1991) military and defense alliance among Albania, Bulgaria, Czechoslovakia, East Germany, Hungary, Poland, Romania, and the Soviet Union. See *North Atlantic Treaty Organization*.

Weapons of Mass Destruction (WMD) Technologically sophisticated weapons that have the potential to kill large numbers of people such as nuclear, chemical, and biological weapons.

World Bank Officially called the International Bank for Reconstruction and Development, the *World Bank* is an international agency with over 150 members. Created by the Bretton Woods agreements in 1944, the *World Bank* originally worked on the reconstruction of Europe after World War II. Today, the *World Bank* makes low-interest loans to *less developed countries* to stimulate economic development.

World Trade Organization (WTO) Successor organization to the *General Agreement on Tariffs and Trade* (GATT).

Yom Kippur War The 1973 war between Israel and several Arab nations in the Middle East.

Zaibatsu Large and powerful family-controlled financial and industrial organization of modern Japan. Among the leading zaibatsu are Sumitomo Mitsubishi, Mitsui, and Yasuda.

Zero-sum game An activity where gains by one party create equal losses for others. See *Positive-sum game*.

Glossary of Acronyms

APEC	Asia-Pacific Economic Cooperation
BOP	Balance of payments
CAP	Common agricultural policy
DFI	Direct foreign investment
EEC	European Economic Community
EU	European Union
EFTA	European free trade area
FDI	Foreign direct investment
FX	Foreign exchange
GATT	General Agreement on Tariffs and Trade
GDP	Gross domestic product
GNP	Gross national product
GSP	Generalized system of preferences
IBRD	International Bank for Reconstruction and Development (also World Bank)
IMF	International Monetary Fund
IOs	International organizations
IPR	Intellectual property rights
ITO	International Trade Organization
LDC	Less developed country
MAD	Mutual assured destruction
MFN	Most favored nation
MITI	Ministry of International Trade and Industry
MNC	Multinational corporation
NAFTA	North American Free Trade Agreement
NATO	North Atlantic Treaty Organization
NGOs	Nongovernmental organizations
NIC	Newly industrialized country
NIEO	New international economic order
NTB	Nontariff barrier
OECD	Organization for Economic Cooperation and Development
OPEC	Organization of Petroleum Exporting Countries
PPP	Purchasing power parity
SALT	Strategic Arms Limitation Treaty
SAP	Structural adjustment programs
USTR	U.S. trade representative
TRIPs	Trade-related intellectual property rights
WIPO	World Intellectual Property Rights Organization
WTO	World Trade Organization

Index